W9-CIH-552
3 6021 00033 1771

The Complete Van Gogh

Paintings, Drawings, Sketches

THE COMPLETE VAN GOGH

Paintings · Drawings · Sketches

Jan Hulsker

Rosendale Library
PO Box 482
Rosendale, NY 12472

HARRISON HOUSE/HARRY N. ABRAMS, INC.
New York

Contents

Editor: Phyllis Freeman

© 1977 Meulenhoff International bv, Amsterdam

Published in 1980 by Harry N. Abrams, Incorporated, New York.
All rights reserved. No part of the contents of this book may be reproduced without the written permission of the publishers.

This 1984 edition published by Harrison House/Harry N. Abrams, Inc., distributed by Crown Publishers, Inc.

Printed and bound in the Netherlands

ISBN: 0-517-44867X

h g f e d c b

Preface

The aim of this book is to provide a clear and comprehensive picture of Vincent van Gogh's path as an artist. In order to achieve this, I have combined a detailed description of that path with illustrations of virtually all his drawings and paintings—a combination never before attempted in any book about Van Gogh. This description follows his artistic career, step by step, from the time he began to make his first series of rather clumsy drawings of figures in the house of his parents—the parsonage in Etten—until the last impressive landscape paintings in Auvers-sur-Oise just preceding the tragic end of his life. His letters to his brother Theo, to his sister Wilhelmina (Wil), and to such painter friends as Anthon van Rappard and Emile Bernard provide us with such a wealth of information that we can pursue the development of Van Gogh's life work from month to month, in many cases even from day to day. However, what he says about his drawings and paintings in those precious letters really comes to life only when we are immediately able to consult reproductions of the works referred to. That is why in this book I have tried to link up text and illustrations as much as possible. This means that generally one will find sketches, drawings, and paintings on the same pages as the text in which they are discussed or mentioned. A commentary accompanying the reproductions traces the chronology of the works, describes the most important events in Van Gogh's life, and indicates the influences of other artists and certain artistic movements on his style.

This commentary is based as much as possible on the oldest authentic documents relating to Van Gogh's life and work. It goes without saying that I also have consulted numerous scholarly studies of a later date, but I have quoted these only where they contain insights that constitute a real contribution to our knowledge of Van Gogh's development.

The illustrations in this book could not have been assembled without the pioneering work of J.-B. de la Faille (1886–1959), who in 1928 published the first catalogue of Van Gogh's paintings and drawings—*L'Oeuvre de Vincent van Gogh, Catalogue raisonné.* Quite on his own, in an effort spanning many years, De la Faille devoted himself to the enormous tasks of gathering together the necessary data about Van Gogh's drawings and paintings and of collecting photographs of them—an achievement hardly to be overestimated considering that there are about two thousand works, half of them outside the Netherlands. His undertaking deserves much admiration and respect, even though many of his findings are now outdated.

A second, corrected edition of De la Faille's catalogue, containing only the paintings, was published more than ten years later, in 1939. Here the paintings were given new numbers, and in some studies about Van Gogh one can still come across these so-called H Numbers (after Hyperion, the publisher). De la Faille continued to work on corrections until his death, in 1959. The third edition of his work had already been announced, but it was not published until 1970. This edition, prepared by a committee of experts under the chairmanship of A.M. Hammacher, was based on De la Faille's manuscript but incorporated many revisions and additions. While De la Faille's first two editions had been published in French, the third was issued in English—a sign of the times!—as *The Works of Vincent van Gogh: His Paintings and Drawings.* In addition to Hammacher, the board that prepared that volume consisted for some years of Jan G. van Gelder, Horst Gerson, W.J. de Gruyter, and Jan Hulsker; later the editors were A.M. Hammacher, Jan G. van Gelder, Sturla J. Gudlaugsson, Jan Hulsker, and Ellen Joosten. Preliminary work was done by members of the staff of the Netherlands Institute for Art History in The Hague. As the intention was to publish a corrected edition of De la Faille's catalogue, the third edition maintained his systems of arranging and numbering the works.

It is precisely with this aspect of De la Faille's catalogue that our volume breaks. De la Faille had divided his catalogues into two parts. First he had described and reproduced all the paintings (about half the works); then he had discussed and reproduced the drawings. Within each of these two main sections, there was a curious kind of subdivision; first the works mentioned in Van Gogh's letters were treated and then the works *not* mentioned in the letters. The information in the letters provided him with firm ground on which to date the first group, but he had to rely on his own insight to date the second group.

From the beginning this division into four groups had the disadvantage of totally obscuring the chronology of Van Gogh's works, but gradually it had become more and more unsatisfactory for other reasons as well. For example, in 1954, letters from Vincent van Gogh to Wil came to light in which many works not mentioned in letters to Theo were referred to or even fully described. Those works henceforth could be dated without difficulty, and thus they no longer belonged in De la Faille's supplementary grouping of works "not mentioned in the letters."

In addition, during the last fifteen years new light thrown on the dating of the letters has made it possible to correct many dates given to works by De la Faille. All in all, so much more has become known about Van Gogh since 1928 that it seemed appropriate to depart from De la Faille's method of classifying the works. I could have limited myself to rearranging each of the two categories of paintings and drawings in chronologically correct order, but I thought it was also justifiable to drop the artificial separation between oil paintings and drawings. In order to demonstrate Van Gogh's artistic development it seemed preferable to arrange all his works chronologically. This has important advantages, especially with an artist such as Van Gogh. He used to fix a subject in a drawing or a watercolor before painting it, and frequently he made more than one version. More often than not Van Gogh also made drawings *after* his painted studies, and in his letters we repeatedly find sketches of works just finished. A group such as a drawing, a painting with variants, and a letter sketch belongs together, especially as in most cases the components were created within a few days. For a better understanding of Van Gogh's way of working, it seemed essential to me to show the parts of a group in their interrelationships, and so in this book there are more than 2,100 illustrations of works placed carefully in a tentative chronological order irrespective of the medium used.

The drawings Van Gogh made as a child and the sketches he executed somewhat later—but before 1881—are represented here by only a few examples. The early drawings were assembled in the *catalogue raisonné* of 1970 in the chapter entitled "Juvenilia" and were accompanied by an expert commentary by Jan G. van Gelder. They can be consulted in that volume, along with the few drawings Van Gogh made during his stays in the Borinage and in Brussels that form the transition to his work as an artist. Also not included here are some sheets that were given a number by De la Faille but that show only the unfinished first draft of a drawing or a few barely decipherable scribbles.

Sketches in letters to relatives or friends—most frequently to Theo or to Anthon van Rappard—are reproduced here, together with other drawings, and each has an individual number. The reason for this is not primarily the *quality* of those sketches, although they often are complete little drawings in their own right, sometimes even more carefully elaborated than many sketchbook scribbles and other sketches. For me the determining factor was that so many letter sketches previously had been included in De la Faille's catalogues. In many instances when Van Gogh had made a sketch for a letter on a separate sheet of paper, the sketch became separated from the letter. Sometimes when De la Faille came across such sketches during the preparation of the catalogues, he must have failed to recognize them as letter sketches; in any case they were treated as ordinary drawings and given a number. We know about twenty-five sketches that originally belonged to letters, and undoubtedly quite a number of the small drawings included in the De la Faille catalogues must also have been made as letter sketches but cannot easily be recognized as such now. We are not sure whether the separate small sketches that have been preserved were Van Gogh's first designs or rough sketches made afterward in order to be sent to Theo or Van Rappard in letters. Under those circumstances I have preferred to include not only the letter sketches with an F Number but the others as well. Obviously they are of primary importance to the identification and dating of Van Gogh's drawings and paintings. They are often the final piece of the series: sketchbook scribble, preliminary drawing, finished picture, letter sketch.

In choosing the illustrations I have not aimed at absolute completeness. Various drawings and paintings that some experts have attributed to Van Gogh are not represented here. For the choice of works I have relied chiefly on the *catalogue raisonné* in its third and final form, as prepared by the committee of experts. I have added a few works that have since come to light and have been identified as authentic and also a number of drawings from a Brabant sketchbook that the committee had not been allowed to publish. On the other hand, I thought it senseless to include once again illustrations of works that the committee had published with such comments as "they do not accept this as an authentic work by Van Gogh" or "they hesitate to accept an attribution to Van Gogh." However, since studying these works and their pedigrees and histories may certainly be worthwhile, the reader is referred to the 1970 *catalogue raisonné*, in which all these data may be found.

Finally, there are some technical questions concerning the material of this book.

Titles. The titles of works as given here do not always correspond with those in the 1970 *catalogue raisonné*. I have tried to bring somewhat more "system" to the titles than has been employed before. Sometimes, for instance, drawings and paintings that are copies of each other or variants with only slight differences were given different titles by De la Faille, but I have preferred to use a uniform title for all copies or variants.

The system I have followed is based on the principle that the title must give a short indication of what one can *see* in a work and not an indication of things one only *knows* about it (even if in a sense this makes the title superfluous so long as the reproduction is at hand). Yet I have not always refrained from giving secondary information. If, for instance, we know with certainty who is represented in certain portraits (for example, Eugène Boch and Joseph Roulin), it seems natural to include the name in the title. In some cases I have adopted title indications that Van Gogh used in his letters. That is why I have used such names as "the Paddemoes" and "the Geest" in the titles of drawings 111 and 112, even though most of the inhabitants of The Hague do not know the names of those old streets in their town. But it seemed illogical to me to go on calling a certain house in Auvers-sur-Oise "the house of Père Eloi" if even the 1970 *catalogue raisonné* found it necessary to comment: "The title is first found in [De la] Faille 1928, and apparently is based on information since lost."

For the rest, the effort to give appropriate titles to long series of works of art may be a fascinating business, but anyone who has played this game will realize that it is sometimes impossible to apply too rigid a logic without falling into absurdities.

Chronology. The chronology of the works in this book is based on the numerous references to the drawings and paintings in the letters; these make it possible to date the works quite accurately, sometimes to the very day. For the dating of the letters themselves, which hardly ever carry a date, I refer to my volume *Van Gogh door Van Gogh* (Van Gogh by Van Gogh, 1973). The correct chronological relationship of other paintings and drawings was based on stylistic similarities with easily datable works.

In most cases the dates ascribed here may be considered as practically certain; in other cases they are only approximate. Of course, I do not suggest that Van Gogh's works were done exactly in the order in which they are reproduced here; in many instances, however, this *was* the case, as the text will prove. The single circumstance that in some periods Vincent worked on several paintings at one time prevents us from establishing their exact order of creation, and in some series of almost identical works, executed in quick succession, such as his studies of peasants' heads and his landscape sketches, stylistic differences are often too slight to permit us to distinguish any certain development. Yet by making use of all the data available, I have attempted to establish as accurately as possible the probable order of origin of Van Gogh's work.

Numbering system. Vincent often used both sides of a sheet of paper for drawings, and in some cases he even used both sides of a canvas for paintings. Where both sides were employed, De la Faille made the distinction—customary in catalogues—of *recto* (front) and *verso* (back). For example, after Van Gogh moved to Paris, he used the other side of a canvas on which he had painted a still life in Nuenen to paint a self-portrait. De la Faille numbered the self-portrait 178 recto and the still life 178 verso. The board of editors of the 1970 edition rightly decided that the side of the canvas that had been used first should be considered the *front* and the side used later the *back*, and they changed the numbers accordingly.

In many cases, however, it has been impossible to decide which of the sketches on the two sides of a sheet of paper was made first, especially when both date from the same period. For that reason I have not used the indications *rectó* and *verso*, but instead I have given each work a separate number. Where both sides of a sheet of drawing paper or a canvas are used, I have added the word *reverse* after the title of each work, followed by that work's particular number. Thus one finds in this volume the above-mentioned still life from the Nuenen period numbered 528, with the indication "reverse: 1198," and the self-portrait numbered 1198, with the indication "reverse: 528."

Letters. The letters of Vincent van Gogh are quoted from the four-volume 1953 edition of the letters in the original languages, which was revised and completed by Dr. V.W. van Gogh and has been reprinted several times. Many letters concerning Van Gogh were subsequently published in the quarterly *Vincent: Bulletin of the Rijksmuseum Vincent van Gogh*, cited in this book as *Vincent*, with the number of volume and issue. Letters to some individuals carry specific designations: B: Letters to Emile Bernard; R: Letters to Anthon van Rappard; T: Letters from Theo van Gogh to Vincent; W: Letters to Wilhelmina van Gogh.

Bibliography. The titles of the books and articles I have consulted and quoted from are given in the footnotes; complete publication data are given in the Selected Bibliography, beginning on page 489. Most books about Van Gogh include a more or less comprehensive bibliography; for extensive bibliographies the reader is referred to J.-B. de la Faille, *The Works of Vincent van Gogh: His Paintings and Drawings* (1970) and John Rewald, *Post-Impressionism* (3d edition, 1978).

For their kindness in letting me study the rich collection of paintings, drawings, and documents in the Rijksmuseum Vincent van Gogh in Amsterdam and the Rijksmuseum Kröller-Müller in Otterlo, I should like to thank the directors and staffs of those museums and the late Dr. V.W. van Gogh, president of the Vincent van Gogh Foundation. I should also like to thank the director and staff of the Netherlands Institute for Art History in The Hague. To this institute I owe much information on the present whereabouts of Van Gogh's works, many of which have changed ownership since the publication of De la Faille's catalogue in 1970. A number of people have been helpful with specific information, and from this group I should like to mention especially Jan G. van Gelder and A.M. Hammacher.

I am also very grateful to the publishers of the Dutch edition of this volume, Meulenhoff of Amsterdam, for the generous way in which they gave form to what I had in mind when planning the book. I particularly want to mention Wim van Hoorn, director of Meulenhoff International, who from the very beginning supervised this publication with great care. Only through his inventiveness and technical knowledge was it possible to solve many problems that resulted from the integration of illustrations and text at which I was aiming. In this and other respects, Joost van de Woestijne's talents as a book designer proved to be of great value.

Finally, I want to thank the editor of the English edition of this book, Phyllis Freeman, for her skill and care in preparing the present volume for publication.

JAN HULSKER

Note on the Captions

Numbers. In this book, paintings, drawings, and letter sketches are numbered in chronological order. In addition, the numbers they had in the *catalogue raisonné* by J.-B. de la Faille, the so-called F Numbers, are also given in the captions at the bottom of the pages. A concordance at the end of this book gives a list of these F Numbers, followed by the new JH Numbers.

In the text the numbers that refer to paintings, drawings, and letter sketches are always JH Numbers. (If a number refers to a letter, the number is always preceded by the word *Letter*.)

Medium. When no mention is made of the medium used, the work is a painting in oil on canvas.

Dimensions. Dimensions are given in centimeters and inches (to the nearest eighth of an inch). Height precedes width.

Ownership. There are continuing changes in ownership of works done by Vincent van Gogh. For this book extensive research was done to check the present whereabouts of works, and the Rijksmuseum Vincent van Gogh, Amsterdam, and the Netherlands Institute for Art History, The Hague, were consulted. However, it was not always possible to ascertain whether changes in ownership had occurred. Therefore, readers are requested to inform the publisher of any corrections concerning the present whereabouts of drawings or paintings.

Canvas Sizes

Very often in his letters from France, Van Gogh makes use of a French numbering system to indicate the size of his paintings. The canvas sizes he most frequently uses are:

Size	Approximate measurement
30	$36 \times 25\frac{1}{2}''$
25	$32 \times 23\frac{1}{2}''$
20	$28\frac{3}{4} \times 21\frac{1}{4}''$
15	$25\frac{1}{2} \times 19\frac{3}{4}''$
12	$24 \times 18''$
6	$16 \times 10\frac{1}{2}''$
5	$13\frac{3}{4} \times 19\frac{1}{2}''$

Van Gogh's Course before 1881

If Vincent van Gogh had died when he was twenty-seven years old instead of at the age of thirty-seven, he would have no place in the history of pictorial art, but he might still be the subject of more or less romanticized biographies and dramatized stories of his life because both his personality and his adventures were exceptional. Henri Perruchot, who has written a sound and reliable biography of Van Gogh, devoted no fewer than a hundred pages—a quarter of his book—to the first part of Van Gogh's life. In Irving Stone's biography, *Lust for Life*, a much more widely known but less accurate work, about a hundred pages out of a total of five hundred are given over to the story of these early years. However, in a volume that is intended essentially to map out the path that Van Gogh followed *as an artist*, it is, of course, impossible to give much space to these early years, and I have limited myself to a condensation of the events of that fascinating and eventful time. Most readers are, in any case, already familiar with the oft-repeated tale of Vincent as a willful assistant in the art trade and a fanatical preacher among the miners of the Borinage. The following paragraphs are a brief summary of the well-known facts of Van Gogh's early years and do not represent any attempt to present them in a new reconstruction.

Vincent Willem van Gogh was born March 30, 1853, in Groot-Zundert, the Netherlands, near the Belgian border. He was the oldest son of the Reverend Theodorus van Gogh (1822–85) and of Anna Cornelia Carbentus (1819–1907). Even his birth date has led his biographers to much comment because exactly one year earlier, March 30, 1852, a first son, who would also have been named Vincent, was stillborn. Psychoanalysts have attributed many of Vincent's difficulties as a child and his later preoccupation with sickness and death to the fact that he was a "replacement child."*

After the birth of Vincent Willem, five more children were born: Anna Cornelia, Theodorus (Theo), Elisabeth Huberta, Wilhelmina Jacoba (Wil or Willemien), and Cornelis Vincent. Of these five Theo occupied the most important place in Vincent's life, not only as his prop and refuge but also as his dearest friend.

Not much is known about Vincent's early youth. What is known we owe to a small memoir written by his sister Elisabeth, then Mrs. E.H. du Quesne-van Gogh, and published by her in 1910 under the title *Vincent van Gogh: Persoonlijke herinneringen aangaande een kunstenaar* (in the English translation *Personal Recollections of Vincent van Gogh*). It is apparent from what she writes that she knew very little about her brother in his later years, but her book does give some insight into his early life, when she knew him more intimately. According to her, he was a retiring sort of boy with a great love of flowers, birds, and insects. She describes him when he was seventeen years old: "the forehead already full of lines, the eyebrows on the large, noble brow drawn together in deepest thought. The eyes, small and deep-set, were now blue, now green, according to the impressions of the moment. But in spite of all awkwardness and the ugly exterior, one was conscious of a greatness, through the unmistakable sign of the deep inner life" (page 4).

Vincent's brothers and sisters, she continues, "felt, however, instinctively, with the delicate sensitiveness of children, that their brother preferred to be alone when home on his vacation from boarding-school. For he sought solitude, not the companionship of his family" (page 6).

*See Albert J. Lubin, *Stranger on the Earth* (1972), chap. 5. For full bibliographical data on all works cited in this text, see the Selected Bibliography, beginning on p. 489.

Elisabeth's small book does not tell us much about what actually occurred in Vincent's boyhood, but we do know that he was educated at the village school as well as at the parsonage until he was eleven, when he was sent to a boarding school in Zevenbergen. Only recently it has become known that he also attended the newly established Hogere Burgerschool (high school) in Tilburg, where he completed the first year and part of the second.†

We do not know why Vincent suddenly left this school in March 1868, when he was fifteen, but since he was getting good marks, it was not because of difficulties with his studies. The school in Tilburg had a very good art teacher, and this may have had some influence on Vincent's subsequent decision to become an artist. It is strange, however, that later in Etten, when he started to draw again, he had great difficulty with perspective and complained that he had to learn all about it on his own.

A number of drawings that Vincent made in his youth have been preserved, but they are the kind of drawings that many children of the same age are capable of making and, in my view, give little indication of the direction in which his talent would lead. For the most part they are carefully executed copies of model drawings.

In 1869, when Vincent was sixteen years old, a position was found for him as junior clerk with the art firm of Goupil & Co. in The Hague, of which his uncle Vincent van Gogh was a partner. His superior there was H.G. Tersteeg, a man eight years his senior, who later played an important part in Vincent's life and was repeatedly mentioned in his letters. Goupil was an important art firm that not only dealt in the paintings of contemporary and traditional artists but also made and sold reproductions of works of art. During the years that Vincent worked at Goupil he acquired the thorough familiarity with nineteenth-century art that is apparent in his letters later on. The years he spent working among the renowned masters in whom Goupil specialized must also have greatly influenced the development of his taste.

Four years later, in June 1873, Vincent was transferred to the Goupil branch in London, the first foreign experience for a man who was to spend many years of his life abroad. In London, he had the opportunity to get a good grounding in English and to become even better acquainted with both English literature and art, in which he always maintained a warm interest. Johanna van Gogh-Bonger, Theo's widow, wrote in her "Memoir" to *The Complete Letters of Vincent van Gogh* that as a result of the unfortunate love he entertained for Ursula Loyer, the daughter of his landlady in London, "his character changed." However, as there is not a single letter or document from Vincent's time substantiating this romantic incident, I shall not discuss it further.‡

In October 1874 Vincent was transferred for a short time to Goupil's headquarters in Paris. The following December he was back in the London branch, but in May 1875 he was permanently assigned to Paris, where he lived in a small room in Montmartre. Gradually, however, his superiors had become dissatisfied with his work, and on April 1, 1876, he was discharged from the firm.

†This discovery was made by H. F. J. M. van den Eerenbeemt; see his article "Van Gogh in Tilburg," *Brabantia*, vol. XX, no. 6 (November 1971).

‡Recently the address of the Loyer family was traced by Paul Chalcroft, and Ken Wilkie discovered a small drawing that Vincent had made of the house. However, the name of the daughter proved not to be Ursula but Eugénie. See *Holland Herald*, vol. VIII, no. 2 (1973).

One of the causes for Vincent's diminishing interest in the art business was undoubtedly his religious zeal, which had gradually assumed the character of fanaticism, as his letters show. Indeed, Vincent's letters to Theo, with whom he had started a regular correspondence in 1872, enable us to see more clearly than before what was going on in his mind. In one of these letters he even went so far as to advise Theo (who had also started working for Goupil, at the branch in The Hague) to get rid of all his books and read only the Bible. It was quite in line with this thinking that, after being discharged from Goupil's and teaching in a boarding school in Ramsgate for a short time, Vincent took a position in Isleworth, near London, where he was allowed not only to teach but also to serve as a kind of assistant preacher. In October 1876 he wrote to Theo in moving words that for the first time he had been allowed to preach in a small church in Richmond: "I felt like someone who has emerged from a dark dungeon below the ground and returns to the kindly light of the day when I stood in the pulpit, and it is a wonderful thought for me that from now on wherever I shall be I will preach the gospel; to do this *well*, one must have the gospel in one's heart. May He create it there" (Letter 79). The nature of his concerns in those days becomes clearly apparent in a document that came to light only in 1975. It is the autograph album kept by the wife of the Reverend Mr. Jones, the head of the school where Vincent taught. Vincent had filled several pages of this book with his carefully formed minuscule characters. Among the texts he had copied out here were a number of psalms and devotional songs in Dutch, a passage from the Bible and religious poems in English, a poem by Friedrich Rückert and some psalms in German (written in German script!), a prose piece by Jules Michelet in French, a long excerpt from *Le Conscrit* (*The Conscript*) by Hendrik Conscience, also in French, and a few more prose passages and the whole of Psalm 107 in French. His education in Tilburg and stay abroad had certainly borne fruit, but spiritually there had clearly been a strong development in a pietistic-religious direction.

It is not surprising that the image of his father occupied Vincent's thoughts more and more and that he longed to follow in his footsteps. But he would first have to undergo another trial. Early in 1877 his parents found a place for him in a bookshop run by the firm of Blussé and Van Braam in Dordrecht. According to the recollections of his employer and of his roommate in Dordrecht, a young schoolteacher, Vincent was again more interested in translating the Bible than in bookkeeping or bookselling and in the evening the business did not exist for him at all. According to his roommate, "Van Gogh spent evening after evening reading the Bible, making excerpts, and writing sermons" (for these recollections, see *The Complete Letters*, Number 94*a*).

In March of that year Vincent wrote Theo very specifically: "As far as we know in our family, which is a Christian family in the true sense of the word, from generation to generation, there has always been someone who was a minister of the Gospel. Why should this voice not also be heard in this and following generations? Why should there not be a member of that family now who feels himself called to that service and with some truth thinks that he may and must declare himself and seek for the means to achieve that aim. It is my prayer and innermost desire that the spirit of my father and grandfather may also rest upon me and that it may be permitted me to be a Christian and a Christian laborer, so that my life may resemble, the more the better—for I see that this old wine is good and I do not desire any that is new—the life of those I have cited here" (Letter 89).

A

B

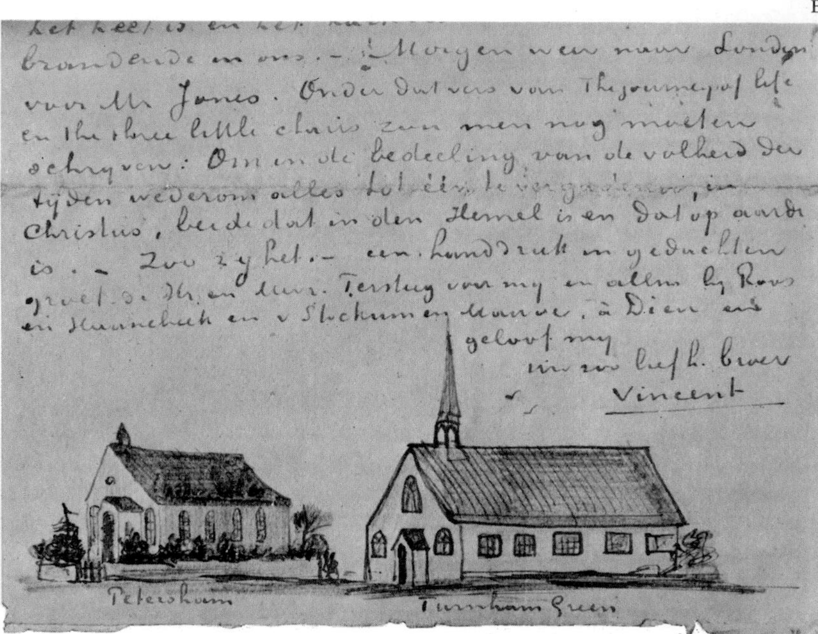
Morgen weer naar Londen voor Mr Jones. Onder dat vers van The journey of life en the three little chairs zou men nog moeten schrijven: Om in de bedeeling van de volheid der tijden wederom alles tot één te vergaderen, in Christus, beide dat in den Hemel is en dat op aarde is. — Zoo zij het. — een handdruk in gedachten

geloof mij

uw zoo liefh. broer

Vincent

A. *Sawmill.* Black chalk, 14 × 18.5 cm ($5\frac{1}{2}$ × $7\frac{3}{8}$"). Annotated: "V. W. van Gogh 2 Oct. 1862." One of Vincent's childhood drawings, undoubtedly copied. Rijksmuseum Vincent van Gogh, Amsterdam

B. *Little Churches of Petersham and Turnham Green.* A typical letter sketch from November 1876, when Vincent attended these churches while serving as a teacher and assistant preacher in Isleworth. Rijksmuseum Vincent van Gogh, Amsterdam

C

C. *Houses in Cuesmes*. Charcoal, 23 × 29.5 cm (9 × 11¾″). One of the drawings Vincent had begun to make in the Borinage as a preliminary stage in his development as an artist. Probably 1879. The Armand Hammer Collection, Los Angeles

D. *The Diggers* (after Millet), F829. Pencil and charcoal, 37 × 62 cm (14⅜ × 24⅜″). Vincent wrote in November 1880: "Have drawn *Les Bêcheurs* by Millet after a photograph by Braun." An example of Vincent's efforts in those years to improve his drawing technique by making copies. Rijksmuseum Kröller-Müller, Otterlo

E. *Miners' Wives Carrying Sacks*, F832. Pen and pencil, washed, 43 × 60 cm (16⅞ × 23⅝″). On the lower right-hand side of this drawing Vincent inscribed a more symbolic title: "The Bearers of the Burden." He wrote Theo in Letter 143, April 12, 1881, that he had sketched this subject at Anthon van Rappard's. The drawing reproduced here may be a more finished version of that sketch done somewhat later. Probably also April 1881. Rijksmuseum Kröller-Müller, Otterlo

Vincent's next step was a logical consequence of these thoughts. In May 1877 he seems to have persuaded his parents (and the family council) to let him go to Amsterdam to prepare himself for theological studies. It would be two years before he would be ready to take the preliminary examination that would determine whether he would start the study itself. I will not go into the details of the failure that was the inevitable result. Vincent's letters to Theo from these years give a clear picture of the zeal with which he embarked on this course and the aversion which slowly grew against a form of study that was so far removed from what inspired him. This picture is filled out by the lively recollections published in 1910 by his tutor in Latin and Greek, Dr. M.B. Mendes da Costa (see *The Complete Letters*, Number 122*a*).

When Vincent gave up his studies, the family decided to let him take a short course in Brussels that enabled him to work in a practical capacity as an evangelist in a poor mining district in Belgium, the Borinage. In the fall of 1878 he started serving in the villages of Pâturages, Wasmes, and Cuesmes. Little is known of the events connected with Vincent's stay in the Borinage, for only a relatively small number of Vincent's letters from that period have come down to us. Many romantic and at first sight hardly credible stories about this period have found their way into print, but some authentic documents from that time confirm that Vincent tried with uncompromising fanaticism to put into practice the Christian life that inspired him profoundly. Particularly important is the unimpeachable testimony of a report by the Union of Protestant Churches in Belgium for the period 1879–80, which is reprinted in *The Tragic Life of Vincent van Gogh*, by Louis Piérard, an inhabitant of the Borinage who collected considerable information about Vincent's stay there. Although the report declares that the experiment of allowing Van Gogh to work as an evangelist did not produce the expected results, it also reveals substantial appreciation of his efforts: "If the gift of eloquence, so indispensable to one who is placed at the head of a congregation, were added to the admirable qualities he displays at a sick-bed or with the injured, to the devotion and self-sacrificing spirit of which he gives constant proof in spending his nights with the sick and in giving them the best of his clothes and linen, M. Van Gogh would certainly be an accomplished evangelist" (Piérard, page 53).

In 1880 Vincent must have gone through a spiritual crisis; there is not a single bit of written evidence about it, but it eventuated in his giving up his work as an evangelist and starting to look upon a career as an artist as his ideal.

In one of his rare letters at this time to Theo he asked him to lend him woodcuts of *Les Travaux des Champs* (*The Labors of the Field*) by Millet as he was making large drawings after Millet's works. In October he wrote from Brussels, where he found lodging in a cheap hotel. He defended this unexpected move in a letter to Theo saying that his room in Cuesmes was too small for him to do his drawings properly, particularly as he had now come to the third series of drawing examples by Charles Bargue, a difficult series with portraits after Holbein and other artists. We see from other letters that he had gone for advice to the painter Willem Roelofs, who had been living in Brussels for many years, and to the much younger painter Anthon van Rappard. As before, Theo had again provided him with the addresses. On Roelofs's advice he had taken steps to enter the Académie des Beaux-Arts, but there is no indication that he ever actually attended it. Dr. Marc E.

Tralbaut published a photograph of a page from the register of the academy* recording Van Gogh's enrollment September 15, 1880, but there is no explanation of the fact that at this date Vincent was still in Cuesmes. And on November 1 he wrote Theo that he had not yet been admitted to the academy. He added: "In Cuesmes, old man, I could not have stood it another month without falling ill from anxiety"; but in Brussels the situation did not seem much better: "You should not imagine that I am living in luxury here, for my meals consist mainly of dry bread and some potatoes or chestnuts, which people here sell on street corners, but by having a better room and eating a somewhat better meal from time to time in a restaurant, whenever I can afford it, I will be able to manage quite well" (Letter 138). He said that he thought he had made some progress in the past months and still hoped to find a painter who might help him go further. However, when he asked Theo's opinion about going to The Hague for a short time to look up Tersteeg and the painter Anton Mauve, Theo hastily replied in an effort to keep him from taking what he regarded as an ill-advised step.

As late as April 2, 1881, it appears, from a letter to Theo, that no decision had yet been taken about Vincent's immediate future. Van Rappard, in whose studio in Brussels Vincent had been working, was going to the Netherlands in May, so Vincent wanted to work in the countryside for a while. In his letter he mentioned as many as eight localities he had in mind, and apparently it was only as he was writing this that he began to consider the advantages of living in Etten (where his father had been called to preach a few years earlier). This seems not even to have been discussed with his father, who had seen him in Brussels only a short while before: "The cheapest way for me would probably be to spend this summer in Etten; there are plenty of subjects there. If you think this advisable, would you write Father about it; I am prepared to resign myself in the matter of clothing or anything else they may want, and quite possibly I might run across C.M. [his uncle Cornelis Marinus, the art dealer, always called C.M. in the correspondence with Theo] there this summer" (Letter 142). The views of Theo, now twenty-three, had obviously become of decisive importance in the family, for Vincent continued: "Since Father said during his visit: 'Just write to Theo and arrange with him what would be best and cheapest,' I hope you will shortly let me know your opinion."

Very soon afterward, the three of them had occasion to discuss the matter together. Father let Vincent know that Theo would be in Etten one Sunday and that Vincent's presence would also be desirable. So Vincent went to the home of his parents April 12, 1881, after a lapse of three years.

Evidently during this meeting it was decided that Vincent could live there for the time being. He probably returned to Brussels to pick up his things, and shortly before the end of the month returned to Etten. Now the important moment had arrived when Vincent, at first with a fairly light heart, could devote himself entirely to what he had now recognized as his true calling. May 1, 1881, he wrote Theo: "I am so glad things have been arranged so that I can work here quietly for some time; I hope to make as many studies as I can, for that is the seed from which later the drawings will come" (Letter 144).

His career as an artist had begun.

D

E

**Van Gogh* (1969), p. 74.

Etten

1

2

April–May 1881

1 Sower (after Millet), F830
Pen, washed, heightened with green and white, 48 × 36.5 cm ($18\frac{7}{8} \times 14\frac{3}{8}$")
Rijksmuseum Vincent van Gogh, Amsterdam

2 Mower (after Millet), F1674
Pencil, washed with sepia, 55.5 × 30.5 cm ($22 \times 12\frac{1}{4}$")
Rijksmuseum Vincent van Gogh, Amsterdam

We have little reliable information about Vincent's first few months in Etten because the few letters he wrote to Theo are difficult to date. The reason that Vincent wrote Theo infrequently was probably that he had seen Theo in the middle of April, written him around May 1, and expected him to be in Etten again in the summer.

Vincent's first letter from Etten (Letter 144) was concerned mainly with his views on an exhibition of watercolors in Brussels, which he had visited some time after April 15, when he returned there. But he also included one somewhat surprising item of news about his own work: "I have meanwhile started on the Millets. *Le Semeur* [*Sower*] is finished and *Les Quatre Heures de la Journée* [*The Four Hours of the Day*] sketched out. And to these there will be added: *Les Travaux des Champs*." These were the woodcuts after Millet, which he had received from Theo or had collected himself, as he had written April 2 (Letter 142). The reason he had started this copying was obviously the weather—which, as he wrote, was not always suitable for working out of doors. Except for a few (1 and 2), all these copies have been lost; the same fate befell most of the many drawings after Bargue—the whole series of sixty, which he had copied as often as three times.

In the next letter, written probably at the end of May, we get a glimpse of the activity he had come to Etten for: "When it is not raining, I go out every day, mostly on the moor. I make my studies fairly large like a few you saw when you were here. One of them is a 'hut at Het Heike [the little moor],' and another a 'barn with moss-grown roof' on the Rozendaal road that is known around here as the Protestant barn. You may remember what I am referring to. Then the mill right across from there in the pasture, and the elms in the graveyard. And yet another, with woodcutters working in a large clearing where a big pine has been cut down. And I also try to draw the implements such as cart, plow, harrow, wheelbarrow, and so on" (Letter 145). Nothing, or next to nothing, has been preserved of the eleven or more studies mentioned here. The "hut at Het Heike" and the "barn with moss-grown roof" are probably 4 and 5, and the "mill ... in the pasture" may be 6. The first two still strongly show the marks of the beginner. The indication that Theo had already seen a few studies during his visit, around April 15, tallies with Vincent's announcement April 12: "I would like to make a few more sketches in Etten on the moor, so I will go a few days sooner" (Letter 143). The drawing in 3 was perhaps one of those, although it might go back even further.

Working with Van Rappard

When Vincent wrote next to Theo, he reported that Van Rappard had been visiting him for about twelve days: "We have been out together quite a lot, several times to places like the moor near Seppe, to the so-called Passievaart, a big marshland" (Letter 146). Since Van Rappard put dates on some of his sketches—*Passievaart near Seppe*, "Seppe, June 13, 1881," and *Parsonage in Etten*, "Etten, June 14"—we know that the visit took place in June, and we can also date some of Vincent's drawings more precisely. "While he was painting, I made a pen-and-ink drawing of another part of the marsh, where a lot of water lilies grow (near the Rozendaal road)." This must refer to drawing 7, which in subject and style is very similar to the larger drawing 8. As the letter goes on to say, "Willemien [Vincent's sister] has now left," and as we know that the drawing of the marsh with the water lilies comes from her holdings, the obvious conclusion is that Vincent gave her this fine example of his art as a farewell present.

The fact that the dating is definitely established is important because otherwise it would be hard to believe that the great progress evident in this admirable drawing as compared with the still rather primitive drawings 4, 5, and especially 3 could have been achieved in so short a time. The dating of this work makes it somewhat more reasonable to place the drawing of the mill (6)—which also exhibits a high degree of technical competence—so early in the Etten period. Affinity of style also argues for assigning the drawings of a garden and orchard (9 and 10) to June.

Willemien's presence induced Vincent to try his hand at portraits. "She is a very good sitter; I have a drawing of her as well as one of another girl who was staying here." The first portrait could be drawing 11, although Marc Edo Tralbaut (in his *Vincent van Gogh* [1969], page 82) takes it to be a portrait of Kee Vos, Vincent's cousin. Contrary to his view, I think it bears a striking resemblance to the portrait of Wilhelmina on page 24 of his book. Furthermore, its oval shape suggests a photograph that Vincent may have copied. (He mentions copying photographs in Letter 147.)

It is a pity that we do not have the drawing of the other girl, for Vincent's description of it is intriguing: "I have put a sewing machine in that one. There are no spinning wheels any more, which is a great pity for artists who paint and draw, but something has taken their place which is no less picturesque and that is the sewing machine." We would very much have liked to see whether Van Gogh succeeded in introducing that remarkable product of the technical-industrial era into modern painting as naturally as Toulouse-Lautrec did when he put the bicycle in his pictures a few years later.

The following passage throws further light on the way in which Vincent continued his technical explorations: "I got a copy of [Armand-Théophile] Cassagne's *Traité d'aquarelle* [Treatise on Watercolors], and am studying it. Even if I did not do any watercolors, it is very likely that I will still find a lot in it, for instance for sepia and ink. Up to now I have been drawing exclusively in pencil, heightening it or drawing it out with the pen or, if need be, a reed pen, which makes broader strokes. The kind of drawing I have been doing lately has called for that technique, for there were subjects that required much *drawing*, also perspective drawing, namely, some workshops in the village here, a smithy, carpenter's shop, and clogmaker's" (Letter 146).

When he says "Up to now I have been drawing exclusively in pencil," this should not be interpreted too literally, for Vincent had already used watercolors in the drawing of a landscape (3), which undoubtedly was earlier. In saying: "Even if I did not do any watercolors," what he must have meant was nothing completely in watercolors, for he had, in fact, not reached that stage.

Summer

The next letter to Theo, presumably written in July, mentions "a drawing in the Liesbosch," which is probably drawing 12. Since it was too hot to sit out on the moor in the daytime, Vincent was working at home "copying drawings by Holbein from Bargue." We know that he was not doing it for the first time. Two copies of one of the examples, *The Daughter of Jacob Meyer*, have by chance come down to us. It was chiefly on the basis of the kind of paper used that in the 1970 *catalogue raisonné* F833 (13) was assigned to the Etten period, while the other version (F847) was assigned to the Brussels series. The catalogue of the Rijksmuseum Kröller-Müller points out the superior draftsmanship in 13, another indication that it is a later work.

Following a suggestion by Theo, Vincent had also attempted "to draw some portraits after photographs" (Letter 147). The fairly large drawing of his father (14) has traditionally been regarded as one of these drawings after photographs. To me, this appears highly improbable. The characteristic, but almost caricaturelike, rendering in profile is

3

4

5

3 Landscape, F874v (reverse: early drawing)
Pen, watercolor, 19 × 28 cm ($7\frac{1}{2} \times 11''$)
The St. Louis Art Museum

4 Hut, F875
Black chalk, 13.5 × 36 cm ($5\frac{1}{2} \times 14\frac{1}{8}''$)
Collection F. Wilson, London

5 Barn with Moss-Grown Roof, F842
Black chalk, pencil, pen, heightened with white and gray, 45.5 × 61 ($18\frac{1}{8} \times 24''$)
Museum Boymans-van Beuningen, Rotterdam

6 Landscape with Mill, F843
Pencil, charcoal, 35.5 × 60 cm ($14\frac{1}{8} \times 23\frac{5}{8}''$)
Rijksmuseum Kröller-Müller, Otterlo
June 1881

7 Marsh with Water Lilies, F845
Pencil, pen, reed pen, 23.5 × 31 cm ($9\frac{1}{2} \times 12\frac{1}{4}''$)
Location unknown

8 Marsh, F846
Pen, pencil, 42.5 × 56.5 cm ($16\frac{7}{8} \times 22\frac{1}{2}''$)
Collection Mrs. M. Feilchenfeldt, Zurich

9 Garden with Arbor, F902
Pencil, black chalk, pen, watercolor, 44.5 × 56.5 cm ($17\frac{3}{4} \times 22\frac{1}{2}''$)
Rijksmuseum Kröller-Müller, Otterlo

6

7

8

9

10

11

12

10 Orchard, F902a
Charcoal, pen, brown ink, heightened with white, 25.5 × 32 cm ($10\frac{1}{4} \times 12\frac{5}{8}''$)
Museum Boymans-van Beuningen, Rotterdam

11 Portrait, F849
Pencil, 35 × 24.5 cm ($13\frac{3}{4} \times 9\frac{7}{8}''$)
Rijksmuseum Kröller-Müller, Otterlo

July 1881

12 Edge of a Wood, F903
Charcoal, heightened with white, 42 × 55 cm ($16\frac{1}{2} \times 21\frac{5}{8}''$)
Rijksmuseum Kröller-Müller, Otterlo

unusual for photographs of that time.* Further, it seems unlikely that Vincent, who saw his father daily, should have done his portrait from a photograph rather than from real life. If the portrait of Willemien (11) was in fact drawn after a photograph, the reason, as appears from Letter 146, was that she had left Etten long before July.

At the beginning of August, Theo came for a stay with his parents, according to the preface to *The Complete Letters*. In Letter 147 Vincent had asked Theo to bring Ingres paper with him, since he had used up his supply. So we read in Letter 148: "I am again busy drawing the *Exercices au Fusain* [Charcoal Exercises] on the Ingres paper that you brought; I have to make quite an effort to keep on with that job." He gave up the outdoor drawing for the time being because he wanted to practice doing the bold lines and simple contours of Charles Bargue's examples. "I have set myself the task of doing them once again, and that will be the last time." Since Bargue's course consisted of sixty large plates, this was a task that would take a great deal of time. Vincent expected that it would be fall before he had completed it, and we may assume that few landscape drawings were made during those summer months. He did, however, start thinking about models: "I also hope to succeed in finding a good model, such as Piet Kaufman, the laborer, but I think it might be better not to let him sit for me here, but rather at the yard, or at his own place, or else in the fields, and let him pose with a shovel or a plow or something else."

In his next letter Vincent reported that he had now done the entire Bargue series all over again; therefore, we may assume that it must have been written no earlier than September. Vincent also reported that he had made a four-day trip to The Hague, shown his copies to Tersteeg, and visited the studios of Anton Mauve and Théophile de Bock. He went with De Bock to see *The Panorama* by the famous painter of seascapes Hendrik Willem Mesdag, and he described in detail an exhibition of drawings by such artists as Mesdag, Mauve, David Artz, and Johannes H. Weissenbruch. He concluded: "Well, I have been to The Hague: maybe this will be a start toward once again getting to know Mauve and others on a serious basis." He also mentioned that on the way to The Hague he had stopped off for a day in Dordrecht because from the train he had seen a row of windmills that he wanted to draw. "Although it was raining, I did manage to do it" (15).

With Mauve

One of the most profitable results of his visit to The Hague proved to be his contacts with Mauve. Mauve, who was married to a cousin of Vincent's, had shown interest in Vincent's "own drawings" (as distinct from his copies after Bargue); and, Vincent wrote, "he has given me many tips I am very pleased with, and we more or less agreed that I would go and see him again quite soon when I have more studies to show him." This did indeed happen a few months later. It meant that Vincent's most cherished wish, which he had nurtured for more than a year—to have the chance to work under the guidance of a more advanced artist—had been fulfilled.

The results became obvious in a short time, as his later work shows. Fortunately, we are better informed about that period than about the months before. In Letter 150, written soon after 149, and probably also in September, he reported: "It was also as the result of some things Mauve told me that I have again started working from a live model. I have fortunately been able to get a few people like Piet Kaufman, the laborer. The careful study-

*Compare this with the photograph of the Reverend Mr. van Gogh in Tralbaut, *Vincent van Gogh* (1966), p. 16.

13

14

15

13 The Daughter of Jacob Meyer (after Holbein), F833
Pen, pencil, 42 × 30 cm ($16\frac{1}{2} \times 11\frac{3}{4}$")
Rijksmuseum Kröller-Müller, Otterlo

14 Theodorus van Gogh (Vincent's Father), F876
Pencil, black ink, washed, heightened with white, 33 × 25 cm ($13 \times 9\frac{7}{8}$")
Collection Mrs. A. R. W. Nieuwenhuizen Segaar-Aarse, The Hague

August 1881

15 Windmills near Dordrecht, F850
Watercolor, pencil, black and green chalk, heightened with white, 26 × 60 cm ($10\frac{1}{4} \times 23\frac{5}{8}$")
Rijksmuseum Kröller-Müller, Otterlo

16

17

18

19

20

21

22

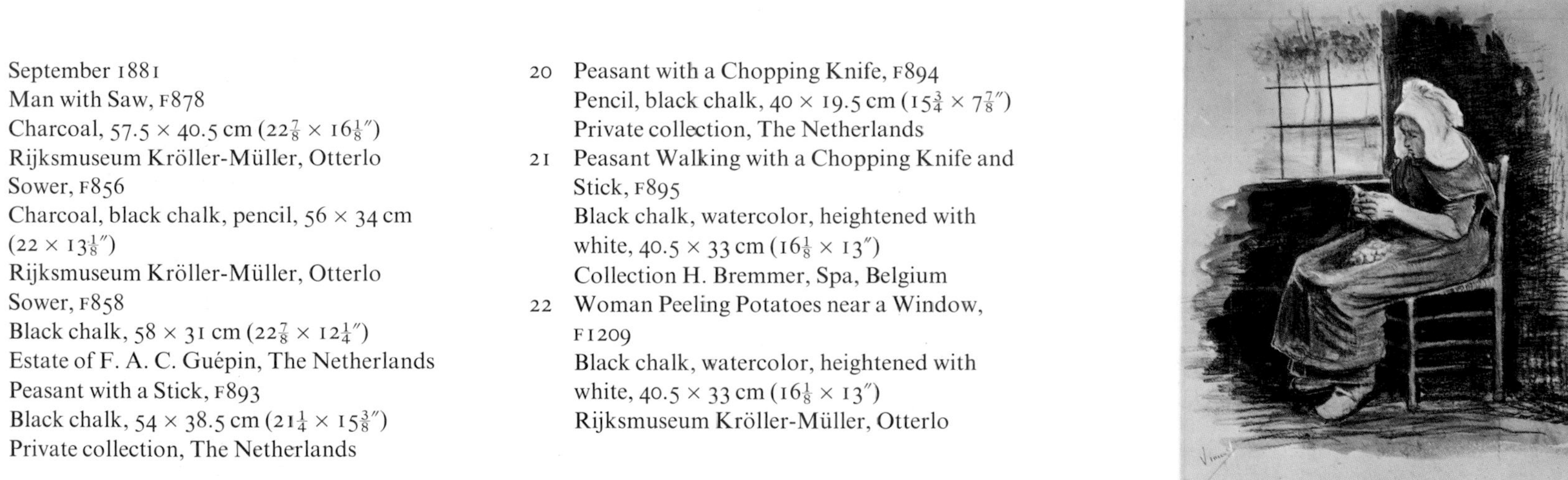

September 1881

16 Man with Saw, F878
Charcoal, 57.5 × 40.5 cm ($22\frac{7}{8} \times 16\frac{1}{8}$″)
Rijksmuseum Kröller-Müller, Otterlo

17 Sower, F856
Charcoal, black chalk, pencil, 56 × 34 cm ($22 \times 13\frac{3}{8}$″)
Rijksmuseum Kröller-Müller, Otterlo

18 Sower, F858
Black chalk, 58 × 31 cm ($22\frac{7}{8} \times 12\frac{1}{4}$″)
Estate of F. A. C. Guépin, The Netherlands

19 Peasant with a Stick, F893
Black chalk, 54 × 38.5 cm ($21\frac{1}{4} \times 15\frac{3}{8}$″)
Private collection, The Netherlands

20 Peasant with a Chopping Knife, F894
Pencil, black chalk, 40 × 19.5 cm ($15\frac{3}{4} \times 7\frac{7}{8}$″)
Private collection, The Netherlands

21 Peasant Walking with a Chopping Knife and Stick, F895
Black chalk, watercolor, heightened with white, 40.5 × 33 cm ($16\frac{1}{8} \times 13$″)
Collection H. Bremmer, Spa, Belgium

22 Woman Peeling Potatoes near a Window, F1209
Black chalk, watercolor, heightened with white, 40.5 × 33 cm ($16\frac{1}{8} \times 13$″)
Rijksmuseum Kröller-Müller, Otterlo

ing that I did and the continuous and repeated drawing after Bargue's *Exercices au Fusain* have given me a better insight into the rendering of the human figure. I have learned to measure and observe and to look for the main outline. As a result, what seemed to me desperately impossible in the past now gradually begins to become possible, thank God." The remainder of the letter consists of a long list of the drawings he had made and ends with a summary of what he regarded as his program for the future: "Diggers, sowers, plowmen, men, and women—these must I now unceasingly draw. Every aspect of country life must I search into and draw—just as many others have done and are still doing. I no longer stand so helpless before nature as I once did."

Balance Sheet
From the sketches in this letter, we are able to deduce which drawings had already been done to that date—September 1881:

22, 23:	Women near a Window (sketch 28)
24:	Man with Winnow (sketch 28)
25, 26:	Sower with Basket (sketch 28)
29:	Digger (facing right) (sketch 30)
31:	Sower (sketches 32 , 33)
34:	Peasant Sitting by the Fireplace (sketch 35)
36:	Field with Thunderstorm (sketch 37)
38:	Digger (facing left) (sketch 39)
40:	Farmer Leaning on His Spade (sketch 41)

No drawing has been preserved of the woman with a broom in sketch 28.

These drawings must certainly be placed in September, and on the basis of the similarity in style, I have also assigned the male figures 16–21 to that month.

It is not surprising that these drawings, the first of this genre that Vincent made, still look somewhat clumsy. He fully realized that himself, although he thought it applied less to the drawings than to the rough sketches made from them in the letter: "I know that there is much to criticize about proportion, certainly more than in the actual drawings anyway" (Letter 150). The fact that the proportions in drawings such as the farmer's wife near a window (22 and 23) and the sower (25) are definitely still not quite right does not seem to have bothered him much. True, the struggle had certainly not been easy. Much later—early in January—Vincent admitted referring to this period: "You may be assured that when I went to Mauve for the first time with my pen-and-ink drawing and M. said: 'You should try it with charcoal and chalk and brush and stump,' I found it damned difficult to work in those new mediums. Although I was patient, it did not seem to help at all; at times I became so impatient that I ground my charcoal under my feet and felt completely discouraged" (Letter 169).

Despite all this, there is undoubtedly a striking improvement in Vincent's draftsmanship. In the long sequence of drawings made in September and October, we now recognize not only many of the themes that would occupy him for many years (people working in the fields, landscapes), but also the characteristic, unromantic, matter-of-fact observation of the real world that was to remain one of the hallmarks of his style. Such progress cannot have remained unnoticed by those around him. In a short letter he reports that his wealthy and influential uncle Vincent in Prinsenhage "is going to The Hague tomorrow and will very likely speak with Mauve about when I should stop off at his place again." In that same letter he had already mentioned something perhaps even more significant: "And last week I got a paint box from Uncle Cent; it is quite good, good enough in any case to start with (they are Paillard paints). I am very happy with it.

23

24

25

26

23 Woman Peeling Potatoes near a Window, F1213
Black and colored chalk, watercolor, 30 × 22.5 cm (11$\frac{3}{4}$ × 9″)
Rijksmuseum Kröller-Müller, Otterlo

24 Man with Winnow, F891
Pencil, black chalk, watercolor, 62.5 × 47.5 cm (24$\frac{3}{4}$ × 18$\frac{7}{8}$″)
Rijksmuseum Kröller-Müller, Otterlo

25 Sower with Basket, F865
Black chalk, watercolor, heightened with white, 62 × 47.5 cm (24$\frac{3}{8}$ × 18$\frac{7}{8}$″)
Rijksmuseum Kröller-Müller, Otterlo

26 Sower with Basket, F1675
Charcoal, black chalk, washed with brownred, 30.5 × 23 cm (12$\frac{1}{4}$ × 9″)
Location unknown

27

28

29

30

31

32

33

27 Sower, F866a
Black chalk, watercolor, washed with brown, 60 × 45 cm ($23\frac{5}{8}$ × $17\frac{3}{4}$″)
Location unknown

28 Woman near a Window (twice), Man with Winnow, Sower, and Woman with Broom
Sketches in Letter 150
Rijksmuseum Vincent van Gogh, Amsterdam

29 Digger, F859
Black chalk, watercolor, 44 × 34 cm ($17\frac{3}{8}$ × $13\frac{3}{8}$″)
Rijksmuseum Kröller-Müller, Otterlo

30 Digger
Sketch in Letter 150
Rijksmuseum Vincent van Gogh, Amsterdam

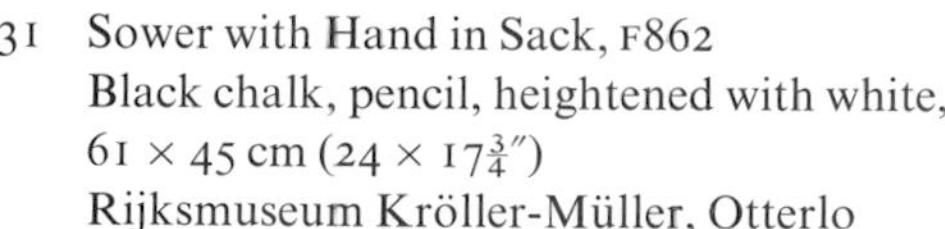

31 Sower with Hand in Sack, F862
Black chalk, pencil, heightened with white, 61 × 45 cm (24 × $17\frac{3}{4}$″)
Rijksmuseum Kröller-Müller, Otterlo

32 Sower with Hand in Sack, F857
Pen, brown ink, heightened with blue, 11.5 × 7 cm ($4\frac{3}{4}$ × $2\frac{3}{4}$″)
Sent with Letter R 1
Private collection, The Hague

33 Sower with Hand in Sack
Sketch in Letter 150
Rijksmuseum Vincent van Gogh, Amsterdam

I immediately tried to make a kind of watercolor, like the sketch above" (Letter 151).

"The sketch above" was the farmhouses on a road with trees (49). Unfortunately, only the sketch in the letter has survived. Drawings 46 and 47 are so close in subject as well as treatment to letter sketches 48 and 49 that I have also placed them in October. The man with broom (45) is clearly a large preliminary study for the figure in landscape 46.

Van Rappard's Criticism

In a letter to Anthon van Rappard of this month—the first that has been preserved from a correspondence that was to last five years—Vincent reported with understandable pride: "I have lately been doing a lot of drawing from models, for I have found a few models who are quite obliging. And I have all sorts of studies of diggers, sowers, and the like, both men and women. I am working a lot with charcoal and conté crayon these days and have also experimented with sepia and watercolor" (Letter R1).

This letter also tells us that Vincent systematically tackled landscapes as well, although once more we do not know the result: "Have made some seven large studies of big tree trunks." At about the same time he also wrote Theo that now and then he "worked with watercolor and sepia" but added that "at the first attempt I am not bringing it off too well right now" (Letter 152). He sent Theo a couple of sketches, one of which corresponds with a drawing that has been preserved (54 and 55), and since the letter was written October 12 to 15, this enables us to date that drawing fairly accurately.

From the next letter it is evident that Van Rappard had expressed some criticism of a small sketch (32) that Vincent had sent him—a criticism that Vincent could hardly disagree with: "Your remark about that figure of the sower when you say 'It is not a man who is sowing, but a man posing as a sower' is quite right." But he added that his drawings were not intended to be anything more than studies after a model: "In a year or two, I will reach the point where I can do a sower who is really sowing" (Letter R2).

Although this series of studies often shows a certain awkwardness in treatment, he did sometimes succeed in creating astonishingly well-observed and well-executed work. Proof of this is the previously mentioned drawing of the peasant sitting by the fireplace (34). On it he wrote rather unobtrusively the title "Worn out" in English. He also used that title in Letter R2, in which he wrote about Van Rappard's trip to Brussels and said that he would like to meet him somewhere: "And I will bring along some drawings, a large one of '*Worn out*' and several others that you do not yet know about." From the way he put this, referring to a drawing that Van Rappard could not yet have seen ("a large one of '*Worn out*' "), I have concluded that the small watercolor after the same subject (51), which also bears this phrase, was enclosed with that letter. This conclusion is supported by the fact that the small sketch comes from Van Rappard's holdings.

It would appear that the meeting between Van Rappard and Vincent was not limited to a short encounter at some railway station,

34

35

36

34 Peasant Sitting by the Fireplace ("Worn out"), F863
Pen, watercolor, 23.5 × 31 cm (9½ × 12¼″)
P. and N. de Boer Foundation, Amsterdam

35 Peasant Sitting by the Fireplace ("Worn out")
Sketch in Letter 150
Rijksmuseum Vincent van Gogh, Amsterdam

36 Field with Thunderstorm, F1676
Pencil, black chalk, washed, heightened with white, 46 × 49 cm (18⅛ × 19¼″)
Private collection, The Netherlands

37 Field with Thunderstorm
Sketch in Letter 150
Rijksmuseum Vincent van Gogh, Amsterdam

38 Digger, F860
Black chalk, 29.5 × 22 cm (11¾ × 8⅝″)
P. and N. de Boer Foundation, Amsterdam

39 Digger and Figure of a Woman
Sketch in Letter 150
Rijksmuseum Vincent van Gogh, Amsterdam

40 Farmer Leaning on His Spade, F861
Black chalk, pen, watercolor, heightened with white, 53 × 23 cm (20⅞ × 9″)
Rijksmuseum Kröller-Müller, Otterlo

41 Farmer Leaning on His Spade
Sketch in Letter 150
Rijksmuseum Vincent van Gogh, Amsterdam

37

38

39

40

41

42

43

44

42 Digger, F860a
Black chalk, heightened with color,
61 × 46 cm (24 × 18$\frac{1}{8}$″)
Private collection, England

43 Digger, F855
Charcoal, watercolor, heightened with white,
52 × 31.5 cm (20$\frac{1}{2}$ × 12$\frac{5}{8}$″)
Rijksmuseum Kröller-Müller, Otterlo

44 Sower (No F Number)
Black chalk, 23.5 × 13.5 cm (9$\frac{1}{4}$ × 5$\frac{1}{4}$″)
Rijksmuseum Vincent van Gogh, Amsterdam

but rather took the form of a conversation at Vincent's parents' home in Etten, for in his next letter to Van Rappard (R3) Vincent wrote: "We all enjoyed your visit very much." On this occasion Vincent must have shown his friend the "large one of '*Worn out*'" (34), but he did not give it to him, for during his stay in The Hague he wrote that he had always kept this drawing (Letter 247). I shall come back to this matter later.

A Love Affair

In the next letters from Etten there is again little information about Vincent's work; nearly all of the space is devoted to lengthy accounts of an affair of an intimate nature. On November 2 Vincent had written (Letter R3) to Van Rappard, who had left for Brussels, that he had again drawn a man digging, a boy cutting grass with a sickle, and a man and a woman at the fireside (54, 61, 63, and 64), but in his letter to Theo on November 3 (Letter 153), he scarcely mentioned his work, saying only that owing to the cold he was now doing almost all his drawing indoors. The rest of the letter was taken up mostly by his love affair. He now told Theo for the first time that in the summer he had fallen in love with a guest, his cousin Kee Vos.* In this and in eight more long letters written to Theo in November, Vincent related in great detail the particulars of his unflagging but unavailing efforts to win Kee's heart. He simply would not accept Kee's "No, at no time, never," and even made a trip to Amsterdam at the beginning of December (after Theo had given him the fare) to visit her at home and to try to win the support of her parents for his efforts. This was all in vain, but the trip did have a bearing on his career as an artist, since after being sent about his business in Amsterdam, he spent a few weeks working in Mauve's studio. This in turn led to his definite decision in January to settle down in The Hague and work there.

A survey of the work done since September discloses that a number of drawings mentioned in Letters 151 and R1, both written on or about October 12, have been lost. Also, we know nothing about the drawings of which there are sketches in these letters (48, 49, and 50). It has already been noted that the closely related landscapes 46 and 47 and the separate figure of a man with a broom (45), a preliminary study for 46, date from this time. Another road with pollard willows is known to us only from the sketch in a letter (58), but the chalk and watercolor drawing of a single pollard willow has been preserved (56). Another watercolor drawing, of the bottom part of a windmill (59), is not mentioned anywhere and is therefore difficult to date, but both style and medium suggest October. The small sketch 51 of the peasant by the fireplace sent with letter R2 of October 15 has already been mentioned. The chalk drawing of a boy on a donkey cart (52) I also assign to this month, on the basis of its atmosphere and style of drawing. Perhaps Vincent was referring to this drawing when he wrote in

*More about this recently widowed young woman, the daughter of the Reverend Mr. Stricker and a sister of Vincent's mother, may be found in *Vincent*, vol. II, no. 4 (1973).

45

47

46

October 1881

45 Man with Broom, F890
Black chalk, watercolor, heightened with white, 55 × 27.5 cm ($21\frac{5}{8} \times 11''$)
Rijksmuseum Kröller-Müller, Otterlo

46 Road with Pollard Willows and Man with Broom, F1678
Pencil, washed, 39.5 × 60.5 cm ($15\frac{3}{4} \times 24''$)
Metropolitan Museum of Art, New York. Robert Lehman Collection

47 Small House on Road with Pollard Willows, F900
Charcoal, heightened with white, 44 × 59.5 cm ($17\frac{3}{8} \times 23\frac{5}{8}''$)
Rijksmuseum Kröller-Müller, Otterlo

48 Road with Pollard Willows
Sketch in Letter 151
Rijksmuseum Vincent van Gogh, Amsterdam

49 Farmhouses on a Road with Trees
Sketch in Letter 151
Rijksmuseum Vincent van Gogh, Amsterdam

50 Road with Pollard Willows
Sketch in Letter R1
Private collection, United States

51 Peasant Sitting by the Fireplace ("Worn out"), F864
Watercolor, 13 × 21 cm ($5\frac{1}{8} \times 8\frac{1}{4}''$)
Sent with Letter R2
Private collection, New York

52 Donkey Cart, F1677
Charcoal, black chalk, washed, heightened with white, 42 × 59.5 cm ($16\frac{1}{2} \times 23\frac{5}{8}''$)
Rijksmuseum Vincent van Gogh, Amsterdam

53 Peasant Woman Sowing with a Basket, F883
Black chalk, watercolor, 62 × 47 cm ($24\frac{3}{8} \times 18\frac{1}{2}''$)
H. Abels Art Gallery, Cologne

54 Digger, F866
Black and colored chalk, watercolor, 62.5 × 47 cm ($24\frac{3}{4} \times 18\frac{1}{2}''$)
Rijksmuseum Vincent van Gogh, Amsterdam

55 Digger
Sketch in Letter 152
Rijksmuseum Vincent van Gogh, Amsterdam

48

49

50

51

52

53

54

55

Letter 151: "I am fooling around with a horse and a donkey." The digger (54) was certainly done in October, as Vincent sent a sketch of it (55) with Letter 152, written around the middle of that month. The peasant woman sowing with a basket (53) is similar in conception to 54. To these I add the girl raking (57), although the distortion of the small figure might suggest the earlier series. The drawing is in black chalk and watercolor and, like 53 and 54, has a landscape as its background.

The boy cutting grass (61) and the man and woman at the fireside (63 and 64) have already been mentioned, and I have grouped the man planting (62) with 60 and 61. Here, as in drawing 27, the model is wearing clothing completely different from that of the other farmers Van Gogh portrayed in Etten. Possibly this man was a "hannikemaaier"—one of the German laborers who came to Holland to mow the grass.

Winter

The difference between this kneeling figure and the other work of this period suggests that it may have been done indoors. I have mentioned that Vincent did work indoors at various times. He explained this in Letter 153, November 3: "I draw a lot and believe it is improving; I use the brush much more than before. It is so cold now that I am indoors almost all the time, drawing figures such as seamstresses, basketmakers and the like." As Vincent's previous letter to Theo was written in the middle of October, a whole series of figures drawn indoors must have been done in the second half of October or, at the latest, in early November. These are drawings 63–75, which, although they are rather laborious studies of figures and interiors, must nonetheless have been done quite rapidly and thus show marked differences in quality. In some we are aware of a disturbing lack of proportion in the figure, as in 69, but at the same time we are struck by the remarkable care with which, for example, the light on the profile has been rendered. Although we do not find a basketmaker among the figures, there are a number of women sewing (67, 69, 70, 71, and 73). It is not difficult to discover the connection between this series and the other figures of women; black chalk and watercolor ("the brush," as Vincent said in Letter 153) are the mediums he chiefly used.

Up to now there was no mention of drawings of children. On November 9 or 10 Vin-

56

57

58

59

60

56 Pollard Willow, F995
Black chalk, watercolor, heightened with white, 58 × 44 cm ($22\frac{7}{8} \times 17\frac{3}{8}$")
Collection Mrs. Julius Joelson, New York

57 Peasant Girl Raking, F884
Black chalk, watercolor, 58 × 46 cm ($22\frac{7}{8} \times 18\frac{1}{8}$")
Museum van Baaren, Utrecht

58 Road with Pollard Willows
Sketch in Letter 152
Rijksmuseum Vincent van Gogh, Amsterdam

59 Bottom Part of a Windmill, F844
Pencil, watercolor, 37 × 55.5 cm ($14\frac{5}{8} \times 22$")
Collection Mrs. M. A. R. van der Leeuw-Wentges, The Hague

61

62

63

64

65

66

67

60 Man Putting Potatoes in a Sack
Sketch in Letter 152
Rijksmuseum Vincent van Gogh, Amsterdam

61 Boy Cutting Grass with a Sickle, F851
Black chalk, watercolor, 47 × 61 cm ($18\frac{1}{2} \times 24''$)
Rijksmuseum Kröller-Müller, Otterlo

62 Kneeling Man, Planting, F879
Charcoal, washed, black chalk, heightened with white, 38.5 × 41.5 cm ($15\frac{3}{8} \times 16\frac{1}{2}''$)
Rijksmuseum Kröller-Müller, Otterlo

63 Farmer Sitting at the Fireside, Reading, F897
Charcoal, watercolor, heightened with white, 45 × 56 cm ($17\frac{3}{4} \times 22''$)
Rijksmuseum Kröller-Müller, Otterlo

64 Woman Sitting at the Fireside, F1216
Black chalk, pencil, watercolor, heightened with white, 45 × 62.5 cm ($17\frac{3}{4} \times 24\frac{3}{4}''$)
Rijksmuseum Kröller-Müller, Otterlo

65 Unfinished Sketch of an Interior with a Pan above the Fire, F888v (reverse: 68)
Black chalk, 32 × 29 cm ($12\frac{5}{8} \times 11\frac{3}{8}''$)
Rijksmuseum Kröller-Müller, Otterlo

66 Woman Peeling Potatoes, F854
Black chalk, watercolor, 59.5 × 47 cm ($23\frac{5}{8} \times 18\frac{1}{2}''$)
Rijksmuseum Kröller-Müller, Otterlo

67 Woman Sewing, F867
Black chalk, watercolor, 49.5 × 31.5 cm ($19\frac{5}{8} \times 12\frac{5}{8}''$)
Location unknown

cent noted: "I am now writing you in the little room with a whole group of men, women, and children from 't Heike ['t Heike—the little moor—was a section of the countryside outside Etten], etc., around me" (Letter 155). Therefore, the only drawings of children (76–79) that are known to us—and were most likely made indoors—may well have been done at the beginning of November, although an earlier date is possible. On the other hand, Vincent wrote shortly before Christmas: "These past few days I have also been drawing children and have found it most enjoyable" (Letter 165). Whether this refers to any of drawings 76–79 cannot be determined with certainty, but it is in any case established from the letter referred to above that Vincent had done some drawings of children by the middle of November.

Only one drawing made in November is specifically mentioned in the letters—the figure of a farmer (80): "I made another one yesterday, a country lad lighting a fire in the morning in the hearth, with the kettle hanging overhead [this drawing has not been preserved], and still another, an old man putting dry twigs on the hearth" (Letter 158, November 18). In spite of the model's rather difficult position, it is one of the most successful of the interior drawings made in October and November. The problems of perspective and proportion have been effectively solved, and Vincent has carefully heightened the drawing with white and red, strikingly rendering the lighting on the farmer's face and clothing.

Apprenticeship with Anton Mauve

In December a distinct change took place in Vincent's work as a result of the instruction he was receiving from Anton Mauve. After his visit to Kee Vos and her parents in Amsterdam, he had gone to The Hague, arriving there November 27, as appears from Letters 162 and 163—written at the beginning of December and about the eighteenth, respectively. In The Hague he spent several weeks working under Mauve's tutelage. Mauve, he wrote, installed him at once before a still life consisting of a couple of old clogs and other objects and made him paint and do watercolors. At the end of his stay in The Hague, Vincent was able to report: "Have now painted five studies and two watercolors and, of course, some rough sketches as well" (Letter 163). We know from the rough sketches drawn in the letter (86–89) and from the descriptions he gave that two of the subjects of the painted studies were: "a terra cotta head of a child with fur cap and a white cabbage with some potatoes, etc." (Letter 163). The rough sketch in the letter (89) is the only evidence we have of the child's head; the still life with the cabbage (in which the clogs he mentioned can be seen) has been preserved (81).In the 1970 *catalogue raisonné* it was suggested, on the grounds of style, that the still life with beer mug and fruits (82) was one of the other painted studies, so it, along with 81, can be regarded as Vincent's first painted works.

The small rough sketches of Scheveningen women sewing and knitting (86–88) were made after watercolors, all three of which have been preserved (83–85). Vincent was quite pleased with these, especially the first

68

69

70

68 Woman Mending Stockings, F888 (reverse: 65)
Black chalk, watercolor, 52 × 32 cm
(20½ × 12⅝″)
Rijksmuseum Kröller-Müller, Otterlo

69 Woman Sewing, F886
Black chalk, watercolor, 59.5 × 44 cm
(23⅝ × 17⅜″)
Collection Martha Stoll, Arlesheim, Switzerland

70 Woman Sewing, F1221
Charcoal, black chalk, watercolor, heightened with white, 62.5 × 47.5 cm (24¾ × 18⅞″)
Rijksmuseum Kröller-Müller, Otterlo

71 Woman Sewing, F885
Black chalk, watercolor, heightened with white, 59 × 45 cm (23¼ × 17¾″)
Rijksmuseum Kröller-Müller, Otterlo

72 Woman Churning Butter, F892
Black chalk, pen, pencil, watercolor, heightened with white, 55 × 32 cm (21⅝ × 12⅝″)
Rijksmuseum Kröller-Müller, Otterlo

71

72

73

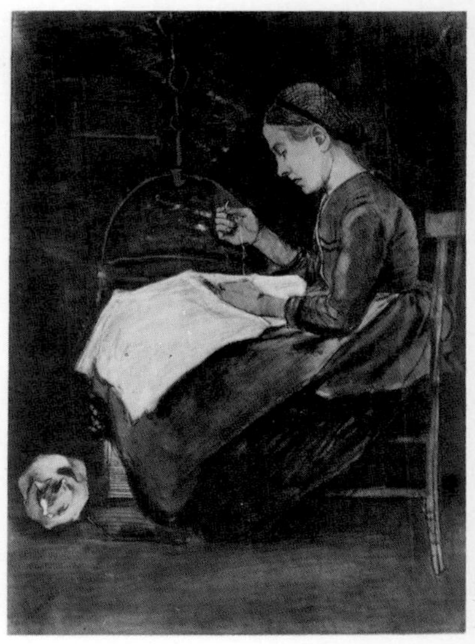

74

76

75

77

73 Young Woman Sewing, F887
Black chalk, watercolor, heightened with white, 60 × 45.5 cm (23⅝ × 18⅛″)
Rijksmuseum Kröller-Müller, Otterlo

74 Mother at the Cradle and Child Sitting on the Floor, F1070
Charcoal, black chalk, watercolor, 46 × 59.5 cm (18⅛ × 23⅝″)
Rijksmuseum Kröller-Müller, Otterlo

75 Woman Grinding Coffee, F889
Pen, pencil, watercolor, heightened with white, 56 × 39 cm (22 × 15⅜″)
Rijksmuseum Kröller-Müller, Otterlo

November 1881

76 Girl Kneeling in Front of a Bucket, F880
Pencil, charcoal, heightened with white, 43 × 55 cm (16⅞ × 21⅝″)
Collection Mr. and Mrs. Leigh B. Block, Chicago

77 Girl Kneeling, F881
Black chalk, pencil, washed, heightened with white, 47.5 × 61.5 cm (18⅞ × 24⅜″)
Private collection, The Hague

two. He felt, he wrote in Letter 163, "that, if it comes to that, these two might just be good enough to sell. Especially one of them, to which Mauve has added a few strokes" (that was 84). Everything indicates that this second trip to The Hague had been extremely profitable for Vincent, thanks to the attention Mauve gave his cousin, fifteen years his junior. Vincent himself wrote: "I cannot tell you how kind and cordial Mauve and Jet [Mauve's wife, and the daughter of one of Vincent's maternal aunts] have been to me during this time. And Mauve has shown me and told me things that I may not be able to do right away but will gradually be able to put into practice" (Letter 163). It was also on Mauve's advice—and because he was running out of money—that he went back to Etten again for a while in order to train himself further in drawing the human figure. His next two letters to Theo once more came from Etten—a long one (Letter 164) and another, written shortly before Christmas (Letter 165), in which he joyfully reported that Mauve had sent him "a paint box with paints, brushes, palette, palette knife, oil, turpentine, in short everything that is needed"—further proof of how well disposed Mauve was toward him at that time. Suddenly, however, a fateful development in Vincent's circumstances wrought a great change in his career.

As early as November, relations between Vincent and his parents had become badly strained as they kept reproaching him about his attitude toward Kee Vos. For a few days the stubborn Vincent had not spoken a single word to them, to make them feel, as he put it, what it meant "to sever ties" (Letter 158). His father had then become very angry and threatened to put him out of the house.

It was probably a soothing letter from Theo that for a while prevented the "protracted and deep-rooted misunderstanding" between them, as Vincent described it (see Letter 161), from leading to an outright break, but at Christmastime the father could take no more. The scene that ensued when Vincent refused to go to church, even as an act of civility as he had done in Etten up to that time, is described in Letter 166: "I became more angry than I can ever remember having been in my life and flatly said that I found the whole system of religion abhorrent. And precisely because I had become too deeply involved in those things during a wretched period of my life, I did not want anything more to do with it and had to be on guard against it as if it were something fatal." What happened next is not hard to understand, for Vincent had attacked the very foundation of his father's life. His father told him that he had better leave the house, and "it was said with such finality that I left the same day."

With the stay at the parsonage in Etten ended, a new and very important period in Vincent's life was dawning: his career as an artist in The Hague.

78

79

80

81

82

83

84

85

86

87

88

89

78 Peasant Girl Standing, F896
Black and red chalk, washed, heightened with blue, 40 × 20.5 cm ($15\frac{3}{4} \times 8\frac{1}{4}$")
Rijksmuseum Kröller-Müller, Otterlo

79 Girl with Black Cap Sitting on the Ground, F873
Black chalk, charcoal, pen, watercolor, heightened with white, 44 × 57 cm ($17\frac{3}{8} \times 22\frac{1}{2}$")
Rijksmuseum Kröller-Müller, Otterlo

80 Farmer Sitting at the Fireplace, F868
Charcoal, washed, heightened with white and red, 56 × 45 cm ($22 \times 17\frac{3}{4}$")
Rijksmuseum Kröller-Müller, Otterlo
December 1881

81 Still Life with Cabbage and Clogs, F1
Paper on panel, 34.5 × 55 cm ($13\frac{3}{8} \times 21\frac{5}{8}$")
Rijksmuseum Vincent van Gogh, Amsterdam

82 Still Life with Beer Mug and Fruits, F1a
44.5 × 57.5 cm ($17\frac{1}{2} \times 22\frac{7}{8}$")
Von der Heydt Museum, Wuppertal

83 Scheveningen Woman Sewing, F869
Watercolor, 48 × 35 cm ($18\frac{7}{8} \times 13\frac{3}{4}$")
P. and N. de Boer Foundation, Amsterdam

84 Scheveningen Woman Knitting, F870
Watercolor, 51 × 35 cm ($20\frac{1}{8} \times 13\frac{3}{4}$")
Private collection, United States

85 Scheveningen Woman Standing, F871
Watercolor, 23.5 × 9.5 cm ($9\frac{1}{2} \times 3\frac{7}{8}$")
Rijksmuseum Vincent van Gogh, Amsterdam

86 Scheveningen Woman Sewing
Sketch in Letter 163
Rijksmuseum Vincent van Gogh, Amsterdam

87 Scheveningen Woman Knitting
Sketch in Letter 163
Rijksmuseum Vincent van Gogh, Amsterdam

88 Scheveningen Woman Standing
Sketch in Letter 163
Rijksmuseum Vincent van Gogh, Amsterdam

89 Sculpture and Still Life with Cabbage and Clogs
Sketches in Letter 163
Rijksmuseum Vincent van Gogh, Amsterdam

The Hague

When Vincent arrived in The Hague, he sought out Anton Mauve. After talking with him, he went to look for a place to live. December 29 he was able to write Theo that he had rented a "studio": "that is, a room with an alcove that is suitable for making into a studio, cheap enough, just outside the city on the Schenkweg, about ten minutes from Mauve's" (Letter 166). He was able to move in on January 1 and up to then had been living in a cheap hotel. In Letter 168, written January 5 or 6, he gave as his address "138 Schenkweg (near the Rhine railway station)." Now, nearly a century later, it has been discovered that this address was not on the Schenkweg (which still exists) but on a side street off the Schenkweg, namely, the Schenkstraat, which at the time was designated as the "third street off the Schenkweg."* The rooms were on the second story in a block of two houses situated in the pastureland along the Schenkweg, which at that time was still a narrow cinder path bordered by trees and a ditch. The sketch in Letter 170(93) and watercolor 99, which present the view from the rear of the house, show the Schenkweg and, behind it, the train sheds of what was then called the Rhine railway, the railroad connection between The Hague and Utrecht. There was a lot of building activity in the area, and this enabled Vincent only a few months later, at the beginning of July, to rent somewhat roomier quarters in a newly built house next door, at 136 Schenkweg.

Vincent's first living quarters—which, as he wrote in Letter 166, he had been "all over the city, as well as in Scheveningen," to find—was a scene of extreme poverty, for he possessed literally nothing. "As to furniture, I will buy just the simplest things, a wooden table, a couple of chairs," he wrote. "For a bed, I would be satisfied with a woolen blanket and the floor. But Mauve insists that I must also have a bed and will lend me the money to buy one, if necessary." Shortly after, the helpful Mauve did in fact advance him the quite considerable sum of 100 guldens to buy furniture. Although the letters do not give any definite information about repayment of this "loan," that debt must have added in no small measure to Vincent's future financial worries.

*For more details, see my article "The Houses Where Van Gogh Lived in The Hague" *Vincent*, vol. I, no. 1 (1970); no. 2 (1971).

Theo's Displeasure

Vincent's stay in The Hague was marked at the outset by a serious disagreement with Theo. When he finally heard from his brother, after having written no fewer than three letters to Paris, it was a sharp rap on the knuckles. "That you have settled in The Hague for good," Theo wrote January 5, "I can fully approve of, and I hope to do all I can to see you through until you are able to earn your keep, but what I do not approve of is the manner you chose to leave Dad and Mom." We know what was in Theo's letter because of an unusual circumstance—Vincent sent it back to him. He did this, he said, not to hurt Theo's feelings, but because he found it to be the quickest way of answering his letter. He put numbers against the main points in Theo's letter and then rebutted them one by one in a lengthy dissertation. This reply (Letter 169) is a remarkable example of Vincent's characteristically clear and independent thinking. In retrospect, one sees that it gives a good insight into the oppressive atmosphere which he felt in his parents' home in Etten. Vincent was particularly incensed at being reproached for not being sufficiently forbearing toward his father and for making life almost impossible for his parents. "Dad is terribly touchy and irritable and completely self-willed around the house and is used to having his own way. . . . Because Dad is an old man, I have been patient with him hundreds of times and have put up with things that are very nearly unbearable." For appearance' sake, Vincent had put matters right by wishing him a happy New Year, but that would have to suffice for the time being so far as he was concerned. "Before it went as far as it did, I suffered much pain and sorrow and had a miserable time of it because things were going so badly between Dad and Mom and me. But now that it has come to pass, well, let it be so, and to tell you the truth, I am not sorry any more, but somehow have a feeling of relief."

After reacting so strongly to Theo's reproaches, Vincent struck another note in the second part of his letter. He thanked Theo for the money he had sent him (for Theo's anger had not kept him from sending the monthly allowance). Since the letter arrived so late, Vincent had had to borrow 25 guldens, this time from Tersteeg. He confessed that he was "going through a period of struggle and despondency, of patience and impatience, of hope and desolation," similar to the year before, when he had had so much trouble putting Mauve's instruction into practice. But he was prepared to fight it out. And the optimism so typical of Vincent seems once more to have gained the upper hand as he continues: "Yet I am enjoying life, and in particular I find it wonderful beyond words that I have my own studio. When are you coming to have coffee or tea with me? Soon, I hope. You could in a pinch stay here, you would find it nice and cozy. I even have some flowers, a few pots with bulbs." One can see the flowers—a few weedy stalks in flowerpots, but at the same time a bit of emerging new life—in various drawings made around that time (90, 92, and 96). What one does not see in the drawings are the other things decorating the studio: Vincent's own drawings from Etten and "marvelous woodcuts" from *The Graphic* and *The Illustrated London News*, which he had bought for 5 guldens from "Blok the second-hand bookdealer"—"an amazing bargain" and "just the thing I have wanted for years."

From a letter written a little more than a week later we learn that he was hard at work. "Mauve has shown me a new way of doing things, namely, painting with watercolors. Well, I am now deeply absorbed in this, and I keep daubing and washing out again, in short, searching and trying" (Letter 170). A pair of sketches in the letter gives an idea of the work that he was in the process of making (91 and 92), but the originals have unfortunately been lost. The third sketch, also in Letter 170, showing the view from the rear of the house, has already been mentioned. Vincent drew this on several occasions, sometimes including details of the foreground, such as the carpenter's work area with the building materials for the new houses and the yard of the laundry that he looked out on. I tend to believe that the sketch in the letter was spontaneously drawn from life and thus independently from the corresponding watercolor (99). The watercolor may have been made somewhat later but at a time when the landscape still had the same wintry look.

Models

In this letter Vincent observed that he was still having a hard time finding models. This indicates that his subsequent housemate, Sien Hoornik, and her little daughter had not yet found their way to the studio. But there may

90

91

92

93

94

95

January 1882

90 Woman at the Window, Knitting, F910a
Watercolor, 33 × 26 cm (13 × $10\frac{1}{4}''$)
Location unknown

91 Girl near the Stove, Grinding Coffee
Sketch in Letter 170
Rijksmuseum Vincent van Gogh, Amsterdam

92 Woman at the Window, Knitting
Sketch in Letter 170
Rijksmuseum Vincent van Gogh, Amsterdam

93 The Schenkweg
Sketch in Letter 170
Rijksmuseum Vincent van Gogh, Amsterdam

94 Waiting Room, F909
Watercolor, 27 × 37.5 cm ($10\frac{5}{8}$ × 15″)
Collection Mrs. J. K. Thannhauser, New York

95 Scheveningen Woman, F946v (reverse: 158)
Watercolor, 32 × 52 cm ($12\frac{5}{8}$ × $20\frac{1}{2}''$) (bottom part of the page torn off)
Collection W. Brinkman, Schipluiden, The Netherlands

have been an initial contact, as suggested by his remark "Although I am now discussing the matter with a mother who has a young child, I am afraid that this will prove to be too expensive for me." January 22 he wrote: "I have already had various models, but they are either too expensive, or they find it too far to come, or they later complain about it and cannot come back on a regular basis. But I think I may have been lucky with this little woman" (Letter 172). He was referring to a "little old woman" shown in sketch 92 and watercolor 90. We must assume that by March 3 Vincent had been working with Sien for some time, because that day he wrote: "Since I received your letter and the money [that is, since Vincent's letter of February 18], I have had a model every single day, and I am up to my ears in work. This one is a new model, although I had made superficial drawings of her before. Or rather, there is more than one model, as I have already had three people from the same house, a woman of about forty-five, who looks just like a figure by Edouard Frère, and also her daughter, thirty or thereabouts, and a younger child of ten or eleven. They are poor people, and I must say that their willingness is boundless" (Letter 178). This was the first mention of the people who were to play such an importat role in the next two years of Vincent's life: Sien (Clasina Maria Hoornik, thirty-two), her mother (Maria Wilhelmina Hoornik, fifty-three), and her youngest sister (Maria Wilhelmina, ten). At this time Vincent makes no mention of Sien's little daughter, also called Maria Wilhelmina, who is often to be seen in later drawings. At the beginning of 1882 she was not yet five years old, so she could not be the "younger child of ten or eleven."

Apart from his financial problems Vincent also had other major worries that at first he kept to himself. From Letter 173, January 26, we learn that he had spent almost three whole days in bed "with fever and nerves," caused, among other things, by the fact that he had only a few guldens left and did not know how he could get through the rest of the week (Letters 171 and 172). But his illness had also to do with the difficulties that had arisen with the man whom he needed almost as much as Theo—Anton Mauve. The tragedy with Mauve—and it was no less than that—comes to us only bit by bit, as we piece together the details from the letters in February and after.

Problems with Mauve

February 13 Vincent wrote Theo that "lately he [Mauve] has treated me most unkindly," but he immediately added, glossing over it, that this was understandable in view of Mauve's illness. Earlier in the letter he had said: "I have to give you bad news, which is that Mauve is again very unwell—the usual, of course." We must assume that this unspecified illness was another attack of depression, from which Mauve had been suffering for years and which made dealing with him far from easy. It also seems significant that the painter Weissenbruch ("about the only one who is still received by Mauve") had come to see Vincent and told him that his visit "was actually motivated by the fact that Mauve, who had some doubt about me, had

96

97

98

96 Scheveningen Woman at Mantelpiece, Sewing
Sketch in Letter 171
Rijksmuseum Vincent van Gogh, Amsterdam

97 Town View of The Hague with New Church, F1680
Watercolor, pen, ink, 24.5 × 35.5 cm ($9\frac{7}{8} \times 14\frac{1}{8}''$)
Private collection, The Netherlands

98 Barren Field, F904
Watercolor, charcoal, black chalk, 45 × 60 cm ($17\frac{3}{4} \times 23\frac{5}{8}''$)
Location unknown
February 1882

99 Meadows near Rijswijk and the Schenkweg, F910
Watercolor, 38 × 56 cm (15 × 22″)
Private collection, London

100 Laundry in The Hague, F1040
Watercolor, 26 × 37.5 cm ($10\frac{1}{4} \times 15''$)
Rijksmuseum Vincent van Gogh, Amsterdam

101 Sien with Umbrella and Prayer Book, F1052
Pencil, black chalk, 45.5 × 22 cm ($18\frac{1}{8} \times 8\frac{5}{8}''$)
Private collection, The Hague

99

101

102

103

104

105

102 Sien under Umbrella with Girl, F 1048
Pencil, heightened with white, 45 × 25.5 cm (17¾ × 10¼″)
Private collection, The Hague

103 Standing Woman, Half-Length, F 840
Black chalk, pencil, watercolor, 42 × 25.5 cm (16½ × 10¼″)
Private collection, Haarlem

104 Sien with Child on Her Lap, F 1071
Pencil, 54 × 41.5 cm (21¼ × 16½″)
Rijksmuseum Kröller-Müller, Otterlo

105 Bending Woman, F 899
Pencil, pen, 40 × 30 cm (15¾ × 11¾″)
Location unknown

sent him in order to get Weissenbruch's opinion regarding my work." We can easily imagine how much Vincent, already worried, must have been upset by all this. Fortunately, Weissenbruch's opinion was favorable, but apparently this did not have any effect so far as Mauve was concerned. "Of late, Mauve has been of almost no help to me at all, and one day he even said to me: 'I am not always in the mood to help you out; sometimes I am so tired that you must, for heaven's sake, wait for a better time'" (Letter 175). It was not until much later, in Letter 189, written in the middle of April, that we get a clearer idea of what had happened: "At the end of January, about two weeks, I believe, after I arrived here, Mauve suddenly started acting very different toward me—his unkindness was just as striking as his kindness had been at first." The anxiety about Mauve's lacking confidence in Vincent's latent abilities appears now as the main cause of the illness he had mentioned in Letter 172: "I attributed this to dissatisfaction with my work, and it made me so worried and tense that it completely upset me and made me ill, as I wrote you at the time."

This, incidentally, is the letter that mentions the anecdote about drawing from plaster casts that has found its way into many books about Van Gogh, mainly with the aim of giving some insight into his character. In my opinion its main value is the light that it sheds on the tense relationship with Mauve. It is probably more typical of Vincent that, despite his aversion to drawing from plaster casts, he did it very patiently for a long time during his stays in Antwerp and Paris. But this is the story in his own words: "In his conversation Mauve became as narrow-minded as he had, if I may put it this way, been broad-minded before. I had to draw from plaster casts, that more than anything else. I was completely fed up with drawing from plaster casts; anyway, I had a couple of hands and feet hanging in the studio—but not for the purpose of drawing from them. He once talked to me about drawing from plaster casts in a way that the worst teacher at the academy would not have done, and I kept my temper. But when I got home I became so angry about this that I threw the poor plaster molds into the coal scuttle, where they smashed to pieces. And I thought to myself: I will draw from plaster casts when you fellows are whole and white again, and there are no more hands and feet of living people to be drawn.

"Then I said to Mauve: Don't talk to me about plaster any more because I can't stand it. After that a note from Mauve that he would not have anything to do with me for two months."

In addition to describing the *fact* of Mauve's changed mood without dissembling, Vincent now also presented the explanation. Mauve, he felt, had been set against him by Tersteeg, who—which was even worse—had also tried to influence Theo. At the end of April, Theo had written a letter in which he attempted to get Vincent to put them both out of his mind, and Vincent thereupon showed himself to be only too ready to assume that "the change in Mauve and Tersteeg was to some extent only apparent" and

107

108

March 1882

106 Woman with White Bonnet (Sien's Mother), Head, F1009a
Black and colored chalk, pencil, 36 × 26 cm (14⅛ × 10¼″)
Gemeentemuseum, The Hague (on loan from Paul Citroen)

107 Girl Standing, Knitting, F983
Pencil, 52 × 25.5 cm (20½ × 10¼″)
Collection A. Hailparn, New York

108 Sitting Girl, Knitting, F984
Pencil, 43 × 26.5 cm (16⅞ × 10⅝″)
Location unknown

109 Old Woman Seen from Behind, F913
Pencil, pen, brown ink, 57 × 32 cm (22½ × 12⅝″)
Rijksmuseum Vincent van Gogh, Amsterdam

110 Old Woman Seen from Behind
Sketch in Letter 178
Rijksmuseum Vincent van Gogh, Amsterdam

111 Old Street (The Paddemoes), F918
Pen, pencil, 25 × 31 cm (9⅞ × 12¼″)
Rijksmuseum Kröller-Müller, Otterlo

112 Bakery on the Geest, F914
Pencil, pen, 20.5 × 33.5 cm (8¼ × 13⅜″)
Private collection, The Hague

601

110

111

112

113

114

115

113 Scheveningen Road, F920
Pencil, pen, 20 × 33.5 cm ($7\frac{7}{8} \times 13\frac{3}{8}''$)
Private collection, The Hague

114 Sand Diggers, F922
Pencil, 27 × 20 cm ($10\frac{5}{8} \times 7\frac{7}{8}''$)
Location unknown

115 Bridge near the Schenkweg, F917
Pencil, 21.5 × 33.5 cm ($8\frac{3}{8} \times 13\frac{3}{8}''$)
Private collection, The Hague

was attributable to his own mood (Letter 195, May 1). Yet his first analysis was undoubtedly correct. This is shown only too clearly by the fact that Mauve, even at the end of the two months, would have nothing more to do with Vincent and made no reply when Vincent wrote him a note in an attempt at reconciliation (he then felt, Vincent said in Letter 190, "as if something were choking him"). A few days later, when they met by chance, and Vincent asked Mauve if he would come and see his work, Mauve retorted: "Come and see you I won't; it is all finished" (Letter 192). Concerning Tersteeg and the part he played, Vincent is too explicit in his language for one to consider it a matter of mere impressions and suppositions: "I found that out from Tersteeg himself, when he made it clear to me that he would see to it that the money you send me would be stopped: 'Mauve and I will make it our business to put an end to that'" (Letter 189, repeated in almost the same words in Letter 191).

Living with Sien

Theo deserves great credit for not letting his brother down, not even when, from a letter written at the beginning of May (Letter 192), he learned something that Vincent had been concealing from him—that he had taken in as a permanent model a woman who was bound to give offense to his family and friends alike. She was a prostitute, the unwed mother of a five-year-old daughter, and was expecting a second child—and Vincent intended to marry her. I will not go too deeply into Vincent's letters about this since they have been quoted frequently, but they are full of dramatic, even pathetic, expressions ("What is more civilized, more sensitive, more manly, to abandon a woman, or to draw someone who has been abandoned to oneself?"). Theo does not seem to have succumbed at once to Vincent's pleas for approval. It was only after letting him wait a considerable time to take a clear stand in this conflict of morals and social conventions that Theo reluctantly accepted Vincent's manner of living. See Letters 192, 194, 197, 198, 193, 199, 200, 202, and 203—written in this sequence, and all in May. An important fact, first of all, is that Theo had sent a letter May 13 in which he expressed disapproval of Vincent's relationship with Sien and tried to dissuade him from marrying her, but nevertheless sent him 50 francs. Another fact is that Vincent was not at all impressed by Theo's admonitions ("I therefore think that, for the most part, your letter was all wrong"), and that without making any concessions, he was able to prevail upon Theo to continue his help. In Letter 204, June 1 or 2, he was able to write: "I need not tell you what a godsend your letter was." Theo had sent 100 francs and, in addition, had even promised to remit from then on 150 francs every month in three installments, on the first, tenth, and twentieth of the month. The good news came at a time when Vincent had been reduced to dire straits. On May 30, fearing that he would be put out of his house and that his meager belongings would be sold if he could not pay his landlord the back rent of 12.50 guldens, he begged his brother: "Do not let it come to this scandal" (Postcard 203). He wrote in English as he sometimes

116

117

118

116 Ditch along the Schenkweg, F921
Pen, pencil, black chalk, heightened with white, 18.5 × 34 cm ($7\frac{1}{2} \times 13\frac{3}{8}$″)
Rijksmuseum Kröller-Müller, Otterlo

117 Factory, F925
Pencil, pen, 24 × 33 cm ($9\frac{1}{2} \times 13$″)
Private collection, Zurich

118 Gas Tanks, F924
Chalk, pencil, 24 × 33.5 cm ($9\frac{1}{2} \times 13\frac{3}{8}$″)
Private collection, The Hague

119 Van Stolkpark, F922a
Black chalk, charcoal, pen, heightened with white, 18 × 33.5 cm ($7\frac{1}{8} \times 13\frac{3}{8}$″)
Collection Mrs. M. Feilchenfeldt, Zurich

120 Backyards, F939a
Charcoal, 24 × 35 cm ($9\frac{1}{2} \times 13\frac{3}{4}$″)
Galerie St. Etienne, New York

121 Bridge near the Herengracht, F1679
Pencil, washed with ink, heightened with white, 24 × 33.5 cm ($9\frac{1}{2} \times 13\frac{3}{8}$″)
Rijksmuseum Vincent van Gogh, Amsterdam

122 Nursery on the Schenkweg, F915
Pencil, heightened with chalk and sepia, 40 × 69 cm ($15\frac{3}{4} \times 27\frac{1}{8}$″)
Collection Mrs. A. R. W. Nieuwenhuizen Segaar-Aarse, The Hague

123 Rhine Station, F919
Pencil and pen, 24 × 33.5 cm ($9\frac{1}{2} \times 13\frac{3}{8}$″)
Private collection, The Hague

124 Country Road in Loosduinen near The Hague, F1089
Black chalk, pen, heightened with white, 26 × 35.5 cm ($10\frac{1}{4} \times 14\frac{1}{8}$″)
Rijksmuseum Vincent van Gogh, Amsterdam

125 Nursery on the Schenkweg, F923
Black chalk, pen, washed, heightened with white, 23.5 × 33 cm ($9\frac{1}{2} \times 13$″)
Stedelijk Museum, Amsterdam
(on loan from the Rijksmuseum, Amsterdam)

126 Pawnshop (No F Number)
Pencil, pen, heightened with white, 24 × 34 cm ($9\frac{1}{2} \times 13\frac{3}{8}$″)
Rijksmuseum Vincent van Gogh, Amsterdam

127 Two Boys near a Cart ("The Dustman"), F1078a
Pencil, 20.5 × 32 cm ($8\frac{1}{4} \times 12\frac{5}{8}$″)
Location unknown (formerly in Leipzig)

119

120

121

122

123

124

125

126

127

did when he had to use a postcard because he did not have the money to buy a stamp for a letter.

How did Vincent's work fare amid all these difficulties? In February, it appears from Letter 175, he seems to have continued making watercolors (99 and 100). He had also worked mainly with models (Letters 177 and 178), such as the child in 107 and 108, and he had certainly started on drawings of Sien and her family. It is difficult to establish which were the first drawings with these models; in my opinion 101–5 must have been among them. However, some of the drawings that are attributed to later months could actually date from as early as February. In March he did a considerable amount of drawing in the streets, sometimes together with the painter George Hendrik Breitner. Letter 178 reports: "Yesterday evening I was out on the street with him again looking for typical figures that could later be studied in the studio" (109 and 110).

Vincent's First Commission

An important event was a visit March 11 by his uncle, the art dealer Cornelis Marinus. When he had seen some small drawings showing views of the city (111, 112, and an unknown drawing of the Vleersteeg, an alleyway in the old part of The Hague), he ordered twelve in the same style. Vincent, who called this "almost miraculous" (Letter 180), was of course glad to accept the order and immediately fixed the price at 1 rijksdaalder (2.50 guldens) apiece. C.M. promised his nephew that he would order a further dozen at a higher price, provided the first group was to his liking. Vincent was able to send off the drawings within two weeks (Letter 183). On the basis of a comparison of all available data (such as which drawings had been in C.M.'s possession), I have been able to determine with a high degree of certainty that the following drawings belonged to this group: 111–19, 121, and 126. These must therefore have been completed before March 24. As Vincent wrote in Letter 183, he went out "almost daily to do these small drawings of city scenes" and probably completed drawings 122 and 123 before the end of the month. Drawing 124, although somewhat different in character since it is a country scene, belongs here. C.M. later expressed disappointment about the outcome of this transaction, but we can only say now that Vincent had made marked and rapid progress in depicting large areas and characteristic details. In most of the drawings there are hardly any human figures, but when he does show people, as in drawings 114 and 126, he strives for a pithy characterization. That this was sometimes preceded by thorough preliminary study is demonstrated by the small figure of the woman with a shawl in the drawing of the bakery on the Geest (112), for he had earlier drawn this same figure separately in a large format (109 and 110).

Of greatest interest to us for documentary reasons is drawing 122, described by Vincent himself in Letter 183 as the "horticultural nursery of the Schenkweg" and simply called "group of houses" in the 1970 *catalogue raisonné*. The interesting point is that the two

128

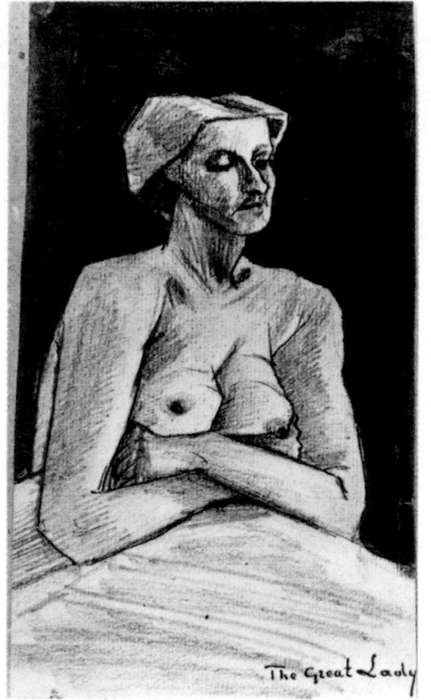

129

130

April 1882

128 Naked Woman, Half-Length
("The Great Lady")
Sketch in Letter 185
Rijksmuseum Vincent van Gogh, Amsterdam

129 "Sorrow," F929 (cf. lithograph 259)
Pencil, washed, 45.5 × 29.5 cm (18⅛ × 11¾")
Private collection, The Hague

130 "Sorrow," F929a
Black chalk, 44.5 × 27 cm (17¾ × 10⅝")
Garman-Ryan Collection, London

131 Torn-Up Street with Diggers, F930a
Pencil, pen, heightened with white and colors, 43 × 63 cm (16⅞ × 24¾")
Nationalgalerie, East Berlin

132 Diggers in Torn-Up Street
Sketch reproduced with Letter 190
(reverse: 133)
Rijksmuseum Vincent van Gogh, Amsterdam

133 Head of a Man
Sketch reproduced with Letter 190
(reverse: 132)
Rijksmuseum Vincent van Gogh, Amsterdam

134 Two Men with a Four-Wheeled Wagon, F1078
Pencil, 21 × 34 cm (8¼ × 13⅜")
Rijksmuseum Kröller-Müller, Otterlo

132

133

134

135

136

137

135 Man and Boy Sitting under a Roof, F 1077
Pencil, 24 × 34 cm ($9\frac{1}{2}$ × $13\frac{3}{8}$″)
Location unknown

136 Saw Mill, F901
Black chalk, heightened with white,
31 × 37.5 cm ($12\frac{1}{4}$ × 15″)
Location unknown

137 Blacksmith Shop, F 1084
Pencil, pen, washed, heightened with
white, 37 × 26 cm ($14\frac{5}{8}$ × $10\frac{1}{4}$″)
Rijksmuseum Kröller-Müller, Otterlo

different apartments in which Vincent lived in 1882 and 1883 were situated in the block of houses extending to the right side of the drawing. His first "studio" was in the somewhat higher building with the four doors and was on the left-hand side of the upper floor. His second apartment, into which he moved in July 1882, was on the upper floor to the left of the first one.

"Sorrow"

In April obviously Vincent was to continue with his drawings for C.M., who had paid him and placed a new order for six detailed views of the city specified in advance (Letter 184, early April). However, during the month, Vincent wrote that he had been unable to make any progress with those drawings because of the raw, wet weather (Letter 191). Another reason was undoubtedly the continuing tension about his situation, evident in Letter 199, written about May 16. We know that at the beginning of April he had again been drawing figures, as can be gathered from the strange, harshly realistic sketch 128 with its sarcastic title—the only surviving example of "many studies of fragments of the figure, heads, neck, breast, shoulders" mentioned by Vincent. We are, however, compensated by a very important drawing that he had titled "*Sorrow*" (129 and 130). After a struggle of scarcely three months in The Hague, Vincent here proved that he was capable of creating a *coup de maître*. He realized himself that this drawing far surpassed his previous work: "Enclosed is what in my opinion is the best figure I have yet drawn, and that is why I thought I would send it to you." Apart from sketches in his letters, this was the first thing he had yet sent Theo from The Hague, and he was somewhat formal in announcing that he was dispatching it: "Today I mailed you 1 drawing, which I am sending you as a token of gratitude for all that you have done for me during this otherwise inclement winter. When you had the large woodcut of Millet's *La Bergère* [*The Shepherdess*] with you last summer, I thought: How much one can do with a single line. I do not, of course, profess to be able to express as much with a single contour line as Millet. Even so I have tried to put some feeling into this figure. I now do hope that this drawing is to your liking" (Letter 186).

Curiously there are two different versions of this drawing: "You ought to know that I had two underlayers beneath my paper. I worked very hard to get the contour right, and when I took the drawing off the board, it had been traced very clearly onto the two underlayers, and so I immediately touched it up from the first study" (Letter 186). The drawing that had been "touched up" is 130, while 129 is one of the other two, which, Vincent wrote, he wanted to keep for himself. It is either the original or the other one that was traced through onto the underlayer. The third one is missing. It appears from Vincent's account that the floral embellishments in 130 do not belong to the original but are part of the "touching up." There is also the somewhat melodramatic quotation from Michelet: "Comment se fait-il qu'il y ait sur la terre une femme seule, délaissée!" ("How can it be that there is on earth a wom-

138

139

140

138 Nursery on the Schenkweg, F930
Pencil, pen, black chalk, heightened with white, 29.5 × 58.5 cm (11$\frac{3}{4}$ × 23$\frac{1}{4}$″)
Metropolitan Museum of Art, New York

139 Man Sitting by a Stove (The Pauper), F1116a (reverse: 499)
Pencil, black chalk, 44 × 35 cm (17$\frac{3}{8}$ × 13$\frac{3}{4}$″)
Location unknown

140 Woman in a Dark Dress (Sien's Mother?), F936
Pencil, pen, brush, sepia, 61 × 37 cm (24 × 14$\frac{5}{8}$″)
Rijksmuseum Kröller-Müller, Otterlo

141 Sien with Cigar Sitting on the Floor near a Stove, F898
Pencil, black chalk, pen, brush, sepia, heightened with white, 45.5 × 56 cm (18$\frac{1}{8}$ × 22″)
Rijksmuseum Kröller-Müller, Otterlo

142 Study of a Tree, F933 (reverse: 371)
Black and white chalk, black ink, pencil, watercolor, 50 × 69 cm (19$\frac{5}{8}$ × 27$\frac{1}{8}$″)
Rijksmuseum Kröller-Müller, Otterlo

141

142

143

144

145

146

147

May 1882

143 Bent Figure of a Woman (Sien?), F935
Pencil, pen, brush, sepia, washed,
58 × 42 cm ($22\frac{7}{8} \times 16\frac{1}{2}''$)
Rijksmuseum Kröller-Müller, Otterlo

144 Bent Figure of a Woman, F937
Pencil, pen, brush, sepia, washed,
58 × 43 cm ($22\frac{7}{8} \times 16\frac{7}{8}''$)
Rijksmuseum Kröller-Müller, Otterlo

145 Figure of a Woman with Unfinished Chair, F932
Pencil, black chalk, washed, 58 × 45.5 cm
($22\frac{7}{8} \times 18\frac{1}{8}''$)
Rijksmuseum Kröller-Müller, Otterlo

146 Sien's Mother's House, F941
Pencil, heightened with white, 29 × 45 cm
($11\frac{3}{8} \times 17\frac{3}{4}''$)
Private collection, The Hague

147 Sien's Mother's House, Closer View, F942
Pencil, pen, heightened with white,
46 × 59.5 cm ($18\frac{1}{8} \times 23\frac{5}{8}''$)
Collection R. M. Light & Co.,
Santa Barbara, California

an alone, forsaken!") But Vincent put this only on the drawing intended for Theo.

A great deal has been written about this large drawing because it is very significant for the background of Vincent's artistic expression, which was influenced to such a large extent by his social concern. The drawing unmistakably represents Sien; Vincent himself said so in a letter in July: "My very best drawing, '*Sorrow*'—at least I consider this the best thing I have done—she posed for that" (Letter 219). At the same time it was more than just a portrait; it was the depiction of a woman's life and a woman's sorrow in a general sense. That same month Vincent drew "*Sorrow*" again, this time on a larger scale (this drawing no longer exists), and sent it, together with a drawing of tree roots, to Theo for his birthday, May 1. In Letter 195 he wrote: "I have now tried to put the same sentiment in the landscape as I have in the figure. It shows the grim tenacity and passionate intensity with which they hold onto the earth although they are half uprooted by the gales. I wanted to express the struggle for life in both that white, slender figure of the woman and those angry, gnarled, black roots." A clear statement of what he intended, which is all the more remarkable because Vincent almost never wrote anything about symbolic intentions in his work.

In a study like this, which places the emphasis on the development of Vincent's work chronologically, it is of particular importance that with this drawing, which can be dated very precisely, before us, we can have no further doubts about his talents as a draftsman. Nor can there be any doubt about the effort he must have made to attain such great technical proficiency and power of expression around the beginning of April 1882—hardly six months after the still somewhat stilted and at times even clumsily drawn figures he did in Etten.

At the same time it should be recognized that "*Sorrow*," from the viewpoint of style, occupies a special place among Vincent's works. This is how he put it himself: "It is obvious that I do not always draw like this. But I very much like the English drawings that have been done in this style, and thus it is not very surprising that I have given it a try myself" (Letter 186).In the matter of a single contour line, he had, of course, already referred to Millet's *La Bergère*. However, in my opinion the strongest influence on the style of drawing came from his recollections of Bargue's *Exercices au Fusain* with their figures in outline on a white background (the comparison here should be made not with the touched-up version of "*Sorrow*," but with the drawing in its original form). Vincent must have been aware of this, for in Letter 185—just before he sent "*Sorrow*" to Theo—he wrote: "I do not yet have many nude studies but there still are some that are very much like the Bargues; are they for that reason less original? Perhaps it could be rather that I learned from the Bargues how to see nature more clearly."

"An Artist"

Soon after he had drawn nudes like "*Sorrow*," Vincent again started to work outdoors a great deal. He mentioned both kinds of

148

149

150

148 Sien, Pregnant, Walking with Older Woman, F988a
Pencil, 45.5 × 26 cm ($18\frac{1}{8} \times 10\frac{1}{4}''$)
Location unknown

149 Woman with Hat, Coat, and Pleated Dress, F1050
Pencil, 32 × 15.5 cm ($12\frac{5}{8} \times 6\frac{1}{4}''$)
Rijksmuseum Kröller-Müller, Otterlo

150 Carpenter's Yard and Laundry, F939
Pencil, pen, brush, heightened with white, 28.5 × 47 cm ($11\frac{3}{8} \times 18\frac{1}{2}''$)
Rijksmuseum Kröller-Müller, Otterlo

151 Fish-Drying Barn, F946a
Pencil, pen, India ink, heightened with white, 27.5 × 46.5 cm ($11 \times 18\frac{1}{2}''$)
Groninger Museum, Groningen

152 Fish-Drying Barn, Seen from a Height, F938
Pencil, pen, brush, heightened with white, 28 × 44 cm ($11 \times 17\frac{3}{8}''$)
Rijksmuseum Kröller-Müller, Otterlo

June 1882

153 Carpenter's Yard and Laundry, F944
Black chalk, heightened with white, 27 × 43.5 cm ($10\frac{5}{8} \times 17\frac{3}{8}''$)
Private collection, New York

154 Fish-Drying Barn, F940
Pencil, pen, heightened with white, 28.5 × 45 cm ($11\frac{3}{8} \times 17\frac{3}{4}''$)
Private collection, Basel

July 1882

155 Cradle
Sketch in Letter 218
Rijksmuseum Vincent van Gogh, Amsterdam

156 Rooftops, F943
Watercolor, heightened with white, 39 × 55 cm ($15\frac{3}{8} \times 21\frac{5}{8}''$)
Private collection, Paris

157 Rooftops
Sketch in Letter 220
Rijksmuseum Vincent van Gogh, Amsterdam

151

152

153

154

155

156

157

work in the same sentence: "I again have a drawing of a female figure like '*Sorrow*,' but larger and I believe better than the first one, and I am making a drawing of a street where they are working on the sewer or the water main and thus there are diggers in a trench" (Letter 189). The first drawing, as already mentioned, has been lost. As to the second (131), the sketch made at the site has been preserved (132). Vincent sent it to Theo with Letter 190, in which he announced with some pride: "I now come to this little sketch—it was made on the Geest, in the drizzle, in a street where I stood in mud amid all that bustle and noise, and I am sending it to you to let you see that my sketchbook proves I try to capture things in action." This remark refers to the criticism from Tersteeg, who had said: "In the past you did not do well and failed, and now it is exactly the same" (Letter 190). Vincent was still feeling his way along, but he was convinced of one thing: he was an artist. "Roaming around lumberyards and alleys and streets and inside houses, waiting rooms, even saloons, that is not a very pleasant occupation, *unless one happens to be an artist*. But as such, one would rather be in the most disreputable neighborhood, provided there is something to draw, than at a tea party with nice ladies" (Letter 190).

The pencil-and-chalk drawing of Sien sitting by the stove (141) seems, in my opinion, to date from April or perhaps a little earlier; it is not mentioned in any letter. The same date would apply to a man by the stove (139), which, I believe, can be identified with *The Pauper*, referred to by Vincent in Letter 195 as a drawing he still had lying about. If these two drawings were actually made in April, then it was before Vincent wrote Letter 188 (which cannot be dated any more precisely than between April 15 and 27), for he then wrote that there was now more space in the studio, "all the more so as the stove is gone." Although the 1970 *catalogue raisonné* has placed *The Pauper* in the Etten period, I am more inclined to regard it as work belonging to the period when Vincent worked in The Hague. The man is wearing shoes rather than the clogs the farmers in Etten wore, and he is sitting by a potbellied stove and a black mantelpiece that can also be seen in sketches and drawings made in The Hague (91, 140, 141, and 155). Furthermore, stylistically it fits The Hague period better.

The study of a tree, 142, presents another problem. In my view it cannot be identified with the drawing *Les Racines* (*The Roots*), which Vincent mentioned in Letter 195, although there certainly is a relationship. There he wrote: "*Les Racines* is some tree roots in sandy soil," and goes on: "Although *Les Racines* is only a pencil drawing, there has been some brushing in with pencil, and this has been scraped off again, in the same way as one works with paint." So neither the description nor the technique provides grounds for identifying *Les Racines* as 142, even though the heavy roots form a very pronounced element of the drawing. Vincent said in Postcard 196 that he could not send *Les Racines* rolled up because it was mounted on cardboard, but he would send a second drawing, *A Root in a Dry Ground*, which was

158

159

160

158 Bleaching Ground, F946 (reverse: 95)
Watercolor, heightened with white, 32 × 52 cm (12⅝ × 20½″)
Collection W. Brinkman, Schipluiden, The Netherlands

159 Fishing Boats on the Beach
Sketch in Letter 220
Rijksmuseum Vincent van Gogh, Amsterdam

160 Fish-Drying Barn, F945
Watercolor, 35.5 × 52 cm (14⅛ × 20½″)
Collection B. E. Bensinger, Chicago

161 Meadows near Rijswijk, F927
Watercolor, 30 × 49 cm (11¾ × 19¼″)
Collection Stephen Hahn, New York

162 Meadow, in the Background New Church and Jacob's Church, F916
Watercolor, heightened with white, 30 × 52.5 cm (11¾ × 20⅞″)
Location unknown

163 Bleaching Ground
Sketch in Letter 220
Rijksmuseum Vincent van Gogh, Amsterdam

164 Pollard Willow, F947
Watercolor, 36 × 56.5 cm (14⅛ × 22¼″)
Location unknown

165 Pollard Willow
Sketch in Letter 221
Rijksmuseum Vincent van Gogh, Amsterdam

161

163

162

164

165

166

167

168

169

166 Iron Mill in The Hague, F 926
Watercolor, 33.5 × 59.5 cm (13⅜ × 23⅝″)
Location unknown

167 Houses in Scheveningen, Seen from the Dunes, F 1041
Pencil, black and white chalk, watercolor, 43.5 × 60 cm (17⅜ × 23⅝″)
Rijksmuseum Vincent van Gogh, Amsterdam

168 Country Lane with Trees, F 1088
Watercolor, 24 × 35 cm (9½ × 13¾″)
Location unknown

169 Woman with White Shawl in a Wood, F 949
Watercolor, 34.5 × 24 cm (13½ × 9½″)
Collection A. Farmanformaian, Tehran

"very similar." This title (given in English) definitely does not fit the subject of 142 (although it does correspond with Vincent's description of *Les Racines* as "some tree roots in sandy soil"), yet Dr. Anna Szymanska has proposed to regard the study of trees as identical with this second drawing.* On the reverse of 142 is the drawing of a blind man (371), which I place in 1883, like the 1970 *catalogue raisonné*. If 142 was indeed sent to Theo May 2, we must presume that Theo returned it later (Vincent often asked for old drawings to be returned so that he could use them as material for study), and that Vincent used the paper a second time in 1883. In my opinion it is more probable that 142 is a *third* drawing, made at the same time and in the same surroundings as *Les Racines* and *A Root in a Dry Ground*.

Woman in a Dark Dress (140), a drawing mentioned in Letter 195, May 1, dates from the end of April. It fits in with drawings 143, 144, and 145, which must date from the beginning of May, in view of a reference to them in Letter 192 (which must have been written between May 3 and 12, that is, after Letter 195). These four very carefully executed drawings demonstrate the mastery Vincent had achieved after four months of working in The Hague.

The Second Series for C.M.

In May, Vincent continued his work on the drawings intended for C.M. This commission resulted in some of the best landscape drawings of The Hague period, such as the view from the back of his lodgings: *Carpenter's Yard and Laundry* (150), well known from many reproductions. He made an almost identical version for Theo (153). In Letter 200 he wrote about the drawings for C.M.: "I can see such drawings only as studies of perspective, and I therefore make them chiefly as a means of getting practice." Drawings like those of the carpenter's yard, as well as those of the fish-drying barn in the adjacent dunes (151, 152, and 154), do indeed strike us with their sense of space and the apparently effortless way in which the many divergent and well-observed details of those complicated compositions have been fitted into the overall scheme. Vincent could justifiably write about the carpenter's yard—and this holds good also for the other drawings of this group—"As you see there are many planes in this drawing, and one may look around in them, or through them, in various holes and corners" (Letter 205).

The chronology of these studies is quite certain as a result of the many references in the letters. The drawing of the view from Vincent's window (150), intended for C.M., is first mentioned in Letter 202 of May 27, in which Vincent writes that Van Rappard had dropped in that day and had seen the drawing. In Letter R8, written the following day, we are told that Vincent had done still more work on it with a pen, so it seems unlikely that the drawing was made much before the second half of May. As to the companion drawing (153), we read in Letter 204 of June

*See the Van Gogh catalogue of the Rijksmuseum Kröller-Müller, which does not, however, take a stand for or against this assumption.

170

171

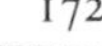

172

170 Four Men Cutting Wood, F950
Black chalk and watercolor, 35 × 45 cm (13¾ × 17¾″)
Rijksmuseum Kröller-Müller, Otterlo

171 Three Woodcutters Walking, F948
Watercolor, 36 × 25 cm (14⅛ × 9⅞″)
Cincinnati Art Museum

172 Scheveningen Women and Other People under Umbrellas, F990
Watercolor, 28.5 × 21 cm (11⅜ × 8¼″)
Gemeentemuseum, The Hague (on loan from the Wibbina Foundation)

August 1882

173 Beach and Sea, F2
Paper on panel, 35.5 × 49.5 cm (14⅛ × 19⅝″)
Collection Mrs. H. van Ogtrop-van Kempen, Aalst, The Netherlands

174 Beach and Sea
Sketch in Letter 224
Rijksmuseum Vincent van Gogh, Amsterdam

175 Potato Field
Sketch in Letter 224
Rijksmuseum Vincent van Gogh, Amsterdam

173

174

175

176

177

179

178

180

181

176 Dunes, F2a
Panel, 36 × 58.5 cm ($14\frac{1}{8} \times 23\frac{1}{4}''$)
Private collection, Amsterdam

177 Sunset over a Meadow
Sketch in Letter 225
Rijksmuseum Vincent van Gogh, Amsterdam

178 Women Mending Nets in the Dunes, F7
Paper on panel, 42 × 62.5 cm ($16\frac{1}{2} \times 24\frac{3}{4}''$)
Gemeentemuseum, The Hague (on loan from Mrs. L. Schokking-Ribbius Peletier)

179 A Girl in the Street, Two Coaches in the Background, F13
Canvas on panel, 42 × 53 cm ($16\frac{1}{2} \times 20\frac{7}{8}''$)
Collection Mrs. L. Jäggli-Hahnloser, Winterthur, Switzerland

180 A Girl in a Wood, F8a
Panel, 35 × 47 cm ($13\frac{3}{4} \times 18\frac{1}{2}''$)
Private collection, The Netherlands

181 Two Women in a Wood, F1665
Paper on panel, 31 × 24.5 cm ($12\frac{1}{4} \times 9\frac{7}{8}''$)
Private collection, Paris

1 or 2: "You will now say: Vincent, you had better concentrate on perspective and the places where they dry flatfish. And to this I say: You are quite right, brother, and that is why I am going to work on those two drawings, which belong to the first group and which you will receive soon." Letter 205, written one or two days later, makes it clear which drawings he was referring to: "Today, Saturday, I am sending you those two drawings: *Fish-Drying Barn in the Dunes, Scheveningen* and *Carpenter's Yard and Laundry* (from the window of my studio)."

Without all these clear signposts one might be inclined to date 150 and 153 earlier in the year, since the trees along the Schenkweg still appear completely bare. It would be reasonable to assume that Vincent had started the two drawings earlier, say in April, and in putting the finishing touches on them in the second half of May had left the somewhat wintry look of the trees. There is no supporting evidence, however.

Just a few words about the other drawings for C.M. In Letter 200, written about May 23, Vincent said that Christien (as he always referred to Sien in the letters up to the end of May) and her mother had moved into a smaller house, since after her delivery, Christien was coming to live with him. It was a little house with a small inner court or yard. He was hoping to make a drawing of it that week. In Letters 202 and R8, written only a few days later, two drawings of the house are mentioned, a larger and a smaller, which Vincent, as it now appears, had intended for C.M. Letter R8 (May 28) states that he was now able to make a parcel of the drawings for C.M. "There are now seven in all." From the enumeration in the letter and other information, it appears that the second series of drawings for C.M. did in fact include two drawings of the little house of Sien's mother, 146 and 147. Also included were: *Nursery* (138), *Fish-Drying Barn* (151), and the view showing the *Carpenter's Yard* (150). In Letter 205 Vincent described the seven drawings as two "large" ones, four like those enclosed (namely, 153 and 154, measuring about 10$\frac{1}{2}$ by 17$\frac{1}{2}$ inches, thus medium-sized) and a small one. The two large drawings were 138 and 147, the four medium-sized ones were 146, 150, 151, and 152. The "small" drawing sent to C. M. must have been *Nursery* (125), which was made at an earlier date.

These drawings did not elicit a cordial response. Vincent got 20 guldens, even less than he had expected, and, according to Letter R9, "with a sort of reprimand into the bargain: 'Did I really think that such drawings could possess the slightest commercial value?' "

Emotions

In June, Vincent's output was suddenly interrupted. Letter 206 of June 8 or 9 reports that he had been admitted to the Municipal Hospital on the Brouwersgracht because he had contracted a venereal disease. Three letters to Theo and one to Van Rappard (R8) tell about his stay in the hospital, where, although condemned to idleness, he had at least the chance to get some rest. One diversion was the view from the ward onto the canal and the town, which he thought mag-

182

183

184

182 A Girl in a Wood, F8
39 × 59 cm (15$\frac{3}{8}$ × 23$\frac{1}{4}$")
Rijksmuseum Kröller-Müller, Otterlo
Colorplate I, opposite

183 A Girl in a Wood
Sketch in Letter 229
Rijksmuseum Vincent van Gogh, Amsterdam

184 Edge of a Wood, F192
Canvas on panel, 34.5 × 49 cm (13$\frac{3}{4}$ × 19$\frac{1}{4}$")
Rijksmuseum Kröller-Müller, Otterlo

Colorplate I, A Girl in a Wood, 182 〉

nificent, while he called the interior of the ward "no less interesting than a third-class waiting room" (Letter 207). One bright spot during this period of illness, which lasted longer than he had expected, was the news that a parcel from home had arrived in his studio, with clothes and underwear, cigars, and 10 guldens (Letter 207). A still greater surprise was a visit by his father, who apparently had come at once after receiving a letter of thanks from Vincent along with the news that he was in the hospital. The visit, however, "had been very short and hurried," and Vincent felt that on both sides they had not enjoyed it very much: "It seemed very strange and somewhat like a dream, as does, indeed, this whole business of lying here sick" (Letter 208).

Sien had meanwhile left for the hospital in Leiden to have her child. When Vincent, just home from his stay in the hospital, wrote Theo on July 1, he told him that everything had been arranged to receive Sien on her return in the new quarters he had rented. Vincent had gone ahead with his plan, about which he had often written Theo, and taken the upper floor of the house next to his. This, as he put it, "was most comfortable" and looked "very smart and handsome." He wrote enthusiastically: "The enormous, completely timbered attic could, if necessary, make a grand studio, although the room facing north would actually have to be used as such. And the price for here is exceptionally low and would be about double in town. Three guldens a week for a large upper story is very little, even by comparison with neighborhoods like the Noordwal or Buitensingels. And for a painter the location is perfect. The view from the attic window is fascinating" (Letter 209). That fascinating view would soon appear in his pictures (156).

The description in the next letters of his visit to the hospital in Leiden, where Sien had given birth on July 2, is quite moving. "I will not soon forget the words 'You may not talk to her for long,' for that meant 'You can still talk to her,' and it might just as easily have been 'You will never speak to her any more'" (Letter 210). A few days later, after he had moved with the assistance of his neighbor the carpenter and the carpenter's helpers, he happily described his new and spacious studio and the small living room with "a large wicker armchair for the woman in the corner

185

186

187

188

189

185 Man Stooping with Stick or Spade, F 12
Paper on panel, 31 × 29.5 cm ($12\frac{1}{4} \times 11\frac{3}{4}$")
Private collection, England

186 Dunes with Figures, F 3
Canvas on panel, 24 × 32 cm ($9\frac{1}{2} \times 12\frac{5}{8}$")
Collection H. R. Hahnloser, Bern

187 Beach with Figures and Sea with a Ship, F 4
Canvas on cardboard, 34.5 × 51 cm ($13\frac{3}{4} \times 20\frac{1}{8}$")
Stedelijk Museum, Amsterdam
(on loan from Miss E. Ribbius Peletier)
Colorplate II, opposite

188 Fisherman on the Beach, F 5
Canvas on panel, 51 × 33.5 cm ($20\frac{1}{8} \times 13\frac{3}{8}$")
Rijksmuseum Kröller-Müller, Otterlo

189 Scheveningen Woman on the Beach, F 6
Canvas on panel, 52 × 34 cm ($20\frac{1}{2} \times 13\frac{3}{8}$")
Rijksmuseum Kröller-Müller, Otterlo

〈 Colorplate II, Beach with Figures and Sea with a Ship, 187

by the window which looks out over the carpenter's yard and the pastures which you know from the drawings. And next to the chair a small iron crib with a green cover." He then continued (and this shows how much domestic life with Sien meant to him): "That last piece of furniture I cannot look at without emotion, for it is a strong and powerful emotion that takes hold of you when you have been sitting next to the woman you love with a little child in the crib nearby" (Letter 213). Small wonder that he made a drawing of it that very month. The drawing "with daubs of color in it" has been lost, but some idea of what it was like is given by the sketch in Letter 218 (155).

Back at Work

Vincent now went back to work with a will, alternately doing watercolors and ecstatically describing the summer landscape that he could see from his windows or that he went looking for in The Hague and Scheveningen. He summed it up when he wrote on July 23: "These are landscapes with a complicated perspective, very difficult to draw, but for that very reason embodying a genuinely Dutch character and feeling. They look like the ones I sent you and are no less scrupulously drawn, only now there is color added to them: the delicate green of the pasture, contrasting with the red roof tiles—the light in the sky which comes out stronger against the dull shades of the foreground, a carpenter's yard with earth and damp wood" (Letter 219).

The work referred to here is the splendid watercolor 156, with a striking red-tiled roof that, with its sweeping perspective, takes up more than a quarter of the entire picture. Vincent's description of how it was made is a fascinating bit of prose, that, better than any lengthy dissertation, brings us closer to the man and artist Van Gogh, with his poetical vision of reality and his pithy power of expression, with words as well as with images: "Just picture me sitting at my little attic window as early as four in the morning, busily studying the pastures and the carpenter's yard with my perspective frame as the fires are lighted inside to make coffee and the first laborer comes sauntering into the carpenter's yard. A flock of white pigeons comes cruising along between the black smoking chimneys. But off behind there is an infinity of a delicate soft green, miles and miles of flat pasture, and a gentle gray sky so very quiet, so peaceful, like a landscape by Corot or Jan van Goyen. That view over the ridges of the roofs where the grass has taken root, very early in the morning, and those first signs of life and awakening, the bird flying, the chimney smoking, the small figure far below sauntering along, that then is the subject of my watercolor. I hope you will like it" (Letter 219.)

The perspective frame mentioned here was a gadget made with the help of the carpenter and the blacksmith that Vincent had been using for some time in drawing (following the example of Albrecht Dürer). He wrote to Theo at the beginning of June that he had incurred some extra expenses "this winter" to have it made. He would continue to rely on this instrument, which he sketched in Letter 222, for quite a long time. Other watercolors

190 The New Church and Old Houses in The Hague, F204
Canvas on cardboard, 35 × 25 cm (13¾ × 9⅞")
Location unknown

September 1882

191 Woody Landscape after the Rain
Sketch in Letter 229
Rijksmuseum Vincent van Gogh, Amsterdam

192 Donkey Cart with Boy and Scheveningen Woman, F1079
Pen, pencil, 11.4 × 20 cm (4¾ × 7⅞")
Destroyed by fire in 1940 (formerly in Rotterdam)

193 Studies of a Horse and Cart, Donkey Cart, and First Sketch of a Donkey Cart, F952 (reverse: 194)
Sketch sent with Letter 230
Pen, pencil, 20.5 × 19.5 cm (8¼ × 7⅞")
Rijksmuseum Kröller-Müller, Otterlo

194 Bench with Four Persons, F952 (reverse: 193)
Sketch sent with Letter 230
Pen, pencil, washed, 19.5 × 20.5 cm (7⅞ × 8¼")
Rijksmuseum Kröller-Müller, Otterlo

195 Bench with Four Persons
Sketch sent with Letter 230
Watercolor
Rijksmuseum Vincent van Gogh, Amsterdam

196 Bench with Three Persons, F1039
Sketch sent with Letter 230
Watercolor, 12.5 × 21 cm (5⅛ × 8¼")
Collection Mrs. M. A. R. van der Leeuw-Wentges, The Hague

197 Bench with Four Persons (and Baby), F951
Watercolor, 25 × 37 cm (9⅞ × 14⅝")
Location unknown

198 Bench with Four Persons (and Baby)
Sketch in Letter R12
Private collection, United States

199 Bench in a Wood, F928
Pencil, pen, brown ink, 28 × 44 cm (11 × 17⅜")
G. J. Nieuwenhuizen Segaar Art Gallery, The Hague

191

192

193

194

195

196

197

198

199

made during this month are *Bleaching Ground* (158), *Fish-Drying Barn* (160), and *Pollard Willow* (164). I believe that watercolor 161 is the one referred to in the description: "As to the Rijswijk pastures, I also have a second one in which a change in eye level and viewpoint gives the same subject an entirely different appearance" (Letter 220). It is apparent that this watercolor depicts the Rijswijk pastures—in other words, Vincent's immediate surroundings—if the buildings in the background are compared with those in the watercolor of the pollard willow. These are the same train sheds of the Rhine railway also visible in the drawings made from Vincent's rear window, that is, from another "viewpoint."

It is a pity that the drawing of the fishing boats on the beach, which Vincent, according to Letter 211, had started before his illness, has not come down to us. To judge from the sketch in Letter 220 (159), it would probably have been impressive.

Working in Oils

At the beginning of August the series of watercolors came to an end as Vincent began working in oils. He had actually tried oils in January (as he wrote in Letter 223), but had given it up because his "drawing was still too hesitant." The impetus for taking up oil painting again was a visit by Theo at the beginning of August. Theo, presumably impressed by the great progress in the work he got to see, had provided Vincent with the necessary funds. In Letter 222, written after Theo left, Vincent said: "I am very grateful to you for having come here; I find it marvelous to be able to look forward again to another year of regular work without any calamities, and what you have given me opens up a new horizon in painting for me." He then enumerated all the things he had bought: new material for watercolors and a good box of paints and "everything that is absolutely essential" for working in oils. It meant a new but laborious beginning, for he had by no means achieved the level in oils that he had already reached in drawing and watercolors.

Much of the work in oils that Vincent did during his stay in The Hague has been lost. Twenty-five studies of that time are known to us, but in Letter 329, from Drenthe, Vincent wrote that he left "more than seventy painted studies" in The Hague. Out of those twenty-five studies, I attribute fourteen to his work during August 1882; a second series of oil paintings would not be done until August of the following year.

200

201

202

203

204

200 Woman Spreading Out Laundry on a Field, F1087
Watercolor, 25.5 × 40 cm ($10\frac{1}{4} \times 15\frac{3}{4}$″)
Location unknown

201 Man Sitting with a Glass in His Hand, F1082
Pencil, black chalk, 32 × 25 cm ($12\frac{5}{8} \times 9\frac{7}{8}$″)
Collection M. Futter, New York

202 Boy with Cap and Wooden Shoes, F1681
Pencil, 31 × 16 cm ($12\frac{1}{4} \times 6\frac{1}{4}$″)
Rijksmuseum Vincent van Gogh, Amsterdam

203 Orphans
Sketch in Letter 232
Rijksmuseum Vincent van Gogh, Amsterdam

205

206

207

208

209

210

211

204 People Walking on the Beach, F980
Pencil, 16 × 25.5 cm ($6\frac{1}{4}$ × $10\frac{1}{4}$″)
Rijksmuseum Kröller-Müller, Otterlo

205 Group of People on the Beach with Fishing Boat Arriving
Sketch in Letter 231
Rijksmuseum Vincent van Gogh, Amsterdam

206 Carpenter, F1043
Pencil, 48.5 × 28 cm ($19\frac{1}{4}$ × 11″)
Private collection, The Hague

207 Carpenter, Seen from the Back, F1042
Pencil, 47.5 × 23.5 ($18\frac{7}{8}$ × $9\frac{1}{2}$″)
Collection H. J. Hyams, England

208 A Carpenter with Apron, F1044
Pencil, 45 × 24 cm ($17\frac{3}{4}$ × $9\frac{1}{2}$″)
Mayfair Kunst, Zug, Switzerland

209 Girl Carrying a Loaf of Bread, F1045
Pencil, 49 × 28 cm ($19\frac{1}{4}$ × 11″)
Formerly collection S. E. Neikrug, New York

210 Orphan Man with Cap, Eating, F956a
Pencil, 51 × 27.5 cm ($20\frac{1}{8}$ × 11″)
Location unknown

211 Orphan Man with Long Overcoat, Cleaning Boots, F969
Pencil, 48.5 × 28 cm ($19\frac{1}{4}$ × 11″)
Private collection, Switzerland

The oil paintings done in August 1882 consist of beach scenes and seascapes (such as 173 and 186–89; studies of trees such as 180–82 and 184; see also colorplates I and II, pages 49 and 50). There are also some other subjects, the most notable being the group of women mending fishing nets in the dunes (178), described in detail in Letter 227. In the same letter Vincent wrote: "For a fortnight now I have so to speak been painting from early in the morning till late in the evening," adding, "and if I went on like this, it would run into too much money unless I sell something." The expense of painting in oils is a theme that keeps recurring in the following letters. This clearly goes hand in hand with a hesitancy about going on with it: "But we are confronted with this question: In order to achieve something higher and better I must still make many studies. What will be the most advantageous, to draw the studies or to paint them?" Whether expense was the main reason to stop oil painting is not clear. One should read the long Letter 227, which is entirely given over to weighing the pros and cons of oils. In my opinion a feeling of disappointment in the results may also have been a reason that in September there are only a few references to studies in oil (the studies in question, incidentally, have all been lost). It is undeniable, however, that working in oils during this period was of immense importance to the emerging artist Van Gogh. This is demonstrated by the following splendid passage—in reference to a forest scene—which describes his struggle with oils: "How I paint *I do not know myself.* I sit down with a white wooden board in front of the spot that caught my eye, I look at what is in front of me, I tell myself: that white board must become something—I come back dissatisfied—I put it away and when I have rested a little, I go to look at it with a kind of fear. I am still dissatisfied because I have that wonderful piece of nature too clearly in my mind for me to be satisfied with it—but yet I see in my work an echo of what struck me, I see that nature has told me something, has spoken to me, and that I have written it down in shorthand. It may be that my shorthand contains words that cannot be deciphered—mistakes or blanks, but there is still something left of what the woods or beach or figure told me, and it is not a lame or conventional language such as came from an acquired mannerism or a system rather than from nature itself" (Letter 228).

Working with Watercolor and Pencil

Watercolor and pencil were the mediums that enabled Vincent to achieve his great production of September. It is clear from the letters that he was still doing studies in oils at the beginning of September, but when he wrote Letter 229, September 9, his paint had run out. When he received Theo's remittance of September 10, the future did not look very bright so far as money was concerned: "What you write about the money you lent and did not get back is certainly a calamity. From this [money] I still have to pay for paint and also buy a new supply, so by September 20 I shall certainly be short of cash. But I will vary the work somewhat and try to make both ends meet" (Letter 230). With the same

212

213

214

212 Orphan Man with Long Overcoat and Stick, F962 (cf. lithograph 256)
Pencil, 50 × 30.5 cm ($19\frac{5}{8} \times 12\frac{1}{4}$")
Rijksmuseum Vincent van Gogh, Amsterdam

213 Orphan Man with Long Overcoat and Umbrella, Seen from the Back, F968
Pencil, 48.5 × 27.5 cm ($19\frac{1}{4} \times 11$")
Location unknown

214 Orphan Man with Long Overcoat and Umbrella, Seen from the Back
Sketch in Letter R14
Private collection, United States

215 Woman with Kettle, Seen from the Back
F1051
Pencil, 46 × 23 cm ($18\frac{1}{8} \times 9$")
Rijksmuseum Kröller-Müller, Otterlo

216 Sien Nursing Baby, Half-Figure, F1062
Pencil, 43.5 × 27 cm ($16\frac{7}{8} \times 10\frac{5}{8}$")
Rijksmuseum Kröller-Müller, Otterlo

217 Sien Nursing Baby, Half-Figure, F1065
Pencil, sepia, washed, China ink, 36.5 × 24 cm ($14\frac{1}{8} \times 9\frac{1}{2}$")
Location unknown

218 Sien Nursing Baby, F1063
Pencil, 49.5 × 27 cm ($19\frac{5}{8} \times 10\frac{5}{8}$")
Rijksmuseum Kröller-Müller, Otterlo

215

216

217

218

219

220

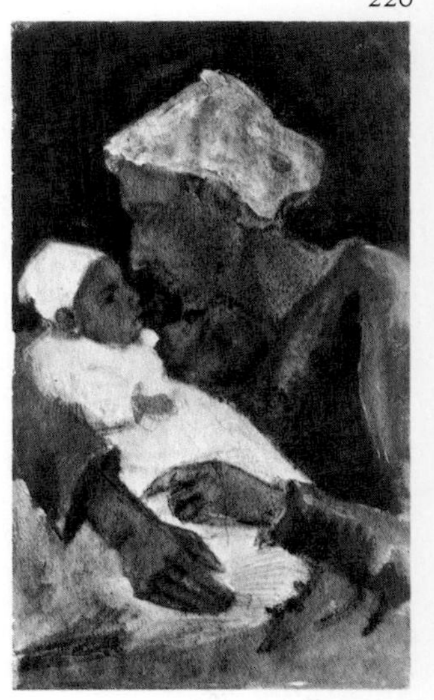

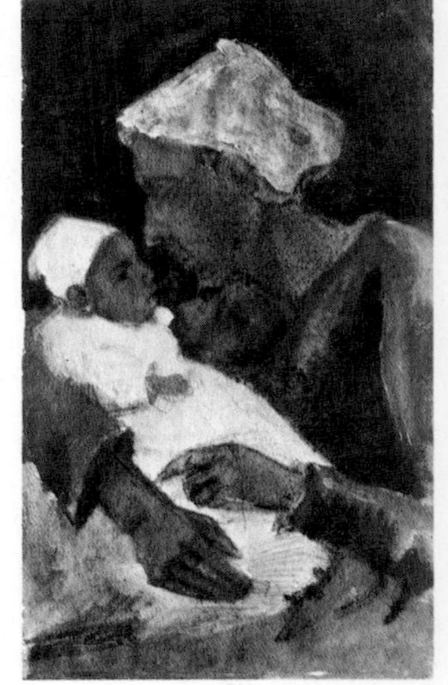

221

219 Sien Nursing Baby. F 1068
Watercolor, black chalk, 47.5 × 30 cm
($18\frac{7}{8} \times 11\frac{3}{4}''$)
Location unknown

220 Woman (Sien?) with Baby on Her Lap, Half-Figure, F 1061
Pencil, watercolor, heightened with white oils, 40.5 × 24 cm ($16\frac{1}{8} \times 9\frac{1}{2}''$)
Rijksmuseum Kröller-Müller, Otterlo

221 Sien Nursing Baby, F 1064
Pencil, black chalk, 48 × 26 cm
($18\frac{7}{8} \times 10\frac{1}{4}''$)
Location unknown

letter he sent along a few watercolors, thus following the advice Theo had given him at the time of his visit, for Vincent had done his best to make something in "the genre that is called 'salable.' " One of the watercolors he sent was a bench in the woods with four people (195); the other was the bench with three people (196). The first corresponded with a larger watercolor; the second with a painted study, both of which have been lost. It is quite apparent that he now expected to have more success with, as he put it, "motifs that have something nice and sociable about them," and this may also have led him to try his hand at sketches and watercolors of larger groups of people. "The enclosed rough sketch will show you what I am aiming at," he wrote in Letter 231 about sketch 205, "with those groups of people who are doing something or other." Various watercolors must have been lost, but that of *The State Lottery Office* (222) gives a good idea of his efforts to capture life, movement, and space involving a large group of people.

It must have been this laborious work with large groups that made Vincent feel the need once more to apply himself vigorously to the rendering of individual figures. "I feel that I need a large number of studies of figures—including the Scheveningen ones," he wrote on September 18 (Letter 232), and he asked Theo to return to him any earlier studies he did not want to keep. But it also appears that at the same time he was already very busy making new studies of figures and that this had certainly been made easier by the "discovery" about this time of what the people in The Hague called "orphan men." These were pensioners from the poorhouse or old people's home, who accounted for a large part of Vincent's work in The Hague, as he wrote to Van Rappard September 18 or 19: "I have also recently been painting and doing watercolors and am likewise drawing a lot of figures from a model and rough sketches on the street. I also recently got a man from the Old Men's Home to serve as a model" (Letter R13).

The Orphan Man Zuyderland

The man introduced into the correspondence in this way is a person whom dozens of drawings have made as familiar to us as Sien and the members of her family. Vincent wrote of this pensioner in Letter 235 (with which he enclosed a small sketch showing the back of his head): "He has a nice bald head—large but deaf ears, and white whiskers." Just re-

222

223

224

225

226

222 The State Lottery Office, F970
Watercolor, 38 × 57 cm (15 × 22½″)
Rijksmuseum Vincent van Gogh, Amsterdam
Colorplate III, p. 67

223 The State Lottery Office
Sketch in Letter 235
Rijksmuseum Vincent van Gogh, Amsterdam

224 Woman with a Broom, F1075
Pencil, watercolor, 45.5 × 23 cm (18⅛ × 9″)
Rijksmuseum Vincent van Gogh, Amsterdam

225 Church Pew with Worshipers, F967
Watercolor, pen, pencil, 28 × 38 cm (11 × 15″)
Rijksmuseum Kröller-Müller, Otterlo

227

228

229

230

231

232

233

226 Church Pew with Worshipers
Sketch in Letter 235
Rijksmuseum Vincent van Gogh, Amsterdam

October 1882

227 Beach and Boats
Sketch in Letter 236
Rijksmuseum Vincent van Gogh, Amsterdam

228 People Strolling on the Beach, F1038
Watercolor, 34 × 49.5 cm ($13\frac{3}{8} \times 19\frac{5}{8}''$)
Baltimore Museum of Art

229 Miners in the Snow ("Winter"), F1202
Sketch sent with Letter 236
Watercolor, 7 × 11 cm ($2\frac{3}{4} \times 4\frac{3}{8}''$)
Rijksmuseum Vincent van Gogh, Amsterdam

230 Orchard ("Spring"), F1245
Sketch sent with Letter 236
Watercolor, 6 × 10.5 cm ($2\frac{3}{8} \times 4\frac{3}{8}''$)
Rijksmuseum Vincent van Gogh, Amsterdam

231 Boy with Spade, F986
Pencil, pen, washed, 50.5 × 31.5 cm
($20\frac{1}{8} \times 12\frac{5}{8}''$)
Location unknown

232 Two Women, F988
Black chalk, pencil, heightened with white,
49 × 27.5 cm ($19\frac{1}{4} \times 11''$)
Location unknown

233 Man and Woman, Arm in Arm, F991
Pencil, 50 × 31 cm ($19\frac{5}{8} \times 12\frac{1}{4}''$)
Rijksmuseum Vincent van Gogh, Amsterdam

cently we have also learned his name. Dr. W.J.A. Visser has pointed out that the "men of the poorhouse"—i.e., the residents of the Dutch Reformed Old Men's and Old Women's Home (then located on the Warmoezierstraat)—wore an identification number on the upper part of their right sleeve, and that such a number, namely 199, is clearly legible on one of Van Gogh's drawings of an orphan man (F954, here 287).* An examination of the inmate register of that institution provided him with the name of Vincent's model: Adrianus Jacobus Zuyderland. Dr. Visser accordingly concluded that drawings F954a and 955 (here 288 and 355) also portrayed Zuyderland.

Dr. Visser did not completely follow up his valuable discovery. Below the sketch of the orphan man with umbrella viewed from the rear, which appears in various editions of the letters to Van Rappard, Van Gogh wrote in bold letters "No. 199," and this number also can be discerned, although not very clearly, on the man's upper right sleeve. Obviously, then, this sketch (here 214) and the virtually identical large drawing from which the small sketch was undoubtedly made (213) both depict the same Zuyderland. This means that Zuyderland is also the orphan man referred to in Letters R13 and 235, and that he was not only the first but also the most frequent of Vincent's models from the Old Men's and Women's Home. Vincent has not always done his best to remain as faithful to the likeness of the original as in the case of the portraits 287 and 355, but once this face with its bald forehead, large hooked nose, and tight mouth has been impressed upon the observer's mind, it will be recognized in many of the drawings.

Besides the figure studies of orphan men (210–13), I also include in this group of figure studies made in September some drawings not mentioned in the letters: those of workmen, (206–8) and those of a boy and a girl (202 and 209). Also, Sien and her baby gradually became Vincent's regular models again (216–21). As late as July 26 he wrote: "As you see, I am still deep in landscapes, since Sien is not yet able to pose for me" (Letter 220).

Groups and Figure Studies

In between the many studies of single figures, Vincent also attempted larger groups. This was near the end of the month when once again he took his box of watercolors in hand. When he sent off a small sketch of such a difficult group—the drawing of people waiting at the State Lottery Office (222 and 223; see also colorplate III, page 67)—he took the opportunity to engage in a lively written discourse on the thoughts the subject aroused in him. It is indicative of the social background of Vincent's life as an artist that he wrote: "The little group of people—and their expression of waiting—struck me, and while I was making it, it assumed a greater and deeper significance for me than in the first moment. It then becomes more meaningful, I think, if it is looked upon as *the poor and*

*In his study "Vincent van Gogh en 's-Gravenhage" ("Vincent van Gogh and The Hague"), *Jaarboek Die Haghe* (1953).

234

235

236

234 Orphan Man Holding Top Hat in His Hand, F953
Pencil, 49 × 23.5 cm (19¼ × 9¼″)
Location unknown

235 Orphan Man with Top Hat and Hands Crossed, F975
Pencil, 49 × 25 cm (19¼ × 9⅞″)
Rijksmuseum Kröller-Müller, Otterlo

236 Orphan Man Holding Top Hat in His Hand, F973
Pencil, washed, 47 × 22 cm (18½ × 8⅝″)
Rijksmuseum Kröller-Müller, Otterlo

237 Orphan Man with Top Hat and Umbrella under His Arm, F972
Pencil, washed, 48.5 × 24.5 cm (19¼ × 9⅞″)
Rijksmuseum Kröller-Müller, Otterlo

238 Orphan Man with Top Hat and Umbrella, Looking at His Watch, F978
Pencil, 48 × 28.5 cm (18⅞ × 11⅜″)
Rijksmuseum Kröller-Müller, Otterlo

239 Orphan Man with Umbrella, Seen from the Back, F972a
Pencil, 49 × 30 cm (19¼ × 11¾″)
Collection M. Huggler, Bern

237

238

239

240

241

242

243

240 Orphan Man with Umbrella, Seen from the Back, F978a
Pencil, 12 × 7.5 cm ($4\frac{3}{4} \times 3\frac{1}{8}$")
Location unknown

241 Orphan Man with Top Hat and Stick, Seen from the Back, F960
Pencil, 47.5 × 26 cm ($18\frac{7}{8} \times 10\frac{1}{4}$")
Rijksmuseum Vincent van Gogh, Amsterdam

242 Orphan Man with Top Hat, Holding Cup, F957
Pencil, 49 × 24.5 cm ($19\frac{1}{4} \times 10\frac{1}{4}$")
Collection Mr. and Mrs. Chapin Riley, Worcester, Massachusetts

243 Orphan Man with Top Hat and Stick, Seen from the Front, F977
Pencil, 47 × 23.5 cm ($18\frac{1}{2} \times 9\frac{1}{2}$")
Rijksmuseum Vincent van Gogh, Amsterdam

money. Thus is it, indeed, with almost all groups of figures: you really have to think about it before you realize what is in front of you: the curiosity and illusion regarding the lottery seems to us somewhat childish—but it becomes serious when one thinks about the contrasting element of poverty and that sort of desperate effort by the poor devils, who imagine that by depriving themselves of food to buy a lottery ticket they can be saved" (Letter 235).

That he nevertheless had also looked at the little group with the true eye of the painter is apparent from the closing lines of the letter: "Needless to say, that group of figures, of which I am sending you a small black-and-white rough sketch, presented a magnificent variety of color—blue blouses and brown jackets, white, black, and yellowish workmen's trousers, faded shawls, an overcoat turned greenish with age, white bonnets and black top hats, muddy paving stones and boots, all contrasting with pallid faces or those weatherbeaten by storm and wind. And that demands painting or working in watercolors."

It must be said that the color is the most attractive element in the watercolor of the State Lottery, although the rendering of a fairly large group of people huddled close and waiting—a completely new task for Van Gogh—has been achieved with surprising success. It is certainly more effective than his handling of a group of some of the same people (a few of Vincent's regular models can be recognized) sitting in a couple of church pews (225 and 226). It is obvious from a few very badly drawn faces that this subject was beyond him.

A few other watercolors from October are known to us (228, 247, 252, and possibly 253; see also colorplate IV, page 68). A number must have been lost, such as the drawing from which the fine sketch 227 was made and a dozen watercolors, mentioned in Letter 239, of the potato market and other street scenes.

Once again, the work produced in this month consists largely of studies of single figures, for as Vincent wrote in Letter 236, October 8, he was working "almost daily with models." No fewer than fifteen times the model was Zuyderland, and occasionally we seem to recognize Sien or her mother. The use of models certainly was due in part to the weather. As early as about October 10 Vincent wrote, "Working out of doors is all over now—the kind of work where you have to sit still—for it is too raw; so we must move into winter quarters" (Letter 238). While it had still been possible toward the end of the month to make a watercolor of the beach (247) and to do some sketching at the potato market, he was confined for the most part to the written word in rendering the effects produced by autumn.

Vincent as a Writer

He certainly did not lack talent in that direction, as is evident in his description of the view from his studio, this time from the front of the house: "At the moment, the view from my studio window makes a wonderful effect. The city, with its steeples and roofs and smoking chimneys, stands out like a dark,

244

245

246

247

248

249

250

251

252

253

254

255

244 Orphan Man with Long Overcoat, Glass, and Handkerchief, F959
Pencil, 49 × 25 cm ($19\frac{1}{4} \times 9\frac{7}{8}$″)
Rijksmuseum Kröller-Müller, Otterlo

245 Orphan Man with Top Hat, Eating from a Plate, F956
Pencil, 46.5 × 24.5 cm ($18\frac{1}{2} \times 9\frac{7}{8}$″)
Collection Irving Mitchell Felt, New York

246 Orphan Man with Top Hat, Standing near the Stove, Seen from the Back, F974
Pencil, heightened with white, 56 × 30 cm (22 × $11\frac{3}{4}$″)
Rijksmuseum Kröller-Müller, Otterlo

247 Beach with People Walking and Boats, F982
Watercolor, 27 × 45 cm ($10\frac{5}{8} \times 17\frac{3}{4}$″)
Private collection, Haarlem

248 Beach with People Walking and Boats
Sketch in Letter 237
Rijksmuseum Vincent van Gogh, Amsterdam

249 Woman with a Broom, F1074
Pencil, pen, heightened with watercolor, 49.5 × 27.5 cm ($19\frac{5}{8}$ × 11″)
Rijksmuseum Vincent van Gogh, Amsterdam

250 Orphan Man, Sitting with a Girl, F971
Pencil, chalk, 48 × 25 cm ($18\frac{7}{8} \times 9\frac{7}{8}$″)
Collection Mary Enole Witt, Knightdale, North Carolina

251 Orphan Man with Cap and Stick, F958
Pencil, 48.5 × 26 cm ($19\frac{1}{4} \times 10\frac{1}{4}$″)
Collection W. Brinkman, Schipluiden, The Netherlands

252 Potato Market, F1091
Watercolor, 35 × 43.5 cm ($13\frac{3}{4} \times 17\frac{3}{8}$″)
Collection D. A. Bennahum, New York

November 1882

253 Women Miners, F994
Watercolor, heightened with white, 32 × 50 cm ($12\frac{5}{8} \times 19\frac{5}{8}$″)
Rijksmuseum Kröller-Müller, Otterlo
Colorplate IV, p. 68

254 Bookseller Blok, Head, F993
Pencil, pen, China ink, watercolor, 38.5 × 26 cm ($15\frac{3}{8} \times 10\frac{1}{4}$″)
Collection R. W. Wentges, Rotterdam

255 Woman with Shawl, Umbrella, and Basket, F934
Watercolor, 66.5 × 37.5 cm ($26\frac{3}{8}$ × 15″)
Collection Prof. Max Stähelin, Binningen, Switzerland

somber silhouette against a horizon of light. This light, however, is no more than a broad streak, and above it a heavy shower hangs, more dense below but above torn by the fall wind into fluffs and masses that drift away. But that streak of light makes the wet roofs gleam here and there in the somber mass of the city (in a drawing these would be delineated with a stroke of body color), and the result is that although the mass has a single tone, it is still possible to distinguish between red tiles and slates. The Schenkweg runs through the foreground like a glistening line through the wet, the poplars have yellow leaves, the sides of the ditches and pastures are deep green, the little figures are black. I would draw it, or rather try to draw it, if I had not been slogging away all afternoon working on figures of peat carriers. My head is so full of these that there is no room for anything new, and they will have to stay there" (Letter 237).

The figures of the peat carriers have disappeared, but the reference to them demonstrates once again how Vincent persevered in his efforts to improve his professional skills. The same letter provides a good insight into his views: "What is drawing? How does one manage to do it? It is working one's way through an invisible iron wall that appears to stand between what one *feels* and what one *can do*. How do you get through that wall—pounding on it won't help—you must undermine it and file through it, slowly and patiently, as I see it, and here you are—how can you persevere in such work without being diverted from it or distracted, unless you reflect on it and govern your life according to principles?"

While governing his life according to the principle of unremitting work, Vincent would have been repeatedly diverted from his main objective by financial worries, but he must have been helped by an apparent improvement in relations with his parents.

In Letter 236, October 8, we read: "Just imagine that this week to my great surprise I received a parcel from home containing a winter coat, a warm pair of trousers, and a warm woman's coat; I was greatly touched." What must have touched him most of all was the woman's coat, for it could not have been easy for the rector and his wife to accept the situation to any extent. The parcel had been preceded a short while before by a visit from his father: "I must now tell you that very unexpectedly I had a very pleasant visit from Dad, who was in the house and in the studio. I find this infinitely better than for him to get news about me secondhand" (Letter 234, September 25). We have to assume that his father also met Sien and the children, but unfortunately Vincent does not say how he reacted.

Experiments with Lithography

At the beginning of November, Theo wrote Vincent about a new kind of paper that made it possible to transmit drawings directly onto stone. The Paris painter and engraver Félix Buhot apparently had promised him a small batch. Vincent's curiosity was immediately aroused, as he saw in this new process an opportunity to get work making illustrations. In Letter 241, November 2 or 3, he pressed

256

257

258

256 Orphan Man, F 1658 (cf. drawing 212)
Lithograph, 61 × 39.5 cm (24 × $15\frac{3}{4}$")
Various collections

257 Young Man with a Broom, F 979a
Pencil, 43 × 29.5 cm ($16\frac{7}{8}$ × $11\frac{3}{4}$")
Gemeentemuseum, The Hague (on loan from the Wibbina Foundation)

258 Digger, F 908
Pencil, ink, 47.5 × 29.5 cm ($18\frac{7}{8}$ × $11\frac{3}{4}$")
Rijksmuseum Vincent van Gogh, Amsterdam

259 "Sorrow," F 1655 (cf. drawing 129)
Lithograph, 38.5 × 29 cm ($15\frac{3}{8}$ × $11\frac{3}{8}$")
Various collections

260 Digger, F 906
Pencil, 50.5 × 31.5 cm ($20\frac{1}{8}$ × $12\frac{5}{8}$")
Rijksmuseum Vincent van Gogh, Amsterdam

261 Digger, F 907
Pencil, 49.5 × 28.5 cm ($19\frac{5}{8}$ × $11\frac{3}{8}$")
Rijksmuseum Vincent van Gogh, Amsterdam

262 Digger, F 1656 (original drawing not known)
Lithograph, 52 × 37 cm ($20\frac{1}{2}$ × $14\frac{5}{8}$")
Various collections

263 Orphan Man with Top Hat, Drinking Coffee, F 1682 (cf. lithograph 266)
Black lithographic chalk, 49.5 × 28.5 cm ($19\frac{5}{8}$ × $11\frac{3}{8}$")
Rijksmuseum Vincent van Gogh, Amsterdam

259

260

261

262

263

264

265

266

264 Orphan Man with Top Hat, Drinking Coffee, F996a (cf. lithograph 266)
Black chalk, washed, heightened with white, 49.5 × 30 cm ($19\frac{5}{8} \times 11\frac{3}{4}''$)
Collection F. Hagemann, Basel

265 Orphan Man with Top Hat, Drinking Coffee, F976
Pencil, black chalk, washed, 49 × 29 cm ($19\frac{1}{4} \times 11\frac{3}{8}''$)
Rijksmuseum Kröller-Müller, Otterlo

266 Orphan Man with Top Hat, Drinking Coffee, F1657 (cf. drawings 263 and 264)
Lithograph, 57 × 37.5 cm ($22\frac{1}{2} \times 15''$)
Various collections

for information, and as Theo did not immediately reply, he kept hammering at this question in the following letters. In Letter 242 his imagination was running so wild that he was talking about a series of thirty lithographs that would form a sort of unit and would require a much larger number of drawings as preliminary studies. Apparently he could not curb his impatience, for Letter 243, November 6 to 8, opens with this announcement: "While awaiting further information regarding the process, I have made a lithograph with the help of the printer from Smulders, and I have the pleasure of enclosing the very first print." It appears from later information that Vincent had used a drawing of the orphan man (256) for this first lithograph. He wrote: "I drew this lithograph on a piece of prepared paper, probably the same kind Buhot was talking about," and he managed to get along with this paper, which he had been able to buy from Smulders, since no reply was forthcoming from Theo (it later turned out that a letter of November 9 with 50 francs had been lost). The little roll of paper from Buhot that had been promised did not arrive until the beginning of December. Meanwhile, Vincent had been making one lithograph after another; in chronological order these were: *Orphan Man* (256), "*Sorrow*" (259), *Digger* (262), *Orphan Man with Top Hat, Drinking Coffee* (266), *Old Man* (268), and *Fisherman Sitting on a Basket, Cutting Bread* (272). Despite his dreams about a long series, that was all for the time being, probably since he regarded the last lithograph, in which the ink had run, as more or less a failure (Letter 250).

The idea of cooperation among artists in a big project, broached in several letters about this time, came very much to the fore again during Vincent's time in France. Although the plan he set forth came to naught, it is very important for us that his letters tell us so completely what he had in mind: "I should think that something along the following lines could be done: Whereas it is useful and necessary for Dutch drawings to be made, printed, and distributed to the homes of the workmen and to farms, in short, for the benefit of every workingman, so let there be some people who will pledge to do their utmost, to give of their best efforts, to achieve this aim." From Vincent's long discourse about this plan (which he also mentioned to Van Rappard), I shall quote only the characteristic detail that "the price of the sheets should not exceed 10, or at the most, 15 cents" (Letter 249).

In connection with these views the following anecdote, which Vincent related to his brother Theo, is typical: "The men at Smulders's other warehouse on the Laan had seen the stone of the *Orphan Man* and asked the printer whether they could get a print to hang up. No result of my work would please me more than for ordinary workmen to hang such sheets in their rooms or workshops." And he appended a reference to one of the British illustrators he most admired: "*For you—the public—it is really done* I regard as a true word spoken by Herkomer" (Letter 245).

The plan for a joint edition, which Vincent continued to discuss in his next letters, was for the time being given the crowning touch

267

269

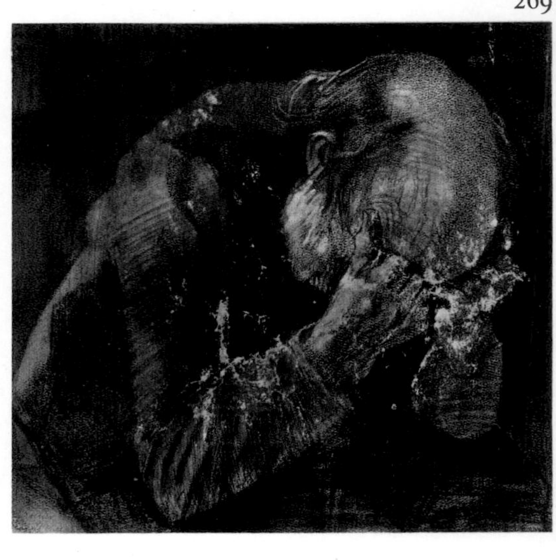

268

267 Old Man with His Head in His Hands, F997 (cf. lithograph 268)
Pencil, 50 × 31 cm (19⅝ × 12¼″)
Rijksmuseum Vincent van Gogh, Amsterdam

268 Old Man with His Head in His Hands ("At Eternity's gate"), F1662 (cf. drawing 267)
Lithograph, 55.5 × 36.5 cm (22 × 14⅝″)
Various collections

269 Old Man with His Head in His Hands, Half-Figure, F998
Black lithographic chalk, pencil, washed, heightened with white, 45.5 × 47.5 cm (18⅛ × 18⅞″)
Rijksmuseum Kröller-Müller, Otterlo

Colorplate III, The State Lottery Office, 222 〉

with the conclusion in Letter 251: "I told myself that what I had to do was obvious: to put my very best into the drawings." Among the new drawings mentioned by Vincent at the beginning of December, the very first were some sowers (274 and 275), one of his regular subjects since the time, nearly two years before, when he had copied the *Sower* by his paragon, Millet. The sowers now seem to have been carefully observed in their movements and to have space around them. This time Van Rappard would not have been able to repeat what he had said about the *Sower* Vincent did in Etten the year before: "It is not a man who is sowing, but a man posing as a sower" (Letter R2). Some of the figures made in December were probably done in haste—sketchily or even carelessly drawn, such as the orphan man in 282 and 283—but in most cases Vincent truly has done "his very best." Full-length figures have been rendered with great care in respect both to postures and to the relationship between light and dark (see 278–81). In heads and half-length figures, the typical characteristics of the old, weatherbeaten faces have been tersely rendered (for example, 284–87). Some of the female heads, like those of Sien and her mother (291 and 296), are also striking by reason of the painstaking manner in which very different types have been rendered. It must be remembered that before doing these heads of women and the orphan men Vincent had virtually never drawn a true portrait. He must indeed have felt it was here that his strength lay; even during his time in France, with its many wonderful landscapes, he often complained that he really preferred to depict people but lacked the money for models.

Only a few drawings were specifically mentioned in his letters. In Letter 253, written about the middle of December 1882, he says: "Again, I now have two drawings, one of a man reading the Bible, and the other of a man saying grace over his midday meal, which is on the table. Both most certainly embody what could be called an old-fashioned feeling, as do figures like the little old man with his head in his hands. The *Bénédicité* [grace before meals] is, I think, the best, although they complement each other."

Three drawings answer to the description of "a man reading the Bible": 278, 279, and 280; the drawing of "a man saying grace," which Vincent also called the *Bénédicité*, must be 281. The little old man with his "head in his hands" is drawing 267, of which he had also made a lithograph (268).

Further on in his letter he explained what his intention had been with these figures, which also clarifies the "old-fashioned feeling": to express the distinctive sentiment of Christmas and New Year's Eve. This led Vincent to one of his rare utterances regarding his own religious feelings. The *form* that religion took did not matter too much to him, but "it is something one respects, provided it is sincere, and for myself I can fully share in it and even have a need for it, at least in the sense that I have a feeling of and belief in *quelque-chose là-haut* [something up there] just as much as such a little old man does, although I am not exactly sure of how it is or of what is there" (Letter 253).

And when in his next letter he came back

270

271

272

273

270 Woman on a Road with Pollard Willows, F 1092
Pencil, black chalk, washed, 35.5 × 60.5 cm ($14\frac{1}{8} \times 24''$)
Rijksmuseum Kröller-Müller, Otterlo

271 Orphan Man, Standing
Sketch in Letter 248
Rijksmuseum Vincent van Gogh, Amsterdam

272 Fisherman, Sitting on a Basket, Cutting Bread, F 1663 (original drawing unknown)
Lithograph, 45 × 29 cm ($17\frac{3}{4} \times 11\frac{3}{8}''$)
Various collections

December 1882

273 Man Carrying Peat, F 964
Pencil, washed, 48 × 22.5 cm ($18\frac{7}{8} \times 9''$)
Location unknown

to his drawings, it was to say once more: "I have been toiling over them again in the last few days, precisely because I was full of that Christmas feeling, and to feel is not enough, you must bring it into your work." And then even the simple large heads (287 and 288) seem to have become involved in these ideas: "So now I am working on two large heads of an orphan man with his white beard and old-fashioned old top hat. He has the kind of old, witty face that you would like to have at a convivial Christmas fire, that fellow."

"I Cannot Make 'Types of Beauty'"

Vincent had explained something of his ideals to Theo earlier when he had sent him part of the Christmas issue of *The Graphic* around Christmastime, apparently a kind of prospectus. He felt that of late the journal was no longer what it had originally promised to be. Just as had happened in other fields of art, according to Vincent, the commercial element had begun to dominate, or, as he expressed it: "*Grandeur morale* [moral greatness] is on the decline and is being replaced by *grandeur matérielle* [material greatness]." He also saw this around him: "Here in The Hague there are able and great men. I will gladly admit that, but in many respects, what a wretched state of affairs, with all the intrigue, quarreling, jealousy. And in the personalities of the artists who are becoming rich, who call the tune with Mesdag at their head, there is also unmistakably a kind of replacement of *grandeur morale* by *grandeur matérielle*" (Letter 252).

Vincent felt that he had perhaps reached the point where, if he put forth his best efforts, he might have a chance of finding employment as an illustrator, possibly in England. "To get this far was my ideal; it was, and after all still is, the thing that spurred me on to overcome those first enormous difficulties. But at times my heart grows heavy within me when I think of how things are going, and the enjoyment fades away. I still want to do my best in my drawings but to go around to all those editorial offices, Lord! it gives me the horrors."

He foresaw that such employment would not really enable him to advance but would lead him in a direction quite different from what he intended. He knew himself well enough to realize that he would eventually be found wanting and be discharged, and he added with self-confidence: "I would also resign of my own accord, as at Goupil's." The individualist (and idealist) that Vincent had always been, and would always be, was true to form even here.

The prospectus of *The Graphic* announced that the journal was going to publish a series entitled "Types of Beauty"; "I suppose to replace 'Heads of the People' by Herkomer, Small, and Ridley," Vincent remarked, sarcastically referring to three English graphic artists he admired—Hubert Herkomer, Matthew White Ridley, and William Small. Vir cent summed up his reasoning pithily: "Look, Theo, old man, I cannot make 'Types of Beauty,' but I do my best on 'Heads of People.' You see, Theo, I would like to do what those who started *The Graphic* did, even though I do not regard myself as their equal, and that is to take a fellow or a girl off the

274

275

276

274 Sower (with Another Sower in the Background), F853
Pencil, 31.5 × 21 cm (12$\frac{3}{8}$ × 8$\frac{1}{4}$″)
Rijksmuseum Vincent van Gogh, Amsterdam

275 Sower, F852
Pencil, brush, China ink, 61 × 40 cm (24 × 15$\frac{3}{4}$″)
P. and N. de Boer Foundation, Amsterdam

276 Sower, F1000
Pencil, 48 × 23.5 cm (18$\frac{7}{8}$ × 9$\frac{1}{4}$″)
Location unknown

277 Sower, F999
Pencil, 49 × 28.5 cm (19$\frac{1}{4}$ × 11$\frac{3}{8}$″)
Collection Mrs. H. Glatt-Kisling, Zurich

278 Man, Sitting, Reading a Book, F1001
Pencil, 47 × 30.5 cm (18$\frac{1}{2}$ × 12$\frac{1}{4}$″)
Rijksmuseum Kröller-Müller, Otterlo

279 Man, Standing, Reading a Book, F1683
Black chalk, pen, brush, washed, dimensions unknown
Location unknown

280 Orphan Man with Cap, Sitting, Reading a Book, F966
Pencil, washed with bister, 48 × 28.5 cm (18$\frac{7}{8}$ × 11$\frac{3}{8}$″)
Rijksmuseum Vincent van Gogh, Amsterdam

277

278

279

280

281

282

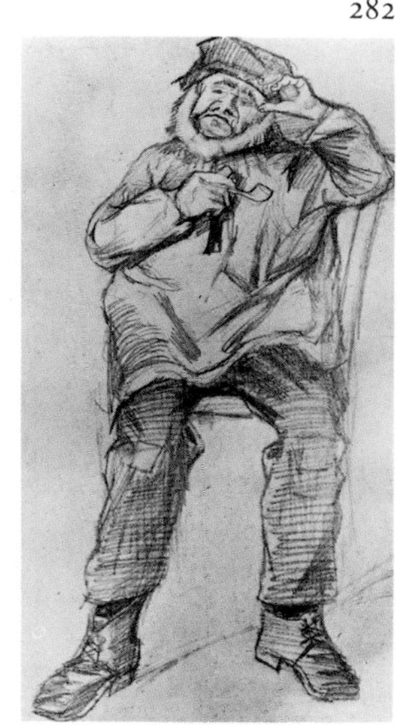

283

281 Prayer before the Meal, F 1002
Pencil, black chalk, ink, heightened with white, 60 × 50 cm ($23\frac{5}{8} \times 19\frac{5}{8}$″)
Collection H. Doyer Family, Chailly-Lausanne, Switzerland

282 Orphan Man, Wearing a Blouse, Sitting with Pipe, F1046
Pencil, 47 × 26 cm ($18\frac{1}{2} \times 10\frac{1}{4}$″)
Collection Mrs. Eva Kobrinsky, Winnipeg

283 Orphan Man, Wearing a Blouse, with Broom and Pipe, F996
Pencil, washed, 50 × 21 cm ($19\frac{5}{8} \times 8\frac{1}{4}$″)
Matthiesen Art Gallery, Geneva

street and draw them in my studio." And thus far he had carried out this program to the letter.

New Year's Eve Reflections

Despite the enthusiasm with which he worked on the drawings of figures, the year's end caused Vincent to put troubled thoughts on paper. After a few words of gratitude ("Before the year comes to an end, I must thank you once again for all your help and friendship"), he wrote: "I feel bad that I have still not succeeded in making a salable drawing this past year; I really do not know what is the reason for this" (Letter 255). A few days later he wrote again to say that he still had so many plans but so little information on how realistic they were that he thought he ought to talk them over with Theo. And this time he added: "In any case, don't let it worry you that this year too I have not made anything that would sell." If Theo should see any improvement in Vincent's work when he came, then he would like to continue working in the same way as before. "If there is bread in the house and I have something in my pocket to pay models, then what more do I want? My pleasure lies in improving my work, and I am engrossed in it more and more" (Letter 256). He must have regained much of his self-confidence the next day when he got a letter from Theo that apparently had some praise for him; it was an incentive to him not to give up. "You say too much in my favor in your letter, but the fact that you think well of me is all the more reason why I should try not to be completely unworthy of it" (Letter 257). Because he felt uncertain about whether he was pursuing the right course, he sent Theo a few of the drawings he had just made, with this letter and the following one, in order to get his opinion. "By working hard, old man, I hope to make something good one day. I haven't yet, but I am pursuing it and fighting for it; I would like something serious, something fresh—something with a soul in it! Onward, onward—" (Letter 257).

In the previous letter, written on New Year's Eve (Letter 256), he had dealt at some length with his efforts to obtain new effects with other mediums, specifically the lithographic chalk he had become familiar with in his experiments with lithography. "I hit on the idea of making a drawing first with a carpenter's pencil and then working lithographic chalk into this and over it, because this chalk (being made of a greasy substance) adheres to pencil—which ordinary chalk does *not*, or only poorly. With the sketch made this way, you can apply the lithographic chalk with a steady hand where it is needed, without too much fumbling or rubbing out." This passage is particularly important to us because of the clue it provides regarding the chronology of a number of drawings not mentioned in the letters. Various studies in which lithographic chalk is recognizable probably date from December or January. And further, the nucleus for the grouping of related studies is formed by some drawings of which we do find descriptions in the letters, such as the old man reading, 278, the man praying, 281, and the "wounded man," 289.

284

285

286

284 Orphan Man with Top Hat, Head, F961
Black chalk, pencil, 45 × 24.5 cm ($17\frac{3}{4} \times 9\frac{7}{8}$")
Hannema-de Stuers Foundation, Heino, The Netherlands

285 Orphan Man in Sunday Clothes with Eye Bandage, Head, F1003
Pencil, lithographic chalk, washed, heightened with black and white, 46.5 × 27.5 cm ($18\frac{1}{2} \times 11$")
Fogg Art Museum, Harvard University, Cambridge, Massachusetts

286 Orphan Man with Top Hat, Head, F985
Pencil, black lithographic chalk, washed, pen, brown ink, 60.5 × 36 cm ($24 \times 14\frac{1}{8}$")
Rijksmuseum Vincent van Gogh, Amsterdam

287 Orphan Man with Top Hat, F954
Pencil, brush, 40 × 24.5 cm ($15\frac{3}{4} \times 9\frac{7}{8}$")
Worcester Art Museum, Massachusetts

288 Orphan Man with Top Hat, Head, F954a
Black chalk, charcoal, heightened with white, 44 × 29 cm ($17\frac{3}{8} \times 11\frac{3}{8}$")
Municipal Art Gallery, Johannesburg

287

288

289

290

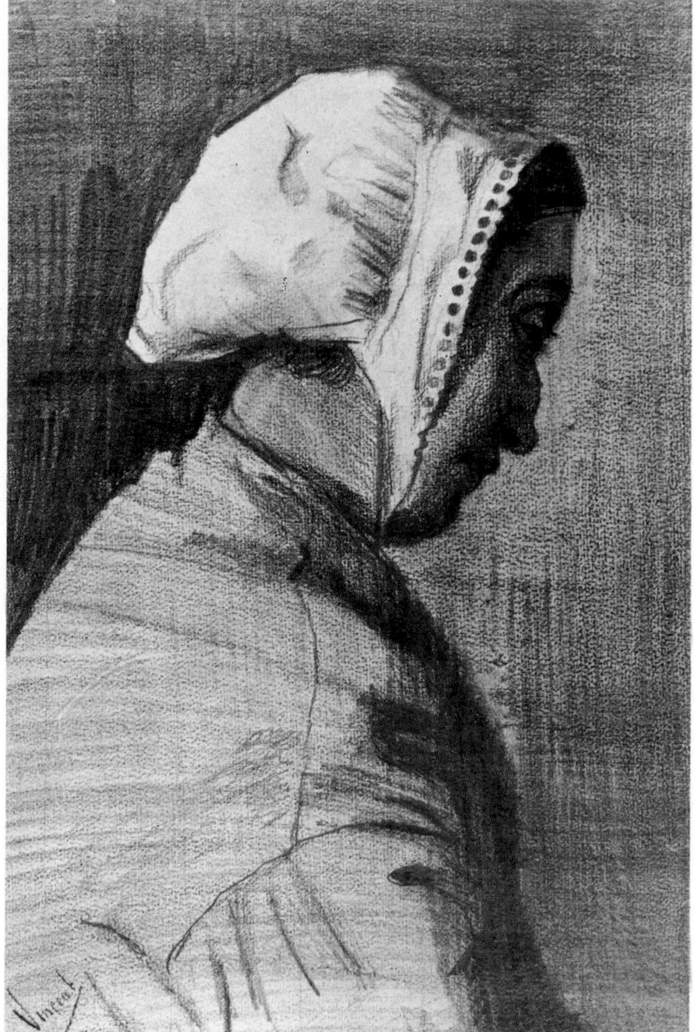

291

292

293

289 Man with Pipe and Eye Bandage, Head, F 1004
Pencil, black lithographic chalk, washed, heightened with white, 45×27.5 cm ($17\frac{3}{4} \times 11''$)
Rijksmuseum Kröller-Müller, Otterlo

290 Sien with White Cap, Head, F 1055
Black chalk, pencil, ink, 43×27 cm ($16\frac{7}{8} \times 10\frac{5}{8}''$)
Rijksmuseum Vincent van Gogh, Amsterdam

291 Sien with White Cap, Head, F 931
Pencil, black lithographic chalk, washed, 47.5×26 cm ($18\frac{7}{8} \times 10\frac{1}{4}''$)
Rijksmuseum Vincent van Gogh, Amsterdam

292 Woman with Dark Cap (Sien's Mother?), Head, F 1005
Pencil, black lithographic chalk, washed with white and black, 45×26.5 cm ($17\frac{3}{4} \times 10\frac{5}{8}''$)
Rijksmuseum Vincent van Gogh, Amsterdam

293 Woman with Hat, Head, F 1054
Black chalk, brush, ink, washed, 46.5×26 cm ($18\frac{1}{2} \times 10\frac{1}{4}''$)
Kunstmuseum, Bern

Life with a Woman and Children

About the middle of January, Vincent wrote about his domestic situation: "At this moment the woman is sitting beside me with the children. There is a great difference when I think of last year. The woman is stronger and more robust, has lost much, very much of her nervousness; the little child is as healthy and cheerful a little fellow as you could possibly imagine, crows like a rooster, is entirely breast-fed but is fat and chubby. And the poor little girl, from the drawing you see that the deep misery of the past is not all gone, and it often worries me, but yet it is quite different from last year; then it was very bad, and now there is something really childlike" (Letter 260). What he says makes clear what life with a woman and children meant to him, but it also shows with how much justifiable pride he could look back on what he had done for them.

The final sentence indicates that one of the drawings he had just sent Theo was a likeness of Sien's little daughter. In my opinion it would have been the girl with the shawl (301) or the girl with the pinafore (300)—more likely the former because in it the misery is certainly not all gone and yet there is also something childlike about the little girl. Even more moving is the expression of the little girl, also with a shawl, in 299. Here the "deep misery" is certainly the dominating element. The face, however, looks so much older that I would be inclined to say that it was not Sien's little daughter, who was five, but rather Sien's youngest sister, who was ten. The sister, whose name, Maria Wilhelmina, was the same as the daughter's, was also one of Vincent's models, according to Letter 178. On the other hand, the older girl, seen in drawing 330, wore her hair in a braid. In any event, as far as power of expression is concerned, the three drawings of children are among the high points of Vincent's stay in The Hague.

Heads—again called "Heads of the People"—continue as the chief element in his production for January. For some reason or other he was fascinated by the sou'wester as a necessary attribute in depicting fishermen, and when at last he was able to get one, he wrote, around January 21: "Fishermen's heads, old and young, are something I have thought about for a long time, and I had already made one of them, and was then unable to get a sou'wester. Now I am getting one of my own, an old one that was weathered by many gales and heavy seas" (Letter 261). Some ten "fishermen" (it is sometimes the orphan man dressed as a fisherman) are the reminder of Vincent's short-lived interest in this subject, which coincided with his experiments with lithographic chalk.

Vincent as a Collector

An event important to Vincent, and described in detail in several letters written in January, was his purchase of a large number of issues of *The Graphic*, the journal he admired so much on account of the wood engravings by a large group of British artists with which it was illustrated. Perhaps because he thought the purchase rather extravagant, he did not write to Theo about it but rather to his friend Van Rappard, whom he had earlier talked

294

295

296

294 Woman with Dark Cap (Sien's Mother?), F 1057
Lithographic chalk, pencil, watercolor, heightened with white, 47.5 × 26 cm ($18\frac{7}{8} \times 10\frac{1}{4}$″)
Groninger Museum, Groningen

295 Woman with Dark Cap (Sien's Mother?), Head, F 1006
Pencil, black lithographic chalk, washed with white, 50 × 28.5 cm ($19\frac{5}{8} \times 11\frac{3}{8}$″)
Rijksmuseum Vincent van Gogh, Amsterdam

296 Woman with Dark Cap (Sien's Mother?), Head, F 1057a
Charcoal, heightened with white, 44 × 23.5 cm ($17\frac{3}{8} \times 9\frac{1}{2}$″)
Collection Mrs. L. Stiennon-de Neuville, Liège

297 Orphan Man with Cap and Walking Stick, F 963
Black chalk, 48 × 24.5 cm ($18\frac{7}{8} \times 9\frac{7}{8}$″)
Museum van Baaren, Utrecht

298 Orphan Man with Cap, Seen from the Back, F 965
Pencil, black chalk, 50 × 28 cm ($19\frac{5}{8} \times 11$″)
Private collection, East Germany

297

298

299

300

301

302

303

January 1883

299 Girl with Shawl, Half-Figure, F 1007
Pencil, black chalk, washed, heightened with white, 43.5 × 25 cm ($17\frac{3}{8} \times 9\frac{7}{8}''$)
Rijksmuseum Kröller-Müller, Otterlo

300 Girl with Pinafore, Half-Figure, F 1685
Pencil, lithographic chalk, pen, brush, ink, heightened with white, 48.5 × 25.5 cm ($19\frac{1}{4} \times 10\frac{1}{4}''$)
Location unknown

301 Girl with Shawl, Half-Figure, F 1008
Pencil, black lithographic chalk, 50.5 × 31 cm ($20\frac{1}{8} \times 12\frac{1}{4}''$)
Rijksmuseum Vincent van Gogh, Amsterdam

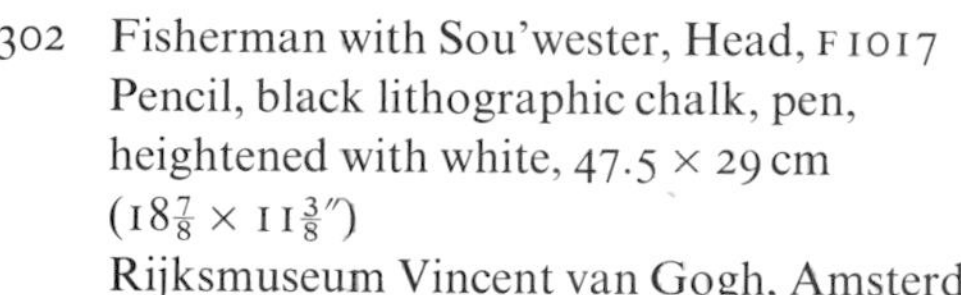

302 Fisherman with Sou'wester, Head, F 1017
Pencil, black lithographic chalk, pen, heightened with white, 47.5 × 29 cm ($18\frac{7}{8} \times 11\frac{3}{8}''$)
Rijksmuseum Vincent van Gogh, Amsterdam

303 Orphan Man with Pickax on His Shoulder, F 987
Black chalk, 45.5 × 21.5 cm ($18\frac{1}{8} \times 8\frac{5}{8}''$)
Collection E. Rogoff, Johannesburg

into collecting prints of this kind. (His words to Van Rappard "my brother helped me get them" [Letter R24] remain difficult to explain.)

About January 15 he announced the big news: "A few days ago I bought twenty-one volumes of *The Graphic*, namely 1870–80. What do you say to that? I hope to get them this week. I got them quite cheap; otherwise, as you can understand, I could not have afforded anything like that" (Letter R22). Some five days later he continued: "*The Graphics* are now in my possession. I was up late into the night looking at them" (R23). The letters, with their page-long observations on the illustrations and their makers, must be read in full to realize what an experience it must have been for Vincent to be absorbed in the work of these artists he admired so much and with whom he felt such a close affinity. Up to the end of March, Van Rappard, with whom Vincent had meanwhile begun an exchange of prints, was kept informed in the letters from Vincent about his collection of "woodcuts." The fact that others considered it a matter of such little importance that he had been able to make this "scandalous purchase" really bothered him: "Although I am glad to have them, I do at the same time feel bad that there is so little enthusiasm for them. I think it wonderful to find such a treasure, but I would have preferred that there were so much enthusiasm that I would not have been able to get them for a while" (Letter R24). It was also characteristic of him to wave away Van Rappard's scruples about accepting prints from him, saying: "You must take these and no nonsense about it, and that also goes for the other ones of which there are duplicates in *The Graphic*. Prints like these, I feel, make up a kind of bible for the artist which he reads from time to time to get into the right mood" (Letter R25).*

Work in the "Studio"

A number of Vincent's letters written during February—a month he spent quietly working on his studies of figures, such as drawings 311, 316, 317, 321, and others—mention a matter connected with his house that was to have a direct influence on his work. When he had rented the new quarters, he had written that the spacious room he used as a "studio" had three large, high windows. In the last week of February he spoke of discussions with his landlord about a plan to improve the situation. He now wrote that he had been able to get the landlord to agree to having shutters fitted to the inside of the windows, which would make it possible to screen off the light from the upper or lower halves. Various sketches in Letter 268 and following letters show the shutters and the effects he was able to achieve when drawing groups of people in the studio. In Letter 270 he explains: "Here you see the windows shuttered at the bottom so that the light strikes the group of figures from above. I am thus able to place them in the studio in such a way that I get, for example, little sidelights falling upon the figures. As in this watercolor." The

*Many interesting details about Vincent's collection and its influence on his work were brought together by Ronald Pickvance in the catalogue issued on the occasion of the exhibition he organized, *English Influences on Vincent van Gogh* (1974).

304

305

306

304 Fisherman with Sou'wester, Pipe, and Firepot, Half-Figure, F1016
Pencil, black lithographic chalk, washed, 47.5 × 29 cm ($18\frac{7}{8} \times 11\frac{3}{8}$")
Rijksmuseum Vincent van Gogh, Amsterdam

305 Fisherman with Sou'wester, Sitting with Pipe, F1013
Sketch reproduced with Letter 262
Pen, pencil, 10.5 × 6.5 cm ($4\frac{3}{8} \times 2\frac{3}{4}$")
Rijksmuseum Vincent van Gogh, Amsterdam

306 Fisherman with Sou'wester, Sitting with Pipe, F1010
Pen, pencil, black chalk, washed, heightened with white, 46 × 26 cm ($18\frac{1}{8} \times 10\frac{1}{4}$")
Rijksmuseum Kröller-Müller, Otterlo

307 Fisherman with Sou'wester, Smoking a Pipe, Head, F1015
Pencil, black lithographic chalk, washed, 41.5 × 26 cm ($16\frac{1}{2} \times 10\frac{1}{4}$")
Rijksmuseum Vincent van Gogh, Amsterdam

308 Fisherman with Sou'wester, Head, F1012
Pencil, lithographic chalk, 44 × 27.5 cm ($17\frac{3}{8} \times 11$")
Norton Simon Foundation, Los Angeles

309 Fisherman with Sou'wester, Head, F1011
Black chalk, brush, heightened with black and white, 43 × 25 cm ($16\frac{7}{8} \times 9\frac{7}{8}$")
Rijksmuseum Kröller-Müller, Otterlo

307

308

309

310

311

312

313

310 Fisherman with Sou'wester, Head, F 1014
Pencil, black lithographic chalk, ink, heightened with black and white, 50.5 × 31.5 cm ($20\frac{1}{8} \times 12\frac{5}{8}$″)
Rijksmuseum Vincent van Gogh, Amsterdam

311 Orphan Man with Cap, Half-Length, F 1019
Pencil, black chalk, pen, washed, 45 × 28 cm ($17\frac{3}{4} \times 11$″)
Collection H. R. Hahnloser, Bern

312 Fisherman in Jacket with Standing Collar, F 1049
Pencil, 48.5 × 22 cm ($19\frac{1}{4} \times 8\frac{5}{8}$″)
Estate of F. A. C. Guépin, London

313 Fisherman with Basket on His Back, F 1083
Pencil, 46.5 × 24 cm ($18\frac{1}{2} \times 9\frac{1}{2}$″)
Location unknown

watercolor he referred to has been lost, but the sketch with the windows shuttered at the bottom is 327, which may be compared with the other sketches of the room 328, 332, and 333. His aim was to introduce more chiaroscuro into his drawings than there had been in his studies of the past winter, and as he wrote: "I now dare in any case to promise you this; tomorrow I will have the house full of people, namely, the woman's mother and youngest sister, and a boy from the neighborhood, and these people, together with the members of my household, will pose for the drawing of which this is the first small rough draft" (Letter 271). The result was the important large drawing 330, which Vincent himself regarded as "not yet properly finished," but still he sent it to Theo the same day (Letter 272). He had now been able to study the scene of the soup kitchen—which he had often had occasion to observe in its actual site—at his ease in the quiet of his studio, thanks to the improvement in the lighting. The drawing demonstrates that he could achieve a surprisingly proficient execution both of individual figures and of total composition. It is forceful and well detailed in spite of the sharp, fairly heavy hatching of some parts that have been kept simple and monumental. What makes the drawing particularly attractive for us is the fact that all the figures have become familiar to us by now: Sien's mother with the baby on her arm, the ten-year-old sister, the little daughter, and Sien herself, whose characteristic features and posture have here been superbly rendered.

Another drawing he had made the same morning—"a watercolor of a boy and a girl in a similar soup kitchen, with the small figure of a woman in the corner" (331)—was less felicitous. The combination of watercolor, pencil, and black mountain chalk resulted in a drawing with an unfinished look in which the figures do not stand out from the background. Vincent himself called the watercolor "stale," with the excuse that it was "partly due to the paper's not being suitable" (Letter 272).

A New Medium

In discussing drawing 331, I mentioned the use of mountain chalk. The (re-)discovery of this medium appears to have been important to Vincent, for in various letters to Theo in March he keeps singing its praises. "Do you remember bringing me some pieces of mountain chalk last summer? I tried working with it then, but without success. So there were still a few pieces lying around that I recently took up again. Enclosed is a rough sketch made with it; as you see, it is a warm, peculiar black" (Letter 270). What he sent was a small, hastily done study of people on a street (323). He had drawn it on the back of an envelope, probably from memory but with earlier drawings in front of him (for example, the figure on the left-hand side can be recognized as the orphan man of drawings 239 and 240. The drawing of the soup kitchen mentioned above (330) was done with mountain chalk, "with the one small piece I had from this summer." And Vincent added: "If you want to do me a *very great* favor, send me a few pieces of mountain chalk by mail."

314

315

316

February 1883

314 Man with a Rake, F979
Pencil, 44 × 22 cm (17⅜ × 8⅝″)
Collection H. J. Nolte, Curaçao

315 Orphan Man Talking with a Woman (Sien?), F989
Pencil, black chalk, 45.5 × 26 cm (18⅛ × 10¼″)
Rijksmuseum Kröller-Müller, Otterlo

316 Orphan Man with Cap, Head, F1018
Pencil, heightened with black, 34.5 × 27.5 cm (13¾ × 11″)
Private collection, The Hague

317 Orphan Man with a Baby in His Arms, Half-Length, F981
Pencil, 36.5 × 25 cm (14⅜ × 9⅞″)
Private collection, The Netherlands

318 Baby, F912
Black lithographic chalk, washed, 31 × 24 cm (12¼ × 9½″)
Collection Mrs. A. Cohen Tervaert-Henny, Zeist, The Netherlands

319 Baby, F911 (reverse: 320)
Sketch sent with Letter 258?
Pen, 10 × 7 cm (3⅞ × 2¾″)
Rijksmuseum Vincent van Gogh, Amsterdam

317

318

319

320

321

322

323

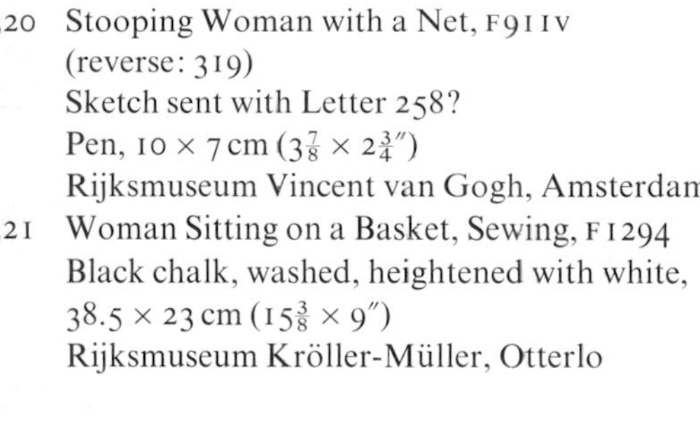

320 Stooping Woman with a Net, F 911 v
(reverse: 319)
Sketch sent with Letter 258?
Pen, 10 × 7 cm ($3\frac{7}{8} \times 2\frac{3}{4}''$)
Rijksmuseum Vincent van Gogh, Amsterdam

321 Woman Sitting on a Basket, Sewing, F 1294
Black chalk, washed, heightened with white,
38.5 × 23 cm ($15\frac{3}{8} \times 9''$)
Rijksmuseum Kröller-Müller, Otterlo

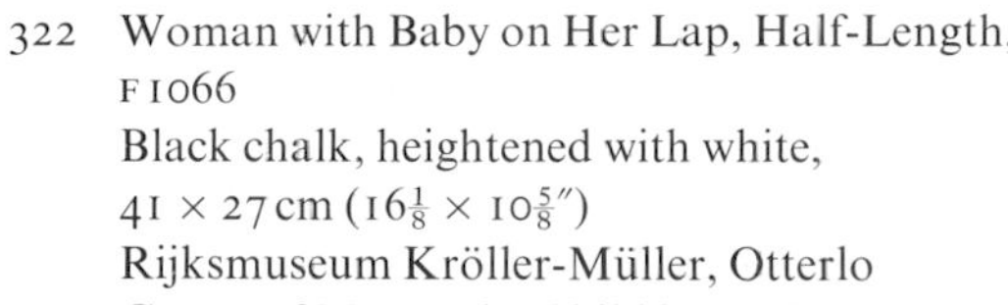

322 Woman with Baby on Her Lap, Half-Length,
F 1066
Black chalk, heightened with white,
41 × 27 cm ($16\frac{1}{8} \times 10\frac{5}{8}''$)
Rijksmuseum Kröller-Müller, Otterlo

323 Group of Men and a Child in the Street
Sketch (on an envelope) sent with Letter 270
Rijksmuseum Vincent van Gogh, Amsterdam

While he saw in conté crayon "something lifeless," he was lyrical in his praise of the medium he was now using: "Mountain chalk understands what you want; I would almost say it listens intelligently and obeys, but conté is indifferent and does not cooperate. Mountain chalk has the true soul of a gypsy; if it is not asking you too much, send me some of it" (Letter 272). We know that Theo did indeed comply with the request. In Letter 277 of March 30 Vincent thanked him for what had been sent, but somewhat earlier, in Letter 274 of March 11, he had been able to write: "I found a little still left at a druggist's, some six pieces or so but all in small bits." It was enough to enable him to go on with the series of drawings in mountain chalk, which he had started early in March. Besides the drawings of the soup kitchen, he also used this medium for the sketch of the baby that was sent to Van Rappard (334), the drawing of Sien seated on a basket with the little girl at her feet (341), the little girl at the cradle (336), the half-length figure of Sien sewing (346), and probably a number of other figure studies of Sien, although the description of the medium used is sometimes given as "black chalk" and not "mountain chalk."

Late Snowfall
When snow had fallen in the middle of March, Vincent made a couple of very typical sketches of the view from his rear window for Theo and Van Rappard (342 and 343). He also made a watercolor of the landscape, seen from the same location, but angled so that part of the tiled roof also came into the picture (344). Another watercolor of the winter landscape—from which the small rough draft 342 was made, as he wrote in Letter 276—was "not sufficiently lively and forceful," to use his own words. This drawing must have been lost, unless Vincent himself disposed of it. Watercolor 344, too, is certainly not "lively" and "forceful" but it can be said to be an effective rendering of the chilly wintry mood.

A few words about the drawing of a woman with her hair hanging down (352). Since this drawing is dated The Hague 1883 in the 1970 *catalogue raisonné*, I have included it here with the other female heads from March, but must say that the style of drawing and the female type depicted hardly seem to fit in this

324

325

326

324 Woman with Folded Hands, Half-Length, F1179
Pencil, ink, watercolor, 47 × 31 cm (18½ × 12¼″)
Rijksmuseum Kröller-Müller, Otterlo

325 Woman Sitting on a Basket, with Head in Hands, F1069
Black chalk, heightened with white, 49 × 30.5 cm (19¼ × 12¼″)
Art Institute of Chicago

326 Woman Sitting on a Basket, with Head in Hands, F1060
Black chalk, washed, heightened with white, 47.5 × 29.5 cm (18⅞ × 11¾″)
Rijksmuseum Kröller-Müller, Otterlo

March 1883

327 People in the Studio
Sketch in Letter 270
Rijksmuseum Vincent van Gogh, Amsterdam

328 The Public Soup Kitchen
Sketch in Letter 271
Rijksmuseum Vincent van Gogh, Amsterdam

329 Woman with White Cap, Half-Length, F1047
Pencil with pink wash, the back of the seat brown, 48 × 30 cm (18⅞ × 11¾″)
Collection S. Sair, Winnipeg

330 The Public Soup Kitchen, F1020a
Black mountain chalk, 57 × 44.5 cm (22½ × 17½″)
Rijksmuseum Vincent van Gogh, Amsterdam

331 The Public Soup Kitchen, F1020b
Pencil, black mountain chalk, watercolor, 34 × 49 cm (13⅜ × 19¼″)
Collection A. Menko, Enschede, The Netherlands

332 The Public Soup Kitchen
Sketch in Letter 272
Rijksmuseum Vincent van Gogh, Amsterdam

333 The Public Soup Kitchen, F1020
Sketch sent with Letter 273
Pen, 10 × 10 cm (3⅞ × 3⅞″)
Rijksmuseum Vincent van Gogh, Amsterdam

334 Baby Crawling, F872
Sketch sent with Letter R 30
Black mountain chalk, 7 × 9 cm (2¾ × 3½″)
Collection Mrs. W. F. Hupkes-de Kanter, Bilthoven, The Netherlands

335 Woman, Bareheaded (Sien's Mother?), Head, F1009
Pencil, black lithographic chalk, washed with black, 39 × 24.5 cm (15⅜ × 9⅞″)
Rijksmuseum Vincent van Gogh, Amsterdam

327

328

329

330

331

332

333

334

335

series or in any other group of Van Gogh drawings, no more than in those from the Antwerp period, to which Vanbeselaere and Tralbaut thought it belonged.

There must be many other works from this month that have been lost. When Vincent drew up the balance sheet at the end of the month, he wrote: "I have a sower—a mower—a woman at the washtub—a *charbonnière* [female coal miner]—a woman sewing—a man digging—a woman with a spade—the orphan man—la bénédicité—a fellow with a wheelbarrow of manure" (Letter 277). Ten subjects, six of which cannot be related to an existing drawing.

In April Vincent continued to draw figures. Although he had said in Letter 277 that he was very happy with the mountain chalk Theo had sent him, we hear very little more about it. However, we do read about an experiment with yet another medium. "I have lately been working with printer's ink; it is diluted with turpentine and put on with a brush. It gives very deep tones of black. Mixed with Chinese white, it also gives good grays" (Letter 278, April 2). Various studies of figures in which printer's ink and brushwork have been used can therefore also be assigned to this period: *Orphan Man* (355), *Woman Feeding Chickens* (349) and man in the same posture (350), *Woman Praying* (357), and others. Only one drawing is specifically mentioned in the letters written this month—a "man kneeling" (Letter 281, April 30), which probably refers to 354.

The painted study of a field of bulbs, 361, is a special case. Although no other painted studies from this time are known to us and no mention of this study is made in the letters, I have placed it here by reason of its subject. The other painted studies date from August 1882 (first series) or August 1883 (second series)—a time of year when bulb fields are not in bloom.

Working Outdoors in Spring

Because of a lack of data I have been able to assign remarkably little of Vincent's work to May. Much of it must have been lost, since next to nothing remains of the many preliminary studies Vincent mentions in connection with the large compositions he was working on at the end of the month: the *Peat Diggers in the Dunes*, 363 and 364. This highly demanding work is first mentioned about May 25 in a letter to Van Rappard, who in a sense made it possible for Vincent to start it by lending him 25 guldens during a visit May 20. Since the drawings were to measure about 19⅝ × 39⅜ inches, Vincent, following Van Rappard's example, had a wooden passe-partout made for working in this format. "As soon as I got back from your place, I started in on it, for it had already more or less taken shape in my head. Like some other compositions, I had already thought about it a great deal and had already made studies for it. However, if I had not gotten the money from you, I would not, for example, have been able to do it at this time" (Letter R36). A few days later, when he sent a small rough sketch of it to Theo, he wrote: "This is *Peat Diggers in the Dunes*—the actual drawing now measures about one meter by one-half meter. It is a really fine scene in the outdoors,

336

337

338

336 Girl Kneeling in Front of a Cradle, F 1024
Black chalk, pencil, heightened with white, 48 × 32 cm (18⅞ × 12⅝")
Rijksmuseum Vincent van Gogh, Amsterdam

337 Woman Digging
Sketch in Letter 275
Rijksmuseum Vincent van Gogh, Amsterdam

338 Girl Kneeling in Front of a Cradle
Sketch in Letter 276
Rijksmuseum Vincent van Gogh, Amsterdam

339 Man with Top Hat in a Village Inn
Sketch in Letter 276
Rijksmuseum Vincent van Gogh, Amsterdam

340 Workman with Spade, Sitting near the Window, F964a
Black chalk, pencil, 59.5 × 41.5 cm (23⅝ × 16½")
Collection F. A. P. Zimmermann, New York

341 Sien, Sitting on a Basket, with a Girl, F 1072
Pencil, ink, black mountain chalk, 56.5 × 30 cm (22¼ × 11¾")
Rijksmuseum Vincent van Gogh, Amsterdam

342 Snowy Yard
Sketch in Letter 276
Rijksmuseum Vincent van Gogh, Amsterdam

339

340

341

342

343

344

345

343 Snowy Yard, F 1023
Sketch sent with Letter R 31
Pencil, pen, 20.5 × 13.5 cm ($8\frac{1}{4} \times 5\frac{1}{2}$")
Collection Mrs. J. E. Greutert-de Kanter, Hengelo, The Netherlands

344 Snowy Yard, F 1022
Watercolor, 39 × 58.5 cm ($15\frac{3}{8} \times 23\frac{1}{4}$")
Location unknown

345 Young Man, Sitting with a Cup in His Hand, Half-Length, F964b
Chalk, pencil, charcoal, 32 × 25 cm ($12\frac{5}{8} \times 9\frac{7}{8}$")
Location unknown

offering an infinite number of motifs; I was there a great deal in recent weeks and have all kinds of studies of it" (Letter 287, about May 30).

Within a week he was able to inform Theo that he had a second large composition: "I was with Van der Weele in Dekkersduin and we came to that sandpit and I have been going there since and had a lot of models day in and day out, and so now the second one is also done" (Letter 288, June 3).

Vincent wrote that the figures in both drawings had been "drawn after detailed studies," and I believe I can identify a few of them. In *Peat Diggers* the woman on the left with the wheelbarrow was probably taken from 362, and the standing figure in the middle with top hat and crossed hands from the earlier drawing 235; in the somewhat indistinct head looming in front of the top-hatted figure, we can recognize one of the fishermen's heads from January (310). In *Sand Diggers in Dekkersduin* only in the digger on the extreme left do we recognize a prototype, 258.

Vincent's enthusiasm for making large compositions of this kind became so great that he started work on several more of them in June. In his letters he mentioned two different studies of the garbage dump (in his eyes "a fine sight"), one of coal loading in the yards of the Rhine railway as he saw it from the window of his studio, and one of a row of men digging. Apart from a few sketches in his letters (369, 370, and 373), nothing remains of these. Indeed, even in connection with *Sand Diggers*, we know of only a few small studies. And if the large drawing *Peat Diggers* exists at all, we do not know its whereabouts. In his *catalogue raisonné* J.-B. de la Faille could reproduce it only because there existed a photograph of it—which Van Gogh had had made in July 1883, together with some others (see Letters 299 and 300; other works reproduced from photographs are the study for the diggers or *Potato Grubbers*, 372, and the *Sower*, 374).

Worrying about Sien

The month of June, which inspired Vincent to this strenuous work outdoors (and, as appears from Letter 294, sometimes to work half the night indoors as well), presented numerous other difficulties.

In the first place he was troubled about the attitude of his parents. After his father had surprised him with a "very short visit" (Letter 285), he wrote to Theo: "When Dad was here he spoke with disapproval about my being with the woman; I then said that I did not refuse to marry her. But Dad *evaded* this and changed the subject. He would not say straight out that I should leave her but regretted that I was having relations with her" (Letter 288). In this letter Vincent actually expressed greater indignation about the fact that his parents objected to *Theo's* intending to marry his woman friend than that they would like to prevent a possible marriage between himself and Sien, the latter being something Vincent could "more or less understand."

Of greater importance was the fact that recently things were not going quite as he might have wished with Sien. After keeping

346

347

348

346 Sien, Sewing, Half-Figure, F 1025
Pencil, black mountain chalk,
53 × 37.5 cm (20⅞ × 15″)
Museum Boymans-van Beuningen, Rotterdam

347 Sien, Sewing, Half-Figure, F 1026
Pencil, washed, 54 × 38.5 cm (21¼ × 15⅜″)
Rijksmuseum Kröller-Müller, Otterlo

348 Two Women, Kneeling, F 1058
Pencil, black chalk, 43 × 28.5 cm (16⅞ × 11⅜″)
Rijksmuseum Kröller-Müller, Otterlo

349 Woman Feeding Chickens, F 1080
Pencil, black ink, heightened with white,
61 × 33.5 cm (24 × 13⅜″)
Rijksmuseum Kröller-Müller, Otterlo

350 Man Feeding Chickens (or Sowing), F 882
Black chalk, washed, pencil, black ink, heightened with white, 62.5 × 41.5 cm (24½ × 16½″)
Rijksmuseum Kröller-Müller, Otterlo

349

350

351

352

353

354

355

351 Woman with Shawl around Her Hair, Head, F 1684
Pencil, black mountain chalk, 28.5 × 18 cm ($11\frac{3}{8} \times 7\frac{1}{8}$″)
Collection H. Claussen, Bergen, Norway

352 Woman with Her Hair Loose, Head, F 1059
Pencil, 27.5 × 17 cm (11 × $6\frac{3}{4}$″)
Private collection, The Hague

353 Woman with Shawl, Sewing, F 1033
Pencil, watercolor, black chalk, 56.5 × 48 cm ($22\frac{1}{2} \times 18\frac{7}{8}$″)
Rijksmuseum Kröller-Müller, Otterlo

April 1883

354 Orphan Man, Kneeling in Prayer, F 1027
Pencil, black chalk, touches of China ink, 56 × 46 cm (22 × $18\frac{1}{8}$″)
Location unknown

355 Orphan Man, Bareheaded, Head, F 955
Pencil, washed with black, 32 × 25 cm ($12\frac{5}{8} \times 9\frac{7}{8}$″)
Collection Mr. and Mrs. Dimitry Jodidio, Summit, New Jersey

silent about her for months, he had given the first signs of uneasiness in Letter 283, written at the beginning of May: "There seems to be something the matter with the woman that has some connection with what I told you about her mother; it may not be anything, but then again it may." In the next letter he wrote more openly: "The great danger—as you will understand—is that she will fall into her former errors," by which he obviously meant prostitution. He was seriously concerned about her wavering "between improving and falling back into her earlier bad habits." And now for the first time he put into words what he had so far kept silent about: "She can be in such a bad mood that it is almost unbearable, even for me, quick-tempered, willfully contrary, indeed I sometimes despair." All the same he defended her, pointing to her "poor upbringing" and the "fatal influence of bad company." And the influence of the mother also: "When a woman behaves badly, it is sometimes the fault of the mother, and when the mother behaves badly, it is sometimes the family that is behind the mother." A little later, in Letter 286, written about May 21, he told Theo that he should not get upset: "Things are now straightened out again, and the time will come, I hope, when everything will be going even better." It would prove to be a vain hope, as is readily understandable in the light of what Vincent was up against. In Letter 288 he explained it to Theo in clearer terms than he had used thus far: the family was trying to get her away from him because he did not earn enough, and her brother, "a notoriously bad character," was trying to get her "to go back to what she used to be."

356

Going to Canossa
A third problem was that Vincent was again faced with a severe shortage of money. In recent months Theo himself had had financial difficulties and therefore was no longer able to send something extra now and then, as he had done the year before. And now the day of reckoning arrived, for Vincent's regular allowance of 150 francs a month was just not enough. The 25 guldens he had borrowed from Van Rappard had given him a short breathing spell to buy material for the large compositions, but those in turn cost him a lot of money for models. "Thus the days are hard to bear and hard to get through for the woman and for me because of our being forced to scrape by," he wrote. In what he called an "effort de perdu" ("act of desperation"), he had decided to go to Tersteeg with a large drawing (the one we do not know depicting a row of diggers) to show him something of his work again and at the same time return the drawing exercises by Bargue that he had borrowed so long ago. All this was obviously intended to regain some of the sympathy he had lost. The sad story of the visit in Letter 295 makes it clear that Tersteeg still did not see anything in Vincent's work and would only repeat what he had said on previous occasions—that Vincent should try to make (salable) watercolors. Ten days later, thinking back on his going to Canossa, Vincent wrote to Theo denouncing Tersteeg's attitude in scathing terms. What Tersteeg had really meant was:

356 Sien with Girl on Her Lap, Half-Length, F 1067
Charcoal, pencil, heightened with white and brown, 53.5 × 35 cm (21¼ × 13¾")
Rijksmuseum Vincent van Gogh, Amsterdam

357 Woman Praying, F 1053
Black chalk, pencil, brush, washed, heightened with white, 63 × 39.5 cm (24¾ × 15¾")
Rijksmuseum Kröller-Müller, Otterlo

358 Sien, Peeling Potatoes, F 1053a
Black chalk, 60 × 37 cm (23⅝ × 14⅝")
Gemeentemuseum, The Hague (on loan from Paul Citroen)

359 Woman on Her Deathbed, F 841
Black chalk, pencil, washed, watercolor, heightened with white, 35 × 62 cm (13¾ × 24⅜")
Rijksmuseum Kröller-Müller, Otterlo

360 Woman on Her Deathbed, Head (after a 17th-century painting), F 1026a
Pencil, black chalk, 25 × 33 cm (9⅞ × 13")
Private collection, The Hague

361 Bulb Field, F 186
Canvas on cardboard, 48 × 65 cm (18⅞ × 25⅝")
Collection Mr. and Mrs. Paul Mellon, Upperville, Virginia
May 1883

362 Scheveningen Woman with Wheelbarrow, F 1021
Pencil, watercolor, 67 × 45 cm (26⅜ × 17¾")
Collection Mrs. S. van Deventer, Oberägeri, Switzerland

363 Peat Diggers in the Dunes, F 1031
Charcoal, black mountain chalk, printing ink, c. 50 × 100 cm (c. 20 × 40")
Location unknown

364 Peat Diggers in the Dunes, F 1030
Sketch sent with Letter 287
Pen, pencil, 11.5 × 21 cm (4¾ × 8¼")
Rijksmuseum Vincent van Gogh, Amsterdam

365 Woman with White Cloth around Her Head, Sitting on a Bench, F 1056
Charcoal, washed, pencil, brush, heightened with white oils, 56.5 × 44 cm (22¼ × 17⅜")
Rijksmuseum Kröller-Müller, Otterlo

357

358

359

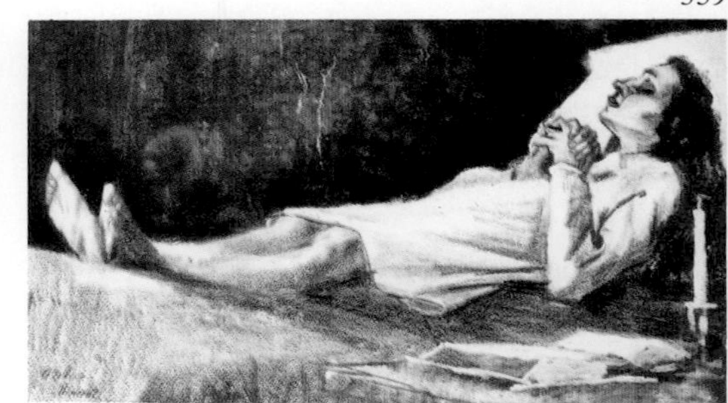

360

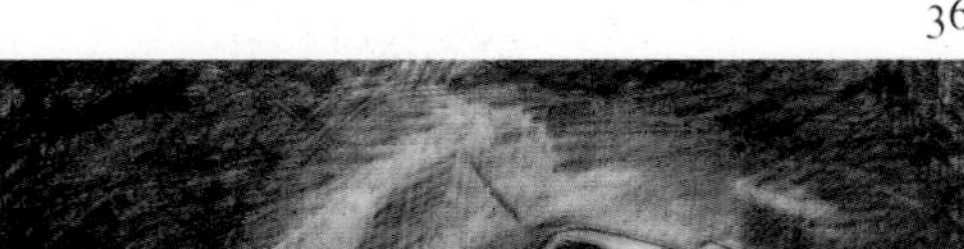

361

362

363

364

365

"You are a mediocrity and it is pretentious of you not to submit and make mediocre little things; you make yourself ridiculous with your so-called 'seeking' and do not work." Tersteeg was to remain for him "the everlasting *no*," but he consoled himself with the thought that almost everyone trying to find his own way has something like that "behind him or next to him like an eternal discourager."

Discouraging it continued to be, and so now we read for the first time a reference to his intended departure from The Hague that two months later would be a fact: "I have lately been thinking of moving entirely out of town, either on the coast or someplace where work in the fields is real, because I think it would save me some money" (Letter 297).

Painting Again

July brought Vincent some new and stimulating contacts, and he renewed his efforts to paint in oils. There is nothing very striking about any of the work done this month. He continued working on the subject of the potato grubbers, for which he again made a new design, but we do not even know of a sketch. He also mentioned a *Sower*, 374 (known only from a photograph made that month), and some studies connected with his work on the potato fields: a *Weed Burner*, 375, and *Three Persons Returning from the Potato Field*, known only in the form of a letter sketch, 378. Vincent apparently considered the study with the weed burner so successful that he made a lithograph of it (377), the first lithograph since those of November. He also took up again the theme he had mentioned in Letter 291, at the beginning of June—the little man in a garden by a gnarled tree. He probably had a sketchbook picture of this and now made a drawing of it. From this drawing, which we know from a letter sketch (380), he again made a lithograph: 379. In Letter 298, July 6 to 8, reference is made to "a pair of landscape studies"; one of these is probably the beautiful *Potato Field in the Dunes*, 390, done with a brush.

The contacts mentioned above were with The Hague painters H.J. van der Weele, Théophile de Bock, and B.J. Blommers; he frequently visited them, and they also came to see him. Vincent said that he had a sort of pied-à-terre at De Bock's place in Scheveningen, so he could keep working for entire days in that area (Letter 298 and following letters). He mentioned that Blommers was encouraging him to continue with his painting (Letter 303), and reported that he was also in touch with G.H. Breitner, who seemed to have broken off all relations with Vincent but had now unexpectedly visited him. In Letter 299 Vincent speaks of his return visit to Breitner's studio, and he is extremely critical of the large canvases he saw there.

In a letter of July 22 (Letter 301) we read that he made "some painted studies" in Scheveningen. "As you know, I did some painting last summer—now I have hung up several of the studies once again because, in making new ones, I recognize that there was something in them after all." And he explained at some length that by painting he hoped to overcome the somewhat meager element in

366

367

368

June 1883

366 Sand Diggers in Dekkersduin near The Hague, F 1029
Pencil, 10 × 20.5 cm ($3\frac{7}{8} \times 8\frac{1}{4}''$)
Private collection, Zurich

367 Sand Diggers in Dekkersduin near The Hague, F 1028
Sketch sent with Letter 288
Pencil, 10.5 × 21 cm ($4\frac{3}{8} \times 8\frac{1}{4}''$)
Rijksmuseum Vincent van Gogh, Amsterdam

368 Horse at the Garbage Dump, F 1032
Pencil, black chalk, washed, 42 × 59 cm ($16\frac{1}{2} \times 23\frac{1}{4}''$)
Location unknown

369 Garbage Dump
Sketch in Letter 289
Rijksmuseum Vincent van Gogh, Amsterdam

370 Garbage Dump
Sketch in Letter 292
Rijksmuseum Vincent van Gogh, Amsterdam

371 Blind Man Sitting in Interior, F933v (reverse: 142)
Black chalk, washed, ink, brush, heightened with white, 69 × 50 cm ($27\frac{1}{8} \times 19\frac{5}{8}''$)
Rijksmuseum Kröller-Müller, Otterlo

372 Potato Grubbers, Four Figures, F 1034
Medium and dimensions unknown (only a photograph has survived)
Location unknown

373 Potato Grubbers, Four Figures
Sketch in Letter 296
Rijksmuseum Vincent van Gogh, Amsterdam

July 1883

374 Sower, F 1035
Medium and dimensions unknown (only a photograph has survived)
Location unknown

375 Weed Burner, Sitting on a Wheelbarrow with His Wife, F 1035a (cf. LIthograph 377)
Watercolor, 20 × 36 cm ($7\frac{7}{8} \times 14\frac{1}{8}''$)
Private collection, Rotterdam

376 Weed Burner, Sitting on a Wheelbarrow with His Wife
Sketch in Letter 299
Rijksmuseum Vincent van Gogh, Amsterdam

377 Weed Burner, Sitting on a Wheelbarrow with His Wife, F 1660 (cf. watercolor 375)
Lithograph, 15.5 × 26 cm ($6\frac{1}{4} \times 10\frac{1}{4}''$)
Various collections

369

370

371

372

373

374

375

376

377

378

379

380

his drawings, the "*sécheresse*" ("dryness"), which had apparently also been pointed out by Theo. He felt that he needed to paint "to achieve more color," in the drawings as well. In this and other letters written in July he had already mentioned various painted works, but none of these has been preserved. We know the subjects of only two from the sketches he made of them in Letter 307—*Path to the Beach*, 382, and *Breakwater*, 381—but we know enough painted works from the following month to give us some idea of the level he had now reached in this medium he had taken up again. The letters do not contain much specific information about the paintings; we find such general remarks as "I am doing my best these days to paint a few more studies" (beginning of August) and "I am still quite busy painting these days" (fourth week of that month). Otherwise, we merely learn that he was still working on the *Potato Grubbers* (Letter 311) and that he was doing "studies in the woods" (Letter 317). The painting of a group of farm buildings can, with a fair degree of certainty, be identified with the study *Farm in Loosduinen* (391). This is supported by Visser's research (see page 60), which has made it possible to identify these buildings as the Dirk van Rijn farm, which was actually located on the Leyweg in Loosduinen. There is somewhat more doubt regarding the painting of a windswept tree, 384. Although it shows only one tree, one is tempted to relate it to a passage in Letter 319, where Vincent says that he came back from Loosduinen "with a study of small gnarled, windswept trees." In any case, we may safely assume that it belongs to this group of painted studies from August or the beginning of September.

In conformity with the 1970 *catalogue raisonné*, I have placed the remaining studies (383, 386, 387, 392, and 393) in 1883. The two studies of a *Cow Lying Down* (388 and 389) are the only ones that I have transferred from 1882 to August 1883. In my opinion they must be related to the study *Cows in the Meadow*, 387. In terms of style, however, not much difference can be discerned between the painted studies of August 1883 and those done a year earlier. There is the further difficulty that we have had to rely on photographs, sometimes of very poor quality, for some of the works mentioned here because their owners are not known.

Difficult Months

In the area of Van Gogh's personal life, the last two months of his stay in The Hague were among the most trying of the entire period. His financial worries, now magnified by the additional costs of canvas and other painting supplies, were great, but even worse was Vincent's feeling that Theo did not have enough confidence in his progress. The short sentence from one of Theo's letters quoted by Vincent in Letter 301—"From now on I can give you little hope"—which probably referred to Theo's own temporary financial difficulties, brought Vincent to the brink of despair. That word, he said, is "for me something like 'the hair that breaks the camel's back at last.' * The burden is indeed so heavy

*In English in Vincent's original letter.

378 Three Persons Returning from the Potato Field
Sketch in Letter 299
Rijksmuseum Vincent van Gogh, Amsterdam

379 Gardener near a Gnarled Apple Tree, F 1659 (original drawing unknown)
Lithograph, 25 × 32.5 cm ($9\frac{7}{8} \times 13''$)
Various collections

380 Gardener near a Gnarled Apple Tree
Sketch in Letter 300
Rijksmuseum Vincent van Gogh, Amsterdam

381 Breakwater
Sketch in Letter 307
Rijksmuseum Vincent van Gogh, Amsterdam

382 Path to the Beach
Sketch in Letter 307
Rijksmuseum Vincent van Gogh, Amsterdam
August 1883

383 Three Figures near a Canal with Windmill, F 1666
Medium and dimensions unknown
Location unknown

384 A Windswept Tree, F 10
35 × 47 cm ($13\frac{3}{4} \times 18\frac{1}{2}''$)
Location unknown

385 Potato Grubbers, Five Persons, F 9
39.5 × 94.5 cm ($15\frac{3}{4} \times 37\frac{3}{8}''$)
Collection Mr. and Mrs. Julian J. Raskin, New York

386 Ditch with Little Bridge, F 189
Canvas on panel, 46 × 34 cm ($18\frac{1}{8} \times 13\frac{3}{8}''$)
Collection Mrs. Gordon Stouffer, Chagrin Falls, Ohio

387 Cows in the Meadow, F 15
Canvas on panel, 31.5 × 44 cm ($12\frac{5}{8} \times 17\frac{3}{8}''$)
Location unknown

381

383

382

384

386

385

387

that the addition of one small hair brings the beast to the ground." Now that those from whom Vincent might have expected support, Mauve, Tersteeg, and Uncle C.M., remained so indifferent toward him, he needed Theo's confidence more than ever. That confidence was even more important to him than financial support: "Even so, Theo, you don't have to spare me if it is only a question of money and if as friend and brother you still have a little sympathy for the work, whether salable or unsalable. If I can only count on your sympathy in this respect, then nothing else will really matter, and then we can calmly and cool-headedly work things out. Therefore, if there is no hope from now on as regards the financial aspect, I would propose a move to the country, to some village, *way out in the country*, where the rent would be cut in half and you can, for the same money you pay here for *bad* food, get *good* and wholesome food needed for the woman and the little ones and, incidentally, for myself as well" (Letter 301).

This was written on a Sunday morning, July 22, and Vincent was so upset about it all, now that he was beginning to see things as they really were, that he wrote another letter that very evening in which he made the shocking statement that he was sorry that "at the time I did not fall ill somewhere in the Borinage and kick the bucket" instead of becoming a painter. "I now take a dark view of things. If it were only myself, but there is the thought of the woman and the children, poor lambs, because you want to look out for them, and you feel responsible for them."

It was to become even worse, for this time Vincent could still write in this letter, "It has been going well with the woman lately," but a few weeks later it was already apparent that her behavior was making it virtually impossible to continue living with her. Of the long, moving letters that Vincent devoted in August to Sien, her character, and the rapidly deteriorating relationship with him, I mention only that again and again he gave evidence of his extraordinary compassion by professing to see in her a pure heart. Somewhere he calls it "strange how pure she is despite her depravity. Just as if deep down something has been spared in the ruins of her soul and heart and mind" (Letter 314). It was therefore not so much her behavior as the pressing financial situation that led him to announce in the second half of August his plan to move to the country (as a result of talks with Van Rappard it was to be Drenthe). And it was only at the last moment, the beginning of September—after some more unpleasant experiences—that he decided to leave the woman and the children behind in The Hague, at least for the time being. Theo, by sending him 100 francs instead of 50 on September 10, helped him with the travel costs, and so on September 11 Vincent left the city where over the past twenty months he had become a highly proficient artist and where, along with heavy cares, he had known moments of domestic bliss that were not to fall to his lot again. He was facing a future in which everything was uncertain—not only the place where he would settle but also the question whether he would remain alone or be united again with the woman and children.

388

389

390

388 Cow Lying Down, F 1b
30 × 50 cm (11¾ × 19⅝″)
Location unknown

389 Cow Lying Down, F 1c
19 × 47.5 cm (7½ × 18⅞″)
Location unknown

390 Potato Field in the Dunes, F 1037
Brush, ink, heightened with white,
27.5 × 42 cm (11 × 16½″)
Rijksmuseum Kröller-Müller, Otterlo

391 Farm in Loosduinen near The Hague, F 16
Canvas on panel, 33 × 50 cm (13 × 19⅝″)
Museum van Baaren, Utrecht

392 Sower (?), F 11
Panel, 19 × 27.5 cm (7½ × 11″)
Location unknown

393 Landscape with Dunes, F 15a
Panel, 33.5 × 48.5 cm (13⅜ × 19¼″)
Hirschl and Adler Galleries, New York

394 Marsh (No F Number)
27 × 45.5 cm (10⅝ × 18⅛″)
Location unknown

391

Drenthe

392

393

394

The external circumstances of Vincent's stay in Drenthe do not call for any special comment. He spent less than three full months there, from September 11 to December 5, 1883. It was a time of great loneliness during a gloomy part of the year in a poor and thinly populated area, and so it is not surprising that he spent the long evenings writing lengthy letters. In the eleven weeks of the Drenthe period, he wrote no fewer than twenty-two letters to Theo; they fill seventy-six closely printed pages in the published edition. A study of them is indispensable to anyone who wants to know more about the psychological aspects of Van Gogh. They contain fascinating reflections on his relationship with Sien and the children, the grand natural beauty of Drenthe, and the simple peasant population—which he greatly preferred to "the darkness of *un*civilization and stupidity and evil" in the cities. Even more important is what he wrote about the nature of the artistic gift in contrast to art dealing. Of all these reflections only his comments about Sien and about his work will be treated here in any detail.

When he arrived, September 11, Vincent found a cheap hotel in the town of Hoogeveen, where—"by the grace of God" and after paying for one week in advance—he was able to stay for 1 gulden a day. Using this as his headquarters, he spent a few weeks making long trips through the peat district and soon after his arrival appears to have made a few painted studies of farms on the moor. By September 24, three of them were dry enough to send to Theo (Postcard 327). Two of these were probably 395 and 397, and it should be noted that the broad landscape, which had made a powerful impression on Vincent, inspired him to make several highly personal little paintings with more atmosphere than in most of the painted studies from The Hague (see 395; colorplate V, page 101).

A few other studies made during those first days have been lost. One was of a cemetery and was reproduced as a small sketch (396) in Letter 325, and another was described in the same letter as "red sun between the little birches standing in a marshy pasture." Also lost were the studies he made before his departure from Hoogeveen, one of which was described in Letter 330 as "a large farm with moss-grown roofs" (unless this refers to study 397).

In Letter 326, about September 22, he wrote that he had also (once again) started doing watercolors. I assume that the drawings of a peat bog, of farms, and of landscapes, 398–403, should be counted among the watercolors made in September.

At the beginning of October, Vincent traveled east by canalboat even farther from the coast and rented a room at an inn in Nieuw-Amsterdam. After that he had to go back to Hoogeveen every now and then to pick up a money order from Theo and cash it, and as a result of this, his stay in Nieuw-Amsterdam caused him much difficulty. Almost from the outset Vincent complained that the trip to Drenthe had been a rather ill-advised venture because his supplies and equipment were quite inadequate, and even in Hoogeveen drawing supplies were virtually unobtainable, and painting supplies not available at all. He even had to have paint sent from The Hague by a friendly dealer named Furnée, but that meant payment in advance. The money from Theo seemed to take longer and longer to arrive, and that often made Vincent worried and upset. On the other hand, there was hardly a letter in which he could not write that he found the countryside, despite the loneliness, magnificent. He also wrote his parents (Letter 334) that they need not worry about his health because he felt better here than in The Hague, where he suffered a great deal from "nervousness."

The separation from Sien and the children, letters indicate, caused him much pain. One example chosen from many can perhaps give some idea of the deep feeling with which he must have struggled for weeks on end. "Theo, when I am on the moor and see a poor wench with a child in her arms or against her bosom, I feel tears welling up in my eyes. I see her in that wench—even her weakness and slovenliness make the likeness more real. *I know she is not good*, I know that I am fully justified in doing what I am doing, that staying with her over there *could not be*, that bringing her along likewise really *could not be*, that what I did was sensible, wise, anything you like, but that does not mean that I hurt any the less when I see such a poor creature, feverish and miserable, or that my heart does not then begin to sink. How much sadness there is in life, but one must not, after all, grow melancholy and must look elsewhere, and working is the right thing, except that there are moments when the only respite is to realize: Misfortune will not spare me either" (Letter 324).

At first Vincent did not want to write to Sien because he knew that she had again moved in with her mother, but he became worried when he had not heard from her for several weeks. In his letters to Theo he called the landlord on the Schenkstraat "a scoundrel" because—obviously thinking he was doing Vincent a favor—he had pretended that he did not know his address when Sien had come asking for it (Letter 332). So he did write to her after all, and heard from her a couple of times, and even went so far as to send her some money out of the paltry funds he had (Letter 343).

The "seemingly endless trip in the canalboat through the moors" from Hoogeveen to Nieuw-Amsterdam (Letter 330) gave Vincent

395

396

397

September 1883

395 Farms, F 17
Canvas on cardboard, 36 × 55.5 cm (14⅛ × 22″)
Rijksmuseum Vincent van Gogh, Amsterdam
Colorplate V, p. 101

396 Cemetery
Sketch in Letter 325
Rijksmuseum Vincent van Gogh, Amsterdam

397 Farms between Trees, F 18
Canvas on panel, 29 × 39 cm (11⅜ × 15⅜″)
Collection F. Meyer-Fierz, Zurich

398 Peat Bog, F 1094
Watercolor, 41 × 54 cm (16⅛ × 21¼″)
Private collection, Amsterdam

399 Landscape at Nightfall, F 1099
Watercolor, 40 × 53 cm (15¾ × 20⅞″)
Location unknown

400 Heath with Wheelbarrow, F 1100
Watercolor, 24 × 35 cm (9½ × 13¾″)
Cleveland Museum of Art

401 Landscape with a Farm, F 1101
Watercolor, 24 × 35.5 cm (9½ × 14⅛″)
Private collection, New York

398

399

400

401

402

403

404

402 Farmhouse, F 1102
Watercolor, 25 × 36.5 cm ($9\frac{7}{8} \times 14\frac{5}{8}$")
Location unknown

403 Group of Farmhouses, F 1103
Watercolor, 25 × 36.5 cm ($9\frac{7}{8} \times 14\frac{5}{8}$")
Von der Heydt Museum, Wuppertal

404 Head of a Woman with Dark Cap, F 1073
Pen, washed, 21 × 13.5 cm ($8\frac{1}{4} \times 5\frac{1}{2}$")
Rijksmuseum Kröller-Müller, Otterlo

the opportunity to produce a fascinating sheet of small pen-and-ink sketches (405) that he sent to Theo with Letter 330 about October 3. Perhaps the drawing of a peasant woman's head (404) done in the same style also belongs here. Because this latter drawing was done in the format (8¼ by 5½ inches) often used for the sketches sent with letters, I believe that it too was a sheet sent with a letter.

Of the work done in October in Nieuw-Amsterdam and the surrounding area, it is probable that again one of the studies in oils mentioned in the letters, as well as the study reproduced in the small letter sketch of the plowman (412), was lost. Although the accompanying text does not expressly say so, other letter sketches such as *Workmen beside a Mound of Peat* (416) and *Farmhouse at Night* (419) were very likely made after painted studies, as studies in oils of the other sketches mentioned in Letter 335—such as *Peat Boat* and *Peasant Burning Weeds*—do exist (see 415 and 417). The motif of *Women Working in the Peat* (letter sketch 410) is also found in the painted study 409. What is more, Vincent had also worked these tiny figures into the background of his drawing of the *Landscape with Bog-Oak Trunks* (406), "being oak trees that had lain buried under the peat for something like a century," as he explains it in describing that drawing in Letter 331 of October 6 or 7.

The motifs of *Plowman* and *Farmhouse at Night* mentioned here are found in drawings that we know of: 411 and 418. Related subjects are also to be found in the drawings *Farmhouse with Barn and Trees* (407) and *Landscape with a Little Bridge* (408), as well as in the painted studies *Landscape at Nightfall* (413) and *Little Farmhouse with Piles of Peat* (421).

Vincent's own work was not the main theme of the letters written in October. A number of them consist largely of attempts to induce Theo to give up art dealing and become an artist himself. This had already been suggested by Vincent in his letters from The Hague. He now renewed the attack with fresh vigor and with his typical obstinate tenacity, which must sometimes have irritated Theo immensely as it did Vincent's later friends in Paris. He did not expect that it would be possible for Theo to remain on good terms with the firm of Goupil & Co. and felt that the time had now come to devote himself to painting as a means of "leaving the world of speculation and convention," as he put it in Letter 336.

There can be no doubt that self-interest played absolutely no part in Vincent's per-

405

406

407

October 1883

405 Sketches
Sent with Letter 330
Rijksmuseum Vincent van Gogh, Amsterdam

406 Landscape with Bog-Oak Trunks, F 1095
Pen, pencil, 31 × 37.5 cm (12¼ × 15″)
Location unknown

407 Farmhouse with Barn and Trees, F 1248
Black chalk, heightened with white, 46 × 60.5 cm (18⅛ × 24″)
Rijksmuseum Kröller-Müller, Otterlo

408 Landscape with a Little Bridge, F 1347
Black chalk, washed, heightened with white, 30 × 44 cm (11¾ × 17⅜″)
Rijksmuseum Kröller-Müller, Otterlo

409 Two Women Working in the Peat, F 19
27 × 35.5 cm (10⅝ × 14⅛″)
Rijksmuseum Vincent van Gogh, Amsterdam

410 Women Working in the Peat
Sketch in Letter 331
Rijksmuseum Vincent van Gogh, Amsterdam

411 Plowman and Three Women, F 1096
Pencil, 21 × 34 cm (8¼ × 13⅜″)
Rijksmuseum Kröller-Müller, Otterlo

412 Plowman and Two Women
Sketch in Letter 333
Rijksmuseum Vincent van Gogh, Amsterdam

413 Landscape at Nightfall, F 188
Cardboard on panel, 35.5 × 52 cm (14⅛ × 20½″)
Private collection, Rotterdam

414 Stooping Woman in Landscape
Sketch in Letter 333
Rijksmuseum Vincent van Gogh, Amsterdam

415 Peat Boat with Two Figures, F 21
Canvas on panel, 37 × 55.5 cm (14⅝ × 22″)
Collection R. W. van Hoey Smith, Rockanje, The Netherlands

408

409

410

411

412

413

414

415

sistent pleas to Theo, but he had great expectations of friendly cooperation between them, for he, as the more experienced of the two, would be able to provide Theo with guidance: " We would have a hard time of it, but the joy of being together, of living together in this wonderfully beautiful countryside and, above all, of realizing that we are both *artisans*, how enormously pleasant that would be, old man" (Letter 339). Devoid of self-interest it certainly was, for by inducing Theo to give up his position with Goupil's, Vincent would be cutting off his only source of income.

Spurring Theo on to action, he made a little drawing to emphasize his point (420). "You must go at it with confidence, with the sure knowledge that you are doing something rational, like the farmer guiding his plow or like our friend in the little rough sketch who is doing his harrowing, all by himself. If you do not have a horse, then you are your own horse. That is what a lot of people here do" (Letter 336).

As Theo reacted indifferently or negatively to his repeated insistence (Letters 336–39*b* are full of the most pressing exhortations), Vincent, in Letter 341, let himself be led into using strong language: "It is my intention to refuse your financial help, should you bind yourself *permanently* to G. & Co." We do not know what Theo's answer to this was, but it is only too clear from Vincent's next letters that the even-tempered Theo, interpreting Vincent's statement as an ultimatum, had become furious. In an apologetic reply (Letter 343), Vincent tried to smooth over the misunderstanding—but for us, viewing the matter dispassionately and remotely, there can be no doubt that Vincent, in an excess of well-intentioned fanaticism, had only expressed himself too strongly. It was literally as he now summed it up: "What I wanted to say is simply this: 'I would not want to bloom if that meant you had to shrivel; I would not want to develop the artist in me if you had to repress the artist in you for my sake.' "

With the gradual onset of winter, life in Drenthe did not become any easier, but Vincent still found the countryside "superb." As an example of the results of his roamings, there is first of all the drawing dating from November of a flock of sheep in front of a small church (423). It was made after a trip in an open farm cart to the picturesque little village of Zweeloo. The trip is described in detail by Vincent in Letter 340—a remarkable example of his talent as a writer. His bent for linking landscapes with recollections of painters he admired is exemplified by what he said about the little church: "I passed by a

416

417

416 Workmen beside a Mound of Peat, and a Peat Boat with Two Figures
Sketches in Letter 335
Rijksmuseum Vincent van Gogh, Amsterdam

417 Peasant Burning Weeds, F 20
Panel, 30.5 × 39.5 cm ($12\frac{1}{4} \times 15\frac{3}{4}$")
Rijksmuseum Kröller-Müller, Otterlo (on loan from T. Bendien)

418 Farmhouse at Night, F 1097
Pen, 22.5 × 29 cm ($9 \times 11\frac{3}{8}$")
Rijksmuseum Kröller-Müller, Otterlo

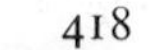

418

419

420

422

421

423

419 Peasant Burning Weeds, and Farmhouse at Night
Sketches in Letter 335
Rijksmuseum Vincent van Gogh, Amsterdam

420 Man Pulling a Harrow
Sketch in Letter 336
Rijksmuseum Vincent van Gogh, Amsterdam

421 Little Farmhouse with Piles of Peat, F22
Canvas on cardboard, 37.5 × 55.5 cm (15 × 22″)
Rijksmuseum Vincent van Gogh, Amsterdam

422 Plowman with Stooping Woman, and a Little Farmhouse with Piles of Peat
Sketches in Letter 339
Rijksmuseum Vincent van Gogh, Amsterdam

November 1883

423 Shepherd with Flock near a Little Church at Zweeloo, F877
Pen, pencil, heightened with white, 25 × 31.5 cm ($9\frac{7}{8} \times 12\frac{5}{8}$″)
Collection R. W. van Hoey Smith, Rockanje, The Netherlands

little old church just exactly, just exactly, like *L'Église de Gréville* in the small painting by Millet in the Luxembourg. But here, instead of the little farmer with the spade in that painting, there was a shepherd with a flock of sheep along the hedge. In the background was a vista, not of the sea itself, but only of a sea of tender wheat, a sea of furrows instead of waves."

In November he also made the strikingly large watercolor of the *Drawbridge in Nieuw-Amsterdam* mentioned in Letter 342 and probably also the fine drawing of a *Landscape with Canal and Sailing Vessel* (424 and 425; see also colorplate VI, page 102). As it is inconceivable that Vincent's entire production in this month consisted of only three drawings, it must be assumed that much of the work from this period has disappeared. As a matter of fact there are indications in his letters to support this view. In Letter 340 Vincent mentioned a sketch of "that little apple orchard which was the subject of Liebermann's large painting" (the fact that the painter Max Liebermann had worked in Drenthe was one of the reasons that Vincent went to that province). In that same letter he also referred to a drawing of "a little old woman at the spinning wheel," and from Letter 342 it appears that the drawbridge was the subject not only of the big watercolor 425 but also of two painted studies.

Apart from the previously mentioned sketch (404), there are no portraits from the Drenthe period. The "little old woman at the spinning wheel" was most likely an exception, for it seemed to be much harder to get models in Drenthe than it had been in The Hague. Even in one of his first letters, Vincent complained about this: "At first I had some trouble here with models on the moor, where people laughed about it and thought I was crazy. And I couldn't finish figure studies I had started because of the unwillingness of the models even though I had paid them well, at least for here" (Letter 326). And despite his early optimism, it appears that this situation did not change, for in the very last letter from Drenthe (Letter 343) Vincent wrote about the "people you would like so much to have as models and cannot get." Small wonder that he referred in that connection to his loneliness as "torture": "*that* loneliness, the kind encountered by a painter in an out of the way district where every Tom, Dick, and Harry regards him as crazy or as a murderer, a vagabond or what not."

That loneliness was certainly a factor in Vincent's decision to leave Drenthe and go to the one place where he felt he would be free from at least some of his worries for a time: his parents' home. The decision must have been made when even on November 26 he had not yet received Theo's letter of November 20. When that letter finally arrived in Nieuw-Amsterdam on December 1, he wrote Theo that he had in the meantime asked his father to advance him some money for the fare home. In a long emotional dissertation he explained how hard pressed he had been and how worried he had become about Theo. The final words of the letter had an unmistakable ring of the irrevocable: "We have now reached a point where I say: Right now, I cannot go on."

424

425

424 Landscape with Canal and Sailing Boat, F 1104
Pen, pencil, washed, 28 × 40 cm (11 × 15¾")
Location unknown

425 Drawbridge in Nieuw-Amsterdam, F 1098
Watercolor, 38.5 × 81 cm (15⅜ × 31⅞")
Groninger Museum, Groningen
Colorplate VI, p. 102

Colorplate V, Farms, 395 〉

Nuenen

Vincent had gone to his parents' home in Nuenen with the intention of giving himself a bit of a breathing spell there and of staying only a short time. One of his first letters to Theo from Nuenen ended in fact with the plea: "Now, old man—if you can do it, try and help me get out of here" (Letter 345*a*). He thought about going from Nuenen to Van Rappard's and from there perhaps to Mauve's. He would not, however, go back to Drenthe again, even though his homecoming had proved disheartening. The feeling of not being welcome ("a dog with muddy paws," a "filthy beast") sometimes led him to express himself in extremely bitter terms, such as: "The dog is only sorry that he did not stay away, for it was less lonely on the moor than in this house, despite all the civility" (Letter 346). The attitude of his father, with whom a complete reconciliation, as he had imagined it, did not seem possible, affected him so deeply the first few weeks of his stay in Nuenen that he could not help confiding to Theo in letter after letter what was going on in his troubled mind. These, too, are important and detailed documents giving an insight into Vincent's personality, mainly because, even as he was writing, he was becoming more clearly aware of the path that he, as both human being and artist, should follow, preferably together with Theo, but if need be, alone, in proud solitude:

"I tell you, I choose the *path of that dog* I mentioned, I will stay a *dog*, I will be *poor*, I will be a *painter*, I want to remain a *human being*—in the midst of nature." And also: "Neither Dad nor Tersteeg has given me anything but a false balm for my conscience, and they have not liberated me, not even acknowledged my longing for freedom and naked truth and my sense of ignorance and darkness. And now that I am thrown back upon myself, I still have not reached the light and succeeded in what I want to do. So be it, but it is just because I have definitely discarded *their* systems that I still have a certain hope and trust that my striving will not prove in vain" (Letter 347).

Two letters had considerable influence: one from Theo, saying he was glad Vincent had gone to Nuenen; and the other from Van Rappard, who earlier had termed it "a great misfortune" for Vincent that he was unable to work at his parents' home but now counseled him "to stay at home a long time." This tipped the scale for Vincent even though he

426

427

428

December 1883

426 Parsonage Garden in the Snow with One Figure, F 1127
Pen, 29 × 21 cm (11⅜ × 8¼″)
Rijksmuseum Vincent van Gogh, Amsterdam

427 Parsonage Garden in the Snow with Three Figures, F 1131
Pen, 28 × 20.5 cm (11 × 8¼″)
Rijksmuseum Vincent van Gogh, Amsterdam

428 Snowy Landscape with the Old Tower, F 1687
Pencil, pen, 20.5 × 28.5 cm (8¼ × 11⅜″)
Collection A. M. Obermayer, Stockholm

‹ Colorplate VI, Drawbridge in Nieuw-Amsterdam, 425

knew that living with his parents would not be easy, and thus he wrote: "I want to tell you now that I have been able to talk Dad into letting me set up a room for my own work here. Provided you agree, *that will be my regular storeroom and my studio so long as we have no money to be anywhere else*" (Letter 348, about December 21). This room was the so-called mangling or laundry room, a small stone shed built against the rear of the parsonage. It was not exactly spacious, and Vincent rented a better studio at the beginning of May, but in any case the arrangement did make it possible for him to decide to stay in Nuenen, which proved to be of the greatest importance to his development as a painter.

First Nuenen Work

Vincent was so troubled over his relations with his father and Theo that not until his tenth letter from Nuenen (Letter 351, about January 2) did he write anything about his *work*. However, we know that he had not been idle in those first weeks. The trip home, which, as he wrote, began with a six-hour walk from Nieuw-Amsterdam to Hoogeveen "on a stormy afternoon with rain, with snow," must have taken place about December 5. By December 7 he had already sent Theo a chalk-and-pen drawing of the snow-covered graveyard in Nuenen, 433 (we know that date because Vincent had simply put the address and a stamp on the back of the drawing!).

A whole series of similar drawings, 426–35, undoubtedly dates from these first and following days in Nuenen, when the wintry weather apparently persisted. This is confirmed by a few excerpts from letters written by his father that are quoted by Mrs. van Gogh-Bonger in her "Memoir" to *The Complete Letters*. As early as the "beginning of December" his father apparently wrote Theo: "Don't you think that pen-and-ink drawing of the old tower which Vincent sent you is beautiful? It seems to come to him so easily." And December 20: "There can be no doubt that he works hard and that he finds plenty of material here for studies; he made a number of them that we admired."*

We are dealing here with quickly noted impressions in an entirely individual style

*The manuscripts of these letters have not yet been located.

429

430

431

429 Snowy Landscape with Stooping Woman, F1232
Pen, pencil, 20.5 × 28.5 cm (8¼ × 11⅜")
Rijksmuseum Kröller-Müller, Otterlo

430 Snowy Landscape with Stooping Woman, F1233 (reverse: 434)
Black chalk, 16 × 25.5 cm (6¼ × 10¼")
Rijksmuseum Vincent van Gogh, Amsterdam

431 Funeral in the Snow near the Old Tower, F1686
Black chalk, pen, brown ink, washed, 16 × 25 cm (6¼ × 9⅞")
Collection Mrs. F. von Werz, Munich

432 Churchyard in the Snow with Two Figures, F1236 (reverse: 436)
Black chalk, pen, brush, 18 × 28 cm (7⅛ × 11")
Rijksmuseum Vincent van Gogh, Amsterdam

433 Churchyard in the Snow with Two Figures, F1237
Black chalk, pen, brush, 16 × 25.5 cm (6¼ × 10¼")
Rijksmuseum Vincent van Gogh, Amsterdam

434 Sketches of Figures in a Landscape, F1233v (reverse: 430)
Black chalk, 16 × 25.5 cm (6¼ × 10¼")
Rijksmuseum Vincent van Gogh, Amsterdam

435 Church in Gerwen with Four Figures, F1238
Pencil, pen, 20.5 × 28.5 cm (8¼ × 11⅜")
Rijksmuseum Vincent van Gogh, Amsterdam

436 Sketch of a Church with Trees, F1236v (reverse: 432)
Black chalk, 15 × 10 cm (6 × 4")
Rijksmuseum Vincent van Gogh, Amsterdam

437 Interior with a Weaver Facing Right, F1110
Pencil, black chalk, pen, watercolor, 24.5 × 29.5 cm (9⅞ × 11¾")
Rijksmuseum Kröller-Müller, Otterlo

438 A Lumber Auction, F1113
Watercolor, 33.5 × 44.5 cm (13⅜ × 17¾")
Rijksmuseum Vincent van Gogh, Amsterdam

439 Interior with a Weaver Facing Right, F1109
Pencil, black chalk, pen, brush, heightened with white, 24.5 × 33.5 cm (9⅞ × 13⅜")
Rijksmuseum Kröller-Müller, Otterlo

January 1884

440 Gardener with a Wheelbarrow
Sketch in Letter 351a
Rijksmuseum Vincent van Gogh, Amsterdam

432

433

434

435

436

437

438

439

440

that splendidly captures the wintry atmosphere. In just a few summary, but characteristic, strokes the people in these scenes were indicated. As his father correctly noted, Vincent did not lack subjects in Nuenen. He found material for his observation of nature and people even in his immediate surroundings, for the old tower (or the "little old church," as Vincent sometimes wrote) was situated right behind the parsonage garden (426 and 427).

The Weavers

Also as early as December, Vincent must have started on other work. In Letter 351, about January 2, 1884, he refers to an "impression" of a lumber auction (438), which thus was probably made in December after the snowy period was over. We also read in the same letter that since he had come to Nuenen, he had become deeply interested "in the weavers." This means that as early as December he had taken up the subject that was to fascinate him for months to come. He was undoubtedly exaggerating somewhat when he wrote about February 1: "Since I have been here I don't think there has been a single day that I did not work with the weavers or farmers from morning to night" (Letter 360). But even before that he had reported that he had been painting studies of weavers "daily." And we keep running across reports of new "weavers" right up to June.

All that activity produced abundant results. We know of ten painted studies of weavers and eighteen drawings, some in watercolors and some in pen and ink or black chalk or a combination of these with watercolors. And there were certainly more.

Two drawings which I consider among the least successful of the series—437 and 439—must have been made as early as December 1883. I deduce this from the complaint voiced by Vincent in his letter of about January 2 concerning the lack of distance between him and the loom in the little rooms, which must often have resulted in failures. In drawings 437 and 439 Vincent's vantage point seems to be above the loom, and in drawing 437 the perspective is, in addition, quite obviously distorted. The complaint just referred to is followed by the news that "However, I have found a room here with two looms where it can be managed" (Letter 351).

I am unable to identify the three watercolors that Vincent, according to this letter, had already made (thus also in December); perhaps he regarded drawing 437—done in mixed techniques—as a watercolor. In Letter 351*a*, written somewhat later, there is a sketch of a weaver (442) that was done in a larger room, and—as he expressly noted—it was made after a watercolor; that is therefore one of the watercolors (by now four) he mentioned here. We do not, however, know of a watercolor that completely matches this sketch, although 445 comes closest. One of the other watercolors mentioned here may be the more or less similar *Weaver*, 444.

Two other subjects represented in letter sketches (440 and 441) point to the existence of other watercolors that must also be presumed lost.

Of the work he did in January we know of a drawing of the little church in Nuenen (not the one with the old tower, but the much smaller Protestant church, which still exists, where his father used to preach). That drawing (446), whose format suggests that it may also have been intended to be sent with one of his letters, corresponds with the small rough sketch in Letter 355 (447). Vincent noted in that letter that he had painted this scene for his mother; the painting has, however, been lost. Another study of this church, with two groups of worshipers (521), should, I believe, be assigned to a later date because of the autumn foliage.

Meanwhile, Vincent was back at work painting the weavers. In Letter 354, January 20 to 24, he wrote that he was doing two studies of a weaver "right in the neighborhood." A few days later, further details were forthcoming. The last study was "the

441

442

444

441 Interior with a Woman Sewing
Sketch in Letter 351a
Rijksmuseum Vincent van Gogh, Amsterdam

442 Weaver Facing Left
Sketch in Letter 351a
Rijksmuseum Vincent van Gogh, Amsterdam

443 Weaver Facing Left, F 1120
Sketch probably sent with Letter 355
Pen, 12.5 × 19.5 cm ($5\frac{1}{8} \times 7\frac{7}{8}$")
Rijksmuseum Vincent van Gogh, Amsterdam

444 Weaver Facing Left, F 1114
Pencil, watercolor, 35 × 45 cm ($13\frac{3}{4} \times 17\frac{3}{4}$")
Rijksmuseum Vincent van Gogh, Amsterdam

445 Weaver Facing Left, F 1107
Watercolor, 33 × 44 cm ($13 \times 17\frac{3}{8}$")
Rijksmuseum Vincent van Gogh, Amsterdam

446 Chapel in Nuenen, with One Figure, F 1117
Pen, 16.5 × 13.5 cm ($6\frac{3}{4} \times 5\frac{1}{2}$")
Rijksmuseum Kröller-Müller, Otterlo

443

445

446

447

448

449

447 Chapel in Nuenen, with One Figure
Sketch in Letter 355
Rijksmuseum Vincent van Gogh, Amsterdam

448 Weaver Facing Right, F1125
Pencil, watercolor, 32 × 44 cm
($12\frac{5}{8} \times 17\frac{3}{8}''$)
Rijksmuseum Vincent van Gogh, Amsterdam

449 Weaver Facing Right, Interior with One Window and High Chair, F1119
Watercolor, 30.5 × 43 cm ($12\frac{1}{4} \times 16\frac{7}{8}''$)
Location unknown

450 Weaver Facing Right, Half-Figure, F26
48 × 46 cm ($18\frac{7}{8} \times 18\frac{1}{8}''$)
Collection H. R. Hahnloser, Bern

February 1884

451 Weaver Facing Right, F1108
Watercolor, 32 × 47 cm ($12\frac{5}{8} \times 18\frac{1}{2}''$)
Galerie Nathan, Zurich

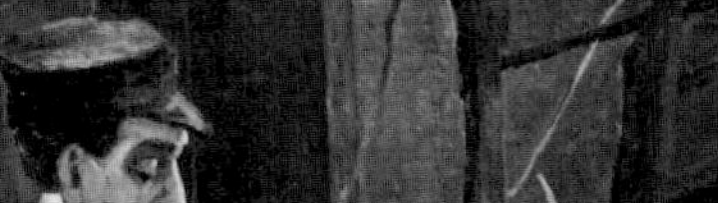

450

451

figure of a man sitting at the loom, by himself, the bust and the hands." This must have been 450. He was also painting a loom next to which there was a child's high chair standing "at a little window through which a small green field can be seen . . . and the little child sits there by the hour watching the shuttle shoot back and forth." Though the canvas has been lost, we can reconstruct this scene with some accuracy because Vincent made a watercolor (449) and a pen-and-ink drawing (452) of it—probably both at about the same time. A further reason for assuming that this was the weaver "right in the neighborhood" is that the old tower which stood behind the parsonage can be seen through the little window in drawing 452.

452

453

Pen-and-Ink Drawings

We know that Vincent's parents were impressed with his pen-and-ink drawings, and Theo quite clearly encouraged him to continue with them. Vincent confirmed this in Letter 355, written about January 24: "Those scenes of the looms with their relatively complicated machinery, with a small figure sitting in the middle, will in my opinion also lend themselves to pen-and-ink drawings, and I shall make a few of them, following the hint you gave me in your letter."

A few weeks after this, Vincent could report: "Just a word to tell you—also in accordance with the letter in which you spoke about pen-and-ink drawings—that I have five weavers for you. I made them after my painted studies, and in treatment they differ somewhat from—and I believe they are pithier than—the pen-and-ink drawings of mine you have seen up to now" (Letter 357, February 18 to 23).

Of those five weavers, we know of four (452–55), all done in the same technique and all approximately the same size (although 454 is smaller, possibly because of its vertical format). Since Van Gogh wrote that the drawings were made after painted studies, we can try to determine which studies these were, but only a few are known to us. The half-length figure 454 clearly corresponds to painting 450. The drawing of the interior with the child's high chair, 452, was undoubtedly made after the lost painting showing the same subject (to which watercolor 449 also corresponds). Drawing 453 is a more detailed version of a painting corresponding to 457, or of 457 itself, assuming that originally the lamp was also part of the picture and was

454

452 Weaver Facing Right, Interior with One Window and High Chair, F 1118
Pencil, pen, brown ink, 32 × 40 cm ($12\frac{5}{8} \times 15\frac{3}{4}''$)
Rijksmuseum Vincent van Gogh, Amsterdam

453 Weaver Facing Right, F 1121
Pencil, pen, brown ink, 27 × 40 cm ($10\frac{5}{8} \times 15\frac{3}{4}''$)
Rijksmuseum Vincent van Gogh, Amsterdam

454 Weaver Facing Right, Half-Figure, F 1122
Pen, washed with bister, heightened with white, 26 × 21 cm ($10\frac{1}{4} \times 8\frac{1}{4}''$)
Rijksmuseum Vincent van Gogh, Amsterdam

455 Weaver Facing Left, F 1123
Pen, heightened with white, 30.5 × 40.5 cm ($12\frac{1}{4} \times 16\frac{1}{8}''$)
Rijksmuseum Vincent van Gogh, Amsterdam

456 Weaver Facing Left, F 1124
Letter sketch?
Pen, washed, 9.5 × 13 cm ($3\frac{7}{8} \times 5\frac{1}{8}''$)
Private collection, The Hague

457 Weaver Facing Right, F 162
37 × 45 cm ($14\frac{5}{8} \times 17\frac{3}{4}''$)
Private collection, The Netherlands

458 The Old Tower of Nuenen with People Walking, F 184
Canvas on panel, 33.5 × 44 cm ($13\frac{3}{8} \times 17\frac{3}{8}''$)
Collection Mrs. H. d'Audretsch-Krop, Amerongen, The Netherlands

459 The Old Tower of Nuenen with a Plowman, F 34
34.5 × 42 cm ($13\frac{3}{4} \times 16\frac{1}{2}''$)
Rijksmuseum Kröller-Müller, Otterlo

460 Woman with Wheelbarrow at Night, F 1106
Letter sketch?
Pen, 21 × 13 cm ($8\frac{1}{4} \times 5\frac{1}{8}''$)
Rijksmuseum Kröller-Müller, Otterlo

March 1884

461 Behind the Hedges, F 1129
Pencil, pen, 40 × 53 cm ($15\frac{3}{4} \times 20\frac{7}{8}''$)
Stedelijk Museum, Amsterdam (on loan from the Rijksmuseum, Amsterdam)

462 Weaver, Seen from the Front, F 1116
Pencil, black and white chalk, pen, 21 × 35 cm ($8\frac{1}{4} \times 13\frac{3}{4}''$)
Rijksmuseum Vincent van Gogh, Amsterdam

463 Parsonage Garden, F 1132
Pencil, pen, 20 × 23.5 cm ($7\frac{7}{8} \times 9\frac{1}{2}''$)
Rijksmuseum Vincent van Gogh, Amsterdam

455

456

457

458

459

460

461

462

463

later painted over (the lamp is also shown in the corresponding watercolor, 451). Finally, drawing 455, showing the weaver facing left, must have been made after one of the paintings done in January and now lost. There is also a small rough sketch (456) of the painting—or of the drawing made from it—which presumably was one of the small sketches intended to be sent with a letter.

At the end of February there were mild days when Vincent painted out of doors. Writing to Van Rappard (Letter R40), he mentioned a small country graveyard; in a letter to Theo he called it "the little old church," which probably refers to the old tower, 459. A similar painting of the tower, 458, in which the surrounding countryside has a distinctly wintry look, can also, I believe, be assigned to February. Letter sketch 460, which has no immediate counterpart, also conveys the winter atmosphere of other February works. Its dimensions suggest that it may have been sent with a letter.

Wintry Landscapes and New Weavers
In March, Vincent's letters report, he continued painting and drawing weavers. In addition, he did a series of drawings of other subjects at this time. He described them most fully to Van Rappard, who must have commented favorably on drawings Vincent had sent him. About the middle of March, Vincent wrote: "Well, I am glad that you liked my little winter garden. That garden set me to dreaming, and I have since made another one with the same motif, and also with a little black ghost, which is there not as an exemplary representation of the structure of the human body, but rather as a patch of contrast" (Letter R44).

Which "winter garden" was the one Van Rappard either possessed or had seen can no longer be determined, but the one with a human figure as a black patch or "little black ghost" must have been the drawing 466. The letter continued: "I am sending you that one too, as well as a few others, namely: sepia sketch *In the Marsh*, pen-and-ink drawings *Pollard Birches*, *Lane of Poplars*, *Behind the Hedges*, *The Kingfisher*, and *Winter Garden*.

There is no sepia sketch *In the Marsh* known to us, but the other five can easily be identified as: 469 (*Pollard Birches*), 464 (*Lane of Poplars*), 461 (*Behind the Hedges*), 468 (*Pond with a Kingfisher*), and 465 (*Parsonage Garden*). Three drawings not mentioned that are similar in subject and style to those made in March are: *Parsonage Garden* (463), *Landscape with Willows and Sun Shining through the Clouds* (467), and *Lane with Trees* (470).*

The pen-and-ink drawings made in these weeks demonstrate a further development of Vincent's ability to render landscapes in an individual—though somewhat dry—manner. In their topographical precision and feeling for space, they are remarkable. The freakish trees in the parsonage garden may recall the touched-up drawing of "*Sorrow*" done two years earlier (130) and Vincent's attempt to convey in a drawing of tree roots "the grim

*Still another winter garden is listed in the 1970 *catalogue raisonné* as F1127a, and dated March–April 1884 there, but the "handwriting" of this drawing differs so much from the Van Goghs of this time that I see no way of assigning it a chronological place.

464

465

466

464 Lane of Poplars with One Figure, F1239
Pen, 54 × 39 cm (21¼ × 15⅜")
Rijksmuseum Vincent van Gogh, Amsterdam

465 Parsonage Garden, F1130
Pen, heightened with white, 51.5 × 38 cm (20½ × 15")
Mücsarnok, Budapest

466 Parsonage Garden, F1128
Pencil, pen, 39 × 53 cm (15⅜ × 20⅞")
Rijksmuseum Vincent van Gogh, Amsterdam

467 Landscape with Willows and Sun Shining through the Clouds, F1240a
Pencil, pen, 34 × 44 cm (13⅜ × 17⅜")
Art Institute of Chicago

468 Pond with a Kingfisher, F1135
Pen, heightened with white, 39 × 53 cm (15⅜ × 20⅞")
Private collection, Wassenaar, The Netherlands

469 Pollard Birches with Woman and Flock of Sheep, F1240
Pencil, pen, 39.5 × 54.5 cm (15¾ × 21⅝")
Rijksmuseum Vincent van Gogh, Amsterdam

470 Lane with Trees and One Figure, F1241
Pen, 19 × 27 cm (7½ × 10⅝")
Estate of M. Frank, New York

471 Weaver Facing Left, with a Spinning Wheel, F29
61 × 85 cm (24 × 33½")
Museum of Fine Arts, Boston

April 1884

472 Ditch, F1243
Pencil, pen, heightened with white, 39 × 33 cm (15⅜ × 13")
Rijksmuseum Vincent van Gogh, Amsterdam

473 Firs in the Fen, F1249
Pen, 34.5 × 44 cm (13¾ × 17⅜")
Rijksmuseum Vincent van Gogh, Amsterdam

474 Houses with Thatched Roofs, F1242
Pencil, pen, heightened with white, 30 × 44 cm (11¾ × 17⅜")
Tate Gallery, London

475 Parsonage, Seen from the Back, F1343
Pen, black chalk, heightened with white, 24 × 36 cm (9½ × 14⅛")
Private collection, Canada

467

469

468

470

471

472

473

474

475

tenacity and passionate intensity with which they hold on to the earth although they are half uprooted by the gales."

The recurrent motif of the sun encircled by rays appears for the first time in a Nuenen landscape (467)—although here it is somewhat muted. The same phenomenon is evident in the drawing *Behind the Hedges*, 461, but the source of light is itself partly hidden behind the trees. Dr. Walther Vanbeselaere in his study of Van Gogh's years in Holland* cleverly remarked that in this drawing we see the three pollard willows and the one pollard birch that Vincent later used as the subject of the famous painting done in the last days of his stay in Nuenen—*Autumn Landscape with Four Trees*, 962.

Two more pictures of weavers date from March 1884—the drawing of a weaver seen head on in a room with one small window, 462; and the painting of a loom on which a piece of red material is being woven, 471. The first we know from Letter 359, written about March 9: "I shall shortly be sending you a new pen-and-ink drawing of a weaver—larger than the other five, the loom seen from the front." Since 462 depicts the only weaver with "the loom seen from the front," we can assume that this is the one referred to here, although in that case the remark about the size does not tally. But I presume that Vincent was mistaken about the measurements, since he had already sent the others off.

The painting of the weaver with the red material, 471, is referred to in Letters 364 and 367, and it is interesting that in the latter Vincent notes that he had already started on this painting "in the winter." The position of the loom in 471 does indeed resemble most closely that in the drawings done in January, 444 and 445, and the letter sketch in 443. These drawings were probably made after the painting in 471, or a companion picture, had been started—and was only now taken up again. The spinning wheel may have been added for compositional reasons.

A Conflict and a "Contract"

In February, March, and April, relations between Vincent and Theo appear once more to have cooled off and finally to have deteriorated quite badly. The crux of the matter was Vincent's growing self-awareness as an artist and his need to be recognized as such. It began with the proposal, calmly formulated in Letter 360, written about February 1, that the money Vincent was receiving from Theo might henceforth be regarded as payment for the work he was sending to Theo, that is, as money *earned*. But when it appeared that Theo could give only faint praise to a few small panels that Vincent had sent him—presumably studies made in Drenthe—and when he had called some drawings "misconceived," Vincent's tone became sharper. In a long letter written about March 1, Vincent upbraided Theo for never having sold anything of his and, according to Vincent, for never even having tried. His pent-up bitterness is epitomized in the often-quoted words:

**De Hollandsche periode (1880–1885) in het werk van Vincent van Gogh* (1853–1890) (The Dutch Period [1880–1885] in the Work of Vincent van Gogh [1853–1890]), published in 1937.

476

477

478

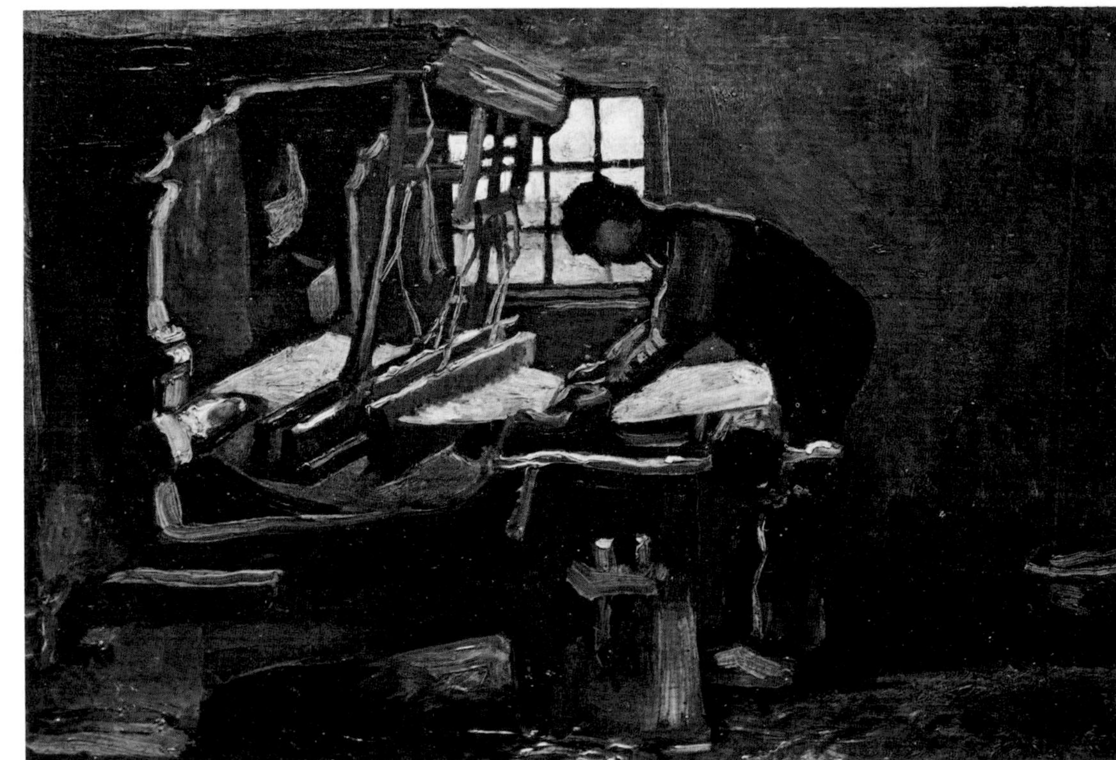

476 Parsonage with Flowering Trees
Sketch in Letter 366
Rijksmuseum Vincent van Gogh, Amsterdam

477 Landscape with Pollard Birches, F31
Canvas on panel, 43 × 58 cm ($16\frac{7}{8} \times 22\frac{7}{8}$")
Private collection, Paris

May 1884

478 Weaver, Arranging Threads, F35
Canvas on panel, 41 × 57 cm ($16\frac{1}{8} \times 22\frac{1}{2}$")
Rijksmuseum Kröller-Müller, Otterlo

479 Weaver, Seen from the Front, F30
70 × 85 cm ($27\frac{5}{8} \times 33\frac{1}{2}$")
Rijksmuseum Kröller-Müller, Otterlo

480 Weaver, Arranging Threads, F32
Panel, 19.5 × 41 cm ($7\frac{7}{8} \times 16\frac{1}{8}$")
Location unknown

481 Weaver, Arranging Threads, F1134
Pencil, pen, heightened with white, 27 × 40 cm ($10\frac{5}{8} \times 15\frac{3}{4}$")
Rijksmuseum Kröller-Müller, Otterlo

482 Weaver, Arranging Threads, F1688
Watercolor, dimensions unknown
Location unknown

483 Weaver with Other Figures in Front of the Loom, F1111
Probably a letter sketch
Pen, washed, 10 × 13.5 cm ($3\frac{7}{8} \times 5\frac{1}{2}$")
Rijksmuseum Kröller-Müller, Otterlo

484 Parsonage Garden, F185
Paper on panel, 25 × 57 cm ($9\frac{7}{8} \times 22\frac{1}{2}$")
Groninger Museum, Groningen

485 Parsonage Garden, F1133
Probably sketch sent with Letter R41
Pen, 9 × 21 cm ($3\frac{1}{2} \times 8\frac{1}{4}$")
Location unknown

479

480

481

482

483

485

484

"A *wife* you cannot give me, a *child* you cannot give me, work you cannot give me. Money, yes. But what good is it to me when I have to go without the rest?" (Letter 358).

When Theo spoke about a letter written "in haste" and "without thinking," Vincent objected and repeated that if he did make anything salable—that is, salable in Theo's eyes—he would rather "sell" it to Theo than to anyone else, but it would have to be "sold" in the literal sense: "What I mean is that I can only accept *that* money which I can dispose of as I see fit without having to ask anyone's opinion" (Letter 361). An explanation for his rebellious attitude can be found in Letter 363*a*; it had become only too clear to him, he said, that the people at home regarded the money he usually received from Theo as something completely *uncertain*, and, he added, "Yes, I'll say it, as a charitable gift to a poor wretch."

Not until the end of April did the tone of Vincent's letters become milder, and even then there seems to be no particular reason for this, such as definite promises or a change in Theo's attitude. One thing is certain: Theo, despite his criticism, did not withhold his financial support in these months and actually sent Vincent more than before.

Work during April

Although in April the theme of the weavers had not been dropped, Vincent did many landscape drawings. Foremost among the works from that month are the drawings sent to Van Rappard: *Ditch* (472), *Firs in the Fen* (473), and *Houses with Thatched Roofs* (474). All three are excellent examples of Vincent's skill in observing and depicting nature. I include here the drawing of the parsonage, viewed from the rear, with Vincent's studio on the right (475), a work somewhat difficult to date. The 1970 *catalogue raisonné* says "probably early 1884," but the blossoming sapling in the foreground, the sparse leaves on the trees at the right, and the presence of a member of the family seated on the rear terrace under a sunshade make me place it rather in early spring.

Vincent also made a painting of the garden behind the house with trees in bloom. Although it has been lost, we can imagine what it looked like from a large letter sketch, (476), in which the garden does not quite give the impression of spring. We do know a study with pollard birches, mentioned in Letter 367 (477).

In the same letter Vincent also mentions the theme of the weavers, writing of a painting of a loom, seen from the front, with "the little figure a dark silhouette against the white wall" (479). This is an important work on which Vincent spent much time; in his next letter, written a few weeks later, he said that he "had lately been busily continuing to paint" it. The other large weaver (471)—the one with the red material—was also a work that he had referred to twice over a period of about a month as being "in hand" (Letters 364 and 367).

The weavers continued to engage Vincent's attention, as is also apparent from Letter 367, in which he set down some of the things that fascinated him about that subject: "I shall still have a lot of work to do on the looms,

486

487

488

486 Old Man at the Bobbin Winder, F 1138
Pencil, black chalk, pen, 22.5 × 23 cm (9 × 9″)
Rijksmuseum Kröller-Müller, Otterlo

487 Old Man at the Bobbin Winder, F 1140
Watercolor, 44 × 34 cm (17⅜ × 13⅜″)
Rijksmuseum Vincent van Gogh, Amsterdam

488 Water Mill, F 48a
Canvas on cardboard, 57.5 × 78 cm (22⅞ × 30¾″)
Collection Mr. and Mrs. S. J. Lefrak, New York

489 Weaver, Standing in Front of the Loom, F 33
Canvas on panel, 55 × 79 cm (21⅝ × 31⅛″)
Location unknown

490 The Old Tower, F 88
Canvas on panel, 47.5 × 55 cm (18⅞ × 21⅝″)
Collection E. G. Bührle, Zurich

491 Portrait of Van Rappard (Upper Part), F 1297 (reverse: 795)
Black chalk, 27 × 45 cm (10⅝ × 17¾″)
Rijksmuseum Vincent van Gogh, Amsterdam

492 Village at Sunset, F 190
Canvas on cardboard, 57 × 82 cm (22½ × 32¼″)
Stedelijk Museum, Amsterdam

June 1884

493 Woman at the Spinning Wheel, F 1137
Sketch sent with Letter 370
Pen, 15 × 21 cm (5⅞ × 8¼″)
Rijksmuseum Vincent van Gogh, Amsterdam

494 Woman at the Spinning Wheel, F 1139
Gouache, 33 × 44 cm (13 × 17⅜″)
Collection Dr. Samuel Karlon, New York

495 Woman at the Spinning Wheel, F 68
Watercolor, heightened with white, 33 × 41 cm (13 × 16⅛″)
Location unknown

496 Woman at the Spinning Wheel, F 1136
Possibly a letter sketch
Pen, 14 × 20 cm (5½ × 7⅞″)
Rijksmuseum Kröller-Müller, Otterlo

497 Spinning Wheel, F 175
Canvas on cardboard, 34 × 44 cm (13⅜ × 17⅜″)
Rijksmuseum Vincent van Gogh, Amsterdam

489

490

491

492

493

494

495

496

497

but the contraptions are by nature so tremendously imposing, all that old oak against the grayish wall, that I certainly believe it is good to do paintings of them."

At the same time he was once again making plans for some others "where the figure will be placed quite differently, that is, where the weaver is not sitting behind it, but is arranging the threads of the cloth." We find this plan carried out in two painted studies, 478 and 480, and in two drawings, 481 and 482. The small sketch 483 was probably also done in the same month, May, but so far as we know it did not lead to any similar paintings or drawings.

A New Studio

The first half of May was entirely devoted to these and other studies in oils, which had kept Vincent so busy that he had "not made a single drawing in between" (Letter 368). Apart from the weavers, he had once more tried his hand at painting the well-known little tower (490). And much time must have been taken up with preparations for doing something about his studio; he had repeatedly expressed his dissatisfaction with it (as in Letter 363*a*). In Letter 368, written to Theo in the middle of May, is his first mention of a move as a *fait accompli*, this probably being attributable to the stand he had previously taken that he was completely free to spend his money as he saw fit. He wrote laconically: "And now let me tell you that today I have just about finished fixing up a roomy new studio I have rented. Two rooms, a big one and a small one, in a suite. I have been quite busy with this the past two weeks. I think I shall be able to work much better there than in the small space at home. And I do hope that when you see it, you will approve of what I have done."

What Vincent did not write, but apparently regarded as obvious, was that the rooms he had rented from the sexton of the Roman Catholic church were really intended to serve only as a studio. He continued to eat and sleep at home, which meant a considerable saving. Not until a year later did he definitely move to the studio and sleep in the attic over it because living together with his mother and sisters was causing too many problems.

498

499

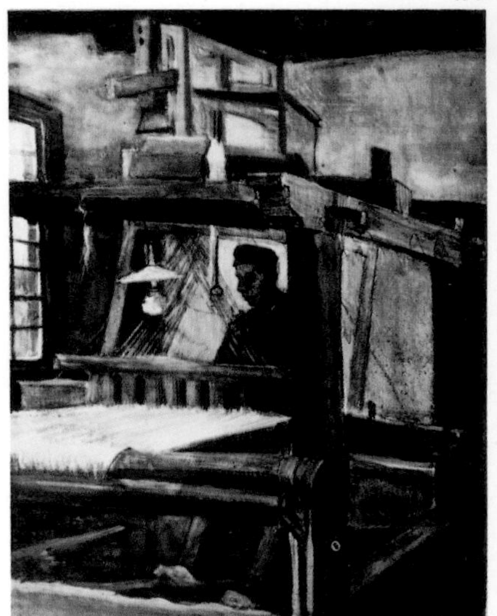

500

Visits by Van Rappard and Theo

In May, in addition to the new studio, there was another pleasant event—a visit by Van Rappard, who stayed at the parsonage for about ten days. Vincent reported on this to Theo at the end of May: "We then, as you can imagine, made quite a few trips together to the weavers and all kinds of attractive spots in the country." He added: "While he was here I did another weaver's cottage in the evening, again in the style of those shanties in Drenthe" (Letter 369). This "cottage in the evening" is not known to us, unless he was referring to the cottage with a little light burning inside that is generally considered to have been done the following year and is identified with the work Vincent in later letters called *La Chaumière* (*Cottage at Nightfall;* 777). He also mentioned a painting of a weaver, again in a somewhat different pose—standing in front of the loom, 489—and another painted study of the parsonage garden, now in full leaf, 484. On the basis of similarity of style and atmosphere, I have also assigned to the end of May the painting showing a village at sunset (492), which is not mentioned in the letters.

The works Van Rappard did during his visit to Nuenen that Vincent mentioned—a weaver and the bust of a girl reeling yarn—are not known to us, but one memento of his visit has been preserved—a portrait drawing by Van Gogh that probably represents Van Rappard (491). The compilers of the 1974 catalogue of Van Rappard's work (J.W. Brouwer, J.L. Siesling, and J. Vis) have advanced the assumption—quite justifiable in my view—that Van Rappard was the subject and that the work was done in Nuenen. Only the upper portion of the work remains; the portrait apparently did not please Van Gogh, for he tore it in two and later used the upper part of the reverse side of the paper for another drawing (795). It should be noted that it is equally possible that Vincent made the portrait at the time of Van Rappard's next visit, in October.

On Pentecost, that is to say, June 1, 1884, Theo paid a visit to his parents and also to Vincent, who in Letter 370 wrote: "I still often think of your pleasant visit." At this time Theo must have seen two studies of "a little old man at the bobbin winder near a small window." Vincent reminds him of this in both Letter 370 and Letter 371. This indicates that these studies, 486 and 487, date from the previous month. Vincent wrote that he hoped to make a painted study of the subject and certainly must have done so, to judge from the color key that he enclosed with the small rough sketch (498) he sent with Letter 371, although we have no knowl-

501

502

503

504

505

506

498 Old Man at the Bobbin Winder
Sketch in Letter 371
Rijksmuseum Vincent van Gogh, Amsterdam

July 1884

499 Weaver Facing Left, F1116a v (reverse: 139)
Watercolor, 44 × 35 cm ($17\frac{3}{8} \times 13\frac{3}{4}''$)
Location unknown

500 Weaver near an Open Window, F24
Canvas on cardboard, 68.5 × 93 cm
($27\frac{1}{8} \times 36\frac{5}{8}''$)
Bayerische Staatsgemäldesammlungen, Munich

501 Weaver, Interior with Three Small Windows, F37
61 × 93 cm ($24 \times 36\frac{5}{8}''$)
Rijksmuseum Kröller-Müller, Otterlo

502 Weaver, Interior with Three Small Windows, F1115
Watercolor, pen, 33.5 × 45 cm ($13\frac{3}{8} \times 17\frac{3}{4}''$)
Rijksmuseum Vincent van Gogh, Amsterdam

503 Weaver, Seen from the Front, F27
Canvas on panel, 48 × 61 cm ($18\frac{7}{8} \times 24''$)
Museum Boymans-van Beuningen, Rotterdam

504 Cart with Red and White Ox, F38
Canvas on panel, 57 × 82.5 cm ($22\frac{1}{2} \times 32\frac{5}{8}''$)
Rijksmuseum Kröller-Müller, Otterlo
Colorplate VII, p. 119

505 Cart with Black Ox, F39
60 × 80 cm ($23\frac{5}{8} \times 31\frac{1}{2}''$)
Collection Julius Fohs, United States

506 Mangle with Two Women and a Man, F1337
Pencil, pen, 23 × 29.5 cm ($9 \times 11\frac{3}{4}''$)
Rijksmuseum Kröller-Müller, Otterlo

507 The Old Tower at Dusk, F40
Canvas on cardboard, 35 × 47 cm
($13\frac{3}{4} \times 18\frac{1}{2}''$)
Private collection, London

507

edge of the painting. The study of a woman at the spinning wheel, made in June and often mentioned in his letters, has likewise failed to come down to us, but we do have drawings of the subject in various mediums (493–96). The first two show a woman with a shawl but no bonnet, and the other two a woman wearing a white bonnet but without a shawl. On the basis of the description given in Letter 370 ("the figure is in blue with a shawl that is somewhat mouse colored"), I assume that the first two correspond to the lost painting. Drawing 493 must therefore be the "small rough sketch" made after the painting and enclosed with Letter 370.

Concern with Color Theories

During Van Rappard's visit the two painters had taken trips to "all kinds of attractive spots in the country," including water mills. Looking back on the visit, Vincent wrote Van Rappard at the end of May that after his departure, he had worked on a water mill: "It is just the same as the two other water mills we went to see together, except that it has two *red roofs* and you see it from the front—with poplars all around" (Letter R50). It is virtually certain from the description that this painting was 488. As we learn from research by Tralbaut, who in 1955 set about to identify the water mills depicted by Van Gogh, this was the mill in Col, a hamlet near Nuenen.* In color and composition it is an exceptionally fine painting, much superior to the other water mills done in the fall. Seeing the unusually warm hues in this landscape, one is not surprised, in reading his letters from this period, to learn how much he was concerned just then with theories of color. After Van Rappard's visit he wrote self-confidently that "so far as color is concerned" he would not at the moment want to change places with him (Letter 369). Vincent read *Les Artistes de Mon Temps* (The Artists of My Time) by Charles Blanc with great interest and copied out a passage from it for Theo that clearly showed Delacroix's opinion that in painting it is not the "local color" that matters but the "tone" in relation to other colors. A relatively dark color may appear light because of the still darker surrounding colors. In his small sketch of the man with the bobbin winder (498) Vincent indicated in the margin how dark he had made a certain spot in the painting, although in the entire composition it constituted the "highest tone." In his letters he repeatedly came back to these matters, which, as he said, had lately very much occupied his thoughts.

He knew that in the world around him, particularly in France, a veritable revolution was taking place right in this very field, and it is moving to read what he writes about it when in his ignorance he artlessly tries to find consolation in the genre painting of his older colleague Jozef Israëls: "The thing with me is that when I hear you talking about many new names, it does not always make sense if I have seen absolutely *nothing* of what they do. And from what has been said by you about 'Impressionism' I have gathered that it was something other than I thought it was, although what is to be understood by it is still

**De Toerist*, June 1955.

508

509

510

511

512

August 1884

508 Wheat Harvest
Sketch in Letter 374
Rijksmuseum Vincent van Gogh, Amsterdam

509 Sower, F1143
Pen, 5.5 × 14 cm (2⅜ × 5½")
Collection R. W. van Hoey Smith, Rockanje, The Netherlands

510 Potato Harvest with Two Figures, F1141
Pen, 5 × 13 cm (2 × 5⅛")
Collection R. W. van Hoey Smith, Rockanje, The Netherlands

511 Oxcart in the Snow, F1144
Pen, 5 × 13.5 cm (2 × 5½")
Collection R. W. van Hoey Smith, Rockanje, The Netherlands

512 Plowman, F1142
Pen, 5.5 × 15 cm (2⅜ × 5⅞")
Collection R. W. van Hoey Smith, Rockanje, The Netherlands
Sketches 509–12 must have been sent, like 508, with Letter 374

Colorplate VII, Cart with Red and White Ox, 504 〉

not too clear to me. Yet as for me, I find so very much in Israëls for example that I am not too curious or eager about other or newer things" (Letter 371).

Vincent's preoccupation with color also left its mark on the new large studies of weavers that he made at the beginning of July. Some are easily identified from his description. The painting showing "a part of the loom with the figure and a small window" must have been 500. The other weaver, in a room with three windows, is 501, a subject he also used for watercolor 502. The terms he used to describe painting 501 clearly indicate how much this meant to him as a study in color: it was "an interior with three small windows looking out on the yellowish green, which contrasts with the blue of the material being woven on the loom and the weaver's blouse, which is still another kind of blue" (Letter 372). Similarity of style with 500 and 501 has led me to include with this group the imposing *Weaver* (503), which is otherwise difficult to date.

The Summer Months

The letters are not of much help in determining the chronology of Vincent's work in July and the next month or two, for we know of only a few written in that period and even those are short: Letter 372, probably written about July 1, and Letters 373 and 374, early August. As Vincent used to write Theo six to eight times a month, it seems plausible that some of the letters written during these months went astray, although there is no indication of this in the material available to us. In any case it is clear that the next letter, 375, must have been preceded by a letter not known to us, since Vincent refers to it in his opening lines. Additional evidence that the correspondence is not complete is a reference at the beginning of Letter 379 to an apparently very sharp letter from Vincent that has been lost or was destroyed.

In existing literature very few of Van Gogh's works have thus far been assigned to the summer months of 1884, although there is no reason why his activity should suddenly have dropped so sharply. I therefore conclude that the lack of information supplied by the letters must have been a factor here. Hence, there is also good reason to assume that several of the many drawings and paintings—especially those showing peasant men and women working in the fields—which in the *catalogue raisonné* have been placed in the summer of 1885 were actually made in 1884. Perhaps the only way to set matters right is a painstaking analysis of style. As I do not now have sufficient data at hand to reassign works from 1885 to a year earlier, I have retained the traditional classification for these months, with the proviso that it probably does not always faithfully reflect the true chronology.

Two works, both studies of an oxcart, were definitely made about the end of July; one shows an oxcart with a red and white ox hitched to the cart, 504 (colorplate VII, page 119), and the other with a black ox, 505. It was an unusual motif for Van Gogh, who was probably fascinated both by the colors and by the "dramatic element" of the sorely tried animals. In the same passage in which

513

514

515

516

517

September 1884

513 Potato Harvest with Figures, F41
66 × 149 cm (26 × 58⅝")
Rijksmuseum Kröller-Müller, Otterlo

514 Plowman and Potato Reaper, F172
70.5 × 170 cm (28 × 66⅞")
Von der Heydt Museum, Wuppertal

515 Wood Gatherer, Figure Study, F1081
Watercolor, 32.5 × 25 cm (13 × 9⅞")
Location unknown

516 Wood Gatherers in the Snow, F43
Canvas on panel, 67 × 126 cm (26⅜ × 49⅝")
Collection Mrs. L. Schokking-Ribbius
Peletier, Doorn, The Netherlands

517 Shepherd with Flock of Sheep, F42
Canvas on cardboard, 67 × 126 cm
(26⅜ × 49⅝")
Location unknown

〈 Colorplate VIII, Lane of Poplars, 522

he told about the oxcart, he also mentioned a study of the old tower at dusk, which we can identify as 507. The small, unfinished drawing showing a mangle (506) stands alone as far as style is concerned and cannot be dated with any certainty.

Vincent was by no means idle during August, as the letter written by him at the beginning of that month clearly shows: "Right now I am writing somewhat in haste because I am busy working. I work quite a bit early in the morning or in the evening, and everything is sometimes so indescribably beautiful then" (Letter 373). Yet all that we know from that month are a few small sketches (508–12). They had to do with a kind of "commission" which would keep Van Gogh busy up to September and which is discussed repeatedly in his letters—including those to Van Rappard.

A Commission
The small sketch of the wheat harvest, 508, that Vincent made in Letter 374 was accompanied by the explanation: "I made this for someone in Eindhoven who wanted to decorate a dining room. He was going to do this with compositions depicting various saints. I suggested to him that a half-dozen scenes of peasant life in the Meierij [a rural area in Brabant]—at the same time symbolizing the four seasons of the year—might do more to sharpen the appetites of the good people who would be dining there than the mystical personages he had in mind. The man has now become quite keen on this after a visit to my studio."

This is how Vincent described this man, whose name was Hermans: "He is a man I would like, if possible, to keep on good terms with—a former goldsmith who on three occasions has brought together and sold a *very* considerable collection of antiques. He is now rich and has had a house built which he has filled with antiques again and is furnishing with some *very* fine oak cupboards and the like" (Letter 374). We are not sure whether the separate small sketches that have been preserved (509–12) were Van Gogh's first designs made for Hermans or letter sketches like the one made in Letter 374 (508). They were probably also sent with this letter. In any case they give us a good notion of four of the subjects he mentioned there: "Sower," "Potato Harvest," "Oxcart in the Snow," and "Plowman." All underwent minor or major changes in the process of being reworked into the large painted studies, of which we only know four (513, 514, 516, and 517).

It had been arranged that Hermans himself would paint the panels in his house and that Vincent would provide him for that purpose, first, with smaller designs, and then with painted prototypes (Letter 374). In a letter to Van Rappard (R47), he described the arrangement (probably further elaborated in the meantime) in some detail: "And after a visit [by Hermans] to the studio, I made him preliminary rough sketches of the six peasants' life motifs: 'Sower,' 'Plowman,' 'Wheat Harvest,' 'Potato Planting,' 'Shepherd,' 'Winter with Oxcart.' And I am now making those. But the way I am doing it is I am making those six canvases *for myself*, although as far as size and other things go, I am naturally making them keeping his room in mind, and he is paying my expenses for models and paint, while the canvases remain my property and I get them back when he has copied them."

It is quite apparent from the letters that Vincent spent a long time working on the "commission." It was not until the second half of September that he completed it, and even that was not the final stage. As he wrote Theo: "Just this past week I have now also designed the last of the six canvases for Hermans: 'Wood Gatherers in the Snow.' So all six are now at his place for copying; when he

518

519

520

October 1884
518 Lane of Poplars at Sunset, F 123
46 × 33 cm ($18\frac{1}{8} \times 13''$)
Rijksmuseum Kröller-Müller, Otterlo
519 Country Lane, F 120
Canvas on panel, 46 × 35 cm ($18\frac{1}{8} \times 13\frac{3}{4}''$)
Collection Mrs. L. Jäggli-Hahnloser, Winterthur, Switzerland
520 Lane of Poplars, F 1246
Pencil, pen, heightened with white, 20.5 × 12.5 cm ($8\frac{1}{4} \times 5\frac{1}{8}''$)
Collection S. Polak, Amsterdam
521 Chapel at Nuenen with Churchgoers, F 25
41 × 32 cm ($16\frac{1}{8} \times 12\frac{5}{8}''$)
Rijksmuseum Vincent van Gogh, Amsterdam

521

522

523

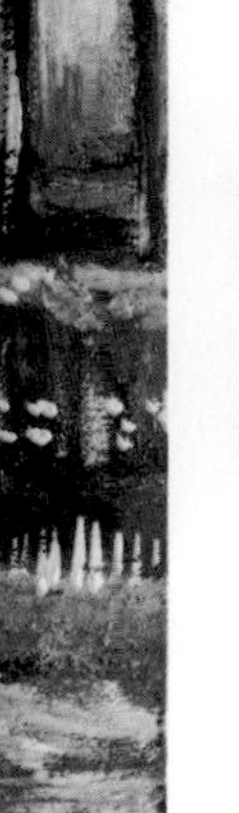

524

525

526

527

522 Lane of Poplars, F 122
Canvas on panel, 99 × 66 cm (39 × 26″)
Rijksmuseum Vincent van Gogh, Amsterdam
Colorplate VIII, p. 120

November 1884

523 Water Mill at Gennep, F 1144a
Watercolor, 30.5 × 47 cm (12¼ × 18½″)
Location unknown

524 Wheels of the Water Mill at Gennep, F 46
60 × 78.5 cm (23⅝ × 31⅛″)
Stedelijk Museum, Amsterdam (on loan from Miss E. Ribbius Peletier)

525 Water Mill at Gennep, F 125
Canvas on panel, 87 × 151 cm (34¼ × 59½″)
Location unknown

526 Water Mill at Gennep, F 47
Cardboard, 75 × 100 cm (29½ × 39⅜″)
Private collection, New York

527 Water Mill at Opwetten, F 48
Canvas on panel, 45 × 58 cm (17¾ × 22⅞″)
Collection Mr. and Mrs. A. T. Smith, London

is finished with them and they have meanwhile had time to become thoroughly dry, I am going to rework them in order to make them into paintings" (Letter 377).

It was Vincent's custom to make preliminary studies for many of the details, and at least one of these has been preserved; it is the central figure of the painting *Wood Gatherers in the Snow* (516) that we see also in watercolor 515. It is also typical of Vincent's method of operation that the ox in his small sketch *Oxcart in the Snow* (511) is a copy of his own large painted black ox (505). But even by October, Vincent was not yet completely finished with the commission; he wrote that Hermans had "already" copied four of the six subjects. And although Hermans proved to be "a very nice, pleasant friend," Vincent nonetheless still grumbled a bit about his stinginess. Hermans had once given him 25 guldens for expenses, perhaps also something for models (Vincent is not very clear about this), but in any case nothing for his time and trouble (Letter 381).

Margo Begemann

Once again there had been a dramatic development in Vincent's personal life that cannot have made his work any easier. His first account of it comes in a letter to Theo written about the middle of September or a little later (Letter 375). After apologizing for not yet having replied to two letters from Theo, one containing 150 francs, he wrote: "Something has happened, Theo, that most of the people around here do *not* know about or suspect, and must never come to know about, so be as silent as the grave—but it is a terrible thing. To tell you everything I would have to write a book—and that I cannot do. Miss Begemann has taken poison, in a moment of despair, after she had spoken to her family, and evil things were being said about her and me. She got so upset that she did it all of a sudden (in my opinion, definitely in a fit of madness)." We are told something about Margo Begemann in Mrs. van Gogh-Bonger's "Memoir" to *The Complete Letters.* We learn that she was the youngest of three sisters who lived next door to the parsonage and was much older than Vincent. It is strange that Vincent said nothing in his letter to Theo of the love affair which must have preceded Margo's attempt at suicide. The inference to be drawn is that Theo had probably been told about it during one of his visits. If this were not so, the way Vincent wrote about a projected marriage without any sort of introduction, would be hard to explain. Laconically and almost incidentally he said "that they put [him] off for two years" (in other words, a marriage was out of the question for two years), to which he added that he would decidedly not agree to that, "since I said that *if* there was to be a question of marriage here, it would have to be very soon or not at all."

There would, of course, be no marriage, whether Vincent wanted it or not. He certainly did not have the burning love for Margo Begemann that he had felt for Kee Vos, about whom he had always written in quite different terms. There can be no doubt that he had felt much sympathy for the woman next door, whom he had gotten to know

528

529

530

531

532

533

534

535

536

537

538

528 Still Life with Pots, Jar, and Bottle, F178 (reverse: 1198)
29.5 × 39.5 cm (11¾ × 15¾″)
Gemeentemuseum, The Hague

529 Still Life with Jars, F50
33 × 41 cm (13 × 16⅛″)
Rijksmuseum Kröller-Müller, Otterlo

530 Still Life with Jars, F56
46.5 × 56 cm (18½ × 22″)
Private collection, The Hague

531 Still Life with Pots, Jar, and Bottle, F58
Canvas on panel, 31 × 41 cm (12¼ × 16⅛″)
Private collection, United States

532 Still Life with Two Sacks and a Bottle, F55
Canvas on panel, 30.5 × 41 cm (12¼ × 16⅛″)
Location unknown

533 Still Life with Pottery, Bottles, and a Box, F61 (reverse: 1302)
Canvas on cardboard, 31 × 42 cm (12¼ × 16½″)
Rijksmuseum Vincent van Gogh, Amsterdam

534 Still Life with Three Beer Mugs, F49
Canvas on cardboard, 32 × 43 cm (12⅝ × 16⅞″)
Rijksmuseum Vincent van Gogh, Amsterdam

535 Still Life with a Bearded-Man Jar and Coffee Mill, F52
Panel, 34 × 43 cm (13⅜ × 16⅞″)
Rijksmuseum Kröller-Müller, Otterlo

536 Still Life with Pottery and Clogs, F54
Canvas on panel, 42 × 54 cm (16½ × 21¼″)
Museum van Baaren, Utrecht

537 Still Life with Bottles and a Cowrie Shell, F64
Canvas on panel, 32 × 41 cm (12⅝ × 16⅛″)
Location unknown

538 Still Life with Pottery and Three Bottles, F53
Canvas on panel, 39.5 × 56 cm (15¾ × 22″)
Rijksmuseum Vincent van Gogh, Amsterdam

539 Still Life with Pottery, Jar, and Bottle, F57
40 × 56 cm (15¾ × 22″)
Collection Arnold Hofland, London

539

much better since his mother's illness and with whom he often went on long walks, according to Mrs. van Gogh-Bonger. But there could have been no question of a great love when he was able to write to Theo so dispassionately about her as in this quite striking passage: "It is a pity I did not meet her *sooner*, say some ten years ago. She now reminds me of a Cremona violin that is out of tune, because of bunglers who tried to repair it in the past. And the way she was when I met her, I had the feeling that there was too much that had been spoiled. But originally it was a rare specimen of great value, *and even now quand même* [despite everything] she still has something of value left" (Letter 377).

From bits here and there in subsequent letters we learn how things later went with Margo Begemann. She had been under medical care in Utrecht after her attempt at suicide, and she recovered fairly rapidly. Vincent continued to correspond with her and even went to see her in Utrecht. In November he wrote that she would "soon" be returning to Nuenen (Letter 385). As we hear no more about her from then on, this must have been the end of a short but very moving episode in Vincent's life, which was otherwise full of dramatic events (see Appendix, note 1).

Works Lost and Works Preserved

Apart from the four landscapes finally made on commission for Hermans and the single preliminary study made in connection with them, none of Vincent's works from September has come down to us. We learn from a letter written at the end of the month that he did make at least one other painting—a *Sower*, which must have been lost; the description of it does not tally with any of the sowers we know. Vincent had sent Theo a photograph of this painting and in a later letter sent him several more photographs of weavers. With the idea of perhaps eliciting some interest from the illustrated journals in what he was doing—in those days many artists worked as journal illustrators—he had had photographs made of about a dozen of his works, but since he was very disappointed in their quality, he sent only a few to Theo and did not bother any more about them.

There are also few works from October that we know of—undoubtedly far fewer than Vincent actually made. Only one of those that have been preserved is described in the letters. It is *Lane of Poplars*, with yellow autumn leaves and patches of sunlight on the ground (522; colorplate VIII, page 120). I have also dated to October the landscapes in 518, 519, and 520 as they are closely related, and I assume that the *Chapel at Nuenen with Churchgoers* (521) was also made about this time. This work has always previously been dated January 1884 and regarded as related to the small sketch (447) in Letter 355. However, as already noted in the comments on that letter sketch, I am inclined to place the present work in late autumn—in view of the sparse brown foliage of the trees (and the brown hedge). Since the little church was part of Vincent's daily surroundings, there is absolutely no reason for this picture with two groups of people to be the study mentioned in Letter 355. That study, to judge from both

540

541

542

543

540 Still Life with Paintbrushes in a Pot, F60
Canvas on panel, 30.5 × 43 cm ($12\frac{1}{4} \times 16\frac{7}{8}$")
Location unknown

541 Vase with Dead Leaves, F200
Canvas on panel, 41.5 × 31 cm ($16\frac{1}{2} \times 12\frac{1}{4}$")
Private collection, The Netherlands

542 Vase with Honesty, F76
Canvas on cardboard, 42.5 × 32.5 cm ($16\frac{7}{8} \times 13$")
Rijksmuseum Vincent van Gogh, Amsterdam

543 Two Rats, F177
Panel, 29.5 × 41.5 cm ($11\frac{3}{4} \times 16\frac{1}{2}$")
Location unknown

545

546

548

549

551

552

December 1884

544 Peasant Woman, Head, F 1192
Pencil, black chalk, washed, 34.5 × 21 cm ($13\frac{3}{4} \times 8\frac{1}{4}''$)
Rijksmuseum Vincent van Gogh, Amsterdam

545 Peasant Woman, Head, F 1180
Black chalk, 41.5 × 29 cm ($16\frac{1}{2} \times 11\frac{3}{8}''$)
Rijksmuseum Vincent van Gogh, Amsterdam

546 Peasant Woman, Half-Figure, Sitting, F 143
Canvas on panel, 36 × 26 cm ($14\frac{1}{8} \times 10\frac{1}{4}''$)
Collection Max Wirth, Basel

547 Peasant Woman, Half-Figure, Sitting, F 1191
Pencil, 35 × 21 cm ($13\frac{3}{4} \times 8\frac{1}{4}''$)
Rijksmuseum Vincent van Gogh, Amsterdam

548 Peasant Woman, Head, F 136a
Canvas on panel, 35 × 26 cm ($13\frac{3}{4} \times 10\frac{1}{4}''$)
Private collection, Japan

549 Peasant Woman, Head, F 1176
Pen, pencil, 12 × 9 cm ($4\frac{3}{4} \times 3\frac{1}{2}''$)
Rijksmuseum Vincent van Gogh, Amsterdam

550 Peasant Woman, Head, F 75
36.5 × 29.5 cm ($14\frac{5}{8} \times 11\frac{3}{4}''$)
Von der Heydt Museum, Wuppertal

551 Peasant Woman, Head, F 146
Canvas on cardboard, 33 × 26 cm ($13 \times 10\frac{1}{4}''$)
Collection Mrs. H. van Ogtrop-van Kempen, Aalst, The Netherlands

552 Peasant Woman, Head, F 1193a
Pencil, pen, washed, 12.5 × 9 cm ($5\frac{1}{8} \times 3\frac{1}{2}''$)
Collection Mr. and Mrs. Clifford Michel, Southampton, New York

the letter sketch and the corresponding drawing 446, showed only a single figure.

Still Lifes

Vincent spent the rest of the month making a series of still lifes, in which he was not only improving his own skills in this field but he was also playing the role of teacher. In Letter 385, written in the first half of November, he reported: "I now have three people in Eindhoven who want to learn to paint, and I am teaching them how to do still lifes." One of them was Hermans, for whom Vincent had worked "on commission." The second was Anton Kerssemakers, a Sunday painter and a tanner, and the third was a postal worker, Willem van de Wakker.* A fourth pupil was added in 1885: Dimmen Gestel, the printer from whom Vincent had ordered the stone for the lithograph of *The Potato Eaters.* From all accounts, Vincent seems to have been able to bring his pupils along with great personal authority and great energy, paying no attention to their views on "technique" and generally working along with them, both indoors and outdoors. Vincent himself wrote of his contact with Kerssemakers: "Yesterday I brought home that study of the water mill at Gennep which I enjoyed working on and which was the occasion for meeting a new person in Eindhoven who is very anxious to learn how to paint. I stopped by to see him, and we started right away. The result was that the same evening he had done a still life, and he had given me his promise that he will try to make about thirty of them this winter. I'll go and look at them from time to time and help him with them" (Letter 386).

Teaching these new pupils was no more remunerative than the work he did for Hermans. In the same letter he wrote: "Little by little, however, I am going to make them pay something—not in money, though, but by telling them '*You have to give me tubes of paint.*' " And in the next letter he said: "Things have not really been going so badly for me lately. It is true that I will not get any money here for what I am doing, but I am making good friends, and I believe they will become even better [friends]" (Letter 387). Besides fostering friendships, which he badly needed at this time, the work in Eindhoven spurred him on to greater creativity, which resulted in a number of attractive studies that offered him wide scope for developing his sense of color: "The past week I have been painting still lifes day after day with the people who are painting in Eindhoven" (Letter 387). Some must have been painted in Kerssemakers's studio, some at Hermans's house, and some in his own studio.

Vincent continued to help his friends from time to time during the next year, as can be gathered from Kerssemakers's and Van de Wakker's reminiscences, but it is reasonable to assume that their still lifes took up

553

554

555

556

557

558

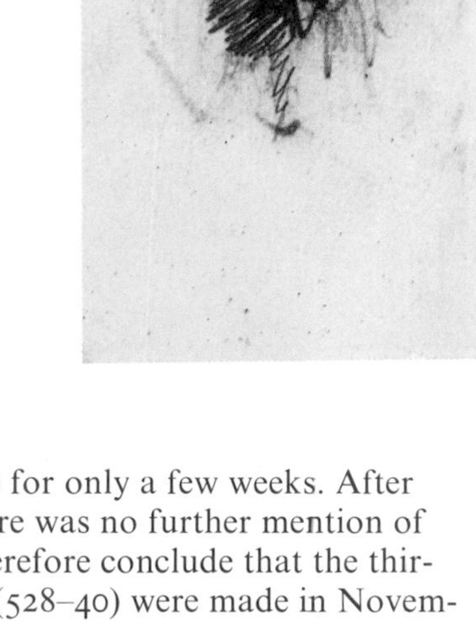

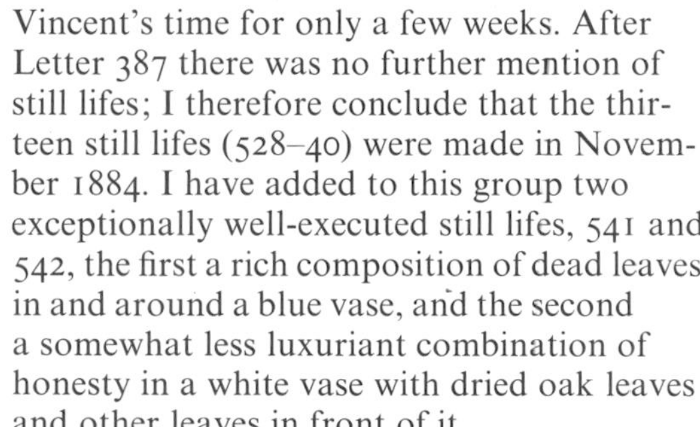

Vincent's time for only a few weeks. After Letter 387 there was no further mention of still lifes; I therefore conclude that the thirteen still lifes (528–40) were made in November 1884. I have added to this group two exceptionally well-executed still lifes, 541 and 542, the first a rich composition of dead leaves in and around a blue vase, and the second a somewhat less luxuriant combination of honesty in a white vase with dried oak leaves and other leaves in front of it.

The dating of these works requires some explanation, since they might be connected with the much later sketch in Letter 398 (726). In the 1970 *catalogue raisonné*, 541 is dated "probably autumn 1884," with the

*Reminiscences of Van Gogh by Kerssemakers were published in 1912; see Number 435c in *The Complete Letters.* Reminiscences by Van de Wakker were also found to exist; they were brought to light by Dr. Benno J. Stokvis, in 1927, as a consequence of the publication of his *Nasporingen omtrent Vincent van Gogh in Brabant* (Research Regarding Vincent van Gogh in Brabant), the preceding year. Van de Wakker's piece is included in the Dutch edition of the letters (Number 435e).

553 Silhouette of a Peasant Woman Digging Carrots
Drawing in sketchbook, pen, washed, 12 × 7 cm (4¾ × 2¾″)
Rijksmuseum Vincent van Gogh, Amsterdam

554 Silhouette of a Man with a Rake
Drawing in sketchbook, pen, washed, 12 × 7 cm (4¾ × 2¾″)
Rijksmuseum Vincent van Gogh, Amsterdam

555 Peasant Woman, Stooping to the Left
Drawing in sketchbook, pencil, 12 × 7 cm (4¾ × 2¾″)
Rijksmuseum Vincent van Gogh, Amsterdam

556 Sower Facing Left
Drawing in sketchbook, pen, 12 × 7 cm (4¾ × 2¾″)
Rijksmuseum Vincent van Gogh, Amsterdam

559

560

561

562

563

564

557 Head of a Man, Bareheaded
Drawing in sketchbook, pencil, 12 × 7 cm ($4\frac{3}{4} \times 2\frac{3}{4}$")
Rijksmuseum Vincent van Gogh, Amsterdam

558 Head of a Man, Bareheaded, F 164
Canvas on panel, 38 × 30 cm ($15 \times 11\frac{3}{4}$")
Rijksmuseum Vincent van Gogh, Amsterdam

559 Head of a Man, Bareheaded
Drawing in sketchbook, pencil, 12 × 7 cm ($4\frac{3}{4} \times 2\frac{3}{4}$")
Rijksmuseum Vincent van Gogh, Amsterdam

560 Peasant with Hat, Head, F 1200
Pen, washed, 14.5 × 8 cm ($5\frac{7}{8} \times 3\frac{1}{8}$")
Rijksmuseum Vincent van Gogh, Amsterdam

561 Peasant Woman, Head, F 144
Canvas on panel, 40.5 × 30.5 cm ($16\frac{1}{8} \times 12\frac{1}{4}$")
Collection Miss Olive Hosmer, Montreal

562 Peasant Woman, Head, F 1174
Pen, 16 × 10.5 cm ($6\frac{1}{4} \times 4\frac{3}{8}$")
Collection P. D. Sanderse, Bentveld, The Netherlands

563 Peasant, Head, F 160a
39 × 30 cm ($15\frac{3}{8} \times 11\frac{3}{4}$")
Location unknown

564 Peasant, Head, F 1198
Pen, pencil, black chalk, brown ink, washed, 14.5 × 10.5 cm ($5\frac{7}{8} \times 4\frac{3}{8}$")
Rijksmuseum Vincent van Gogh, Amsterdam

comment "stylistically related to F76"; this is 542, which the 1970 work dates "before 26 March 1885. Probably autumn 1884."

The notation "before 26 March 1885" was based on the fact that Theo had visited Nuenen on that date and that, according to Letter 398, he had taken with him a painting of honesty: "Enclosed is a rough sketch . . . of a still life with honesty done in the same style as the one you took with you." The painting after which this sketch (726) was made has been lost, but the one Theo took with him may well have been still life 542, which can certainly be said to be "in the same style" as the small sketch.

Since there is nothing to indicate that Vincent had been working on still lifes during the months immediately preceding Theo's visit, it is my assumption that the work Theo had selected to take with him had been done in the fall of 1884, when Vincent had in fact been making many still lifes. The stylistically related painting of the vase with dead leaves, 541, could thus very well have been made at the same time.

In my opinion the small painting with the two rats, 543, fits in best with this period insofar as color and treatment are concerned, although the exceptional nature of the subject makes it difficult to tie it in with other groups of works that can more easily be dated.

What is certain is that as early as October, Vincent had already started painting heads. In Letter 383, written at the end of that month, he harked back to a wish he had expressed before—to work for a while in Antwerp—but to this he added: "However, if I first paint about thirty heads here, I will be able to profit more from Antwerp, and I am now starting on those thirty heads or rather I have already started on the bust of a shepherd." This shepherd, which has unfortunately been lost, had already been described in Letter 382: "I am working on the figure of a shepherd wearing a big cloak, which is in the same format as the *Woman at the Spinning Wheel*." Although this picture has also disappeared, Vincent had mentioned the format in Letter 371; it was 39⅜ by 29½ inches, so the *Bust of a Shepherd* (assuming that this is identical to the *Figure of a Shepherd*), the first of the series of heads, was a remarkably large painting. Vincent must also have made smaller heads during that month, since he wrote in Letter 384 of about November 1: "What I have gained with this is that I can, for instance, now easily paint a head after a model in a single morning and that my color is becoming better and more precise and my technique is acquiring more character."

It is not possible to trace which of the many heads of countryfolk, both men and women, were made in October and it is debatable whether even a thoroughgoing stylistic analysis could enable us to determine which of these should be regarded as of an earlier date and be shifted from December or later to October or to the beginning of November. When Vincent writes in his next letter about "two heads of dike workers," I feel that it is again impossible to decide which of the heads represent farmers and which show dike workers.

Vincent's other work in early November included yet another important painting of what he called "an old water mill in Gennep, on the other side of Eindhoven" (Letter 385). This must be 525, and it is probably not too farfetched to suppose that during the days he worked there he also painted the detail of the wheel (524) as well as the smaller study of the entire mill (526). Because of the similarity in subject and treatment I also place the study of the *Water Mill at Opwetten* (527) in this period, although it is not mentioned in the letters.

Rebelliousness

The grim tenacity with which Vincent devoted himself to painting heads in December

565

566

567

565 Peasant Woman, Head, F146a
43.5 × 37 cm (17⅛ × 14⅝″)
Location unknown

566 Peasant Woman, Head, F1193
Black chalk, pen, washed, 11.5 × 8 cm
(4¾ × 3⅛″)
Private collection, Amersfoort, The Netherlands

567 Peasant Woman, Head, F1148
Black chalk, pen, washed, 13 × 10 cm
(5⅛ × 3⅞″)
Location unknown

568 Peasant Woman, Head
Drawing in sketchbook, pencil, 12 × 7 cm
(4¾ × 2¾″)
Rijksmuseum Vincent van Gogh, Amsterdam

568

569

570

571

572

573

574

575

576

577

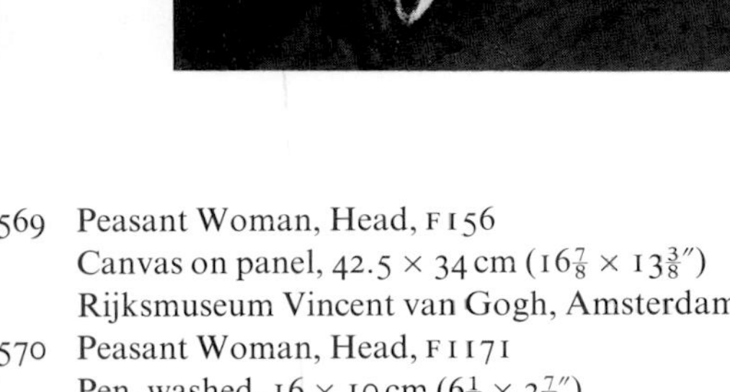

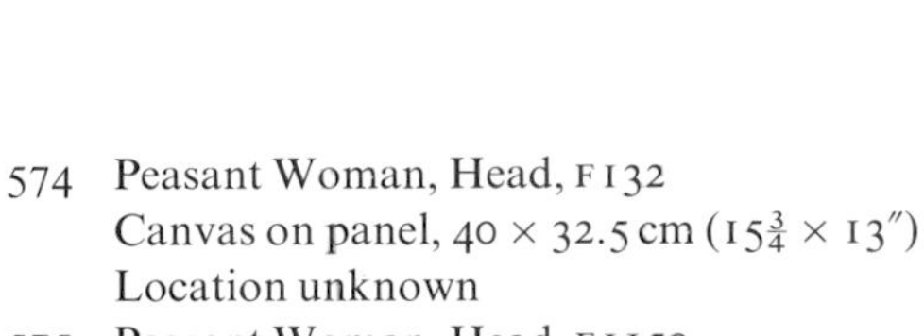

569 Peasant Woman, Head, F 156
Canvas on panel, 42.5 × 34 cm ($16\frac{7}{8} \times 13\frac{3}{8}$")
Rijksmuseum Vincent van Gogh, Amsterdam

570 Peasant Woman, Head, F 1171
Pen, washed, 16 × 10 cm ($6\frac{1}{4} \times 3\frac{7}{8}$")
Rijksmuseum Vincent van Gogh, Amsterdam

571 Peasant Woman, Head, F 1172
Pen, 8 × 6.5 cm ($3\frac{1}{8} \times 2\frac{3}{4}$")
Rijksmuseum Vincent van Gogh, Amsterdam

572 Peasant Woman, Head, F 1173
Pen, 14.5 × 10 cm ($5\frac{7}{8} \times 3\frac{7}{8}$")
Rijksmuseum Vincent van Gogh, Amsterdam

573 Head of a Peasant Woman, Bareheaded
Drawing in sketchbook, pencil, 12 × 7 cm ($4\frac{3}{4} \times 2\frac{3}{4}$")
Rijksmuseum Vincent van Gogh, Amsterdam

574 Peasant Woman, Head, F 132
Canvas on panel, 40 × 32.5 cm ($15\frac{3}{4} \times 13$")
Location unknown

575 Peasant Woman, Head, F 1150
Pen, washed, 12.5 × 8 cm ($5\frac{1}{8} \times 3\frac{1}{8}$")
Rijksmuseum Vincent van Gogh, Amsterdam

576 Sketches of Heads, F 1151
Pen, washed, 16.5 × 10 cm ($6\frac{3}{4} \times 3\frac{7}{8}$")
Rijksmuseum Kröller-Müller, Otterlo

577 Head of a Girl, Bareheaded, and Head of a Man with Beard and Cap
Drawings in sketchbook, pen, 7 × 12 cm ($2\frac{3}{4} \times 4\frac{3}{4}$")
Rijksmuseum Vincent van Gogh, Amsterdam

578

579

580

was probably connected with another worsening of relations with Theo.

I shall merely sketch the main outline of the new wave of rebelliousness that becomes evident in Vincent's letters during the fall. As early as September the relationship appeared once again to be in a state of complete turmoil. As I mentioned on page 121, no trace has been found of a very caustic letter that must have preceded Letter 379, which in itself could not have been more explicit (in *Van Gogh door Van Gogh* I explain that Letter 378 is out of sequence and dates from October). Vincent declared that Theo and himself, in 1884, stood in the same relationship to one another as had Louis Philippe and his conservative minister Guizot, for example, in 1848, to people like the historian Jules Michelet or Victor Hugo and the students. In other words, they were in opposition—not intentionally but through the workings of fate—and found themselves in different camps on opposite sides of the barricades. "Neither you nor I concern ourselves with politics, but we are in the world and in society, and people line up with different groups through no will of their own" (Letter 379). And when Theo in his reply had called what divided them not a barricade but a "mere ditch," Vincent sharply retorted: "There happens to be an old society which, *through its own fault in my view*, is perishing—[and] there is a new society which has arisen and has grown and is continuing to do so" (Letter 381).

Letter 378 in October is more specific in taking Theo to task for doing too little on behalf of his work ("you flatly refuse to look out for my affairs") and for not doing enough to help when he needed something extra, for he still was unable to sell anything regardless of how hard he worked. He talked about the possibility of coming to Paris (Letter 378), or of working for a short while in Antwerp, in The Hague, or in Den Bosch with a sculptor who was also director of the Academy of Art there (Letter 381). After Theo had failed to reply to his previous letter, he lamented in Letter 382: "Perhaps you don't care about my having to strike out on my own for the sake of my work, and to become my own dealer."

The ten days he spent in October with Van Rappard must have been a welcome diversion during these troubled months, but in November and December the acid tone in Vincent's letters to Theo had returned in full force. Just one example of many: "It seems to me *in our mutual interest* to go our separate ways. Your position does not allow us, does it, to associate with one another on an intimate and active and cordial basis. Your position—just to mention one thing—would keep me, say, from possibly living with you in Paris, whether for study, or for financial reasons, no matter how useful and necessary, if things came to that, such a step might increasingly prove to be. Because—regarding my person, manners, clothes, speech—you, like so many others, find things to say that are sufficiently important and clearly without redress, which have wilted and weakened our personal brotherly relationship more and more for years now. Add to this my past and the fact that with G. & Co. you are the dainty gentleman and I am a *bête noire* and *mauvais coucheur*"* (Letter 386*a*, one of those that, for understandable reasons, were omitted by Mrs. van Gogh-Bonger from her 1914 edition and did not come to light until 1953).

Vincent pressed Theo to agree to his staying on in Nuenen for a while and keeping his studio, because he felt he still needed that very much "for his painting," and he added, repeating the condition he had earlier laid down: "Please understand once and for all that if I ask you for money, I am not asking it for *nothing*. The work I produce with it you

*"*Bête noire*": bugbear; "*mauvais coucheur*": nuisance, a person who is hard to get along with.

January 1885

578 Young Peasant with Pipe, Head, F 1147
Pen, black chalk, 32.5 × 21 cm (13 × 8¼″)
Rijksmuseum Vincent van Gogh, Amsterdam

579 Young Peasant with Pipe, Half-Figure, F 1199
Pencil, washed, 39 × 28.5 cm (15⅜ × 11⅜″)
Rijksmuseum Vincent van Gogh, Amsterdam

580 Young Peasant, Head, F 1146
Pencil, 35 × 21.5 cm (13¾ × 8⅝″)
Rijksmuseum Vincent van Gogh, Amsterdam

581 Young Peasant, Head, F 1145
Pencil, 35 × 21 cm (13¾ × 8¼″)
Rijksmuseum Vincent van Gogh, Amsterdam

582 Young Peasant, Head, F 1156v (reverse: 613)
Black chalk, 33 × 19.5 cm (13 × 7¾″)
Rijksmuseum Vincent van Gogh, Amsterdam

581

582

583

584

585

586

587

583 Peasant, Head, F 169a
35.5 × 26 cm ($14\frac{1}{8} \times 10\frac{1}{4}$″)
Stavros S. Niarchos Collection

584 Peasant Woman, Head, F 133
Canvas on panel, 39.5 × 30 cm ($15\frac{3}{4} \times 11\frac{3}{4}$″)
Location unknown

585 Peasant Woman, Head, F 135
Canvas on panel, 37.5 × 24.5 cm ($15 \times 9\frac{7}{8}$″)
Cincinnati Art Museum

586 Peasant Woman, Head, F 153a
Canvas on panel, 25 × 19 cm ($9\frac{7}{8} \times 7\frac{1}{2}$″)
Collection Mrs. Donald B. Stralem, New York

587 Peasant Woman, Head, F 153
Canvas on panel, 26 × 20 cm ($10\frac{1}{4} \times 7\frac{7}{8}$″)
Rijksmuseum Kröller-Müller, Otterlo

can have in return, and if I am *now* behind in this, I am well on the way to getting *ahead* in it" (Letter 390).

Theo kept sending him money and even added something extra at the end of the year, which Vincent said he appreciated greatly because during the winter months, when he could get the farmers to pose for him more readily, he needed more money than at other times (Letter 391). Yet, about January 20, he felt constrained to write: "I have hardly ever started a year that offered a more somber aspect in a more somber mood, and so I do not foresee a future of success but a future of struggle." His surroundings matched that gloomy mood: "It is sad outside, the fields look like marble with clods of black earth and some snow, mostly interspersed with a few days of fog and mud, the red sun in the evening and the morning, crows, withered grass and wilted rotting green-black bushes and branches of poplars and willows showing angrily like strands of wire against the sad sky" (Letter 392).

A Sketchbook

In the work done in the winter months—consisting mainly of portraits depicting heads—a small sketchbook played a considerable part. In the Rijksmuseum Vincent van Gogh, in Amsterdam, there is a small pocket sketchbook from the Nuenen period measuring $4\frac{3}{4}$ by $2\frac{3}{4}$ inches that has been preserved in its entirety with all its 160 pages still affixed to the spine except for one loose page at the back. The sketches, published here for the first time,* consist mainly of heads and figures, along with a few landscapes, and relate to work done in the middle of the Nuenen period. There is, however, no way that the drawings in the sketchbook can be *accurately* dated. Even their sequence presents difficulties, something quite unexpected inasmuch as the sheets are still firmly attached. Vincent seems to have used the sketchbook in a very haphazard manner, only for jotting things down hastily. He would make drawings in the front of it, then in the middle and then in the back of it, would repeatedly skip over a number of pages at a time and would often hold it upside down in his hand in order to use any available space for small rough sketches, which then ended up standing on their heads in relation to the others.

Although there is little to go on in trying to determine the sequence in which the sketches were made, there are some clues to aid us in dating the sketchbook as a whole and some of the individual sketches in it. First, there are two sketches on pages 18 and 19 of the sketchbook (in this book, 598 and 599) that correspond to two paintings that we know, *The Old Tower in the Snow* (600) and *The Parsonage Garden in the Snow* (603). They undoubtedly were initial studies made outdoors for these paintings; the canvases themselves could certainly not have been painted outside with the weather being what it was. It had snowed in January 1885 according to Letters 392 and 398, and painting 603 was probably the one meant when, in February, Vincent wrote: "I painted two more studies of our garden when the snow was on the ground" (Letter 394).

From this it is evident that the little sketchbook was certainly being used in January 1885. A clue of an entirely different kind is that one of the little sheets (page 38) contains nothing but the words "Illustration No. 2174 25 Oct. 84." This is a reminder related to what he wrote in Letter 393, of about January 24, in which he asked Theo to get him this issue of *L'Illustration* ("a back issue"), which contained a drawing much admired by Vincent, by Paul Renouard, depicting a strike

*Six were included (without explanatory text) as illustrations in the later editions of *The Complete Letters:* 598, 599, 606, 635, 636, and 638.

588

589

590

588 Peasant Woman, Head, F 1194
Watercolor, 25 × 18 cm ($9\frac{7}{8} \times 7\frac{1}{8}$")
Formerly Jacques O'Hana Ltd. Collection, London

589 Peasant Woman, Head
Drawing, reproduced with Letter 392
Original unknown

590 Peasant Woman, Head, F 1182
Black chalk, 40 × 33 cm ($15\frac{3}{4} \times 13$")
Rijksmuseum Vincent van Gogh, Amsterdam

591 Peasant Woman, Head
Drawing in sketchbook, black chalk, 12 × 7 cm ($4\frac{3}{4} \times 2\frac{3}{4}$")
Rijksmuseum Vincent van Gogh, Amsterdam

591

592

593

594

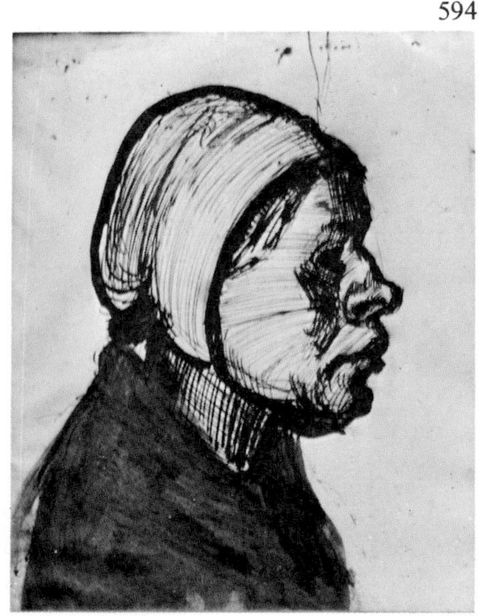

595

596

597

592 Peasant Woman, Head
Drawing in sketchbook, black chalk,
12 × 7 cm ($4\frac{3}{4} \times 2\frac{3}{4}$")
Rijksmuseum Vincent van Gogh, Amsterdam

593 Peasant Woman, Head, F 137
40 × 30.5 cm ($15\frac{3}{4} \times 12\frac{1}{4}$")
Collection Arend Nordin, Stockholm

594 Peasant Woman, Head, F 1178
Pen, washed, 17.5 × 13.5 cm ($7\frac{1}{8} \times 5\frac{1}{2}$")
Rijksmuseum Kröller-Müller, Otterlo

595 Peasant Woman, Head, F 1185
Black chalk, 34 × 20 cm ($13\frac{3}{8} \times 7\frac{7}{8}$")
Rijksmuseum Vincent van Gogh, Amsterdam

596 Peasant Woman, Head, F 1183
Black chalk, 31 × 21 cm ($12\frac{1}{4} \times 8\frac{1}{4}$")
Collection Mrs. L. S. Pollock, Dallas

597 Peasant Woman, Head, F 1184
Pencil, 33.5 × 21 cm ($13\frac{3}{8} \times 8\frac{1}{4}$")
Rijksmuseum Vincent van Gogh, Amsterdam

of weavers in Lyons. Vincent could not in any event have made this note until after October 25, but he probably did so shortly before writing the letter of about January 24. Thus, this piece of information, too, points to the final months of 1884 and the beginning of 1885 as the period during which Vincent used the pocket sketchbook.

An effort has been made to place these sketches with the drawings and paintings to which they seem to be related. In the case of several heads it is clear that the sketches, serving as preliminary studies, must have immediately preceded the final work.

Studies of Heads

During the winter months Vincent repeatedly mentioned these studies of heads. In the middle of December he wrote that he was very busy with "the series of heads of the people" (Letter 390); the English title "Heads of the People," in *The Graphic*, must undoubtedly still have been on his mind. About January 24 he said: "I am working all the time on various heads and hands" (Letter 393), and in February he reported that he was "very busy" painting heads and in the evening making drawings of them, and then, summing up, he wrote: "In this way I have surely already painted about thirty of them and done an equal number of drawings" (Letter 394).

Because he worked almost continuously on the same kinds of subjects, it is obviously not easy, and perhaps even impossible, to determine satisfactorily in what sequence the heads were made.

Yet even here there are some pointers to help us. The most important is Vincent's announcement at the end of December (Letter 391) that he was going to send Theo "twelve small pen-and-ink drawings made after studies of heads." When these drawings are compared with the heads, it becomes apparent that eight studies can be placed in December on the basis of the corresponding pen sketches. In these instances the sketches do not precede the painted studies, but follow them. These eight studies and the corresponding pen sketches are: the female heads 548 (549), 550 and 551 (552), 561 (562), 565 (566 and 567), 569 (570), 574 (575), and the male head 563 (564).

It is clear that Vincent, who had *drawn* many heads during his time in The Hague but had still lacked experience in *painting* portraits, had now made rapid progress. In most of the portrait studies mentioned here the characterization of the heads is very well done, but what is most noteworthy is that he has done things entirely his own way; he is not seeking a romantic idealization of the subjects, but rather a forceful and realistic rendering of them, a striving that in a few months would find its culmination in his famous *The Potato Eaters*.

Vincent's Models

As a result of Vincent's emphasis on the unvarnished features of the people he portrayed, it is possible to identify some of his regular models; I shall mention here only those most frequently portrayed. Previous attempts to identify them have been greatly hampered by the arbitrary order in which the

598

599

600

598 The Old Tower in the Snow
Drawing in sketchbook, black chalk, 7 × 12 cm ($2\frac{3}{4} \times 4\frac{3}{4}$″)
Rijksmuseum Vincent van Gogh, Amsterdam

599 The Parsonage Garden in the Snow
Drawing in sketchbook, black chalk, 7 × 12 cm ($2\frac{3}{4} \times 4\frac{3}{4}$″)
Rijksmuseum Vincent van Gogh, Amsterdam

600 The Old Tower in the Snow, F87
Canvas on cardboard, 30 × 41.5 cm ($11\frac{3}{4} \times 16\frac{1}{2}$″)
Stavros S. Niarchos Collection

601 Garden in the Snow
Drawing in sketchbook, black chalk, 7 × 12 cm ($2\frac{3}{4} \times 4\frac{3}{4}$″)
Rijksmuseum Vincent van Gogh, Amsterdam

602 The Old Station at Eindhoven, F67a
15 × 26 cm ($5\frac{7}{8} \times 10\frac{1}{4}$″)
Rijksmuseum Kröller-Müller, Otterlo (on loan from Mrs. J. Hendrikx-Korting)

603 The Parsonage Garden in the Snow, F194
Canvas on panel, 59 × 78 cm ($23\frac{1}{4} \times 30\frac{3}{4}$″)
Norton Simon Foundation, Los Angeles

604 The Parsonage Garden in the Snow, F67
Canvas on panel, 53 × 78 cm ($20\frac{7}{8} \times 30\frac{3}{4}$″)
Location unknown

605 Winter Landscape with Hut and Wood Gatherer, F1126
Black and colored chalk, 22.5 × 29 cm ($9 \times 11\frac{3}{8}$″)
Rijksmuseum Vincent van Gogh, Amsterdam

606 The St. Catharina Church at Eindhoven
Drawing in sketchbook, pencil, 12 × 7 cm ($4\frac{3}{4} \times 2\frac{3}{4}$″)
Rijksmuseum Vincent van Gogh, Amsterdam

607 Peasant Woman, Head
Drawing in sketchbook, pencil, 12 × 7 cm ($4\frac{3}{4} \times 2\frac{3}{4}$″)
Rijksmuseum Vincent van Gogh, Amsterdam

608 Peasant Woman, Head, F154
40 × 30 cm ($15\frac{3}{4} \times 11\frac{3}{4}$″)
Rijksmuseum Kröller-Müller, Otterlo

609 Peasant Woman, Head, F1177
Pencil, pen, brown ink, washed, 14 × 10.5 cm ($5\frac{1}{2} \times 4\frac{3}{8}$″)
Rijksmuseum Vincent van Gogh, Amsterdam

601

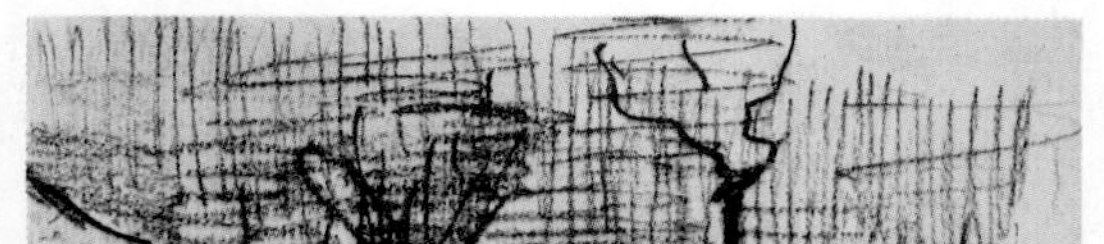

602

604

603

605

606

607

608

609

portraits were presented in De la Faille's catalogue.

A–D. First, there are the members of the De Groot family, in whose cottage Vincent later painted *The Potato Eaters*. We owe this name to the research conducted by Dr. Benno J. Stokvis.* Vincent must have been a regular visitor at the cottage, and the daughter, Sien, in particular sat for him quite often, at least about twenty times if the drawings are counted. She is the young woman with the clean open face and big eyes, pointed nose, and dark hair parted in the middle. In the painting *The Potato Eaters* (764; colorplate IX, page 169), she is seated on the left-hand side. She is seen in a white cap in 568–70, 691–95, 745, 783, and 784, and in a dark cap in 591, 593, 642, 644, 645, and 650.

The older woman in *The Potato Eaters*, who is pouring the coffee, must be Mother de Groot. This woman, with a broad face, broad nose, and very thick lips, is also seen, with a white cap, in 565–67, 679–82, 704 (knee length), 747, and 782. She is probably also the one seen in the profile portrait 676. The older man in *The Potato Eaters*, Father de Groot, also appears alone in 563 and 564, and the son is seen in studies 687, 688, and 689.

E. In Letter 397, about March 28, 1885, Vincent wrote: "The first two heads did not turn out well at all; the one today is a head of a young girl, almost a child's head," and he added a small sketch (723) showing this girl's head alongside a rough sketch of Sien in her white cap. His description of "a juxtaposition of flaming red and pale green against the color of the face" certainly leaves no room for doubt that this small rough sketch refers to the painted head in 722, although it takes some effort to regard it as "a child's head." This girl is also portrayed in paintings 724 and 725, again with a dark cap.

F. Another fairly young model is a woman with a bony, sunken face and sharply protruding nose and mouth. She is shown bareheaded in 573–76 and 589. She is again seen in a painted profile portrait (785), which was intended by Vincent to record an impression he had received from reading Emile Zola's *Germinal* (see below, page 174).

G. A model portrayed even more often was a woman of about fifty, also with a pointed nose, thick protruding lips, a receding but heavy double chin, and a somewhat puffy face. We see her in the drawings and paintings 584–88 (all with dark bonnet), 683 and 684 (also with dark bonnet), and 685 (with white bonnet).

H. The woman just referred to shows some likeness to Sien de Groot and her mother (perhaps she was related to the De Groots) and also to a young woman with an even more sharply pointed nose, but less puffy face, who also frequently served as a model

*In his *Nasporingen omtrent Vincent van Gogh in Brabant* (1926). Part of the text has been reprinted in the Dutch edition of the letters under Number 435*d*, together with some additions by Dr. Stokvis under Number 435*e* (in the Dutch edition of the letters only). He referred to the daughter as Stien de Groot. Tralbaut referred to her in various publications as Gordina de Groot, the name on her birth certificate. I have kept to the name "Sien" because Vincent used that name himself, although only once, in Letter W1.

610

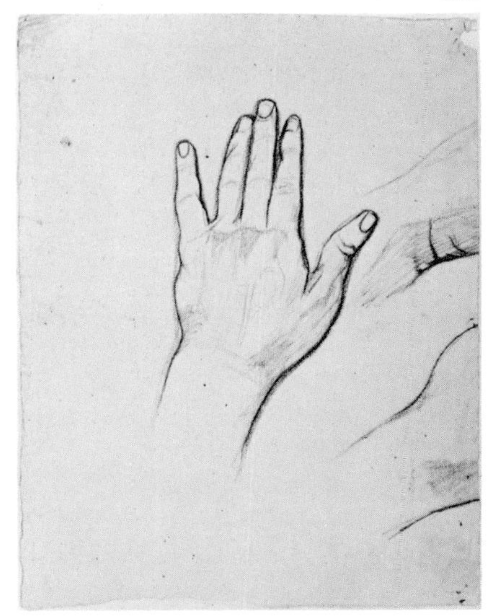

611

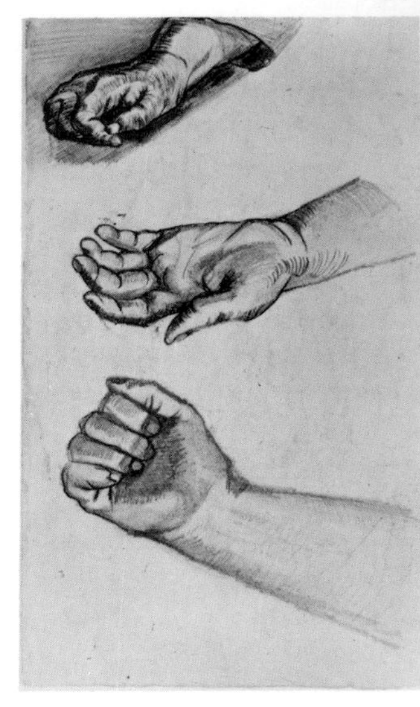

612

610 Hand, F1727
Pencil, black chalk, 31 × 24 cm (12¼ × 9½″)
Rijksmuseum Vincent van Gogh, Amsterdam

611 Hands, F1164v (reverse: 615)
Pencil, pen, brown ink, 35 × 21 cm (13¾ × 8¼″)
Rijksmuseum Vincent van Gogh, Amsterdam

612 Hands, F1154
Pencil, 21 × 34.5 cm (8¼ × 13¾″)
Rijksmuseum Vincent van Gogh, Amsterdam

613 Hands, F1156 (reverse: 582)
Black chalk, 19.5 × 33 cm (7¾ × 13″)
Rijksmuseum Vincent van Gogh, Amsterdam

614 Hands, F1159 (reverse: 742)
Pencil, 20 × 33 cm (7⅞ × 13″)
Rijksmuseum Vincent van Gogh, Amsterdam

615 Hands, F1164 (reverse: 611)
Pencil, 21 × 35 cm (8¼ × 13¾″)
Rijksmuseum Vincent van Gogh, Amsterdam

616 Hands, F1726
Pencil, black chalk, 24 × 32 cm (9½ × 12⅝″)
Rijksmuseum Vincent van Gogh, Amsterdam

617 Hands, F1725
Black chalk, 23.5 × 32 cm (9½ × 12⅝″)
Rijksmuseum Vincent van Gogh, Amsterdam

618 Hands, F1608v (reverse: 1962)
(The digger must have been added in Saint-Rémy)
Black chalk, 23.5 × 32 cm (9½ × 12⅝″)
Rijksmuseum Vincent van Gogh, Amsterdam

619 Hands, F1360 (reverse: 621)
Black chalk, 32 × 24 cm (12⅝ × 9½″)
Rijksmuseum Vincent van Gogh, Amsterdam

620 Feet, F1724
Pencil, black chalk, 33 × 25 cm (13 × 9⅞″)
Rijksmuseum Vincent van Gogh, Amsterdam

621 Studies of a Dead Sparrow, F1360v (reverse: 619)
Black chalk, 24 × 32 cm (9½ × 12⅝″)
Rijksmuseum Vincent van Gogh, Amsterdam

613

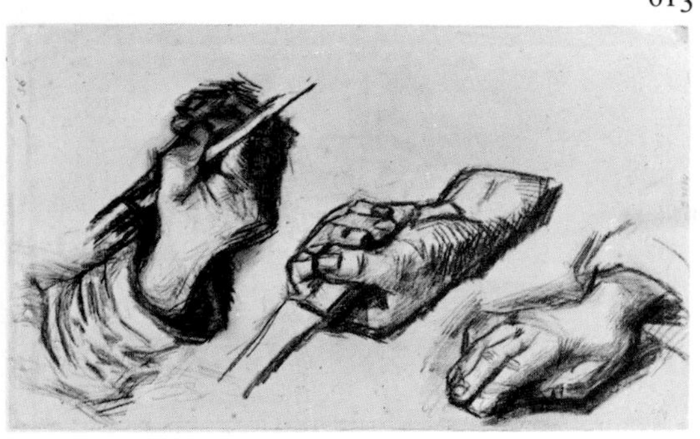

614

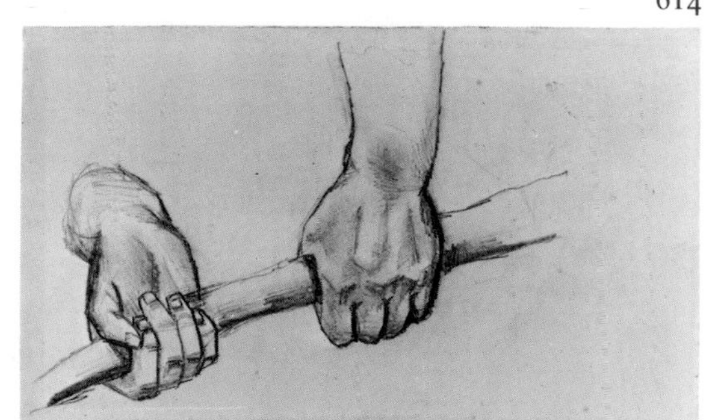

615

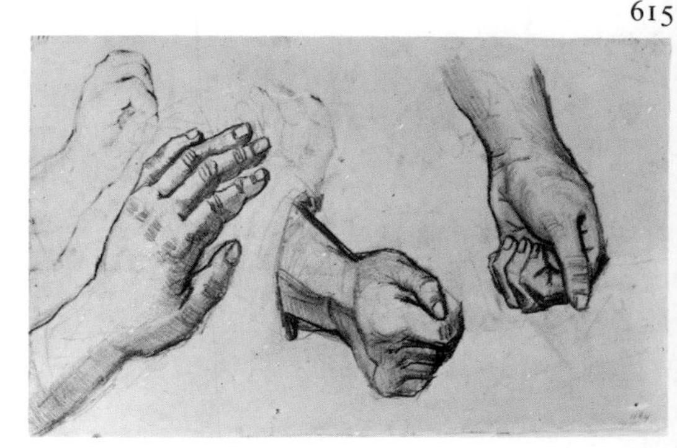

616

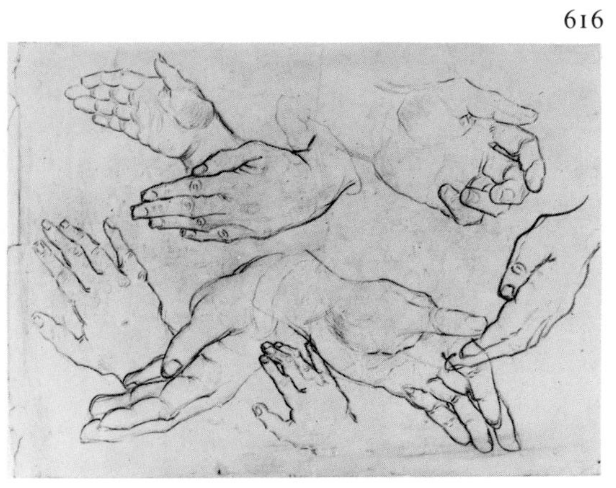

619

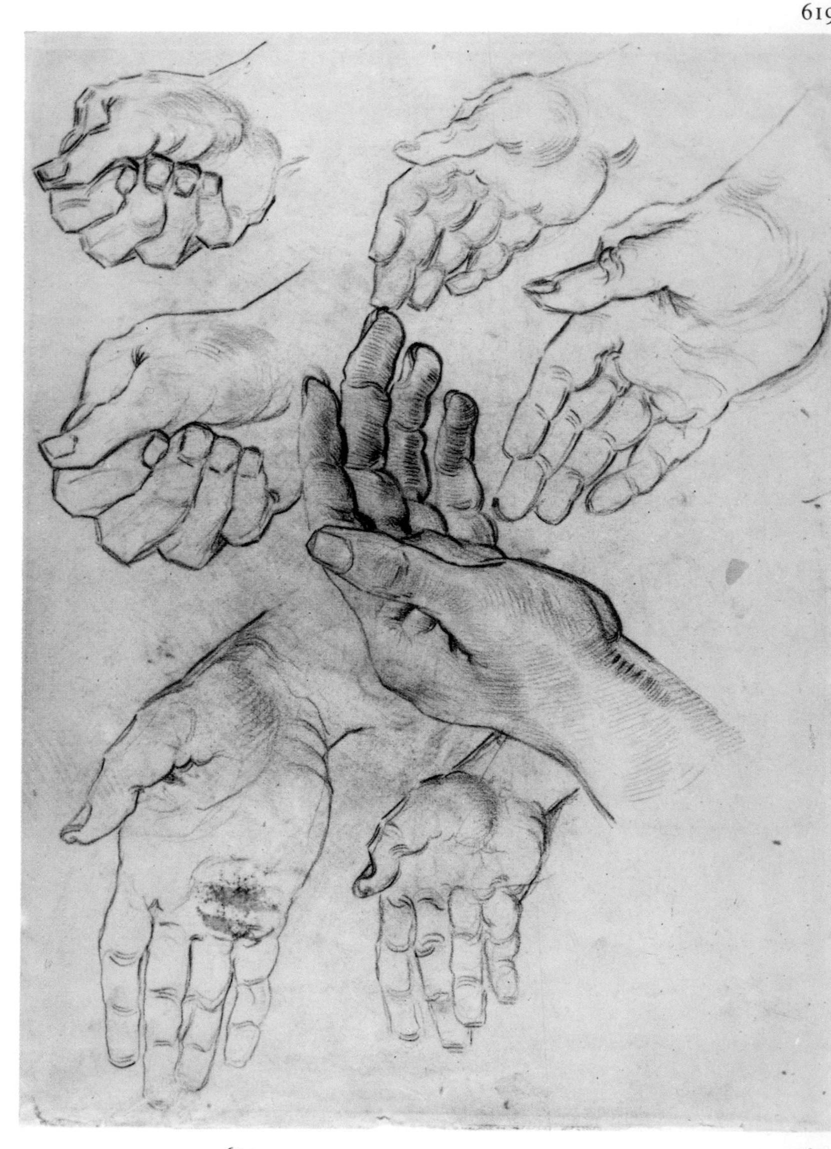

617

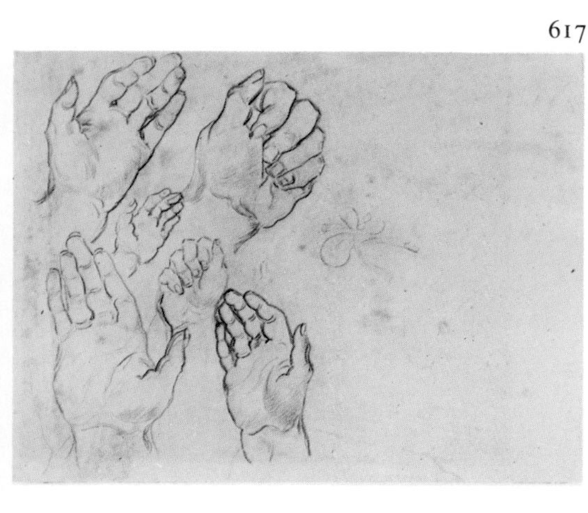

618

620

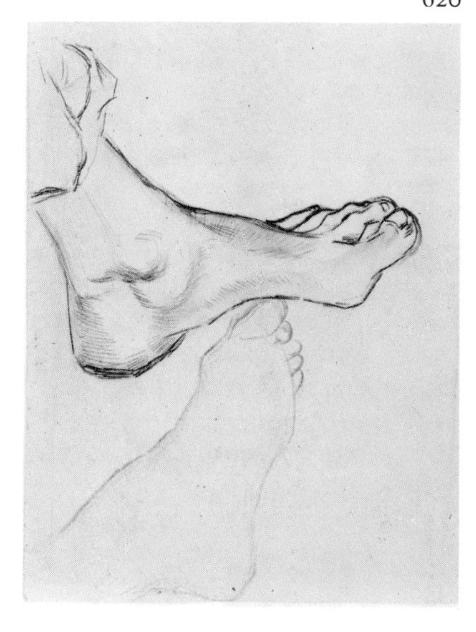

621

for Vincent. She is seen in 594–97 (with white bonnet—the crudely done small rough sketch 594 is probably a first note made for the much larger drawing 595) and in 630 and 631 (with dark bonnet). Despite the similarity to Model G, I still assume that this is another woman.

I. There is also a somewhat older woman, about sixty, with a broad face and closely spaced eyebrows, who is not to be found among the models from December but does appear in the portraits made a short while later: in 608 and 609 (with dark bonnet), 627 and 628 (with hair combed down over her forehead and a white bonnet), and 629 (also with hair down over her forehead but with a dark cap).

J. And last, the old woman with the long, somewhat curved nose, who was portrayed by Vincent in December with a white cap, in 550–52, and somewhat later with a dark cap, in 646–49.

The originals of pen-and-ink drawings 589 and 628 have not thus far been traced. They are to be found only as reproductions in Letters 392 and 393.

1885
As mentioned on page 134, Vincent entered upon the new year in a very gloomy mood. There is a letter, presumably written at the beginning of January 1885, which Mrs. van Gogh-Bonger had omitted from her 1914 edition of the letters, undoubtedly because it revealed serious turmoil in his relationship with Theo. When the letter was included in the 1953 edition, it was erroneously assumed to have been written earlier and was given the number 355*a*. In it Vincent reacted quite violently to a letter from Theo asking him to start paying their father for room and board. Theo undertook to see to it that Vincent would be able to do so. We know the main sentence in Theo's letter because Vincent himself quoted from it: "and so I ask you to give Dad from now on 50 francs out of the 150 francs I shall keep sending you, *as was agreed when we were good friends* and *was approved by both of us*." Vincent retorted: "Although I do appreciate your offer to add another 50 francs a month to the 100 francs I request, intended to reimburse Dad for the cost of my staying here, I must absolutely *reject* it." He was particularly indignant because, as he saw it, there was no such agreement. He remembered very well having a talk about it "in the garden" with Theo (this must have been during a visit by Theo in August), and "what I said is just the opposite, namely, that for the time being I had too many other things to pay for and that I *could* not do it yet." In his opinion it was not the appropriate time "to make a kind of contract with Dad," because in the circumstances he could not plan on staying there much longer. But: "I cannot give up the studio yet; I must have some kind of fixed place, and in any case I cannot be expected just to leave the village. Since, however, it is likely that I must prepare for this, that is exactly the thing that *makes me sorry I did not recognize last year that our agreement was mutually untenable*." In a long postscript Vincent reiterated his point of view in strong

622

623

624

622 Hands, F 1162
Pencil, 35 × 21 cm (13¾ × 8¼″)
Rijksmuseum Vincent van Gogh, Amsterdam

623 Hands, F 1167v (reverse: 625)
Black chalk, 34 × 21 cm (13⅜ × 8¼″)
Rijksmuseum Vincent van Gogh, Amsterdam

624 Hands Holding a Bowl, F 1165
20.5 × 34.5 cm (8¼ × 13¾″)
Rijksmuseum Vincent van Gogh, Amsterdam

625 Hands in Repose, F 1167 (reverse: 623)
Black chalk, 21 × 34 cm (8¼ × 13⅜″)
Rijksmuseum Vincent van Gogh, Amsterdam

626 Hands, F 1158
Black chalk, pen, brown ink, 21 × 34.5 cm (8¼ × 13¾″)
Rijksmuseum Vincent van Gogh, Amsterdam

627 Peasant Woman, Head, F 65
38 × 30 cm (15 × 11¾″)
Location unknown

628 Peasant Woman, Head
Sketch reproduced with Letter 393
Location unknown

629 Peasant Woman, Head, F 1667
Canvas on panel, 41 × 31 cm (16⅛ × 12¼″)
Collection Mrs. E. de Ridder-Pierson, Scheveningen, The Netherlands

630 Peasant Woman, Head, F 1170
Black chalk, 34.5 × 20.5 cm (13¾ × 8¼″)
Rijksmuseum Vincent van Gogh, Amsterdam

631 Peasant Woman, Head, F 1169
Black chalk, 26 × 21 cm (10¼ × 8¼″)
Collection Mrs. L. S. Pollock, Dallas

February 1885

632 Peasant, Head, F 168
47 × 30 cm (18½ × 11¾″)
Rijksmuseum Kröller-Müller, Otterlo

633 Peasant with Pipe, Head, F 169
44 × 32 cm (17⅜ × 12⅝″)
Rijksmuseum Kröller-Müller, Otterlo

625

626

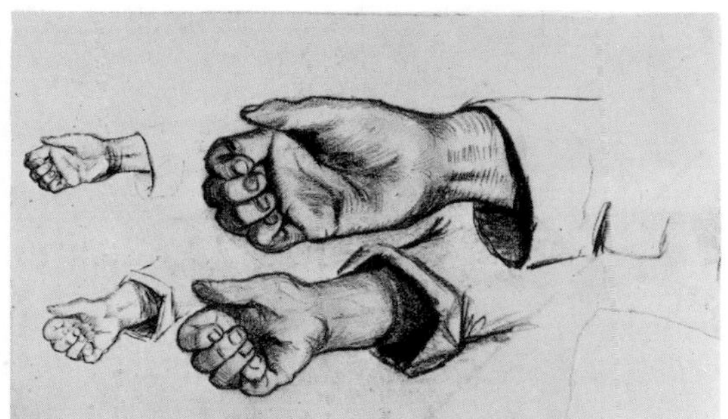

627

628

629

630

631

632

633

language, and then, somewhat resigned, he concluded: "Let us separate, old man, for a while, as friends. That can do no harm, either to you or to me. If we go on together, it would end badly if things went on like this."

Fortunately, it did not come to that, although the sharp exchanges continued in their letters for a time (from Vincent's side Letters 392, 393, 394, 388*a*, 388*b*, and 355*b*—in that sequence). After that, Vincent did not mention the dispute again, perhaps because, as he wrote in Letter 355*b*: "It did not bother me any more." He simply announced in that letter that he was counting on 100 francs a month and would return anything Theo sent over that amount. What had annoyed him most of all was Theo's remark in one of his letters that he felt a kind of suspicion toward Vincent; Vincent then kept harping on the words "suspicion" and "distrust." It is not quite clear what basis Theo had for suspicion. In any case Vincent defended himself in Letter 388*a*, dated (something Vincent rarely bothered to do) January 31, 1885: "I have written you at great length that the painting of some fifty heads that I am planning to do is costing me more than would otherwise be the case." And at the end of the next letter (388*b*), he summarized it again: "For me the work is expensive, I have to paint a lot and I need models for this all the time, and that is all the more reason why, at a time when the work is hard and trying and thankless too, it is really abominable to get suspicion in return."

January and February Heads

If Theo had been able to see the amount of work produced by his brother during these months—as we can today—he would not have had to worry about Vincent's use of his time and his money, assuming that this was the basis of his "suspicion," as Vincent supposed. In addition to the more than thirty portraits of heads done in December, there were certainly another thirty done in January and February, alternating with studies of hands and landscapes.

In the matter of chronological exactness and dating by month, I must make the same reservation as in the case of the heads done in December (see page 136). There are, however, a few clues. If the previously mentioned sketch of Model F, 589, really belongs to Letter 392, with which it has been reproduced since the first edition of *The Complete Letters*, this would indicate that Vincent was at that time doing portraits against a *light* background, with the shape of the face or profile often delineated by means of a fairly heavy outline. A number of the portraits that have some affinity with 589 are placed together here in January (578–97).

In Letter 394, written in February, Vincent said: "I am busy painting those heads. I paint during the day and draw at night. In this way I have already made at least thirty paintings and as many drawings, with the result that in a little while, I hope, I will be able to do it quite differently. I think that it will help me for the figure in general." And after a fine passage about the delicate blue of the farmers' home-woven linen clothing which had impressed him: "But this is a question of color, whereas at the stage I have now reached, it is the question of form that matters more to me. I believe that to express form, the best way is to use almost monochrome color, with the tones differing mainly in intensity and value."

It is apparent here, as in so many other of Vincent's comments addressed to his brother, how much work to him meant study—a self-imposed task carried out with great dedication for the purpose of making further progress. It can also be gathered from what he says that studies of *figures* represented for him a stage beyond heads; this means that the figures studies can probably be dated somewhat later than at least the first series of heads, that is, in the second half of January.

634

635

636

637

638

639

634 Head of a Man, Bareheaded
Drawing in sketchbook, pencil, 12 × 7 cm ($4\frac{3}{4} \times 2\frac{3}{4}''$)
Rijksmuseum Vincent van Gogh, Amsterdam

635 Peasant, Walking with a Wheelbarrow
Drawing in sketchbook, pencil, 7 × 12 cm ($2\frac{3}{4} \times 4\frac{3}{4}''$)
Rijksmuseum Vincent van Gogh, Amsterdam

636 Man with Bowler, Head
Drawing in sketchbook, black chalk, pen, 12 × 7 cm ($4\frac{3}{4} \times 2\frac{3}{4}''$)
Rijksmuseum Vincent van Gogh, Amsterdam

637 Two Heads: Man with Beard and Hat; Peasant with Cap
Drawing in sketchbook, pencil, 12 × 7 cm ($4\frac{3}{4} \times 2\frac{3}{4}''$)
Rijksmuseum Vincent van Gogh, Amsterdam

640

641

642

643

644

645

638 Town House with Three Stories
Drawing in sketchbook, pencil, 7 × 12 cm ($2\frac{3}{4} \times 4\frac{3}{4}$″)
Rijksmuseum Vincent van Gogh, Amsterdam

639 Parsonage Garden at Dusk
Drawing in sketchbook, pencil, 7 × 12 cm ($2\frac{3}{4} \times 4\frac{3}{4}$″)
Rijksmuseum Vincent van Gogh, Amsterdam

640 St. Martin's Church at Tongelre
Drawing in sketchbook, pencil, black chalk, 7 × 12 cm ($2\frac{3}{4} \times 4\frac{3}{4}$″)
Rijksmuseum Vincent van Gogh, Amsterdam

641 Head of a Peasant with Cap
Drawing in sketchbook, pen, washed, 12 × 7 cm ($4\frac{3}{4} \times 2\frac{3}{4}$″)
Rijksmuseum Vincent van Gogh, Amsterdam

642 Peasant Woman, Head
Drawing in sketchbook, black chalk, 12 × 7 cm ($4\frac{3}{4} \times 2\frac{3}{4}$″)
Rijksmuseum Vincent van Gogh, Amsterdam

643 Peasant Woman, Head
Drawing in sketchbook, black chalk, 12 × 7 cm ($4\frac{3}{4} \times 2\frac{3}{4}$″)
Rijksmuseum Vincent van Gogh, Amsterdam

644 Peasant Woman, Head, F 138
33 × 23 cm (13 × 9″)
Location unknown

645 Peasant Woman, Head, F 1175
Pencil, black chalk, 32 × 19 cm ($12\frac{5}{8} \times 7\frac{1}{2}$″)
Collection H. Levine, New York

Studies of Hands

At the same time, Vincent was continuing his winter landscapes and embarking on studies of hands. He mentions the latter subject in Letter 393, about January 24, which also contains the characteristic statement: "Every day I become more convinced that the people who do not see the struggle with nature as the major issue are just *not* going to succeed," and a little further on: "In any case whether or not people approve of what I am doing and how I am doing it, for myself the only way I know is to keep on struggling with nature until she discloses her secret." And in this connection, he adds: "I am working constantly on various heads and hands. I have again drawn a number of them, perhaps you will see something in them, then again perhaps not, what can I do about it. Once more, it is the only way I know."

January was not the only time that in his struggle with nature Vincent drew hands. Some of these drawings are directly related to the painting of *The Potato Eaters* and must therefore be dated April. A comparison of those hands with the other studies provides a fairly reliable basis for distinguishing between the later and earlier drawings. The later ones have more character and less of an academic look, and just as was true of the heads, they have a more "expressive"—or, if you will, a more "Expressionistic"—appearance. In Letter 406 Vincent called it "the rustic" but also "a sort of passionate" element. To what extremes of characteristic exaggeration this led him can be seen in the final version of *The Potato Eaters* (764; colorplate IX, page 169), in which Vincent tried "to portray the peasants in their coarseness" (Letter 404) and to avoid above all "sentimental" effects.

On the basis of these considerations I have placed 610–19 and 622–26 in January. In the 1970 *catalogue raisonné* ten of these fifteen sheets were dated between January and March 1885 (one is given as January–February 1885 and another as March 1885); the other five (610, 616, 617, 618, and 619) were included under Saint-Rémy and are dated April–May 1890—one as an exception being dated winter–spring 1890. This was done because of the fact that some sheets with studies of hands did show motifs from the Saint-Rémy period. On page 444 below, I explain, however, that in my opinion the studies of hands on these sheets date from the Nuenen period, and that when Vincent was in Saint-Rémy, he filled in the space remaining on the sheets with the kinds of figure he was concerned with at that time. The careful, studied manner in which the hands on all these sheets were drawn corresponds closely with the work done in Nuenen and stands in striking contrast to the far from realistic manner in which the small human figures from the first months of 1890 were depicted.

Where the Saint-Rémy elements predominate, I have catalogued the sheets under that period (1936, 1937, 1956); the others, in my view, have more in common with the studies of hands from the Nuenen period. That is why I have also catalogued under the Nuenen period the drawing showing a small figure of a digger that must have been added by Vincent in the Saint-Rémy period (618).

646

647

648

Finally there is the sheet with two sketches of a foot (620), which was also assigned to Saint-Rémy in the *catalogue raisonné*, but which I have included with the studies of hands in the Nuenen period.

Winter landscapes

A few comments are needed regarding the landscapes. On page 134 I quoted Vincent's words indicating that he had painted two studies of the garden about January 20, when the snow was on the ground. These studies are probably the view of the parsonage gar-

646 Peasant Woman, Head
Drawing in sketchbook, pen, 12 × 7 cm ($4\frac{3}{4} \times 2\frac{3}{4}$″)
Rijksmuseum Vincent van Gogh, Amsterdam

647 Peasant Woman, Head, F 1149
Pencil, pen, 10 × 9 cm ($3\frac{7}{8} \times 3\frac{1}{2}$″)
Rijksmuseum Vincent van Gogh, Amsterdam

648 Peasant Woman, Head, F 74
37.5 × 28 cm (15 × 11″)
Rijksmuseum Kröller-Müller, Otterlo

649 Peasant Woman, Head, F 151
Canvas on panel, 36 × 25.5 cm ($14\frac{1}{8} \times 10\frac{1}{4}$″)
Rijksmuseum Kröller-Müller, Otterlo

649

650

651

652

653

654

655

650 Peasant Woman, Head, F 150
39×26 cm ($15\frac{3}{8} \times 10\frac{1}{4}$″)
Rijksmuseum Kröller-Müller, Otterlo

651 Peasant Woman, Sitting, Half-Figure, F 127
Canvas on panel, 45×27 cm ($17\frac{3}{4} \times 10\frac{5}{8}$″)
Location unknown

652 Peasant Woman, Peeling Potatoes, Three-Quarter Length, F 1208
Black chalk, 29×22.5 cm ($11\frac{3}{8} \times 9$″)
Rijksmuseum Vincent van Gogh, Amsterdam

653 Peasant Woman, Peeling Potatoes, Half-Figure, F 145
Canvas on panel, 42×32 cm ($16\frac{1}{2} \times 12\frac{5}{8}$″)
Formerly Jacques O'Hana Ltd. Collection, London

654 Peasant Woman, Peeling Potatoes, Three-Quarter Length, F 365 (reverse: 1354)
41×31.5 cm ($16\frac{1}{8} \times 12\frac{5}{8}$″)
Metropolitan Museum of Art, New York

655 Peasant Woman, Sewing, F 126a
41×32 cm ($16\frac{1}{8} \times 12\frac{5}{8}$″)
Collection Georg Schäfer, Schweinfurt, Germany

den in the snow with the little old church in the background (604) and the more confined view of the parsonage garden fence and hedge with the gardener shoveling the snow (603). I have added to these several other studies painted or drawn also on days when there was snow. These are the little old tower from close by (600), the railway station (602), and the landscape with hut and wood gatherer (605; see also the corresponding scenes from the sketchbook: 598 and 599). The study of the little railway station in Eindhoven is mentioned in Anton Kerssemakers's "Reminiscences,"* which relates some amusing details about it. Speaking about the inexpertly prepared paints Vincent had to use because of lack of money, Kerssemakers tells us: "I still have a small study as a reminder of that intractable paint. He painted it in great haste to teach me, through the window of my house in the winter when the snow was melting, and the thin white flowed all over the landscape." (The small painting 602 did indeed come to us from Kerssemakers.)

In the last letter written by Vincent in January (Letter 388*a*), he made a significant remark in passing. His critical attitude toward Theo led him to say that his brother was well on the way to becoming a Parisian through and through. Then, somewhat sarcastically declaring that he did indeed consider "the sidewalks of Paris and the people who knew their Paris well" to be "great," he assured Theo that it was his personal conviction that "There are various things in the world that are *great*—the sea with its fishermen—the furrows and the farmers—the mines and the coal diggers." This remark tells us more about Vincent's views, as man and artist, than any lengthy reflections and explains why Vincent continued to devote his energies to depicting the farmers and their land that were part of his immediate surroundings. In doing this, he found the *people* even more fascinating than what he called "the furrows," that is, the landscape. Since the snow had left the garden, he wrote in February, the landscape had changed considerably. "We now have marvelous evening skies of lilac and gold above dark silhouettes of houses among the masses of the copses, which have a reddish color, surmounted by the spidery black poplars, while the foregrounds are a faded pale green, relieved by strips of black soil and dry, pale rushes along the narrow canals. I do see all that—to me it is just as magnificent as to anyone else—but what interests me even more are the proportions of the human figure, the sectioning of the oval shape of a head, and I have nothing firm to go by for the rest until I master the figure more fully" (Letter 394).

Self-Imposed Limitations

It is typical of Vincent that he imposed a rather curious limitation on his *choice* of figures. He could well understand, he wrote in Letter 395, about March 1, that there were artists—for example, James Whistler, J.E. Millais, A.B. Boughton, in England, and Henri Fantin-Latour, in France "who painted heads of girls such as, for instance, our own sisters. In my case, however, I do not have the kind of personality that would stand me much chance of being on close enough terms with such girls for them to want to pose for me. Particularly not with my own sisters." It was not only that he was unable to do so, but also that he did not want to, Vincent admitted: "Perhaps I am also prejudiced against women who wear dresses. And those who wear jackets and skirts are more my territory." What was more, a painter such as Chardin, whom he greatly admired, was a French man and painted French women.

*See *The Complete Letters*, Number 435*c*.

656

657

658

656 Peasant Woman, Sweeping the Floor, F152
Canvas on panel, 41 × 27 cm (16⅛ × 10⅝")
Rijksmuseum Kröller-Müller, Otterlo

657 Peasant, Making a Basket, F171a
41 × 33 cm (16⅛ × 13")
Location unknown

658 Peasant, Making a Basket, F171
41 × 35 cm (16⅛ × 13¾")
Private collection, Switzerland

659 Head of a Man
Drawing in sketchbook, pencil, 12 × 7 cm (4¾ × 2¾")
Rijksmuseum Vincent van Gogh, Amsterdam

659

660

661

662

663

664

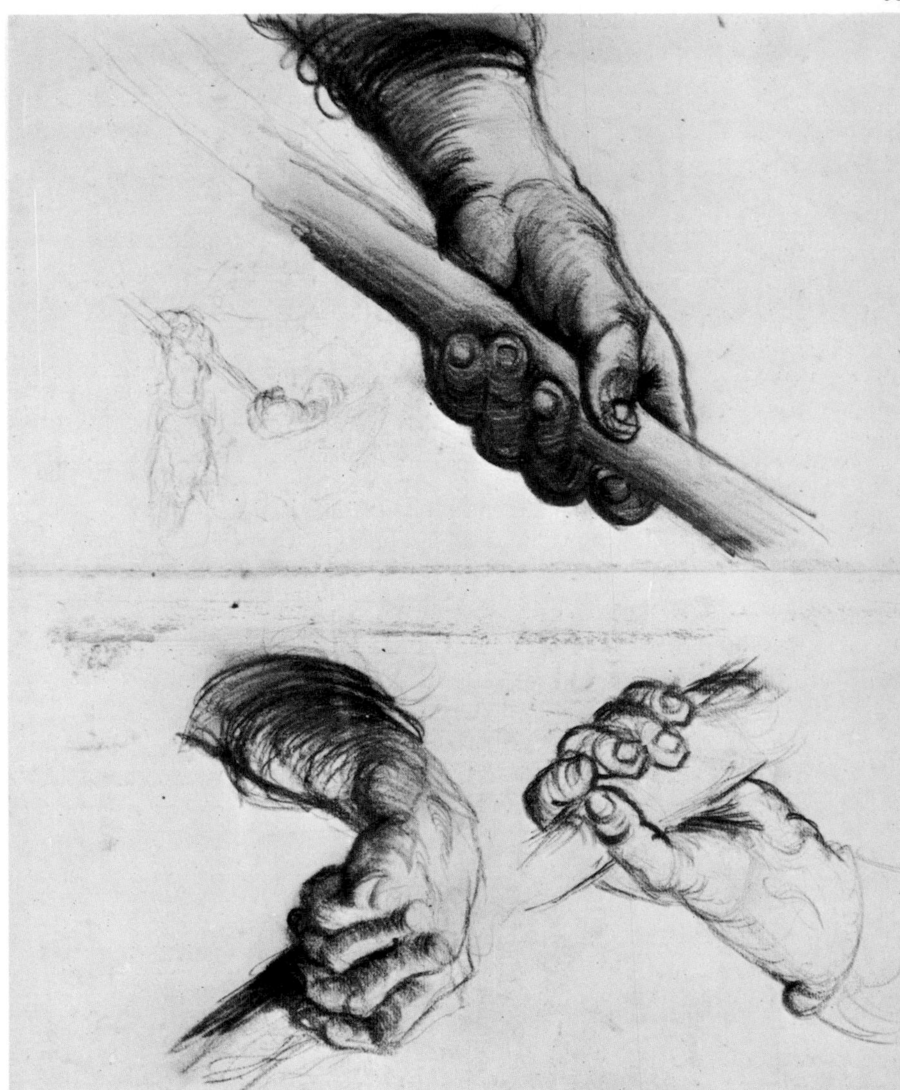

665

660 Two Heads of Men
Drawing in sketchbook, pencil, 12 × 7 cm ($4\frac{3}{4} \times 2\frac{3}{4}''$)
Rijksmuseum Vincent van Gogh, Amsterdam

661 Head of a Man
Drawing in sketchbook, pencil, 12 × 7 cm ($4\frac{3}{4} \times 2\frac{3}{4}''$)
Rijksmuseum Vincent van Gogh, Amsterdam

662 Head of a Man with Straw Hat
Drawing in sketchbook, pencil, 12 × 7 cm ($4\frac{3}{4} \times 2\frac{3}{4}''$)
Rijksmuseum Vincent van Gogh, Amsterdam

663 Head of a Man with Cap
Drawing in sketchbook, pencil, black chalk, 12 × 7 cm ($4\frac{3}{4} \times 2\frac{3}{4}''$)
Rijksmuseum Vincent van Gogh, Amsterdam

March 1885

664 Hands, F 1168v
Black chalk, 42 × 34.5 cm ($16\frac{1}{2} \times 13\frac{3}{4}''$)
Rijksmuseum Vincent van Gogh, Amsterdam

665 Cottage at Dusk, F 1152v (reverse: 749)
Black chalk, 17 × 21 cm ($6\frac{3}{4} \times 8\frac{1}{4}''$)
Rijksmuseum Vincent van Gogh, Amsterdam

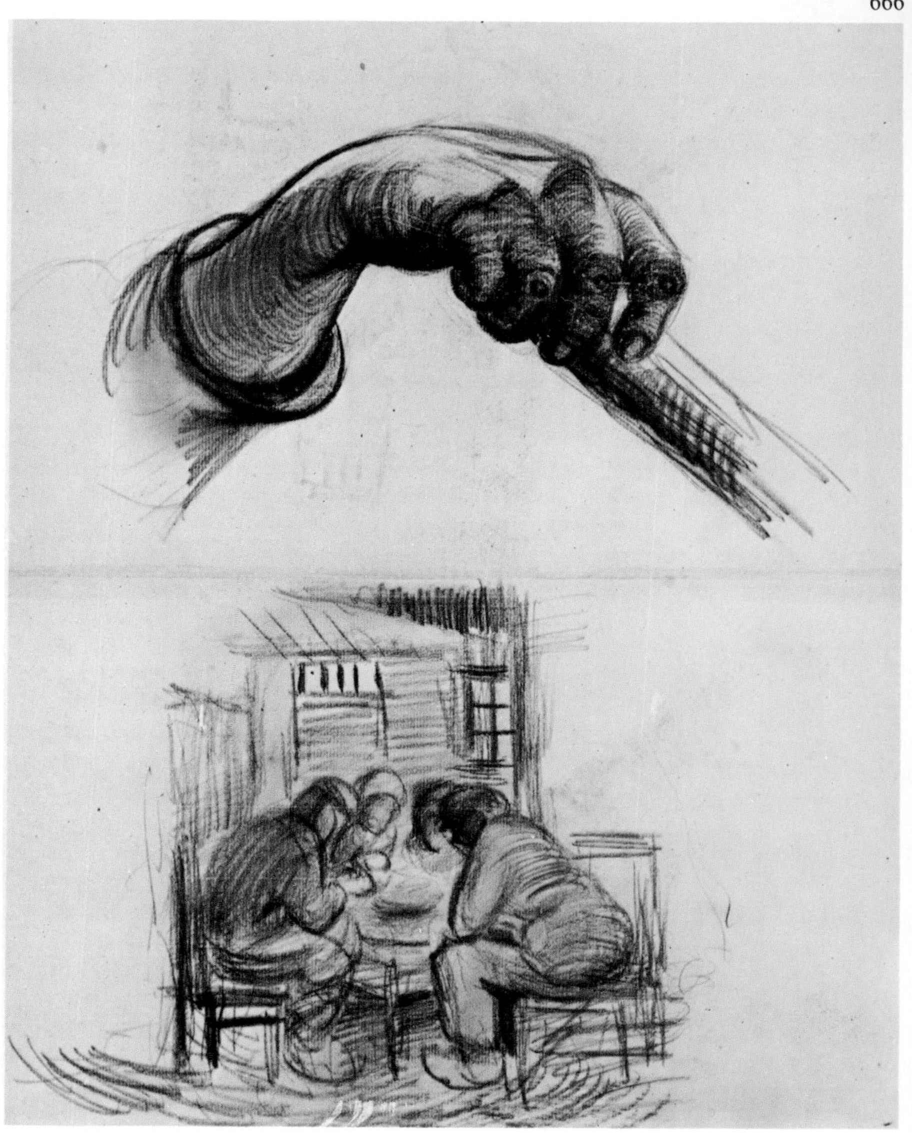

"And the *respectable Dutch* women, in my opinion, only too often are lacking in that charm that French women so frequently possess. Consequently, the so-called respectable portion of Dutch womanhood is not attractive enough to paint or think about. On the other hand, some ordinary servant girls are very Chardin-like."

It is also important to note Vincent's modesty about his own achievements. He still made a sharp distinction—and would continue for years to do so—between what he called studies and what he classed as real paintings. Regardless of how many "heads" he had already made, he still considered himself at the "studies" stage. When Theo asked him whether he might have something to send in to the Paris Salon (possibly in an effort to bring about a better relationship after the polemics of the past months), Vincent replied: "As to your writing that if I had something ready I thought was good, you would try to send it in to the Salon, I appreciate your wanting to do this. First of all—and there are other things too—if I had known this six weeks earlier, I would have tried to send you something for this purpose. Now, however, I do not have anything I myself would care to send in; I have, as you know, been spending most of my time lately painting heads. And those are *studies* in the literal sense of the word, that is, they are intended for the studio. However, today I have started making some that I shall send you. Because I think that it might possibly be worthwhile so that if you happen to meet any people at the Salon, you could let them see something—even if it is only *studies*. So you will receive an old and a young female head, and probably more than one of those two models" (Letter 395).

Coming back to this matter a short time later, Vincent admitted that it was hard to say "where a study ended and a painting began," but he emphatically repeated: "As far as I am concerned, I cannot show a single *painting* and, when it comes right down to it, not a single drawing." He started off this letter by saying: "Some of the heads I promised you are finished but not completely dry yet. But as I wrote before, they were painted in a dark cottage, and they are studies in the strict sense of the word" (Letter 396).

Painting by Lamplight

Returning to Vincent's production in February, I would point out first of all that he undoubtedly continued making studies of heads, at least in the first half of the month. I have brought together a few of these (644–50) in which the manner of painting seems somewhat more daring, more forceful, and richer in contrast than in the earlier ones. The evolution becomes clear if, for example, the portrait of the old woman in 648, with its broad, vigorous brushstrokes, is compared with the equally well characterized but more smoothly brushed portrait of the same woman in 551. Before these later studies of heads I have inserted a few of the little sketchbook drawings, but with considerable reservations regarding the chronology.

We are on firmer ground in dating the February work when we deal with some of the studies of figures. Here again a passage in

666 A Hand, and Four Persons at a Meal, F 1168
Black chalk, 42 × 34.5 cm (16½ × 13¾″)
Rijksmuseum Vincent van Gogh, Amsterdam

667 Peasant Girl, Half-Figure
Drawing in sketchbook, black chalk, 12 × 7 cm (4¾ × 2¾″)
Rijksmuseum Vincent van Gogh, Amsterdam

668 Peasant Girl, Half-Figure
Drawing in sketchbook, black chalk, 12 × 7 cm (4¾ × 2¾″)
Rijksmuseum Vincent van Gogh, Amsterdam

669 Peasant Woman, Half-Figure
Drawing in sketchbook, black chalk, 12 × 7 cm (4¾ × 2¾″)
Rijksmuseum Vincent van Gogh, Amsterdam

670 Peasant Woman, Walking
Drawing in sketchbook, black chalk, 12 × 7 cm (4¾ × 2¾″)
Rijksmuseum Vincent van Gogh, Amsterdam

671 Peasant Woman, Sitting with Chin in Hand
Drawing in sketchbook, pen, 12 × 7 cm (4¾ × 2¾″)
Rijksmuseum Vincent van Gogh, Amsterdam

672 Four Persons at a Meal, F 1227 (reverse: 811)
Black chalk, 21 × 35 cm (8¼ × 13¾″)
Rijksmuseum Vincent van Gogh, Amsterdam

673 Peasant, Stooping, Seen from the Back
Drawing in sketchbook, black chalk, 12 × 7 cm (4¾ × 2¾″)
Rijksmuseum Vincent van Gogh, Amsterdam

674 Two Peasant Women, Seen from the Back
Drawing in sketchbook, black chalk, 12 × 7 cm (4¾ × 2¾″)
Rijksmuseum Vincent van Gogh, Amsterdam

675 Woman in Dark Dress, Walking
Drawing in sketchbook, black chalk, 12 × 7 cm (4¾ × 2¾″)
Rijksmuseum Vincent van Gogh, Amsterdam

667 668 669

670 671 673

674 672

675

a letter shows us the way. Letter 395, quoted earlier, was written about March 1 and is thus concerned with the work done in February. In it Vincent wrote: "Nowadays I paint not only while there is still daylight, but even at night by lamplight, in the cottages, when I can hardly distinguish anything on my palette, to capture if possible at least something of the peculiar effects of artificial light at night with, for instance, a large shadow cast on the wall." Examples of such night effects are 653–58 (drawing 652 seems to be a preliminary sketch for 653) and must therefore have been made in February. The painted study 651 has been included here on the basis of similarity in composition.

The canvases 653–58 certainly do not belong to Vincent's best work of this period. Some, such as 653 and 655, are extremely sketchy in execution and betray the difficult conditions under which Vincent reported they were made. He would, in fact, have regarded these canvases, too, as "studies in the strict sense of the word." One rather curious thing is the existence side by side of two almost identical and scarcely distinguishable small paintings of the basket weaver, 657 and 658. The explanation might possibly be that the study done in the cottage (probably 657) was copied by Vincent in his studio very carefully, even to the extent of imitating the original brushstrokes in strategic places. Why he did this, however, is hard to guess; it is not revealed in the letters.

The small sketch of a peasant cottage in the evening (665) stands alone and is difficult to date. Although the *catalogue raisonné* places it in November 1885, the drawing has such a wintry look compared to the November paintings that I would opt rather for February or the beginning of March; I would also say, though, that it could have been made even earlier in the winter. The drawings of hands, 664 and 666, are a continuation of the studies made in January. The small sketch of the peasant family around the table leads me to place both these drawings at the beginning of March, which was when Vincent was thinking about "making a couple of larger, more detailed things," as he put it in Letter 396, written in March.

The small rough sketches 666 and 672 are of particular importance to us because they represent the first formulations of Vincent's later painting *The Potato Eaters*. Sketch 666 was undoubtedly made in the cottage of the De Groot family; the arrangement featuring the window and the door with the little windows at the top corresponds exactly to what is seen in the two painted versions of *The Potato Eaters*, 734 and 764.

Working in the Cottages

We have little information on what Vincent was doing in March; we know of only a few short letters written that month. Letter 395 was written about March 1;. Letter 396 must have been written much later, for at the end of it he said: "I did not want to wait any longer before writing again." Letter 397 was written around the end of March or perhaps even April 1 or 2. One thing is certain: Vincent was very active in March, and much of his work must therefore be assigned to that month.

676

677

678

First of all, he continued to paint heads. I have already quoted his statement in Letter 396 that the heads he had promised were finished. He felt that he should now show Theo more and more of his work, and the way he put it gives us some notion of how self-assurance and lack of self-confidence were still struggling for mastery within him: "I am working hard, and even if only one out of ten or twenty studies I make has something that makes it worth looking at—those few, whether more or less in number, although they are *not* worth anything *now*, may possibly be so later on. Not so much by

676 Peasant Woman, Sitting, Three-Quarter Length, F 1190
Pencil, pen, brown ink, 35 × 21 cm (13¾ × 8¼")
Rijksmuseum Vincent van Gogh, Amsterdam

677 Peasant Woman, Sitting, Three-Quarter Length, F 1189
Pencil, pen, brown ink, 32 × 20.5 cm (12⅝ × 8¼")
Rijksmuseum Vincent van Gogh, Amsterdam

678 Peasant Woman, Three-Quarter Length, F 1224
Pencil, 34.5 × 21.5 cm (13¾ × 8⅝")
Rijksmuseum Vincent van Gogh, Amsterdam

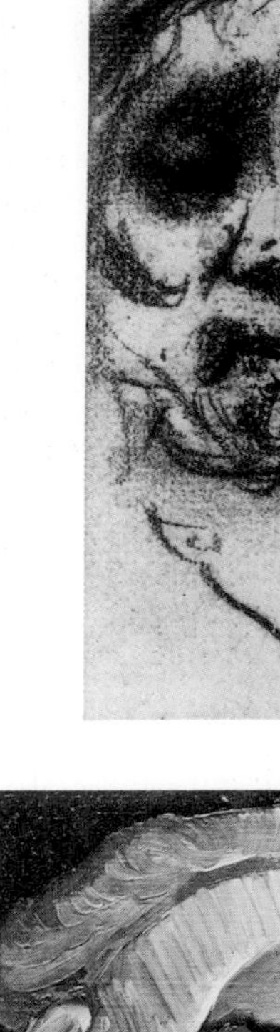

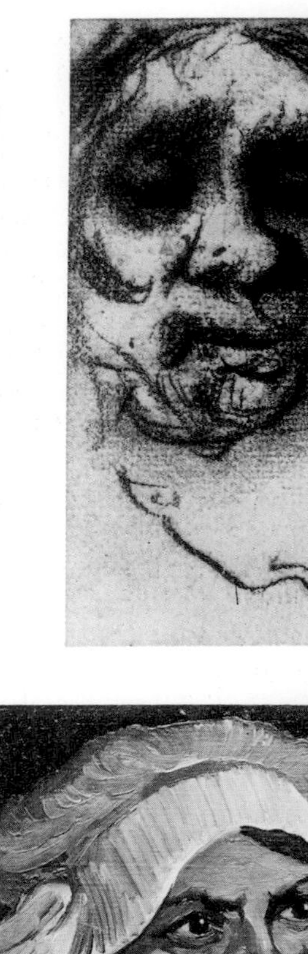

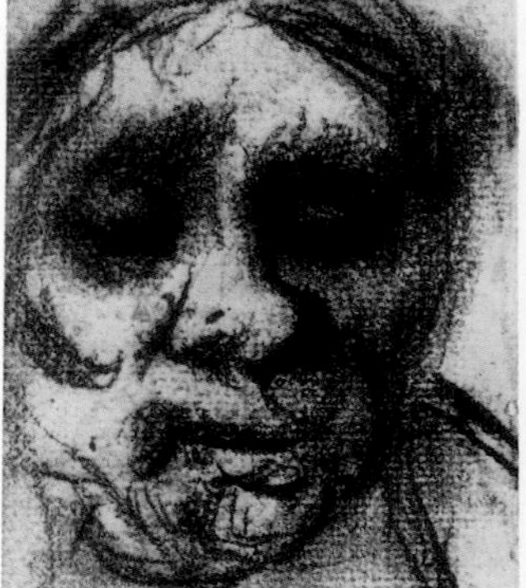

683

679 Peasant Woman, Head, F 1181
Black chalk, pen, washed, 29.5 × 20 cm ($11\frac{3}{4} \times 7\frac{7}{8}''$)
Collection D. Bührle, Switzerland

680 Peasant Woman, Head
Drawing in sketchbook, black chalk, 12 × 7 cm ($4\frac{3}{4} \times 2\frac{3}{4}''$)
Rijksmuseum Vincent van Gogh, Amsterdam

681 Peasant Woman, Head, F 80
Canvas on panel, 41 × 31.5 cm ($16\frac{1}{8} \times 12\frac{5}{8}''$)
Collection E. G. Bührle, Zurich

682 Peasant Woman, Head, F 80a
42 × 35 cm ($16\frac{1}{2} \times 13\frac{3}{4}''$)
Rijksmuseum Vincent van Gogh, Amsterdam

683 Peasant Woman, Head, F 136
Canvas on panel, 40 × 30 cm ($15\frac{3}{4} \times 11\frac{3}{4}''$)
Galerie Dufresne, Paris

684 Peasant Woman, Head, F 134
Canvas on panel, 38.5 × 26.5 cm ($15\frac{3}{8} \times 10\frac{5}{8}''$)
The Louvre, Paris

685 Peasant Woman, Head, F 131
Canvas, formerly canvas on panel, 41 × 34 cm ($16\frac{1}{8} \times 13\frac{3}{8}''$)
Location unknown

themselves, but in connection with other studies. However it may be—I want to try it again, and so as soon as they are completely dry and I can varnish them, I'll send you a couple of heads and also a small sketch of a bobbin winder" (Letter 396).

This letter provides a good insight into Vincent's artistic ideal when he expresses his admiration for Léon-Augustin Lhermitte, the French painter of peasants. Reminding Theo of "those marvelous woodcutters" by Lhermitte, he wrote that he fully realized he had a long way to go before he could "make anything like that myself. But considering my views and the way I set about things—always going right outside or into the poor, smoky cottages—I feel encouraged when I look at his work."

Vincent could tell from the detail in the work of artists like Lhermitte that they must have studied the peasant figure at very close range, and that was precisely what he himself was doing. This is, of course, most apparent from the numerous painted (and some drawn) heads that I believe were made about this time (676–95, among which are also some studies of figures). To the extent that they lend themselves to generalizations, we would say that they are more forceful in expression, but with a bolder brushstroke, and even less romanticized, than the earlier studies of heads. We are certain that at least one of these heads (692) should be placed here; this provides a definite clue to the chronology. In a later letter, Vincent referred to this head when he wrote about the small sketch 723: "In my opinion the head I made today is certainly as good as the one with a big white cap you have," and he had drawn an arrow to the left-hand head in the sketch (Letter 397). That small head resembles most closely the painted study in 692 (the more or less similar portraits 691, 693, 694, and 695 show Sien de Groot without a shawl but wearing a sort of white collaret). Study 692 must accordingly be the one Vincent had sent Theo in March, thus redeeming the promise he had made in Letter 395, written about March 1 (see page 148).

Although the study of a woman with a tot on her lap, 690, does not really fit into this series, it seems to me to have been made at about this time because of the bold brushstroke and the accents of light on a very dark background. Of greater importance to us is the expressive figure of a peasant sitting at a table (689), certainly also of March. Vincent used this study a few weeks later when he was doing a group portrait of peasants at a table. In the preliminary version of *The Potato Eaters*, 734, this man is seen from the knees up, in the very same posture and with the same strong lighting of the face. The model, who probably also sat for the portraits of heads 687 and 688, must therefore be Sien de Groot's brother, whose name, according to the previously mentioned research by Dr. Stokvis, was Gijsbertus de Groot. In the final version of *The Potato Eaters*, 764, Van Gogh exaggerated the "ugliness" of this head even more. The very sketchy small painting 686 is significant in quite a different way because it is obviously a first rough draft made for *The Potato Eaters*, showing only four figures instead of the later five.

686

687

688

Studies of Figures

Vincent's plan to make "larger, more detailed things" was unveiled later in the month in Letter 396, in which he made a pair of small sketches (713 and 714) as examples of his aim: "figures made against the light from a window." In this letter he reported that he had made studies of heads for this purpose, front posed both against the light and with the light falling on the subject, "and several times I have worked on full-length figures: winding yarn, sewing, or peeling potatoes.

686 Four Persons at a Meal, F77 (reverse: 1304)
Canvas on cardboard, 33.5 × 45 cm ($13\frac{3}{8}$ × $17\frac{3}{4}$")
Rijksmuseum Vincent van Gogh, Amsterdam

687 Peasant, Head, F163
39 × 30.5 cm ($15\frac{3}{8}$ × $12\frac{1}{4}$")
Musées Royaux des Beaux-Arts de Belgique, Brussels

688 Peasant, Head, F165
Panel, 44.5 × 33.5 cm ($17\frac{3}{4}$ × $13\frac{3}{8}$")
William Rockhill Nelson Gallery and Atkins Museum of Fine Arts, Kansas City, Missouri

689

690

691

692

693

694

695

689 Peasant, Sitting at a Table, F 167
44 × 32.5 cm (17⅜ × 13″)
Rijksmuseum Kröller-Müller, Otterlo

690 Peasant Woman with Child on Her Lap, Three-Quarter Length, F 149
Canvas on cardboard, 43 × 34 cm (16⅞ × 13⅜″)
Formerly Jacques O'Hana Ltd. Collection, London

691 Peasant Woman, Head, F 1668
Canvas on panel, 41 × 32.5 cm (16⅛ × 13″)
Collection Mrs. A. M. Pierson, Zurich

692 Peasant Woman, Head, F 130
Canvas on panel, 45 × 36 cm (17¾ × 14⅛″)
Rijksmuseum Vincent van Gogh, Amsterdam

693 Peasant Woman, Head, F 85
44 × 36 cm (17⅜ × 14⅛″)
Rijksmuseum Kröller-Müller, Otterlo

694 Peasant Woman, Head, F 85a
Canvas on panel, 47 × 34.5 cm (18½ × 13¾″)
Collection David Bakalar, Boston

695 Peasant Woman, Head, F 81
Canvas on panel, 41 × 31.5 cm (16⅛ × 12⅝″)
Kunstmuseum, Basel

Full face and profile, it is a difficult effect." We know of more than twenty studies of full-length figures, both drawn and painted, which Vincent must have turned out at incredible speed within a few weeks (696–712). It is clear that the two painted studies of heads viewed against a window, 715 and 716, must have served as examples for the sketches in Letter 396 (713 and 714). The full-length figure positioned against the light that is discernible in the small letter sketch 713 is not to be found in exactly this form in the studies that have been preserved. These consist of three painted sketches and one drawn sketch, 717–20, in all of which the problem of a figure viewed against a window has been dealt with by Vincent in much the same fashion. The picture in 721 is actually the reverse image of the one in 720, which apparently showed through the paper and was reworked by Vincent with a few chalk lines.

In another group of drawings and paintings the figures are placed not right against the window, but in the interior, often with the window just within the picture surface, as in many of the series 699–712. These works, as was the case with previous series, vary in quality. Some are quite superficial and appear to be hasty rough sketches, for example, 700 and 709; in others much greater care has been devoted to composition and the rendering of the small figures. In the more detailed works, one can clearly see how Vincent strove to master the difficult problem of working against the light and chiaroscuro (see 707, 710, and 712). Even in sketchy drawings such as the chalk study of Mother de Groot at the spinning wheel, 699, it is truly striking how lively and forcefully the posture and action of the woman are rendered with a few lines and how effortlessly volume is suggested.

A Tragedy

The month of March ended with a tragedy for the Van Gogh family: the sudden death of the father. Our only source for details about it is Mrs. van Gogh-Bonger's "Memoir" to *The Complete Letters;* the letters and documents from which, about 1914, she drew her information no longer exist or are inaccessible. On page xxxviii of the *Letters* we read: "'May he meet with success anyhow,' are the last words he wrote about Vincent in a letter of March 25. Two days later, coming home from a long walk across the heath, he fell down on the threshold of his home and

696

697

698

696 Peasant Woman at the Spinning Wheel, F1290
Black chalk, 30 × 23 cm (11¾ × 9″)
Rijksmuseum Vincent van Gogh, Amsterdam

697 Peasant Woman Standing in a Room, F128
Canvas on panel, 41 × 26 cm (16⅛ × 10¼″)
Narodni Muzej, Belgrade

698 Woman at the Spinning Wheel, F36
Canvas on cardboard, 41 × 32.5 cm (16⅛ × 13″)
Rijksmuseum Vincent van Gogh, Amsterdam

699 Peasant Woman at the Spinning Wheel, F1290a
Black chalk, 28 × 36 cm (11 × 14⅛″)
Collection H. J. de Koster, Wassenaar, The Netherlands

700 Interior with Peasant Woman Sitting near the Fireplace, F1217
Black chalk, 22 × 29.5 cm (8⅝ × 11¾″)
Rijksmuseum Kröller-Müller, Otterlo

701 Interior with Peasant Woman Sitting near the Fireplace, F1218
Black chalk, 43.5 × 28.5 cm (17⅜ × 11⅜″)
Rijksmuseum Kröller-Müller, Otterlo

702 Interior with Peasant Woman Shelling Peas, F1214
Black chalk, 42 × 26 cm (16½ × 10¼″)
Rijksmuseum Vincent van Gogh, Amsterdam

703 Interior with Peasant Woman Sewing, F1220
Black chalk, 44 × 30 cm (17⅜ × 11¾″)
Rijksmuseum Kröller-Müller, Otterlo

704 Peasant Woman, Sitting, Three-Quarter Length, F144a
Paper on panel, 36 × 27 cm (14⅛ × 10⅝″)
Noordbrabants Museum, 's-Hertogenbosch (on loan from the state)

705 Interior with Peasant Woman Sewing, F1206
Black chalk, 29 × 26 cm (11⅜ × 10¼″)
Rijksmuseum Kröller-Müller, Otterlo

706 Interior with Peasant Woman Sewing, F1207
Black chalk, 28.5 × 22 cm (11⅜ × 8⅝″)
Rijksmuseum Kröller-Müller, Otterlo

707 Interior with Peasant Woman Knitting, F1207a
Black chalk, 32.5 × 25 cm (13 × 9⅞″)
Mücsarnok, Budapest

699

700

701

702

703

705

704

706

707

was carried lifeless into the house." (Actually, the date of his death was not March 27, but March 26, 1885.)

The *Personal Recollections* of Vincent's sister Elisabeth, Mrs. E. H. du Quesne-van Gogh, gives even fewer particulars of her father's death. She writes merely: "The sudden death of the father, who had been suffering from heart disease without anyone's knowledge, caused the younger brother to return from Paris."

The fact that Theo naturally came to Nuenen immediately is the reason that we have no written record of Vincent's reaction to his father's death. Vincent's first letter to Theo after it happened, Letter 397, must have been written a few days after the funeral, when Theo was back in Paris—about the end of March or the beginning of April. Theo had even written to Nuenen in the meanwhile. Vincent begins the letter with a few simple statements that reveal little emotion; the most important feelings had probably already been expressed when they had met: "It was the same with me as with you when you write that the first few days things had not yet got back to normal; that was my experience too. They were, after all, days we shall remember, and yet the general impression was not so much the shock of it as its gravity. Life is not long for anyone, and the only thing that matters is what you do with it." It was not to be expected that a person as sincere as Vincent would indulge in excessive sentimentality; furthermore, relations between his father and himself had gone poorly for years. Except for a single sentence in the next letter, Vincent would never mention the event again.

His father's death had no immediate effect on Vincent's way of life. However, although his mother and the children still living at home—Wil, twenty-three, and Cor, eighteen—were allowed to remain in the parsonage for another year, it does appear that Vincent had arranged with Theo to leave the house, for in Letter 398 he refers to this: "There are certainly still a lot of things that will be confronting us all. You will, of course, understand that, for me, living in the studio will not be a matter of convenience. Doing this will make things all the harder again for me, but I am convinced that it is to their advantage for me to leave, especially in view of Mom's intention, if possible, this summer to take in a lodger who would like to be in the country for reasons of health—or if that did not work out, they would then be freer to have guests and the like." He actually carried out this intention a month later, on May 1, when he started using the studio as his sleeping quarters as well.

In the same letter Vincent explained that he was not going to let himself be discouraged by this new setback. He firmly intended to stay in Brabant even if the others moved to Leiden the following year. "I desire nothing more than to put my roots deep in the country and paint the life of the peasants. I feel that I can make a career for myself here, and so I will calmly keep my hand on the plow and cut my furrow." He hoped to be able to count on Theo's support, and pending the completion of "more important

708

709

710

708 Interior with Peasant Woman Sewing, F 1204
Black chalk, heightened with white, 24.5 × 28.5 cm ($9\frac{7}{8} \times 11\frac{3}{8}$″)
Rijksmuseum Vincent van Gogh, Amsterdam

709 Interior with Peasant Woman Peeling Potatoes, F 1210
Black chalk, 30 × 22.5 cm ($11\frac{3}{4} \times 9$″)
Rijksmuseum Vincent van Gogh, Amsterdam

710 Interior with Peasant Woman Sewing, F 1203
Black chalk, 39 × 23.5 cm ($15\frac{3}{8} \times 9\frac{1}{4}$″)
Rijksmuseum Vincent van Gogh, Amsterdam

711 Interior with Peasant Woman Sewing, F 1205
Black chalk, 34.5 × 28 cm ($13\frac{3}{4} \times 11$″)
Rijksmuseum Vincent van Gogh, Amsterdam

712 Interior with Peasant Woman Sewing, F 157
Canvas on panel, 28.5 × 18.5 cm ($11\frac{3}{8} \times 7\frac{1}{2}$″)
Location unknown

713 Peasant Woman, Seen against the Window, Head and Whole Figure
Sketches in Letter 396
Rijksmuseum Vincent van Gogh, Amsterdam

714 Peasant Woman, Seen against the Window, Two Heads
Sketch in Letter 396
Rijksmuseum Vincent van Gogh, Amsterdam

711

712

713

714

715

716

717

715 Peasant Woman, Seen against the Window, Head, F70
Canvas on cardboard, 41 × 32 cm ($16\frac{1}{8} \times 12\frac{5}{8}''$)
Collection Mrs. G. A. de Wolff Peereboom-Eece, Bergen, The Netherlands

716 Peasant Woman, Seen against the Window, Head, F70a
38.5 × 30.5 cm ($15\frac{3}{8} \times 12\frac{1}{4}''$)
Rijksmuseum Vincent van Gogh, Amsterdam

717 Peasant Woman, Peeling Potatoes, Seen against the Window, F73
Canvas on panel, 36.5 × 25 cm ($14\frac{5}{8} \times 9\frac{7}{8}''$)
Collection H. Doyer Family, Chailly-Lausanne, Switzerland

compositions," he would send him the studies "as they came straight from the cottages." He had in fact already begun to show Theo somewhat more of his work. We know in any case that he sent him a first version of *The Potato Eaters* (see Letter 408) and a few heads, as he had promised in Letter 395. Theo had already had an opportunity to look at his brother's most recent work when he had come for his father's funeral, and it appears from Vincent's first letter to Theo after his departure (Letter 397) that Theo took some of it with him to Paris. This was presumably at Vincent's request so it could be shown to others; in Letter 398 he wrote: "Of course, they will say it's unfinished or ugly and so on and so on, but—the way I see it, *have them look anyway.*"

Back to Work

The relevant passage in Letter 397—quoted in part on page 138—supplies important information regarding Vincent's work: "Painting went better again today. The first two heads did not turn out well at all; the one today is a head of a young girl, almost a child's head. As to color, there is a juxtaposition of flaming red and pale green against the color of the face; there is already a head like it among those [studies] you took with you." To the sketch at the end of the letter (723) he added the words: "In my opinion the head I made today is certainly as good as the one with a big white cap you have; this last one is somewhat like this [sketch], and might serve as a pendant to it."

From the sketch it is clear that the portrait of the young girl is 722, while the one with the white cap must have been 692.

In the same letter Vincent had said: "I would like to know whether the ones that were rolled up got there all right." This may refer to a roll sent by mail, but it is more probable that Theo had taken some canvases back to Paris rolled up. Apart from the portrait head mentioned before these included also a still life. This appears from Vincent's next letter: "Enclosed is a rough sketch of a male head* and one of a still life with honesty done in the same style as the one you took with you with a tobacco pouch and one of Dad's pipes in the foreground. If you would like to have it sometime, you are certainly welcome to it."

From the first edition of *The Complete Letters* on, the small sketch of the still life (726) has been reproduced, in color, along with Letter 398, but the original of this sketch appears to have been lost. Even worse is that the important still life itself cannot be traced, as I pointed out on page 130, where I also advanced the theory that the canvas Theo took with him was still life 542. However, an argument against this is to be found in Vincent's Letter 397, in which he had spoken of a *blue* background, which does not tally with 542. He put it thus: "I am also going to start a new still life of the honesty and dry leaves against blue, because he [Uncle C. M.] said something about that, too." Perhaps, though, this should not be taken too literally.

*This sketch is unknown to us, which makes identification of the painting impossible.

718

719

720

718 Peasant Woman at a Meal, Seen against the Window, F 72
42 × 29 cm (16½ × 11⅜″)
Rijksmuseum Kröller-Müller, Otterlo

719 Peasant Woman, Sewing, Seen against the Window, F 71
43.5 × 34.5 cm (17⅛ × 13¾″)
Rijksmuseum Vincent van Gogh, Amsterdam

720 Interior with Peasant Woman Cutting Bread, F 1219 (reverse: 721)
Black chalk, pen, brown ink, washed, 30 × 22 cm (11¾ × 8⅝″)
Rijksmuseum Vincent van Gogh, Amsterdam

721 Sketch of Interior with Peasant Woman Cutting Bread, F 1219v (reverse: 720)
Black chalk, 30 × 22 cm (11¾ × 8⅝″)
Rijksmuseum Vincent van Gogh, Amsterdam

April 1885

722 Peasant Woman, Head, F 160
42.5 × 29.5 cm (16⅞ × 11¾″)
Rijksmuseum Vincent van Gogh, Amsterdam

723 Peasant Women, Two Heads
Sketch in Letter 397
Rijksmuseum Vincent van Gogh, Amsterdam

721

722

723

724

725

726

724 Peasant Woman, Head, F69
Canvas on cardboard, 44 × 30.5 cm
($17\frac{3}{8} \times 12\frac{1}{4}''$)
Rijksmuseum Vincent van Gogh, Amsterdam

725 Peasant Woman, Head, F269 (reverse: 1301)
41 × 33 cm ($16\frac{1}{8} \times 13''$)
Rijksmuseum Vincent van Gogh, Amsterdam

726 Honesty in a Vase
Sketch in Letter 398
Rijksmuseum Vincent van Gogh, Amsterdam

The fact that Vincent's father's pipe and tobacco pouch have been worked into this canvas strikes me as an act of filial respect that underscores how deeply the sudden death of his father affected him. On the other hand, I would not go so far as the psychoanalyst Humberto Nagera, who, in connection with this still life (and the later painting with the empty chair, 1636), speaks of Vincent's guilt feelings, whether repressed or not, concerning the death of his father.*

"Peasants around a Dish of Potatoes"
In contrast with the scanty information about March, in April we are able to keep track of Van Gogh's activities on a week-by-week and even a day-by-day basis. This is all the more important because it is the month in which the various versions of *The Potato Eaters* came into being. It is understandable that apart from this great project, which demanded almost all his time and attention, there are only a few other studies that can also be assigned to April.

To begin with, there is the previously mentioned head of a young girl (722) painted about April 1 and both referred to and sketched in Letter 397. He must have done 724 and 725 about the same time; they give the impression of being variations after the same model. I similarly date the portrait of Sien de Groot in a white bonnet, 745, on the basis of a somewhat later remark. In Letter 409, about the middle of May, Vincent made a small sketch after a study of the same model, and commented: "You received the same one with the last studies that were sent; it was the largest among them. That one was smoothly painted. This time I did not smooth out the brushstroke, and the color, for that matter, is also quite different." The head corresponding most closely to the small sketch and to the study referred to (784 and 783)—apart from, indeed, being much more "smoothly" painted—is portrait 745, which Vincent most probably used as a preliminary study for the final version of *The Potato Eaters*.

Although Vincent had already made a first study of this important painting in March (686; see page 152), it was not until April 5 that he wrote Theo about his definite intention of beginning the work itself; the wording of his announcement suggests that he had mentioned the subject earlier, probably when Theo had visited Nuenen: "I intend to start this week on that scene of those peasants around a dish of potatoes in the evening or—maybe I will make it with daylight, or both, or, you might say, 'neither of the two.' But whether it succeeds or whether it fails, I am going to start on the studies of the different figures" (Letter 398).

The communications that followed, and that, it happens, can be accurately dated, indicate that very soon Vincent was working not merely on the studies for the figures but also on the composition as a whole. While he had to do this mostly in the evenings when the peasants were at home, he worked in the daytime on a few studies in the field. This is apparent from a postcard, dated April 9 (Thursday), sent to Anton Kerssemakers. Adding a little sketch (728), he wrote: "I am not sure whether I can come next Saturday to paint because I am making a few studies—of potato planting—on which I may have to keep working that day." He promised that in any case he would come to Eindhoven on Monday (that is, April 13). This postcard shows that Vincent had kept in touch with Kerssemakers, whom we had lost sight of since November of the previous year, and that he still went to Eindhoven to paint with him in his studio.

The little sketch on the postcard enables us to identify at least one of the studies referred to here; it is 727, although the position of the head of the farmer shown digging differs somewhat in the study. The other study has probably been lost. In Letter 399, written a few days later, Vincent also included two small sketches (729 and 730) of the outdoor studies. The one with two peasant women (730) also gives us some idea of what the second study was like.

The few days that it took Vincent to work on "that scene of those peasants around a dish of potatoes" must have been April 9, 10, and 11, for on Monday, April 13, he wrote in Letter 400: "I painted continuously for three days from early until late, and Saturday

727

728

729

*Psychoanalysts can be expected to assume that the subjects of their investigation will have guilt feelings (subconscious) toward a deceased father. With regard to Vincent, I would point out that in the hundreds of pages of self-analysis that have come down to us, there is *not a single statement* indicative of such feelings. When, moreover, Nagera states: "His [father's] sudden death had been preceded by weeks of intense quarrelling and accusations" (*Vincent van Gogh* [1967], p. 139), I must counter this by saying that in the letters—not only of the final *weeks*, but of the final *months*—*not a single indication* of this is to be found.

730

731

732

733

734

735

727 Peasant Man and Woman Planting Potatoes, F 129a
33×41 cm ($13 \times 16\frac{1}{8}''$)
Kunsthaus, Zurich

728 Peasant Man and Woman Planting Potatoes
Sketch on Postcard 399*a*
Rijksmuseum Vincent van Gogh, Amsterdam

729 Peasant Man and Woman Planting Potatoes, F 1225
Sketch sent with Letter 399
Pen, 6.5×9 cm ($2\frac{3}{4} \times 3\frac{1}{2}''$)
Rijksmuseum Vincent van Gogh, Amsterdam

730 Two Peasant Women Working in a Field, F 1228
Sketch sent with Letter 399
Pen, 6×8.5 cm ($2\frac{3}{8} \times 3\frac{1}{2}''$)
Rijksmuseum Vincent van Gogh, Amsterdam

731 Clock, Clog, and Spoon Rack, F 1349 (reverse: 732)
Black chalk, 34.5×20.5 cm ($13\frac{3}{4} \times 8\frac{1}{4}''$)
Rijksmuseum Vincent van Gogh, Amsterdam

732 Plate, Knives, and Kettle, F 1349v (reverse: 731)
Black chalk, 34.5×20.5 cm ($13\frac{3}{4} \times 8\frac{1}{4}''$)
Rijksmuseum Vincent van Gogh, Amsterdam

733 Kettle, and a Cottage in a Frame, F 1153v (reverse: 741)
Black chalk, 34.5×21 cm ($13\frac{3}{4} \times 8\frac{1}{4}''$)
Rijksmuseum Vincent van Gogh, Amsterdam

734 Five Persons at a Meal (The Potato Eaters), F 78
Canvas on panel, 72×93 cm ($28\frac{3}{8} \times 36\frac{5}{8}''$)
Rijksmuseum Kröller-Müller, Otterlo

735 Five Persons at a Meal
Sketch in Letter 399
Rijksmuseum Vincent van Gogh, Amsterdam

evening the paint was already starting to get to the state where no further work was possible until it had completely dried."

The progress of the piece in that one week can be easily followed, for Vincent made small rough sketches of it in letters. In Letter 399, written Friday or Saturday, he said: "I have just come back home from there and have been continuing to work on it by lamplight, although this time it was daylight when I started. See what the composition looks like now" (735). Letter 400 begins with the words: "Many thanks for your registered letter of yesterday and what it contained. In reply I am writing at once and enclose a rough sketch after my latest study more detailed than the previous one" (736). Having been done on a separate small sheet, the sketch became detached from the letter and was thus not reproduced with it in *The Complete Letters*. Although Vincent added at the end of the letter that this small sketch had been made in great haste and served only to give Theo a better idea of effect and composition than the first one, it is actually so clear as to permit a detailed comparison to be made with the painted study (734). This version, in the Rijksmuseum Kröller-Müller in Otterlo, directly preceded the final one (764), in the Rijksmuseum Vincent van Gogh in Amsterdam.

A Lithograph

Vincent's remarks about what he had in mind when he made the picture—frequently quoted later—do not appear in these early letters (399 and 400). Evidently, only gradually, as he worked on the different versions of it, did he become aware of its unconventional nature. In Letter 400 he did recognize—emphatically—how much it was an expression of his ideal: "When I say I am a painter of peasants, that is really true, and you will see even more as time goes on that that is where I feel at home. And it is not for nothing that I have spent so many evenings musing at the fireside with the miners and the peatmen and the weavers and farmers here, unless I had no time to think because of working."

Many parts of painting 734 were quite sketchily done, and it could certainly not have been regarded by Vincent as definitive. Indeed, he tackled the subject again a short time later. Before that happened, however, an intermezzo followed that had rather important consequences for Vincent and particularly for his relationship with his painter friend Van Rappard. Apparently he decided on the spur of the moment to have a lithograph made of the painting just as it was; it is likely that he regarded this composition as the culmination of an endeavor spread out over many months and considered it so important that he wanted to give others some idea of it. He was thinking, for example, of the Parisian art dealer Arsène Portier, and he asked Theo to supply Portier with a number of the resulting prints. This was Vincent's first lithograph since the small series he had made in The Hague, and it would also be his last—although at this particular moment he was thinking of doing "a series of rural motifs." In Letter 400, April 13, he reported: "I went to Eindhoven today to order a small stone, as this is to be the first of a series of

736

737

738

739

740

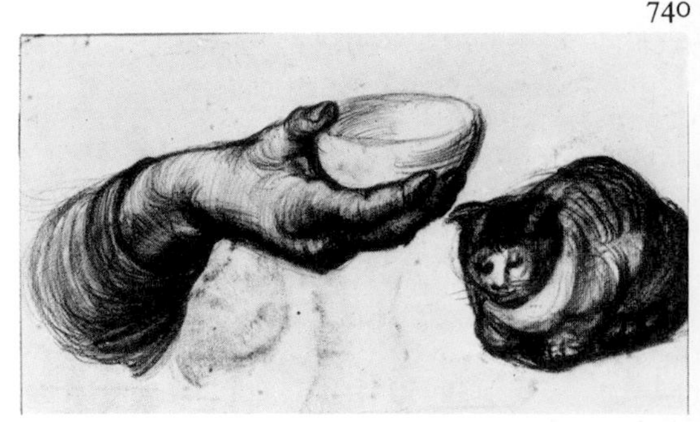

741

742

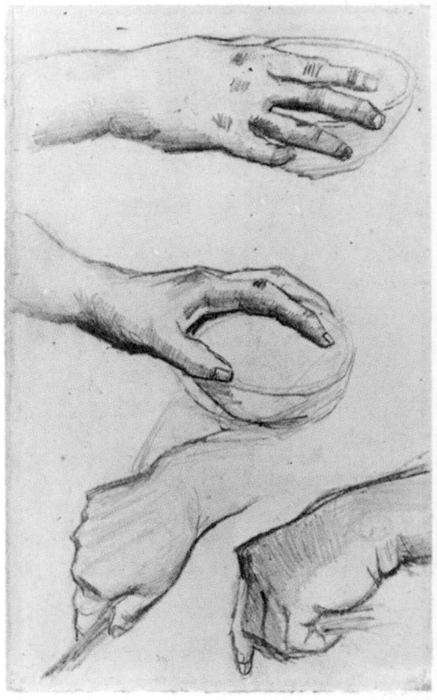

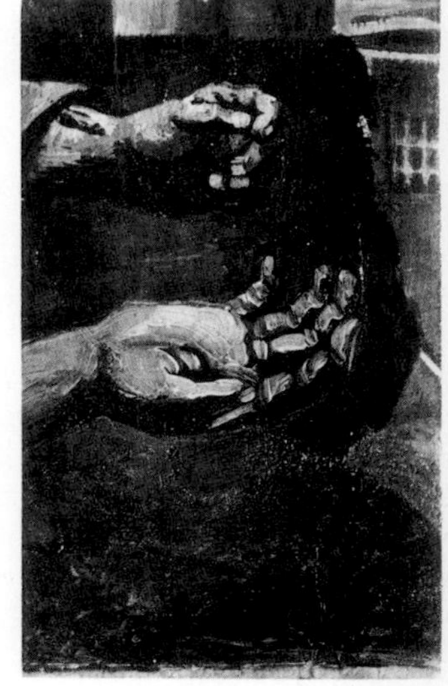

743

744

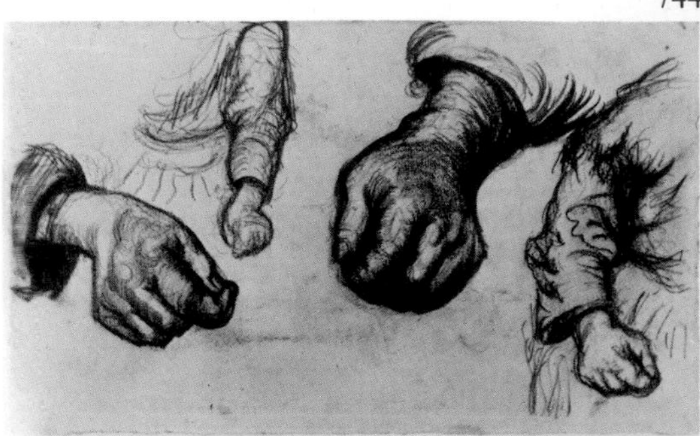

736 Five Persons at a Meal, F 1226
Sketch sent with Letter 400
Pen, lithographic chalk, 11 × 18 cm
($4\frac{3}{8} \times 7\frac{1}{8}$")
Rijksmuseum Vincent van Gogh, Amsterdam

737 Five Persons at a Meal (The Potato Eaters), F 1661
Lithograph after 734
Various collections

738 Kettle and Two Bowls, F 202
Panel, 23 × 34 cm ($9 \times 13\frac{3}{8}$")
Collection J. E. van der Meulen, Utrecht

739 Hand with Handle of a Kettle, F 1157
Black chalk, 21 × 34.5 cm ($8\frac{1}{4} \times 13\frac{3}{4}$")
Rijksmuseum Vincent van Gogh, Amsterdam

740 Hand with Bowl and Cat, F 1229 (reverse: 775)
Black chalk, 20 × 33 cm ($7\frac{7}{8} \times 13$")
Rijksmuseum Vincent van Gogh, Amsterdam

741 Two Hands, F 1153 (reverse: 733)
Black chalk, 21 × 34.5 cm ($8\frac{1}{4} \times 13\frac{3}{4}$")
Rijksmuseum Vincent van Gogh, Amsterdam

742 Hands, F 1159v (reverse: 614)
Pencil, 33 × 20 cm ($13 \times 7\frac{7}{8}$")
Rijksmuseum Vincent van Gogh, Amsterdam

743 Two Hands, F 66
Canvas on panel, 29.5 × 19 cm
($11\frac{3}{4} \times 7\frac{1}{2}$")
Private collection, The Hague

744 Two Hands and Two Arms, F 1155
Black chalk, 20 × 33 cm ($7\frac{7}{8} \times 13$")
Rijksmuseum Vincent van Gogh, Amsterdam

lithographs I intend to start again." As early as the next letter (Letter 401), probably written a few days later, Vincent announced: "You will receive with this mail a few prints of a lithograph" (737).

Theo had evidently told him about an appreciative comment by Portier, and in the same letter we find Vincent's reaction: "What you write about Mr. Portier certainly made me feel very good" and "The fact that he felt that it has '*personnalité*' really gives me much pleasure, and as a matter of fact, I am trying more and more to be myself and to remain indifferent to what others think—whether it is very ugly or an improvement." But Portier's comment could not have referred to the lithograph, for it had been sent with the same mail as Letter 401; presumably Theo had shown him the sketch of the composition sent with Letter 400. In any case the little compliment, coming from a professional, meant a great deal to Vincent. He clung to it eagerly and came back to it time and again in subsequent letters. He even wrote a long letter to Portier right away, as appears from Letter 402, written at the beginning of the following week: "You will receive in the same mail a number of prints of the lithograph. Please give Mr. Portier as many of them as he might want. And I enclose a letter for him that you, I think, will regard as somewhat lengthy and consequently impractical. But I thought that what there was to say could not be compressed into fewer words and that what mattered most was to give him reasons for his own instinctive feelings."

How the lithograph came into being is clearly described in a somewhat later letter to Van Rappard (Letter R53, written about the middle of June): "About the lithograph, this is my explanation: I made it, entirely from memory and in one day, when, casting about for a composition, working with an entirely different process, I tried to think of something new to put it together." It is surprising to learn that Vincent had drawn the group on the stone *from memory* and it shows to what extent, helped along by making the letter sketches, he had let the composition become a part of him. His strong visual memory also stood him in good stead in making the final version: "I have such a feel of the thing that I can literally dream it" (Letter 405).

The quotation from the letter to Van Rappard betrays a somewhat defensive tone. There was good reason for this. Van Rappard had reacted in a singularly offensive way when Vincent sent him a copy of the lithograph, so offensively that Vincent simply returned his letter (R51*a*) without comment. Among the things Van Rappard had written was: "You must admit that such work is not meant seriously," and he added all kinds of critical remarks concerning the construction of the figures. This matter need not detain us here too long, but Vincent was very annoyed about it and was driven to revert to it in letter after letter to Van Rappard, on the one hand, to seek satisfaction from him and, on the other, to convince him that he was in the wrong. It was not until September that Vincent reported to Theo that the dispute had been settled (Letter 421), but nevertheless, no further letters from Vincent to Van Rappard have been preserved after September, and in the letters to Theo, there is no indication that any were written.

745

746

747

The Final Version

Around the middle of April, in the letter notifying Theo that copies of the lithograph were being sent to him, Vincent wrote: "I would like to take that sketch I made in the cottage and rework it with some changes into the definitive form of a painting. And it might be one that Portier could show or we could enter in an exhibition" (Letter 401). This is the first announcement of *The Potato Eaters* as a painting in its final form. The term "rework" is apt to cause misunderstanding (and has done so in the past), but from everything else that is known, Vincent's intention does not seem to have been to change the existing version by painting over it, but simply to make a new painting. The intensity with which he set about working this time is apparent in particular from Letter 403, about

748

749

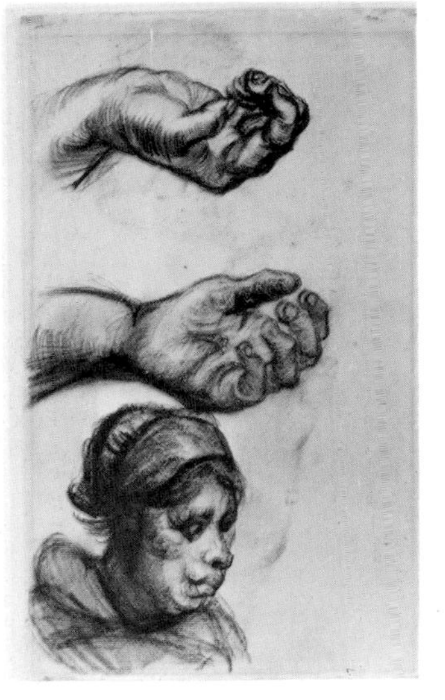

750

751

752

753

745 Peasant Woman, Head, F 140
Canvas on cardboard, 47.5 × 35.5 cm ($18\frac{7}{8} \times 14''$)
National Gallery of Scotland, Edinburgh

746 Three Hands, Two with a Fork, F 1161 (reverse: 760)
Black chalk, 20 × 33 cm ($7\frac{7}{8} \times 13''$)
Rijksmuseum Vincent van Gogh, Amsterdam

747 Peasant Woman, Head, F 1194a
Black chalk, 23 × 17 cm ($9 \times 6\frac{3}{4}''$)
Location unknown

748 Head of a Woman, F 1186
Black chalk, 30 × 18 cm ($11\frac{3}{4} \times 7\frac{1}{8}''$)
Rijksmuseum Vincent van Gogh, Amsterdam

749 Two Hands, and Head of a Woman, F 1152 (reverse: 665)
Black chalk, 35.5 × 21 cm ($14 \times 8\frac{1}{4}''$)
Rijksmuseum Vincent van Gogh, Amsterdam

750 Peasant, Seen from the Back, and Three Hands Holding a Stick, F 1330v (reverse: 780)
Black chalk, 34 × 19 cm ($13\frac{3}{8} \times 7\frac{1}{2}''$)
Rijksmuseum Kröller-Müller, Otterlo

751 Two Hands, with Tongs or Shovel, F 1166
Black chalk, 21 × 34.5 cm ($8\frac{1}{4} \times 13\frac{3}{4}''$)
Rijksmuseum Vincent van Gogh, Amsterdam

752 Study of Two Peasants, F 1333v (reverse: 753)
Black chalk, 21 × 35 cm ($8\frac{1}{4} \times 13\frac{3}{4}''$)
Rijksmuseum Kröller-Müller, Otterlo

753 Study of Two Peasants, F 1333 (reverse: 752)
Black chalk, 35 × 21 cm ($13\frac{3}{4} \times 8\frac{1}{4}''$)
Rijksmuseum Kröller-Müller, Otterlo

April 26, in which he describes his mode of operation: "Just wanted to tell you I am working hard on *The Potato Eaters* and have once again painted studies of the heads and especially changed the hands a great deal.* I am not going to send you *The Potato Eaters* unless *I know for certain* that it has *something* to offer. But it is coming along, and I think that something more is going to come of it than from anything else of mine you have seen yet. At least so clearly. What I mean is *life.* I am painting this *out of my head onto the painting itself.* But you know yourself how many times I have painted the heads! And what is more, I keep going over to look every evening in order to draw bits of it over again on the spot." An important fact provided here is that he also painted this much more detailed version of *The Potato Eaters* in his studio from memory and at the most went back to check details on the spot in the evening. Many studies of detail have been preserved, mostly sketches of hands, with or without forks, of the coffee pot, the wall clock, the spoon rack, and so forth, besides some individual painted studies (731–33, 738–44, and others). It has not been possible to determine whether these were made before or after the provisional version of *The Potato Eaters*, 734.

Despite the complications of working in this way and Vincent's great care in painting the heads and other details, the painting was finished in an amazingly short time. Referring to Theo's birthday (May 1), Vincent wrote on April 30 (Letter 404): "I would have liked to send you the painting of *The Potato Eaters* by that day, but although it is coming along well, it is still not completely finished." But nearly finished, and Vincent rightly pointed out how thorough the preparations had been. "Although I shall have painted the actual painting in a relatively short time, and mostly from memory, it took a whole winter of studies of heads and painting of hands."

There was thus not much more to be done to the painting. "Yesterday I took it over to the house of someone I know in Eindhoven who is painting. In about three days I will go there and finish it with some egg white and touch up a few details at his place" (Letter 404). A week later, on May 6, he wrote: "Yesterday I sent a number of painted studies by mail and today, Wednesday, a case marked 'VI POSTPAID' containing the painting." Three weeks after he had written he was going to start this new version, *The Potato Eaters*, Vincent's masterpiece from the Nuenen period, was on its way to Theo.

I must say something about other studies that were probably made in April. The drawing of the female head, 748, is difficult to date and is in a style hardly characteristic of Van Gogh. I have placed it here because I believe there is some similarity to the small head on the study sheet 749. We are on firmer ground with the painted landscape 763. I see a connection between this work and Vincent's remark in Letter 402 when he was working on the final version of *The Potato Eaters*: "Am, in addition, also working on a red sunset. To paint the life of the peasants there is such an awful lot one has to master." In view of the strong similarity in conception and treatment I have assumed that landscapes 762 (also with a setting sun) and 761, both with almost bare trees, were made at about the same time as 763.

*Studying the manuscript of the letter, I discovered that important words were left out in the printed text. After "I am working hard on *The Potato Eaters*," the text goes on: "I have started them again on a new canvas." This confirms what is said above about the term "rework."

Statement of Principles

Vincent himself was quite aware that with *The Potato Eaters* he had reached a high

754

755

756

754 Peasant Boy, F 1328 (reverse: 757)
Black chalk, 35 × 21 cm ($13\frac{3}{4} \times 8\frac{1}{4}''$)
Rijksmuseum Kröller-Müller, Otterlo

755 Study of Three Peasants, One Sitting, F 1329v (reverse: 756)
Black chalk, 35 × 21 cm ($13\frac{3}{4} \times 8\frac{1}{4}''$)
Rijksmuseum Kröller-Müller, Otterlo

756 Peasant, F 1329 (reverse: 755)
Black chalk, 35 × 21 cm ($13\frac{3}{4} \times 8\frac{1}{4}''$)
Rijksmuseum Kröller-Müller, Otterlo

757 Studies of Three Peasants and a Head, Seen from the Back, F 1328v (reverse: 754)
Black chalk, 21 × 35 cm ($8\frac{1}{4} \times 13\frac{3}{4}''$)
Rijksmuseum Kröller-Müller, Otterlo

757

758

759

760

761

762

758 Short-Legged Man with Frock Coat, F 1332 (reverse: 781)
Black chalk, 34.5 × 21 cm ($13\frac{3}{4} \times 8\frac{1}{4}$″)
Rijksmuseum Vincent van Gogh, Amsterdam

759 Short-Legged Man with Frock Coat, F 1331
Black chalk, 34.5 × 21 cm ($13\frac{3}{4} \times 8\frac{1}{4}$″)
Rijksmuseum Vincent van Gogh, Amsterdam

760 Door and Window (seen at the back of 734 and 764), and Sketch of 764 in a Frame, F 1161v (reverse: 746)
Black chalk, 33 × 20 cm ($13 \times 7\frac{7}{8}$″)
Rijksmuseum Vincent van Gogh, Amsterdam

761 Landscape with Church and Farms, F 185a
22 × 37 cm ($8\frac{5}{8} \times 14\frac{5}{8}$″)
Location unknown

762 Landscape with Sunset, F 191
Canvas on cardboard, 35 × 43 cm ($13\frac{3}{4} \times 16\frac{7}{8}$″)
Thyssen-Bornemisza Collection, Lugano-Castagnola, Switzerland

point in his development. There is no work about which he wrote so often and at such great length as this. Even two years later he would write to his sister Wilhelmina (Letter W1): "What I think of my own work is that the painting of the peasants eating potatoes, which I made in Nuenen, is, *après tout*, the best thing I have made." Even before he had shipped it off, he filled many pages of what became an important letter to Theo (Letter 404) explaining what the work was intended to show and relating with justifiable pride that an acquaintance in Eindhoven (naturally, Kerssemakers), who had also seen the preliminary study, was "especially taken" with the final version; he "said that he had not expected that I would have intensified both the color and the composition to such an extent." Vincent was well aware that he could easily be faulted on the grounds of ungainliness and coarseness, but he made it clearly understood that everything was the result of conscious deliberation. "The whole winter long," he wrote, in his usual metaphorical style, "I have held the threads of this fabric in my hands and sought the final pattern, and although now it may be a fabric with a coarse, rough look, the threads were nonetheless chosen with care and according to certain rules."

It is tempting to keep quoting from Vincent's brilliant statement of principles, but I shall confine myself to the two most important passages: "I have wanted so very much to implant the thought that these people, eating their potatoes by the light of their little lamp, have themselves dug the earth with the very hands they are now putting into the dish; it thus speaks of *work with the hands* and of honestly *earning* the food that they eat. I wanted it to give the idea of a way of life quite different from that of ours, of civilized people. What, then, I absolutely would not want is for everyone to consider it just beautiful or good."

And finally: "It might very well seem to be a *genuine peasant painting. I know that that is what it is.* But if anyone would prefer to see the peasants in a sentimental way, let him. I myself am convinced that in the long run to portray the peasants in their coarseness gives better results than introducing conventional sweetness. ... If a peasant painting smells of bacon, smoke, potato steam, very well, that's not unhealthy; if a stable smells of manure, all right, that's why it is a stable; if a field smells of ripe grain and potatoes or of guano and manure, that's quite healthy, especially for city people."

What Van Gogh was trying to do can best be understood by observing the metamorphosis undergone by the heads at the various stages of the composition. His aim could not have been to achieve a better likeness. The members of the De Groot family may well have had such peculiar features that, according to Dr. V.W. van Gogh, they were called "the pikes."* The fact remains, however, that what we have here, as I have already pointed out, is a conscious Expressionistic exaggeration that is graphically exemplified in the form given to the face of the young peasant in the successive group portraits 734, 736,

*In *Vincent at Nuenen* (1974), p. 47.

763

764

763 Landscape with Sunset, F79
27.5 × 41.5 cm (11 × 16½")
Collection R. Graber, Rüschlikon, Switzerland

764 Five Persons at a Meal (The Potato Eaters), F82
82 × 114 cm (32¼ × 44⅞")
Rijksmuseum Vincent van Gogh, Amsterdam
Colorplate IX, opposite

Colorplate IX, Five Persons at a Meal (The Potato Eaters), 764 ›

and 764, as well as in the individual portrait 689. It is striking to note that the young woman, Sien de Groot, for whom Vincent must have had a warm spot in his heart in view of the many portraits of her, came off rather well in this regard, although her head, with the full lips and the strong side lighting, is still far from "sentimental." The scant heed Vincent paid to a strict photographic rendering of color is also noteworthy. Initially, he had painted flesh color, for example, as flesh color, using a mixture of yellow ocher, red ocher, and white. "But that was *much too light* and just not suitable. What to do about it? I had already finished the heads, and had done them carefully, but I went right ahead and ruthlessly painted them out, and the color they are painted now is *somewhat like the color of a good dusty potato, unpeeled of course*" (Letter 405, and see Appendix, note 2).

Shortly before finishing *The Potato Eaters* Vincent introduced one further but minor variation into the motif that fascinated him. This is apparent from a sketch in Letter 405 (776), in which he wrote: "Can't you imagine how marvelous the scene I am sketching here was? When I went over to the cottage this evening, I found the people [at table,] eating by the light of the small window instead of under the lamp, and oh, it was so amazingly beautiful. The color also had a strange look; you remember those heads painted against the light from the window—the effect was just like that, only somewhat darker." We do not know whether he ever painted this little group in De Groot's cottage, but there is a black-chalk drawing (775) that roughly corresponds with the sketch in the letter.

About May 1, Van Gogh moved to the rooms he had been using as a studio for a year (see page 156). As late as the end of April he wrote, "I have been so absorbed in painting that I literally almost forgot about the moving, which must, however, also be taken care of" (Letter 404). A week later he reported: "The moving is now behind me," and while he had really wanted to make it easier for his mother by moving out of the house, he could not help now adding, with a touch of bitterness: "At home they are quite different from what you imagine, and what they are saying is that I have had 'my own way.' Well, it is all right as far as I am concerned, and I would rather not talk about it" (Letter 407). The move would, to be sure, have some advantages for him, even though living was going to be more expensive because of it, and thus he noted in his next letter: "I think that in the long run I will save quite a bit of time by living in the studio because, for example, I can get started early in the morning right away, whereas at home I could not do this" (Letter 408). For us the most important thing is that we actually see what is perhaps even greater productivity on Vincent's part than before. This would be evident mainly in the summer months, but even in May, he made a considerable number of drawings.

Renewed Production of Drawings

The primary reason for the increase in Vincent's drawing activities was the demolition of the old church tower, surrounded by a small graveyard, that stood directly behind the parsonage and had appeared in many of his works. He reported to Theo about May 11: "I have lately been toiling away making drawings. The old tower in the fields is being torn down. There was a sale of lumber, slate, and old iron, including the cross. I have finished a watercolor of it, done in the same style as the one of that lumber auction, but, I think, better." And after mentioning several unsuccessful attempts to make a second watercolor of the graveyard, he said: "If you

765

766

767

May 1885

765 Three Studies of a Peasant Woman, F 1298 (reverse: 766)
Black chalk, 21.5 × 35 cm ($8\frac{5}{8} \times 13\frac{3}{4}$")
Rijksmuseum Vincent van Gogh, Amsterdam

766 Peasant Woman, F 1298v (reverse: 765)
Black chalk, 35 × 21.5 cm ($13\frac{3}{4} \times 8\frac{5}{8}$")
Rijksmuseum Vincent van Gogh, Amsterdam

767 Sketches of the Old Tower and Figures, F 1336 (reverse: 773)
Black chalk, 35.5 × 20.5 cm ($14\frac{1}{8} \times 8\frac{1}{4}$")
Rijksmuseum Kröller-Müller, Otterlo

〈 Colorplate X, Peasant Cemetery, 772

want, you can nevertheless have the one of the sale" (Letter 408). (By "the one of that lumber auction" he meant the December 1883 watercolor, 438.) Even more fascinating than the watercolor of the sale itself (770)—a complicated subject because of the large number of figures—are the many chalk drawings that must have served as preliminary studies for it or were made in conjunction with it. These are undoubtedly the drawings he said he was "toiling away" on. Some details of the watercolor can be recognized immediately in drawings of the tower (771 and 774) and of the people attending the sale and the auctioneer (768 and 769). It is also possible to pick out individual figures, such as 766 (the woman at the extreme right in the watercolor) and 765 (a few of the women, with backs turned, who are standing in the front row of the group). Of the drawings intended merely as exercises (such as 752–59), some are nothing more than hasty rough sketches; others, however, reveal a high degree of skill in the characteristic rendering of the human figure or can even be termed masterly. Take, for example, the portrayal of the peasant lad with his hands in his pockets, 754, which although sketchily done—apart from the head—is quite impressive. The mutual relationship among these drawings is obvious from the frequency with which the same little figures keep recurring. The strange and seemingly half-witted little man in 758 and 759 is met with again on the sketchbook sheets 755 and 757—in which the peasant lad from 754 also appears—and there are a number of similar examples.

"I begin the figures in these new drawings with the trunk of the body"—Vincent told Theo—"and it seems to me that in this way they become fuller and broader" (Letter 408). The method of starting a drawing from the trunk, which clearly influenced the sketches originating in May, was a notion that had engaged Vincent's attention for some time, ever since he had read about it in a book Theo obtained for him about Delacroix, written by the French painter Jean Gigoux. Vincent mentions it in Letters 401, 403, and especially R58. As he often tended to do, Vincent built up a whole program on the basis of this new idea: "If fifty is not enough, I shall draw a hundred of them, and if that is still not enough, then even more until I definitely have what I want, namely, that everything is round, and there is, as it were, neither beginning nor end anywhere on the form, which instead becomes one harmonious living whole" (Letter 408). This striving to make everything round can be detected in such examples of his work as the three small figures of women, 765, in particular the one standing farthest to the left, and the odd little figure of a peasant, 780.

768

769

770

"God Remains"

The old church tower was the subject of the important painting 772. In the previously mentioned letter in which Vincent had reported its demolition, he added: "The spire is already gone; I am working on a painting of it." Much more information was provided, however, in a letter written a few weeks later, at the beginning of June (Letter 411), which makes it clear that the title he intended to give the painting was not *Old Tower* but *Peasant Cemetery*. I shall quote the relevant part of this letter in full because it is one of the few instances where Vincent dwells at some length on the conscious symbolic meanings he sometimes tried to convey through his work.* This excerpt also throws considerable light on his outlook on life and his religious views.

"Today I sent off the little box I mentioned, containing, in addition to what I wrote you about, another painting, *Peasant Cemetery*. I have left out some details—I wanted to express how those ruins show that *for centuries* the peasants were laid to rest in that spot in the very fields which in their lifetime they dug and tilled—I wanted to express how very simple dying and being buried are, as simple as the falling of an autumn leaf—nothing but some earth dug up—a small wooden cross. The fields around it—they make a last small line above the little wall where the grass of the graveyard ends, a line against the horizon—like a horizon of a sea. And that ruin now tells me how a creed and religion have moldered away—even though founded on solid ground—how nev-

*H.R. Graetz, in his book *The Symbolic Language of Vincent van Gogh* (1963), an imaginative work based on sound scholarship and penetrating study, has curiously failed to treat this painting.

771

772

773

774

775

776

768 Sketches for the Drawing of an Auction, F 1112 (reverse: 774)
Black chalk, 35 × 21 cm ($13\frac{3}{4} \times 8\frac{1}{4}$″)
Rijksmuseum Kröller-Müller, Otterlo

769 Auction of Crosses near the Old Tower, F 1231 (reverse: 771)
Black chalk, 21 × 34.5 cm ($8\frac{1}{4} \times 13\frac{3}{4}$″)
Rijksmuseum Vincent van Gogh, Amsterdam

770 Auction of Crosses near the Old Tower, F 1230
Watercolor, 37.5 × 55 cm ($15 \times 21\frac{5}{8}$″)
Rijksmuseum Vincent van Gogh, Amsterdam

771 Auction of Crosses near the Old Tower, F 1231v (reverse: 769)
Black chalk, 21 × 34.5 cm ($8\frac{1}{4} \times 13\frac{3}{4}$″)
Rijksmuseum Vincent van Gogh, Amsterdam

772 Peasant Cemetery, F 84
63 × 79 cm ($24\frac{3}{4} \times 31\frac{1}{8}$″)
Rijksmuseum Vincent van Gogh, Amsterdam
Colorplate X, p. 170

773 Sketches of a Man with a Ladder, of Other Figures, and of a Cemetery, F 1336v (reverse: 767)
Black chalk, 35.5 × 20.5 cm ($14\frac{1}{8} \times 8\frac{1}{4}$″)
Rijksmuseum Kröller-Müller, Otterlo

774 Entrance to the Old Tower, F 1112v (reverse: 768)
Black chalk, 35 × 21 cm ($13\frac{3}{4} \times 8\frac{1}{4}$″)
Rijksmuseum Kröller-Müller, Otterlo

775 Three Persons Sitting at the Window, F 1229v (reverse: 740)
Black chalk, 20 × 33 cm ($7\frac{7}{8} \times 13$″)
Rijksmuseum Vincent van Gogh, Amsterdam

776 Three Persons Sitting at the Window
Sketch in Letter 405
Rijksmuseum Vincent van Gogh, Amsterdam

ertheless the living and dying of the small farmers is always the same and remains so, calmly sprouting up and withering away like the grass and the little flowers growing there in the soil of that graveyard.

" 'Les religions passent, Dieu demeure' ['Religions pass away, God remains'], said Victor Hugo, who has also just been buried."

In the letter announcing that he was working on the *Old Tower* (Letter 408), Vincent also wrote: "I am also working on a large study of a cottage at nightfall. And some six heads."

The *Cottage at Nightfall* is very likely the well-known and frequently reproduced painting 777, which shows the cottage under a very dark evening sky with greenish and orange-yellow streaks of light and a small red lamp shining through the middle window. It is indeed quite large: 24¼ by 30¾ inches. He sent it to Theo at the end of May under the title *La Chaumière (Cottage at Nightfall)*. In the letter saying that he was sending it (Letter 410), he also mentioned a watercolor on the same subject, but this has been lost.

Only two of the heads he was working on can be identified with any degree of certainty. We are sure that one is that of Sien de Groot (783) because Vincent began Letter 409, about May 15, with a fairly large, clear sketch of it (784). Referring to a "smoothly painted" study he had sent earlier, he wrote: "This time I did not smooth out the brushstroke, and the color, for that matter, is also quite different. No head I have yet made has been 'peint avec de la terre' ['painted with earth'] to such an extent, and there will certainly be more to follow." The expression "peint avec de la terre" is an allusion to a comment on Millet that Van Gogh had run across somewhere and had quoted approvingly in several earlier letters (such as Letters 402 and 405): "Ses paysans semblent peints avec la terre qu'ils ensemencent" ["His peasants seem to be painted with the earth they sow"].

The other head that certainly belonged to the group is 785, for this striking head—which I believe to be one of the high points of Van Gogh's Expressionistic stage—is commented on in some detail in Letter 410, written about June 1, when he announced that he was sending twelve painted studies, along with some other things. Quoting at length from *Germinal*, Zola's novel about miners, which he had just read, he told about a head he had painted as the result of being influenced by that book. He then wrote: "You will find a variation of this enclosed—a profile—a background consisting of 'la plaine rase des champs de betteraves, sous la nuit sans étoiles, d'une obscurité et d'une épaisseur d'encre' ['the flat surface of the beet fields, under a starless sky, as dark and thick as ink']. Standing out from this a head of an *hercheuse* or *sclôneuse* [female miner], with something like a cow lowing as far as expression goes," and so on. The two trees make it easier for us to see a landscape as background in 785 (an exception in Van Gogh's portraits of heads), and the night sky also points the way to the quotation referred to. The daring of the simile used to describe the facial expression ("with something like a cow lowing") is matched by the manner in which the head—with its forceful chiaroscuro in bold brushstrokes—was painted. This woman's features have been so coarsened that the face could easily be taken for that of a man, and although De la Faille, as early as 1929, described the work as "tête de paysanne" ("head of a peasant woman"), it is not hard to understand how a recent Italian catalogue could have mistakenly referred to it as a "contadino" ("peasant man"). The model we recognize from various earlier studies: 573–76 and 589.

777

778

779

777 Cottage at Nightfall, F83
64 × 78 cm (24¼ × 30¾")
Rijksmuseum Vincent van Gogh, Amsterdam

778 Peasant, Sitting, F1201 (reverse: 779)
Black chalk, 33 × 19.5 cm (13 × 7⅞")
Collection R. W. Wentges, Rotterdam

779 Peasant, Digging, F1201v (reverse: 778)
Black chalk, 33 × 19.5 cm (13 × 7⅞")
Collection R. W. Wentges, Rotterdam

780 Peasant with Walking Stick, and Little Sketch of the Same Figure, F1330 (reverse: 750)
Black chalk, 34 × 19 cm (13⅜ × 7½")
Rijksmuseum Kröller-Müller, Otterlo

780

781

782

783

784

785

781 Peasant and Peasant Woman, Sitting at the Table, F 1332v (reverse: 758)
Black chalk, 21 × 34.5 cm (8¼ × 13¾″)
Rijksmuseum Vincent van Gogh, Amsterdam

782 Peasant Woman, Head, F 388 (reverse: 1307)
42.5 × 35.5 cm (16⅞ × 14⅛″)
Rijksmuseum Vincent van Gogh, Amsterdam

783 Peasant Woman, Head, F 141
41 × 34.5 cm (16⅛ × 13¾″)
Collection Mrs. M. C. R. Taylor, Santa Barbara, California

784 Peasant Woman, Head
Sketch in Letter 409
Rijksmuseum Vincent van Gogh, Amsterdam

785 Peasant Woman, Head, F 86
40.5 × 34 cm (16⅛ × 13⅜″)
Rijksmuseum Kröller-Müller, Otterlo

The other head that Vincent mentioned as inspired by *Germinal* is supposed to represent a woman in Russia awaiting execution. One of the characters in the book, Souvarine, says: "I got up on a post and she saw me; our eyes never left each other." We might say that this is the head portrayed in 788, but that would be venturing onto the dangerous ground of conjecture. The haunting look and strange garb, with the shawl pulled over the head, support this view, but then some of the peasant women also wear shawls (787 is a variant or preliminary study).

Solely on grounds of style, I have included 782 and 786 among the six heads mentioned in Letter 408 and the seven referred to in Letter 409. The most forceful is 782, again a portrait of Mother de Groot. It is not only what is probably a good likeness, but is at the same time unbelievably unconventional and "modern" with its unmixed touches of color; the face built up with vivid red, dark red, and bright yellow strokes of paint on a ground of brownish green. The male head 786 is hard to classify, and it is also especially hard to date because the figure differs in both type and dress from the other studies of portraits dating from 1884 and 1885.

"Human Nests"

The painting of the *Cottage at Nightfall* (777) appears to have been a source of inspiration for Vincent's work in June. At the beginning of the month he had written—again with a brief reference to the symbolism of the piece: "I am really thinking about doing the painting of the cottage once more. The thing made a terrific impression on me; those two half-decayed cottages under a single thatched roof made me think of a couple of old, worn people who have virtually become one single being and are seen supporting one another" (Letter 410).

As early as the next letter we read: "Tomorrow I am going to paint a scene in another village—also a cottage—in a smaller format," and in Letter 412 he wrote: "I also wanted to tell you that I have another subject of the same kind, a white mud hut, somewhat wider in format." Later in June, in Letters 414 and 415, he incidentally mentioned painting the cottages, and also in Letters 417 and 418 in July, but the references are too vague to relate them to specific works. Only the white mud hut in a "somewhat wider" format can be identified with some degree of probability with the one in 809. We must therefore be content simply to note that the studies of cottages (801–10 and 823–25) date from June and July. I have included in this group a few drawings that are difficult to date: 802 and the closely related landscape 804.

This is an attractive and quite varied group of studies that makes us realize how much a man like Van Gogh must have felt compelled to portray a number of these simple, sometimes even dilapidated dwellings typical of the beloved countryside that surrounded him. It would be an injustice to call them merely picturesque. Vincent, in any case, always saw them in relation to the people living in them, and he even depicted some of those people at work in and around their cottages. In Letter 411 he wrote: "Working on the cottages ... and looking for subjects, I have found some

786

787

788

786 Peasant, Head, F 179 (reverse: 1300)
41.5 × 31 cm (16½ × 12¼″)
Rijksmuseum Vincent van Gogh, Amsterdam

787 Peasant Woman with Green Shawl, Head, F 155
45 × 35 cm (17¾ × 13¾″)
Musée des Beaux-Arts, Lyons

788 Peasant Woman with Green Shawl, Head, F 161
45.5 × 33 cm (18⅛ × 13″)
Rijksmuseum Vincent van Gogh, Amsterdam

June 1885

789 Woman, Stooping by the Fire, F 1287
Black chalk, 30 × 22.5 cm (11¾ × 9″)
Rijksmuseum Vincent van Gogh, Amsterdam

790 Woman, Sitting by the Fire, Peeling Potatoes, F 1212
Black chalk, heightened with white, 27.5 × 25.5 cm (11 × 10¼″)
Location unknown

791 Woman, Sitting by the Fire, Peeling Potatoes; Sketch of a Second Figure, F 1211
Black chalk, charcoal, 57 × 78.5 cm (22½ × 31⅛″)
Rijksmuseum Kröller-Müller, Otterlo

792 Peasant Woman, Sitting by the Fire, F 158
Canvas on panel, 29.5 × 40 cm (11¾ × 15¾″)
Private collection, Paris

789

790

791

793

792

794

795

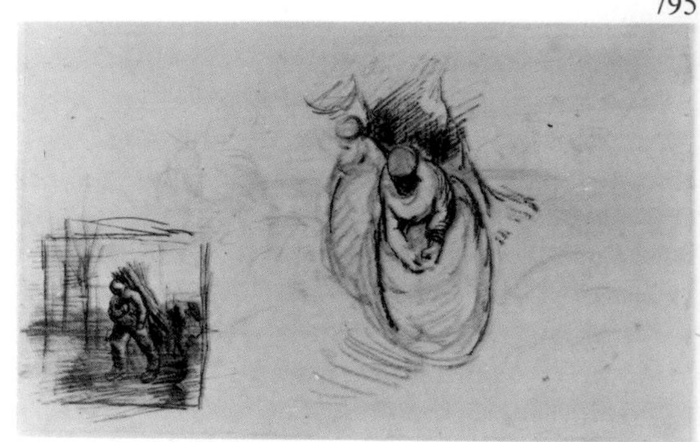

793 Peasant Woman, Half-Figure, F 1297a (reverse: 794)
Black chalk, pen on an envelope, 12.5 × 7 cm ($5\frac{1}{8} \times 2\frac{3}{4}$")
Collection Paul Citroen, Wassenaar, The Netherlands

794 Peasant Woman, Sweeping, F 1297av (reverse: 793)
Black chalk, pen on an envelope, 12.5 × 7 cm ($5\frac{1}{8} \times 2\frac{3}{4}$")
Collection Paul Citroen, Wassenaar, The Netherlands

795 Sketches of Two Women and a Man with a Faggot, F 1297v (reverse: 491)
Black chalk, 27 × 45 cm ($10\frac{5}{8} \times 17\frac{3}{4}$")
Rijksmuseum Vincent van Gogh, Amsterdam

that are so beautiful and that look so much like the nests of the wrens that I feel I must go bird's-nesting—in other words, must paint a few variations of these 'human nests.'" In an even more lighthearted vein he wrote a few weeks later about the people living in a couple of the cottages: "One of them is the residence of a gentleman who is popularly known as 'the little farmer in mourning'; the person living in the other one is an honest soul, who, when I was there, was engaged in no more mysterious an activity than tending to her potato pit but must also be able to perform magic, since she is called Witch Face" (Letter 418).

As regards color, in the case of some of the cottages a development can be detected of which Vincent himself was also aware. After the darker "green-soap colors" (as he himself called them) of *The Potato Eaters* and many of the heads, a tendency to use lighter tints was apparent in the *Peasant Cemetery* (772; colorplate X, page 170). Now, various studies of cottages appear also to have been painted in a lighter gamut of colors (for example, 809, 810, and 823). In the second half of June, when the painter L. W. R. Wenckebach of Utrecht had been to visit him, Vincent wrote Theo: "I also showed him that, so far as color is concerned, I am not *always* partial toward dark painting. A few of the cottages are even very light. But what I do is to take the primary colors, red, blue, and yellow, as the basis, as the point of departure, and not gray" (Letter 415).

Indefatigable Draftsman

Apart from the paintings of the cottages, Vincent's production in June must have consisted mainly of drawings. At the beginning of the month he wrote: "I am otherwise busy drawing in order to send a few full-length figures in a little while" (Letter 411). And in Letter 416 (which brings us to the beginning of July) there is a short list that gives us an idea of some of the subjects that had kept him busy all that time: "I have a few figures here, a woman with a shovel viewed from the rear, another one bending down to pick up ears of grain, and another one viewed from the front, with her head almost on the ground pulling up carrots."

Some of the drawings of interiors with female figures (789–800) date from the beginning of June, I assume, and were presumably done after the numerous heads and in conjunction with the work on *The Potato Eaters*. They probably represented some of the promised "full-length figures." The three painted studies 792, 799, and 800 were clearly made after or from the drawings or are closely related to them.

The full-length drawings of figures 811–19 make up a group that must also have been made at this time, probably together with the work on the cottages. Almost the same comments can be made concerning these drawings as were made about the little peasant figures done the previous month as preliminary studies for the watercolor of the lumber sale. Again, the drawings are extremely clever evocations of the unusual models, where the objective is not photographic exactness but rather the characterization of a unique type or attitude.

796

797

798

796 Peasant Woman, Sitting by the Fire, F 1291
Pen, 10 × 13.5 cm ($3\frac{7}{8} \times 5\frac{1}{2}$″)
Rijksmuseum Kröller-Müller, Otterlo

797 Peasant Woman, Sitting by the Fire, F 1288
Black chalk, washed, 43 × 35 cm ($16\frac{7}{8} \times 13\frac{3}{4}$″)
Rijksmuseum Vincent van Gogh, Amsterdam

798 Interior with Woman Baking Pancakes, F 1215
Black chalk, heightened with white, 29 × 35.5 cm ($11\frac{3}{8} \times 14\frac{1}{8}$″)
Rijksmuseum Vincent van Gogh, Amsterdam

799 Woman Baking Pancakes, F 176
44 × 38 cm ($17\frac{3}{8} \times 15$″)
Formerly collection Mr. and Mrs. Mortimer Hays, Norwalk, Connecticut

800 Peasant Woman, Sitting on a Chair, F 126
Panel, 34 × 26 cm ($13\frac{3}{8} \times 10\frac{1}{4}$″)
Location unknown

801 Cottage, F 1344
Black chalk, 10 × 13.5 cm ($3\frac{7}{8} \times 5\frac{1}{2}$″)
Rijksmuseum Vincent van Gogh, Amsterdam

802 Two Cottages between the Trees, F 1345
Black chalk, 22.5 × 30 cm ($9 \times 11\frac{3}{4}$″)
Rijksmuseum Vincent van Gogh, Amsterdam

803 Cottage with Woman Digging, F 89
Canvas on panel, 30.5 × 40 cm ($12\frac{1}{4} \times 15\frac{3}{4}$″)
Location unknown

804 Trees and Windmill under Storm Clouds, F 1346
Black chalk, heightened with white, 29 × 22.5 cm ($11\frac{3}{8} \times 9$″)
Rijksmuseum Vincent van Gogh, Amsterdam

805 Cottage, F 93
Canvas on panel, 32 × 46 cm ($12\frac{5}{8} \times 18\frac{1}{8}$″)
Collection Mr. and Mrs. T. Plate-Elink Schuurman, Rotterdam

799

800

801

802

803

804

805

The Judgment of a Painter

In these months Vincent was very much aware of his drawing skills, and particularly of his personal style of drawing. He became most keenly alive to this in his efforts to enlist the support of the French painter Charles-Emmanuel Serret for his work.

By a stroke of good fortune some letters from this period written by Theo van Gogh to his family have been preserved.* On May 19, 1885, Theo wrote to his mother about Vincent: "Various people saw his work, either at my place or at Mr. Portier's, and the painters in particular consider it promising. Some find much beauty in it, just because his types are so true to life. For there is, after all, a certain truth in it that among the peasant men and women of Brabant you find more people whose faces bear the sharp lineaments reflecting hard work and, yes, poverty too, than those with sweet little faces." What he wrote in a letter around June 1 is even more important: "I do hope that things will eventually work out with Vincent. One *cannot* expect him to be entirely like an òrdinary person, but the best thing is just to let him do as he wants and, if possible, to see what is good in him. I showed his work again to an old painter (by the name of Serret), who has seen and experienced a great deal of his lifetime and also has a good heart and a clear head. He told me he could see from his work that it was done by someone who has not been working long, but he saw much in it that was good. He even said that if he persevered and could succeed in channeling his ideas, he thought that in his power of expression he would surpass Millet—who, as you know, was one of the greatest painters in history. But as for success with the public, he thought that would be a slow, very slow, process. 'But,' he added, 'if it would make him happy, tell him that he has *my* entire sympathy.' So we just have to wait, and if he produces beautiful work that great men consider good and admirable, try to forgive his peculiarities in everyday life. The money I give him I regard as payment for his work, and as such he earns it. It may take a long time, but one day it will be valuable; I only wish it would be soon, because then people would look at him differently than they do now."

This letter is, of course, of incalculable value primarily because it contains completely reliable evidence of Theo's own thoughts about Vincent (and what is striking is that he appears to have given in completely to Vincent's condition that the financial support be regarded as payment for his work). For the moment we are mainly interested in what Theo said about Serret. His mother and sisters did not, of course, let Vincent read Theo's confidential letter, but they do seem to have told him the good news. "I heard from them at home that you had written them something about Serret; from what they said, I can be assured of his sympathy, etc." (Letter 412).

For some time after that it was always Serret whom Vincent thought about when he was doing his work and theorizing about it.

*Excerpts from these letters were published by me in *Vincent*, vol. III, no. 2 (1974).

806

807

808

"I also wanted to enclose here a little word for Serret, which you should read first, as I write in it about what I was going to send shortly, mainly because I want Serret to look at some of my finished figure studies" (Letter 413). "I would also like Serret to see the studies of the harvest" (Letter 414). Speaking of the studies of cottages: "I would like to send them to you, together with a few studies of figures, to let Serret have a look at the latter" (Letter 417).

The fact that Vincent was sending work to Paris with the intention of having it shown to Serret may explain why some of the drawings have annotations in French: the inscription

806 Cottage, F92a
22.5 × 34 cm (9 × 13⅜″)
Location unknown

807 Cottage with Woman Digging, F142
Canvas on cardboard, 31 × 41 cm
(12¼ × 16⅛″)
Art Institute of Chicago

808 Cottage with Trees and Peasant Woman, F187
47.5 × 46 cm (18⅞ × 18⅛″)
Location unknown

809 Cottage, F91
35.5 × 67 cm (14⅛ × 26⅜″)
Collection John P. Natanson, Harrison, New York

809

810

811

812

813

814

815

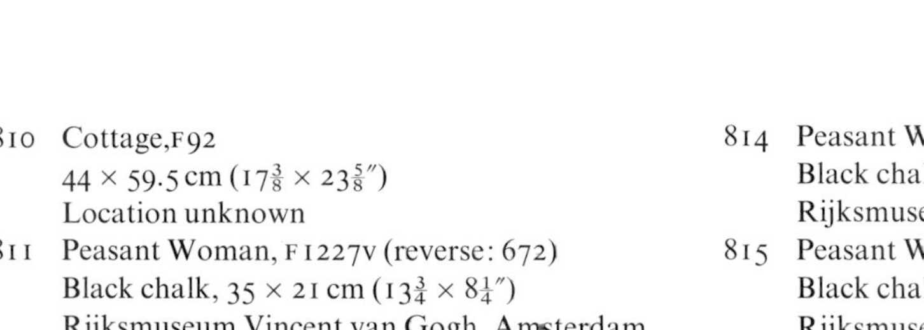

810 Cottage, F 92
44 × 59.5 cm ($17\frac{3}{8} \times 23\frac{5}{8}''$)
Location unknown

811 Peasant Woman, F 1227v (reverse: 672)
Black chalk, 35 × 21 cm ($13\frac{3}{4} \times 8\frac{1}{4}''$)
Rijksmuseum Vincent van Gogh, Amsterdam

812 Peasant Woman, Seen from the Back, F 1187 (reverse: 813)
Black chalk, 35 × 21 cm ($13\frac{3}{4} \times 8\frac{1}{4}''$)
Rijksmuseum Vincent van Gogh, Amsterdam

813 Peasant Woman, F 1187v (reverse: 812)
Black chalk, 35 × 21 cm ($13\frac{3}{4} \times 8\frac{1}{4}''$)
Rijksmuseum Vincent van Gogh, Amsterdam

814 Peasant Woman, F 1289 (reverse: 815)
Black chalk, 34.5 × 21 cm ($13\frac{3}{4} \times 8\frac{1}{4}''$)
Rijksmuseum Kröller-Müller, Otterlo

815 Peasant Woman, F 1289v (reverse: 814)
Black chalk, 34.5 × 21 cm ($13\frac{3}{4} \times 8\frac{1}{4}''$)
Rijksmuseum Kröller-Müller, Otterlo

on drawing 821 is: "Planteuse de betteraves—Juin" ("Woman planting beets—June"), and that on 822: "Planteuse de betteraves—Juin—Vincent" ("Woman planting beets—June—Vincent"). According to the 1970 *catalogue raisonné*, these annotations are by Van Gogh himself. Assuming that this is correct, I have placed both these drawings in June. Two other drawings with annotations in French are 835 and 845. The inscription on both is "arracheuse de carottes (hiver)" ("woman pulling up carrots [winter]"). If these titles too are attributable to Vincent, they present at first sight something of a mystery, for the drawings without the slightest doubt date from the summer, just as do many other black-chalk studies that correspond with these exactly. An explanation does emerge if the drawings are considered in conjunction with Letter 418, written sometime in July, which in itself is equally obscure: "I am slogging away these days at a drawing of a woman I saw last winter pulling up carrots in the snow." In my opinion Vincent must have meant the same thing here as he did with the inscription on drawings 835 and 845—something along the following lines: "I am having a woman pose for me in the same way as someone pulling carrots out of the ground, just as they do in winter and as I saw it last winter, in the snow."

Vincent's Program

Thinking about Serret is what led Vincent to make some of his most important statements of principle. They appear in a very long letter about art and artists, only a small part of which can be quoted here, and they are an outcome of his understandable expectation that he would meet with criticism. "When I send you and Serret some sketches of people digging, or peasant women weeding, gleaning, and so on, *as the first part* of a whole series on all kinds of work in the fields, it may happen that either Serret or you will find faults in them which it would be useful for me to know about and which I will probably admit." But although he may admit "faults," he is prepared to defend them, and in a spirited dissertation he arrives at the following impressive formulation—with perhaps more self-assurance than he had ever evinced in any similar statement addressed to Theo: "Tell Serret that I would be *desperate if my figures were good*, tell him that I do not *want* them academically correct, tell him what I am driving at is that if you take a *photograph* of a man digging, then he *would surely not be digging at all.* Tell him that I think Michelangelo's figures are magnificent, even though the legs are definitely too long, the hips and buttocks too broad. Tell him that, as I see it, Millet and Lhermitte are the real painters because they do not paint things as they are, dryly analyzing and investigating them, but as *they*—Millet, Lhermitte, Michelangelo—feel them to be. Tell him that it is my great desire to learn how to make such inaccuracies, such deviations, refashionings, changes in reality that they might become, well, lies if you like, but—truer than the literal truth" (Letter 418). And after explicitly arguing once again that the main object of his "passionate" perseverance in the drawing of figures is to "present the figure of the peasant in action," he concludes: "The figure of the peasant and the laborer began as genre, but today, with Millet as the eternal master leading the way, it is the very heart of modern art and will continue to be."

Vincent had made the figure of the peasant the heart of *his* art, and for that we can be grateful. However, it would be no more than a year before he, in Paris, would observe that the "heart of modern art" was to be found elsewhere. But it should not be forgotten that for five years he had been too isolated in the Netherlands and particularly in Brabant, from the world of art to see it differently then.

At this time he displayed a talent for giving

816

817

818

816 Peasant Woman with Shawl over Her Head, Seen from the Back, F1196
Charcoal, 35 × 21 cm (13¾ × 8¼")
Rijksmuseum Kröller-Müller, Otterlo

817 Old Peasant Woman with Shawl over Her Head, F1197
Black chalk, 34.5 × 20.5 cm (13¾ × 8¼")
Rijksmuseum Vincent van Gogh, Amsterdam

818 Peasant Woman with Shawl over Her Head, Seen from the Side, F1195 (reverse: 819)
Black chalk, 35 × 21 cm (13¾ × 8¼")
Rijksmuseum Kröller-Müller, Otterlo

819 Peasant Woman with Shawl over Her Head, Seen from the Side, F1195v (reverse: 818)
Black chalk, 35 × 21 cm (13¾ × 8¼")
Rijksmuseum Kröller-Müller, Otterlo

819

820

821

822

823

824

825

820 Peasant Woman, Half-Figure, F 1188
Black chalk, 30.5 × 19 cm ($12\frac{1}{4} \times 7\frac{1}{2}''$)
Rijksmuseum Vincent van Gogh, Amsterdam

821 Peasant Woman, Planting Beets, F 1270
Black chalk, 53.5 × 44 cm ($21\frac{1}{4} \times 17\frac{3}{8}''$)
Museum Boymans-van Beuningen, Rotterdam

822 Peasant Woman, Planting Beets, F 1272a
Black chalk, 45 × 52 cm ($17\frac{3}{4} \times 20\frac{1}{2}''$)
Collection E. R. Schaible, Easton, Pennsylvania

July 1885

823 Cottage and Woman with a Goat, F 90
60 × 85 cm ($23\frac{5}{8} \times 33\frac{1}{2}''$)
Städelsches Kunstinstitut, Frankfurt

824 Cottage with Peasant Coming Home, F 170
64 × 76 cm ($25\frac{1}{4} \times 29\frac{7}{8}''$)
Collection Mrs. M. Q. Morris, London

825 Cottage with Decrepit Barn and Stooping Woman, F 1669
62 × 113 cm ($24\frac{3}{8} \times 44\frac{1}{2}''$)
Collection Luigi Grosso, London

clear expression to his views not only on art but also on life. He was prompted by a masterly passage in *Germinal* that had impressed him so deeply that he had copied it out for Theo in its entirety (Letter 410; see also pages 174 and 176). It was a reflection by Hennebeau, a character in the book, who would have given all his wealth to be just for once *a peasant among the peasants*. Referring back to this, Vincent acknowledged that the reason that passage meant so much to him was that he, too, "literally had almost the same desire to be something like a grass mower or a dike worker," and he, too, "was fed up with the *boredom* of civilization." And then come the lines which, more than anything else uttered by him during his years in Nuenen, can be taken as his credo: "And it is *something*—something good to be out in the snow in the winter, out in the yellow leaves in the fall, out in the ripened grain in the summer, out in the grass in the spring; it is *something*—always to be with the women reaping the grain and the peasant girls; with the great sky above in summer, and beside the black hearth in winter. And to feel that it has always been and always will be. So what if then you may have to sleep on straw and eat rye bread—in the long run it will be better for you" (Letter 413).

Theo's Difficulties

We know that Theo paid a visit to his family's home in the summer, and although we cannot determine exactly when he came, we have reason to assume that it was at the beginning of August. There is a short letter from Vincent about this visit, and it is my belief that it was not sent to Paris but was delivered to the parsonage in Nuenen. It is indicative of the misgivings Vincent harbored against his mother and her household that although he lived in the same village, he did not go to meet his brother with the others, but, on the pretext of being too busy, welcomed him in the following curious note:

"Just a short word to bid you welcome.

"If it is convenient, I would like you and your friend Bonger to drop by here for a little visit sometime this afternoon before supper, let us say between three and five. I thought that perhaps this would work out best, as you will then have all evening to visit at home.

"As they are reaping the grain in the fields, I am rather busy, for you know this lasts only a few days and is certainly one of the most beautiful sights of all. But I will be certain to be in my studio today between three and five. I shall also, of course, stop by Mom's in the evening for a chat.

"Apart from that, please forgive me if I keep on working" (Letter 419).

It appears from later letters, as I have mentioned, that Theo did go to Vincent's studio and looked at his work. It appears also that the brothers took the opportunity to discuss the prospects of selling some work and of further financial support. The outcome of the talk does not seem to have been encouraging, particularly as Theo's own future with the Goupil firm was somewhat uncertain. Summing it up, Vincent wrote: "Your visit did not really leave me feeling very reassured; I am more convinced than ever that the next few years will bring you more difficulties than you expect" (Letter 420).

There is nothing to tell us what Theo's difficulties were. It may be that even by then his relations with Messrs. Boussod and Valadon, the owners of the Goupil firm, had begun to deteriorate, although it would be another five years before the situation really became critical.

As to Vincent's financial troubles, however, there is no dearth of information. Although in fact his financial difficulties were always great, in the summer of 1885 they seem to have become almost unbearable. That was probably due to his frequent use of

826

827

828

826 Peasant Woman, Digging, Seen from the Back, F1255
Black chalk, 55.5 × 40.5 cm (22 × 16⅛")
Rijksmuseum Vincent van Gogh, Amsterdam

827 Peasant Woman, Digging, Seen from the Back, F95
Canvas on panel, 41.5 × 32 cm (16½ × 12⅝")
Location unknown

828 Peasant Woman with a Bucket, F1283 (reverse: 846)
Black chalk, 33.5 × 20 cm (13⅜ × 7⅞")
Rijksmuseum Kröller-Müller, Otterlo

829 Peasant Woman, Digging, F1257 (reverse: 830)
Black chalk, 33 × 20 cm (13 × 7⅞")
Rijksmuseum Vincent van Gogh, Amsterdam

829

830

831

832

833

834

835

830 Peasant Woman, Digging, Seen from the Back, F 1257v (reverse: 829)
Black chalk, 33 × 20 cm (13 × 7⅞″)
Rijksmuseum Vincent van Gogh, Amsterdam

831 Peasant Woman, Stooping, Seen from the Back, F 1262
Black chalk, washed, 44.5 × 58.5 cm (17¾ × 23¼″)
Rijksmuseum Kröller-Müller, Otterlo

832 Peasant Woman, Stooping, Seen from the Back; Sketch of Other Figures, F 1269
Black chalk, washed, 52.5 × 43.5 cm (20⅝ × 17⅜″)
Rijksmuseum Kröller-Müller, Otterlo

833 Peasant Woman, Stooping and Gleaning, F 1265
Black chalk, washed, 52 × 38 cm (20½ × 15″)
Rijksmuseum Kröller-Müller, Otterlo

834 Peasant Woman, Stooping and Gleaning, F 1265a
Black chalk, 52 × 43 cm (20½ × 16⅞″)
Collection Charles Clore, London

835 Peasant Woman, Stooping with a Spade, Digging Up Carrots, F 1691
Black chalk, 53 × 44 cm (20⅞ × 17⅜″)
Colecţia de Artĕ Comparată, Bucharest

models and the greater expense of living in his own rented quarters. His cry of distress in the middle of July bears this out: "What has the money situation been with you this month? I hope it went better than you thought it would because it worried me when you wrote that you expected to be short yourself. I *had* to pay a lot out at the beginning of this month, and all I have left is exactly 5 guldens. And the end of the month is still a long way off" (Letter 417). It is clear why he was short of money: "There is no way that I can avoid spending quite a bit on models. It is the same here as everywhere else, people are far from eager to pose for me, and if it were not for the money, *no one* would." In the next long, and contemplative, letter, fairly cheerful in tone, he was still able to speak about it with something like sardonic humor: "I am forced into being one of the most unpleasant of people by having to ask for money." But further on in the letter the tone becomes more serious: "The expenses I *have to meet if I want to work* are sometimes overwhelming when compared with what I have at my disposal. I can assure you that if my constitution had not become almost like that of a peasant through the effects of wind and weather, I would not be able to stick it out, for there is simply nothing left over for my comfort. But what I want is not for myself, any more than many peasants want to live any differently from the way they do. But what I ask for I want for paint and mostly for models" (Letter 418).

Vincent's Creditors

Just how bad things could sometimes get is seen from a letter Vincent sent August 5 to the paint dealer Furnée in The Hague. He asked Furnée, who had apparently threatened him with "collection proceedings," not to resort to extreme measures because the sale of his belongings would yield practically nothing. Vincent was prepared to send him some of his work in order that Furnée himself might show it to prospective buyers. He naïvely added that this might lead to his buying more paint. In any case, he assured Furnée: "*You will be paid* if you will either try yourself to sell some of my work for me or will wait until I sell some of what I have on hand" (Letter 419*a*).

Furnée's reaction is not known, but later (in Letter 420) Vincent announced that yet another creditor, the paint dealer Leurs, had agreed to a similar request and had said he was willing to exhibit some of Vincent's work in the two show windows of his shop on the Molenstraat in The Hague. Then, however, Vincent had to ask his brother to send some money so that he could have a case made and pay to have it shipped. Letter 422 reports that Theo had actually sent 20 francs and Vincent had shipped a case with seven "different subjects" and twelve small studies to Leurs. Meantime Vincent had explained his financial situation at length (in Letter 420), making it quite clear how difficult it was going to be for him to make ends meet in the coming months on the 150 francs (75 guldens) he received monthly from Theo. Out of this he had to pay 25 guldens for rent (covering a period of six months!) and try to do something about the claims of his paint dealers (of which there were three) to whom he owed a total of 100 guldens.

How the difficulties were solved—if they ever were—is not clear from the correspondence. Apart from a single comment by Vincent in Letter 426, wondering whether he would be able to keep afloat until the end of October, we find no further complaint about his tight financial situation up to the time he leaves Nuenen. It may be that his desire to earn something extra was a factor in his decision to go and try his luck in Antwerp.

836

837

838

836 Peasant Woman, Stooping and Gleaning, F 1279
Black chalk, 51.5 × 41.5 cm (20½ × 16½″)
Museum Folkwang, Essen

837 Peasant Woman, Stooping, F 1276v (reverse: 900)
Black chalk, 56.5 × 45 cm (22¼ × 17¾″)
Rijksmuseum Kröller-Müller, Otterlo

838 Peasant Woman, Stooping, F 1262a
Black chalk, washed with gray, heightened with white, 52.5 × 42 cm (20⅞ × 16½″)
Location unknown

Colorplate XI, Still Life with Open Bible, Candlestick, and Novel, 946 〉

839

840

841

Harvest Scenes

The drawings of the grain harvest should for the most part be dated August, to judge from what Vincent said in a letter written to Theo when he came to Nuenen at the beginning of that month, explaining that he had to take advantage of the brief opportunity to catch the harvesters at work (Letter 419, quoted in full on page 184).

To begin with, these drawings naturally include the peasants cutting the stalks of grain with their sickles (854 and many others) and the women helping them by gathering up the bundles of stalks, binding them into sheaves, and so on (868–73). I have added five sketches of women engaged in similar tasks in the fields (880–82, 884, and 887). Of these the small rough sketch 882 (similar in style to 884—note the horizontal hatching) was probably done as a letter sketch. The same must have been true of the small rough pen-and-ink sketch of the farmer with the little cart, 883, which is also similar in style to 882 and identical with it in size. We can reasonably assume that several studies, in the form of drawings or paintings, of two figures shown digging (874–78) date from the second half of August. They must belong here, since Vincent made a small rough sketch of this subject (879) in a letter to Van Rappard (Letter R57), which must have been written in the second half of August and immediately precedes Letter 421. In the case of the two women who are digging, Vincent apparently made a preliminary drawing (875) and then a painted study (876). He did the same thing with the two women, turning to each other and talking, the preliminary sketch here being in the form of a small watercolor (877 and 878). In 888–93 Vincent depicted women "digging up potatoes." Here again there is a painted study (893) done after a drawing (892), even though differing slightly, but no drawing corresponding to the painted study 891 has been preserved. This series is continued in 900 and 901—901 depicting one of the subjects rendered in oils—and 909 and 910, in a more complicated form, with more "entourage" (I shall return to this shortly). It is clear that Vincent's intention in all these figures (even in such an extremely closed form as the one in 899, where the relief depends solely on the light) was to portray *action*, in conformity with his theory that to "present the figure of the peasant in action" was the essence of modern art.

The three watercolor studies of a woman in her cubbyhole by the fireplace (894–96), which are difficult to date, I have also placed in August, because in Letter 421, written in the second half of August, Vincent mentions "also studies of interiors" without, however, providing any further details that might enable us to pinpoint the subject and medium. I have also included here three drawings of another woman bending over, this time while doing the washing (906–8), and three action drawings of a peasant chopping wood (902–4). There can be little doubt that these six studies, too, date from Vincent's summer working season.

Development in Composition

We learn something more about the *background*—the "entourage," as Vincent called it—against which some of the men and women working in the field were depicted from a letter written in the second half of August: "Since you left I have made another small painting, about the size of the one showing the women pulling up turnips in the snow. This one shows the grain harvest—a man reaping, a woman binding up sheaves, the sheaves themselves and the windmill—just like the drawings you saw. An effect of evening after sundown" (Letter 421). What is presumably meant here is that the reaper, the

839 Peasant Woman, Kneeling, Seen from the Back, F 1280
Black chalk, 43 × 52 cm ($16\frac{7}{8} \times 20\frac{1}{2}$")
Nasjonalgalleriet, Oslo

840 Peasant Woman, Kneeling, Possibly Digging Up Carrots, F 1262b
Black chalk, 37 × 46 cm ($14\frac{5}{8} \times 18\frac{1}{8}$")
Collection Constance B. and Carroll L. Cartwright, New York

841 Peasant Woman with Pitchfork, F 1251
Black chalk, 49.5 × 40 cm ($19\frac{5}{8} \times 15\frac{3}{4}$")
Rijksmuseum Vincent van Gogh, Amsterdam

‹ Colorplate XII, Lane with Poplars, 959

woman, the sheaves, and the windmill are shown in the small painting of the grain harvest, but this, of course, is not quite sure. If it is, then the small painting in question has been lost. A drawing is, however, known to us that fits this description closely, except for the windmill; it is 917. The windmill and the sheaves, on the other hand, do appear in various drawings, such as 911, 913, 915, 918, and 919. Therefore, some of them presumably date from the beginning of the month, as Theo is supposed to have seen them and his visit took place early in August.

In the second half of August, Vincent was working on somewhat more complicated compositions than the simple, isolated figures of farmers reaping, women binding sheaves, and the like, where often hardly anything of a background can be discerned. This tallies with a passage in Letter 422, probably dating from the last week of August and written after Theo had suggested something to him in this connection. We may assume that he considered drawings with more background detail more attractive or easier to sell. Vincent appeared favorably disposed: "To reply for the present to what you write concerning drawings of figures with entourage, I sent a few of them off today. I doubt whether they are suitable for framing, and if I am lucky enough to find anything better in the fields, I shall try to add a few new ones fairly soon."

The supposition advanced here—that, generally speaking, Van Gogh in his harvest drawings concentrated initially on isolated figures and then made the somewhat more complicated compositions with a background later on—is confirmed in a rather unexpected way. This is that 885 and 886 obviously represent the two halves of the same drawing. For some reason or other, probably because it did not please him, Vincent tore the drawing in two and used the reverse side of the two halves to make other drawings. These drawings—made later, of course—are 915 and 917, and it can be seen that whereas the original drawing portrayed simply a single figure, the latter two give prominence to the "entourage."

Vincent's concentration on *drawings* probably explains why there are no paintings of any significance known to us that were made by him in the latter part of the summer. The few painted studies dating from that period—a peasant youth (850), two women (876 and 878), and a woman digging alone (891)—cannot, of course, be regarded as significant. These were really "studies in the literal sense of the word," to borrow a phrase from Vincent, and they cannot be compared with works such as the *Peasant Cemetery* (772: colorplate X, page 170), the *Cottage at Nightfall* (777), or some of the other paintings of cottages. But in his drawings Vincent's creativity entered a new phase. Those centered about the demolition of the old tower (765 and following) gave evidence of his highly trained powers of observation by his mastery in presenting the villagers somewhat caricatured in a few rapid strokes. After that group he had now built up a grandiose panorama of work in the fields in a long series of men and women in action. He did not observe these people with cool detachment but rather with an admiring and even adoring eye. Particularly in some of the women, standing and bending down as they worked at the harvest, he had attained a stature one might term monumental.

842

843

844

Monumental Drawings

As early as 1937 Dr. Walther Vanbeselaere quite aptly pointed out: "In August—at the height of the harvest season—Vincent's black-chalk drawings of peasant men and women in the fields mark the high point of his Dutch period. Those drawings, almost of themselves, force a comparison with Michelangelo."* Fortunately, Vanbeselaere did not let his enthusiasm carry the comparison with Michelangelo beyond the statement that Van Gogh and Michelangelo both "laid absolute emphasis upon man."

He continued: "Michelangelo, and as such he is essentially of the Renaissance, takes the nude figure. Vincent chooses the farmer, almost grown into his rough clothes. The rendering of the firmly outlined, yet plastic form by which he, like Michelangelo, sought to express the action of the figure constitutes a single momentary problem in Vincent's career as an artist, whereas for Michelangelo it remains the essential problem of his art form."†

** De Hollandsche periode in het werk van Vincent van Gogh* (1937), p. 387.

†Ibid., p. 388.

845

846

847

848

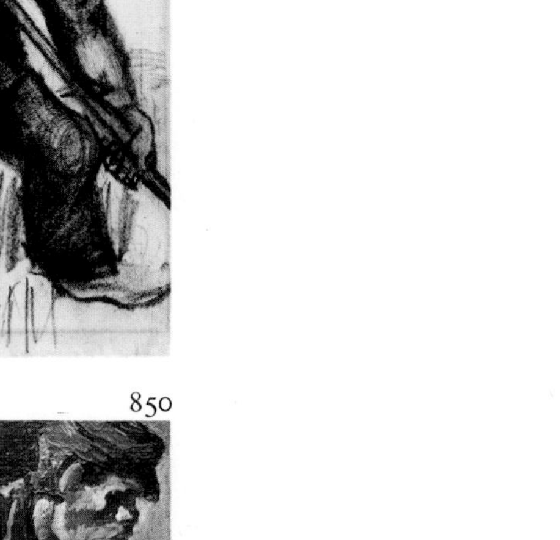

849

850

851

842 Peasant Woman with Spade, F 1250
Black chalk, 53 × 42 cm ($20\frac{7}{8} \times 16\frac{1}{2}''$)
Rijksmuseum Vincent van Gogh, Amsterdam

843 Peasant Woman, Kneeling with Chopper, F 1281
Black chalk, 36 × 40 cm ($14\frac{1}{8} \times 15\frac{3}{4}''$)
Rijksmuseum Kröller-Müller, Otterlo

844 Peasant, Digging, F 1308
Black chalk, 29.5 × 22.5 cm ($11\frac{3}{4} \times 9''$)
Rijksmuseum Vincent van Gogh, Amsterdam

845 Peasant Woman, Stooping with Spade, Possibly Digging Up Carrots, F 1690
Black chalk, 52 × 41.5 cm ($20\frac{1}{2} \times 16\frac{1}{2}''$)
Location unknown

846 Peasant Woman with Broom, F 1283v (reverse: 828)
Black chalk, 33.5 × 20 cm ($13\frac{3}{8} \times 7\frac{7}{8}''$)
Rijksmuseum Kröller-Müller, Otterlo

847 Peasant, Digging Up Potatoes, F 1304
Black chalk, 28 × 22 cm ($11 \times 8\frac{5}{8}''$)
Location unknown

848 Peasant, Digging, F 1311
Black chalk, 35 × 21 cm ($13\frac{3}{4} \times 8\frac{1}{4}''$)
Rijksmuseum Kröller-Müller, Otterlo

849 Peasant, Digging, F 1305
Black chalk, 53 × 35.5 cm ($20\frac{7}{8} \times 14\frac{1}{8}''$)
Rijksmuseum Vincent van Gogh, Amsterdam

850 Peasant, Digging, F 166
45.5 × 31.5 cm ($18\frac{1}{8} \times 12\frac{7}{8}''$)
Rijksmuseum Kröller-Müller, Otterlo

851 Peasant Boy, Digging, F 1306
Black chalk, 52 × 39 cm ($20\frac{1}{2} \times 15\frac{3}{8}''$)
Nasjonalgalleriet, Oslo

When Vanbeselaere says of the *Peasant Woman, Tossing Hay* (872) that he finds it to be "perhaps Vincent's most classical drawing" (page 389), I am unable to agree with him. The way in which the turning of the body is rendered is unfortunate, because it produces a tendency for the viewer to see the woman's right foot as her left foot, since the left is positioned behind the right. But in general I agree with Vanbeselaere when he says that Vincent has achieved his "most classical" moment in his peasant women because, as he puts it, "with their low-hanging, heavy skirts" they form "a more plastically closed, massive whole than do the peasant men" (page 389). And he has in my opinion made the keen observation that all the peasant women are not of equal quality. After pointing out that some of the figures of women bear a close resemblance to the work of Millet (he mentions 832, 833, 881, and 890), he says: "But generally, the peasant women who are bending over, with skirts drawn up and buttocks turned toward us, raised high in the air, are portrayed much more daringly" (page 391). Indeed, a comparison of the drawings 831 and 839 with, for example, one apparently at least quite similar, such as 832, is certainly enlightening. This obliges us to conclude that those "portrayed ... more daringly" are the most characteristic at this stage of Van Gogh's development.

Difficulties with Models

One day near the beginning of September, just after receiving his monthly allowance from Theo, Vincent reported a new kind of trouble that had crossed his path. The somewhat tragicomic narrative is too odd not to be recounted in his own words: "For the past couple of weeks I have had quite a bit of trouble with the reverend fathers, the priests, who informed me, with, of course, the best of intentions, and believing, no less than others would, that they were obliged to concern themselves with the matter—who, I say, informed me that I should not get too familiar with people below my station. That is the way they spoke to *me*, but to the 'people of lower station' they spoke in an entirely different tone, namely, with threats not to allow themselves to be painted. This time I went right down to the burgomaster and told him exactly what had happened and pointed out that this was no concern of the priests, who should stay in their own area of more abstract things. In any case I have not for the time being had any more opposition, and I think it may very well stay this way."

Further on he added the following significant details: "The priest even went so far as to *promise* the people money if they would not let themselves be painted, but they cockily replied that they would rather earn it from me than ask anything from him."

What lay behind the behavior of the priest(s) he describes quite matter-of-factly: "It must have been because of a girl I had often painted who got pregnant; they suspected me, although I was not to blame. However, knowing how matters stood from the girl herself and it being a case in which one of the Nuenen priest's own parishioners had behaved rather badly, they cannot, this

852

853

854

852 Peasant, Digging, F 1310
Black chalk, 44 × 28 cm ($17\frac{3}{8} \times 11''$)
Rijksmuseum Vincent van Gogh, Amsterdam

853 Peasant Boy, Digging, F 1307
Black chalk, 44 × 30 cm ($17\frac{3}{8} \times 11\frac{3}{4}''$)
Rijksmuseum Vincent van Gogh, Amsterdam

August 1885

854 Peasant with Sickle, Seen from the Back, F 1312
Black chalk, pen, 44 × 28 cm ($17\frac{3}{8} \times 11''$)
Stedelijk Museum, Amsterdam (on loan from the Rijksmuseum, Amsterdam)

855 Peasant, Digging, F 1309
Black chalk, 23 × 32.5 cm ($9 \times 13''$)
Rijksmuseum Vincent van Gogh, Amsterdam

856 Peasant with Sickle, Seen from the Back, F 1315
Black chalk, 44.5 × 57 cm ($17\frac{3}{4} \times 22\frac{1}{2}''$)
Rijksmuseum Kröller-Müller, Otterlo

857 Peasant with Sickle, F 1319 (reverse: 911)
Black chalk, 56.5 × 44.5 cm ($22\frac{1}{2} \times 17\frac{3}{4}''$)
Rijksmuseum Vincent van Gogh, Amsterdam

858 Peasant with Sickle, F 1316
Black chalk, 43.5 × 55.5 cm ($17\frac{3}{8} \times 22''$)
Rijksmuseum Vincent van Gogh, Amsterdam

859 Peasant, Digging, Seen from the Back, F 1302
Black chalk, 54 × 41 cm ($21\frac{1}{4} \times 16\frac{1}{8}''$)
Rijksmuseum Vincent van Gogh, Amsterdam

860 Peasant, Digging, Seen from the Back, F 1303
Black chalk, 53 × 41 cm ($20\frac{7}{8} \times 16\frac{1}{8}''$)
Rijksmuseum Vincent van Gogh, Amsterdam

855

856

857

858

859

860

861 Peasant with Sickle, Seen from the Back, F1314
Black chalk, 44.5 × 28.5 cm ($17\frac{3}{4} \times 11\frac{3}{8}$″)
Rijksmuseum Kröller-Müller, Otterlo

862 Peasant with Sickle, Seen from the Back, F1323
Black chalk, 52.5 × 37 cm ($20\frac{7}{8} \times 14\frac{5}{8}$″)
Rijksmuseum Kröller-Müller, Otterlo

861

862

time at least, hold anything against me" (Letter 423).

Nevertheless, this posed a serious threat to his work as an artist: "In the fields I have not been able to get anybody these days." As a result, nearly all the harvest drawings showing the peasant men and women working must have originated in the first half of August. Only the drawings (and the one painted study) of the field with the sheaves of grain (911–19) can be presumed to have been made later, and he had only a meager output to show for the time: "a few new drawings."

Ultimately Vincent gives the impression that the matter turned out fairly well. Exactly one month later he wrote: "The problem I had with the priest has not given me much more trouble. There may, however, be some god-fearing natives of the village who still suspect I was to blame, for it is certain that the priest would be very happy to pin the matter on me. Since, however, I am not the guilty party, gossip from that quarter does not bother me at all; as long as they do not hamper me in my painting, I just ignore them altogether. I am still on good terms with the peasants where I used to go a lot to paint and where the whole thing happened, and I can go and see them just as easily as I did before" (Letter 425).*

A New Series of Still Lifes

Despite Vincent's reassuring remarks it appeared later that this new setback contributed to his leaving Nuenen sooner than he had originally intended. He was not the man to take things lying down, and while we can see that his harvest "campaign" had fully supplied what he had needed for his development as a draftsman, we can also go so far as to say that what had happened had given new impulse to his creative urge, for he turned to other subjects and another medium—the painting of still lifes. Because only two letters to Theo and one to Van Rappard are known to have been written in September, we have little information on the work done in that month. In a short letter written toward the end of the month Vincent reported: "I just wanted to tell you that I have a few things

*The girl in question must have been Sien de Groot. This can be gathered from a question addressed by Vincent to his sister Wil in Letter W1, sent from Paris: "How did that business end, did Sien de Groot marry her cousin? And did her child live?"

863

864

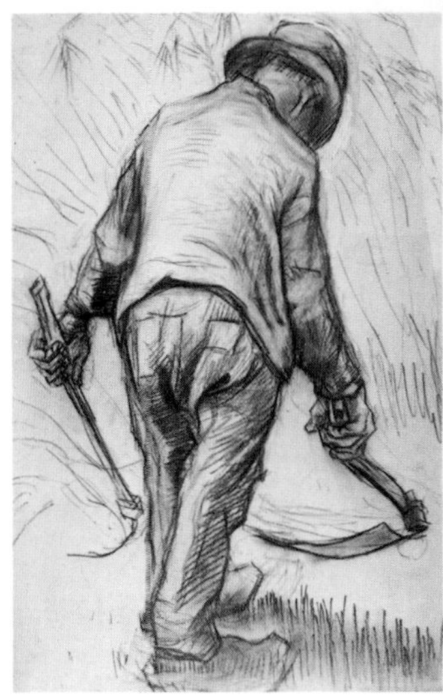

865

866

867

863 Peasant with Sickle, Seen from the Back, F1317
Black chalk, 43 × 55 cm (16 7/8 × 21 5/8")
Rijksmuseum Vincent van Gogh, Amsterdam

864 Peasant with Sickle, Seen from the Back, F1313
Black chalk, heightened with white, 56 × 38 cm (22 × 15")
Rijksmuseum Kröller-Müller, Otterlo

865 Peasant with Sickle, Seen from the Back, F1322v (reverse: 916)
Black chalk, 41.5 × 58 cm (16 1/2 × 22 7/8")
Rijksmuseum Kröller-Müller, Otterlo

866 Peasant with Sickle, Seen from the Back, F1318
Black chalk, 41 × 51 cm (16 1/8 × 20 1/8")
Rijksmuseum Vincent van Gogh, Amsterdam

868

869

870

871

872

873

874

867 Peasant with Sickle, F 1320
Black chalk, 43 × 54 cm ($16\frac{7}{8} \times 21\frac{1}{4}''$)
Collection Mrs. D. Hahnloser-Gassmann, Zurich

868 Peasant Woman, Picking Up a Sheaf of Grain, F 1266
Black chalk, 56.5 × 44.5 cm ($22\frac{1}{2} \times 17\frac{3}{4}''$)
Rijksmuseum Vincent van Gogh, Amsterdam

869 Peasant Woman, Picking Up a Sheaf of Grain, F 1264
Black chalk, 45 × 53 cm ($17\frac{3}{4} \times 20\frac{7}{8}''$)
Rijksmuseum Kröller-Müller, Otterlo

870 Peasant Woman, Carrying a Sheaf of Grain, F 1267
Black chalk, washed, 57 × 42 cm ($22\frac{1}{2} \times 16\frac{1}{2}''$)
Nasjonalgalleriet, Oslo

871 Peasant Woman, Binding a Sheaf of Grain, F 1263
Black chalk, 55.5 × 43 cm ($22 \times 16\frac{7}{8}''$)
Rijksmuseum Kröller-Müller, Otterlo

872 Peasant Woman, Tossing Hay, Seen from the Back, F 1261
Black chalk, 53 × 43 cm ($20\frac{7}{8} \times 16\frac{7}{8}''$)
Rijksmuseum Kröller-Müller, Otterlo

873 Peasant Woman, Stooping between Sheaves of Grain, F 1275a
Black chalk, 30 × 46 cm ($11\frac{3}{4} \times 18\frac{1}{8}''$)
Location unknown

874 Peasant Man and Woman, Digging, F 1299
Black chalk, watercolor, 20 × 33 cm ($7\frac{7}{8} \times 13''$)
Rijksmuseum Kröller-Müller, Otterlo

ready that I was going to send you" (Letter 424). Further on he became more specific: "What I have for you are some still lifes of a basket of potatoes, fruit, a copper kettle, and so on, but these I just made in connection with modeling with different colors [he had just read something about this in a book by Félix Bracquemond], and I would like Portier to see them."

We know eighteen still lifes fitting this description, and I have placed them in September (920–37), subject, however, to a reservation. That this many pieces done with such careful detail could have been made in a single month is hard to believe, and we must therefore allow for the possibility that the series of still lifes extended into the following few weeks.

As the two still lifes 920 and 922 differ somewhat from the others in subject, their dating must be regarded as less than certain. Vanbeselaere, solely on the criterion of style, dates them March 1885, but it should be noted that he regarded the series of still lifes done a year earlier (528–42) as continuing on into March and even April, so that in his opinion the two still lifes did not stand by themselves. The detailed Van Gogh catalogue of the Rijksmuseum Kröller-Müller, the repository of these two paintings, draws attention to the higher degree of technical mastery evidenced in them compared with the earlier works done in Eindhoven and concludes that, on the basis of the smooth, meticulous brushwork with which they were painted and the fine shading of colors, they should be dated summer 1885. The editorial board of the 1970 *catalogue raisonné*, concurring with this view, gives "probably summer 1885" for 920 and 922. I assume that the summery straw hat in 922 was a factor in their decision. My principal objection to these dates is that neither during the first three months of 1885 nor in the summer is there the slightest hint that Vincent was working on still lifes. The lost still life with honesty (726), made at the beginning of April, is an isolated case and, to judge from the sketch, differs sharply from 920 and 922. Also, the few still lifes made later in April were preliminary studies for *The Potato Eaters*. Consequently it seemed to me more plausible that the two being considered here also belonged to the series Vincent started working on at the beginning of September, and I think they also fit in very well from the point of view of style.

875

876

877

879

878

875 Two Peasant Women, Digging, F 1295
Black chalk, washed, 20 × 32 cm (7⅞ × 12⅝″)
Rijksmuseum Kröller-Müller, Otterlo

876 Two Peasant Women, Digging, F 97
Canvas on panel, 31.5 × 42.5 cm (12⅝ × 16⅞″)
Rijksmuseum Kröller-Müller, Otterlo

877 Two Women Talking to Each Other While Digging, F 1296
Watercolor, 23 × 42 cm (9 × 16½″)
Collection H. Doyer Family, Chailly-Lausanne, Switzerland

878 Two Women Talking to Each Other While Digging, F 96
Canvas on panel, 41 × 56 cm (16⅛ × 22″)
Location unknown

880

881

882

883

884

885

886

879 Two Peasant Women, Digging
Sketch in Letter R57
Private collection, United States

880 Peasant Woman, Working with a Long Stick, F1277
Black chalk, 54.5 × 37 cm (21$\frac{5}{8}$ × 14$\frac{5}{8}$″)
Rijksmuseum Kröller-Müller, Otterlo

881 Peasant Woman, Carrying Wheat in Her Apron, F1268
Black chalk, washed, 58.5 × 38 cm (23$\frac{1}{4}$ × 15″)
Rijksmuseum Kröller-Müller, Otterlo

882 Peasant Woman, Standing near a Ditch or Pool, F1292
Pen, washed, 17.5 × 10.5 cm (7$\frac{1}{8}$ × 4$\frac{3}{8}$″)
Rijksmuseum Kröller-Müller, Otterlo

883 Man Loading a Cart, F1335
Pen, washed, 10.5 × 17.5 cm (4$\frac{3}{8}$ × 7$\frac{1}{8}$″)
Rijksmuseum Kröller-Müller, Otterlo

884 Peasant Woman, Pitching Wheat or Hay, F1260
Black chalk, 57 × 44.5 cm (22$\frac{1}{2}$ × 17$\frac{3}{4}$″)
Rijksmuseum Kröller-Müller, Otterlo

885 Peasant, Working, Upper Part of Drawing, F1321v (reverse: 915)
Black chalk, 27 × 39.5 cm (10$\frac{5}{8}$ × 15$\frac{3}{4}$″)
Rijksmuseum Vincent van Gogh, Amsterdam

886 Peasant, Working, Bottom Part of Drawing, F1301v (reverse: 917)
Black chalk, 27 × 38.5 cm (10$\frac{5}{8}$ × 15$\frac{3}{8}$″)
Rijksmuseum Kröller-Müller, Otterlo

In the Rijksmuseum

Van Gogh now became engrossed once more with everything connected with *painting*—colors, blending of colors, and brushwork. Not only did he devote long letters to the subject, but he also permitted himself what in his circumstances was the almost reckless luxury of a trip to Amsterdam with his friend Kerssemakers to study the paintings in the Rijksmuseum there.

We have considerable detailed information about this visit because Vincent himself reported it very fully to Theo in Letters 426 and 427, and in addition we have Kerssemakers's reminiscences.* Clearly for Vincent, who had complained in his letters that he never saw paintings any more, it must have been an exceptional experience to stand once again in front of the great masters, particularly now that his own experience in the technique of painting in oils enabled him to "decipher" them, as he put it, so much differently from the way he had before (Letter 426). In a somewhat amusing anecdote Kerssemakers described how deeply affected Vincent was; he would not be torn away from Rembrandt's *Jewish Bride*, Kerssemakers recalled: "He sat down beside it and made himself comfortable while I went off to look at other things. 'You will find me right here,' he said. When I returned after quite a while and asked whether we should not get a move on, he looked up surprised and said: 'Would you believe, and I really do mean it, that I would give ten years of my life if I could sit in front of this painting for two weeks with nothing but a crust of dry bread to eat?' "

Vincent himself wrote with great enthusiasm not only about Rembrandt but also about Frans Hals. It must have meant a great deal to him to find confirmation in their work that he, with the freedom he had gained in painting, was on the right road. Seeing the old masters like Hals, Rembrandt, Ruisdael, and many others once again, it had struck him that their canvases had mostly been painted quickly, as far as possible *de premier coup*, without premeditation, and that, if it came out right, they left it alone. After all, that was what he had set for himself in recent months as the ideal, even to the extent of sometimes taking a painting to Kerssemakers's to keep himself from continuing to work on it (*The Potato Eaters*, for example; see Letter 404). "What I particularly admired were hands, those by Rembrandt and Hals—hands that were alive, but *not finished* in the sense that today we insist on doing this at all costs—certain hands in *The Syndics* (*The Sampling Officials of the Drapers' Guild*), even in *The Jewish Bride*, in Frans Hals. And heads too—eyes, nose, mouth done with the first strokes of the brush, without any retouching at all." And again, a little further on: "What a joy it is to see something like a Frans Hals, how entirely different it is from the paintings—there are so many of them—where everything is carefully smoothed out the same way" (Letter 427).

He also found support there for his view that it was permissible to use *black*. Reacting with his customary vehemence and obstinacy to something Theo had written about the use of black ("You, who look to see whether there are dark shadows anywhere and think that if the shadows are dark, indeed black, then it is wrong, isn't that it?"), he could now fall back on what he had seen: "Frans Hals has twenty-seven blacks" (Letter 428). Theo hastened to explain what he meant, and it was apparent from his next letter that Vincent was satisfied. "I was very pleased to read your letter about black. And it convinces me, moreover, that you are not prejudiced against black" (Letter 429).

*See *The Complete Letters*, 435c.

887

888

889

887 Peasant Woman, Pitching Wheat or Hay, F 1259
Black chalk, 54 × 41 cm ($21\frac{1}{4} \times 16\frac{1}{8}''$)
Dordrechts Museum, Dordrecht

888 Peasant Woman with Spade, F 1254
Black chalk, 35.5 × 21 cm ($14\frac{1}{8} \times 8\frac{1}{4}''$)
Rijksmuseum Kröller-Müller, Otterlo

889 Peasant Woman with Broom, F 1278
Black chalk, 35 × 21 cm ($13\frac{3}{4} \times 8\frac{1}{4}''$)
Rijksmuseum Kröller-Müller, Otterlo

890 Peasant Woman, Digging, F 1252
Black chalk, 47 × 31 cm ($18\frac{1}{2} \times 12\frac{1}{4}''$)
Israel Museum, Jerusalem

890

891

892

893

894

895

896

891 Peasant Woman, Digging Up Potatoes, F 147
Canvas on panel, 41 × 31 cm ($16\frac{1}{8} \times 12\frac{1}{4}$″)
Private collection, Amsterdam

892 Peasant Woman, Digging, Seen from the Back, F 1258
Black chalk, 29 × 22.5 cm ($11\frac{3}{8} \times 9$″)
Rijksmuseum Vincent van Gogh, Amsterdam

893 Peasant Woman, Digging, Seen from the Back, F 94
Canvas on panel, 36 × 25 cm ($14\frac{1}{8} \times 9\frac{7}{8}$″)
Location unknown

894 Woman by the Fireplace, F 1223
Watercolor, 32 × 43 cm ($12\frac{5}{8} \times 16\frac{7}{8}$″)
Location unknown

895 Woman by the Fireplace, F 1222
Watercolor, 34.5 × 44.5 cm ($13\frac{3}{4} \times 17\frac{3}{4}$″)
Rijksmuseum Vincent van Gogh, Amsterdam

896 Woman with Kettle by the Fireplace, F 1293
Watercolor, 42 × 31 cm ($16\frac{1}{2} \times 12\frac{1}{4}$″)
Staatsgalerie, Stuttgart

Lumpiness

As we have already seen, he had made his own still lifes at this time "in connection with modeling with different colors," or, as he expressed it in Letter 426: "The still lifes I am sending are studies for color." At the same time they were something else as well; they were the expression of a vague striving to endow the objects being portrayed with plastic form and solidity, a striving that was linking him—unbeknown to him, of course—with what Cézanne was doing at the same time with his still lifes of fruit: "You will receive a large still life of potatoes to which I have tried to give *body*, I mean, to give expression to the material in a way that it becomes lumps that have weight and are firm, which you would feel if it were thrown at you for example" (Letter 425).

The painting Vincent had in mind here is probably 933, the largest of the three still lifes portraying baskets with potatoes, but what he says applies also to the two others, 931 and 934, and for that matter, to the still lifes with apples and other fruit. They can all be recognized by this "lumpy" quality, and most of them also by their simple design, devoid of any aesthetic pretensions and quite different from the still lifes of a year earlier, when the picturesqueness of Hermans's "old jugs and other antiques" (see page 122 and the following pages and Letter 387) and the various ways in which they could be arranged were the essence of the practice material. Something of that striving toward an effect of beauty through the choice and arrangement of objects is to be found again in 920–25, particularly in 921 and 924. In the other still lifes there is almost no trace of "airs and graces" ("Don't try to be all airs and graces, don't make it 'chic' " was what Van Gogh taught his pupils Kerssemakers and Van de Wakker; see the Dutch edition of the letters under 435*e*. The predominating elements here are clearly a striving toward the tangible, as Vincent himself termed it, and his experiments with color.

When he had sent a few still lifes and Theo had made some appropriate remarks about the colors, Vincent, in his reaction, showed the most insufferable side of his character by inquiring of Theo—who, Vincent remarked, had never noted such things in the past—whether he had arrived at those observations all by himself. At the same time, he delivered himself of a long explanation that shows how

897

898

899

900

901

897 Peasant Woman with a Dung Fork, Seen from the Back, F1256
Black chalk, pen, 28.5 × 22.5 cm (11⅜ × 9″)
Rijksmuseum Vincent van Gogh, Amsterdam

898 Peasant Woman, Digging, Seen from the Side, F1253
Black chalk, 30 × 23 cm (11¾ × 9″)
Rijksmuseum Kröller-Müller, Otterlo

899 Peasant Woman, Digging, F95a
Canvas on panel, 42 × 32 cm (16½ × 12⅝″)
Barber Institute of Fine Arts, University of Birmingham, England

900 Peasant Woman, Digging, F1276 (reverse: 837)
Black chalk, washed, 45 × 56.5 cm (17¾ × 22¼″)
Rijksmuseum Kröller-Müller, Otterlo

902

903

904

905

906

907

908

901 Peasant Woman, Digging Up Potatoes, F 98
Paper on panel, 31.5 × 38 cm ($12\frac{5}{8}$ × 15″)
Koninklijk Museum voor Schone Kunsten, Antwerp

902 Peasant, Chopping Wood, F 1327
Black chalk, 44 × 54.5 cm ($17\frac{3}{8}$ × $21\frac{5}{8}$″)
Rijksmuseum Vincent van Gogh, Amsterdam

903 Peasant, Chopping, F 1325
Black chalk, 44 × 33.5 cm ($17\frac{3}{8}$ × $13\frac{3}{8}$″)
Rijksmuseum Kröller-Müller, Otterlo

904 Peasant, Chopping, F 1326
Black chalk, 43 × 32 cm ($16\frac{7}{8}$ × $12\frac{5}{8}$″)
Rijksmuseum Kröller-Müller, Otterlo

905 Peasant Woman with Long Stick, Seen from the Side, F 139
38.5 × 26.5 cm ($15\frac{3}{8}$ × $10\frac{5}{8}$″)
Collection Mr. and Mrs. P. Schweitzer, New York

906 Peasant Woman at the Wash Tub, F 1282
Black chalk, 54.5 × 43.5 cm ($21\frac{5}{8}$ × $17\frac{3}{8}$″)
Rijksmuseum Kröller-Müller, Otterlo

907 Peasant Woman at the Wash Tub and Peasant Woman Hanging Up the Laundry, F 1284
Pen, pencil, black chalk, 32 × 25.5 cm ($12\frac{5}{8}$ × $10\frac{1}{4}$″)
Formerly collection Robert von Hirsch, Basel

908 Peasant Woman, Spreading Out the Laundry, F 148
29.5 × 36 cm ($11\frac{3}{4}$ × $14\frac{1}{8}$″)
Location unknown

methodically he went about his work: "Just to say *how* that study was painted, it is simply this: green and red are complementary. Now there is of course a really bold red in the apples themselves and beside them some greenish things. But there are also one or two apples of a different color, a kind of pink, which makes the whole thing right. That pink is the compound color, obtained by blending the first red and the first green. There you have the reasons that there is a connection between the colors. A second contrast has been added to this. The background forms a contrast with the foreground; the one is a neutral color, obtained by mixing blue with orange, the other is the same neutral color, only modified by adding some yellow" (Letter 428). And in commenting on the three studies of baskets with potatoes, 931, 933, and 934, he said: "Further, it is most certainly the case that one of the studies seemed to you to be a variation on the brown-gray theme, only that goes for all three studies of the potatoes, except that one is a study in raw sienna, another in burnt sienna, and the third in yellow ocher and red ocher."

Although Vincent may speak of all these still lifes as experiments in color, we cannot entirely detach ourselves from their subjects. It was Vanbeselaere who aptly pointed out that "the choice of these subjects is so intimately linked with his absorption in the life of the peasants that we detect a smell of products of the earth equally in the peasant, the cottages, the potatoes, and the nests."* In this light it almost seems as if Vincent, in the large rich canvas 937—one of the later ones, I assume—wanted to show that a true symphony of colors and forms can be composed on the basis of such mundane, "prosaic" motifs as a few cabbages, dry leaves, and a wicker basket with potatoes.

Birds' Nests

The birds' nests have been mentioned here, and it should come as no surprise that Vincent, as an extension of his work with fruit and potatoes, should also want to try his hand at this subject. We know from his contemporaries about his enthusiasm for collecting birds' nests himself and having them collected for him by the village boys. His sister Mrs. du Quesne-van Gogh wrote about a dead tree he had in his studio that was full of birds' nests the painter had collected in the course of his wanderings about the countryside. According to Kerssemakers, the studio had "a cupboard with some thirty birds' nests, all kinds of moss and plants found on the moor, some stuffed birds," and so on. Vincent himself wrote in September 1885 to Van Rappard: "Today I sent to your address a basket containing birds' nests. I also have quite a collection of them in my studio, and I am sending you some of those I have more than one of" (Letter R58). At the beginning of October he wrote Theo: "I am now working on still lifes of my birds' nests and have finished four of them. I believe that those, because of the colors of the moss, dry leaves and grasses, clay, etc., might prove appealing to some people who know nature well" (Letter 425). The letter was accompanied by a small sketch showing such a nest on a branch (943), and a few lines had been written under the sketch. These lines have not been reproduced in *The Complete Letters*, but they do have some value as a statement typical of Vincent's thought: "With the onset of winter, when I have more time for it, I shall make some drawings of things like this. *La nichée* et *les nids* [the brood and the nests], that is what I care for—especially those *human* nests, those cottages on the moor and the people who live in them."

We know of five painted still lifes of nests, 938–42. They have become very personal little works, some of them shaded with striking dark touches of the brush, which have perhaps darkened further with the passage of time. But, with all that, they effectively express the loving attention Vincent gave to such widely varied forms of nature. As to what Vincent's intentions were with the dark

***De Hollandsche periode* (1937), page 346.

909

910

911

909 Peasant Woman, Digging Up Potatoes, F 1273
Black chalk, 40.5 × 46.5 cm (16⅛ × 18½")
Rijksmuseum Vincent van Gogh, Amsterdam

910 Peasant Woman, Planting Potatoes, F 1272
Black chalk, 42 × 44.5 cm (16½ × 17¾")
Städelsches Kunstinstitut, Frankfurt

911 Wheat Field with Sheaves and a Windmill, F 1319v (reverse: 857)
Black chalk, 44.5 × 56.5 cm (17¾ × 22½")
Rijksmuseum Vincent van Gogh, Amsterdam

912 Wheat Field with a Peasant Binding Sheaves, F 1339
Black chalk, 20 × 33 cm (7⅞ × 13")
Rijksmuseum Vincent van Gogh, Amsterdam

913 Wheat Field with Sheaves and a Windmill, F 1340
Black chalk, heightened with white, 22.5 × 29.5 cm (9 × 11¾")
Rijksmuseum Vincent van Gogh, Amsterdam

914 Sheaves of Wheat in a Field, F 193
40 × 30 cm (15¾ × 11¾")
Rijksmuseum Kröller-Müller, Otterlo

912

913

914

915

916

917

915 Wheat Field with Mower, Stooping Peasant Woman, and a Windmill, F 1321 (reverse: 885)
Black chalk, 27 × 39.5 cm (10⅝ × 15¾″)
Rijksmuseum Vincent van Gogh, Amsterdam

916 Wheat Field with Trees and a Mower, F 1322 (reverse: 865)
Black chalk, 41.5 × 58 cm (16½ × 22⅞″)
Rijksmuseum Kröller-Müller, Otterlo

917 Wheat Field with Mower and a Stooping Peasant Woman, F 1301 (reverse: 886)
Black chalk, heightened with white, 27 × 38.5 cm (10⅝ × 15⅜″)
Rijksmuseum Kröller-Müller, Otterlo

918 Wheat Field with Sheaves and a Windmill, F 1341
Black chalk, 25 × 34 cm (9⅞ × 13⅜″)
Rijksmuseum Vincent van Gogh, Amsterdam

919 Wheat Field with Sheaves and a Windmill, F 1342
Black chalk, 25 × 34 cm (9⅞ × 13⅜″)
Rijksmuseum Vincent van Gogh, Amsterdam

918

919

backgrounds, he himself has given the answer: "Now the nests have also been painted on a dark background, quite intentionally, because I want to be frank in admitting that in these studies the objects are not in their natural surroundings but are seen against a conventional background. A *living* nest in nature is something quite different, one scarcely sees the nest itself, one sees the birds" (Letter 428).

City Scenes
Two small works, entirely different in character, also date from the first half of October, 944 and 945. They are studies of little importance as regards either size or treatment, but the anecdotal element in the painting of them is too amusing for us to pass them by. They are "souvenirs" of Vincent's visit to Amsterdam October 6 to 8, as he indicated in Letter 426: "The two small boards I painted in Amsterdam were done in a great hurry; the one, mark you, in the waiting room of the station when I was somewhat early for the train, the other in the morning before I went to the museum around ten o'clock. Even so, I am sending them to you as though they were little tiles on which something has been thrown with a few sweeps of a brush."

Kerssemakers recalled some details of how the second small painting came about: "Because circumstances at home at the time prevented me from spending the night away from the house, he went the day before and arranged to meet me the next day in the third-class waiting room of the Central Station. When I went in there, I saw a large crowd of people of all kinds, conductors, laborers, travelers, and so on, standing in the front part of the waiting room near the windows, and there, surrounded by this pack, he sat completely at his ease in his shaggy ulster and inseparable fur cap, industriously working on some scenes of the city (he had brought along a small tin box of paints), taking not the slightest notice of the sarcastic and noisy remarks and observations of the esteemed (?) public. When he caught sight of me, he very calmly packed everything up, and we went off to the museum."

It is not entirely certain that 945 does represent one of the two small works described here. Vanbeselaere has expressed some doubt about it, noting simply: "It is not the second sketch mentioned: the format is not that of a 'small board.'"* In my opinion the expression "as though they were little tiles" should give even greater cause for hesitation, but I do not think too much importance should be attached to this phrase; why could Van Gogh not have referred to a small panel of 13¾ by 18½ inches as a "small board"? ("Board" does not enter into the matter at all.) In any case 945 does answer to the description "done in a great hurry" and "on which something has been thrown with a few sweeps of a brush."

Because of the similarity of subject I have also included here 947. The site has not been identified, and opinions concerning the date vary. De la Faille, in his first edition (1928), gives: "Antwerp?"; and in his second edition (1939): "Nuenen 1885." Vanbeselaere does

* *De Hollandsche periode* (1937), p. 303.

920

921

922

September 1885

920 Still Life with Earthen Pot and Clogs, F63
Canvas on panel, 39 × 41.5 cm (15⅜ × 16½″)
Rijksmuseum Kröller-Müller, Otterlo

921 Still Life with Two Jars and Two Pumpkins, F59
Canvas on panel, 58 × 85 cm (22⅞ × 33½″)
Private collection, Switzerland

922 Still Life with Straw Hat and Pipe, F62
36 × 53.5 cm (14⅛ × 21¼″)
Rijksmuseum Kröller-Müller, Otterlo

923 Still Life with Ginger Jar and Fruit, F104
Canvas on panel, 30.5 × 46.5 cm (12¼ × 18½″)
Location unknown

924 Still Life with Ginger Jar and Onions, F104a
34 × 49.5 cm (13⅜ × 19⅝″)
Private collection, Great Britain

925 Still Life with a Jar and Copper Kettle, F51
65 × 80 cm (25⅝ × 31½″)
Rijksmuseum Vincent van Gogh, Amsterdam

926 Still Life with an Earthen Bowl and Pears, F105
33 × 43.5 cm (13 × 17⅜″)
Museum van Baaren, Utrecht

927 Still Life with a Basket of Apples, F101
33 × 43.5 cm (13 × 17⅜″)
Rijksmuseum Vincent van Gogh, Amsterdam

928 Still Life with Cabbage and Fruit, F103
Canvas on cardboard, 32.5 × 43 cm (13 × 16⅞″)
Rijksmuseum Vincent van Gogh, Amsterdam

929 Still Life with a Basket of Vegetables, F212a
35.5 × 45 cm (14⅛ × 17¾″)
Collection Mrs. Anneliese Brand, Landsberg, Germany

930 Still Life with a Basket of Apples, F99
43 × 59 cm (16⅞ × 23¼″)
Rijksmuseum Vincent van Gogh, Amsterdam

931 Still Life with a Basket of Potatoes, F100
44.5 × 60 cm (17¾ × 23⅝″)
Rijksmuseum Vincent van Gogh, Amsterdam

923

924

926

925

927

928

929

930

931

not mention it at all, which means that he does not ascribe it to the Brabant period.

Still Life with the Bible

More important in every respect is 946 (colorplate XI, page 187), a still life that we can date with certainty, for this much-discussed and frequently reproduced piece was announced by Vincent himself very explicitly in his long letter at the end of October dealing with other painters' theories of color and his own efforts in this area: "In reply to your description of the study by Manet, I am sending you a still life of an open—thus a broken white—Bible, bound in leather against a black background with a yellow-brown foreground, with also a touch of lemon yellow. I painted this *at one go* in a single day" (Letter 429).

It is noteworthy that this painting, too, is described by Vincent as an experiment in color. However, just as in the case of the still lifes discussed above, and in even greater measure, we must not lose sight of the subject of this work. The Bible, which Vincent sent in a case to Theo with a number of studies, was, as he wrote, "a Bible they gave me at home for you" (Letter 430), thus, we can assume, his father's Bible. It was, I believe, Jean Leymarie who, in connection with the motif of the candlestick with its burned-out candle, was the first to recall the *vanitas* motifs of the seventeenth century—of the transitoriness of human glory—themes with which Vincent, in view of his years in the book trade, was certainly familiar. But even without this motif, it would be clear that the imposing, almost crushingly large Bible represents his dead father and his world, in opposition to which is the much-read, familiar little book put there by the painter and representing his world. It is not only a daub of yellow paint, it is also Zola; it is *La Joie de Vivre* (*The Joy of Living*), a novel published the year before. The contrast is all the starker (and all the more deliberate) if one notices—as Leymarie has done—that the Bible does not lie open at just any page, but at a page at the top of which one can clearly read: *Isaïe, cap. LIII.* (The French *Isaïe*, instead of the Dutch *Jesaja*, for *Isaiah*, was intended, I believe, for the benefit of those who would see the painting in Paris.)*

*Jean Leymarie wrote: "Une inscription très distincte: *Isaïe, cap LIII, xx*" ("very distinct lettering: Isa. 53:20"). However, chapter 53 has only 12 verses. *Van Gogh* (1951), p. 26.

932

933

934

932 Still Life with an Earthen Bowl with Potatoes, F 118
44.5 × 57 cm ($17\frac{3}{4} \times 22\frac{1}{2}''$)
Collection Mrs. E. Brugmans-Beukema, Groningen

933 Still Life with Two Baskets of Potatoes, F 107
66 × 79 cm ($26 \times 31\frac{1}{8}''$)
Rijksmuseum Vincent van Gogh, Amsterdam

934 Still Life with a Basket of Potatoes, F 116
51 × 66 cm ($20\frac{1}{8} \times 26''$)
Rijksmuseum Vincent van Gogh, Amsterdam

935 Still Life with a Basket of Apples, F 115
30 × 47 cm ($11\frac{3}{4} \times 18\frac{1}{2}''$)
Gemeentemuseum, The Hague (on loan from the Estate of H. P. Bremmer)

936 Still Life with a Basket of Apples and Two Pumpkins, F 106
59 × 84.5 cm ($23\frac{1}{4} \times 33\frac{1}{2}''$)
Rijksmuseum Kröller-Müller, Otterlo

937 Still Life with a Basket of Potatoes, Surrounded by Autumn Leaves and Vegetables, F 102
75 × 93 cm ($29\frac{1}{2} \times 36\frac{5}{8}''$)
Collection F. C. Graindorge, Liège

October 1885

938 Still Life with Birds' Nests, F 112
33 × 42 cm ($13 \times 16\frac{1}{2}''$)
Rijksmuseum Kröller-Müller, Otterlo

939 Still Life with Birds' Nests, F 111
38.5 × 46.5 cm ($15\frac{5}{8} \times 18\frac{1}{2}''$)
Rijksmuseum Vincent van Gogh, Amsterdam

940 Still Life with Birds' Nests, F 108
33.5 × 50.5 cm ($13\frac{3}{8} \times 20\frac{1}{8}''$)
Rijksmuseum Kröller-Müller, Otterlo

941 Still Life with Birds' Nests, F 110
Canvas on panel, 43 × 57 cm ($16\frac{7}{8} \times 22\frac{1}{2}''$)
Gemeentemuseum, The Hague (on loan from the Wibbina Foundation)

942 Still Life with Birds' Nests, F 109 (reverse: 1303)
Canvas on cardboard, 31.5 × 43.5 cm ($12\frac{5}{8} \times 17\frac{3}{8}''$)
Rijksmuseum Vincent van Gogh, Amsterdam

943 Birds' Nests
Sketch in Letter 425
Rijksmuseum Vincent van Gogh, Amsterdam

935

936

937

938

939

940

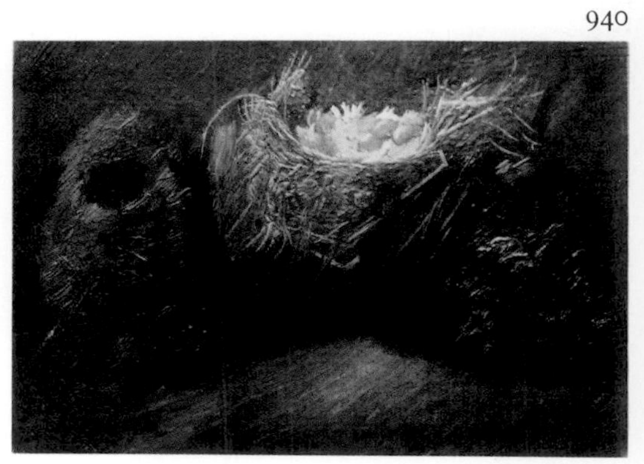

941

942

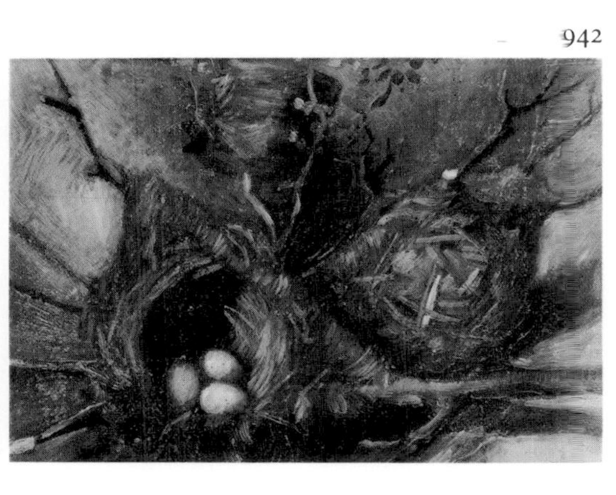

943

als ik meer tijd er voor heb
Tegen den winter zal ik van dit soort gevallen eenige
teekeningen maken.
— vooral die menschen
die hutten op de hei en heuvel bewonen —

Fall Studies

In the same breath in which he talked about his still life of the Bible, Vincent wrote: "I have lately been making some studies of the fall landscape out of doors." These might be the somewhat similar small panels 949 and 950. They are quiet, sedate landscapes, not presenting any new facet in Vincent's development. More characteristic is his rendering of the parsonage in fall colors—the house linked with memories so important to him, which he would soon be taking leave of forever (948). The canvas was probably made some time during these weeks, as was perhaps also pencil sketch 951, which is actually difficult to date.

There are also significant personal associations in the study of the parsonage viewed from the rear (952), which, to judge from the barer look of the trees, was probably painted somewhat later, perhaps in November. It makes one think of a last farewell to the house and to the now long deserted studio behind it that stands there grim and closed in the center of the picture.

We have now come to November 1885, the last month of Vincent's stay in Nuenen. The fall colors enticed him into working out of doors as much as possible. Announcing that he was making two studies of the autumn foliage, he reported November 4: "I have also made a fall study of the pond in the garden at home. There is certainly a painting to be made in that spot. Last year, too, I tried to get one out of it.* The one I have made now is a rather tight composition, two trees, orange and yellow, on the right; two bushes, gray-green, in the center; two trees, brown-yellow, on the left" (Letter 430). This study is undoubtedly 955, and we can assume that the corresponding watercolor (954) was made immediately before or after it. Some other fall landscapes not further identified in the letters probably date from the same time; 956 and 957, and a watercolor that was inscribed by Vincent "un dimanche à Eindhoven" ("a Sunday in Eindhoven") also has an autumnal look.

The studies of autumn foliage 959 and 962 are better documented. At the beginning of the month Vincent had written: "You will shortly be getting two studies of autumn foliage, one in yellow—poplars; the other in orange—oaks" (Letter 430). Subsequent letters provided further particulars—Letter 431, about the orange oaks, and Letter 434, about the yellow poplars—shortly before and about the middle of the month.

Especially striking and deeply felt is Vincent's description of the magnificent painting 962, generally regarded today as one of the principal works of the Nuenen period: "You know the three pollard oaks behind the garden at home; I have slogged away at them for the fourth time. I had sat in front of them for three days with a canvas about the same size, for example, as that *Cottage* and the *Peasant Cemetery*, which you have. It was those clusters of tobacco-colored leaves, to shade them and to give them form, color, and tone. In the evening I took it along to that acquaintance of mine in Eindhoven who has a rather fine large room where we hung it (gray wallpaper, furniture black with gold). Well, never have I been so convinced that I shall make things that turn out right, that I shall succeed in so figuring out my colors that I will have control over effect. This was tobacco, soft green and white (gray), even *pure* white right out of the tube" (Letter 431).

It is typical of Vincent's character that the satisfaction and even emotion he felt at seeing his successful painting hanging there made him feel that "he could not sell" it, as he himself related further on in his letter, even though his friend in Eindhoven (Anton Kerssemakers) "had money" and "wanted

*This landscape, mentioned in Letter 369, is not known and may not have been finished.

944

945

946

944 View in Amsterdam, F113
Panel, 19 × 25.5 cm ($7\frac{1}{2} \times 10\frac{1}{4}$″)
P. and N. de Boer Foundation, Amsterdam

945 View in Amsterdam, F114
Canvas on panel, 35 × 47 cm ($13\frac{3}{4} \times 18\frac{1}{2}$″)
Collection H. R. Hahnloser, Bern

946 Still Life with Open Bible, Candlestick, and Novel, F117
65 × 78 cm ($25\frac{5}{8} \times 30\frac{3}{4}$″)
Rijksmuseum Vincent van Gogh, Amsterdam
Colorplate XI, p. 187

947 Town View with Drawbridge, F210
Panel, 42 × 49.5 cm ($16\frac{1}{2} \times 19\frac{5}{8}$″)
Collection Mrs. E. A. E. M. van Meeteren-van Diemen Arbeiter, The Hague

947

948

949

950

951

952

953

948 The Parsonage at Nuenen, F 182
33 × 43 cm (13 × $16\frac{7}{8}$″)
Rijksmuseum Vincent van Gogh, Amsterdam

949 Autumn Landscape, F 119
Canvas on panel, 64 × 87 cm ($25\frac{1}{4}$ × $34\frac{1}{4}$″)
Garman-Ryan Collection, London

950 Lane with Two Figures, F 191a
Canvas on panel, 30 × 38 cm ($11\frac{3}{4}$ × 15″)
Location unknown

951 The Parsonage at Nuenen, F 1343a
Pencil, pen, 7.5 × 10 cm ($3\frac{1}{8}$ × $3\frac{7}{8}$″)
Location unknown
November 1885

952 The Parsonage at Nuenen at Dusk, Seen from the Back, F 183
41 × 54.5 cm ($16\frac{1}{8}$ × $21\frac{5}{8}$″)
Galeries Stoliar, Cannes, France

953 Landscape with Pollard Willows, F 1247
Black chalk, heightened with blue and red, 47.5 × 30.5 cm ($18\frac{7}{8}$ × $12\frac{1}{4}$″)
Location unknown

very much to have it." Therefore, what might have been one of his first sales did not take place; Vincent simply gave it away as a gift.

Finally, painting 959 (colorplate XII, page 188) was described in detail in the letter announcing Vincent's intended departure for Antwerp. The sketch (960) enclosed with the letter was later erroneously reproduced alongside a passage about an avenue of poplars in Letter 383 in the edition of the letters published by Mrs. van Gogh-Bonger in 1914. This error was not corrected in later printings, or in the American or French editions. This is what Vincent said about the work: "The one landscape that I am taking with me, and possibly both, but the one with the yellow leaves, I believe it would also please you. I am enclosing a hasty sketch of it. The horizon is a dark band against a light band of white and blue sky. In the dark band there are red, bluish, and green or brown specks, forming the silhouette of the roofs and the orchards, the field greenish. The sky higher up gray, and against this the slender black trunks and yellow leaves. Foreground completely covered with fallen yellow leaves and in it three little figures, two black and one blue. To the right the trunk of a birch, white and black, and a green trunk with reddish-brown leaves" (Letter 434; and see Appendix, note 3).

Off to Antwerp

The reader may wonder how Vincent came to decide that he wanted to settle in Antwerp. It was something he had been thinking about for a long time. As early as February 1884 he had written: "Well, maybe I will try to sell something in Antwerp" (Letter 358), and in the letters from October of that year he had repeatedly returned to the subject as on the occasion when he had spoken about it with Van Rappard (Letters 382 and 383). Antwerp was the nearest big city, and as later proved to be the case, Vincent hoped that at the Antwerp academy he would be able to qualify to work from the nude model—which was not possible in Brabant. The difficulties in November 1885 were what decided the matter.

Since Vincent had intended to go to Antwerp for only a few months, he left the greater part of his household effects behind in a rented room. "When in May [1886] his mother also left Nuenen," Mrs. van Gogh-Bonger recounts, "everything belonging to Vincent was packed in cases, left in the care of a carpenter in Breda and—forgotten! After several years the carpenter finally sold everything to a junk dealer." In this way hundreds of drawings and paintings by Van Gogh were lost, intentionally destroyed, or sold for a song.*

*In her "Memoir" to *The Complete Letters*, p. xxxix. This story, which sounds incredible but is perfectly true, is also told in Stokvis, *Nasporingen omtrent Vincent van Gogh in Brabant* (1926).

954

955

956

954 The Parsonage Garden with Figures, F 1234
Watercolor, 38 × 49 cm (15 × 19¼″)
Collection B. Meijer, Wassenaar, The Netherlands

955 The Parsonage Garden with Figures, F 124
Panel, 92 × 104 cm (36¼ × 41″)
Destroyed in Rotterdam in 1944

956 Autumn Landscape at Dusk, F 121
Canvas on panel, 51 × 93 cm (20⅛ × 36⅝″)
Centraal Museum, Utrecht

957 Landscape with Leaning Trees, F 196
Paper on panel, 32 × 50 cm (12⅝ × 19⅝″)
Location unknown

958 Street in Eindhoven in the Rain, F 1348
Watercolor, 21 × 29.5 cm (8¼ × 11¾″)
Rijksmuseum Vincent van Gogh, Amsterdam

959 Lane with Poplars, F 45
78 × 97.5 cm (30¾ × 38⅝″)
Museum Boymans-van Beuningen, Rotterdam
Colorplate XII, p. 188

960 Lane with Poplars
Sketch in Letter 434
Rijksmuseum Vincent van Gogh, Amsterdam

961 Pollard Willow, F 195
Panel, 42 × 30 cm (16½ × 11¾″)
Haso Art Gallery, Ottawa

962 Autumn Landscape with Four Trees, F 44
64 × 89 cm (25¼ × 35″)
Rijksmuseum Kröller-Müller, Otterlo

957

959

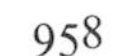

962

961

Antwerp

963

964

965

Vincent's three-month stay in Antwerp was a continuous heroic struggle against poverty and sickness. From that period there are twenty-three letters to Theo, most of them quite long, and I must conclude that they are far more important than the work he did there. Vincent rarely expressed himself in a more direct, penetrating, and emotional way about his conditions of life, his views and projects, than he did during these months.*

In Letter 435 Vincent informed Theo that he was leaving for Antwerp on Tuesday (which was November 24), and in my opinion there is no reason to assume that he did not arrive there the same day, that is, the twenty-fourth. (Tralbaut set the probable date of arrival at November 27 or 28 and repeated this in his *Van Gogh le mal aimé* [Van Gogh the Unloved] of 1969.) Vincent's first letter from Antwerp (Letter 436), in which he reported that he had already made "various tours" of the city and had already seen all sorts of things, such as the museum of old masters and the modern museum, must therefore have been written on November 26 or 27. He said that for 25 francs a month he had rented a small room above a paint shop, at 194 Rue des Images. In the next letter (Letter 437, Saturday, November 28) he said that his things had arrived from Nuenen that day, and as a result he was now able to use his painting equipment and could think about making some portraits. The first few days he had just been able to do a bit of drawing, sometimes in the park.

He added that he had pinned "a number of little Japanese prints" on the walls. This is the first time that we hear of those colored Japanese woodcuts in which in the Paris period, too, he was extremely interested. He did not say that he had bought them in Antwerp, and this letter indicates that he had just enough money left for a few days' supply of bread. Since he mentions them in the same breath as the things of his that had arrived from Nuenen that day, I am inclined to believe that he had had them in Nuenen.

Exploring the Terrain

In the first days of his stay in Antwerp, Vincent seems to have confined himself to making sketches of his new surroundings. We know of four of these, 963–66, none of which is more than a quick note in a sketchbook.

More important, both because of the subject, which was unusual for Van Gogh, and because of the keen observation and lively presentation, are the sketchbook sheets 967, 968, and 969. The first shows two women in the box of a theater or, more likely, one woman in two different attitudes. The other two are dance hall scenes.

Vincent's many exploratory jaunts throughout the city during the first week of December seem also to have brought him to its entertainment spots: "Yesterday I was in the Scala café concert, something like the Folies-Bergère; I found it dull and, of course, trite, but—the spectators were a lot of fun. There were magnificent female heads, really extraordinarily beautiful, among the good burghers on the benches in the rear, and generally speaking I think it is quite true

* That it is possible to write 368 pages about this period was demonstrated by Tralbaut in his 1948 dissertation *Vincent van Gogh in zijn Antwerpsche periode* (Vincent van Gogh's Antwerp Period). I have essentially had to restrict myself to the work Vincent did in Antwerp.

966

967

968

969

970

971

972

December 1885

963 Square with People Walking, F 1354
Pencil, black chalk, 11 × 20 cm (4⅜ × 7⅞″)
Rijksmuseum Vincent van Gogh, Amsterdam

964 Walking Couple, F 1338
Pencil, pen, 7 × 12.5 cm (2¾ × 5⅛″)
Private collection, The Netherlands

965 Landscape with People Walking, F 1093
Black chalk, 13 × 21 cm (5⅛ × 8¼″)
Location unknown

966 Town View, F 1355
Black chalk, 9.5 × 16.5 cm (3⅞ × 6¾″)
Rijksmuseum Vincent van Gogh, Amsterdam

967 Two Women in a Box at the Theater, F 1350v
(reverse: 976)
Black and colored chalk, 9 × 16 cm (3½ × 6¼″)
Rijksmuseum Vincent van Gogh, Amsterdam

968 Dance Hall, F 1350a
Black and colored chalk, 9 × 16 cm (3½ × 6¼″)
Rijksmuseum Vincent van Gogh, Amsterdam

969 Dance Hall with Dancing Women, F 1350b
Black and colored chalk, 9 × 16 cm (3½ × 6¼″)
Rijksmuseum Vincent van Gogh, Amsterdam

970 Houses, Seen from the Back, F 260
44 × 33.5 cm (17⅜ × 13⅜″)
Rijksmuseum Vincent van Gogh, Amsterdam

971 Head of an Old Man, F 205
44 × 33.5 cm (17⅜ × 13⅜″)
Rijksmuseum Vincent van Gogh, Amsterdam

972 Woman with Her Hair Loose, Head, F 206
35 × 24 cm (13¾ × 9½″)
Rijksmuseum Vincent van Gogh, Amsterdam

what they say about Antwerp, that the women there are beautiful" (Letter 438).

Another work done in the first days of Vincent's stay in Antwerp is canvas 970: "The past week I have also painted three studies, one showing the backs of old houses, seen from my window, two in the park" (Letter 438). The scenes in the park have not been preserved, but the third study can definitely be identified as 970. This small painting of houses brings to mind the drawings and the watercolor that Vincent made from the back of his house on the Schenkweg in The Hague (150, 153, and 156). There, too, he produced a naïve, realistic representation of what the eye saw, without the slightest concern for traditional beauty.

This is an instance of a method in which the composition is determined as though by the merciless lens of a camera, the result being a scene of arbitrary chaos. The jumble of rear walls of houses crowding against one another, the little outbuildings, and the dividing walls in the yards form a classic example of the antiaesthetic which had always been carefully avoided in pictorial art before Van Gogh's time. It took a totally original artist like Vincent to come to grips with a subject like this. He had, after all, already demonstrated—for example, in *The Potato Eaters* and in many of the heads made in connection with it—that he had a sensitive eye even for the picturesque in what was ugly.

973

Portraits and Views of the City

A few days later he did his first portraits in Antwerp, which he mentioned in Letter 439, written in the second week of December: "Wanted to write and tell you that I have been continuing on with models. I have made two fairly large heads as sort of experiments in portraits. First, that old man I already wrote you about, a kind of head in the style of V[ictor] Hugo's, and then I also have a study of a woman." The first one, taking into account the type of the head, must be the fine portrait in profile 971; the second, to judge from the description that follows in the letter, is undoubtedly the full-face portrait 972. That description is important for a reason other than that of identification: "In the portrait of the woman I have put lighter tones into the flesh, *white*, tinted with carmine, vermilion, yellow, and a background of gray-yellow, from which the face is separated only by the black hair. Lilac tones in the clothes." When we read in the very next sentence: "Rubens does make a strong im-

974

975

973 Quay with Ships, F 211
Panel, 20.5 × 27 cm ($8\frac{1}{4} \times 10\frac{5}{8}$")
Rijksmuseum Vincent van Gogh, Amsterdam

974 Spire of the Church of Our Lady, F 1356
Black chalk, 30 × 22.5 cm ($11\frac{3}{4} \times 9$")
Rijksmuseum Vincent van Gogh, Amsterdam

975 De Grote Markt, Antwerp, F 1352
Black chalk, heightened with white, 22.5 × 30 cm ($9 \times 11\frac{3}{4}$")
Rijksmuseum Vincent van Gogh, Amsterdam

976 Kasteel Het Steen, Antwerp, F 1350 (reverse: 967)
Black and colored chalk, 9 × 16 cm ($3\frac{1}{2} \times 6\frac{1}{4}$")
Rijksmuseum Vincent van Gogh, Amsterdam

977 Kasteel Het Steen, Antwerp, F 1351
Pencil, pen, heightened with colored chalk, 13 × 21 cm ($5\frac{1}{8} \times 8\frac{1}{4}$")
Rijksmuseum Vincent van Gogh, Amsterdam

978 Woman with White Bonnet, Head, F 174
50 × 40 cm ($19\frac{5}{8} \times 15\frac{3}{4}$")
Rijksmuseum Vincent van Gogh, Amsterdam

979 Woman with a Scarlet Bow in Her Hair, F 207
60 × 50 cm ($23\frac{5}{8} \times 19\frac{5}{8}$")
Collection Alfred Wyler, New York
Colorplate XIII, p. 221

January 1886

980 Man with Apron, Half-Length, F 1358
Black chalk, 16.5 × 9 cm ($6\frac{3}{4} \times 3\frac{1}{2}$")
Rijksmuseum Vincent van Gogh, Amsterdam

981 Head of a Woman, F 1357
Charcoal, black and red chalk, 51 × 39 cm ($20\frac{1}{8} \times 15\frac{3}{8}$")
Rijksmuseum Vincent van Gogh, Amsterdam

982 Head of a Man with Hat and Pipe, F 1372 (reverse: 983)
Black chalk, 19.5 × 11 cm ($7\frac{7}{8} \times 4\frac{3}{8}$")
Rijksmuseum Vincent van Gogh, Amsterdam

983 Head of a Man, F 1372v (reverse: 982)
Black chalk, 19.5 × 11 cm ($7\frac{7}{8} \times 4\frac{3}{8}$")
Rijksmuseum Vincent van Gogh, Amsterdam

984 Head of a Man with Pipe, F 1359
Black chalk, 16.5 × 9 cm ($6\frac{3}{4} \times 3\frac{1}{2}$")
Rijksmuseum Vincent van Gogh, Amsterdam

976

977

978

981

979

980

982

983

984

pression on me," it is quite obvious what led to the further brightening of Vincent's palette and his use of white and carmine, a combination that he had previously avoided. And it brought him another step further in the use of white in the next portraits, 978 and 979. In the second portrait (colorplate XIII, page 221) the carmine is also employed in a way previously unthinkable for Vincent: the woman has cherry-red lips and a red bow in her hair that dominates the entire picture.

Apart from the portraits, Vincent also worked on views of the city in December. Letter 440, written about the middle of the month, reports that he had done a painting of Antwerp's castle, Het Steen, and had taken it to various dealers without success. This painting has unfortunately been lost, but we do have two small drawings (976 and 977) that were probably preliminary studies and can give some idea of the work that disappeared. The first one is a small sketchbook sheet in black chalk heightened by some red, green, and blue chalk; the second one is a larger and more carefully executed drawing, done in pencil and pen and also enlivened by colored chalk, in a much brighter tonality.

The view of the quay that Vincent announced in Letter 439 has been preserved: "I hope in the final days of the month, when I have a few more heads, to make a view of the Scheldt, for which I have already bought a canvas." This became the small panel 973, a highly impressionistic study, painted with great determination, in which the quay and ships, done almost entirely in black and brown under heavy rain clouds, make a somber contrast with the milky-white light reflected on the water.

Two drawings of city views (974 and 975) belong here; they are mentioned by Vincent in Letter 441, about December 19: "Yesterday, for instance, I drew a pair of studies for a scene showing the cathedral." Whether he also did this "scene," that is, a painted study, we do not know.

In addition to the portraits in oils, we also know of a few, in a variety of sizes, that were drawn: 980–85. With the exception of the large female head 981, they are small sketchbook sheets such as Vincent often used while he was in Antwerp, and the characterization of the subjects, particularly in sketches 982, 983, and 984, has been skillfully achieved with a few lines of black chalk. The portrait of the woman, 981, is, however, the most important of the group. This is much more than a sketch; it is a finely executed portrait in the unusually large size of $20\frac{1}{8}$ by $15\frac{3}{8}$ inches, in which some red chalk was used to enliven the black and white background.

When Dr. Tralbaut was permitted to study the sketchbook sheets in the possession of Dr. V. W. van Gogh, he also came across the small sketches 996 and 997. In 1948, when he published them in his dissertation, he termed them "a couple of self-portraits" (page 272). In his detailed commentary he did not discuss what had led to the conclusion that they were *self*-portraits. There is probably no other evidence to support this than the sharply piercing look out of the corner of one eye. Later writers have always classified the sketches as self-portraits. If they are, the fact that they bear hardly any resemblance to the portrait of Vincent done in Antwerp by the English painter H. M. Livens is rather surprising.

Entering the Academy

At the beginning of January 1886, Vincent, under the pressure of lack of money and the difficulties encountered in doing portraits, considered a new step: "Because of the models, I think I shall go this month to see Verlat, who is the head of the academy here —and I will see what kind of regulations they have and to what extent it would be possible to work from the nude model; I shall take a portrait and drawings along" (Letter 443). This led to his enrollment, which, ac-

985

986

987

988

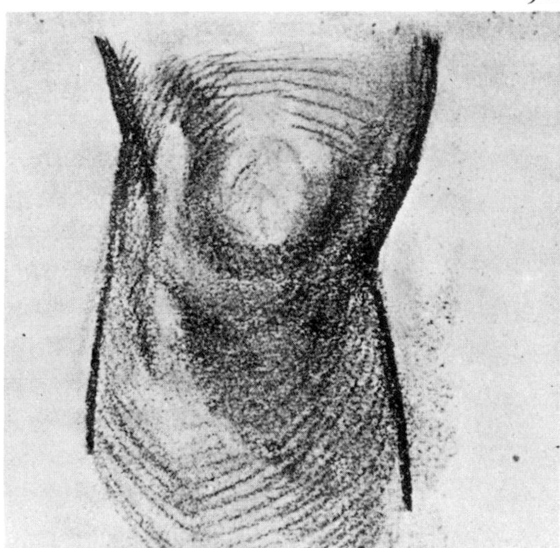

989

990

985 Woman with Hat, Half-Length, F 1357a
Pen, brush, pencil, 13 × 9.5 cm ($5\frac{1}{8} \times 3\frac{7}{8}''$)
Estate of Dr. J. Wiegersma, Deurne, The Netherlands

986 Head of a Woman, F 1693e
Pencil, black chalk, 9 × 11.5 cm ($3\frac{1}{2} \times 4\frac{3}{4}''$)
Rijksmuseum Vincent van Gogh, Amsterdam

987 Sketch of a Knee, F 1693c
Black chalk, 11.5 × 9 cm ($4\frac{3}{4} \times 3\frac{1}{2}''$)
Rijksmuseum Vincent van Gogh, Amsterdam

988 Sketch of a Knee, F 1693d
Black chalk, 11.5 × 9.5 cm ($4\frac{3}{4} \times 3\frac{7}{8}''$)
Rijksmuseum Vincent van Gogh, Amsterdam

989 Sketch of a Left Hand, F 1693f
Black chalk, 11.5 × 9 cm ($4\frac{3}{4} \times 3\frac{1}{2}''$)
Rijksmuseum Vincent van Gogh, Amsterdam

991

992

993

994

995

996

997

990 Sketch of a Left Hand, F 1693g
Black chalk, 11.5 × 9 cm ($4\frac{3}{4} \times 3\frac{1}{2}''$)
Rijksmuseum Vincent van Gogh, Amsterdam

991 Two Women on a Quay, F 1693b
Black chalk, 9 × 11.5 cm ($3\frac{1}{2} \times 4\frac{3}{4}''$)
Rijksmuseum Vincent van Gogh, Amsterdam

992 Field with Cart and Two Rabbits, F 1693a
Black chalk, 9 × 11.5 cm ($3\frac{1}{2} \times 4\frac{3}{4}''$)
Rijksmuseum Vincent van Gogh, Amsterdam

993 Street with Figures (Market Scene?), F 1692
Pencil, blue chalk, 21 × 30 cm ($8\frac{1}{4} \times 11\frac{3}{4}''$)
Rijksmuseum Vincent van Gogh, Amsterdam

994 Head of a Woman with Her Hair Loose, F 1695
Pencil, 8 × 9 cm ($3\frac{1}{8} \times 3\frac{1}{2}''$)
Rijksmuseum Vincent van Gogh, Amsterdam

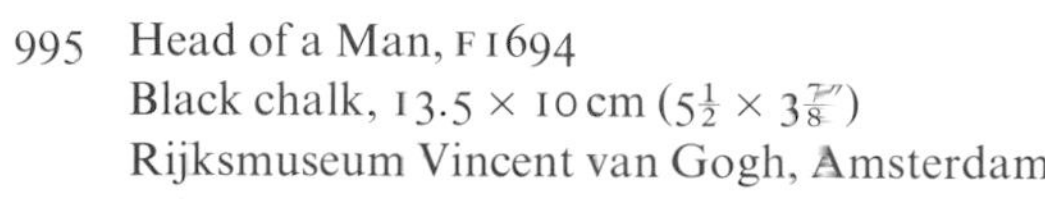

995 Head of a Man, F 1694
Black chalk, 13.5 × 10 cm ($5\frac{1}{2} \times 3\frac{7}{8}''$)
Rijksmuseum Vincent van Gogh, Amsterdam

996 Self-Portrait with Cap, F 1354av (reverse: 997)
Black chalk, 20 × 11 cm ($7\frac{7}{8} \times 4\frac{3}{8}''$)
Rijksmuseum Vincent van Gogh, Amsterdam

997 Self-Portrait with Cap, F 1354a (reverse: 996)
Black chalk, 20 × 11 cm ($7\frac{7}{8} \times 4\frac{3}{8}''$)
Rijksmuseum Vincent van Gogh, Amsterdam

cording to Tralbaut's research, took place on January 18. Besides the painting class in the daytime, there was a drawing class in the evening, but that was not all. A little over a week later he reported to Theo: "I have been terribly busy this week, because apart from the painting class I also go in the evening to draw, and after that, from nine-thirty to eleven-thirty, I go and work from the model in a club. For I have even joined two of these clubs" (Letter 447). This sudden, intensive working from models must have had a great influence on Vincent's technical development, particularly the opportunity to paint and draw from "the nude and the antique" (from plaster casts). However, it was an activity that lasted only a very short time. Even before the end of February, thus after four or five weeks, he had to write that, because of the examinations, courses were over, and apart from the "day class for the antique," there was nothing more to do (Letter 458).

The small canvas 999 brings to mind the weeks spent at the academy. It shows the upper part of a skeleton with a cigarette between the teeth—a macabre joke that the teachers at the academy were not likely to have approved of. It is improbable, however, that Vincent himself would have had a skeleton at his disposal, so some connection with the academy must be assumed.

Drawings 980–1018, which I believe were made in January and February, fall into three main categories: small sheets (approximately $3\frac{1}{2}$ by $4\frac{3}{4}$ inches) belonging to a sketchbook that Vincent probably had with him most of the time and was still using when he was in Paris; sheets from a somewhat larger sketchbook (approximately $4\frac{3}{8}$ by $7\frac{7}{8}$ inches) that were also used for earlier Antwerp drawings depicting city views and dance hall scenes; and larger drawings. The larger nudes (1007–16)—and certainly the female nudes—must for the most part have been made at the sketching club. In Letter 453 Vincent complained that at the academy "they hardly use female nude models at all." These ungainly figures make it easy to understand that the instructors found much fault with the newcomer from the Netherlands.

More typical of the work done at the academy are the two studies of an arm (1004 and 1005) and particularly the very large charcoal drawing 1015—even though this is a *female* nude. This last is a technically more advanced, more "distinguished" drawing, to use Vincent's own term, although it displays little individuality, and I even suspect that the

998

999

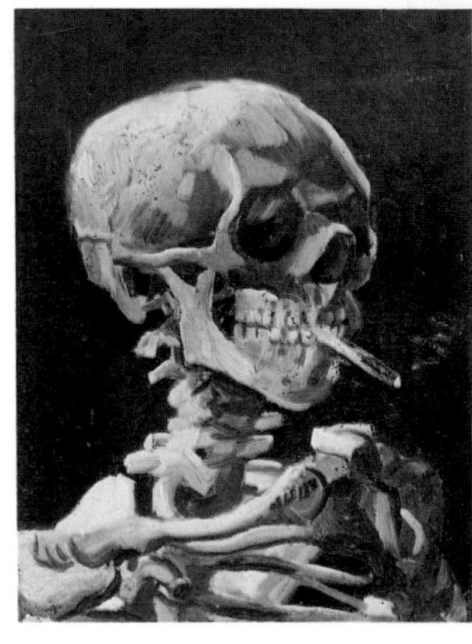

1000

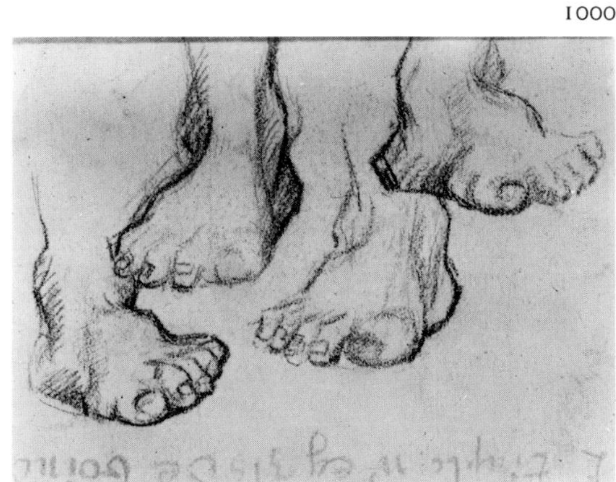

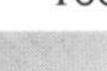

1001

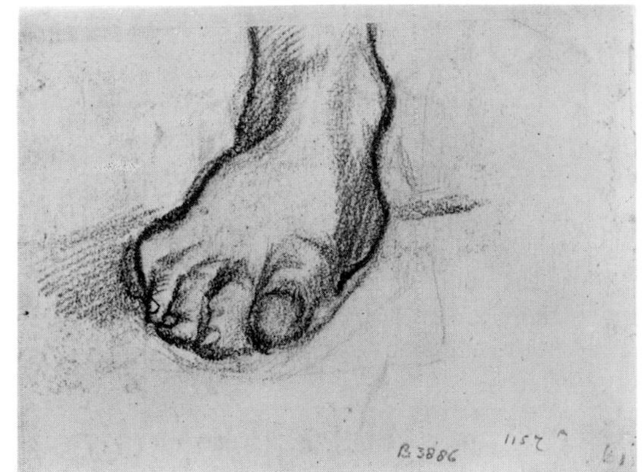

1002

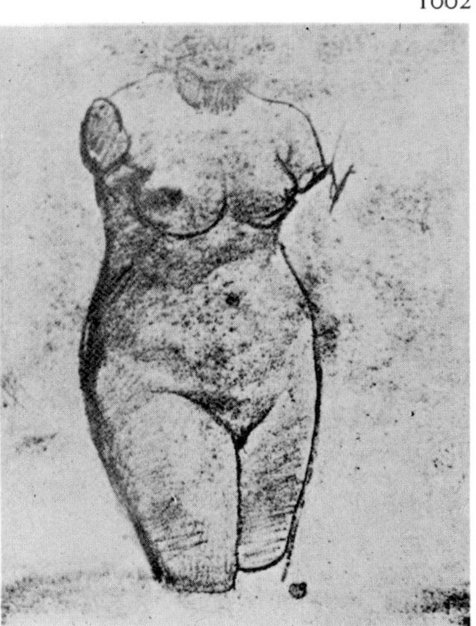

1003

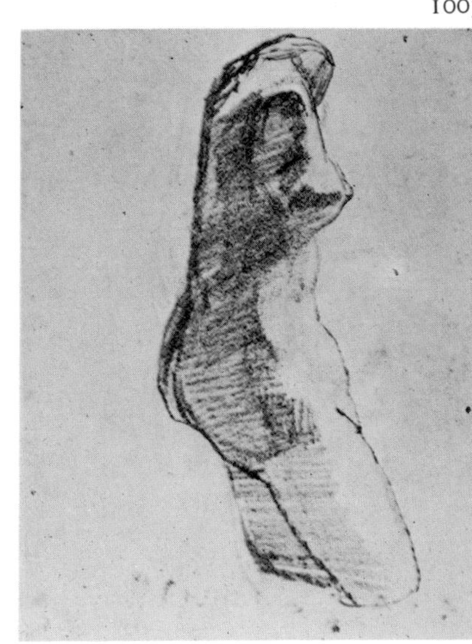

February 1886

998 Hanging Skeleton and Cat, F 1361
Pencil, 10.5 × 6 cm ($4\frac{3}{8} \times 2\frac{3}{8}''$)
Rijksmuseum Vincent van Gogh, Amsterdam

999 Skull with a Burning Cigarette between the Teeth, F 212
32.5 × 24 cm ($13 \times 9\frac{1}{2}''$)
Rijksmuseum Vincent van Gogh, Amsterdam

1000 Four Sketches of a Foot, F 1697 (reverse: 1001)
Black chalk, 10 × 13.5 cm ($3\frac{7}{8} \times 5\frac{1}{2}''$)
Rijksmuseum Vincent van Gogh, Amsterdam

1001 Sketch of a Foot, F 1697v (reverse: 1000)
Black chalk, 10 × 13.5 cm ($3\frac{7}{8} \times 5\frac{1}{2}''$)
Rijksmuseum Vincent van Gogh, Amsterdam

1002 Plaster Torso of a Woman, F 1693h
Pencil, 11.5 × 9 cm ($4\frac{3}{4} \times 3\frac{1}{2}''$)
Rijksmuseum Vincent van Gogh, Amsterdam

1003 Plaster Torso of a Woman, Seen from the Side, F 1693i
Pencil, 11.5 × 9 cm ($4\frac{3}{4} \times 3\frac{1}{2}''$)
Rijksmuseum Vincent van Gogh, Amsterdam

1004 Sketch of a Right Arm, F 1160v (reverse: 1005)
Black chalk, 19.5 × 33 cm ($7\frac{7}{8} \times 13''$)
Rijksmuseum Vincent van Gogh, Amsterdam

1005 Sketch of a Left Arm, F 1160 (reverse: 1004)
Black chalk, 19.5 × 33 cm ($7\frac{7}{8} \times 13''$)
Rijksmuseum Vincent van Gogh, Amsterdam

1006 Sketch of a Right Arm and Shoulder, F 1693j
Black chalk, 11.5 × 9 cm ($4\frac{3}{4} \times 3\frac{1}{2}''$)
Rijksmuseum Vincent van Gogh, Amsterdam

1007 Male Nude, Standing, F 1364-1
Black chalk, 47 × 31 cm ($18\frac{1}{2} \times 12\frac{1}{4}''$)
Rijksmuseum Vincent van Gogh, Amsterdam

1008 Male Nude, Standing, F 1364-2
Black chalk, 47.5 × 30.5 cm ($18\frac{7}{8} \times 12\frac{1}{4}''$)
Rijksmuseum Vincent van Gogh, Amsterdam

1009 Male Nude, Standing, Drawn over a Sketch of a Peasant, Digging, F 1362
Pen, pencil, 21.5 × 13 cm ($8\frac{5}{8} \times 5\frac{1}{8}''$)
Rijksmuseum Vincent van Gogh, Amsterdam

1010 Female Nude, Sitting, F 1700
Pencil, 47.5 × 31 cm ($18\frac{7}{8} \times 12\frac{1}{4}''$)
Rijksmuseum Vincent van Gogh, Amsterdam

1004

1005

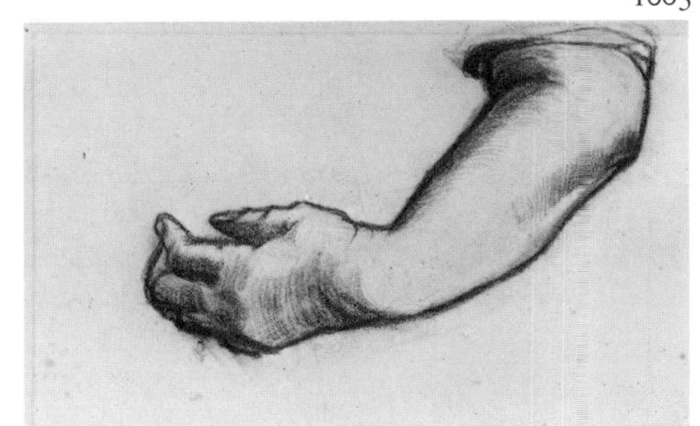

1006

1007

1008

1009

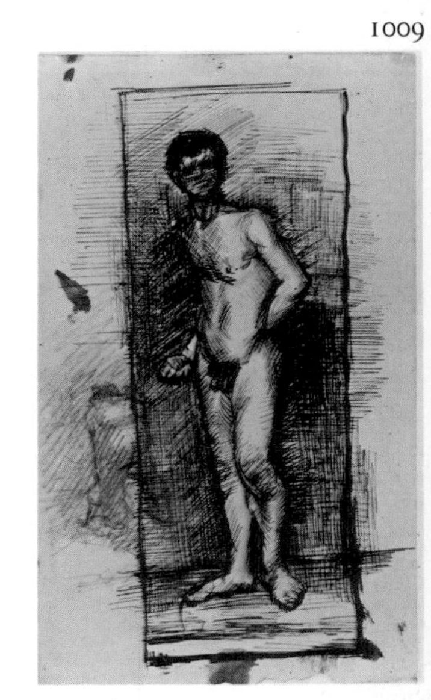

1010

1011

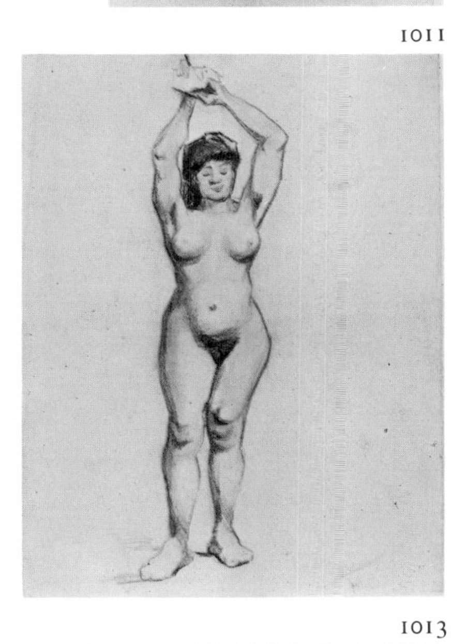

1012

1013

1014

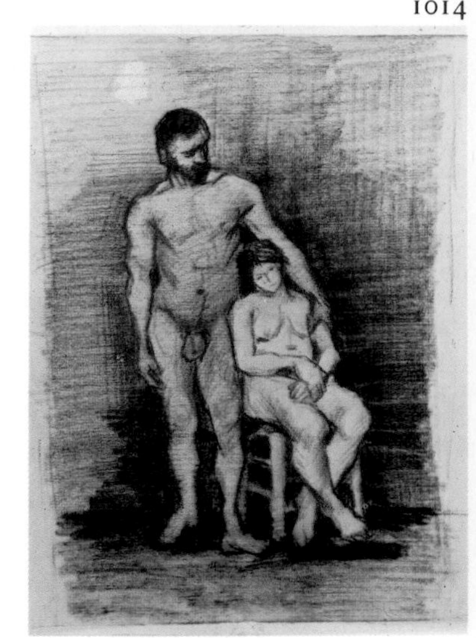

1011 Female Nude, Standing with Raised Arms, F 1696
Black, blue, and red chalk, 50 × 39 cm ($19\frac{5}{8} \times 15\frac{3}{8}''$)
Rijksmuseum Vincent van Gogh, Amsterdam

1012 Female Nude, Standing, Seen from the Back, F 1698
Pencil, 51 × 39.5 cm ($20\frac{1}{8} \times 15\frac{3}{4}''$)
Rijksmuseum Vincent van Gogh, Amsterdam

1013 Female Nude, Standing, Seen from the Side, F 1699
Pencil, 50 × 39.5 cm ($19\frac{5}{8} \times 15\frac{3}{4}''$)
Rijksmuseum Vincent van Gogh, Amsterdam

1014 Male Nude, Standing, and Female Nude, Sitting (partial), F 1363a (reverse: 1063)
Black chalk, charcoal, 30.5 × 21.5 cm ($12\frac{1}{4} \times 8\frac{5}{8}''$)
Rijksmuseum Vincent van Gogh, Amsterdam

flowing curves betray the correcting hand of a teacher. The two large drawings of the clothed model (1017 and 1018) seem to me to be more characteristic of Van Gogh. Here the experience he brought with him from Brabant, combined with what he had learned in recent weeks, produced, in my opinion, a much more successful result.

Vincent certainly did not spend much time entertaining feelings that he was inferior to the students who had been taking the courses a great deal longer than he had. He was even more explicit on this point further on in Letter 452: "Just yesterday I finished a drawing I made for the competition being held in the evening class. It is the figure of Germanicus, with which you are familiar. Well, I know for sure that I will certainly come out last because all the drawings of the others are alike, and mine is completely different from them. But the drawing that will be judged the best —I have seen it being made; I was sitting right behind it, and it is correct, it is all you might want, but it is *dead*, and that goes for all the drawings I saw." Whether he actually did come out "last," we do not know, but we do know that as a result of the examination, he, together with some other students, was put back into the beginners' class.

Off to Paris

Vincent's desire to go to Paris is a recurrent theme in many of his letters from Antwerp. This is a complex matter that becomes clear only after careful reading and rereading; differing interests came into play, and Vincent's own ideas about his future took form gradually during the months in Antwerp (see Appendix, note 4).

At the beginning of February, in Letter 449, Vincent wrote Theo "categorically" that he was literally overworked and exhausted. Since he had moved into his own studio in Nuenen, May 1, he had permitted himself a hot dinner only six or seven times, he reported. Theo sent 25 francs, but by the middle of February, Vincent again had to call for help: "If you could send me something more this month, whether a lot or a little, even if it's only 5 francs, don't fail to do so" (Letter 453). His health was not good ("I am sick, although I still keep going"—Letter 454), and he had to write again just a few days later: "I would also like very much to have the work on my teeth finished. What am I to do? All I have left is 1.50 francs, and as far as food goes, I still have credit for 5 francs up to the end of the month" (Letter 455). We shall never know whether Vincent's last letter—in which he repeated his request that arrangements be made as speedily as possible for him to enroll in the painters' class at Fernand Cormon's studio in Paris—had any effect. The next document we have is the now famous scrawled note in which he announced his arrival in Paris. There is, of course, at least some possibility that Theo, in the letter with which he sent the monthly allowance (regarded by Vincent primarily as train fare) on or about March 1, gave his consent for Vincent to come to Paris. The wording of the note announcing his arrival seems, however, to belie this. Vincent, with his typical tenacity, appears this time too to have mapped out his own course of action.

1015

1016

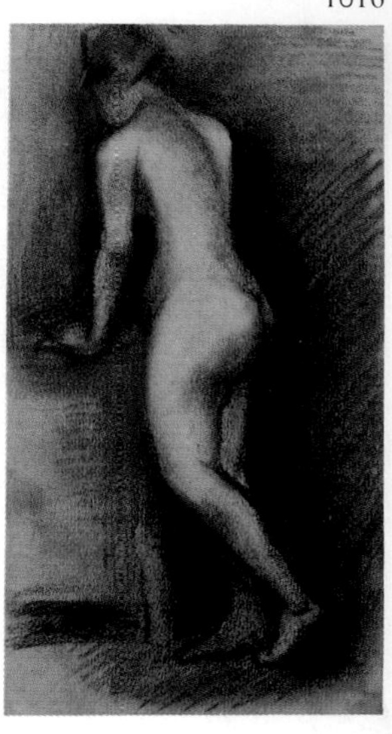

1017

1018

1015 Female Nude, Sitting, F1368
Charcoal, 73.5 × 59 cm ($29\frac{1}{8} \times 23\frac{1}{4}$")
Rijksmuseum Vincent van Gogh, Amsterdam

1016 Female Nude, Standing, F1353
Black chalk, 19.5 × 11 cm ($7\frac{7}{8} \times 4\frac{3}{8}$")
Rijksmuseum Vincent van Gogh, Amsterdam

1017 Man with Cap, Sitting, F1369 (reverse: 1018)
Black chalk, charcoal, 74.5 × 58 cm ($29\frac{1}{2} \times 22\frac{7}{8}$")
Rijksmuseum Vincent van Gogh, Amsterdam

1018 Man with Beard, Sitting, F1369v (reverse: 1017)
Black chalk, charcoal, 74.5 × 58 cm ($29\frac{1}{2} \times 22\frac{7}{8}$")
Rijksmuseum Vincent van Gogh, Amsterdam

Colorplate XIII, Woman with a Scarlet Bow in Her Hair, 979 〉

Paris

1019

1020

1021

1022

Although this has been said so often as hardly to need repeating, we can never be sufficiently grateful to Theo van Gogh for having preserved his brother's letters with such care. It seems almost a miracle—which can be explained only by the tidiness of Theo's mind—that even the note informing him of Vincent's arrival in Paris has been saved. It was no more than a few lines written in black chalk on a slip of paper, which not many people would have thought worth filing away and keeping. But to us its contents are particularly important precisely because they give some insight into a train of events that is far from clear. The entire text is as follows:

"Dear Theo, please forgive me for showing up so suddenly. I have thought about it a great deal and feel that we will save time this way. Will be in the Louvre from twelve o'clock on, or earlier if you like. Please reply so I know what time you could be in the Salle Carrée. As to expenses, I repeat that it comes to the same thing. I still, of course, have money left and before spending any would like to talk to you. We'll work things out, you'll see. So come as quickly as you can. With a handshake."

It thus appears (but see the reservation noted on page 220) that Vincent had come to Paris quite unexpectedly, that he had not gone to Theo's apartment, and that he had not tried to look him up at the Goupil branch on the Boulevard Montmartre, of which Theo was in charge—apparently not wanting to be seen by his former employer. Vincent had obviously wanted to arrange an encounter on "neutral ground" and, in any case, at a place very important to him, where he need not get bored however late Theo might arrive. Vincent may have dropped the note off at Goupil's or had it taken there. It all seems to point to a "bad conscience"—in any case to a psychologically very tense situation.

Although the date of Vincent's arrival in Paris cannot be fixed with any accuracy, it must have been around February 28, since Vincent had to give up his room in Antwerp before the rent for March became due. Theo's reaction cannot be traced in any way either. He probably took his brother into his small apartment in the Rue de Laval, thus sparing him the need to go live in a "mansard" (i.e., attic) room of his own, as he had proposed in some of his letters from Antwerp. This is not evident from letters or other documents, but Mrs. van Gogh-Bonger mentions it in her "Memoir" to *The Complete Letters* (page xl). She gives no source, but it is one of the things she may have remembered from what her husband had told her: "After the meeting in the Louvre Vincent moved into Theo's apartment on the Rue de Laval. As there was no room for a studio, he worked during the first month at Cormon's studio." But we know now that lack of space was not the only reason for Vincent's working at Cormon's studio; he had repeatedly expressed his eagerness to do just that. One problem that arises in a study of Vincent's biography is that his correspondence with Theo almost ceased

March 1886

1019 Street with People Walking, F 1380 (reverse: 1020)
Black chalk, washed, 10 × 17 cm ($3\frac{7}{8} \times 6\frac{3}{4}$")
Rijksmuseum Vincent van Gogh, Amsterdam

1020 Man on Bench, F 1380v (reverse: 1019)
Pencil, pen, 10 × 17 cm ($3\frac{7}{8} \times 6\frac{3}{4}$")
Rijksmuseum Vincent van Gogh, Amsterdam

1021 The Garden of the Tuileries, F 1384
Pencil, 11 × 20 cm ($4\frac{3}{8} \times 7\frac{7}{8}$")
Rijksmuseum Vincent van Gogh, Amsterdam

1022 A Public Garden with People Walking, F 1386
Pencil, 10 × 17 cm ($3\frac{7}{8} \times 6\frac{3}{4}$")
Rijksmuseum Vincent van Gogh, Amsterdam

< Colorplate XIV, Plaster Statuette, 1059

1023

1024

1025

completely during the two years Vincent spent in Paris, which is understandable, since they saw each other daily. There are a few letters from Vincent written during the summer months of 1886 and 1887, when Theo was on vacation in the Netherlands, and a few letters to friends. However, that is all we have in the form of testimony from Vincent himself (see Appendix, note 5).

This, of course, does not make it any easier to catalogue the large body of work that Vincent produced during these years. It is an almost impossible task to establish a reliable chronology; the writers who have dealt with this problem are in full agreement on this point (A.M. Hammacher and Jean Leymarie, to name only two). Because of this generally accepted lack of concrete data, I have departed from my practice elsewhere in this book, and for the Paris period I have made no attempt at an *accurate* dating of the work but have applied a broad classification on a more or less quarterly basis. In this I follow the procedure of the 1970 *catalogue raisonné*, which for many works uses designations such as "summer 1886" or "autumn 1887," although my dating does not always agree with that in the catalogue.

There will be little disagreement about the dating of drawings 1019–30. With a single exception, to be dealt with shortly, these are small sheets from a sketchbook that correspond in format and style to the series of sketches made in Antwerp. We may assume that they constitute a sort of reconnoitering of the new surroundings, random notes, as it were, made at the very beginning of the Paris period, and thus probably in March, which may also be deduced from the bareness of the trees in a number of the sketches. The artist has not bothered about details in pictures of such small size, but the posture or movement of the people resting on benches or walking has been well observed, and these seemingly casual smudges in black chalk display an undeniable virtuosity. The format of 1026 is somewhat different and fairly large ($12\frac{5}{8}$ by $18\frac{1}{8}$ inches). With its small thin lines it would appear to be the unfinished first draft of a drawing to be done in greater detail later or perhaps the composition sketch for a painted study to be made of presumably the same spot in a park as is recorded in the sketchbook jotting 1027. On the opposite side of 1026 appears a drawing of feet (1083), which must have been made at Cormon's. There is no way of determining which side of the paper was used first.

The studies of a burial in the rain (1031 and 1032) differ sharply from the Paris drawings mentioned thus far. Assuming that they should indeed be dated Paris 1886, as was done in the 1970 *catalogue raisonné*, they fit in best with the earliest drawings (the small dark silhouettelike figures, the bare trees). They must be regarded as the expression of something that stands apart, the rendering of a strongly anecdotal subject that obviously had a special significance for Van Gogh. He embodied it first in the fairly large pencil-and-ink drawing 1031 and then redid the whole thing with pen and brush in a still larger format and heightened it with white and colored chalk (the use of colored chalk—which harks back to the Antwerp period—is one of my reasons for ascribing the drawing to Paris).

Of the three views of the city of Paris 1033, 1034, and 1035, the last is probably again a sheet from a sketchbook. It is somewhat more carefully detailed than the other two and is heightened with colored chalk. Emphasis is given to the caricaturelike figure of the fat woman who is described in a rhyming inscription: "De son métier elle ne faisait rien./Le soir elle baladait son chien./La Villette" ("At a calling she did not work./In the evening her dog she did walk"). I imagine that this was taken from a Paris ditty of the time, which might well have inspired Vincent to make the drawing. (La Villette is a quarter of Paris bordering on Montmartre.) Although 1033 is rather small (it was drawn on the border of a menu), it is charming and remarkably successful. Here, drawn in black ink enlivened with a bit of violet ink, we meet the same little groups of walkers that we know from other small sketches such as 1019, 1021, and 1022. The menu (which offers a choice of main dishes for about half a franc!) is dated April 8, 1886, and thus provides a good starting point for dating this and a number of related small sketches.

If only because of the format (15 by $20\frac{1}{2}$ inches), drawing 1034 is the most important of this group. It shows a *guinguette* (café in the suburbs), which Vincent also *painted* in the autumn (1178); it is seen here almost deserted in the chill of winter. The starkness

1026

1027

1028

1029

1030

1031

1032

1023 A Public Garden with People Walking in the Rain, F 1381 (reverse: 1024)
Pencil, 10 × 14 cm (3⅞ × 5½″)
Rijksmuseum Vincent van Gogh, Amsterdam

1024 Woman, Half-Length, F 1381v (reverse: 1023)
Pencil, 10 × 14 cm (3⅞ × 5½″)
Rijksmuseum Vincent van Gogh, Amsterdam

1025 Terrace of the Tuileries with People Walking, F 1383
Pencil, 10 × 16 cm (3⅞ × 6¼″)
Rijksmuseum Vincent van Gogh, Amsterdam

1026 Pond in a Park, F 1703v (reverse: 1083)
Blue chalk, 32 × 46 cm (12⅝ × 18⅛″)
Rijksmuseum Vincent van Gogh, Amsterdam

1027 Pond in a Park, F 1382
Black chalk, 6 × 10.5 cm (2⅜ × 4⅛″)
Rijksmuseum Vincent van Gogh, Amsterdam

1028 Walking Couple, F 1705
Pencil, black chalk, 11 × 8 cm (4⅜ × 3⅛″)
Rijksmuseum Vincent van Gogh, Amsterdam

1029 Walking Couple, F 992
Pencil, 11 × 9.5 cm (4⅜ × 3⅞″)
Rijksmuseum Vincent van Gogh, Amsterdam

1030 Quay on the Seine, F 1385
Pencil, 11 × 20 cm (4⅜ × 7⅞″)
Rijksmuseum Vincent van Gogh, Amsterdam

1031 Cemetery in the Rain, F 1399
Pencil, pen, 23 × 37 cm (9 × 14⅝″)
Albertina, Vienna

1032 Cemetery in the Rain, F 1399a
Pen, brush, colored chalk, heightened with white, 36.5 × 48 cm (14⅝ × 18⅞″)
Rijksmuseum Kröller-Müller, Otterlo

of the bare tables and benches and of the bizarre trunks and thin branches of the trees links this small work with some of the drawings of the parsonage garden in Nuenen in the wintertime. But the starkness is somewhat offset by the slightly mysterious atmosphere of the arbors and the presence of a few visitors in the background.

At Work at Cormon's

In a long series of drawings and some paintings (1036–88), we get an idea of what Vincent was doing at Cormon's studio. From the very first of these, it is apparent that they are a mixture of studies from a live model, from anatomical drawings, and from plaster casts. They must all have been made during the few months that Vincent worked at Cormon's—I will say more about the length of his stay at the studio later—and it is therefore virtually impossible to determine a chronological sequence within this group of studies. It would be logical to suppose that Vincent had begun by working from plaster casts and that only after becoming proficient at this would he have ventured to work with a live nude model. However, a careful study of the available data has led me to conclude that that was not the case. To understand this, one must first of all look at 1036. There can be no doubt that this represents two pieces of a single drawing depicting a standing female nude viewed from the rear. It is a drawing that Vincent, for some reason or other—probably it did not please him—had torn in two. On the reverse side there are two drawings: one (1048) of a standing male nude (with sketches of plaster casts), and the other (1051) a sketch of a plaster cast with top hat. It is clear that these two drawings were not made until after the paper had been separated into two sheets; in other words, they are of a later date than the drawing of the female nude. It thus appears that at least some of the plaster casts were drawn after a drawing from a live model had already been made. Furthermore, in an effort to introduce some order into the many drawings and painted studies made from plaster casts, I have grouped together the drawings made after each of the different models. (In the 1970 *catalogue raisonné*, they are to be found in random order in three different locations under F numbers 216–216h, 1363–66, and SD [Supplementary Drawings] 1697–1716.) I based my reasoning on the assumption that Vincent made all his drawings from one plaster cast before proceeding on to another plaster cast. Not only does this fit in with his frequent habit of producing "repetitions" or "variants" of a subject, but an actual demonstration of it can be seen on the right side of 1048, where he sketched the same plaster cast three times. There is, of course, *no way* of determining in what sequence he worked with the various plaster figures. Everything points to a considerable amount of "study" activity on Vincent's part as he devoted himself to one subject after another and covered his paper on both sides.

The drawings of the anatomical model provide us with clues to other subjects with which he was concerned either at the same time or a little later. The fact that the anatomical model and the four successive

1033

1034

1035

April–June 1886

1033 Boulevard with People Walking, F 1377
Sketch on the border of a menu, dated April 8, 1886
Pencil, pen, violet and black ink, 11 × 23 cm ($4\frac{3}{8} \times 9''$)
Rijksmuseum Vincent van Gogh, Amsterdam

1034 Terrace of a Café (La Guinguette), F 1407
Pen, pencil, heightened with white, 38 × 52 cm ($15 \times 20\frac{1}{2}''$)
Rijksmuseum Vincent van Gogh, Amsterdam

1035 Street with Woman Walking a Dog and with Other People, F 1704
Pen, colored chalk, 17 × 10 cm ($6\frac{3}{4} \times 3\frac{7}{8}''$)
Rijksmuseum Vincent van Gogh, Amsterdam

1036

1037

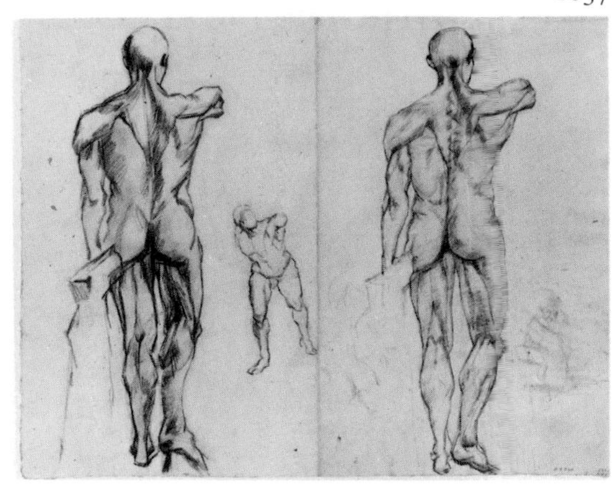

1038

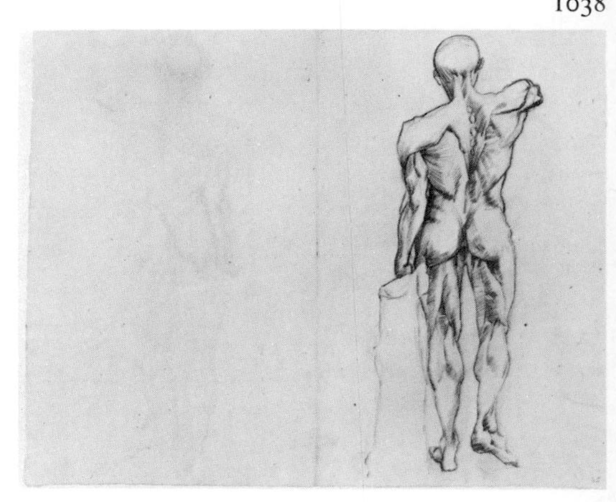

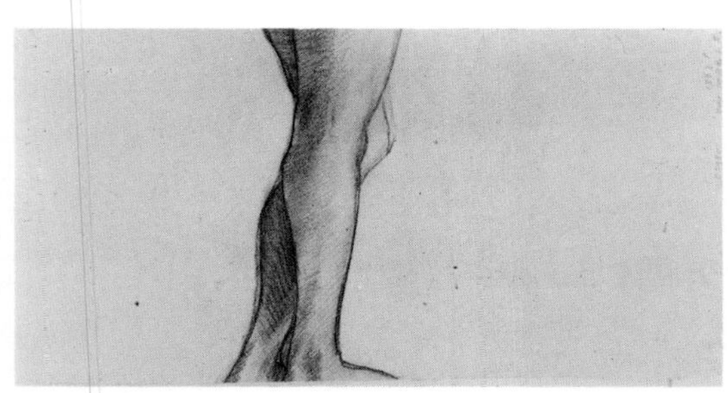

1039

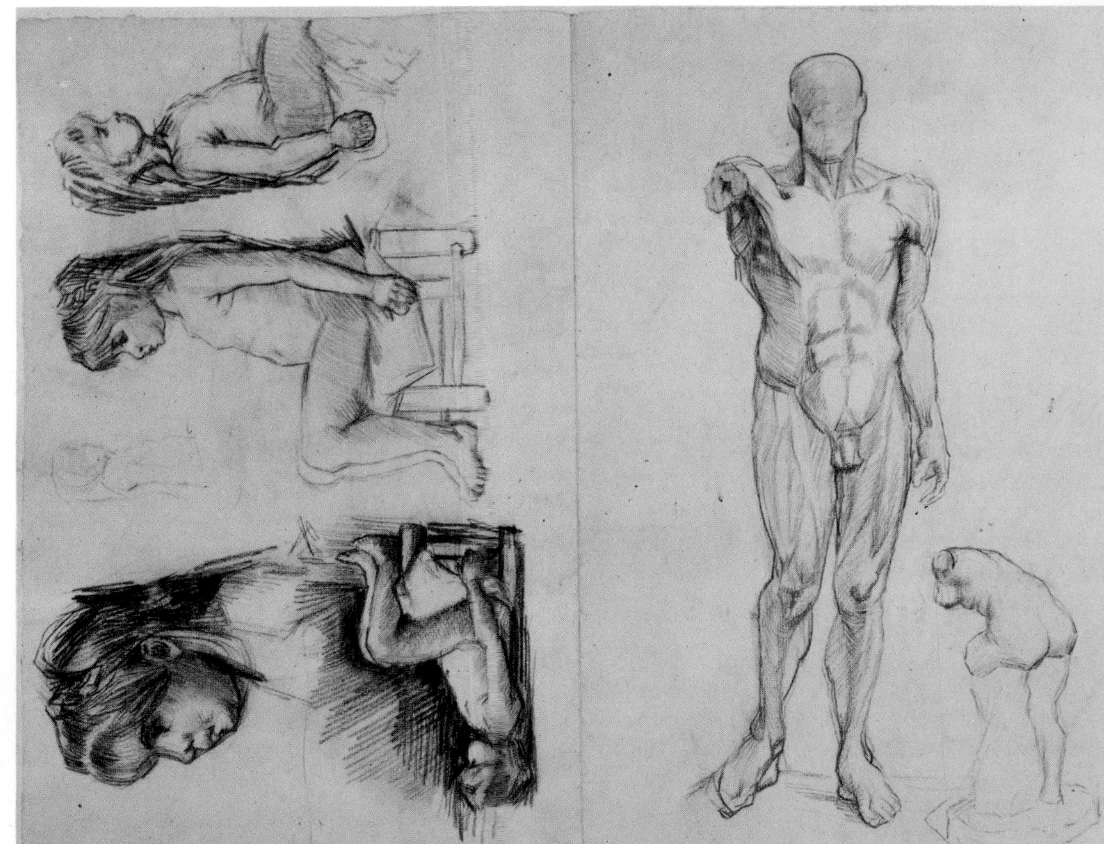

1040

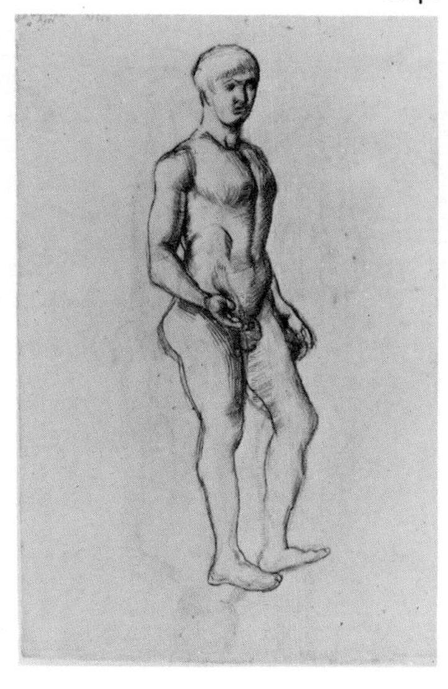

1041

1036 Female Nude, Standing, Upper Part, F1710 (reverse: 1048)
Lower Part, F1363fv (reverse: 1051)
Black chalk, 35 × 46 cm ($13\frac{3}{4} \times 18\frac{1}{8}''$) and 19 × 38 cm ($7\frac{1}{2} \times 15''$)
Rijksmuseum Vincent van Gogh, Amsterdam

1037 Drawing Model: the Muscles of the Male Body, Back (with Sketch of a Plaster Model), F1702 (reverse: 1038)
Black chalk, 47.5 × 63 cm ($18\frac{7}{8} \times 24\frac{3}{4}''$)
Rijksmuseum Vincent van Gogh, Amsterdam

1038 Drawing Model: the Muscles of the Male Body, Back, F1702v (reverse: 1037)
Black chalk, 47.5 × 63 cm ($18\frac{7}{8} \times 24\frac{3}{4}''$)
Rijksmuseum Vincent van Gogh, Amsterdam

1039 Drawing Model: the Muscles of the Male Body, Front (with Sketch of Plaster Statuette—Type A—and Five Sketches of Sitting Nude Girl), F1366 (reverse: 1044)
Black chalk, 47.5 × 61.5 cm ($18\frac{7}{8} \times 24\frac{3}{8}''$)
Rijksmuseum Vincent van Gogh, Amsterdam

1040 Nude Young Man, Standing, F1364dv (reverse: 1047)
Black chalk, 45 × 29 cm ($17\frac{3}{4} \times 11\frac{3}{8}''$)
Rijksmuseum Vincent van Gogh, Amsterdam

1041 Nude Young Man, Standing, Seen from the Back, F1364a
Black chalk, 47.5 × 30.5 cm ($18\frac{7}{8} \times 12''$)
Rijksmuseum Vincent van Gogh, Amsterdam

1042

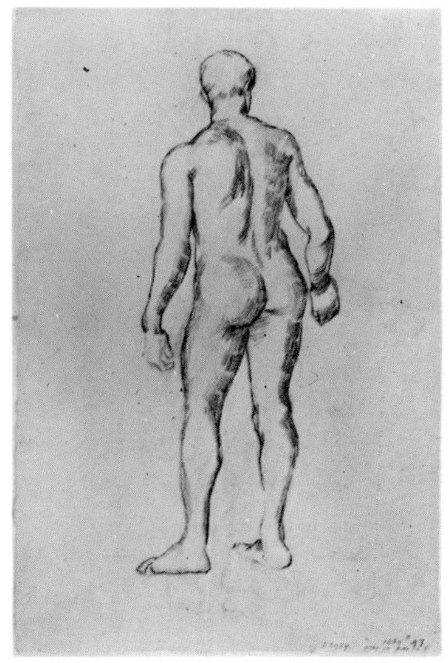

1043

1044

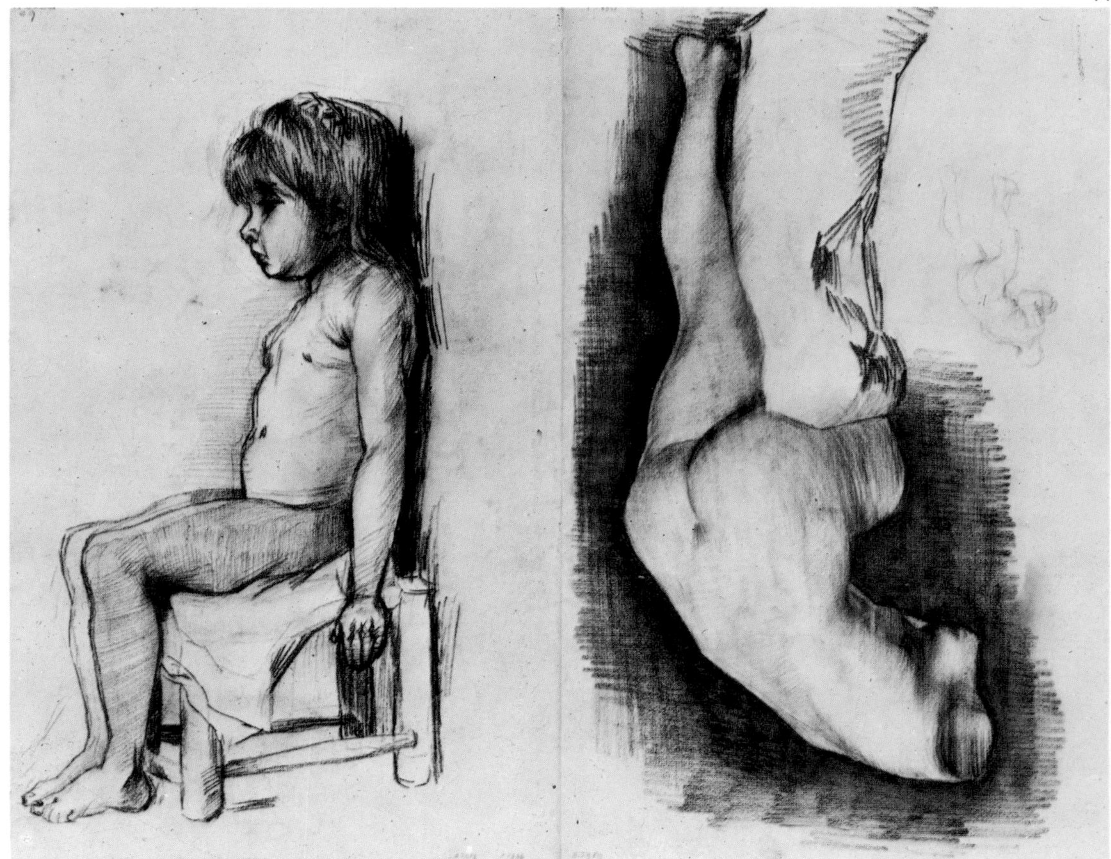

sketches of the nude girl in 1039 are on the same sheet of paper indicates that these two entirely different subjects were the focus of his attention at approximately the same time. These quick sketches of the nude child—a live model—were actually preliminary studies for the somewhat more detailed drawings of the child in 1043 and 1044 and for the painted study 1045, which may well have been the final objective of all these preliminary studies. Accordingly, there is good reason to believe that he did not put off his *painting* activity at Cormon's until the end of all his *drawing* activity, but rather that a subject was sometimes started in oils after the way had been prepared for it by a series of drawings.

The Plaster Casts

An examination of the studies from plaster casts shows that some of the models served for only a single drawing, whereas others were drawn and painted by Vincent several times. The ones used most often are four plaster casts of a female torso that I shall refer to as Types A to D.

Some exist in painted form while others do not. Plaster cast B, for instance, was painted by Vincent three times (1058, 1059, and 1060) in approximately the same posture as sketch 1057 and always with a blue background—blue-green, sky blue, and dark blue, respectively. It is probable that painting 1060 was intended as the final version of 1059 (colorplate XIV, page 222), in a format twice as large. Painting 1058, while smaller than 1060, is somewhat more carefully detailed and the contrasts are not so sharp.

Plaster cast D similarly appears in three drawings and two painted studies: 1070–74. It is a female torso, bending to the right, with the left thigh merely a stump and the right leg, minus the foot, resting on a pedestal. In 1071, a study in oils on a blue background, the figure is viewed from the front. These figures are strikingly reminiscent of the lumpy, almost caricaturelike features of some of the nudes from the Antwerp period. This is less evident in 1072, a study in oils—in which there is also a fair amount of drawing—on a green-gray background. Sketches 1073 and 1074, done on both sides of a small sheet of paper, probably from a sketchbook, do not really fit with this series of sketches from Cormon's studio. They seem to have been drawn in a mischievous mood, perhaps a mood in which Vincent felt he had more than enough of drawing from plaster casts—as he had when he worked with his teacher Mauve (Letter 189)—because, like a recalcitrant schoolboy, he has added female sexual characteristics to the untidy drawing of the small plaster cast, again introducing an absurd element. In 1073 he also covered the page with some undecipherable notes.

Incidentally, it may be noted that the composition sketch of the Montmartre hill at the edge of 1053 might indicate that even in the Cormon period, Vincent was working on that particular landscape, but it does not correspond to any painting that we know.

An exceptional attention to detail is demonstrated in the drawings of feet in 1083, and here again Vincent's high degree of professionalism is striking. Finally, there is a rough sketch of a nude in 1086, but this unfinished and obviously partially erased drawing has been included here merely for the sake of completeness. Also, the hastily sketched figures sitting around a table seem to be a somewhat later addition. The *catalogue raisonné* links them with a series of sketches of musicians (1153 and following; see also page 252). Among the work done at Cormon's I also include two drawings of a clothed model (1087 and 1088), although here we are treading on unsure ground. The figure in 1088 certainly makes one think of a posing model; the seated figure might also be

1042 Nude Young Man, Standing, Seen from the Back, F 1364bv (reverse: 1046)
Black chalk, 47.5 × 31 cm ($18\frac{7}{8} \times 12\frac{1}{4}''$)
Rijksmuseum Vincent van Gogh, Amsterdam

1043 Nude Girl, Sitting, F 1367
Black chalk, 30.5 × 23.5 cm ($12\frac{1}{4} \times 9\frac{1}{2}''$)
Rijksmuseum Vincent van Gogh, Amsterdam

1044 Nude Girl, Sitting, and Plaster Statuette (Type A), F 1366v (reverse: 1039)
Black chalk, 47.5 × 61.5 cm ($18\frac{7}{8} \times 24\frac{3}{8}''$)
Rijksmuseum Vincent van Gogh, Amsterdam

1045 Nude Girl, Sitting, F 215
27 × 22 cm ($10\frac{5}{8} \times 8\frac{5}{8}''$)
Rijksmuseum Vincent van Gogh, Amsterdam

1045

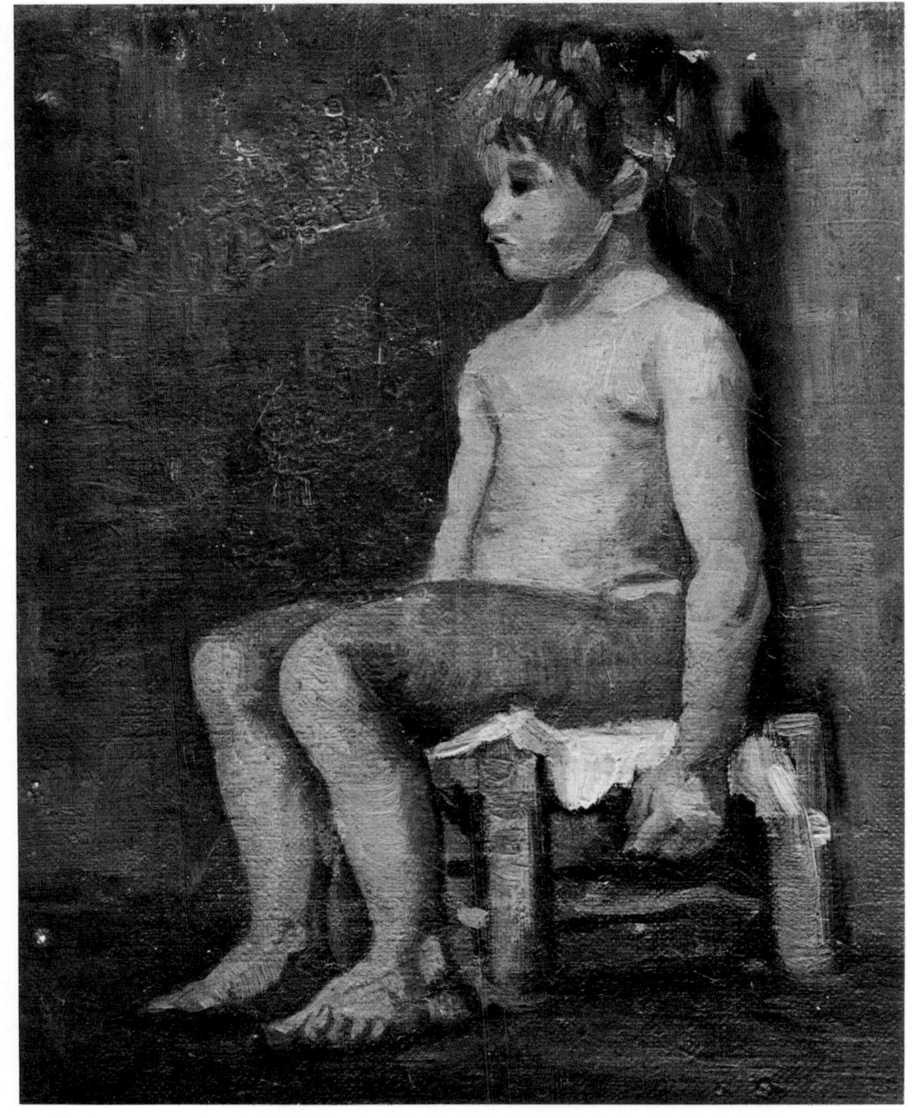

1046

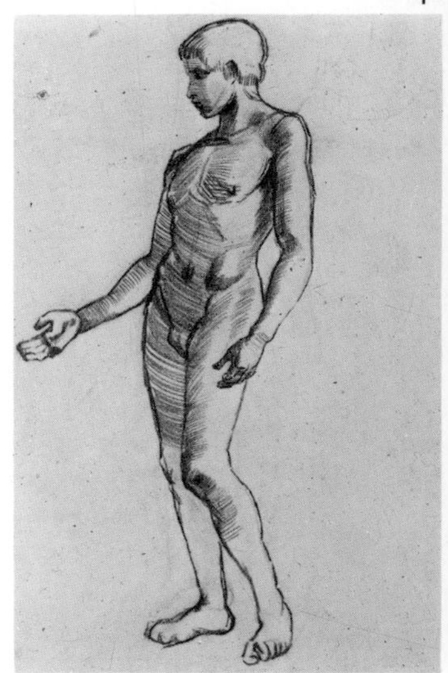

1047

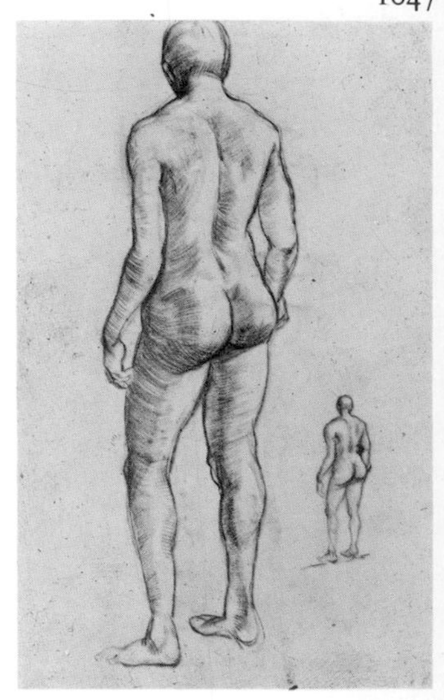

1048

1049

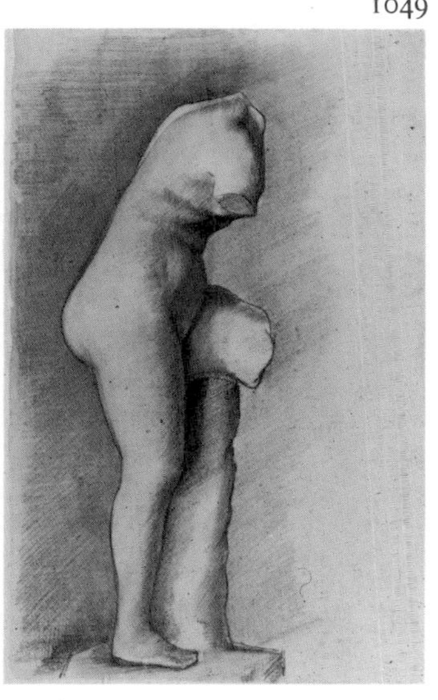

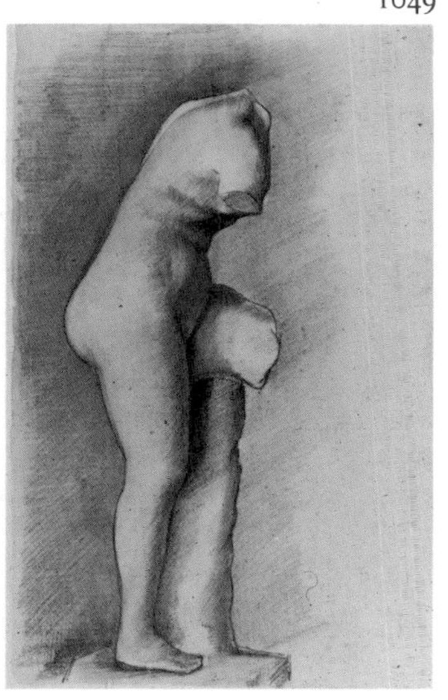

1050

1051

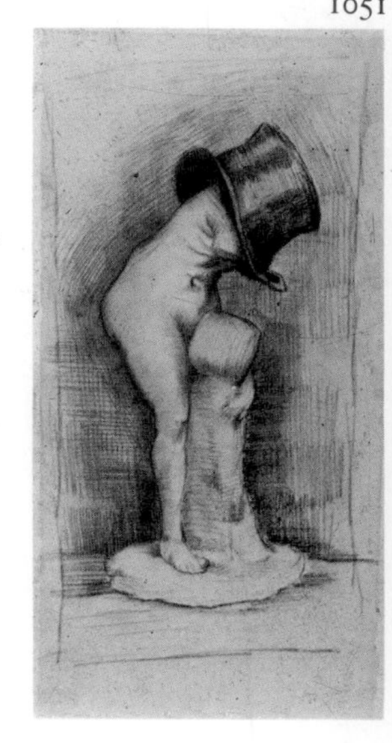

1046 Nude Young Man, Standing, F 1364b (reverse: 1042)
Black chalk, 47.5 × 31 cm ($18\frac{7}{8} \times 12\frac{1}{4}$")
Rijksmuseum Vincent van Gogh, Amsterdam

1047 Nude Young Man, Standing, Seen from the Back (with Small Sketch of the Same), F 1364d (reverse: 1040)
Black chalk, 45 × 29 cm ($17\frac{3}{4} \times 11\frac{3}{8}$")
Rijksmuseum Vincent van Gogh, Amsterdam

1048 Nude Young Man, Standing, Seen from the Back (with Three Small Sketches of Plaster Statuette—Type A), F 1710v (reverse: 1036)
Black chalk, 46 × 35 cm ($18\frac{1}{8} \times 13\frac{3}{4}$")
Rijksmuseum Vincent van Gogh, Amsterdam

1049 Plaster Statuette (Type A), F 1363e
Black chalk, 48 × 31 cm ($18\frac{7}{8} \times 12\frac{1}{4}$")
Rijksmuseum Vincent van Gogh, Amsterdam

1050 Plaster Statuette (Type A), F 1709v (reverse: 1066)
Pencil, 47.5 × 31 cm ($18\frac{7}{8} \times 12\frac{1}{4}$")
Rijksmuseum Vincent van Gogh, Amsterdam

1051 Plaster Statuette (Type A), with Top Hat, F 1363f (reverse: 1036)
Black chalk, 38 × 19 cm ($15 \times 7\frac{1}{2}$")
Rijksmuseum Vincent van Gogh, Amsterdam

a somewhat later drawing done by Vincent as a portrait. At all events, this latter work in particular gives witness to a masterly level of craftsmanship.

Cormon's Studio

Now that we have seen the result of Vincent's activity at Cormon's studio, it is fitting to look into what is known about the atmosphere in which that activity took place. There is only one short statement by Vincent himself concerning the Cormon period. It is to be found in a letter Vincent wrote (in English) to the British painter Livens, whom he had known in Antwerp (Letter 459*a*): "I have been in Cormon's studio for three or four months but I did not find that so useful as I expected it to be. It may be my fault however, anyhow I left there too as I left Antwerp and since [then] I [have] worked alone, and fancy that since I feel my own self more." The earliest account from others comes from Emile Bernard, who, as a nineteen-year-old fellow pupil, had seen Vincent at work at Cormon's and had become one of his best friends. Shortly after Vincent's death he wrote in an obituary notice: "I met Vincent van Gogh for the first time at Cormon's studio; and what laughter there was behind his back, which he deigned not to notice."*

This impression is confirmed by the much later account from another fellow pupil, François Gauzi. It appears in a charming little book of reminiscences of Toulouse-Lautrec *(My Friend Toulouse-Lautrec)*, which, although not published until 1954 (the English translation was published in 1957), had been written much earlier, in 1933, shortly before Gauzi's death. Writing on Lautrec and Van Gogh he begins: "In March 1886, Vincent Van Gogh suddenly left Anvers to join his brother in Paris, and in June he entered Cormon's. At that time he insisted on being called by his Christian name, and for ages we were in the dark as to his real name. He was an excellent fellow whom it was necessary to leave in peace. He came from the North, and did not appreciate Parisian humour, while the studio's practical jokers avoided him as a victim—they were rather frightened of him."†

A few years after Vincent's death, when Bernard wrote about him again, he once more reverted to the times at Cormon's: "At the noon hour when all the pupils were out and the studio had become a sort of study cell. He is sitting there in front of an antique plaster cast copying the beautiful contours with angelic patience. He wants to master those contours, those masses, those reliefs. He corrects himself, begins passionately anew, rubs out and finally makes a hole in his

Les Hommes d'Aujourd'hui, vol. VIII, no. 390 (1891).

†P. 12. Less reliable is the next part of his account, the anecdote about what is supposed to have been Van Gogh's first painting at Cormon's. It was the study of a nude in which he had replaced the stool on which the model was seated by a couch draped with a bright blue cover. A note by the publisher says that this "undoubtedly" refers to the reclining nude 1212 (F328), but this painting has nothing to do with the Cormon period; it is dated 1887 by Vincent himself. After so many years, Gauzi's memory must have played him false so far as this anecdote is concerned.

1052

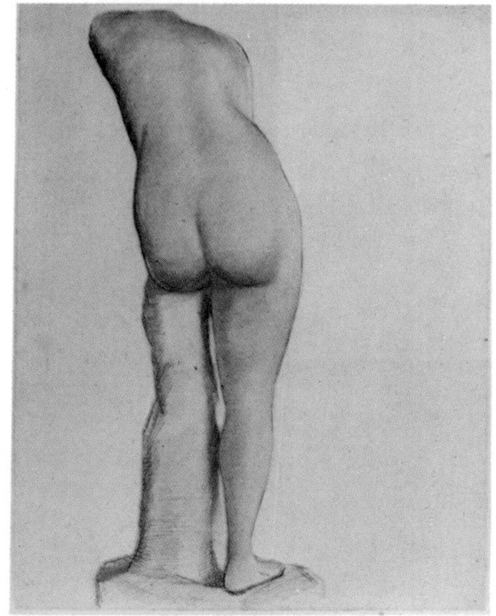

1053

1054

1055

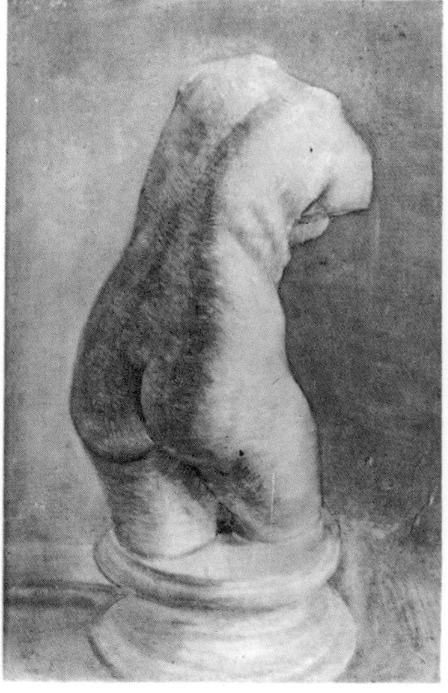

1056

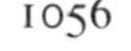

1057

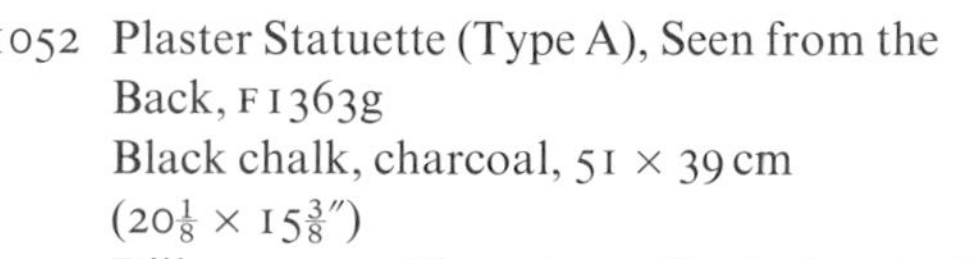

1052 Plaster Statuette (Type A), Seen from the Back, F1363g
Black chalk, charcoal, 51 × 39 cm (20⅛ × 15⅜″)
Rijksmuseum Vincent van Gogh, Amsterdam

1053 Plaster Statuette (Type B) and Composition Sketch of Landscape, F1712v (reverse: 1056)
Black chalk, pen, 32 × 24.5 cm (12⅝ × 9⅞″)
Rijksmuseum Vincent van Gogh, Amsterdam

1054 Plaster Statuette (Type B), Seen from the Back, F216a
Cardboard, 47 × 38 cm (18½ × 15″)
Rijksmuseum Vincent van Gogh, Amsterdam

1055 Plaster Statuette (Type B), Seen from the Back, F216g
40.5 × 27 cm (16⅛ × 10⅝″)
Rijksmuseum Vincent van Gogh, Amsterdam

1056 Plaster Statuette (Type B), F1712 (reverse: 1053)
Black chalk, 32 × 24.5 cm (12⅝ × 9⅞″)
Rijksmuseum Vincent van Gogh, Amsterdam

1057 Plaster Statuette (Type B), F1711v (reverse: 1062)
Black chalk, 31.5 × 24.5 cm (12⅝ × 9⅞″)
Rijksmuseum Vincent van Gogh, Amsterdam

1058

1059

1060

1061

1062

1063

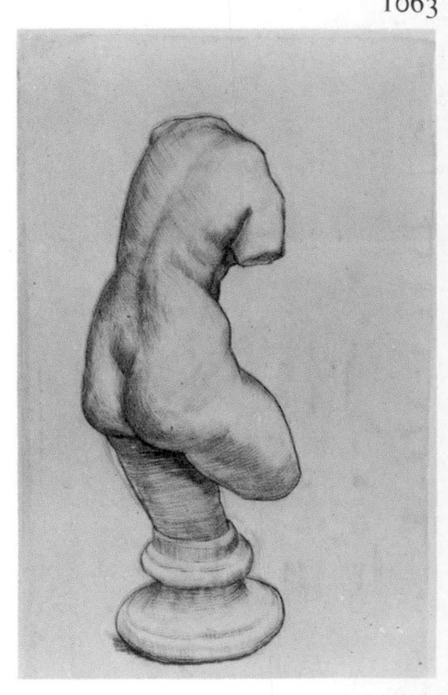

1064

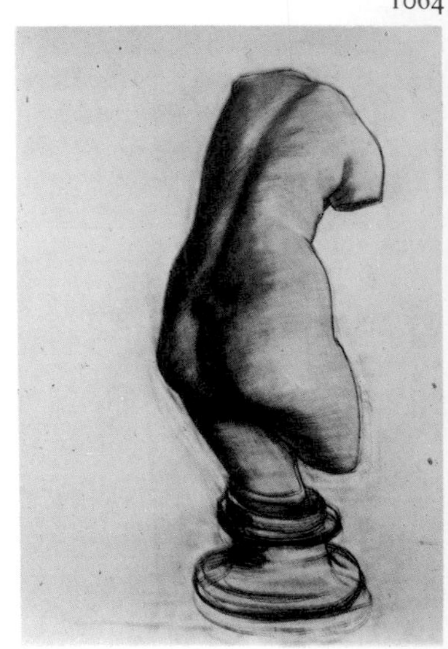

1058 Plaster Statuette (Type B), F216h
41 × 32.5 cm (16⅛ × 13″)
Rijksmuseum Vincent van Gogh, Amsterdam

1059 Plaster Statuette (Type B), F216j
Cardboard, 35 × 27 cm (13¾ × 10⅝″)
Rijksmuseum Vincent van Gogh, Amsterdam
Colorplate XIV, p. 222

1060 Plaster Statuette (Type B), F216b
Cardboard, 47 × 38 cm (18½ × 15″)
Rijksmuseum Vincent van Gogh, Amsterdam

1061 Plaster Statuette (Type B), F1713 (reverse: 1077)
Black chalk, 32 × 24.5 cm (12⅝ × 9⅞″)
Rijksmuseum Vincent van Gogh, Amsterdam

1062 Plaster Statuette (Type B), F1711 (reverse: 1057)
Black chalk, 31.5 × 24.5 cm (12⅝ × 9⅞″)
Rijksmuseum Vincent van Gogh, Amsterdam

1063 Plaster Statuette (Type C), Seen from the Back, F1363av (reverse: 1014)
Black chalk, 47 × 30.5 cm (18½ × 12¼″)
Rijksmuseum Vincent van Gogh, Amsterdam

1064 Plaster Statuette (Type C), Seen from the Back, F1708 (reverse: 1065)
Charcoal, 61 × 45 cm (24 × 17¾″)
Rijksmuseum Vincent van Gogh, Amsterdam

sheet by his vigorous use of the India rubber."*

The most detailed and vivid reminiscences of the Cormon studio are to be found in the autobiography of the British painter A.S. Hartrick, who also became friendly with Van Gogh. Although he did not arrive at Cormon's until November 1886, when Vincent was no longer there, things would not have changed very much in the meantime. The book also contains the reproduction of an excellent portrait that Hartrick made of Vincent.†

Hartrick's Reminiscences

In the chapter on Van Gogh, Hartrick relates that upon his return to Paris from Pont-Aven in Brittany in the autumn of 1886, he had become acquainted with the Australian painter John P. Russell.

"He had been working for some time in the Atelier Cormon, which was situated in the Clichy quarter, where, I learnt, were the homes of the painters with new ideas. Russell also had his studio in the neighbourhood.

"Here it was, then, that guided by pure chance I first set eyes on Van Gogh, or 'Vincent' as he was generally known and signed himself in Paris, because the French could not pronounce Van Gogh. It so happened that he, too, had been working *chez* Cormon, up to the summer of 1886, when that atelier was suddenly closed down by Cormon himself on account of a disturbance among the pupils there. In spite of certain quite erroneous theories, which appeared in the press when his work was first exhibited in this country, that Van Gogh was of robust appearance (to fit the fury of his painting, no doubt), I can affirm that to my eye Van Gogh was a rather weedy little man, with pinched features, red hair and beard, and a light blue eye. He had an extraordinary way of pouring out sentences, if he got started, in Dutch, English and French, then glancing back at you over his shoulder, and hissing through his teeth. In fact, when thus excited, he looked more than a little mad; at other times he was apt to be morose, as if suspicious. To tell the truth, I fancy the French were civil to him largely because his brother Theodore was employed by Goupil and Company and so bought pictures" (pages 39–40).

After a short summary of Vincent's life up to the Antwerp period, Hartrick continues: "Soon after this he entered the Atelier Cormon, most probably because it was near his brother's flat in the rue Lepic. He was now about thirty-three years of age, and though he had had no success in selling any of his work, there is no doubt he had at last come to an environment in which he could expand. I saw him first in Russell's studio in the Impasse Hélène, Clichy quarter. Russell had just painted that portrait of him in a striped blue suit, looking over his shoulder, which is now, I believe, in the Modern Gallery of Amsterdam, together with the Van Gogh

Lettres de Vincent van Gogh à Emile Bernard (1911), p. 10.

† A. S. Hartrick, *A Painter's Pilgrimage through Fifty Years* (1939). The portrait is reproduced in black and white in the Dutch edition of letters, in color in the English and French editions.

1065

1066

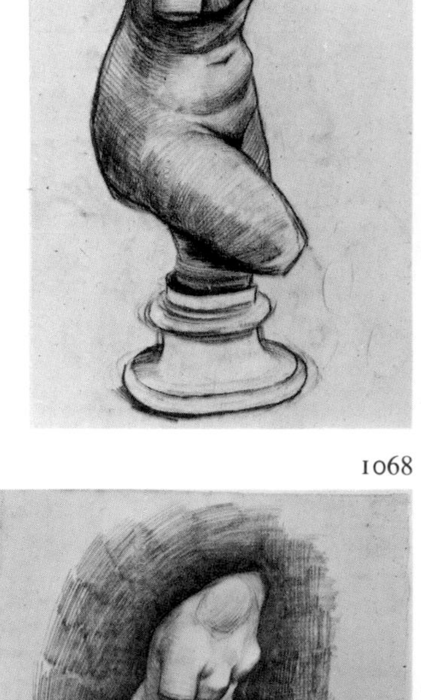

1067

1068

1069

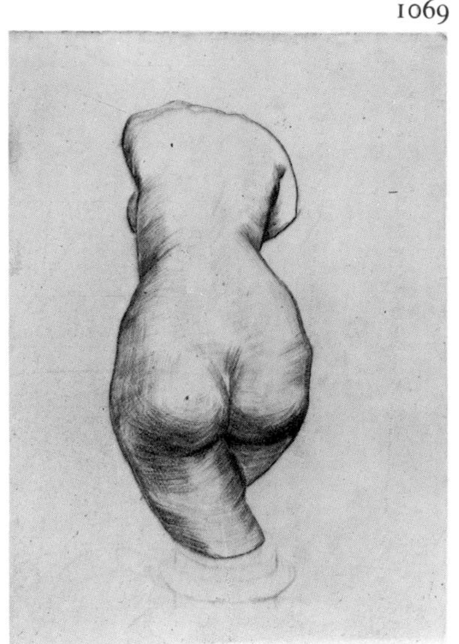

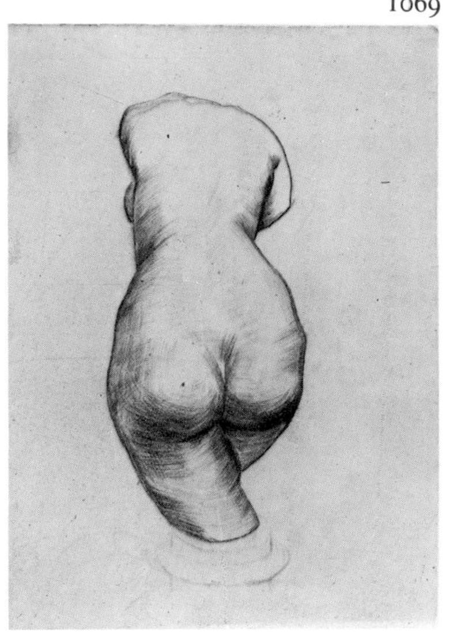

1070

1065 Plaster Statuette (Type C), F 1708v (reverse: 1064)
Charcoal, 61 × 45 cm (24 × $17\frac{3}{4}$″)
Rijksmuseum Vincent van Gogh, Amsterdam

1066 Plaster Statuette (Type C), F 1709 (reverse: 1050)
Black chalk, 47.5 × 31 cm ($18\frac{7}{8}$ × $12\frac{1}{4}$″)
Rijksmuseum Vincent van Gogh, Amsterdam

1067 Plaster Statuette (Type C), F 1707
Pencil, 49 × 31.5 cm ($19\frac{1}{4}$ × $12\frac{5}{8}$″)
Rijksmuseum Vincent van Gogh, Amsterdam

1068 Plaster Statuette (Type C), F 1371
Black chalk, 48 × 31.5 cm ($18\frac{7}{8}$ × $12\frac{5}{8}$″)
Rijksmuseum Vincent van Gogh, Amsterdam

1069 Plaster Statuette (Type C), Seen from the Back, F 1363b
Black chalk, 43 × 31 cm ($16\frac{7}{8}$ × $12\frac{1}{4}$″)
Rijksmuseum Vincent van Gogh, Amsterdam

1070 Plaster Statuette (Type D), F 1363c (reverse: 1079)
Black chalk, charcoal, 30 × 24.5 cm ($11\frac{3}{4}$ × $9\frac{7}{8}$″)
Rijksmuseum Vincent van Gogh, Amsterdam

1071 Plaster Statuette (Type D), F 216d
Cardboard, 35.5 × 27.5 cm ($14\frac{1}{8}$ × 11″)
Rijksmuseum Vincent van Gogh, Amsterdam

1071

1072

1073

1075

1074

1076

1077

1072 Plaster Statuette (Type D), F216i
Cardboard, 32.5 × 24 cm (13 × $9\frac{1}{2}$″)
Rijksmuseum Vincent van Gogh, Amsterdam

1073 Plaster Statuette (Type D), Page of Scribbles, F1716 (reverse: 1074)
Blue and black chalk, pencil, 20.5 × 13 cm ($8\frac{1}{4}$ × $5\frac{1}{8}$″)
Rijksmuseum Vincent van Gogh, Amsterdam

1074 Plaster Statuette (Type D), Page of Scribbles, F1716v (reverse: 1073)
Pencil, black chalk, 20.5 × 13 cm ($8\frac{1}{4}$ × $5\frac{1}{8}$″)
Rijksmuseum Vincent van Gogh, Amsterdam

1075 Plaster Statuette of Kneeling Man, F1363d
Pencil, pen, 32.5 × 24.5 cm (13 × $9\frac{7}{8}$″)
Rijksmuseum Vincent van Gogh, Amsterdam

1076 Plaster Statuette of Kneeling Man, F216f
Cardboard, 35.5 × 26.5 cm ($14\frac{1}{8}$ × $10\frac{5}{8}$″)
Rijksmuseum Vincent van Gogh, Amsterdam

1077 Plaster Statuette (Man) and Sketch of a Sitting Woman, F1713v (reverse: 1061)
Black chalk, 24.5 × 32 cm ($9\frac{7}{8}$ × $12\frac{5}{8}$″)
Rijksmuseum Vincent van Gogh, Amsterdam

Collection there. It was an admirable likeness, more so than any of those by himself or Gauguin" (page 42).

Still Lifes of Flowers

We have a firsthand description of Vincent's condition and activities in a letter Theo wrote their mother, probably late in July 1886: "We are fortunately all right in our new apartment. You wouldn't recognize Vincent so much he has changed and it strikes others even more than me. He has had a major operation to his mouth, for he had nearly lost all his teeth as a result of the bad state of his stomach. The doctor says that he has now completely got over it. He is progressing tremendously in his work and this is proved by the fact that he is becoming successful. He has not yet sold paintings for money, but is exchanging his work for other pictures. In that way we obtain a fine collection which, of course, also has a certain value. There is a dealer in pictures who has now taken four of his paintings and has promised him to arrange for an exhibition of his work next year. He is mainly painting flowers—with the object to put a more lively colour into his next pictures. He is also much more cheerful than in the past and people like him here. To give you proof: hardly a day passes or he is asked to come to the studios of wellknown painters, or they come to see him. He also has acquaintances who give him a collection of flowers every week which may serve him as models. If they are able to keep it up I think his difficult times are over and he will be able to make it by himself."*

Since what Vincent was "mainly painting" at the end of July was flowers and he had been doing so for some time, he must have started on them directly after the Cormon period, that is, May or perhaps June. This means that the earliest of the long flower series should be dated May–July, though some might date from even earlier. The still lifes 1091–94 would, in my opinion—particularly because of the varieties of flowers depicted—belong to the works painted in the spring. The dating of 1091 is uncertain, as is noted in the 1970 *catalogue raisonné* (in his 1928 catalogue De la Faille ascribed the piece to Nuenen; Vanbeselaere transferred it to Paris; and the editors of the 1970 De la Faille left it in Nuenen with the reservation mentioned). If the flowers portrayed in this simple but charming little painting are really Christmas roses—as the piece is always described—then Vincent must have painted it very soon after his arrival in Paris, say in March.

I have placed two self-portraits (1089 and 1090) between the work of the Cormon period and the still lifes of flowers. Expert opinion on their date has attributed them alternately to the Nuenen and Antwerp periods. In accord with the 1970 *catalogue raisonné*, I assume that they were done in Paris, but that they are the earliest of the long series of self-portraits we know from that period. In many respects these canvases remind us of the Nuenen style with its dark colors and chiaroscuro effects. However, the way Van Gogh is pictured here makes it impossible for me to imagine him either in Nuenen (where he was often criticized for his unconventional appearance) or in Antwerp. While he was still at the academy in Antwerp, his fellow student Victor Hageman expressed surprise at his strange appearance in a blue smock like those worn by Flemish cattle salesmen and a fur cap (according to Piérard).† Now the felt

*The relevant part of this letter was published for the first time in *Vincent*, vol. III, no. 2 (1974). Two short passages had been quoted—rather freely, incidentally—in Mrs. van Gogh-Bonger's "Memoir" to *The Complete Letters*, p. xli. The beginning of the letter, with the date, is missing, but to judge from the text itself the letter must have been written shortly after the move to the new quarters, thus late in July 1886.

†Piérard, *The Tragic Life of Vincent van Gogh* (1925). p. 92.

1078

1079

1080

1081

1082

1078 Plaster Statuette (Man), F216e
Cardboard, 35 × 27 cm (13¾ × 10⅝″)
Rijksmuseum Vincent van Gogh, Amsterdam

1079 Plaster Statuette of Male Nude and Smaller Sketch of the Same, F1363cv (reverse: 1070)
Black chalk, 30 × 24.5 cm (11¾ × 9⅞″)
Rijksmuseum Vincent van Gogh, Amsterdam

1080 Plaster Statuette of "The Discus Thrower," Seen from the Back, F1364e
Black chalk, 56 × 44 cm (22 × 17⅜″)
Rijksmuseum Vincent van Gogh, Amsterdam

1081 Plaster Copy of a Bust by Antonio del Pollaiuolo, F1701 (reverse: 1085)
Charcoal, black chalk, 61.5 × 47.5 cm (24⅜ × 18⅞″)
Rijksmuseum Vincent van Gogh, Amsterdam

1083

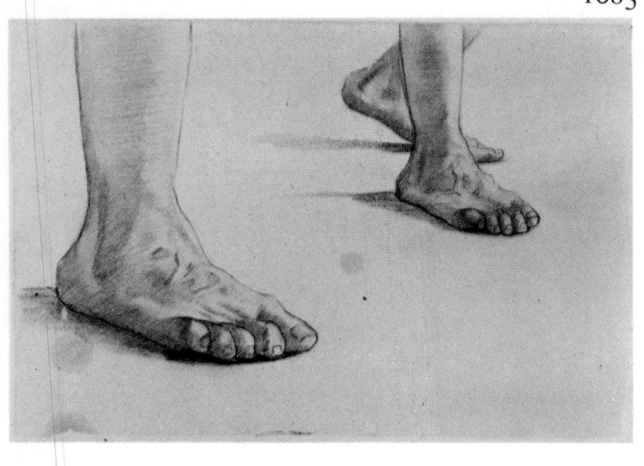

1084

1085

1086

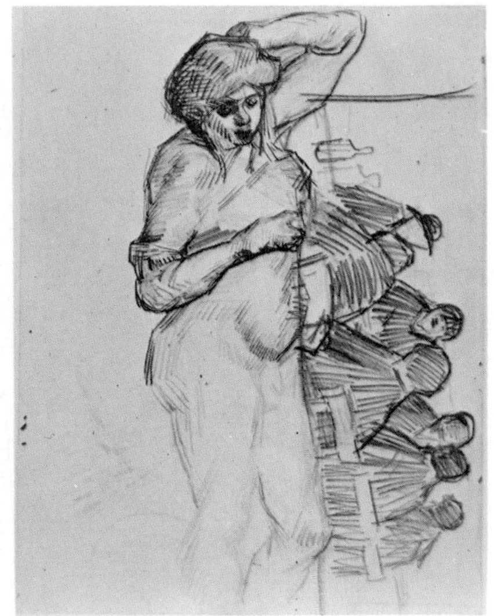

1088

1087

1082 Plaster Statuette of a Horse, F216c
Cardboard, 33.5 × 41 cm ($13\frac{3}{8} \times 16\frac{1}{8}''$)
Rijksmuseum Vincent van Gogh, Amsterdam

1083 Studies of a Foot and of a Pair of Feet, F1703 (reverse: 1026)
Black chalk, 32 × 46 cm ($12\frac{5}{8} \times 18\frac{1}{8}''$)
Rijksmuseum Vincent van Gogh, Amsterdam

1084 Male Nude, Standing, F1364c
Pencil, charcoal, washed, 48.5 × 31 cm ($19\frac{1}{4} \times 12\frac{1}{4}''$)
Rijksmuseum Vincent van Gogh, Amsterdam

1085 Nude Man, Sitting on a Stool, F1701v (reverse: 1081)
Black chalk, 61.5 × 47.5 cm ($24\frac{3}{8} \times 18\frac{7}{8}''$)
Rijksmuseum Vincent van Gogh, Amsterdam

1086 Sketch of a Nude and Figures around a Table, F1365
Dark blue ink, pencil, blue chalk, 35 × 25.5 cm ($13\frac{3}{4} \times 10\frac{1}{4}''$)
Rijksmuseum Vincent van Gogh, Amsterdam

1087 Sitting Man (Dressed Model), F1370
Black chalk, 51 × 39.5 cm ($20\frac{1}{8} \times 15\frac{3}{4}''$)
Rijksmuseum Vincent van Gogh, Amsterdam

1088 Standing Man (Dressed Model), Seen from the Back, F1706
Pencil, black chalk, 50 × 39 cm ($19\frac{5}{8} \times 15\frac{3}{8}''$)
Rijksmuseum Vincent van Gogh, Amsterdam

hat seems to indicate that he had adapted himself to his brother's environment. The fact of that adaptation is documented not only by the later self-portraits but also by Hartrick's reminiscences: "When in Paris he did not appear so poverty-stricken to me as one would suppose from the various tales written of him. He dressed quite well and in an ordinary way, better than many in the atelier" (page 45).

While these two self-portraits—and a few others—can be regarded as a continuation of the mastery achieved in Brabant, the still lifes of flowers, on the other hand, stand in stark contrast to them as attempts to break new ground. Van Gogh himself, in what he wrote to his friend Livens (Letter 459*a*), has left us in no doubt on this score (although the exact date of the letter is not known, the approximation "August–October 1886" given in *The Complete Letters* seems acceptable): "And now for what regards what I myself have been doing, I have lacked money for paying models else I had entirely given myself to figure painting. But I have made a series of colour studies in painting, simply flowers, red poppies, blue corn flowers and myosotis, white and rose roses, yellow chrysanthemums —seeking oppositions of blue with orange, red and green, yellow and violet seeking *les tons rompus et neutres* to harmonise brutal extremes. Trying to render intense colour and not a grey harmony."

Vincent's Painter Friends

Although Vincent had already written a great deal about colors and color oppositions even in the Nuenen period, he was now systematically engaged in trying to achieve bright colors and intense contrasts. In doing this, he was of course greatly influenced by the new art that he saw about him. In the sentence before the preceding quotation, he wrote: "In Antwerp I did not even know what the impressionists were, now I have seen them, and though *not* being one of the club yet I have much admired certain impressionists' pictures —*Degas* nude figure—*Claude Monet* landscape." What is striking here is that he mentions only Degas and Monet. There were certainly many other influences that came into play. Theo's letter of the end of July in which he spoke of Vincent's almost daily visits to the studios of well-known painters, who in their turn also came to see him, leaves us in no doubt on this point.

It would be useful to examine somewhat more closely the position of the two brothers in the Paris art world. As far as Theo is concerned, his widow wrote in her "Memoir" in *The Complete Letters:* "His own work was very strenuous and exhausting, he had made the gallery on the Boulevard Montmartre a centre of the impressionists; there were Monet, Sisley, Pissarro and Raffaëlli, Degas—who exhibited nowhere else—Seurat, etc. But to introduce that work to the public, which filled the small entresol every afternoon from five until seven, what discussions, what endless debates, had to be held. On the other hand, how he had to defend the rights of the young painters against *ces messieurs*, as Vincent always called the heads of the firm" (page xli). There is no reason to doubt the accuracy of this account, but one should bear in mind that it describes the situation as it existed somewhat later than the time of Vincent's arrival in Paris. A good insight into Theo van Gogh's position has been provided by John Rewald on the basis of his examination of the books of Goupil—which had been in the hands of Boussod and Valadon since 1875. Rewald found that in the two years before Vincent's arrival, Theo had sold a total of four paintings by Impressionists; in 1884 one Pissarro; in 1885 one Sisley, one Monet, and one Renoir. For the entire year 1886 Rewald discovered only one sale, that

1089

1090

1091

1089 Self-Portrait with Dark Felt Hat, F208a
41 × 32.5 cm (16⅛ × 13″)
Rijksmuseum Vincent van Gogh, Amsterdam

1090 Self-Portrait with Dark Felt Hat in Front of the Easel, F181
45.5 × 37.5 cm (18⅛ × 15″)
Rijksmuseum Vincent van Gogh, Amsterdam

1091 Glass with Christmas Roses, F199
Canvas on panel, 31 × 22.5 cm (12¼ × 9″)
Location unknown

1092 Fritillarias, F214
38 × 55 cm (15 × 21⅝″)
Location unknown

1092

1093

1094

1095 1096

1097

1098

1093 Bowl of Pansies, F 244
46 × 55 cm ($18\frac{1}{8} \times 21\frac{5}{8}''$)
Rijksmuseum Vincent van Gogh, Amsterdam

1094 Scabiosa and Ranunculus, F 666
26 × 20 cm ($10\frac{1}{4} \times 7\frac{7}{8}''$)
Location unknown

1095 The Roofs of Paris, F 1388
Brownish-black chalk, heightened with white,
24.5 × 31.5 cm ($9\frac{7}{8} \times 12\frac{5}{8}''$)
Rijksmuseum Vincent van Gogh, Amsterdam

1096 The Roofs of Paris and Notre-Dame, F 1389
Charcoal, black, white, and red chalk,
24.5 × 31.5 cm ($9\frac{1}{2} \times 12\frac{5}{8}''$)
Location unknown

1097 View of Paris with the Opéra, F 1390
Black, white, and brownish-red chalk,
22.5 × 30 cm ($9 \times 11\frac{3}{4}''$)
Rijksmuseum Vincent van Gogh, Amsterdam

1098 View of Paris with the Panthéon, F 1387
Red, black, and white chalk, 22.5 × 30 cm
($9 \times 11\frac{3}{4}''$)
Rijksmuseum Vincent van Gogh, Amsterdam

of a Manet, but in 1887 there was clearly much more activity; not only did Theo manage to sell two Pissarros, four or five Sisleys, one Renoir, one Gauguin, and no fewer than eight Manets, but he also managed to get hold of works by these and other painters in order to exhibit them on the entresol.* Vincent, by his enthusiasm for the new form of painting and the friends he soon made among the artists, doubtless contributed in large measure to making the store on the Boulevard Montmartre in fact "a center of the impressionists."

Theo greatly appreciated this, as is apparent from several frank statements he made. February 24, 1888, after Vincent had left for Arles, he wrote his sister Wil: "Through him I got to know many painters who regarded him very highly."† And sometime later in a letter to Vincent himself: "If you want to do something for me, you can keep on creating for us, as you did before, a following of artists and friends which I am quite incapable of doing all by myself but which you have more or less taken care of since you have been in France" (October 27, 1888).

Quite apart from his personal contacts with artists, Vincent found a wealth of things to be experienced in the Paris of 1886. We can certainly assume, given his eager interest, that he visited all the exhibitions, where he was able to become acquainted with the Impressionists, who were still new to him, and with the "accepted" painters, such as Pierre Puvis de Chavannes and Albert Besnard. But he also must have seen the work of the even more progressive painters who had already turned away from Impressionism, seeking to move off in new directions such as Pointillism, or Divisionism, but who would soon come to be known simply as Neo-Impressionists. The large painting by Seurat *A Sunday Afternoon on the Island of La Grande Jatte*, one of the major Pointillist works, was to be seen at the eighth Impressionist group exhibition, to which Signac had also been invited and where Gauguin was represented by no fewer than nineteen canvases. The *Grande Jatte* was shown again at the Salon des Indépendants, as were paintings by Signac. Thus, Vincent had already had ample opportunity by August 1886 to familiarize himself with the methods of the Pointillists to the extent that he had not yet been initiated into their theories by friends such as the fifty-six-year-old Impressionist Camille Pissarro, who followed the new trends with interest and was on very good terms with the Van Gogh brothers.

These new trends, to which I shall return further on, appear to have had no impact on Vincent during the first few months. His efforts "to render intense colour and not a grey harmony" did, however, mean for him an almost complete break with the past. There is soon an abundance of color in the still lifes of flowers, aided by the choice of very colorful varieties, such as fritillarias

*"Theo van Gogh, Goupil and the Impressionists," *Gazette des Beaux-Arts*, vol. LXXXI (January–February 1973).

†See the article previously referred to in *Vincent*, vol. III, no. 2 (1974).

1099

1100

1101

1102

1099 View of Roofs and Backs of Houses, F231
Cardboard, 30 × 41 cm (11¾ × 16⅛″)
Rijksmuseum Vincent van Gogh, Amsterdam

1100 The Roofs of Paris, F265
44.5 × 37 cm (17¾ × 14⅝″)
Private collection, Germany

1101 The Roofs of Paris, F261
54 × 72 cm (21¼ × 28⅜″)
Rijksmuseum Vincent van Gogh, Amsterdam
Colorplate XV, opposite

1102 The Roofs of Paris, F262
38.5 × 61.5 cm (15⅜ × 24⅜″)
Kunstmuseum, Basel

Colorplate XV, The Roofs of Paris, 1101 〉

(1092), poppies (1104), peonies and roses (1105 and 1107), and so on, although there are in addition fairly sober harmonies of color, such as the bowl with purple pansies (1093). In the large canvas 1103 (colorplate XVI, page 240) with its lush composition (numerous flowers of various kinds in a vase and strewn over the table), the riot of colors of vivid red, white, pink, and blue is so pronounced that one simply no longer recognizes the Van Gogh of the Netherlands period. Because of the profusion of red poppies, which constitute the dominant color element of the painting, there is no doubt in my mind that it should be considered one of the works done in the early summer. As such, it provides striking evidence of the rapid pace at which Van Gogh was achieving full stature as an artist.

Other Still Lifes and Landscapes
Theo's report at the end of July that what Vincent was "mainly painting" were "flowers" indicates that they were not his only subject. Vincent's letters showed that he regarded it as his most important subject at that time, and it was also a still life that he had given Theo to take to the Netherlands as an example of his work ("as to work, I have a companion piece for that bouquet you have with you," Letter 460). Even if Mrs. van Gogh-Bonger did not say it in her "Memoir" (see page xli), it should be obvious that, as soon as he had moved, Vincent would start recording impressions of his new surroundings. Consequently, we have the splendid views from Butte Montmartre and from his room high over the roofs of Paris portrayed in several chalk sketches, 1095–98. In these a few important buildings can be recognized such as Notre-Dame (1096), the Opéra (1097), and the Panthéon (1098). There are, in addition, several painted studies of these scenes—the somewhat sketchily done small canvas 1100, and the larger panoramas 1101 (colorplate XV, page 223) and 1102, which are more detailed works done in fine tints of brown, gray, and gray-blue. The study of the backs of houses (1099), probably not made from the apartment, recalls his work of an earlier period because of its gamut of brown-green and gray-green tones.

The small canvas 1108 shows an entirely different coloring. This picture portraying festively decorated streets must be an impression of the Quatorze Juillet (Fourteenth of July—Bastille Day) celebration, and has always been titled accordingly. It is so daring in its vivid color contrasts that it might more readily be taken for the work of one of the Fauves in the Paris of twenty years later than for a Van Gogh. This is partly because it is a sketch that has not been reworked later, purely a fleeting impression of what could be brightly colored flags, laid on with heavy broad brushstrokes.

Although this small painting is both unusual and unexpected in Van Gogh's work in July 1886, it does not stand entirely alone. There is a still smaller sketch with similar very rough indications of the subject in broad sweeps of color, 1114. This also dates from July, according to an annotation in Vincent's handwriting on the back of the cardboard: "8 heures soir 27 Juillet pour le crépuscule

〈 Colorplate XVI, Vase with Poppies, Daisies, Cornflowers, and Peonies, 1103

1103

1104

1105

July–September 1886

1103 Vase with Poppies, Daisies, Cornflowers, and Peonies, F278
99 × 79 cm (39 × 31⅛″)
Rijksmuseum Kröller-Müller, Otterlo
Colorplate XVI, opposite

1104 Vase with Poppies, F279
56 × 46.5 cm (22 × 18½″)
Wadsworth Atheneum, Hartford, Connecticut

1105 Vase with Peonies and Roses, F249
59 × 71 cm (23¼ × 28″)
Rijksmuseum Kröller-Müller, Otterlo

orage" ("8 P.M. July 27 for the twilight thunderstorm"); "*pour* le crépuscule" is not at all clear. A moderate impasto effect is also encountered in other landscape paintings done at this time, such as 1110–13 (by contrast to painting 1109, a colorful but more graphically rendered Seine landscape).

Small paintings such as 1110 and 1111, depicting strollers in a park and on the terrace of the Tuileries, are strongly reminiscent of Vincent's earliest Paris sketches of street scenes, such as 1025. In these later pictures, however, the rich foliage of the trees points unmistakably to summer.

The views of the Montmartre hill again take us back a little in time. It was noted on page 228 that the small rough sketch of a landscape (1053) might indicate that Vincent was drawing or painting in Montmartre even in the Cormon period. It is quite certain that some of his windmills were done very soon after Theo had moved to the Rue Lepic, in other words in June. The famous Moulin de la Galette, a subject immortalized also by Renoir and Lautrec, to name a few, was right near the new apartment, and the other windmills were also in the immediate vicinity. Various paintings and drawings of those other windmills also used to be known as the "Moulin de la Galette," but in his biography* Pierre Leprohon has pointed out that the real name of the windmill depicted most often by Vincent was the "Moulin de Blute-Fin." This windmill can be recognized by a sort of balcony at the top and the small belvedere next to it. It was not far from the windmill that, according to Leprohon, should properly have been called the Moulin du Radet, but was commonly referred to by Vincent and others at that time as the Moulin de la Galette. Vincent painted it three times: 1170, 1171, and 1172. The Moulin de Blute-Fin is seen in the small paintings 1115 and 1116, amid a rather messy group of small gardens with sheds, laid out against the steep incline surmounted by the windmill. On page 193 of Leprohon's book there is a photograph of this spot dating from Vincent's time.

A whole series of still lifes of subjects other than flowers must also be ascribed to the second half of 1886 on the basis of their style. Here, too, no precise sequence of dates can be determined; it is uncertain whether they were painted before, after, or at the same time as the still lifes of flowers. Writing to Theo in August (Letter 460), Vincent mentioned only pictures of flowers, and in the letter to Livens (Letter 459*a*), probably written a little later, he reported: "I did a dozen landscapes too, frankly *green* frankly *blue*"—but there is nothing about other still lifes. This group, representing a somewhat different kind of subject, has been placed together here (1117–24). They are mostly simple compositions consisting of objects that are among the daily necessities of life, such as apples, meat, and bread (1117), meat and vegetables (1119), and most often, mackerels and herrings (1118, 1120, 1122, and 1123). Vincent's predilection for fish as the subject was doubtless based on the picturesqueness of the light effects to which the gold and silver-colored scales lend themselves. And his concern with

**Vincent van Gogh* (1971), p. 350.

1106

1107

1108

1106 Vase with Myosotis and Peonies, F243a
Cardboard, 34.5 × 27.5 cm (13¾ × 11″)
Rijksmuseum Vincent van Gogh, Amsterdam

1107 Vase with Peonies, F666a
55 × 46 cm (21⅝ × 18⅛″)
Location unknown

1108 Street Scene in Celebration of Bastille Day, F222
44 × 39 cm (17⅜ × 15⅜″)
Collection Mrs. L. Jäggli-Hahnloser, Winterthur, Switzerland

1109 The Pont du Carrousel and the Louvre, F221
31 × 44 cm (12¼ × 17⅜″)
Collection F. Herman, Los Angeles

1110 A Public Garden with People Walking, F225
37.5 × 45.5 cm (15 × 18⅛″)
Private collection, United States

1111 Terrace of the Tuileries with People Walking, F223
27.5 × 46 cm (11 × 18⅛″)
Sterling and Francine Clark Art Institute, Williamstown, Massachusetts

1109

1110

1111

1112

1113

1114

1112 The Bois de Boulogne with People Walking, F224
46.5 × 37 cm ($18\frac{1}{2} \times 14\frac{5}{8}''$)
Private collection

1113 A Path in Montmartre, F232
Cardboard, 22 × 16 cm ($8\frac{5}{8} \times 6\frac{1}{4}''$)
Rijksmuseum Vincent van Gogh, Amsterdam

1114 Stormy Night (July 27, 1886), F1672
Cardboard, 15 × 10 cm ($5\frac{7}{8} \times 3\frac{7}{8}''$)
Collection G. Darrieutort, Paris

color studies in these still lifes, too, is clearly apparent from a work such as 1121, where the deep-red wine in a bottle and two glasses and the bright yellow of a slab of cheese and a piece of bread are set in simple but striking contrast to the dark green of the background.

The most widely discussed still life in this series is the one of the two shoes, 1124, the first portrayal of a subject that Vincent repeated a number of times in several variations (1233–36, 1364, and 1569). It is only too easy to see in this a symbol of Vincent's own journey through life, his craving always to settle somewhere else, his "goût de l'errance" ("taste for roving"), as Leprohon called it (page 194)—and so we find this thought in several books on Van Gogh. Tralbaut has simply pointed out that Vincent had always been a great walker and said that it was therefore hardly surprising that he depicted his shoes, "his companions on these wanderings."* What many have seen in a work like 1124 has been aptly summed up by Frank Elgar: "Old, worn, gaping and down at heel, the articles exhibited tell a story of poverty, wretchedness and weary, endless tramping. They reveal the plight of the man who wore them out so utterly and, through his adversity, the toil and fatigue of the whole world."†

More Still Lifes of Flowers

During the summer Vincent continued to paint still lifes of flowers (1125–30). In this lengthy succession of colorful, sometimes even festive canvases we are struck by Vincent's ingenuity in varying this intrinsically simple subject. Although a particular vase or ginger jar may reappear from time to time, the arrangement and color combination of the bouquets they hold are almost always different. All kinds of summer flowers are represented here, in addition to those mentioned by Vincent in Letters 459*a* and 460: red and white carnations (1126, 1129, 1130), zinnias and geraniums (1132, 1134, 1140), hollyhocks and roses (1136 and 1144), gladioli (1128, 1131, and many others), and so on. Although we do not meet with the exact combination mentioned by Vincent in Letter 460: "red gladiolus in a blue vase against pale yellow," we do find the bright colors and color oppositions that he described: "oppositions of blue with orange, red and green, yellow and violet," while the "soft-soap colors" have completely disappeared.

A somewhat difficult case among these pictures of flowers is 1125, a ginger jar with what appear to be daisies. The careful manner in which the ginger jar has been painted —rather more conventional than, for instance, the similar jar in 1164—is characteristic of a somewhat earlier style, and the *catalogue raisonné* has accordingly dated this piece "autumn 1885," thus Nuenen. Vanbeselaere, however, ascribed the work to the Paris period, and I am inclined to agree more with him, as I have not found a single indication that Vincent had done still lifes of flowers in the autumn of 1885.

*Tralbaut, *Van Gogh* (1969), p. 199.

†Frank Elgar, *Van Gogh: A Study of His Life and Work* (1958), p. 44.

1115

1116

The still life showing white carnations and small red roses in a blue vase next to a bottle of wine with a red label (1133) provides the occasion for telling about one of the earliest influences Vincent must have come under in Paris. Many years ago, when A.M. Hammacher was still director of the Rijksmuseum Kröller-Müller, he hung a flower piece by Monticelli next to this canvas in order to draw attention to the close affinity between the two. Letters by Vincent from Arles and Saint-Rémy will show how great, in fact, his admiration was for the Marseilles painter Adolphe-Joseph-Thomas Monticelli, whose

1115 The Moulin de Blute-Fin, F274
46×38 cm ($18\frac{1}{8} \times 15''$)
Glasgow Art Gallery and Museum

1116 The Moulin de Blute-Fin, F273
46.5×38 cm ($18\frac{1}{2} \times 15''$)
Collection J. S. Lasdon, New York

1117 Still Life with Apples, Meat, and a Roll, F219
46×55 cm ($18\frac{1}{8} \times 21\frac{5}{8}''$)
Rijksmuseum Kröller-Müller, Otterlo

1118 Still Life with Mackerels, Lemons, and Tomatoes, F285
39×56.5 cm ($15\frac{3}{8} \times 22\frac{1}{2}''$)
Collection Oskar Reinhart, Winterthur, Switzerland

1117

1118

1119

1120

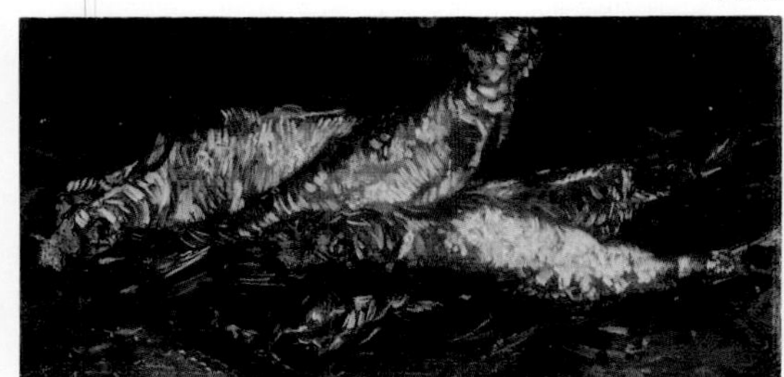

1121

1122

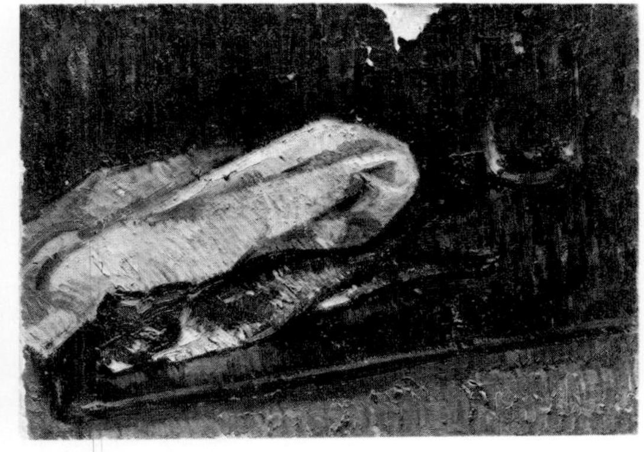

1123

1119 Still Life with Meat, Vegetables, and Pottery, F 1670
33.5 × 41 cm (13⅜ × 16⅛″)
Location unknown

1120 Still Life with Red Herrings, F 283
21 × 42 cm (8¼ × 16½″)
Kunstmuseum, Basel (on loan from the Rudolf Staechelin Foundation)

1121 Still Life with a Plate, Glasses, and a Wine Bottle, F 253
37.5 × 46 cm (15 × 18⅛″)
Rijksmuseum Vincent van Gogh, Amsterdam

1122 Still Life with Red Herrings, a Cloth, and a Glass, F 1671
32.5 × 46 cm (13 × 18⅛″)
Private collection, United States

1123 Still Life with Red Herrings, F 203
45 × 38 cm (17¾ × 15″)
Rijksmuseum Kröller-Müller, Otterlo

work he first came to know in Paris. Not only does he mention Monticelli in his letters more than fifty times, but he says in unmistakable terms that he regards him (together with Delacroix) as his master. Theo had five Monticellis (Letter 464), among them a flower painting that Vincent particularly praised ("as to color, a first-rate piece," Letter 617; it is now in the Rijksmuseum Vincent van Gogh). Vincent also spoke about landscapes that he, together with Theo, had seen at the galleries of Reid and Delarebeyrette (Letters 471, 488, and 610). He repeatedly mentions Monticelli's "*empâtements*" ("impastoes") (Letters 552, 597, and 626) and his "vibrating" color (Letter 519), characteristics that he had in common with Monticelli. To the Australian painter John Russell he wrote that Monticelli "gives us something passionate and eternal—the rich colour and rich sun of the glorious South in a true colourist way parallel with Delacroix' conception of the South" (Letter 477*a*). On more than one occasion Vincent wrote Theo that he felt he was the continuation of Monticelli in Provence: "Sometimes I really do believe I am continuing that man, only I have not yet made any amorous little figures as he did" (Letter 541, also Letters 542 and 570 among others). His admiration for Monticelli—in whose life he also recognized his own difficulties—is most forcefully expressed in what he wrote Wil at the end of August 1888: "I think a great deal about Monticelli here. He was a very strong man—a little crazy, and even very much so—who dreamed of sun and love and gaiety, but who was always harassed by poverty; an extraordinary taste as a colorist, a man of rare breed, who carried on the best of the old traditions. He died in Marseilles in a rather sad way and probably after having gone through a true Gethsemane. Well, I am sure that I am a continuation of him here, as if I was his son or his brother." And so strong was his need to identify with his predecessor that he continued: "When friend Gauguin is here and we go to Marseilles, I intend to go strolling along the Cannebière, dressed exactly as I saw him in a portrait, with an enormous yellow hat, a black velvet jacket, white trousers, yellow gloves and a bamboo cane, passing myself off as a real Southerner [avec un grand air méridional]" (Letter W8).

It is quite apparent that Vincent maintained his admiration for Monticelli for a long time, so Monticelli's influence, too, can be expected to last right through the years 1888–90, as Ellen Joosten pointed out.* But there is also the question here of an immediate and spontaneous reaction of the electrifying moment of coming face to face with Monticelli's work in Paris. His *empâtements* of small brushstrokes by which the flowers are, as it were, molded and his richness of color are also to be found in many of the flower paintings Van Gogh made in 1886.

Vincent and Theo

Some information about Vincent's personality during the Paris period and his relationship with Theo was provided at a very early

*"Het rijke begrip 'invloed,'" *Museumjournaal*, vol. V, no. 4 (1959), pp. 73–76.

1124

1125

1126

1124 A Pair of Shoes, F255
37.5 × 45.5 cm (15 × 18⅛″)
Rijksmuseum Vincent van Gogh, Amsterdam

1125 Ginger Jar with Daisies (?), F198
Canvas on panel, 40 × 29.5 cm (15¾ × 11¾″)
Collection Howard J. Lepow, New York

1126 Jug with Red and White Carnations, F327
40 × 52 cm (15¾ × 20½″)
Rijksmuseum Kröller-Müller, Otterlo

1127 Vase with Asters and Other Flowers, F286
70.5 × 34 cm (28 × 13⅜″)
Gemeentemuseum, The Hague

1128 Vase with Gladioli and Lilacs, F286a
69 × 33.5 cm (27⅛ × 13⅜″)
Collection Mr. and Mrs. Edwin McClellan Johnston, St. Louis

1129 Glass with White, Pink, and Red Carnations, F243
46 × 38 cm (18⅛ × 15″)
Collection Mrs. Charles B. Murphy, New York

1130 Vase with White and Red Carnations, F236
58 × 45.5 cm (22⅞ × 18⅛″)
Location unknown

1127

1128

1129

1130

1131

1132

1131 Vase with Gladioli and Wallflowers, F237
65.5 × 35 cm (26 × 13¾″)
Museum Boymans-van Beuningen,
Rotterdam

1132 Vase with Carnations and Zinnias, F259
61 × 49 cm (24 × 19¼″)
Location unknown

stage by Theo's friend Andries Bonger (who in 1889 also became his brother-in-law). Writing in the *Nieuwe Rotterdamsche Courant* of September 5, 1893, he recalled his intimate acquaintance with the brothers in Paris seven years earlier. Although Bonger's piece is interesting as an eyewitness report, its fragmentary and somewhat one-sided nature demands that it be treated with circumspection. Here is part of what Bonger wrote: "However close Vincent and Theo were—and they could not get along without each other—they were never able to live together. Within the first week Vincent embarked on interminable discussions, brought on by Impressionism but branching off into every imaginable topic. One day Theo left the house in desperation and swore that he would not return until Vincent had found a place of his own in which to live. Shortly after this Vincent left for the South. Although Vincent was a stimulant for Theo in his work, cooperation between them was out of the question. Vincent always wanted to dominate his brother. Theo often opposed Vincent's theories vigorously."

Of far greater significance than this little article, with its limited audience, were the observations by Theo's widow, Johanna (Jo) van Gogh-Bonger, on the Paris period in her "Memoir" to the 1914 edition of the letters. Of greatest importance was what she was able to quote from several letters written by Theo to Wil, which shed considerable light on the life together of the two brothers, since they were an even more immediate source than the article by her brother Andries. They partly confirmed and partly clarified what Andries had written, and for sixty years not much more information became known than what she had vouchsafed in those few pages. In 1974, however, the actual letters she had quoted from became available (and the most important passages were published in *Vincent*, vol. III, no. 2 [1974]). I shall therefore rely on this original source rather than on Mrs. van Gogh-Bonger's rather free rendering in what follows.

Although Vincent and Theo's life together was indeed sometimes difficult, it hardly seems to justify the assertion that "they were never able to live together." In the beginning there appear to have been few if any problems, as was, moreover, evident from Theo's letter to his mother in July (an excerpt appears on page 234)—that is, at least four months after Vincent's arrival. (We may then ask what precisely is meant by Andries Bonger's "Within the first week.") Gradually, though, the situation does seem to have become hard for Theo to bear, for on March 11, 1887, he wrote his brother Cor: "Vincent continues his studies and he works with talent. But it is a pity that he has so much difficulty with his character, for in the long run it is quite impossible to get on with him. When he came here last year he was difficult, it is true, but I thought I could see some progress. But now he is his old self again and he won't listen to reason. That does not make it too pleasant here and I hope for improvement. It will come, but it is a pity for him, for if we had worked together it would have been better for both of us."

1133

1134

1135

1133 Vase with Carnations and Bottle, F246
40 × 32 cm (15¾ × 12⅝″)
Rijksmuseum Kröller-Müller, Otterlo

1134 Vase with Zinnias and Geraniums, F241
63 × 46 cm (24¾ × 18⅛″)
National Gallery of Canada, Ottawa

1135 Vase with Carnations and Other Flowers, F596
61 × 38 cm (24 × 15″)
Collection Mr. and Mrs. D. L. Kreeger, Washington, D.C.

1136 Vase with Hollyhocks, F235
94 × 51 cm (37 × 20⅛″)
Kunsthaus, Zurich

1137 Vase with Different Kinds of Flowers, F324a
65 × 54 cm (25⅝ × 21¼″)
Property of the Government of Egypt

1138 Vase with Carnations, F220
40 × 32.5 cm (15¾ × 13″)
Willem van der Vorm Foundation, Rotterdam

1136

1137

1138

1139

1141

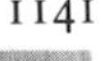

1140

1139 Geranium in a Flowerpot, F201
46 × 38 cm (18⅛ × 15″)
Location unknown
1140 Bowl with Zinnias, F252
61 × 45.5 cm (24 × 18⅛″)
Collection Mr. and Mrs. D. L. Kreeger, Washington, D.C.
1141 Vase with Roses and Other Flowers, F258
37 × 25.5 cm (14⅝ × 10⅛″)
Location unknown

Theo's Troubles

A few days later, on March 14, Theo wrote Wil telling her in somewhat more detail about the situation in a letter that was probably not the first one to her on this subject but is the first that has been preserved. After saying that he sometimes had the feeling of standing alone and of being unable to cope with difficulties, Theo continued: "Your letter proves to me that I am wrong. This is such a special case. If he was someone who did different work, I would certainly have done what you advise me a long time ago and I have often asked myself whether it was not wrong always to help him and I have often been on the verge of letting him muddle along by himself. After getting your letter I have again seriously thought about it and I feel that in the circumstances I cannot do anything but continue. It is certain that he is an artist and what he makes now may sometimes not be beautiful, but it will surely be of use to him later and then it may possibly be sublime and it would be a shame if one kept him from his regular studies.

"However impractical he may be, when he becomes more skilful the day will undoubtedly come when he will start to begin selling. You should not think either that the money side worries me most. It is mostly the idea that we sympathise so little any more. There was a time when I loved Vincent a lot and he was my best friend but that is over now. It seems to be even worse from his side, for he never loses an opportunity to show me that he despises me and that I revolt him. That makes the situation at home almost unbearable. Nobody wants to come and see me, for that always leads to reproaches and he is also so dirty and untidy that the household looks far from attractive. All I hope is that he will go and live by himself and he has talked about this for a long time, for if I told him to leave that would only give him a reason to stay on. Since I cannot do any good for him I only ask for one thing and that is that he won't do any harm to me and that is what he does by staying, for it weighs heavily on me. It appears as if there are two different beings in him, the one marvellously gifted, fine and delicate and the other selfish and heartless. They appear alternatively so that one hears him talk now this way and then that way and always with arguments to prove pro and contra. It is a pity that he is his own enemy, for he makes life difficult not only for others but also for himself. I have firmly decided to continue as I have done up to now, but I hope that for some reason or other he will move to other quarters and I will do my best for that."

It is a sad letter but one that leaves little to the imagination. Not only was the artist's slovenliness around the house almost too much for the orderly Theo to bear and Vincent's difficult character extremely irritating to him, but even more the tension between them had apparently now reached the point where Theo had come to feel—undoubtedly wrongly so—that Vincent even "despised" him and that he "revolted" Vincent. There can be no doubt that at this stage Theo hoped Vincent would move out, but it also appears from the letter that—despite Wil's advice to him to do something—he had "firmly decided to continue as [he had] done up to now."

Easing of Tension

That this was a relatively short-lived crisis and not a situation that lasted a couple of years is apparent from a letter written to Wil less than six weeks later. On April 25 Theo reported: "A lot has changed since I wrote you last. We have made peace, for it didn't do anybody any good to continue in that way. I hope it will last. So there will be no change and I am glad. It would have been strange for me to live alone again and he would not have gained anything either. I

1142

1143

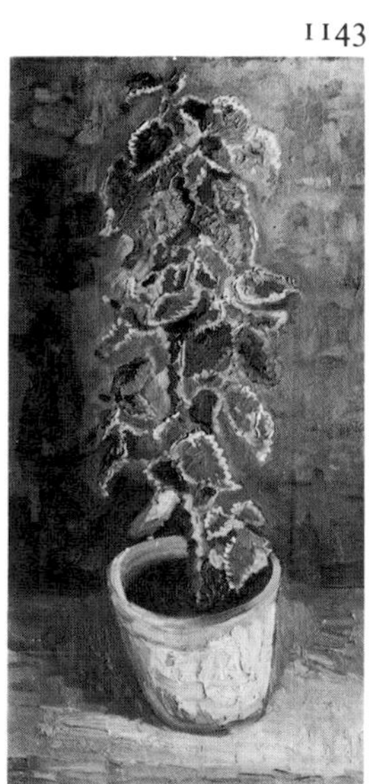

1144

1142 Bowl with Zinnias and Other Flowers, F251
49.5 × 61 cm (19⅝ × 24")
Winnipeg Art Gallery

1143 Coleus Plant in a Flowerpot, F281
42 × 22 cm (16½ × 8⅝")
Rijksmuseum Vincent van Gogh, Amsterdam

1144 Glass with Roses, F218
Cardboard, 35 × 27 cm (13¾ × 10⅝")
Rijksmuseum Vincent van Gogh, Amsterdam

1145 Vase with Carnations, F245
46 × 37.5 cm (18⅛ × 15")
Stedelijk Museum, Amsterdam

1146 Vase with Red Gladioli, F248
50.5 × 39.5 cm (20⅛ × 15¾")
Location unknown

1145

1146

1147

1148

1149

1150

1147 Vase with Gladioli and Other Flowers, F242
78.5 × 40.5 cm (31⅛ × 16⅛″)
Location unknown

1148 Vase with Gladioli, F248a
48.5 × 40 cm (19¼ × 15¾″)
Rijksmuseum Vincent van Gogh, Amsterdam

1149 Vase with Gladioli, F247
65 × 40 cm (25⅝ × 15¾″)
Location unknown

1150 Vase with Red Gladioli, F248b
65 × 35 cm (25⅝ × 13¾″)
Collection J. Planque, Pully, Switzerland

asked him to stay. That will seem strange after all I wrote you recently, but it is no weakness on my side and as I feel much stronger than this winter, I am confident that I will be able to create an improvement in our relationship. We have drifted apart enough than that it would serve any purpose to make the rift any larger."

Andries Bonger's "Shortly after this Vincent left for the South" gave the erroneous impression that Vincent's departure from Paris was connected with, and perhaps even directly resulted from, the atmosphere of conflict. The fact is that the conflict, for all practical purposes, had ended in March or April of 1887, and once Vincent had actually moved away, Theo's only feelings, in looking back on his stay in Paris, were those of wistfulness and gratitude. There is another letter to Wil that confirms this: "When he came here two years ago I had not expected that we would become so much attached to each other, for now that I am alone in the apartment there is a decided emptiness about me. If I can find someone I will take him in, but it is not easy to replace someone like Vincent. It is unbelievable how much he knows and what a sane view he has of the world. If he has still some years to live I am certain that he will make a name for himself. Through him I got to know many painters who regarded him very highly. He is one of the avant-garde for new ideas, that is to say, there is nothing new under the sun and so it would be better to say for the regeneration of the old ideas which through routine have been diluted and worn out. In addition he has such a big heart that he always tries to do something for others. It's a pity for those who cannot or refuse to understand him" (February 24, 1888; a sentence from this letter was quoted above, on page 238).

Drawings of the Human Figure

Among the work Vincent did in Paris there is a series of hastily done sketches of musicians and other figures and heads (1151–63), a rather unexpected new subject. The only things really comparable are a few sketchbook sheets from the Antwerp period, such as the scenes in a dance hall (968 and 969) and male heads, such as 982–84. As Tralbaut has suggested, these Paris sketches were probably made in August, and may have been prompted by an article in the Paris *Illustré* of August 1, 1886 (no. 50), which was illustrated with somewhat similar drawings by the French Impressionist painter Jean-François Raffaëlli.*

They are somewhat humorous rough sketches, probably done very rapidly, with forceful parallel lines that aptly render the subjects and their attitudes. Of special note is the use of colored chalk: blue (as in 1155 and 1156), green (as in 1153 and 1157), or blue and green (as in 1154 and 1159).

For the sake of completeness in the matter of dating it should be mentioned that the *Head of a Man with Hat*, 1161, is dated 1887 in the 1970 *catalogue raisonné*. I see no connection with drawings made that year, but

*M.E. Tralbaut, *Vincent van Gogh in het caf' conc' of het raakpunt met Raffaëlli* (Vincent van Gogh in the café concert or the point of contact with Raffaëlli) (1955).

1151

1152

1153

1154

1155

1156

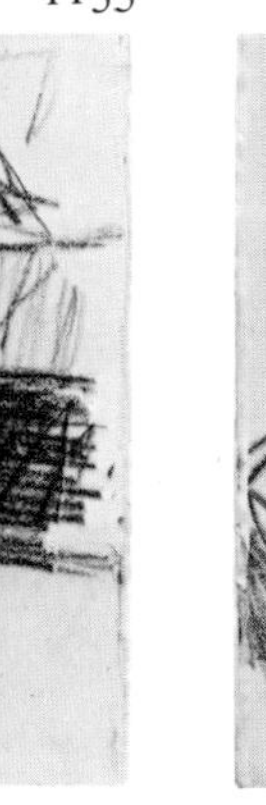

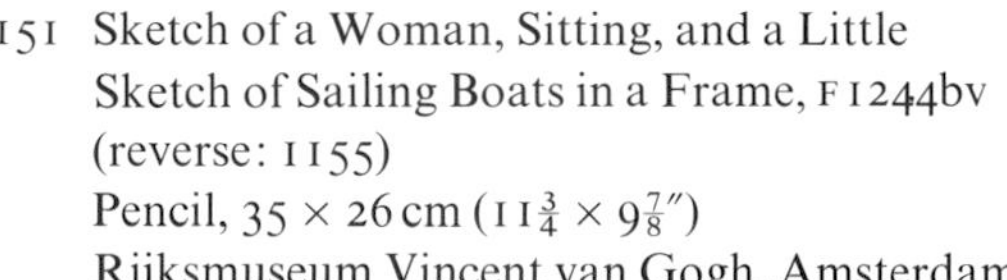

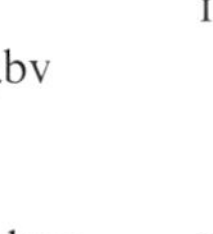

1151 Sketch of a Woman, Sitting, and a Little Sketch of Sailing Boats in a Frame, F 1244bv (reverse: 1155)
Pencil, 35 × 26 cm ($11\frac{3}{4} \times 9\frac{7}{8}$″)
Rijksmuseum Vincent van Gogh, Amsterdam

1152 Sketch of a Woman, Sitting While Dressing, F 1718
Pencil, 30 × 25 cm ($11\frac{3}{4} \times 9\frac{7}{8}$″)
Rijksmuseum Vincent van Gogh, Amsterdam

1153 Double Bass Player, F 1244cv (reverse: 1157)
Green chalk, 34 × 25.5 cm ($13\frac{3}{8} \times 10\frac{1}{8}$″)
Rijksmuseum Vincent van Gogh, Amsterdam

1154 Violinist, F 1244a (reverse: 1156)
Blue and green chalk, 35 × 26 cm ($13\frac{3}{4} \times 10\frac{1}{4}$″)
Rijksmuseum Vincent van Gogh, Amsterdam

1155 Clarinetist and Flutist, F 1244b (reverse: 1151)
Blue chalk, 26 × 35 cm ($10\frac{1}{4} \times 13\frac{3}{4}$″)
Rijksmuseum Vincent van Gogh, Amsterdam

1156 Violinist, F 1244av (reverse: 1154)
Blue chalk, 26 × 35 cm ($10\frac{1}{4} \times 13\frac{3}{4}$″)
Rijksmuseum Vincent van Gogh, Amsterdam

1157 Pianist, F 1244c (reverse: 1153)
Green chalk, 25.5 × 34 cm ($10\frac{1}{8} \times 13\frac{3}{8}$″)
Rijksmuseum Vincent van Gogh, Amsterdam

1158 Head of a Man, Profile, F 1244d (reverse: 1159)
Charcoal, colored chalk, 35 × 26 cm ($13\frac{3}{4} \times 10\frac{1}{4}$″)
Rijksmuseum Vincent van Gogh, Amsterdam

1157

1158

1159

1160

1161

1162

1163

1159 Head of a Man with Top Hat, F1244dv
(reverse: 1158)
Blue and green chalk, 26 × 35 cm ($10\frac{1}{4} \times 13\frac{3}{4}''$)
Rijksmuseum Vincent van Gogh, Amsterdam

1160 Violinist and Pianist, F1714
Pencil, 14 × 21 cm ($5\frac{1}{2} \times 8\frac{1}{4}''$)
Rijksmuseum Vincent van Gogh, Amsterdam

1161 Head of a Man with Hat, F1715
Black chalk, dimensions unknown
Location unknown

1162 Nude Woman, Squatting, F1376
Sketch on the back of a menu of the
Restaurant du Chalet
Pencil, 21 × 13.5 cm ($8\frac{1}{4} \times 5\frac{1}{2}''$)
Rijksmuseum Vincent van Gogh, Amsterdam

1163 Nude Woman, Sitting, F1717
Pencil, 31 × 20 cm ($12\frac{1}{4} \times 7\frac{7}{8}''$)
Rijksmuseum Vincent van Gogh, Amsterdam

the boldly drawn hatching lines in chalk, each standing apart from the others—as, for example, on the brim of the hat and on the wreathlike frame around the face—have traits in common with this group of drawings dating from 1886, particularly 1158 and 1159. I similarly see an affinity of style between the pencil drawings 1151 and 1152, specifically in the capricious experiment of indicating the outline of the figures not by a line, but in a more Impressionistic manner by means of short hatching strokes drawn perpendicularly and diagonally across an imaginary line. Note, for instance, the shoulder of the woman in 1151, and the arms and legs of the woman in 1152.

For the same reason I have included the two unimportant sheets of a female nude, 1162 and 1163, with these other sketchbook sheets, although both have been dated 1887 in the *catalogue raisonné*. For one thing, the shadows and background rendered by the harsh and somewhat untidy pencil lines seem to me more typical of this earlier period; they are recognizable in sketches such as 1158 and 1160. In sketch 1162, which is remarkable by reason of the unusual treatment of the subject (like a deliberate flouting of academic conventions), the fagotlike background detracts too much from the rather carefully drawn figure. Sketch 1163 represents nothing more than a first attempt, and a completely abortive one as far as the raised left shoulder and forearm are concerned.

In the late summer and fall of 1886, Van Gogh also seems to have continued the series of still lifes of flowers. In many that in the *catalogue raisonné* are dated fall 1886, there are flowers that look like those of late summer or fall: chrysanthemums and asters (1164 and 1168), sunflowers and roses (1166), daisies (1167), cinerarias (1165), and so on. Most of them are warm in color and fairly rich in composition and betray a painter's skilled hand in suggesting what is typical of form and substance in the widely assorted varieties of flowers, and sometimes also of leaves (as in 1165), without any attempt being made to achieve a literal fidelity to nature.

1164

1165

1166

The Windmills of Montmartre

Vincent undoubtedly also continued to scout for subjects in Montmartre and vicinity in the fall of 1886. First of all, he did the three previously mentioned almost identical studies of the Moulin de la Galette, 1170–72. Through a sort of coincidence it has been learned that they almost certainly date from October. The source of this information is a short letter from Van Gogh that only recently came to light.* In this interesting document, postmarked October 25, 1886, Vincent reports that he had spoken to the American painter Frank Boggs about the possibility of an exchange of paintings between Boggs and Charles Angrand and that he himself would also like to be taken into account for an exchange with Angrand. He wrote: "I also recommend myself for an exchange. Right now I have two views of the Moulin de la Galette that I could part with."

*Bogomila Welsh-Ovcharov, *The Early Work of Charles Angrand and His Contact with Vincent van Gogh* (1971), p. 37.

As I see it, two of the studies 1170–72 must be the ones referred to here, the third probably being intended for Theo and Vincent's own collection. These are the only ones in which the Moulin de la Galette is actually depicted, as is, moreover, apparent from the legends *Moulin de ... Galette* on the windmill structure and *Buvette Moulin de la Galette* on the café door. The studies have been painted in an Impressionist style, with buildings and people roughly defined in broad brushstrokes and in a rather dark gamut of red-brown and brown-yellow, but with a yellow-gray light sky. That Vincent attached more than ordinary importance to these studies is obvious from the fact that they were the particular ones he had in mind for an exchange.

It may incidentally be noted that this letter

1164 Bowl of Little Chrysanthemums, F217
46 × 61 cm (18⅛ × 24″)
Location unknown

1165 Cinerarias in a Flowerpot, F282
54.5 × 46 cm (21⅝ × 18⅛″)
Museum Boymans-van Beuningen, Rotterdam

1166 Bowl of Sunflowers, Roses, and Other Flowers, F250
50 × 61 cm (19⅝ × 24″)
Städtische Kunsthalle, Mannheim

1167 Vase with Daisies, F197
Paper on panel, 40 × 56 cm (15¾ × 22″)
Collection Mr. and Mrs. William Coxe Wright, St. David's, Pennsylvania

1168 Vase with Asters and Phlox, F234
61 × 46 cm (24 × 18⅛″)
Rijksmuseum Vincent van Gogh, Amsterdam

1167

1168

1169

1170

1171

1172

October–December 1886

1169 Mussels and Shrimps, F256
27 × 34 cm ($10\frac{5}{8} \times 13\frac{3}{8}$″)
Rijksmuseum Vincent van Gogh, Amsterdam

1170 The Moulin de la Galette, F227
38.5 × 46 cm ($15\frac{3}{8} \times 18\frac{1}{8}$″)
Rijksmuseum Kröller-Müller, Otterlo

1171 The Moulin de la Galette, F228
38 × 46.5 cm ($15 \times 18\frac{1}{2}$″)
Nationalgalerie, East Berlin

1172 The Moulin de la Galette, F226
38 × 46 cm ($15 \times 18\frac{1}{8}$″)
Collection John Brown, Baden, Switzerland

1173 The Moulin de Blute-Fin, F1397
Black chalk, watercolor, 31 × 25 cm
($12\frac{1}{4} \times 9\frac{7}{8}$″)
P. and N. de Boer Foundation, Amsterdam

1173

confirms what has already been said about Vincent's contacts with artists in Paris and about the position of the two brothers. This is especially evident from the postscript: "Do also go and see my brother (Goupil & Co., 19 Boulevard Montmartre); right now he has a very fine Degas." Thus, once again, the initiative clearly came from Vincent.

The hill with the windmills and the vegetable gardens is also portrayed in other drawings (1173 and 1174) and paintings (1175–77). The tiny drawing 1181, a sketchbook sheet measuring $3\frac{7}{8}$ by $6\frac{3}{4}$ inches, gives the impression of embodying a combination of three motifs: the silhouettelike foreground to the right, the distant view of the windmills, and the small rough sketch in the lower left-hand corner, drawn in another perspective. In the finely executed drawing 1173 we again find the Moulin de Blute-Fin, which is also the largest of the three windmills seen in the panoramic view 1174. An almost identical composition appears in the imposing painting 1175 (colorplate XVII, page 257), which, however, is much better balanced by reason of the greater attention given to the little gardens and sheds in the foreground. The canvases 1176 and 1177 present a side view of the same windmill viewed from the bottom of the hill, 1176 being identical with the central portion of 1177, in which Vincent shows the same landscape as seen from a much greater distance. In the latter work he has brought a quarry at the foot of the steep hillside into the composition as the principal motif in the foreground of the painting, and has placed a pair of small dark figures there who stand out as silhouettes against the lighter stone. The three canvases have all been painted in light, delicate tints of brown, green, and gray with the skies a soft blue, white, and gray. They thus present a striking contrast to the lavish color experiments in Vincent's still lifes of flowers. One also gets the feeling, however, that a characterization of these landscapes—certainly far from "beautiful" in the traditional sense—was not his only aim, but that he was trying at the same time to achieve a careful composition of color harmonies in delicate and subdued shades.

This observation also applies to a certain extent to the landscapes 1179 and 1180, the latter apparently being another view of the hill of Montmartre and an even less "picturesque" spot. This small canvas—truly a study, exhibiting little detail and done with broad brushstrokes—is Vincent's only attempt at this subject. The considerably larger piece 1179, again done in a broad-brushed, sketchy style, also stands pretty much by itself as far as the subject is concerned. Through his peculiar composition portraying a single lamppost set right in the center of the picture, the solitary little man in the foreground, and the two small groups of people moving away from him, Vincent seems to have succeeded admirably in making one feel the dreariness of this kind of open tract on the outskirts of the city under gray skies.

In 1178 (colorplate XVIII, page 258) we come back again to the *guinguette* of 1034, now in fall colors and with somewhat more activity. In its treatment this, too, is very sketchy and Impressionistic (the figure of the waiter is built up merely of a few brushstrokes in white and black and reddish brown), but it is certainly a color study as well. Although the principal colors are gray-green and brown, Vincent has set the whole composition against the delicate blue-gray of the clouded sky and introduced some sharp contrasts in color, such as the bright green of the lamppost and the strong red of the small female figure.

The windmills, especially the now familiar Moulin de Blute-Fin, reappear as an attractive central motif in some of the paintings

1174

1175

1176

1174 The Hill of Montmartre with Windmills, F1398
Charcoal, black chalk, 39 × 47.5 cm ($15\frac{3}{8} \times 18\frac{7}{8}''$)
Rijksmuseum Vincent van Gogh, Amsterdam

1175 The Hill of Montmartre with Windmills, F266
36 × 61 cm ($14\frac{1}{8} \times 24''$)
Rijksmuseum Kröller-Müller, Otterlo
Colorplate XVII, opposite

1176 The Hill of Montmartre with Quarry, F229
32 × 41 cm ($12\frac{5}{8} \times 16\frac{1}{8}''$)
Rijksmuseum Vincent van Gogh, Amsterdam

Colorplate XVII, The Hill of Montmartre with Windmills, 1175 >

and drawings dating from the final months of the year (1182, 1184–86, and 1188). Curiously, the Theo van Gogh collection in the Rijksmuseum Vincent van Gogh possesses a painting by A. H. Koning, a Paris friend of the Van Goghs, a work that exactly corresponds with Vincent's study of the Moulin de Blute-Fin and the long stairway leading up to it. It does not seem too farfetched to suppose that Koning and Vincent could have sat there painting side by side.

These painted landscapes, and the beautiful watercolor of a city scene, 1187, are further examples of what are primarily studies in refined, soft color harmonies. This applies particularly to the small painting 1183, which is remarkable for its composition. It apparently depicts the belvedere that stood next to the Moulin de Blute-Fin and can be seen in several of the studies of that windmill, such as 1115 and 1182. A few people standing on the hill and the belvedere are looking out over the city of Paris, enveloped in haze and scarcely distinguishable from the delicate soft gray-blue sky above it. The ground, delineated by a few broad brushstrokes, has also been done in various nuances of grayish blue. The representation of the transparent lanterns in dark gray lines is extremely delicate, and all this blue-gray is set off by the warm brown of the paling of the belvedere, by the fence on the left, and by some of the items of clothing. One might say that a painting like this showed Vincent to be worthy of being ranked among the French Impressionist painters, whom he had hardly even heard about a half year earlier.

Stuffed animals also occupied Vincent in a small group of drawings and paintings (1189–93) depicting an owl, a kingfisher, a kalong bat, and a green parrot. They have been brought together here because they have something in common in subject, but even remotely accurate dating seems impossible. In the 1970 *catalogue raisonné* the first four are dated Paris 1886. In the case of the green parrot (1193), which De la Faille ascribed to Nuenen and Vanbeselaere to Paris, the editors of the 1970 *catalogue* commented: "The date and period seem uncertain." The kingfisher shown in the small painting 1191 appears to have been observed in the natural state, but the editors of the *catalogue raisonné* state: "V.W. van Gogh has identified the kingfisher as a stuffed bird, still in his possession, which Vincent bought in Paris." The owls (1189 and 1190) are cleverly done drawings with a somewhat academic look which I surmise were done in the Cormon atelier, assuming that the students there also worked from stuffed animals. Most striking is the large painting of the "flying dog," 1192. It is a daring picture, primarily because of the bright red, orange, and green colors applied in broad brushstrokes to portray the outspread wings, but also because of the unusual composition in which the animal, apparently viewed against the light, fills almost the entire surface of the canvas.

Second Series of Self-Portraits

At about this time Vincent appears to have embarked on another series of self-portraits, 1194–98. There is much difference of opinion about the dating of the first two. De la Faille

1177

1178

1179

1180

1177 The Hill of Montmartre with Quarry, F230
56 × 62 cm (22 × 24⅜")
Rijksmuseum Vincent van Gogh, Amsterdam

1178 Terrace of a Café (La Guinguette), F238
49 × 64 cm (19¼ × 25¼")
The Louvre, Paris
Colorplate XVIII, opposite

1179 A Suburb of Paris, F264
Canvas on cardboard, 46.5 × 54.5 cm
(18½ × 21⅝")
Location unknown

1180 The Hill of Montmartre with Quarry, F233
22 × 33 cm (8⅝ × 13")
Rijksmuseum Vincent van Gogh, Amsterdam

〈 Colorplate XVIII, Terrace of a Café (La Guinguette), 1178

originally ascribed 1194 to Nuenen, while the very similar self-portrait 1195 was assigned by him to Antwerp. Tralbaut ascribed both works to Antwerp, and other experts have opted for either the Antwerp or the Nuenen period. The 1970 *catalogue raisonné* places them both in "Paris first half of 1886," which, strictly speaking, means that they must have been made during the period March to June. Because of the looser manner of painting, I think they should be placed later in 1886 than the self-portraits with felt hat 1089 and 1090, and I have further tried to link them with self-portrait 1199, painted in a similar style, in which Vincent appears with the same calm look, in the same suit, and also with his pipe.

This last self-portrait now bears the signature "Vincent" and the date "'87." In his book on the self-portraits (1969) Fritz Erpel has suggested that this signature and date may have been forged, but this is contradicted in the 1970 *catalogue raisonné*, where it is said: "The editors accept the authenticity of the signature and date of F263a [that is, 1199]. The painting could have been executed in 1886, then reworked in 1887." I regard this as the most acceptable explanation, since the painting passed directly from Mrs. van Gogh-Bonger to her son, and thus ended up in the Rijksmuseum Vincent van Gogh. Accordingly there seems to have been no stage at which any tampering of this kind could have taken place and no reason why anyone should have wanted to do so.

The three self-portraits 1194, 1195, and 1199 together give a good picture of Van Gogh as we must imagine him in the second half of 1886 and the beginning of 1887: full of relaxed self-assurance, well dressed (compare this with what is said on page 266), and possessing sufficient mastery of the technique of painting a convincing portrait. If the self-portraits 1195 and 1199, which are almost like an image and its reflection in a mirror, are compared more closely, 1199 does seem to have been done at a somewhat later stage, either because in fact it was not done until 1887 or because it was "reworked." In comparison, the thinly painted self-portrait 1195, with the "flat" background, appears to be the work of a less experienced hand.

The well-known and frequently reproduced drawing 1197 represents a self-portrait of masterly stature. It was done on the same sheet as a less successful first draft of another self-portrait in the lower right corner and a rough sketch of some details in the upper right. These extra sketches make it clear that Vincent did not consider the first drawing important as an independent effort and probably regarded it only as a preliminary study for a painted portrait. In addition, the sheet has unfortunately been mutilated: a rectangular piece has been cut away from the upper left corner—by whom and for what reason is not known. In referring to this drawing the 1970 *catalogue raisonné* notes: "Compare painting F380" (here, 1225), thus suggesting that this painting is the study made after the drawing. The painted self-portrait 1225 was considered to have been made in the summer of 1887, and thus drawing 1197 has similarly been dated "summer 1887" in the *catalogue raisonné*. As I see it, the draw-

1181

1182

1183

1181 The Hill of Montmartre, F1394
Pen, colored chalk, 10 × 17 cm ($3\frac{7}{8} \times 6\frac{3}{4}''$)
Rijksmuseum Vincent van Gogh, Amsterdam

1182 The Moulin de Blute-Fin, F348
61 × 50 cm ($24 \times 19\frac{5}{8}''$)
Museo Nacional de Bellas Artes, Buenos Aires

1183 Belvedere Overlooking Montmartre, F272
Canvas on panel, 44 × 33.5 cm ($17\frac{3}{8} \times 13\frac{1}{4}''$)
Art Institute of Chicago

1184 Windmill on Montmartre, F349
55 × 38.5 cm ($21\frac{5}{8} \times 15\frac{3}{8}''$)
Collection Mrs. Charles W. Engelhard, Newark, New Jersey

1185 The Moulin de Blute-Fin, F1396a
Pen, black chalk, 53 × 39 cm ($20\frac{7}{8} \times 15\frac{3}{8}''$)
Collection Miss E. Hudson, Syracuse, New York

1186 The Moulin de Blute-Fin, F271
46.5 × 38 cm ($18\frac{1}{2} \times 15''$)
Destroyed by fire in 1967

1184

1185

1186

1187

1188

1189

1190

1187 View in Paris, F 1405
Watercolor, 34 × 51 cm ($13\frac{3}{8} \times 20\frac{1}{8}''$)
Rijksmuseum Vincent van Gogh, Amsterdam

1188 The Moulin de Blute-Fin, F 1395
Pencil, 11 × 20 cm ($4\frac{3}{8} \times 7\frac{7}{8}''$)
Rijksmuseum Vincent van Gogh, Amsterdam

1189 Stuffed Owl, F 1373v (reverse: 1190)
Pencil, pen, blue ink, 35.5 × 26 cm
($14\frac{1}{8} \times 10\frac{1}{4}''$)
Rijksmuseum Vincent van Gogh, Amsterdam

1190 Stuffed Owl, F 1373 (reverse: 1189)
Pencil, pen, blue ink, 35.5 × 26 cm
($14\frac{1}{8} \times 10\frac{1}{4}''$)
Rijksmuseum Vincent van Gogh, Amsterdam

ing is a preliminary study, not for 1225 (nor for 1224, as suggested by K. Bromig-Kolleritz in her study on the self-portraits),* but for 1198. The position of the head, details such as the shorter growth of beard, and particularly the intense expression of the eyes correspond much more closely, in my opinion, with 1198 than with 1225. Self-portrait 1198 is in any case the earlier of the two by far, as is apparent just from the plain background. Self-portrait 1225 exhibits a hatching technique and a patchy background—both relatively late characteristics. Thus, if my surmise is correct, the drawing would have to be dated considerably earlier than "summer 1887." One complication is that there is an amazingly wide divergence of views among the experts in dating painting 1198. De la Faille, in his 1928 and 1939 editions, dated it Nuenen; Bromig-Kolleritz: "late Antwerp," which would mean about February 1886; Erpel: Paris, March–April 1886. Nuenen, in my opinion, is out of the question, for, quite apart from the style in which the canvas was painted, the Van Gogh depicted here, with his neat blue jacket and its narrow velvet collar, seems to me to bear little relationship to the tales about his appearance in Brabant, and very much the same is the case for Antwerp. In my opinion, both the preliminary study and the painting (1197 and 1198) must be dated late in 1886.

The Self-Portraits of 1887

One of the first paintings that Van Gogh did in 1887 is probably self-portrait 1199 (which even bears the painted numeral "'87," referred to above). Because of its dark brown-red and green colors, it would seem to be a step backward even in comparison with 1198. An even wider gap separates it from the self-portraits 1209–11, which have been painted in quite a different gamut of colors, including much light blue and violet.

In view of these somewhat inexplicable elements, a few general remarks about the 1887 self-portraits may be in order. In addition to 1199, there are another twenty-one self-portraits that should be assigned to that year. It has not yet been possible, even in the few studies devoted entirely to the self-portraits, to determine in a completely satisfactory manner the sequence in which these works were produced. My efforts to arrive at an acceptable chronology have been based on the following considerations:

As these twenty-two self-portraits were done in the course of one year, they must have been made at fairly close intervals. Furthermore, the self-portraits from a particular moment will naturally be similar in style and technique to other works done at the same time. An additional fact of some importance is that the last self-portrait Vincent did in the Paris period—the famous portrait at the easel (1356)—was dated "'88" by Vincent himself. This work must therefore have been painted in January or February 1888, since Vincent left for Arles at the end of February. Certainly the last of the paintings in that series could not have differed very much in style and treatment from the self-portrait at the easel.

In studying and comparing the twenty-two self-portraits, I was struck by the fact that they nearly always appear in *pairs*. One gets the impression that after Vincent made a self-portrait according to a certain conception as to brushwork, background, and so on, he almost immediately did a repetition or variant. Consequently, the self-portraits seem to fall into a number of small groups consisting of two or three works (in only one group are there more than this) that follow the same pattern of style. The eight groups I have thus been able to distinguish (and which I have labeled to indicate a salient characteristic) are as follows:

Elegant	1209–11
Soft-colored	1224–25
Pointillist	1248–49
Blue	1299–1304
Cloudy	1309–10
Wild	1333–34
Transitional	1344–45
Multicolored	1353–54

*K. Bromig-Kolleritz, "*Die Selbstbildnisse Vincent van Goghs*" (The Self-Portraits of Vincent van Gogh) (1955).

1191

1192

1193

1194

1195

1196

1197

1198

1191 Kingfisher, F28
19 × 26.5 cm ($7\frac{1}{2} \times 10\frac{5}{8}''$)
Rijksmuseum Vincent van Gogh, Amsterdam

1192 Stuffed Kalong Bat (Flying Dog), F177a
41 × 79 cm ($16\frac{1}{8} \times 31\frac{1}{8}''$)
Rijksmuseum Vincent van Gogh, Amsterdam

1193 Stuffed Green Parrot, F14
Canvas on panel, 48 × 43 cm ($18\frac{7}{8} \times 16\frac{7}{8}''$)
Collection R. W. van Hoey Smith, Rockanje, The Netherlands

1194 Self-Portrait with Pipe, F180
46 × 38 cm ($18\frac{1}{8} \times 15''$)
Rijksmuseum Vincent van Gogh, Amsterdam

1195 Self-Portrait with Pipe, F208
27 × 19 cm ($10\frac{5}{8} \times 7\frac{1}{2}''$)
Rijksmuseum Vincent van Gogh, Amsterdam

1196 Self-Portrait, F1379
Pencil, 19 × 21 cm ($7\frac{1}{2} \times 8\frac{1}{4}''$)
Rijksmuseum Vincent van Gogh, Amsterdam

1197 Two Self-Portraits and Several Details, F1378
Pencil, pen, 32 × 24 cm ($12\frac{5}{8} \times 9\frac{1}{2}''$) (upper-left corner cut out)
Rijksmuseum Vincent van Gogh, Amsterdam

1198 Self-Portrait, F178v (reverse: 528)
39.5 × 29.5 cm ($15\frac{3}{4} \times 11\frac{3}{4}''$)
Gemeentemuseum, The Hague

1199

Vincent and Neo-Impressionism

By the time Vincent arrived in Paris and became acquainted with Impressionism, the movement had already passed its peak; the eighth exhibition of the Impressionists, held in 1886, was also the last one of those painters as a group. Younger painters with ideas that deviated from the theories of Impressionism—all of them artists Vincent would eventually get to know—were beginning to attract attention, although initially only among a small group. Very little indication of how Vincent felt about Impressionism—beyond a few random remarks addressed to Wil in June 1888—is found in his letters. These observations were made after Theo had sent a consignment of paintings by Impressionists, including one by Vincent, to Tersteeg, and Tersteeg "had found nothing in it." They met with the same lack of response from the Dutch artists to whom Tersteeg had apparently shown the paintings. In a resigned tone, Vincent commented: "That is really quite understandable, for it is always the same story. One has heard about the Impressionists and expects a lot, and ... when one sees them for the first time, there is bitter disappointment, and it all seems slapdash, ugly, badly painted, badly drawn, bad in color, and just plain wretched. That was also my own first impression when I came to Paris with the ideas of Mauve, Israëls, and other able painters" (Letter W4).

Yes, disappointment, but a disappointment that must have turned very soon into admiration. For a proper understanding of the matter, however, we must realize that "Impressionists," for Vincent, was a collective term for "the new painters," embracing also what we refer to as the Neo-Impressionists. In a few letters (Letters 468, 500, and others) he did make a distinction between the painters of the "Grand Boulevard" and those of the "Petit Boulevard." This distinction was explained by Mrs. van Gogh-Bonger in a note to Letter 468: "Vincent called Monet, Sisley, Renoir, Degas, etc., whose work was shown by Theo on the Boulevard Montmartre: 'The Painters of the Grand Boulevard,' whereas he called himself, Bernard, Anquetin, Gauguin and Lautrec, who once exhibited in the restaurant on the Boulevard de Clichy,* 'The Painters of the Petit Boulevard.'"

What Vincent considered the common trait of the Impressionists, as appears from the letter to Wil, was the rapid pace at which they worked, and he imagined that "this decisive working without hesitation, the exact measuring in one glance, the nimble blending of colors, the delineation at lightning speed" were things that a later generation would be better able to appreciate. Speaking of "those twenty or so painters who are called Impressionists," he told Wil that a few of them had become fairly rich, but that "the majority [were] poor devils who live in cafés, stay at cheap inns, and exist from day to day." But, he added, "in a single day all those twenty I mentioned paint anything they see in front of them and better than many a great figure in the world of art who has a big name."

*In the Restaurant du Chalet, 43 Avenue de Clichy. (Mrs. van Gogh-Bonger's note was quoted from the original [Dutch] edition of the letters.)

The "Elegant" Group

The self-portraits 1209–11 differ from the previously discussed self-portrait 1199 (see page 260) because they disclose the influence of Impressionism much more clearly. They are not yet Pointillist but are much more colorful than his earlier work. The red-brown backgrounds of the paintings 1089, 1198, and 1199 have now given way to a background of blue or blue-green in various tints against which the figure, in related or contrasting color, is set off. In the latter three portraits Vincent has shown himself wearing a hat and

January–March 1887

1199 Self-Portrait with Pipe and Glass, F263a
61 × 50 cm (24 × 19⅝″)
Rijksmuseum Vincent van Gogh, Amsterdam

1200 Portrait of a Man, F288
55 × 41 cm (21⅝ × 16⅛″)
Location unknown

1201 Portrait of a Man, F209
Canvas on panel, 31 × 39.5 cm (12¼ × 15¾″)
National Gallery of Victoria, Melbourne

1202 Portrait of Père Tanguy, F263
47 × 38.5 cm (18½ × 15⅜″)
Ny Carlsberg Glyptotek, Copenhagen

1203 Portrait of a Man with a Skullcap, F289
65.5 × 54 cm (26 × 21¼″)
Rijksmuseum Vincent van Gogh, Amsterdam

1200

1201

1202

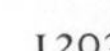

1203

a trim suit, and in 1209 and 1210 he is even wearing a smart-looking light blue bow tie. He presents himself here—in these three portraits of what I have called the "elegant" group—as a well-dressed man of the world.

The suit shown in 1209 is dark blue, piped with light blue, but the suit in 1210 and 1211 is brown with blue piping (I assume that in all these cases it was actually the same brown suit, but that the lighter, almost mauve color of 1209 was the result of the artist's conscious striving to achieve a harmony of soft colors). Instead of a soft felt hat, the painter is seen wearing a straw hat in 1209—the hat that would appear in many self-portraits of the coming summer. Although such a hat is out of place in the winter months (and the 1970 *catalogue raisonné* has accordingly dated the piece "summer 1887"), I am convinced that this self-portrait was done at about the same time as 1210, with which it has in common not only the somewhat stiff pose, but also the material (cardboard) and the strikingly small format ($7\frac{1}{2}$ by $5\frac{1}{2}$ inches). Vincent may have used the yellow straw hat solely to provide a complementary color.

In the much larger portrait 1211 I see something of a further development. More than in 1210, the plastic quality of the face has been achieved by touches of paint that have not been smoothed out; the brim of the hat and the piping of the suit have been rendered by short lines; the suit is rather more stippled than in 1210; and lastly, the background has been enlivened by broad diagonal brushstrokes. It is undoubtedly a more important work than 1209 and 1210, not only because of its size but also because it exhibits a freer and more controlled design. The expression is searching and worried. Behind the elegant façade the tense and fanatical artist shows through.

From a few portraits that can be assumed to have been done in the first months of 1887, it is apparent that Vincent's Pointillist friends probably still did not influence him very much at that time. One portrait, which is dated "janvier 87," serves as a good reference point for the chronology. It is a portrait of the famous Père Tanguy (1202)—a work particularly surprising from a psychological standpoint because it captures so well the kindly, lively understanding of this essentially simple man who was so important to many painters. I have grouped together with 1199 and 1202 the portraits 1200–1208 even though they differ to a fair degree among themselves. Four of them have been dated somewhat earlier in the 1970 *catalogue raisonné*: 1200, 1201, 1204, and 1205. The portrait of a woman 1204 was dated as early as the Antwerp period by Tralbaut, but in comparison with the female portraits 978 and 979 done in Antwerp, the much easier style of painting and the delicate touches in this portrait make me think rather of Paris. In view of the scarcity of data I attach much importance to what Theo wrote to his mother (see the previously mentioned article in *Vincent*, vol. III, no. 2), which indicates that Vincent did not resume making portraits until 1887. Theo wrote on January 12, 1887: "He seems to be setting himself to doing portraits," and again on February 28: "He has painted a couple of portraits which have turned out well." This tallies with the date Vincent put on the portrait of Tanguy.

The portrait of an unidentified man 1203 bears some resemblance to the portrait of Tanguy because of its location in the picture plane and the forceful, massive figure. In addition, some similarities to Impressionist painting can be detected in the soft tints of the jacket and skullcap and in the light background, which gives the impression of being plain but has been built up from delicate blue-green and soft pink touches of paint.

The portrait of a man 1207, which, again, has been painted in a somewhat more pronounced "short-stroke style," is known definitely to represent the British painter and art dealer Alexander Reid, whom Vincent had known from his London days and who, like Vincent himself, had a keen interest in Monticelli. Since he was more or less in competition with Theo, his name cropped up frequently in Vincent's letters to Theo.

The portrait of a woman 1208 is of even greater anecdotal interest—in addition to its great importance as a work of art. The tambourine-shaped top of the café table and the two tambourines in the lower left and right corners of the picture make it reasonable to

1204

1205

1206

1207

1204 Portrait of a Woman in Blue, F207a
46 × 38 cm ($18\frac{1}{8} \times 15''$)
Rijksmuseum Vincent van Gogh, Amsterdam

1205 Portrait of a Woman, F215b
26.5 × 21 cm ($10\frac{5}{8} \times 8\frac{1}{4}''$)
Rijksmuseum Vincent van Gogh, Amsterdam

1206 Lady, Sitting by a Cradle, F369
61 × 46 cm ($24 \times 18\frac{1}{8}''$)
Rijksmuseum Vincent van Gogh, Amsterdam

1207 Portrait of Alexander Reid, Sitting in an Easy Chair, F270
Cardboard, 41 × 33 cm ($16\frac{1}{8} \times 13''$)
Collection Mrs. Aaron Weitzenhoffer, Oklahoma City

1208 Woman at a Table in the Café du Tambourin, F370
55.5 × 46.5 cm ($22 \times 18\frac{1}{2}''$)
Rijksmuseum Vincent van Gogh, Amsterdam

1209 Self-Portrait with Straw Hat, F294
Cardboard, 19 × 14 cm ($7\frac{1}{2} \times 5\frac{1}{2}''$)
Rijksmuseum Vincent van Gogh, Amsterdam

1210 Self-Portrait with Gray Felt Hat, F296
Cardboard, 19 × 14 cm ($7\frac{1}{2} \times 5\frac{1}{2}''$)
Rijksmuseum Vincent van Gogh, Amsterdam

1211 Self-Portrait with Gray Felt Hat, F295
Cardboard, 41 × 32 cm ($16\frac{1}{8} \times 12\frac{5}{8}''$)
Stedelijk Museum, Amsterdam (on loan from the Rijksmuseum, Amsterdam)

1208

1209

1210

1211

assume that the Café du Tambourin, situated at 62 Boulevard de Clichy, is the establishment depicted here. This cabaret and restaurant was a favorite haunt of writers and artists and played an important part in Vincent's life in Paris. He exhibited paintings by himself and friends here and likewise a collection of the Japanese prints that were very much in vogue. The vaguely defined representation of a female figure on the wall to the right is perhaps one of the Japanese prints he had hung there himself.

Vincent is believed to have been the lover of the café proprietress, Agostina Segatori, an Italian woman who was also an artist's model. The woman with the curious red headdress (perhaps a hat made of feathers), sitting at the small table with a quietly pensive expression, may indeed be La Segatori, as is generally assumed, but there is nothing really to confirm this. There is a much later portrait of a woman in a colorful dress (1355) that is always described in catalogues as "the Italian woman" and is likewise often assumed—but I think wrongly so—to portray La Segatori.

I have also included in this group the portrait 1206, showing an unidentified woman sitting next to a cradle. The work is hard to date; the 1970 *catalogue raisonné* assigns it to the spring of 1887. What is more significant here is that Vincent, in this only slightly Pointillist and very carefully painted canvas done in subtle colors, has demonstrated in a style entirely his own that he could paint a portrait that can hold its own with the work of most of his Impressionist friends and yet show a personal touch. In atmosphere and layout it reminds me of the fine painting *The Cradle*, by Berthe Morisot (1873), now in the Louvre, which Vincent may have consciously or unconsciously had in mind while making his portrait. The composition differs by reason of the prominence given to the cradle by Berthe Morisot, whereas Vincent has merely hinted at it in a very subtle way through the tulle curtain and the blue bow on the right-hand side of the canvas.

Nudes and Landscapes

The nudes 1212–15, which are not easy to date, are also generally ascribed to the first half of 1887. They show the influence of Vincent's new manner of painting, without being distinctly Pointillist. Drawing 1213 is clearly a preliminary study for the oval painting 1214; in 1215 the posture of the model (right arm) and the position on the page are somewhat different. The exaggeration of the coarse features of the woman, who has kept on only her stockings (in 1215, also her shoes), and her provocative pose, may indicate that the model was a prostitute and that Vincent also wanted to make that clear. In the beautiful composition of a nude, with hanging pigtail, seen from the back, 1212—whether or not it is the same model is not known—Vincent has succeeded in obtaining a less shocking and aesthetically more pleasing result. Here the clear contrast between the silvery white of the bedclothes and the light brown of the skin has been achieved with a high degree of refinement.

I have also put with this group the portrait of a woman 1216 because the model in this

1212

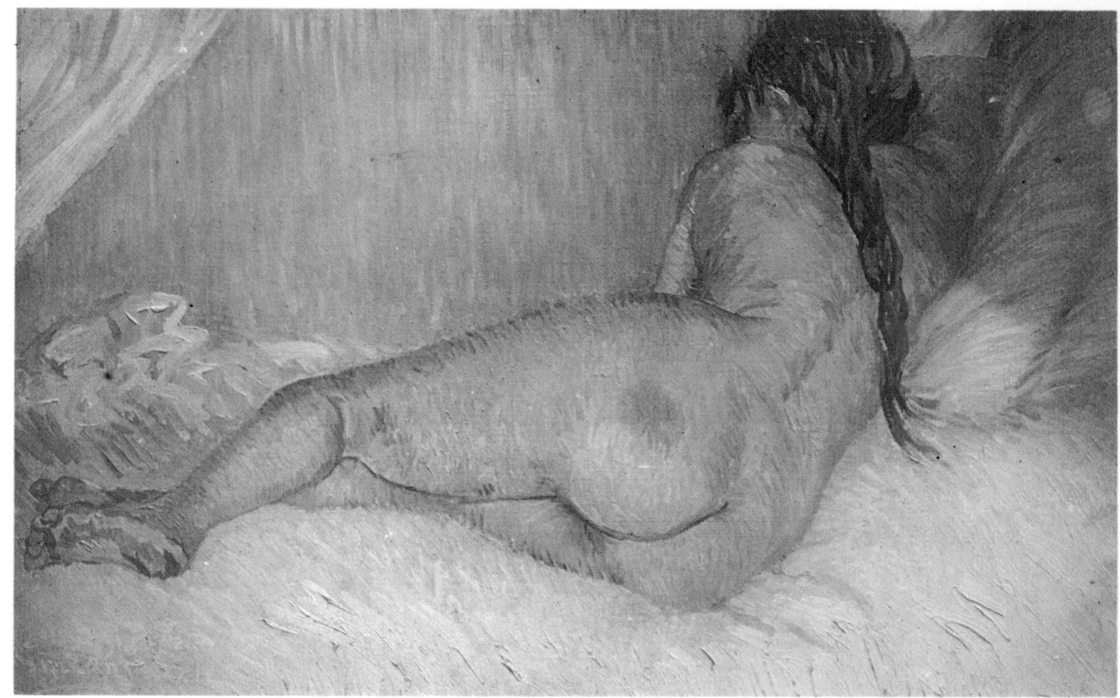

1213

1214

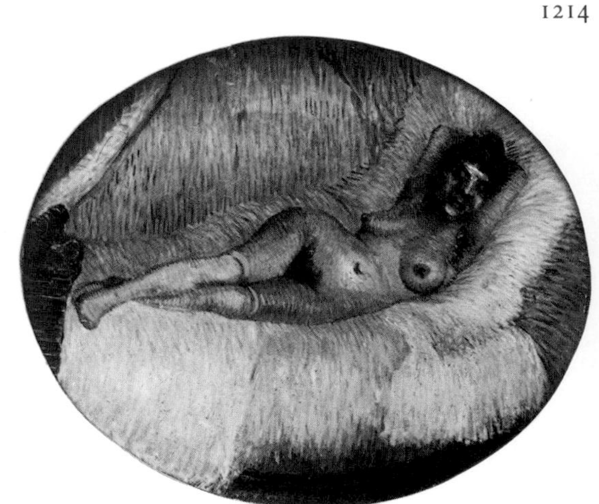

1212 Nude Woman, Reclining, Seen from the Back, F328
38 × 61 cm (15 × 24″)
Private collection, Paris

1213 Nude Woman, Reclining, F1404
Pencil, 24 × 31.5 cm (9½ × 12⅜″)
Rijksmuseum Vincent van Gogh, Amsterdam

1214 Nude Woman, Reclining, F330
Oval, 59.5 × 73 cm (23⅝ × 28¾″)
© The Barnes Foundation Museum of Art, Merion, Pennsylvania

1215 Nude Woman, Reclining, F329
24 × 41 cm (9½ × 16⅛″)
Collection Mrs. S. van Deventer, Oberägeri, Switzerland

1216 Portrait of a Woman, Head, F357
42 × 35 cm (16½ × 13¾″)
Kunstmuseum, Basel (on loan from the Rudolf Staechelin Collection)

1217 Street Scene (Boulevard de Clichy), F1393
Pen, colored chalk, 40 × 54 cm (15¾ × 21¼″)
Rijksmuseum Vincent van Gogh, Amsterdam

1215

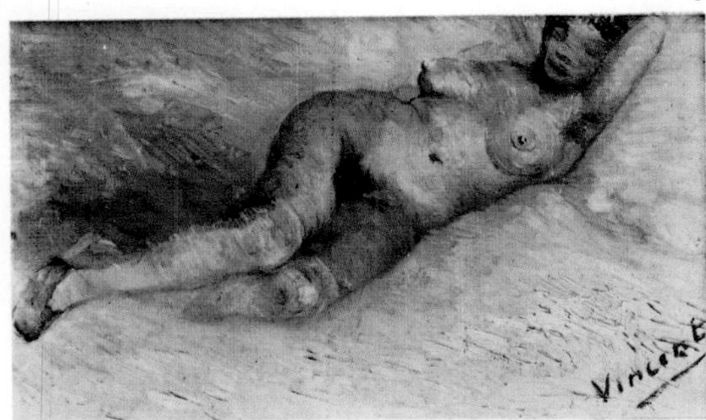

1217

1216

1218

1218 View from a Window (Restaurant Chez Bataille), F 1392
Pen, colored chalk, 54 × 40 cm ($21\frac{1}{4} \times 15\frac{3}{4}$″)
Rijksmuseum Vincent van Gogh, Amsterdam

case seems to me to be the same as the nude in 1213–15; both have the same hair style and strikingly broad nose. Vincent obviously made the portrait of this woman during the same period that he painted the nudes. The style is here again somewhat more decidedly Pointillist than in 1212 and 1215, and the vigorous contrast between the glaring green of the dress and the blood-red background is especially noteworthy.

The city scenes and landscapes 1217–23 should also be dated early 1887, specifically in the *winter months* because of the bare trees. Both 1217 and 1219, which show the Boulevard de Clichy, were strongly influenced by Impressionism; 1219 was done in a markedly graphic style with small unmixed strokes of paint in soft colors. Drawing 1217, heightened with colored chalk—a preliminary study for the painting—exhibits the same subdued coloring, but there is an even warmer play of light on the façades of the buildings. The two female figures in the lower right-hand corner cut off from below, a typical Neo-Impressionist compositional element, were omitted by Vincent in the painting, perhaps because he thought they were too prominent, but the foreground has become noticeably empty as a result.

Done in an Impressionist style like that in 1217, with short thin lines, the drawing of the *View from Vincent's Window* on the Rue Lepic (1220) is impressive in its daring composition and plastic effect.

The ink-and-chalk drawing 1218, showing an interior with a glimpse of the street, is also Impressionist in character. It is an attractive scene, caught with an appearance of speed and bravado, which effectively renders both the indoor and the outdoor atmospheres with virtually nothing but yellow and blue. It also has autobiographical significance, for on the table top in the lower right-hand corner Vincent has written: "La fenêtre chez Bataille Vincent 87" ("the window at Bataille's"), giving the name of a restaurant near the Rue Lepic where the Van Gogh brothers used to dine.

The landscapes with the windmills 1221 and 1222—in which the Moulin de Blute-Fin and the belvedere next to it can be recognized from the works of the previous year—present a rather wintry look. The drawing technique in 1222 is similar to that in 1217, 1218, and 1220. Painting 1221, by reason both of its composition and the brightness of the colors, is somewhat more Impressionist in nature than the similar paintings of windmills dating from 1886. Finally, the wintry landscape with the moon, 1223, which is difficult to date precisely, is again entirely different in character with its simple composition and delicate building up of colors in three horizontal bands: the dark-green foreground, the blue middle strip with the vaguely defined factories, and the blue-green sky with yellowish streaks of light and the orange-red orb of the moon. The little canvas is fascinating, more for its purely artistic merits than for any experiments in technique.

The self-portraits 1224 and 1225 must also, in my opinion, be assigned to these months. They represent the second small group of self-portraits done in 1887—what I have called the "soft-colored" group. They are

1219

1220

1221

1219 Street Scene (Boulevard de Clichy), F292
46.5 × 55 cm (18½ × 21⅝")
Rijksmuseum Vincent van Gogh, Amsterdam

1220 View from Vincent's Window, F1391
Pencil, pen, washed, 39.5 × 53.5 cm (15⅝ × 21¼")
Rijksmuseum Vincent van Gogh, Amsterdam

1221 The Moulin de Blute-Fin, F348a
46 × 38 cm (18⅛ × 15")
Museum of Art, Carnegie Institute, Pittsburgh

1222 The Moulin de Blute-Fin, F1396
Pencil, colored chalk, 40 × 54 cm (15¾ × 21¼")
Rijksmuseum Vincent van Gogh, Amsterdam

1223 View of a Town with Factories, F266a
20.5 × 46 cm (8⅛ × 18⅛")
Rijksmuseum Vincent van Gogh, Amsterdam

April–June 1887

1224 Self-Portrait, F267
Cardboard, 19 × 14 cm (7½ × 5½")
Rijksmuseum Vincent van Gogh, Amsterdam

1222

1223

1224

1225

1226

1227

1228

1225 Self-Portrait, F380
Paper, 32 × 25.5 cm ($12\frac{5}{8} \times 10\frac{1}{8}''$)
Rijksmuseum Kröller-Müller, Otterlo

1226 Three Novels, F335
Oval panel, 31 × 48.5 cm ($12\frac{1}{4} \times 19\frac{1}{4}''$)
Rijksmuseum Vincent van Gogh, Amsterdam

1227 A Basket with Bulbs, F336
Oval panel, 31.5 × 48 cm ($12\frac{5}{8} \times 18\frac{7}{8}''$)
Rijksmuseum Vincent van Gogh, Amsterdam

1228 A Basket with Sprouting Bulbs, F334
32.5 × 41 cm ($13 \times 16\frac{1}{8}''$)
Rijksmuseum Vincent van Gogh, Amsterdam

not yet markedly Pointillist as are many of the spring landscapes 1240–46, and their coloring seems for the most part to fall between the earlier landscapes, also done mainly in fairly delicate colors, and the series of still lifes 1226–39 , to be discussed later. The small sketch ($7\frac{1}{2}$ by $5\frac{1}{2}$ inches) on cardboard 1224 is, in my opinion, only a first, unfinished draft, not quite identical with 1225, but closely related to it in the position of the head and the expression. In 1225 the face has been built up from still clearly visible separate touches of color, and this reveals a greater measure of freedom and technical mastery than is apparent in the earlier series of self-portraits, 1209–11. The facial expression in this fine piece is quietly searching and fairly relaxed, in harmony with the unusually soft colors of the mauve jacket with gray-green piping, the light blue necktie, and the soft green speckled background.

Still Lifes

A decided brightening of Vincent's palette is evident in the still lifes of early 1887 (1226–39), and they can accordingly be dated on this basis with some assurance. In the 1970 *catalogue raisonné* they have almost all been dated "spring" or "early spring 1887" or "first half of 1887." On one of the paintings of *A Pair of Shoes* (1236), Vincent himself provided the date: "87," although the bright blue of the material on which the shoes have been placed here is in itself sufficient to indicate that this piece could never have been painted in 1886. From the standpoint of composition the still life of shoes 1233 is the counterpart of 1236, and although the shoes in 1235 are portrayed against a beige ground, this piece, too, has been executed in the same manner—with short isolated, sharply contrasting brushstrokes—as 1236. (The psychological significance of these still lifes with shoes was discussed on page 244.)

With the exception of the still life in which Van Gogh, contrary to his custom, seeks an aesthetic effect by depicting a vase with flowers, a coffee pot, and fruit (1231), the other still lifes of this group, like those just discussed, all portray simple, humble objects, such as the little baskets with bulbs, 1227 and 1228; a flowerpot with chives, 1229; little dishes with fruit, 1237 and 1239 (colorplate XIX, page 275); or some plain bread and rolls or a few herrings, 1232 and 1230. It is as though Vincent went through a period of continual wonderment at the reality of simple things and felt the need to reexperience their form, color, and tangibleness through the magic of his brushes and paints. While there is occasionally still a conscious effort to create color compositions—as in 1229 and 1239, where he brings the reddish-orange and green bands of the backdrop into play—often there is not even anything like this at all, and, as in 1237, all that remains, in Cézannesque simplicity, are the bare objects themselves in their concreteness.

The still life with the glass of absinthe and a carafe of water, 1238, is strongly reminiscent—because of its graphic style featuring delicate brushstrokes in soft blue, violet, and reddish-brown tints—of city scenes like those in 1217–20. A glass of absinthe, certainly a favorite drink with artists of that time, was a

1229

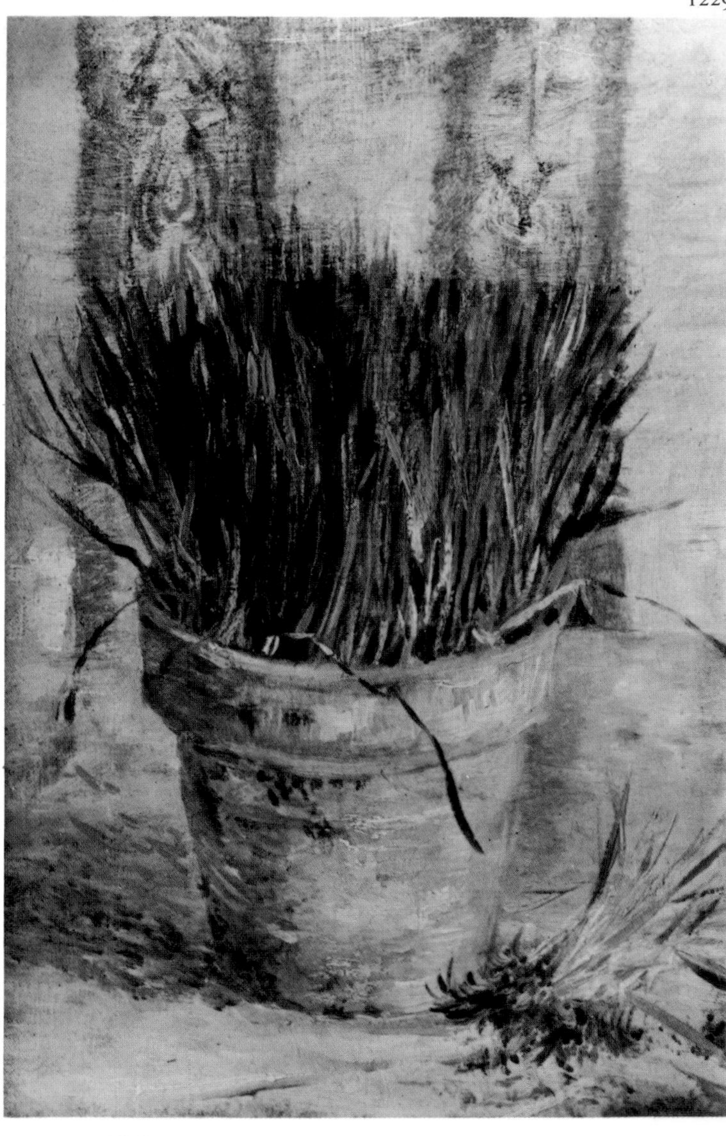

1230

1231

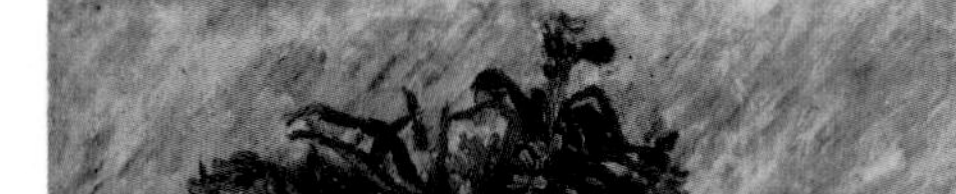

1229 Flowerpot with Chives, F337
32 × 22 cm ($12\frac{5}{8} \times 8\frac{5}{8}$″)
Rijksmuseum Vincent van Gogh, Amsterdam

1230 Three Red Herrings and a Garlic Bulb, F283b
37 × 44.5 cm ($14\frac{5}{8} \times 17\frac{3}{4}$″)
Bridgestone Museum of Art, Tokyo

1231 Vase with Flowers, Coffee Pot, and Fruit, F287
41 × 38 cm ($16\frac{1}{8} \times 15$″)
Von der Heydt Museum, Wuppertal

1232 A Plate with Rolls, F253a
31.5 × 40 cm ($12\frac{5}{8} \times 15\frac{3}{4}$″)
Rijksmuseum Vincent van Gogh, Amsterdam

1233 A Pair of Shoes, One Shoe Upside Down, F332a
37.5 × 45.5 cm ($15 \times 18\frac{1}{8}$″)
Collection E. Schumacher, Brussels

1234 Three Pairs of Shoes, One Shoe Upside Down, F332
49 × 72 cm ($19\frac{1}{4} \times 28\frac{3}{8}$″)
Fogg Art Museum, Harvard University, Cambridge, Massachusetts

1235 A Pair of Shoes, F331
Cardboard, 33 × 41 cm ($13 \times 16\frac{1}{8}$″)
Rijksmuseum Vincent van Gogh, Amsterdam

1232

1233

1234

1235

1236

1237

1238

1236 A Pair of Shoes, One Shoe Upside Down, F333
34 × 41.5 cm ($13\frac{3}{8} \times 16\frac{1}{2}''$)
Baltimore Museum of Art

1237 A Plate with Lemons, F338
21 × 26.5 cm ($8\frac{1}{4} \times 10\frac{5}{8}''$)
Rijksmuseum Vincent van Gogh, Amsterdam

1238 A Table in Front of a Window with a Glass of Absinthe and a Carafe, F339
46.5 × 33 cm ($18\frac{1}{2} \times 13''$)
Rijksmuseum Vincent van Gogh, Amsterdam

motif that appeared in many an Impressionist painting, probably also because of the yellowish-green color. The most famous is surely the work by Degas in the Louvre, *L'Absinthe* (1876), in which a glass, in a situation of tragic drama, stands on a small café table at which two persons are seated. In the pastel portrait that Toulouse-Lautrec made of Vincent in 1887, there, too, unobtrusively, a glass of absinthe sits in front of Vincent.

Books in Van Gogh's Still Lifes

Finally, a few words about the still life with books, 1226. In the first place, it shows Vincent's penchant at the time for oval compositions. (Incidentally, 1226 and 1227, also ovals, were done on the wooden cover of a tea chest; a third oval composition, 1214, was done on canvas and in a much bigger format.)

More important was the reason for his choice of the books in 1226; they were chosen not solely because of their form and color, not solely because of the contrast between the brown and red of the book in the rear and the bright yellow of the modern covers on the books in front, but also because of their intellectual connotations. Vincent apparently felt the need to record his literary preferences of the moment in this manner, depicting Emile Zola's *Au Bonheur des Dames*, Jean Richepin's *Braves Gens*, and Edmond de Goncourt's *La Fille Elisa*.

In connection with this painting and other still lifes with books from Van Gogh's Paris period A.M. Hammacher has pointed out that the influence of Paul Signac must have been important here: "The works produced by Signac around 1883 show a remarkable resemblance to still-lifes done by Van Gogh from the end of 1886 to 1888. As far as we know, nothing can be found in contemporary work by other painters which can be said to be so nearly related."* Among the examples Hammacher referred to were two still lifes by Signac. One, portraying a book and other objects on a table, dates from 1883. The other, probably dating from 1884, depicts a book entitled *Au Soleil*—African travel impressions by Guy de Maupassant, published in 1884.

But it is even more striking to observe that as early as 1885—at a time when Vincent knew next to nothing about the Impressionists and had certainly not seen the still lifes by Signac referred to here—Vincent had made the large still life of the Bible, 946, in which he had portrayed the recently published French novel *La Joie de Vivre* in almost the same position as *Au Soleil* in Signac's still life and likewise bearing a legible title. I can find no rational explanation for this. One can only say that in October 1885, Vincent, working in an isolated environment in Nuenen, had with a rare intuition for "what was in the air" spontaneously done the same thing as the Impressionists in Paris who were later to become his friends. Without impugning the soundness of Hammacher's assertion regarding Signac's

*A. M. Hammacher, *Van Gogh's Life in His Drawings/Van Gogh's Relationship with Signac* (1962, exhibition catalogue), p. 92.

1239

1240

1241

1239 A Plate with Lemons and a Carafe, F340
46 × 38 cm (18⅛ × 15″)
Rijksmuseum Vincent van Gogh, Amsterdam
Colorplate XIX, opposite

1240 Street Scene in Montmartre (No F Number)
46 × 61 cm (18⅛ × 24″)
Private collection, Copenhagen

1241 Street Scene in Montmartre, F347
35 × 64.5 cm (13¾ × 25⅝″)
Rijksmuseum Vincent van Gogh, Amsterdam

Colorplate XIX, A Plate with Lemons and a Carafe, 1239 〉

Vincent
87

influence in 1887, one might equally well hazard the opinion that, in depicting recent French books in his still lifes of that year, Vincent was carrying forward an idea he had hit upon in 1885.

Pointillism

Vincent, too, must have gradually been won over to the new trends, such as working with unmixed dots, short lines, and strokes in bright and mostly even primary colors. We see that technique applied in many of his paintings made in 1887 and the beginning of 1888, sometimes fairly consistently and sometimes very freely. It is clear that he was very much taken by this system and liked to experiment with it because it fortified the color and brightness of his work, but it is equally clear that he did not let himself be led into a strictly scientific application of it in the manner of Georges Seurat. There is a great diversity of style in Vincent's paintings of those years that makes it difficult to set up a reliable chronology. In the absence of any written testimony from the Paris years, what Pointillism meant to him must be determined from what he wrote to Theo in August 1888: "As regards pointillé, aureoling [that is, circling or haloing objects with a line in a complementary color], and the like, I consider them to be real discoveries, but there is little likelihood of that technique, any more than any other, becoming a universal dogma. One reason more why Seurat's *Grande Jatte*, the landscapes by Signac done in thick dots, and Anquetin's boat will in time come to seem more personal and more strange" (Letter 528).

The two closely related street scenes of Butte Montmartre, 1240 and 1241, must also have been done in the early part of spring in 1887, since there are almost no leaves on the trees. The first one does not appear in the *catalogue raisonné* because De la Faille did not know of its existence.* This work, like 1241, shows a pair of strollers and two small children but views the subject at closer range.

The views of Paris, 1242 and 1243, and the Montmartre landscape, 1244, would seem, in my opinion, to have been done at a somewhat later date. An emphatically Pointillist technique begins to dominate here, as is, for example, clearly apparent from the roofs and walls of the buildings in 1242 and 1243. The landscape with the Moulin de Blute-Fin, 1244, is painted in much softer colors. The lateral faces of the small sheds in the center and to the right are made up entirely of tiny blue dots, while the small plots in the foreground are covered with yellow, orange, and green dots, contrasting with the uniformly painted blue and white sky.

The landscapes 1245 and 1246, certainly done even later in the spring, also belong here. The fields show a little more green, and the paintings have a bit more force and color. They are still marked by a strongly Pointillist style, but the dots of paint are gradually taking on the character of *short lines*. The landscape with the windmill, 1245, has practically the same motif as Vincent painted about a half year before, when he did 1175.

*It was first described and reproduced by A.M. Hammacher in *Vincent*, vol. II, no. 2 (1972).

‹ Colorplate XX, People Walking in a Public Garden at Asnières, 1258

1242

1243

1244

1242 View from Vincent's Window, F341
46 × 38 cm (18⅛ × 15″)
Rijksmuseum Vincent van Gogh, Amsterdam

1243 View from Vincent's Window, F341a
Cardboard, 46 × 38 cm (18⅛ × 15″)
Collection Millicent Rogers, New York

1244 Vegetable Gardens in Montmartre and the Moulin de Blute-Fin, F346
43 × 80 cm (16⅞ × 31½″)
Rijksmuseum Vincent van Gogh, Amsterdam

But what a distance separates the newer work, sparkling with light and color, from the earlier one, which has the atmosphere of fall and is reminiscent of the color of Van Gogh's Dutch landscapes. The landscape with the little gardens and the distant view of a suburb of Paris, 1246, is noteworthy because of its singular composition—a kind of anticomposition—with the aggressively protruding plot of flowers and the empty foreground with paths that run out of the picture to the left and the right. Despite the bright colors in the central part, this forlorn landscape does not create a sunny or cheerful impression. Three years later we shall encounter the dynamics of this composition in excessive form in the famous painting of the wheat field with crows.

There can be little doubt that there was a direct connection between all these Pointillist works and the self-portraits 1248 and 1249 (my third group of 1887 self-portraits, the "Pointillist" group) as well as the closely related portrait 1250. In self-portrait 1249, for example, one is struck by the profusion of red and blue dots swarming over the dark-green background and by the manner in which the reddish brown of the jacket is achieved by a kind of painted mosaic of dark blue-green, orange-red, and yellow dots. The bright red beard and yellow-brown hair have been built up from separate brushstrokes in forceful colors, and Vincent has not hesitated to leave touches of unmixed complementary green in the eyebrows, hair, and beard. In self-portrait 1248, the Pointillist effect is, if anything, even more pronounced. Here the background has not been completely filled in, but the dots of color have been arranged in an irregular wreathlike pattern about the face. Both are excellent self-portraits that give the impression of complete control and assurance in spite of the disquieting Pointillist technique.

The subject of 1250 is the art dealer Alexander Reid, whom we recognize from the earlier portrait by Vincent, 1207. The background had been treated in the same way as in self-portrait 1249, with bright touches of paint, but now the total impression is one of brick-red instead of dark green. The jacket—a lighter brown—is suggested by a mass of yellow, green, and brown dots. Face, hair, and beard have been rendered even more daringly than in the two self-portraits by bright and unmixed short strokes of paint.

Spring

A long series of works clearly exhibiting springtime or early summer motifs (1251–78) must be assigned to the spring of 1887. These canvases, portraying the banks of the Seine, park scenes, and other themes much in favor with the Impressionists, offered Vincent the opportunity—just as the many still lifes of flowers had done earlier—to make his palette lighter and more colorful. In these paintings Van Gogh, with varying degrees of success and by means of various techniques, practiced outdoor painting in the spirit of his Impressionist friends. In some he still employed a definite Pointillist technique, very likely encouraged by his friend Signac as a zealous proponent of Pointillism, or "Divisionism," as he and the leaders of the move-

1245

1246

1247

1245 Vegetable Gardens in Montmartre, F350
96 × 120 cm ($37\frac{3}{4} \times 47\frac{1}{4}''$)
Stedelijk Museum, Amsterdam

1246 The Gardens of Montmartre, F316
81 × 100 cm ($31\frac{7}{8} \times 39\frac{3}{8}''$)
Rijksmuseum Vincent van Gogh, Amsterdam

1247 Fritillarias in a Copper Vase, F213
73.5 × 60.5 cm ($29\frac{1}{8} \times 24''$)
The Louvre, Paris

1248 Self-Portrait, F356
41 × 33 cm ($16\frac{1}{8} \times 13''$)
Rijksmuseum Vincent van Gogh, Amsterdam

1249 Self-Portrait, F345
Cardboard, 42 × 34 cm ($16\frac{1}{2} \times 13\frac{3}{8}''$)
Art Institute of Chicago

1250 Portrait of Alexander Reid, F343
Cardboard, 41.5 × 33.5 cm ($16\frac{1}{2} \times 13\frac{3}{8}''$)
Glasgow Art Gallery and Museum

1251 Restaurant de la Sirène at Asnières, F313
57 × 68 cm ($22\frac{1}{2} \times 26\frac{3}{4}''$)
The Louvre, Paris

1248

1249

1250

1251

ment preferred to call it. Genuinely Pointillist works, for example, are the park scenes 1259 and 1260, and more particularly 1258 (colorplate XX, page 276), which can be seen as a frankly Pointillist experiment. With the figures placed frontally in the foreground and the "naïve" symmetrical composition, this work shows some affinity with the strangely "frozen" atmosphere of Seurat's *Grande Jatte*, which may have inspired Van Gogh, but it has failed to approach even remotely the grandeur and originality of that example.

Although the interior of a restaurant, 1256, has often been described and reproduced as an example of Van Gogh's Pointillism, it is, as a matter of fact, only one of many such examples. However, it is justly famous for the remarkably effective rendering of the flat rear walls of the restaurant, and to a somewhat lesser degree also the floor, by means of a confettilike shower of white, yellow, green, and reddish-brown spots of color. It is clear that in this way Vincent achieved exactly what he obviously intended: to give the interior a light, cheerful, and springlike atmosphere, which is enhanced by the bright yellow chairs and the flowers on the neatly set tables in the small room.

Typically Impressionist studies in light and color are to be found in 1261 and 1262, both depicting a woman in a park or meadow. In each case, Van Gogh must have had a model, something that happened only rarely during his stay in Paris. The identity of these women is not known, any more than is that of the woman sitting next to a cradle in painting 1206 (see page 266). Among Vincent's circle of acquaintances in Paris, there is, apart from Agostina Segatori, only one woman that we know of by name. This was the Countess de la Boissière, who lived at Asnières, close by the Voyer d'Argenson Park on the bank of the Seine. He spoke about her and her daughter in a letter from Arles in which he asked Theo to give her two small paintings he had sent him. "She is staying at the Boulevard Voltaire, second floor of the first house at the end of the Pont de Clichy. On the ground floor is Père Perruchot's restaurant. Would you be kind enough to take them to her personally in my name and tell her that I had hoped to see her again this spring and that I have not forgotten her here; I also gave her and her daughter two small ones last year. . . . Perhaps I am entertaining illusions, but I cannot help thinking about it, and perhaps it will please them, and you too, if you get to know them" (Letter 489). We would, of course, like very much to know more about Vincent's relationship with these two people whom he apparently knew quite well, but there is nothing more than what this letter discloses.

Many river views, such as 1268–71, and the pictures of the Restaurant de la Sirène, 1251 and 1253, have been executed in a technique of "strokes"—consisting of fairly broad, long brushstrokes in bright colors placed next to but separate from each other—which was appearing more and more frequently in the work of Van Gogh. These strokes, often *small dabs* of paint (as distinct from *dots*), are sometimes intended to provide an Impressionistic rendering of objects, but occasionally they are strewn in random fashion

1252

1253

1254

over the canvas in order to produce an effect of light—as, for example, in 1270.

This magnificent painting of a sunny spring day seems to me to be without a doubt the high point of this series of landscapes. The theme of the riverbank scene, a somewhat traditional one among the Impressionists and Neo-Impressionists, has taken the form here of a very personal variant owing its charm equally to the intimate atmosphere and to the soft but yet bright colors—"frankly *green* frankly *blue*," as Vincent had put it in an earlier letter to Livens (Letter 459*a*).

One of the most personal and—from the standpoint of our times—most advanced works in the series seems to me to be the painting of the chestnut tree in bloom (1272). Here, broad strokes of paint in light to dark green, white, yellow, and brown have been used to produce a glittering surface of colors, but one that has neither perspective nor depth and is almost completely abstract (so much so that it is doubtful whether the traditional title "chestnut" aptly describes this tree).

With Bernard in Asnières

During this time Vincent often used to go painting in Asnières with a nineteen-year-old artist friend, Emile Bernard. There is even a photograph (probably taken in winter) in which we see Bernard and Van Gogh sitting opposite one another on the riverbank with the bridge they have both painted in the

1255

1256

1257

1258

1259

1260

1261

1252 Restaurant de la Sirène at Asnières, F 1408
Pencil, green chalk, 40 × 54 cm ($15\frac{3}{4} \times 21\frac{1}{4}''$)
Rijksmuseum Vincent van Gogh, Amsterdam

1253 Restaurant de la Sirène at Asnières, F 312
51.5 × 64 cm ($20\frac{1}{4} \times 25\frac{1}{4}''$)
Ashmolean Museum, Oxford

1254 Road along the Seine at Asnières, F 299
49 × 66 cm ($19\frac{1}{4} \times 26''$)
Rijksmuseum Vincent van Gogh, Amsterdam

1255 A Suburb of Paris, F 351
38 × 46 cm ($15 \times 18\frac{1}{8}''$)
Formerly collection Mrs. Salman Schocken, New York

1256 Interior of a Restaurant, F 342
45.5 × 56.5 cm ($18\frac{1}{8} \times 22\frac{1}{2}''$)
Rijksmuseum Kröller-Müller, Otterlo

1257 The Seine with a Rowboat, F 298
55 × 65 cm ($21\frac{5}{8} \times 25\frac{5}{8}''$)
Private collection, Paris

1258 People Walking in a Public Garden at Asnières, F 314
75.5 × 113 cm ($29\frac{7}{8} \times 44\frac{1}{2}''$)
Rijksmuseum Vincent van Gogh, Amsterdam
Colorplate XX, p. 276

1259 Lane in a Public Garden at Asnières, F 276
59 × 81 cm ($23\frac{1}{4} \times 31\frac{7}{8}''$)
Yale University Art Gallery, New Haven, Connecticut

1260 A Suburb of Paris with a Man Carrying a Spade, F 361
48 × 73 cm ($18\frac{7}{8} \times 28\frac{3}{4}''$)
Collection Karen Carter Johnson, Fort Worth, Texas

1261 Woman, Sitting in the Grass, F 367
41.5 × 34.5 cm ($16\frac{1}{2} \times 13\frac{3}{4}''$)
Private collection, New York

background—but unfortunately Vincent is sitting with his back to us. In her introduction of 1914, Mrs. van Gogh-Bonger, without giving any source, supplies all kinds of details concerning the friendship with Bernard. Her information was derived from Bernard's own reminiscences, which he incorporated in the introduction to his publication containing the letters written to him by Vincent. Here is the story in his own words, which are more detailed, more vivid, and more authentic than her condensed version. After mentioning that Vincent's expeditions ranged as far as Asnières and that he was a regular visitor to the Ile de la Grande Jatte, Bernard continues:

"He started off with a large canvas fastened to his back. This he divided into as many sections as the number of motifs [he happened across]; in the evening he brought it back completely filled, and it was like a little walking museum in which all the emotions of the day had been recorded. There were little sketches of the Seine filled with boats, islands with blue swings, fashionable restaurants with multicolored sunshades, with pink sweetbrier; deserted little corners of a park or country houses for sale. Those little sketches, wrested as it were by the artist's brush from the fleeting hours, breathed a springlike poetry. I reveled in their charm, all the more because I then lived in those surroundings, because they were the object of my own solitary wanderings, and because they reflected the spirit of what I sensed in them. Vincent often came to see me in the wooden studio that had been built in the garden of my parents in Asnières. It was there that we made a portrait of Tanguy together; he even started one of me, but when he got into a quarrel with my father, who refused to listen to his advice about my future, he became so enraged that he just left my portrait as it was and picked up the unfinished portrait of Tanguy and took it with him still wet under his arm. He then left without once looking back and never set foot in our door again. So from then on I went to the apartment at 54 Rue Lepic, where the two brothers lived."*

In 1923 Gustave Coquiot published some recollections of Van Gogh by Signac that expand upon the picture given by Bernard: "Yes, I got to know Van Gogh at Père Tanguy's. At other times I ran into him in Asnières and Saint-Ouen [a quarter bordering on Asnières to the east]; we painted on the banks of the river and ate in a country café, and we returned to Paris on foot, through the streets of Saint-Ouen and Clichy. Van Gogh wore a blue zinc worker's smock and had painted colored smudges on the sleeves. Pressed closely against me, he walked along, shouting and gesticulating, waving his freshly painted oversize canvas, smearing paint on himself and the passersby."†

1262

1263

1264

New Subjects in the Summer

Spring must have merged into summer by the time Van Gogh made the landscapes 1273–78. The delightful and important canvas 1274, which has been frequently discussed and reproduced, depicts a field with yellow stubble, yellow-green wheat stalks, and poppies under a blue and white sky. Similar green and blue-green wheat stalks and poppies and a blue sky with white clouds are to be seen in 1273. This vertical composition is a livelier counterpart to the quiet, poetic, horizontal landscape with a bird rising up into the air.

Something of the range of colors of these skies and the wheat field is to be found again in the charming watercolor 1277, which probably depicts a bit of rural life in Montmartre. Although this watercolor was formerly called *Quatorze Juillet*, the 1970 *catalogue raisonné* points out that despite the flag there is no justification for this title. This seems to me to be correct but not for the reason given, namely, that the flag is Dutch. The fact that Van Gogh painted the color bars of the flag in the Dutch pattern rather than the French, appears to me to have been a slip. There is something else. I believe that the spot shown is the same as the one in 1241, or is at any rate the entrance to a similar observation point or place of interest. On the crossbar above the entry gate in 1241, Vincent has quite clearly painted the words "Point de vue." There is no shortage of flags there (and the flag above that entrance is undoubtedly French); furthermore, to judge by the bare trees, it was most certainly not quatorze juillet (the fourteenth of July).

***Lettres de Vincent van Gogh à Emile Bernard* (1911), pp. 11–12.

† Gustave Coquiot, *Vincent van Gogh* (1923), p. 140.

1265

1266

1267

1268

1269

1270

1262 Woman, Strolling in a Garden, F 368
48×60 cm ($18\frac{7}{8} \times 23\frac{5}{8}''$)
Private collection, United States

1263 Pasture in Bloom, F 583
31.5×40.5 cm ($12\frac{5}{8} \times 16\frac{1}{8}''$)
Rijksmuseum Kröller-Müller, Otterlo

1264 Undergrowth with Flowers, F 362
50×65 cm ($19\frac{5}{8} \times 25\frac{5}{8}''$)
Singer Memorial Museum, Laren (N.H.), The Netherlands

1265 Two Ladies at the Gate of a Public Park at Asnières, F 305
55×67 cm ($21\frac{5}{8} \times 26\frac{3}{8}''$)
Collection Mrs. Charles Gilman, New York

1266 Restaurant Rispal at Asnières, F 355
72×60 cm ($28\frac{3}{8} \times 23\frac{5}{8}''$)
Collection Mrs. Hugo L. Moser, New York

1267 Viaduct, F 239
Cardboard on panel, 31.5×40.5 cm ($12\frac{5}{8} \times 16\frac{1}{8}''$)
Justin K. Thannhauser Collection, Solomon R. Guggenheim Museum, New York

1268 Bridge across the Seine at Asnières, F 240
53×73 cm ($20\frac{7}{8} \times 28\frac{3}{4}''$)
Menil Foundation, Houston, Texas

1269 Bank of the Seine, F 293
32×45.5 cm ($12\frac{5}{8} \times 18\frac{1}{8}''$)
Rijksmuseum Vincent van Gogh, Amsterdam

1270 Two Boats near a Bridge across the Seine, F 354
49×58 cm ($19\frac{1}{4} \times 22\frac{7}{8}''$)
Art Institute of Chicago

1271 Bank of the Seine with Boat, F 353
48×55 cm ($18\frac{7}{8} \times 21\frac{5}{8}''$)
Farkas Foundation, Palm Beach, Florida

1271

Another view of the Seine is 1276, one of the few pencil drawings from this period. The sheet contains some color notes, indicating that Vincent intended to make a painting of this subject too.

The walls of the city of Paris were an unusual source of inspiration for Vincent during this summertime; they represented a sort of transition between the landscapes and the city scenes he had been doing earlier, under the influence of his Impressionist friends. It is also conceivable that the Japanese colored woodcuts exerted some influence here, for Vincent depicted the walls of the city in little multicolored anecdotal prints in flat colors, with many small figures. There is, despite all the differences, a certain affinity between the bridge based on Hiroshige (1297) and the bright-yellow Paris street with the small figures of pedestrians and a horsecar in 1284.

Apart from the works done with watercolors, or with watercolors and colored chalk, 1280, 1281, 1283, and 1284—some with only a few figures, but all portraying roughly the same spot—there are three rough drafts, all in pencil, which are clearly nothing more than composition sketches: 1279 intended for 1280, 1282 for 1283, and 1285 for either finished or uncompleted variants of 1283 or 1284. Closely related to all the foregoing is the well-nigh monumental watercolor with a view of Asnières, 1286, which must certainly be regarded as one of the most important of Vincent's Paris drawings. In the foreground he has probably depicted the leveling of the city of Paris wall, and we are struck by the same graphic and topographically accurate representation as in the watercolors just mentioned, but here the artist's high vantage point enables him to exploit the massive wall in the foreground to achieve a much more powerful effect than in the earlier drawings of this site. Later, in Arles and Auvers, drawings and paintings of panoramas like the one Vincent presents here would be repeated on numerous occasions (see, for example, landscape 1440 and its variations). Equally remarkable in 1286 is the Spartan use of color—mainly bright blue and red, alternating with a great deal of white.

The city scenes include two works differing somewhat from the others: the painted studies of factory buildings, probably also in Asnières, 1287 and 1288. Here Vincent seems not to be concerned with the rural and picturesque aspects of the suburb where he went so often to work, but rather with the threatening ugliness of its seamier side.

There is virtually no basis for determining from the two drawings of swallows in flight, 1289 and 1290, when they were made. The pencil drawing 1290 appears on the reverse side of the washed pen-and-ink drawing 1289 and is probably an unfinished preliminary study for it.

The rough pencil sketch 1291, which, for want of a better place, is mentioned incidentally here, shows a street with tall buildings and, like 1308, depicts a shining sun. Here, again, the presence of color notes supports the assumption that this was the composition sketch for an intended work, although we do not know of a watercolor or painting corresponding to this subject.

1272

1273

1274

Among the works done in the summer of 1887, I include also some still lifes of flowers, 1292–95. To take first the still life with the clusters of cut flowers (lilacs?) 1294, this, too, is difficult to date, but the Impressionistic treatment with fairly broad brushstrokes points strongly, in my opinion, to the summer of 1887 (*catalogue raisonné*: "spring 1887"). The others seem even more clearly to belong to the summer or late summer of that year. Apart from the canvases not yet discussed with cut sunflowers, these still lifes, I believe, represent the limit of what Vincent had wanted to achieve with his flower pieces in the

1272 Chestnut in Bloom, F270a
56 × 46 cm (22 × 18⅛")
Rijksmuseum Vincent van Gogh, Amsterdam

1273 Edge of a Wheat Field with Poppies, F310a
Canvas on cardboard, 40 × 32.5 cm
(15¾ × 13")
Collection Mrs. William Herman, Boston

1274 Edge of a Wheat Field with Poppies and a Lark, F310
54 × 64.5 cm (21¼ × 25⅝")
Rijksmuseum Vincent van Gogh, Amsterdam

1275 View of a River with Rowboats, F300
52 × 65 cm (20½ × 25⅝")
Private collection, Aberdeen, Scotland

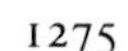

1277

1278

1280

1279

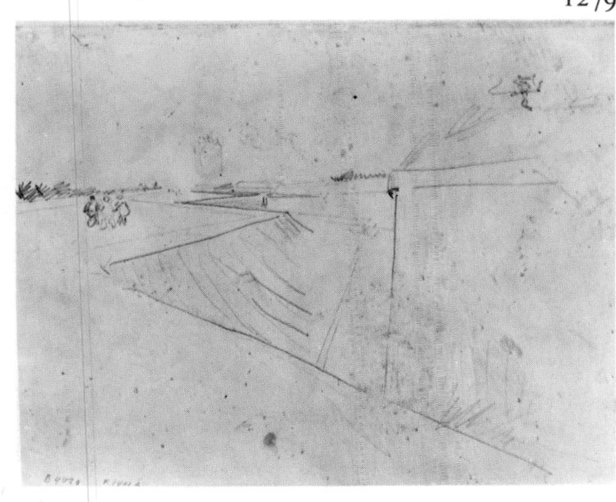

1281

1276 Sailboat on a River, F 1409
Pencil, 53.5 × 39.5 cm ($21\frac{1}{4} \times 15\frac{3}{4}$″)
Rijksmuseum Vincent van Gogh, Amsterdam

1277 Path to the Entrance of a Belvedere, F 1406
Black chalk, watercolor, 31.5 × 24 cm
($12\frac{5}{8} \times 9\frac{1}{2}$″)
Rijksmuseum Vincent van Gogh, Amsterdam

1278 Lane in a Public Garden at Asnières, F 275
Canvas on cardboard, 32.5 × 42 cm
($13 \times 16\frac{1}{2}$″)
Rijksmuseum Vincent van Gogh, Amsterdam

July–September 1887

1279 Composition Sketch of the Ramparts of Paris, F 1719 (bottom part; reverse: 1285)
Pencil, 23 × 29 cm ($9 \times 11\frac{3}{8}$″)
Rijksmuseum Vincent van Gogh, Amsterdam

1280 The Ramparts of Paris, F 1402
Watercolor, colored chalk, 39.5 × 54 cm
($15\frac{3}{4} \times 21\frac{1}{4}$″)
Private collection, London

1281 The Ramparts of Paris, F 1403
Watercolor, 39.5 × 53.5 cm ($15\frac{3}{4} \times 21\frac{1}{4}$″)
Whitworth Art Gallery, University of Manchester, England

Paris period. They are festive portrayals, all light and color: light blue vases on a speckled table top in light brown against bright blue backgrounds, rendered in Pointillist style with white or colored dots.

The Japanese Prints

The curious paintings 1296–98 clearly reflect Vincent's admiration for Japanese colored woodcuts; they are in fact enlarged copies in oil of some of those prints. During his stay in Paris he had built up a large collection of the prints (the collection has been preserved and can still be seen in the Rijksmuseum Vincent van Gogh in Amsterdam). It will be recalled that Vincent had decorated his room with Japanese prints even while he was in Antwerp (see page 212). When he arrived in Paris, he could not fail to notice that *japonisme*, as it was called, was all the rage. Not only was he able to learn much about Japanese art from all kinds of books and magazines, but he also had the opportunity to see and study countless numbers of these colorful prints, which he found so appealing, at the homes of friends and collectors—and perhaps even at his brother's. In letters to Theo from Arles, Vincent reminisced about the wonderful times he had spent at the shop of the famous dealer Samuel Bing, who, in addition to thousands of bound volumes of prints, had an immense supply of colored woodcuts (in Letter 510 Vincent speaks of a hundred thousand, and in Letter 511 of ten thousand). There he had often rummaged about, trying to add to his and Theo's collection: "Let me tell you this: I for one have searched through the pile [at Bing's] four or five times; the sheets we have at home are the result of our having replenished our stock every so often" (Letter 511). And he urged Theo to keep on looking in Bing's inexhaustible loft for prints that would improve their collection.

In Paris, Vincent showed his admiration for the "*crépons*," as he always called the prints, not only by the exhibition of the Japanese colored woodcuts he held in the Café du Tambourin (see page 268)—an exhibition that he described a year later as "such a disaster"(Letter 510)—but also by working them into the background of some portraits. A vaguely defined representation of one of them can be seen behind the figure of La Segatori in the Café du Tambourin (1208), and in two portraits of Père Tanguy (1351 and 1352), in which the entire background is occupied by quite accurately copied Japanese prints. In 1296–98, however, these prints have become the principal motif. This I see as an attempt to make these small works of art—which were so far removed from everything he himself had made up to that time but yet fascinated him so much—a part of his own intellectual heritage by re-creating them in his own medium.

They were significant for Vincent's artistic development mainly because they enabled him, to an even greater degree than had some of the flower pieces, still lifes, and landscapes, to experiment with setting off forceful colors against one another in large, virtually flat areas: red, orange, yellow, and green in 1296, blue, dark green, and light green in 1297. In *Flowering Plum Tree*, 1296, he must have been further attracted by the compositional effect of the bizarre-looking tree as a silhouette in the foreground; those branches must have reminded him of the gnarled trees—drawn by him often—in the garden behind the parsonage in Nuenen (see 426, 465, and 466); and the silhouette motif he would return to a year later in one of his pictures of a sower (see 1627–29). In the case of the bridge (1297), his object must have been to render the simplicity of the composition with only a few large planes of color, with the diagonal of the yellow bridge as a contrast to the blue and green of the water and the landscape.

1282

1283

1284

1282 Composition Sketch of the Ramparts of Paris, F 1719 (upper part)
Pencil, 23 × 29 cm ($9 \times 11\frac{3}{8}$")
Rijksmuseum Vincent van Gogh, Amsterdam

1283 Street with People Walking and a Horsecar near the Ramparts, F 1400
Watercolor, heightened with white, 39.5 × 53.5 cm ($15\frac{3}{4} \times 21\frac{1}{4}$")
Rijksmuseum Vincent van Gogh, Amsterdam

1284 Street with People Walking and a Horsecar near the Ramparts, F 1401
Watercolor, pen, pencil, 24 × 31.5 cm ($9\frac{1}{2} \times 12\frac{5}{8}$")
Rijksmuseum Vincent van Gogh, Amsterdam

1285

1286

1287

1288

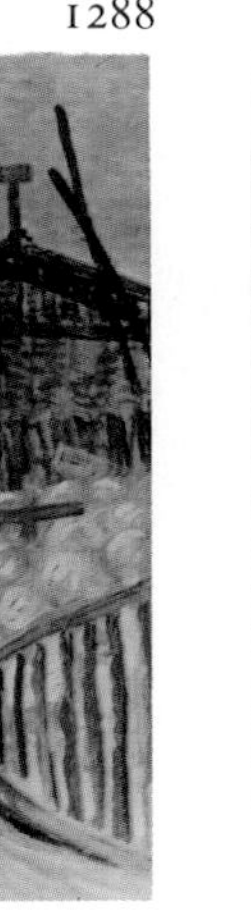

1289

1290

1291

1285 Composition Sketch of the Ramparts of Paris, F1719v (reverse: 1279)
Pencil, 23 × 29 cm ($9 \times 11\frac{3}{8}''$)
Rijksmuseum Vincent van Gogh, Amsterdam

1286 A Suburb of Paris, Seen from a Height, F1410
Watercolor, heightened with white, 39.5 × 53.5 cm ($15\frac{3}{4} \times 21\frac{1}{4}''$)
Stedelijk Museum, Amsterdam

1287 Factories at Asnières, F317
54 × 72 cm ($21\frac{1}{4} \times 28\frac{3}{8}''$)
The St. Louis Art Museum

1288 A Factory at Asnières, F318
46.5 × 54 cm ($18\frac{1}{2} \times 21\frac{1}{4}''$)
© The Barnes Foundation Museum of Art, Merion, Pennsylvania

1289 Swallows in Flight, F1244 (reverse: 1290)
Pen, washed, 26.5 × 35 cm ($10\frac{5}{8} \times 13\frac{3}{4}''$)
Rijksmuseum Vincent van Gogh, Amsterdam

1290 Swallows in Flight, F1244v (reverse: 1289)
Pencil, 26.5 × 35 cm ($10\frac{5}{8} \times 13\frac{3}{4}''$)
Rijksmuseum Vincent van Gogh, Amsterdam

1291 Sketch for a Painting of Blocks of Houses, F1374
Pencil, 29 × 23 cm ($11\frac{3}{8} \times 9''$)
Rijksmuseum Vincent van Gogh, Amsterdam

1292

1293

1294

More Self-Portraits and Summer Landscapes
Despite all the differences in treatment and expression exhibited by the self-portraits 1299–1304, they seem to me to constitute a group, which I call the "blue" group. In them Vincent has broken away from Pointillism, and he combines a very free style of brushwork with sharp concentration on the rendering of the model in a variety of moods. There is a common denominator in the dark-blue backgrounds, nearly all horizontal, with occasional broad, upward-slanting brushstrokes. In 1299, the background is almost uniformly blue, but the painter's blouse displays the same coarse, indistinct strokes on a beige-yellow ground as are seen in the other self-portraits.

The variation in facial expression is remarkable. In 1299, the expression is fierce, almost hostile. It most closely resembles the frequently reproduced portrait that the painter John Russell made of Vincent (now in the Rijksmuseum Vincent van Gogh in Amsterdam). Russell's portrait shows the same attitude, although in mirror image, and the same rather suspicious look. There is also a marked similarity with the portrait by Hartrick, reproduced in his reminiscences.

The same tense, penetrating look is to be found again in the self-portraits 1301 and 1303—although in these the eyes are turned slightly away from the viewer—and in 1304. In 1301 the model suddenly appears some years younger, but in my opinion this self-portrait, too, must be reckoned to belong to this group by reason of the brushwork. The portraits 1300 and 1302 not only impress us as more relaxed, but they differ from the others mainly because of the large yellow straw hat, which was obviously brought into the picture for the purpose of achieving a forceful color contrast. The conspicuous, hastily applied broad brushstrokes with which the head, the painter's smock, and the background were done are to my mind unmistakable evidence that these portraits belong to this group.

Although the self-portraits 1309 and 1310 (colorplate XXI, page 293) are in a sense allied to those in the series just discussed, they nonetheless seem to me to form a separate small group (which, on page 262, I refer to as the "cloudy" group). In both portraits Van Gogh is wearing his beloved large straw hat, and in both the peering look is about the same, while the hawklike form of the nose is more accentuated than in the previous group. The most remarkable thing, however, is the color, which is lighter and more forceful than before. Against the bright yellow of the straw hat, Vincent has placed the light colors of the painter's smock—brownish beige with bright red piping in 1310, and light blue in 1309. In both portraits attention is drawn to the background because it is strewn with bright, randomly placed strokes of paint—splashes of color, one might call them. In 1310 these consist of blue and green touches on a beige foundation, and in 1309 they are bright red spots on a light green, and also "cloudy," foundation. Despite the curious experiment with the background (which one might say reinforces the vividness of the term "Expressionist"), the paintings 1309 and 1310 are undeniably among the most impressive self-portraits of this year.

Sunflowers—later to become one of Van Gogh's favorite motifs—appear in a few small works presumably done in the late summer or early fall: 1305–8. A fresh, sunny landscape, where a single sunflower, however subordinate its part in the total composition, still attracts attention as the sole warm yellow note, is watercolor 1305. Off in the distance to the left, the same kind of factory town with smokestacks as appears in drawing 1286 gives reason to believe that 1305 may

1292 Vase with Lilacs, Daisies, and Anemones, F322
46.5 × 37.5 cm ($18\frac{1}{2}$ × 15″)
Private collection, Switzerland

1293 Vase with Cornflowers and Poppies, F324
80 × 67 cm ($31\frac{1}{2}$ × $26\frac{3}{8}$″)
Location unknown

1294 Lilacs, F286b
27 × 34.5 cm ($10\frac{5}{8}$ × $13\frac{3}{4}$″)
The Armand Hammer Collection, Los Angeles

1295 Vase with Daisies and Anemones, F323
61 × 38 cm (24 × 15″)
Rijksmuseum Kröller-Müller, Otterlo

1295

1296

1297

1298

1299

1300

1301

1296 Japonaiserie: Flowering Plum Tree (after Hiroshige), F371
55 × 46 cm ($21\frac{5}{8} \times 18\frac{1}{8}$″)
Rijksmuseum Vincent van Gogh, Amsterdam

1297 Japonaiserie: Bridge in the Rain (after Hiroshige), F372
73 × 54 cm ($28\frac{3}{4} \times 21\frac{1}{4}$″)
Rijksmuseum Vincent van Gogh, Amsterdam

1298 Japonaiserie: Oiran (after Kesaï Yeisen), F373
105 × 61 cm ($41\frac{3}{8} \times 24$″)
Rijksmuseum Vincent van Gogh, Amsterdam

1299 Self-Portrait, F268
41 × 33.5 cm ($16\frac{1}{8} \times 13\frac{3}{8}$″)
Wadsworth Atheneum, Hartford, Connecticut

1300 Self-Portrait with Straw Hat and Pipe, F179v (reverse: 786)
41.5 × 31 cm ($16\frac{1}{2} \times 12\frac{1}{4}$″)
Rijksmuseum Vincent van Gogh, Amsterdam

1301 Self-Portrait, F269v (reverse: 725)
41 × 33 cm ($16\frac{1}{8} \times 13$″)
Rijksmuseum Vincent van Gogh, Amsterdam

have been made from the same high point (perhaps the hill of Montmartre).

A giant sunflower plant is the principal motif in 1307, which is remarkable in both concept and composition. Although the rather melancholy colors are reminiscent of 1886 (the *catalogue raisonné*, incidentally, dates the painting 1887), my opinion is that, despite the fairly heavy impasto, this work should be classified with 1305 and 1306. The dark range of colors is explainable by the fact that Vincent has depicted an evening effect.

Finally, the small pencil sketch 1308, where a little couple is seen walking past some sunflowers taller than they, is probably a quick impression jotted down in the same location. The sun is shown in this picture, just as in the small rough sketch in 1291, but here it is much larger and bears a direct relationship to the flowers bending toward their image in the sky.

With the following long series of landscapes we are still in the summer and probably for the most part in the late summer. An impression of a warm summer's day is certainly imparted by painting 1311 with which the series starts. It shows a façade, probably the exterior of a restaurant, decorated with flower boxes. The summery impression is due principally to the coloring: the straw yellow of the façade itself, a color that is continued in the pavement and is offset only by the green and blue-green of the window shutters and the oleanders and by the few orange and pinkish-red spots of color representing the blossoms. Here for once is a picture that does not express torment or worry, but rather sunny restfulness and harmony.

A number of works represent scenes in the interiors of woods—*sous-bois* as French painters liked to call this type of landscape—(1312–19). Van Gogh's object here has obviously been to render the cool atmosphere and intimate character of the woods in a range of colors consisting almost exclusively of greens, browns, and yellows. The result at times is a somewhat dull effect, but often the sparkling light that filters through the foliage overhead has been rendered most beautifully, as in 1312. The use of separate white, yellow, green, and reddish-brown spots of color has here become an effective means of expression that is in no way forced.

Van Gogh endeavored to express both space and depth in 1316, which shows an avenue of trees in a park and thus is related to the impressions of what probably was the Voyer d'Argenson Park—such as 1261, 1262, 1264, and 1265. And here too the depiction of the interplay of light and shadow must also have been a paramount aim.

The forest landscape 1319 is somewhat of a special case. It is similar in subject to the canvases 1312 and 1315, but the brushwork seems quite different. That is why this painting was formerly ascribed to the Auvers period—and still is in the revised *catalogue raisonné* of 1970, although the editors have added the comment that they do not exclude the possibility of its having been made in the summer of 1887 in Paris. I, too, consider the dating to be a doubtful point.

In the landscapes 1320–27, the river and the bridges constitute a secondary motif or

1302

1303

1304

1302 Self-Portrait with Straw Hat, F61V (reverse: 533)
Canvas on cardboard, 42 × 31 cm
($16\frac{1}{2} \times 12\frac{1}{4}$″)
Rijksmuseum Vincent van Gogh, Amsterdam

1303 Self-Portrait, F109v (reverse: 942)
Canvas on cardboard, 43.5 × 31.5 cm
($17\frac{3}{8} \times 12\frac{5}{8}$″)
Rijksmuseum Vincent van Gogh, Amsterdam

1304 Self-Portrait, F77v (reverse: 686)
41 × 33 cm ($16\frac{1}{8} \times 13$″)
Rijksmuseum Vincent van Gogh, Amsterdam

1305 Path in Montmartre with Sunflowers, F1411
Pencil, pen, watercolor, 30.5 × 24 cm
($12\frac{1}{4} \times 9\frac{1}{2}$″)
Rijksmuseum Vincent van Gogh, Amsterdam

1306 Path in Montmartre with Sunflowers, F264a
35.5 × 27 cm ($14\frac{1}{8} \times 10\frac{5}{8}$″)
Fine Arts Museums of San Francisco

1307 Garden with Sunflowers (in Montmartre?), F388v (reverse: 782)
42.5 × 35.5 cm ($16\frac{7}{8} \times 14\frac{1}{8}$″)
Rijksmuseum Vincent van Gogh, Amsterdam

1305

1306

1307

1308

1309

1308 Couple Walking beside a Group of Sunflowers, F 1720
Sketch on the back of a menu of the Restaurant du Chalet
Pencil, 13.5 × 21 cm ($5\frac{1}{2} \times 8\frac{1}{4}''$)
Rijksmuseum Vincent van Gogh, Amsterdam

1309 Self-Portrait with Straw Hat, F 526
Canvas on panel, 35.5 × 27 cm ($14\frac{1}{8} \times 10\frac{5}{8}''$)
Detroit Institute of Arts

even the main subject. The summer landscapes 1321 and 1322, which are virtually companion pieces in subject and composition, are closely related to the forest scenes. Although a small corner of a bridge (probably the Pont de Clichy) is shown here, what Van Gogh was mainly concerned with in these paintings was the luxuriant abundance of trunks, stems, and foliage in a wide variety of colors that are warmer than those in the comparable spring scene 1270. In a canvas such as 1321, with its almost abstract pattern of heavy white, yellow, green, and brick-red dabs of paint, Vincent has, in my opinion, reached a new pinnacle of prowess as a painter in a completely personal style that can be called as fervent and dynamic as it is disciplined.

In 1325 Vincent depicts a wide barge, presumably used as a bathhouse, seen at close hand. With its bold brushstrokes it has the rough, sketchy look characteristic of some of the notes dating from these months that give the impression of having been done casually and hastily. It is fairly small (7½ by 10⅝ inches) and was probably intended as no more than a preliminary study, but the technique it exhibits was also used in larger paintings, such as the view of the riverbank 1322 and the vigorous, colorful river view 1326. (In the latter work, however, the perspective is a bit awry, making it appear that the three parts of the bridge do not fit together.)

The last of this series, 1327, shows the railroad bridge at Asnières and, in the distance, the Pont de Levallois. The brushwork is just as rugged as in 1326, but the space effect and the remarkable composition with its many intersecting lines make it a much more fascinating work. It has been rendered in a warm range of colors with much reddish brown, yellow, and brownish green; the highest note on the color scale is the woman on the embankment, with a brick-red dress and a glaring red parasol. It is interesting to note that in this same year, 1887, Vincent's young friend Bernard also made a painting, from almost the same point, showing the Pont de Levallois as well as the railroad bridge in the foreground with a train passing over it.* What is even more interesting is to see how differently the two paintings have turned out and consequently to realize how much the two friends, even though collaborating closely, retained their individuality.

Sunflowers and Other Still Lifes

Vincent's familiar sunflowers form another clearly related group (1328–31) in this Paris period. In all four pictures Vincent has depicted cut sunflowers that have almost passed the flowering stage. The small, sketchy piece 1328 (7⅞ by 10⅝ inches) must certainly be regarded as a preliminary study for the much larger and more detailed work 1329 (16⅞ by 24 inches), which is almost identical in composition, although in 1328 the ground is dark green, whereas in 1329 it is deep blue. Vincent must have felt that the blue provided a better contrast to the yellow or orange-yellow of the sunflowers, for he also employed it in

*A color reproduction of Emile Bernard's painting, which is privately owned, was published by John Rewald in the first chapter of his book *Post-Impressionism*.

1310

1311

1312

1310 Self-Portrait with Straw Hat, F469
Cardboard, 41 × 33 cm (16⅛ × 13″)
Rijksmuseum Vincent van Gogh, Amsterdam
Colorplate XXI, opposite

1311 Exterior of a Restaurant with Oleanders in Pots, F321
19 × 26.5 cm (7½ × 10⅝″)
Rijksmuseum Vincent van Gogh, Amsterdam

1312 Undergrowth, F309a
46 × 55.5 cm (18⅛ × 22″)
Rijksmuseum Vincent van Gogh, Amsterdam

Colorplate XXI, Self-Portrait with Straw Hat, 1310 〉

1330 and 1331, which otherwise differ considerably from each other. In the latter the small red strokes of color in the background are particularly eye-catching, and in the even richer still life 1330, the red splashes of paint reminiscent of the self-portraits 1309 and 1310 are to be found mainly in the left-hand corner, where the blue has been replaced by gray. The contrast in colors between the straw yellow and the cobalt blue, running from dark to light, is at the same time both spirited and disciplined. What is strange here is the quality of unreality in the depiction of the subject. In the other three pictures the sunflowers can be visualized as resting on a somewhat ill-defined blue surface, but in 1330 they seem to be floating in some kind of mysterious space. The greater degree of freedom the artist has allowed himself in dealing with his objects and with the arrangement of planes and colors has resulted in a painting that is highly personal and unique, deserving to be ranked with the most mature works of Van Gogh's Paris period.

Gustave Coquiot relates that a fellow painter, Armand Guillaumin, had admired some of Vincent's work that was being stored by the art dealer Arsène Portier, who lived in the same building on the Rue Lepic as the Van Goghs. Portier took Guillaumin to visit Vincent, and they came upon him "painting the *Books*—also known as the *Romans Parisiens*—the famous canvas painted entirely in yellow, and depicting the books spread about [on a table] with a rose in a glass to brighten things up."*

Quite apart from its cheerful coloring in warm yellow, this painting (1332) is a remarkable and very personal work. It is not just a large number of books piled together in a rather untidy way and Vincent's own title, *Romans Parisiens*, is significant. Clearly, in this painting—done at the time during his Paris period when he was at the peak of his powers—he wanted to express even more explicitly than he had done before his affection and gratitude for the French novels that meant so much to him at that time. Here they are piled up in almost inexhaustible abundance around a single opened book that lies in the foreground like an invitation to read. In his use of color here he permitted himself a large measure of nonnaturalistic freedom—in the bright green to indicate the printed text in the open volume, for instance. In order to create the effect of perspective and to heighten the color, Vincent apparently used the same backdrop with the orange-red bands and green figures as in the still lifes 1229 and 1239, but now this motif has been treated much more freely, with bold hatching in separate brushstrokes.

New Developments

The self-portraits 1333 and 1334 (referred to on page 262 as the "wild" group) have been assigned to the final months of 1887 because of the brushwork and, more particularly, the hatching, which was becoming increasingly harsh, with the spaces between the brushstrokes often being wider than the strokes themselves. It is a stylistic trait also found in the still lifes that I have assigned to this

*Coquiot, *Vincent van Gogh* (1923), p.125.

1313

1314

1315

1313 Undergrowth, F308
46 × 38 cm (18⅛ × 15″)
Rijksmuseum Vincent van Gogh, Amsterdam

1314 Trees on a Slope, F291
37 × 45.5 cm (14⅝ × 18⅛″)
P. and N. de Boer Foundation, Amsterdam

1315 A Path in the Woods, F309
46 × 38.5 cm (18⅛ × 15⅜″)
Rijksmuseum Vincent van Gogh, Amsterdam

‹ Colorplate XXII, Portrait of Père Tanguy, 1351

period. Although blue is the dominant color of the smock or jacket and of the background in the "wild" self-portraits (blue hatching in 1333 and blue-green in 1334), this striking brushwork is what prevents them from being classified with what I have called the "blue" group (1299–1304). In my view the effects of this experiment in brushwork are so marked in the latter pair of self-portraits that it detracts a great deal from their unity and harmony. In 1334 the expression lacks the force of many other self-portraits of this year, and in 1333 the face has a masklike character, caused mainly by the light edging of the dark deep-set eyes.

A more important innovation, I believe, is to be found in the group of still lifes depicting autumn fruits (1336–43). To a much greater extent than the earlier series of still lifes of flowers, these are pure studies in color—studies in which Vincent, in a completely personal manner, limited himself almost entirely to the primary colors, virtually avoiding intermediate tones. A typical example is the still life with apples 1340, in which the framework of the wicker basket is rendered solely by short lines in vermilion on an off-white ground. No attempt has been made to represent the local color of the wicker. The apples, too, have been outlined in vermilion, and this color appears again in the dedication "à l'ami Lucien Pissaro" (the son of Camille Pissarro, whose surname Vincent misspelled), which is to be seen in the lower left-hand corner of the painting. The off-white of the ground and the light blue hatching of the wall give this work a joyful effect with an abundance of light hues that is in direct contrast to the heavy palette he had brought with him to Paris, which had still been evident in much of his work in 1886.

Speaking of the still life *Romans Parisiens*, Vincent's English friend Hartrick called it "the first of a series of yellow pictures."* Perhaps the still life with apples, 1340, is one of the canvases he had in mind, for here at least there is a strong yellow in the apples. In any event, the important still life 1339 does match his description. It depicts yellow pears (quince pears, Vincent himself called them), lemons, white grapes, and a solitary orange, and it also has a yellow background. It can be assumed from the fact that he inscribed it "à mon frère Theo" that Vincent attached special importance to it and probably even regarded it as one of his most successful canvases.

Colorful apples, one green pear, bunches of red and violet grapes, and yellow lemons, spread out on an off-white surface with blue hatching and surrounded as it were by a halo of blue light, make up the colorful composition of still life 1337. In the companion piece 1336, the principal motif consists of blue and white grapes strewn in rich profusion partly in a dish and partly over the table. The experiment in style that characterizes these still lifes was carried to the extreme limit in 1338. Here, not only have the fruits traditionally regarded as picturesque been replaced by prosaic onions and pieces of red cabbage, but even these objects have become

*Hartrick, *A Painter's Pilgrimage through Fifty Years* (1939), p.46.

1316

1317

1318

1316 Lane in a Public Garden, F277
55 × 67 cm (21⅝ × 26⅜″)
Collection Mrs. Charles Gilman, New York

1317 Undergrowth, F306
32 × 46 cm (12⅝ × 18⅛″)
Museum van Baaren, Utrecht

1318 Trees, F307
46 × 38 cm (18⅛ × 15″)
Rijksmuseum Vincent van Gogh, Amsterdam

1319 Trees, F817
73 × 92 cm (28¾ × 36¼″)
Collection Mr. and Mrs. Joseph H. Hazen, New York

1320 Corner of a Public Garden, F315
49 × 65 cm (19¼ × 25⅝″)
Location unknown

1321 The Seine with the Pont de Clichy, F352
50 × 60 cm (19⅝ × 23⅝″)
Private collection, Texas

1322 Bank of the Seine with the Pont de Clichy, F302
Cardboard, 30.5 × 39 cm (12¼ × 15⅜″)
Stavros S. Niarchos Collection

1319

1320

1321

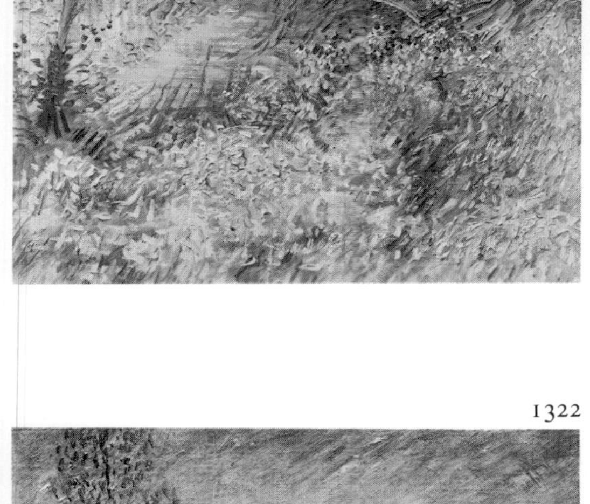

1322

1323

1324

1323 The Seine with the Pont de Clichy, F 303
55 × 46 cm (21⅝ × 18⅛″)
Collection F. H. Hirschland, Harrison, New York

1324 The Seine with the Pont de Clichy
Sketch in Letter 471
Rijksmuseum Vincent van Gogh, Amsterdam

almost unrecognizable in a welter of detached brushstrokes that bear little relationship to the local color: the onions done in chrome yellow, orange, green, and white strokes; the red cabbage in bright red, yellow, green, and gray-blue strokes.

The blue-green underpainting and background of the still life with apples, 1342, give a much darker impression, but the short brushstrokes in many colors arranged more or less like a halo around the mass of the fruit link this work with the others in this series. The same is true of the still life with the warm-yellow pears, 1343, in which the table top and the background are rendered by strokes of equally intense color.

The treatment of the self-portraits 1344 and 1345 is more relaxed than in the earlier pair, 1333 and 1334. They give less evidence of experimentation with the "stroke" technique, and Vincent seems once more to have concentrated on likeness and expression. I see them as a "transitional" stage on the way to the mature self-portrait 1353. From a general impression of the stylistic means employed, I would say that the self-portraits 1344 and 1345 are most closely allied to the work done in the fall of 1887 or the winter of 1887–88.

A further development of the stylistic traits already discussed in connection with the still lifes 1336–43 is met with in the frequently reproduced work 1349 and the somewhat related painting of a plaster cast, 1348. There can be no doubt that 1349 belongs with the last of the works done in the Paris period. The curious technique of rendering shadows by means of isolated brushstrokes in blue and green forms a clear link with the group 1336–43. A relationship might also be established with the "yellow" group mentioned previously, in view of the large lemon-yellow plane of the ground and the added note of intense yellow provided by one of the books depicted against the ground. It also shows Vincent's fondness for the complementary pairing of yellow and blue that was to continue on into the Arles period and later.

Finally, the small plaster cast, whose somewhat misshapen form seems to have been intentionally accentuated, will be remembered from Vincent's work during the Cormon period (see 1070 and subsequent numbers), where I have described it as plaster cast Type D. What induced Vincent to incorporate this small plaster cast, which apparently belonged to him, into another still life a year and a half later is hard to fathom. For that matter, the almost Surrealistic combination of disparate objects in this painting, however fine the color effect may be, remains in all other respects somewhat of an enigma.

A plaster cast that we do not know from the Cormon period is the subject of the large canvas 1348, with a striking light blue background. The picture does not give even an approximate idea of the actual size of this plaster cast, which may have been as small as the one depicted in 1349. Despite the massively protruding lower part, there is no distortion here. On the contrary, the painting is compelling and impressive; it is in a certain sense an idealized female nude serving as a substitute for the live model.

With these still lifes I include the pictures

1325

1326

1327

1325 Bathing Boat on the Seine, F311
19 × 27 cm ($7\frac{1}{2} \times 10\frac{5}{8}$″)
Collection Mr. and Mrs. Paul Mellon, Upperville, Virginia

1326 The Seine with the Pont de la Grande Jatte, F304
32 × 40.5 cm ($12\frac{5}{8} \times 16\frac{1}{8}$″)
Rijksmuseum Vincent van Gogh, Amsterdam

1327 Bridges across the Seine at Asnières, F301
52 × 65 cm ($20\frac{1}{2} \times 25\frac{5}{8}$″)
Collection E. G. Bührle, Zurich

1328 Two Cut Sunflowers, One Upside Down, Sketched, F377
20.5 × 26.5 cm ($8\frac{1}{8} \times 10\frac{5}{8}$″)
Rijksmuseum Vincent van Gogh, Amsterdam

1329 Two Cut Sunflowers, One Upside Down, F375
43 × 61 cm ($16\frac{7}{8} \times 24$″)
Metropolitan Museum of Art, New York

1330 Four Cut Sunflowers, One Upside Down, F452
60 × 100 cm ($23\frac{5}{8} \times 39\frac{3}{8}$″)
Rijksmuseum Kröller-Müller, Otterlo

1331 Two Cut Sunflowers, F376
50 × 60 cm ($19\frac{5}{8} \times 23\frac{5}{8}$″)
Kunstmuseum, Bern

1328

1329

1330

1331

of a skull, 1346 and 1347, which are difficult to date. Both are shown on a yellow background, and the one in 1346 particularly reminds us of the more complicated still life 1349 because of the pronounced height of the vantage point and the slanting background line in the composition. The two skulls probably belong best with the group of still lifes just discussed, which are characterized by a sometimes bizarre preference for unusual objects.

It was probably during the very last months of Vincent's stay in Paris that he did one of his most important portraits: the woman with two carnations in her hand, the so-called Italian woman (1355). As I mentioned on page 268, I am unconvinced by the attempts to identify this woman with the subject of the portrait in 1208, generally regarded as La Segatori. The red kerchief and the curious costume suggest rather an actress or a singer from one of the Paris cabarets frequented by Vincent. What is more significant is that the colorful appearance of this woman, with her wide skirt and ample blouse, inspired Vincent to paint a Neo-Impressionist interpretation that constitutes a highly individual companion piece to the Japanese portraits of actors that he greatly admired.

Regardless of who "the Italian woman" might have been, Vincent has here created an unforgettable figure, one of those compelling portrayals worthy to be numbered among the great works he produced in Arles.

I have also assigned to the winter of 1887–88 the subsequently famous portraits of Père Tanguy, which present a background of Japanese prints, 1351 (colorplate XXII, page 294) and 1352. It will be recalled that Vincent painted a portrait of this good friend of the Impressionists as early as January 1887 (1202); it was one of the first paintings made in his Paris period. Just how great a distance Van Gogh covered as a Neo-Impressionist painter in this one year is evident, so far as color and composition are concerned, from these much more original and daring portraits. They are a tribute both to the good Tanguy and to the world of the Japanese "*crépons*" which Vincent so greatly admired. The same prints have not been used as background in both pictures, probably for the sole reason that the effect was not entirely to Vincent's liking the first time. The only details of the prints that are identical are the head of an actor on the left and, below this, the group of red and blue flowers with green leaves on a yellow background (which cannot with certainty be identified as a Japanese print). Various writers have tried to determine what prints have been depicted. The most thorough research conducted thus far was done by Fred Orton, whose findings are summarized in the 1970 *catalogue raisonné* under items F363 and F364 (see Appendix, note 6).

The Final Self-Portraits

Of the Paris *oeuvre*, three paintings, all self-portraits, are still to be considered: the undated 1353 and 1354 (the "multicolored" group) and the self-portrait of the artist before the easel, 1356, dated with the numeral "'88." Since Van Gogh left Paris on Sunday, February 19, 1888,* this last self-portrait must have been completed before that date. It is hard to imagine that this was the only painting he did in the first six or seven weeks of the new year, but there is, of course, no way of determining even roughly how many such works there may have been. The advent of the new year could hardly have marked a turning point for Vincent, even though for some reason or other he saw fit to put a date on this important large self-portrait.

Of all the self-portraits dating from 1887 (or 1888), 1354—apart from the summer straw hat, which I believe Vincent put on merely for its color—bears the closest resemblance to the very famous and frequently reproduced portrait with the gray soft felt hat, 1353.

Although the attitude of head and body in the two portraits is identical, there is a marked difference in expression. The color combination also differs: in 1353 it is deep blue and light blue; in 1354 the dominant tones are soft violet-brown and sea green. The latter has a disquieting effect. The

*See *Vincent*, vol. III, no. 3 (1947), p. 13.

1332

October–December 1887

1332 Piles of French Novels and a Glass with a Rose (Romans Parisiens), F359
73 × 93 cm (28¾ × 36⅝")
Private collection, Baden, Switzerland

1333 Self-Portrait, F319
44 × 35 cm (17⅜ × 13¾")
Kunstmuseum, Basel (on loan from the Dr. Emile Dreyfus Foundation)

1334 Self-Portrait, F320
47 × 35 cm (18½ × 13¾")
The Louvre, Paris

1335 Little Chrysanthemums and Other Flowers in a Vase, F588
65 × 54 cm (25⅝ × 21¼")
Collection Mr. and Mrs. W. Averell Harriman, New York

1336 Plate with Blue and White Grapes, F603
34 × 47.5 cm (13⅜ × 18⅞")
Rijksmuseum Vincent van Gogh, Amsterdam

1337 Blue and White Grapes, Apples, Pears, and Lemons, F382
44 × 59 cm (17⅜ × 23¼")
Art Institute of Chicago

1338 Red Cabbages and Onions, F374
50 × 65 cm (19⅝ × 25⅝")
Rijksmuseum Vincent van Gogh, Amsterdam

1333

1334

1335

1336

1337

1338

look (strikingly different in each eye) is that of a person who is fearful or suspicious, and the pronounced angularity of the right cheekbone and the socket of the right eye have something about them that gives the face a lean, unhealthy appearance. Judged by itself, the portrait is undoubtedly impressive and highly characteristic; but when it is viewed together with the portrait with the felt hat 1353, I cannot help feeling that it is a preliminary study for that work or a less masterly repetition of it. That is because the portrait with the felt hat is undoubtedly a masterstroke; here Van Gogh is revealed as serious, perhaps a little melancholy, but with a degree of self-assurance to be found in few of the many self-portraits done earlier. We are moved by the strength he has exhibited in portraying Van Gogh the *man*, but at the same time we are amazed at the mastery he has displayed in assimilating the influences of the Paris environment in entirely his own way and bringing them to a high level of fulfillment.

Finally, the self-portrait of the artist at the easel, 1356. Others have seen this as the true finale of the Paris period, and it is certainly the powerful expression of a great painter—yet even with all the scintillation of color, its general effect is more subdued in tone than the others. Pure, unmixed, primary colors in good-sized daubs have been put on the palette in the lower left-hand corner of the painting, and on closer inspection the vivid colors, in the form of small touches of paint, are rediscovered everywhere except in the gray background and the yellow and grayish blue of the wood and the linen. They twinkle in the light falling on the painter's blue smock from behind; they sparkle in his hair and beard and even in the shaded areas of his forehead and cheeks. The expression of the face is more reflective than in the self-portrait 1353, in keeping with the more generally subdued mood of the color.

Jean Leymarie in his *Van Gogh* (1951) asserted that "the composition was directly inspired by Cézanne's famous *Self-Portrait with Palette* (1885–87), and others have repeated this. Vincent may have seen Cézanne's painting somewhere, for instance at Tanguy's, but it should not be forgotten that he had employed the same composition earlier, namely, in his self-portrait 1090. Therefore, in deciding on what composition to use for self-portrait 1356, he needed only to look at his earlier self-portrait at the easel, which was still in his studio.

Farewell to Paris

It is not hard to guess why Vincent finally took leave of Paris to go to the South. His artist friends—in particular, Toulouse-Lautrec—must certainly have sung the praises of the Midi, and cities such as Marseilles and Aix-en-Provence were closely linked with the names of predecessors such as Monticelli and Cézanne whom he admired. It is apparent from his letter to the English painter Livens, which must have been written in the fall of 1886, that he had plans even then to go to sunnier climes: "In the spring—say February or even sooner I may be going to the South of France, the land of the *blue* tones and gay colors" (Letter 459*a*). A year later he wrote

1339

1340

1341

Winter 1887–1888

1339 White Grapes, Apples, Pears, Lemons, and Orange (Dedicated to Theo van Gogh), F383
49 × 65 cm (19$\frac{1}{4}$ × 25$\frac{5}{8}$″)
Rijksmuseum Vincent van Gogh, Amsterdam

1340 Basket with Apples (Dedicated to Lucien Pissarro), F378
50 × 61 cm (19$\frac{5}{8}$ × 24″)
Rijksmuseum Kröller-Müller, Otterlo

1341 Basket with Apples, F379
46 × 55 cm (18$\frac{1}{8}$ × 21$\frac{5}{8}$″)
The St. Louis Art Museum

1342 Apples, F254
45.5 × 61 cm (18$\frac{1}{8}$ × 24″)
Rijksmuseum Vincent van Gogh, Amsterdam

1343 Quince Pears, F602
46 × 59.5 cm (18$\frac{1}{8}$ × 23$\frac{5}{8}$″)
Gemäldegalerie, Staatliche Kunstsammlungen, Dresden

1344 Self-Portrait, F1672a
46 × 38 cm (18$\frac{1}{8}$ × 15″)
Kunsthistorisches Museum, Vienna

1342

1343

1344

1345

1346

1347

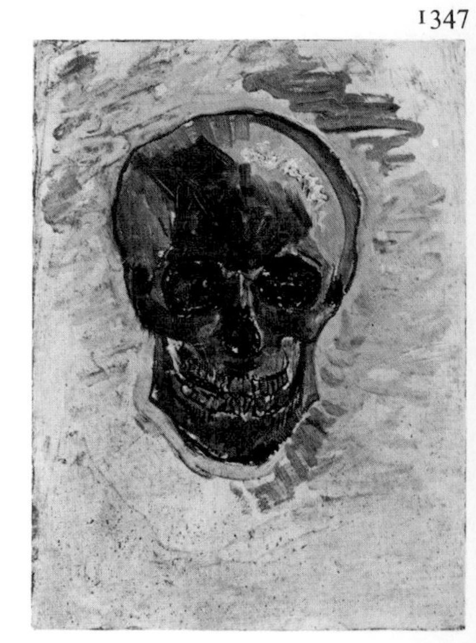

1348

1345 Self-Portrait, F366
46.5 × 35.5 cm ($18\frac{1}{2} \times 14\frac{1}{8}$")
Collection E. G. Bührle, Zurich

1346 Skull, F297
42.5 × 30.5 cm ($16\frac{7}{8} \times 12\frac{1}{4}$")
Rijksmuseum Vincent van Gogh, Amsterdam

1347 Skull, F297a
41.5 × 31.5 cm ($16\frac{1}{2} \times 12\frac{5}{8}$")
Rijksmuseum Vincent van Gogh, Amsterdam

1348 Plaster Statuette, F216
73 × 54 cm ($28\frac{3}{4} \times 21\frac{1}{4}$")
Private collection, Tokyo

Wil: "I intend as soon as possible to spend some time in the South, where there is even more color and more sun" (Letter W1).

But there was more to it than that. He had had enough of Paris. How bad it was becomes clear only when we read in a letter to Gauguin: "When I left Paris, very miserable, quite ill, and almost addicted to drink, which I resorted to in order to shore up my flagging strength—I crawled back into myself, without daring to hope" (Letter 553*a*), a sentiment that was repeated in almost the same words in the accompanying letter to Theo. It was expressed scarcely less strongly in an incidental passage in a later letter to Theo in which he recollected that he had arrived in Arles "tired and in a state of almost complete mental collapse [*presqu'évanoui cérébralement*]" (Letter 564). Thus, what he had long been planning to do was finally realized, but more in the form of an escape.

Nearly all biographies of Van Gogh contain accounts of two events connected with his departure from Paris. The first is based on the following recollection by Bernard as related in the introduction to his edition of Vincent's letters to him published in 1911: "One evening Vincent said to me: 'I am leaving tomorrow, let us both arrange the studio in such a way that my brother will think I am still here.' He nailed Japanese prints to the walls and placed canvases on the easels, while leaving others in a pile. He had a roll ready for me which I opened. It consisted of Chinese paintings, one of his finds saved from a second-hand dealer who used them to wrap up the purchases of his customers. He next told me that he was going to the South, to Arles, and that he hoped I would come to be with him there, 'because,' he said, 'the Midi is now the place where one should set up the studio of the future.' I walked with him to the Avenue de Clichy—which he so aptly called the 'Petit Boulevard'—I shook his hand, and it was all over forever. I shall never see him again, we shall never be together again except with death in between us" (page 12).

No matter how often it has been repeated in all sorts of versions, Bernard's account has continued to have something puzzling about it, something that not even the psychoanalysts who have concerned themselves with Van Gogh have ever been able to explain. Why would Vincent have wanted to make Theo believe he was still there when in fact he had left for Arles? Or is this suggestion that one could gather from Bernard's striking account off the mark, and did Vincent merely mean: "Let us arrange the studio in such a way that, when I am gone, it will look to Theo as if I am still here"—in other words, that there would not suddenly be such complete emptiness for him. One should certainly not get the impression (although Bernard's account gives grounds for this) that Vincent left the house in a stealthy manner, without letting Theo know. The facts tell a different story. Theo even took his brother to the station, as is unmistakably apparent from his reference to the leave-taking in Letter 544: "When I left you at the Gare du Midi . . . ."

The other frequently mentioned event that occurred on the last day of Vincent's stay in Paris was his visit to Seurat. The information about this is drawn from Letter 553*a*. What is usually not mentioned is that, here too, he was accompanied by his brother. Also, in October, when he had made a number of large pictures to decorate the walls of his house in Arles, he asked Theo, on his behalf, to tell Seurat about this because: "What often encourages me in this work is the remembrance of his personality and the visit we paid to his studio to look at his fine large canvases" (Letter 553).

However unpleasant the circumstances of Vincent's departure from Paris may have been, the relationship with his brother at that time seems to have been quite harmonious.

1349

1350

1351

1352

1349 Still Life with Plaster Statuette (Type D), a Rose, and Two Novels [Guy de Maupassant, *Bel-Ami*, and Jules and Edmond de Goncourt, *Germinie Lacerteux*], F360
55 × 46.5 cm (21$\frac{5}{8}$ × 18$\frac{1}{2}$″)
Rijksmuseum Kröller-Müller, Otterlo

1350 Portrait of Père Tanguy, Head, F1412
Sketch on the back of a menu of the Restaurant du Chalet
Pencil, 21.5 × 13.5 cm (8$\frac{5}{8}$ × 5$\frac{1}{2}$″)
Rijksmuseum Vincent van Gogh, Amsterdam

1351 Portrait of Père Tanguy, Half-Length, F363
92 × 75 cm (36$\frac{1}{4}$ × 29$\frac{1}{2}$″)
Musée Rodin, Paris
Colorplate XXII, p. 294

1352 Portrait of Père Tanguy, Half-Length, F364
65 × 51 cm (25$\frac{5}{8}$ × 20$\frac{1}{8}$″)
Stavros S. Niarchos Collection

1353 Self-Portrait with Gray Felt Hat, F344
44 × 37.5 cm (17$\frac{3}{8}$ × 15″)
Rijksmuseum Vincent van Gogh, Amsterdam

1354 Self-Portrait with Straw Hat, F365v (reverse: 654)
41 × 31.5 cm (16$\frac{1}{8}$ × 12$\frac{5}{8}$″)
Metropolitan Museum of Art, New York

1353

1354

1355

1356

1355 Portrait of a Woman with Carnations (La Segatori?), F381
81 × 60 cm (31⅞ × 23⅝″)
The Louvre, Paris

1356 Self-Portrait in Front of the Easel, F522
65 × 50.5 cm (25⅝ × 20⅛″)
Rijksmuseum Vincent van Gogh, Amsterdam

Arles

The most remarkable thing about Vincent's arrival in Provence was that he had gone for the sun but found it was covered with a thick blanket of snow. In his first letter from Arles—written probably February 21, the day after his arrival—he said: "There are at least two feet of snow all over, and it is still snowing." But he also wrote: "And the landscapes in the snow with white hill-tops against a sky as bright as the snow were really like the winter-landscapes of the Japanese" (Letter 463). Japan was the ideal against which Provence, in the near future, would always be measured.

He found lodgings in a small hotel not far from the station; "Restaurant Carrel, 30 Rue Cavalerie" was the address he gave Theo. And he set to work at once. In the next letter to Theo, which must have been written about February 25, he was already able to report: "I have completed three studies . . . an old woman from Arles, a landscape with snow, a view of a small part of a street with a butcher's shop" (Letter 464). These are 1357–59.

It is curious that Vincent began with three different kinds of subjects, but that is probably because he had encountered a spell of bad weather. The landscapes would very soon become his principal subject, and he would not resume doing portraits until June.

During the first weeks the weather continued to be unusually bitter. Even in his fourth letter (about March 3), he reported: "It is freezing cold, and the snow is still on the ground" (Letter 466). As a result he was mostly working indoors again. Referring once more to the landscape with snow (1358), he wrote: "I have a study of a white field with the city in the background. Also two small studies of a sprig from an almond tree, which is already in bloom." Those small studies were 1361 and 1362, and he indicated in a somewhat later letter to Wil that one was intended for her: "As I would like to give you something of my work that you might find pleasing, I am putting aside for you a small study of a book and a flower [meaning 1362]" (Letter W3).

There is still another winter landscape, 1360, which I assume was made when the snow was beginning to disappear. According to Letter 467, that would have been during the week of March 4 to 10. In that letter Vincent also wrote: "I have just finished a study like the one of mine Lucien Pissarro has, but this time it is oranges." The work he is referring to here is the painting that he had dedicated to Pissarro, 1340. The new companion piece was 1363. Although he does not mention them in the letters, I assume that the two still lifes with the clogs and a pan with potatoes, 1364 and 1365, also date from this time. Both exhibit the striking bird's-eye perspective characteristic of the later Paris period, and they share with 1363 the distinctive broad, individual brushstrokes by which the cast shadows have been rendered.

After Vincent had painted the small basket with oranges, he wrote: "That now makes eight studies I have done. But that still does not mean anything because I have not yet been able to work in warmth and at my leisure" (Letter 467). For the same reason it is understandable that his thoughts were less occupied with the landscape than with other matters. In his letters to Theo he dealt especially with the problems of the art trade, which had naturally been a frequent topic of conversation between them during the past two years. He gave his imagination free rein concerning the possibilities of selling the work of Impressionist painters in the Netherlands and England. Their friend the art dealer Alexander Reid, whose specialties included the works of Monticelli, should, in Vincent's opinion, be given a free hand so far as those painters were concerned, but Theo should press for Impressionist art to be imported into England, and in addition, he should try to get Tersteeg, the manager of the Goupil branch in The Hague, to take a greater interest in these painters. In his enthusiasm Vincent even went so far as to send Theo the draft of a letter that, by adding to it a little, he could send to Tersteeg, something that Theo actually did.

When the weather in March did improve, Vincent was again able to work outdoors. On March 10 he wrote that he not only had made two landscapes, but also hoped to start four or five works that week (Letter 468). Landscapes 1366 and 1367 were among them.

The Drawbridges

At the end of the week, about March 17, he wrote: "Today I brought home a size-15 canvas*; it is a drawbridge with a little horse and carriage crossing it, which stands out against a blue sky—the river also blue, the

*For an explanation of Van Gogh's use of canvas sizes, see p. 7.

1357

1358

February 1888

1357 An Old Woman of Arles, F 390
55 × 43 cm ($21\frac{5}{8} \times 16\frac{7}{8}$")
Rijksmuseum Vincent van Gogh, Amsterdam

1358 Landscape with Snow, F 391
50 × 60 cm ($19\frac{5}{8} \times 23\frac{5}{8}$")
Private collection, Basel

1359 A Pork Butcher's Shop Seen from a Window, F 389
Canvas on cardboard, 39.5 × 32.5 cm ($15\frac{3}{4} \times 13$")
Rijksmuseum Vincent van Gogh, Amsterdam

1359

1360

1361

1362

1363

1364

1365

March 1888

1360 Landscape with Snow, F290
38 × 46 cm (15 × 18⅛″)
Justin K. Thannhauser Collection, Solomon R. Guggenheim Museum, New York

1361 Blossoming Almond Branch in a Glass, F392
24 × 19 cm (9½ × 7½″)
Rijksmuseum Vincent van Gogh, Amsterdam

1362 Blossoming Almond Branch in a Glass with a Book, F393
24 × 19 cm (9½ × 7½″)
Private collection, Switzerland

1363 Basket with Oranges, F395
45 × 54 cm (17¾ × 21¼″)
Collection Mr. and Mrs. Basil P. Goulandris, Lausanne

1364 A Pair of Leather Clogs, F607
32.5 × 40.5 cm (13 × 16⅛″)
Rijksmuseum Vincent van Gogh, Amsterdam

1365 Bowl with Potatoes, F386
39 × 47 cm (15⅜ × 18½″)
Rijksmuseum Vincent van Gogh, Amsterdam

banks a sort of orange covered with green, a group of washerwomen with brightly colored jackets and bonnets" (Letter 469). This is important news, for the *Drawbridge with Carriage* (1368) is generally acknowledged to be one of Vincent's first masterpieces of the Arles period. The canvas has the simple but effective composition, the sunny character, and clear, richly contrasting colors that today, a century later, still make it one of Van Gogh's most popular works. The drawbridge motif, which must have reminded him of his own country, was to fascinate Vincent for some time to come, and his personal satisfaction with this first of the drawbridge paintings is quite apparent from the fact that it was the one he chose when a little later he wanted to send a specimen of his work to the Netherlands: "[Tersteeg] has to have one of my paintings in his own collection. I have been thinking about this lately and have found something nice of a kind I won't be making every day. It is the drawbridge with the little yellow carriage and the group of washerwomen, a study in which the earth is deep orange, the grass very green, the sky and water blue" (Letter 473).

In April he made a copy of it for Theo (1392) and set himself to drawing and painting still more works from the same subject. In his second study he combined it with a new experiment that he would attempt many times more: the bold venture of bringing the bare disk of the sun into the picture. While he was engaged in doing this, he wrote Emile Bernard: "At the top of this letter I am sending you a small sketch of a study that is keeping me occupied in an attempt to make something out of it: sailors with their sweethearts walking back to the city, which, with the strange silhouette of its drawbridge, is outlined against an enormous yellow sun" (1370). However, as he told Theo, it did not work out: "I had bad luck with the sunset with figures and a bridge that I told Bernard about. Since the bad weather prevented me from working at the site itself, I completely ruined that study when I tried to complete it at home" (Letter 471, March 24). What happened to the canvas is not known, but a fragment of it has been preserved (1369).

Vincent did not leave it at that: "I started the same subject once again, but because the weather was entirely different, I did so in an entirely different range of colors and without figures" (1371).

Another interesting point is what the drawbridge was called. Vincent referred to it as the "Pont de l'Anglais," but this was because he had misheard the name. Actually it was called "Pont de Langlois" after a former bridge keeper. The bridge no longer exists but was replaced by another built in 1962 at a location two miles farther from Arles.*

Vincent had also started on a series of small landscape drawings in March. One of these, depicting a small lane running past two bare pollard willows (1372), is inscribed by Vincent himself "Arles mars 88." The style of this minutely executed, somewhat delicate pen-and-ink drawing with its wide perspective leads me also to assign other comparable drawings to the month of March (1373–75).

*See Leprohon, *Vincent van Gogh* (1972), pp. 356ff.

1366

1368

1367

1366 Lane with Plane Trees, F398
45 × 49 cm ($17\frac{3}{4} \times 19\frac{1}{4}$")
Musée Rodin, Paris

1367 Landscape with Rustic Bridge, F396
46 × 49 cm ($18\frac{1}{8} \times 19\frac{1}{4}$")
Private collection

1368 Drawbridge with Carriage, F397
54 × 65 cm ($21\frac{1}{4} \times 25\frac{5}{8}$")
Rijksmuseum Kröller-Müller, Otterlo

1369 Walking Couple (fragment), F544
32.5 × 23 cm (13 × 9")
Collection J. E. Werenskiold, Lysaker, Norway

1370 Drawbridge with Walking Couple
Sketch in Letter B2
Private collection, Paris

1371 Drawbridge without Figures, F400
58.5 × 73 cm ($23\frac{1}{4} \times 28\frac{3}{4}$")
Rijksmuseum Vincent van Gogh, Amsterdam

1372 Landscape with Path and Pollard Trees, F1499
Pencil, pen, brown ink, 25.5 × 35 cm ($10\frac{1}{4} \times 13\frac{3}{4}$")
Rijksmuseum Vincent van Gogh, Amsterdam

1373 Field with Factory, F1500
Pencil, chalk, pen, 25.5 × 35 cm ($10\frac{1}{4} \times 13\frac{3}{4}$")
Courtauld Institute Galleries, London

1369

1371

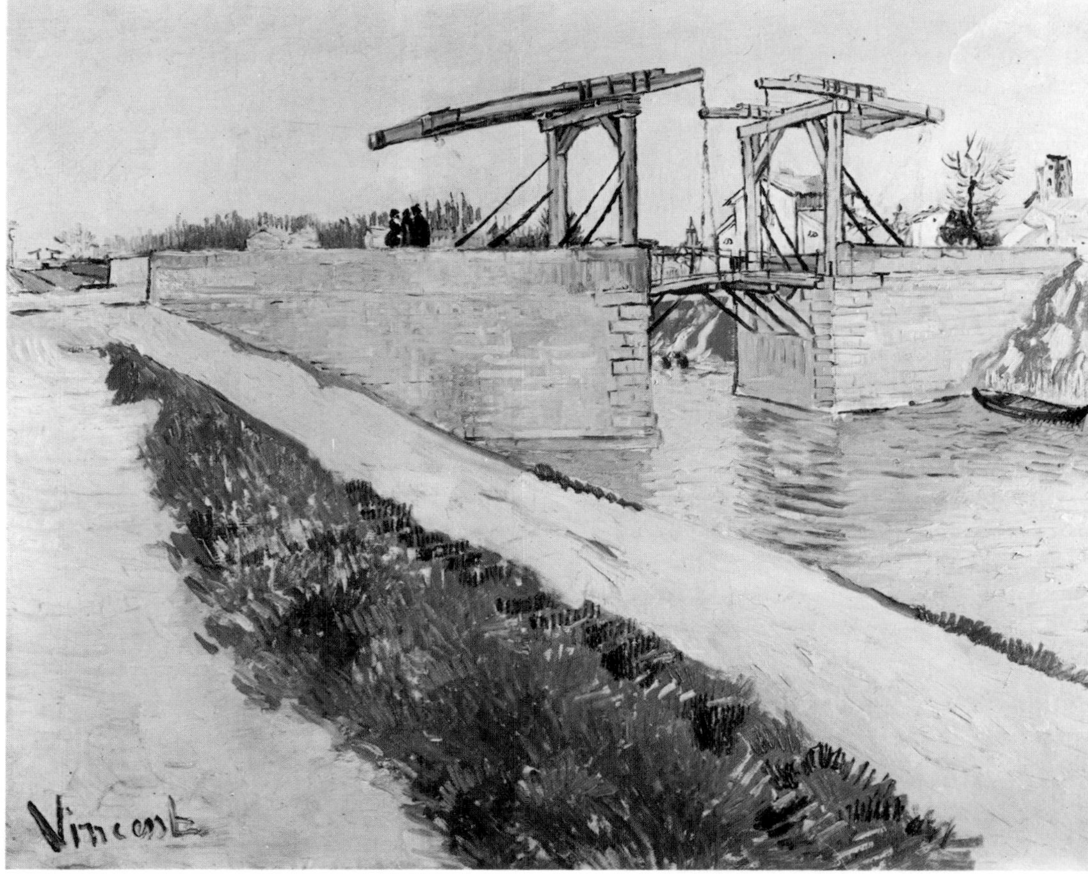

1370

1372

1373

1374

1375

1374 Landscape with Two Trees, Plowman, and Houses, F 1517
Pencil, reed pen, 25 × 34 cm ($9\frac{7}{8} \times 13\frac{3}{8}$″)
Collection Mr. and Mrs. Paul Mellon, Upperville, Virginia

1375 Field with Houses under a Sky with Sun Disk, F 1506
Pencil, pen, reed pen, brown ink, 24.5 × 35.5 cm ($9\frac{7}{8} \times 14\frac{1}{8}$″)
Rijksmuseum Vincent van Gogh, Amsterdam

A New Subject: Orchards

Before the month's end Vincent's attention had shifted to a new theme that was to occupy him completely for many weeks. The fruit trees had begun to blossom, and as early as March 24, in the same letter in which he reported his setback with the drawbridge, he wrote: "I have a large group of blossoming apricot trees in a small bright-green pasture" (Letter 471). This was 1380.

The blossoming of the trees brought on what he called a frenzy of work ("un rage de travail"), and since in his enthusiasm for what he was doing he regularly reported on his progress to Theo, Wil, and Emile Bernard, his letters enable us to get a fairly good idea of the number of studies and the sequence in which they were made. March 30—scarcely a week after his first mention of the blossoming orchards in the letter to Theo—he reported to Wil: "Now, for instance, I am working on six paintings of blossoming fruit trees" (Letter W3). It appears that Vincent had started several different studies at the same time, which took a while to complete, for three weeks had passed before he wrote: "I have nine orchards in work" (Letter B4, about April 21), and to Theo, about the same date: "I now have ten orchards, three small studies, and in addition to these, a large one of a cherry tree that I botched" (Letter 478).

On the basis of the descriptions, eight of the fifteen painted orchards that have been preserved can be dated fairly accurately, and the remainder can be inserted into more or less their proper place in the series without great difficulty. The sequence cannot, of course, be determined with absolute certainty because of the fact that work was being done on several canvases simultaneously.

From the letter to Wil (W3) it appears that apart from the apricot trees mentioned in Letter 471 (1380), five more orchards, not mentioned in the letters, were in production. In my opinion, 1378, 1381, and 1383 were among this group of five that were being worked on during the last week of March. Since 1378 appears in one of the three small sketches in Letter 477, written in the second week of April (1393), we know that it was in existence as a painting at that time. As Vincent mentioned in his letter of March 30, he brought home the canvas with the pink peach trees (1379; colorplate XXIII, page 311) on that day. When this important work—to which I shall return shortly—had been completed, he made a watercolor sketch of it for Theo, just as he did of the *Drawbridge*. In Letter 474, April 9, he wrote: "I have sent you sketches of the paintings which are intended for the Netherlands" (1382 and 1384, from, respectively, 1368 and 1379).

Meanwhile, he continued to do orchards. On March 30 or 31 he wrote: "I am going to start a size-30 canvas of the same subject" (Letter 472). This must refer to 1386, for it is the only size-30 canvas among the orchards. This must also be the canvas he had in mind when he wrote: "I have a new *Orchard* that is just as good as the pink peaches; this one is apricot trees in a very soft pink" (Letter 474). In this letter he also mentioned 1387: "I am now working on *Plum Trees*, in which the trees are yellowish white with countless black branches." In a letter to Bernard the same

1376

1377

1378

1379

1376 Orchard with Arles in the Background, F 1516
Pencil, pen, black and violet ink,
53.5 × 39.5 cm ($21\frac{1}{4} \times 15\frac{3}{4}$″)
Hyde Collection, Glens Falls, New York

1377 Drawbridge with Road, F 1470
Pen, reed pen, 35.5 × 47 cm ($14\frac{1}{8} \times 18\frac{1}{2}$″)
Graphische Sammlung, Staatsgalerie, Stuttgart

1378 Orchard with Blossoming Plum Trees, F 403
60 × 80 cm ($23\frac{5}{8} \times 31\frac{1}{2}$″)
Rijksmuseum Vincent van Gogh, Amsterdam

1379 Pink Peach Trees, F 394
73 × 59.5 cm ($28\frac{3}{4} \times 23\frac{5}{8}$″)
Rijksmuseum Kröller-Müller, Otterlo
Colorplate XXIII, opposite

Colorplate XXIII, Pink Peach Trees, 1379 ›

Souvenir de Mauve
Vincent

day, he sketched yet another orchard on which he was working at the same time (1389 and 1390), and wrote: "For that matter, here is a small sketch, the entrance to a Provençal orchard with its yellow fencing, with its windbreak (against the mistral) of dark cypresses, with its typical vegetables in various kinds of green: yellow lettuce, onions, garlic, emerald-green leeks" (Letter B3).

Tribute to the Memory of Mauve

Of the six studies of orchards that Vincent was already working on in March, he singled out the *Pink Peach Trees* (1379) "as probably the best landscape I have painted yet" (Letter 472). He wrote Wil: "And what I brought home today would possibly please you—it is a tilled bit of soil in an orchard, a rush fence, and two peach trees in full bloom. Pink against a brilliant blue sky with white clouds and in sunshine" (Letter W3). He was so pleased with the success of the canvas, which, in contrast to the other orchards, had apparently been completed in one sitting, that he immediately decided it should be devoted to a special purpose. He had learned more than a month before that Anton Mauve—once his teacher—had died on February 8, and he had written to Theo that they ought to send a painting to Mauve's widow as a tribute to his memory (Letter 467). On the very day that he came home with the study of the peach trees, he found that Wil had sent him a publication prepared as a memorial to Mauve (this was an article by H.A.C. Dekker, reprinted from *De Portefeuille*, and it has been preserved and is now in the Rijksmuseum Vincent van Gogh). When Vincent saw this, he immediately knew what he had to do. He considered the article "trite and poorly done" and the portrait of Mauve its only redeeming feature, and he wrote to Theo: "Something that I cannot describe took hold of me and made me choke up with feeling and I wrote on my painting: 'Souvenir de Mauve Vincent & Theo,' and if you agree, we shall send it like that from both of us to Mauve's widow. I have purposely taken the best study I have made here; I don't know what they will say about it in Holland, but we need not worry about that; it seemed to me that in memory of Mauve I had to make something tender and at the same time quite cheerful and not a study in a more somber mood" (Letter 472).

The picture did indeed go to the Netherlands—on May 10, as appears from Letter 486 and Letter W4—but the inscription read simply "Souvenir de Mauve Vincent." Why Theo's name is missing—despite Vincent's very explicit mention of its inclusion to Theo, which is also found in the letter to his sister, W3—we now have no way of knowing, but I am convinced that Vincent himself eliminated the words "& Theo," probably at Theo's request. Was it not, after all, a gift in memory of Mauve that Vincent himself had thought of and made? In order still to have this very successful painting for himself and Theo, he made a very carefully executed, somewhat larger replica of it: 1391 (see letter 477). He also made a smaller version (1388) of the important landscape 1389, and he made two more visits to the same orchard to paint two parts of it viewed from different

1380

1381

1382

1380 Orchard with Blossoming Apricot Trees, F555
65.5 × 80.5 cm (26 × $31\frac{7}{8}$")
Rijksmuseum Vincent van Gogh, Amsterdam

1381 Orchard with White Blossoms, F552
74 × 55 cm ($29\frac{1}{8}$ × $21\frac{5}{8}$")
Metropolitan Museum of Art, New York

April 1888

1382 Drawbridge with Carriage, F1480
Watercolor, 30 × 30 cm ($11\frac{3}{4}$ × $11\frac{3}{4}$")
Private collection

〈 Colorplate XXIV, Field with Flowers, 1416

angles: 1396 (this is the view to the left of the one in 1389) and 1398 (this is the left-hand portion of the picture in 1389 with an additional peach tree close by). His cherished *Pink Peach Trees* (1379; colorplate XXIII, page 311) was, I believe, painted in this same orchard, judging from the view in 1396, in which these trees are to be seen in the foreground against the same rush fences.

Vincent wrote about his six orchards in Letter 477: "Every day I try to improve them in some way and bring them together into one whole." The small sketch 1393 reveals how he proposed to do this by combining three views; these sketches relate to canvases 1380, 1379, and 1378. The titles he wrote under the sketches help us to identify the paintings: "verger rose pâle (abricotiers)," "pêcher rose," and "verger blanc (pruniers)," meaning "pale pink orchard (apricot trees)," "pink peach tree," and "white orchard (plum trees)." The small pear tree, 1394, was to be the middle view in another group of three, and he hoped to get still another group of three pictures that fitted together, "but those are still only in an embryonic state," he wrote. Scherjon and De Gruyter, in their book *Vincent van Gogh's Great Period* (1937), have tried to reconstruct the other two sets of three that Van Gogh had in mind, but in my opinion that is impossible because of the lack of reliable data. It seems fairly certain to me that the flanking panels of the third group—which was to show "a very large orchard, bordered by cypresses and large pear and apple trees" (Letter 477)—must have been 1396 and 1388, but we have no clues to identify the middle panel. The small canvas 1398, although showing the center of the orchard, cannot be the one because it is considerably lower than the two flanking panels.

The last of the blossoming orchards done in 1888 is 1399, described and sketched in Letters 478 and B4, both written about April 21 (the sketches in these letters are 1400 and 1401). Vincent wrote to Theo: "Here is a small rough draft of an orchard I had ... particularly intended for you on the occasion of the first of May [Theo's birthday]. It is absolutely bright and was absolutely done at one go. A frenzied piling up of paint with hardly a trace of yellow or mauve in the first white layer of paint." But, he added, "I must now turn to a different subject because most of the orchards are no longer in bloom."

We know of only one *drawing* of an orchard that Vincent did during the preceding weeks. This large drawing, 1385, corresponds to painting 1378. It was probably intended to give Theo at least some idea of the work he was doing while the painted studies were still drying. This drawing, together with another one that is not known to us, must have been sent to Theo about the middle of April (see Letter 478).

Small Drawings

During the final days of April, Vincent spent his time drawing, which was cheaper than painting. He was worried because Boussod and Valadon were displeased with Theo's efforts to promote the work of the Impressionists. "I have continued with a series of pen-and-ink drawings, the first two of which you already have, but smaller in size," he

1383

1384

1385

1383 Orchard with Blossoming Apricot Trees, F556
55×65.5 cm ($21\frac{5}{8} \times 26''$)
Private collection, Switzerland

1384 Pink Peach Trees, F1469
Charcoal, watercolor, 45.5×30.5 cm ($18\frac{1}{8} \times 12\frac{1}{4}''$)
Rijksmuseum Vincent van Gogh, Amsterdam

1385 Orchard with Blossoming Plum Trees, F1414
Reed pen, heightened with white, 39.5×54 cm ($15\frac{3}{4} \times 21\frac{1}{4}''$)
Rijksmuseum Vincent van Gogh, Amsterdam

1386 Orchard, F511
72.5×92 cm ($28\frac{3}{4} \times 36\frac{1}{4}''$)
Rijksmuseum Vincent van Gogh, Amsterdam

1387 Orchard with Blossoming Plum Trees, F553
55×65 cm ($21\frac{5}{8} \times 25\frac{5}{8}''$)
National Gallery of Scotland, Edinburgh

1388 Orchard Surrounded by Cypresses, F554
32×40 cm ($12\frac{5}{8} \times 15\frac{3}{4}''$)
Private collection, New York

1389 Orchard Surrounded by Cypresses, F513
65×81 cm ($25\frac{5}{8} \times 31\frac{7}{8}''$)
Rijksmuseum Kröller-Müller, Otterlo

1390 Orchard Surrounded by Cypresses
Sketch in Letter B3
Private collection, Paris

1386

1387

1388

1389

1390

said in Letter 479 (about April 24 to 27). "For I said to myself that a quarrel with these people would make it desirable that you have fewer expenses on my account." I assume that the drawings 1403–11—which are actually smaller (roughly 10 by 13¾ inches) than the drawing of the white orchard, 1385, sent to Theo in the middle of April—belong to this series. Drawing 1403 shows the view from Vincent's room at that time, on the Rue Cavalerie, and the others are probably the result of his scouting expeditions about the neighborhood. In Letter 479 Vincent wrote: "I shall shortly be sending you pen-and-ink drawings, I already have four of them"; on May 1 he wrote: "I have just sent off a roll of small pen-and-ink drawings, a dozen I think" (Letter 480).

The small painted landscape 1402 must date from before May 1, because it was made from one of these drawings (1372). As Vincent said later: "There is a small landscape with a little white, red, and green house next to a cypress; you have the drawing of this, and I made the painting of it entirely at home" (Letter 484).

The May 1 letter contained still another important piece of news: Vincent had rented a house, actually the right wing of the building he had sketched in the letter (1413). It had two regular-sized and two small rooms; the rent was 15 francs a month. One of the reasons for this move was the poor food he was getting in the cheap hotel where he had been staying, instead of getting nourishing things like strong broth, as he wrote. He was not able to occupy the "little yellow house," as it was always referred to afterward, because he did not have any furniture for it, but he would use it as his studio and for storage. He now took his meals in a restaurant—a better place than before where he could eat for 1 to 1.50 francs a day—and slept at an inn for 1 franc a night. All the same, he could now say with some pride that his address was 2 Place Lamartine, and as soon as he could get some furniture, he planned to share the studio with another artist, perhaps Paul Gauguin.

Across from the house there was a public garden with a small pond (which can be seen clearly in drawing 1412), and even before he rented the house, Vincent had made several drawings of this garden, which was the source of inspiration for a great many more drawings and for a series of paintings called "The Poet's Park."

About a week later Vincent had written Theo that he had sent him a roll of small drawings: "There has been a lot of mistral here and that was when I made the dozen small drawings which I sent. The weather is now marvelous; I have made two more large drawings and five small ones" (Letter 483). He added that he would send the *small* drawings to Theo—who was in Brussels for a few days—that same day.

Of these seventeen small drawings, most can be identified with a high degree of certainty. In the first place, they must have included the drawings he had done in March—1372–75. Also, possibly four drawings of the public garden across from the little yellow house; Vincent had announced May 1 that he was sending "a hurried sketch on yellow paper" of the lawn in the park and "two more drawings" of the public garden, while a fourth may have gone with the second consignment. I have in mind 1409–11 and 1414 (not 1412, because that is a much larger drawing).

1391

1392

1393

The *Canal with Bridge and Women Washing* (1405) was certainly part of one of these consignments, because Vincent specifically referred to it in Letter 504, reporting that he had made a painted study of the subject.

I likewise assume that five additional drawings in the same small format (about 10 by 13¾ inches) and exhibiting a very similar style of drawing were included in the two consignments of early May and must therefore have been made in April or at the beginning of May: the tiled roof (1403), the river view (1404), the laborers in the field (1406), and the two small landscapes (1407 and 1408). This accounts for fourteen of the seventeen drawings.*

Reed-Pen Drawings

Apart from the fact that these drawings give us—as they must also have given Theo—a good idea of Vincent's new environment, they can also be said to represent an important new element in his development as an artist. The few drawings made in Paris were different in character; they did not display this somewhat dry but pithy and highly illustrational manner. This was partly due to the technique he used. In Letter 478, about April 21, commenting on two drawings he had sent Theo, he wrote: "These drawings were made with a reed, cut like a goose quill; I am thinking of making a series of them, and I hope better than the first two. It is a technique I tried in Holland at the time, but I did not have reed quite as good as here." One of the two drawings referred to, which, according to

*Mark W. Roskill included with this series of early drawings F1502, F1509, F1518, and F1518a (in this book, 1492, 1494, 1493, and 1495), which I have dated somewhat later because of their more summery atmosphere (see "Van Gogh's Exchanges of Work with Emile Bernard in 1883," *Oud Holland*, vol. LXXXVI, no. 2–3 [1971], p. 167). I have dealt in greater detail with the dating of the drawings made in Arles in the article "The Intriguing Drawings of Arles," *Vincent*, vol. III, no. 4 (1974), pp. 24–32.

1394

1395

1396

1397

1398

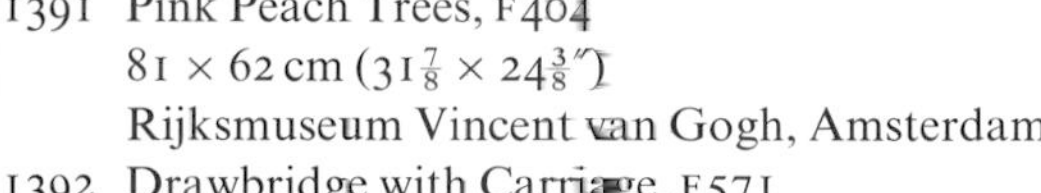

1391 Pink Peach Trees, F 404
81×62 cm ($31\frac{7}{8} \times 24\frac{3}{8}$″)
Rijksmuseum Vincent van Gogh, Amsterdam

1392 Drawbridge with Carriage, F 571
60×65 cm ($23\frac{5}{8} \times 25\frac{5}{8}$″)
Private collection, Paris

1393 Three Orchards (1380, 1379, and 1378)
Sketch in Letter 477
Rijksmuseum Vincent van Gogh, Amsterdam

1394 Blossoming Pear Tree, F 405
73×46 cm ($28\frac{3}{4} \times 18\frac{1}{8}$″)
Rijksmuseum Vincent van Gogh, Amsterdam

1395 Blossoming Pear Tree
Sketch in Letter 477
Rijksmuseum Vincent van Gogh, Amsterdam

1396 Orchard with Cypresses, F 551
65×81 cm ($25\frac{5}{8} \times 31\frac{7}{8}$″)
Private collection, New York

1397 Almond Tree, F 557
50.5×38 cm ($20\frac{1}{8} \times 15$″)
Rijksmuseum Vincent van Gogh, Amsterdam

1398 Peach Tree in the Orchard Surrounded by Cypresses, F 399
41×33 cm ($16\frac{1}{8} \times 13$″)
Collection Continental Art Holdings Ltd., Johannesburg

Letter 479, were larger than the dozen sent later, must have been the orchard 1385. As previously noted, the other one is not known to us and has probably been lost.

Speaking about their mutual friend the painter A. H. Koning, he went on: "I will write him to explain the technique and I will send him some cut reeds so that he can also make them" (that is, reed-pen drawings). Most of the previously mentioned series of small drawings were also done with the reed pen, or with standard pen and reed pen, and it is clear that Vincent quickly developed great virtuosity in the new technique. The reed pen generally produces heavier lines than an ordinary pen—frequently also double lines—and so we see in these drawings how Vincent worked with a determination and energy not previously witnessed but also with a bare minimum of means. Drawing 1408, to take just one example, graphically illustrates how skillfully the landscape has been caught with comparatively few short lines to depict the white farmhouse and the waving stalks of grain around it. The impression one gets from all these drawings is one of precision, control, and drive; one clearly senses how swiftly and unhesitatingly the essence of a landscape has here been put down on paper (one need only look at the short bold lines suggesting the storm clouds and the angry waters in 1404). The omission of all superfluous details is probably best seen in 1406, where a few converging lines are used to create a suggestion of great depth and breadth around the laborers and their overseers, who are depicted in summary yet expressive fashion in a variety of attitudes. Another thing that we see here is Van Gogh developing the drawing technique that, in the course of the Arles period, he would carry forward to masterly heights and that would prove to be one of the most typical characteristics of his graphic work at this time: the rendering of various planes and textures by means of a system of shorter or longer lines and lighter or heavier dots. A good example is the view of the park, 1411, in which the foreground is rendered by dots and the curb by short vertical lines, whereas, in contrast, in a landscape such as 1408 the lines depicting the wheat stalks fade away and are replaced by dots in the distance.

One might be inclined to view this stippling technique as a last remnant of Pointillism, but it is a kind of Pointillism that Vincent—this time as a draftsman—had developed in an entirely personal way. There is no longer any question of a more or less naturalistic rendering of the real world; the little lines and dots are an imaginative representation rather than an accurate depiction of reality, but in a surprising way this is not at the expense of the subject matter.

"A Japanese Dream"

In Letter 483, about May 8, Vincent mentioned "two *large* drawings" in addition to the dozen smaller ones that he sent. He was presumably referring here to the drawing of the public garden in front of the house, 1412, and to the one of the pasture in bloom, 1415. There is no painted counterpart that we know of to the first of these, but there is to the second, namely 1416 (colorplate XXIV, page 312). This painting is mentioned in Letter 487, about May 12, and can therefore be accurately dated: "At the moment I have two new studies as follows: you already have a drawing of a farmhouse by the side of the road in the wheat fields. [Also] a pasture full of bright yellow buttercups, a ditch with irises with green leaves and violet flowers; in the background, the city, a few gray pollard willows, a band of blue sky."

As he made a small rough sketch of the two subjects in the letter (1418), their identification presents no problem. The small drawing referred to, whose composition appears slightly different, was 1408; the painting was 1416. Vincent must have been very fond of that picture, for he continued: "Provided they do not mow the pasture, I would like to do that study over again, for the subject was very beautiful and I had difficulty in arranging the composition. A little city, surrounded by

1399

1400

1401

1402

1399 Orchard and House with Orange Roof, F406
72 × 58 cm ($28\frac{3}{8} \times 22\frac{7}{8}$")
Collection Mrs. E. Friedlaender, Manchester, England

1400 Orchard and House with Orange Roof
Sketch in Letter 478
Rijksmuseum Vincent van Gogh, Amsterdam

1401 Orchard and House with Orange Roof
Sketch in Letter B4
Private collection, Paris

1402 Landscape with Path and Pollard Trees, F407
31 × 38.5 cm ($12\frac{1}{4} \times 15\frac{3}{8}$")
Location unknown

1403 Tiled Roof with Chimneys and Church Tower, F1480a
Pencil, reed pen, 25.5 × 34.5 cm ($10\frac{1}{4} \times 13\frac{3}{4}$")
Galerie Berggruen, Paris

1404 The Rhône with Boats and a Bridge, F1472
Pen, 22.5 × 34.5 cm ($9 \times 13\frac{3}{4}$")
Staatliche Graphische Sammlung, Munich

1403

1404

1405

1406

1407

1408

1405 Canal with Bridge and Women Washing, F 1473
Pen, 22.5 × 34.5 cm (9 × $13\frac{3}{4}$″)
Staatliche Graphische Sammlung, Munich

1406 Farmers Working in a Field, F 1090
Reed pen, 26 × 34.5 cm ($10\frac{1}{4}$ × $13\frac{3}{4}$″)
Rijksmuseum Vincent van Gogh, Amsterdam

1407 Meadow with Flowers, F 1474
Pencil, pen, brown ink, 25.5 × 34.5 cm ($10\frac{1}{4}$ × $13\frac{3}{4}$″)
Rijksmuseum Vincent van Gogh, Amsterdam

1408 Farmhouse with Wheat Field along a Road, F 1415
Pencil, pen, reed pen, brown ink, 25.5 × 34.5 cm ($10\frac{1}{4}$ × $13\frac{3}{4}$″)
Rijksmuseum Vincent van Gogh, Amsterdam

1409 Public Garden with a Corner of the Yellow House, F 1476
Pen, reed pen, 35 × 26 cm ($13\frac{3}{4}$ × $10\frac{1}{4}$″)
Rijksmuseum Vincent van Gogh, Amsterdam

1409

a completely yellow and violet field in bloom; it would, you know, be a real Japanese dream." I have put the two landscapes 1422 and 1423 in one group with 1416 because of their similarity in style. In the 1970 *catalogue raisonné* 1423 is dated September 1888, but the bright green grass and the abundance of fiery red poppies in the foreground (which incidentally lend charm to the otherwise rather empty picture) unmistakably point to spring.

In the meantime, another change had occurred in Vincent's domestic circumstances. Because he had been dissatisfied with his small hotel, he had moved to an inn, but he then became involved in a dispute over the amount of his bill. The matter then had to go to court because the innkeeper had seized Vincent's baggage, and although the verdict was partly in Vincent's favor, these were very trying days (see Letters 484–88). He explained that he had almost no money left, because he had had to buy something so that he could make coffee and broth "at home" (that is, at the yellow house), and he had also bought two chairs and a table. "I am sorry I did not take this studio sooner; with what those people overcharged me, I could have had it furnished by now. I only hope that I have now paid my dues to misfortune, and it is better for this to come at the beginning rather than at the end of the undertaking" (Letter 485).

By happy coincidence it was precisely during these difficult days that for the first time since his arrival in Arles Vincent was able to show Theo what he had achieved as a painter. After having written several times about his attempts to find a case to send the pictures in, he could finally write, in Letter 486, May 10, that they would be on their way that evening. Even before that, in Letter 484, he had had an important announcement to make: "I am now sending you in the case all the studies that I have made, except for some I have destroyed, but I have not signed them all; there are twelve which I have taken off their stretchers and fourteen on stretchers." This is firm evidence that during the first two months of his stay in Arles Vincent had painted more than twenty-six studies, an average of one every two days, and how many masterpieces among them!

In the middle of May Vincent reported: "I have two new studies, a bridge and a roadside scene" (Letter 488). He was probably referring to the new version—remarkable for its beautiful color—of the drawbridge, 1421, and to landscape 1419. He also made a drawing of the drawbridge (1420) in which the simple but striking interplay of lines was reduced to its absolute essentials—a small miracle in drawing technique. He mentioned the landscape again a few days later in his letter to Bernard (Letter B5): "And also two studies of a roadside, made later in the full force of the mistral"; and a small rough sketch of this (1464) appears in Letter B6, June 24. The other of the "studies of a roadside" is undoubtedly 1417, a sketch of which is also to be found in Letter B6; as previously noted, there is also a small sketch of this (1418) in Letter 487. This road, with its massive trees and farmhouses, was obviously a motif that Vincent was very fond of; it also appears in 1495, in which the road with the house is seen at closer range.

1410

1411

1412

Still Lifes as Color Studies

About May 19 Vincent reported on work that was quite different in character but would prove to be no less significant: "This week I have made two still lifes. A coffee pot of blue enameled iron, to the left a cup in royal blue and gold, a milk pitcher in a light-blue and white checkered pattern, to the right a white cup with a blue and orange design, standing on a yellowish-gray earthenware plate, a blue pitcher of glazed earthenware or majolica with designs in red, green, and brown; finally, two oranges and two lemons; the table is covered with a blue cloth, the background is yellow-green, so there are six different blues and four or five yellows and oranges. The other still life is the majolica jar with wild flowers" (Letter 489).

1410 Public Garden with Benches, F 1487
Pen, reed pen, 26 × 35 cm (10¼ × 13¾")
Location unknown

1411 Public Garden with Fence, F 1477
Pencil, pen, brown ink, 32 × 24.5 cm (12⅝ × 9⅞")
Rijksmuseum Vincent van Gogh, Amsterdam

1412 Public Garden with Vincent's House in the Background, F 1513
Pencil, reed pen, brown ink, 31.5 × 49.5 cm (12⅝ × 19⅝")
Rijksmuseum Vincent van Gogh, Amsterdam

May 1888

1413 Vincent's House
Sketch in Letter 480
Rijksmuseum Vincent van Gogh, Amsterdam

1414 Field of Grass with a Round Clipped Shrub, F 1421
Pencil, reed pen, brown ink, 25.5 × 34.5 cm (10¼ × 13¾")
Rijksmuseum Vincent van Gogh, Amsterdam

1413

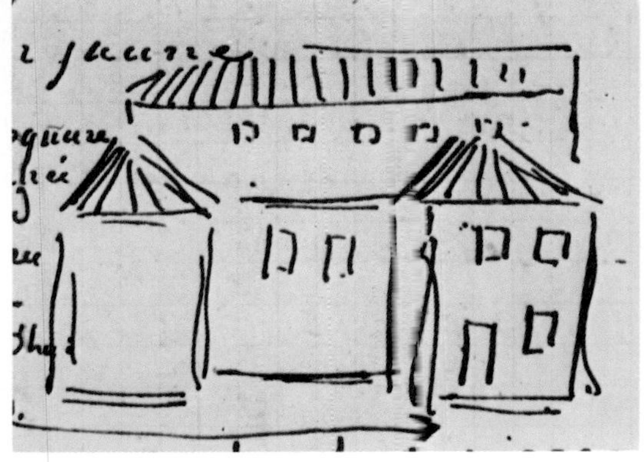

1414

1415

1416

1417

1418

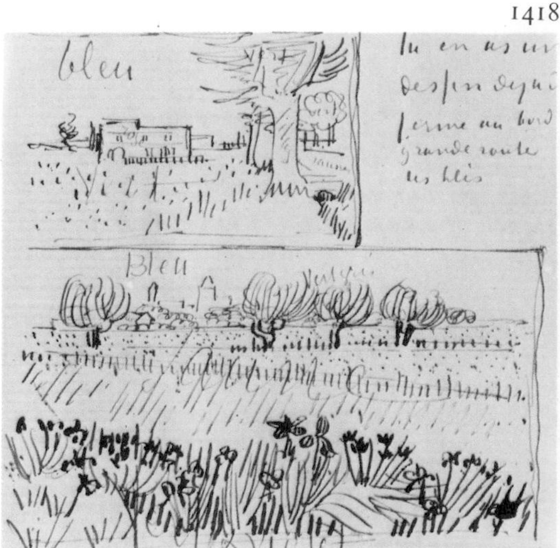

1419

1415 Field with Flowers, F 1416
Reed pen, 43.5 × 55.5 cm ($17\frac{3}{8}$ × 22″)
Museum of Art, Rhode Island School of Design, Providence

1416 Field with Flowers, F 409
54 × 65 cm ($21\frac{1}{4}$ × $25\frac{5}{8}$″)
Rijksmuseum Vincent van Gogh, Amsterdam
Colorplate XXIV, p. 312

1417 Farmhouse with Wheat Field along a Road, F 408
45 × 50 cm ($17\frac{3}{4}$ × $19\frac{5}{8}$″)
Rijksmuseum Vincent van Gogh, Amsterdam

1418 Farmhouse with Wheat Field along a Road and Field with Flowers
Sketches in Letter 487
Rijksmuseum Vincent van Gogh, Amsterdam

1419 Landscape with Edge of a Road, F 567
61 × 50 cm (24 × $19\frac{5}{8}$″)
Coburg, Germany

Apparently Vincent himself had a special affection for the important still life with the coffee pot, which is 1426. He made a sketch of it in the letter to Theo (1427) and a similar one, but including many color notes (1428), in a letter he wrote to Bernard (Letter B6). A short time later, after he had painted the ambitious composition *Harvest Landscape* (1440), he wrote Theo that the still life with the coffee pot was the only one that could bear comparison with it (Letter 497). Subsequently, not only *Harvest Landscape*—perhaps his most famous work today—but also this unassuming still life, which is fascinating precisely because of its simplicity of composition and marvelous color, has come to be regarded as evidence of Van Gogh's mastery during the Arles period.

The still life with wild flowers referred to in Letter 489 is 1424. From what Vincent wrote to Bernard, he appears to have made not just two, but three, still lifes at that time: "I also have another still life, lemons in a basket on a yellow background" (Letter B5, about May 19). This piece—1425—which is another, but richer and more balanced variant of the earlier still lifes 1340 (with apples) and 1363 (with oranges), is also essentially a study in color with its yellow on yellow. (To this small series of still lifes I have added still another, depicting a pot with daisies, 1429, whose dating is open to question.)

The Crau and Montmajour

The works in the following group, 1430–40, owe their origin to Vincent's walks in the region of the Crau and the Abbey of Montmajour in the vicinity of Arles. On May 26 he wrote Theo: "Today I have again sent you some drawings and I am adding two more. They are panoramic views, which were made on a rocky hill that overlooks the Crau (a district from which very good wine comes), the city of Arles, and the Fontvieille area. The contrast between the desolate and romantic foreground and the view off into the distance, with its broad and tranquil lines fading away into the chain of the Alpines so famous because of the heroic ascents by Tartarin P.C.A.* and by the Alpine Club—that contrast is most picturesque. The two drawings I am now adding will give you an idea of the ruins surmounting the rocks" (Letter 490). Which of the drawings are the ones referred to cannot be determined with any certainty, but we may assume that 1430–32, which fit the description in every respect, must have been among them. In drawing 1435 the city of Arles can indeed be clearly seen in the distance. Drawing 1436, done in exactly the same style, must, in my opinion, also have belonged to this small group. The two drawings of the ruins are easier to identify; 1433 and 1434 must be the ones referred to.

The energetic drawing 1437 can also be identified from the information in the letters. On June 9 Vincent wrote Theo about a drawing larger than the ones he had sent thus far: "If the roll is not too big for mailing, you will

*Tartarin of Tarascon, a character in a series of stories by Alphonse Daudet, was notorious for his boasts about his feats of courage and vigor; P.C.A. means Président du Club des Alpines (President of the Alpine Club).

1420

1421

1422

1420 Drawbridge with Lady with Parasol, F1471
Pen, 23.5 × 31 cm ($9\frac{1}{2}$ × $12\frac{1}{4}$")
Los Angeles County Museum of Art, Mr. and Mrs. George Gard de Sylva Collection

1421 Drawbridge with Lady with Parasol, F570
49.5 × 64 cm ($19\frac{5}{8}$ × $25\frac{1}{4}$")
Wallraf-Richartz Museum, Cologne

1422 Meadow with Flowers under a Stormy Sky, F575
60 × 73 cm ($23\frac{5}{8}$ × $28\frac{3}{4}$")
Collection Mr. and Mrs. Louis Franck, Gstaad, Switzerland

1423 Meadow with Poppies, F576
23 × 34 cm (9 × $13\frac{3}{8}$")
Rijksmuseum Vincent van Gogh, Amsterdam

1424 Majolica Jar with Wild Flowers, F600
55 × 46 cm ($21\frac{5}{8}$ × $18\frac{1}{8}$")
© The Barnes Foundation Museum of Art, Merion, Pennsylvania

1425 Basket with Lemons, F384
53 × 63 cm ($20\frac{7}{8}$ × $24\frac{3}{4}$")
Rijksmuseum Kröller-Müller, Otterlo

1426 Still Life with Coffee Pot, F410
65 × 81 cm ($25\frac{5}{8}$ × $31\frac{7}{8}$")
Collection Mr. and Mrs. Basil P. Goulandris, Lausanne

1427 Still Life with Coffee Pot
Sketch in Letter 489
Rijksmuseum Vincent van Gogh, Amsterdam

1428 Still Life with Coffee Pot
Sketch in Letter B6
Private collection, Paris

1429 Pot with Flowering Plant (Daisies?), F591
33 × 42 cm (13 × $16\frac{1}{2}$")
Collection Mr. and Mrs. Paul Mellon, Upperville, Virginia

1423

1424

1425

1426

1427

1428

1429

be getting another large pen-and-ink drawing" (Letter 495). And in a letter to Koning, sent at the same time (Letter 498*a*), he gave a detailed description of it: "I have just made a drawing, even larger than the first two, of a group of pine trees on a rock seen from a hill. Behind that first plane a distant view of pasture, a road lined with poplars, and far in the distance, the city. The trees very dark against the sunlit pasture; perhaps you will see that drawing. I did it with very thick reed pens on thin Whatman [paper] and worked up the distant detail with a quill pen for the finer lines."

In the next letter, June 12, come the first reports on the painting that would prove to be one of the masterpieces of Vincent's stay in Arles—even in his own judgment: "I have embarked on a new motif, endless green and yellow fields which I have already drawn twice and am now starting on again as a painting" (Letter 496). This is *Harvest Landscape* (1440), done in the same area. Such was the mastery that Vincent had developed now that it allowed him to incorporate a wealth of anecdotal detail in the painting of a landscape without disturbing its pictorial harmony. Because of the dry heat, nature was beginning to look parched and so this *Harvest Landscape* has little atmosphere, but it is warm in color and forceful in its perspective. This is how Vincent described it: "In everything you could say there is now old gold, bronze, copper, and that, with the greenish azure of a white-hot sky, gives a marvelous color, extraordinarily harmonious, with broken tints just like in Delacroix" (Letter 497).

There are two watercolor drawings and two pen-and-ink drawings of *Harvest Landscape*. Roskill has convincingly demonstrated that the drawings Vincent mentioned as having preceded the painting (he wrote about the "endless green and yellow fields which I have already drawn twice") must have been the pen-and-watercolor drawings 1438 and 1439. (The pen-and-ink drawings, done somewhat later, will be discussed further on.) Both differ only slightly from the painting, although clearly 1439, which Roskill regarded as the second of the preliminary studies, is closer to the final work.*

Vincent followed the same procedure when he made the painting of a farmhouse with haystacks. Here, too, he started with a drawing in color as a preliminary study, 1441. Speaking about *Harvest Landscape*, he wrote in Letter 497: "And I have another motif, *Haystacks near a Farm*, which will probably be its counterpart." In his next letter he reported: "Today I mailed you three drawings. You will find the one with the haystacks in the farmyard too bizarre, but it was made very hurriedly as a draft for a painting and to show you the subject" (Letter 498). Whether or not the drawing should now be called bizarre, the painting certainly cannot be, and as a study in golden yellow and deep blue it may indeed be seen as a counterpart to *Harvest Landscape*, although it is undeniably less balanced in composition and less carefully detailed.

It is undoubtedly the same farm with the

*"Van Gogh's 'Blue Cart' and His Creative Process," *Oud Holland*, vol LXXXI, no.1 (1966), pp. 3–19.

1430

1431

1432

1430 The Plain of the Crau, F 1419
Pen, reed pen, black chalk, 29 × 47 cm ($11\frac{3}{8} \times 18\frac{1}{2}''$)
Museum Folkwang, Essen

1431 Landscape with Tree in the Foreground, F 1418
Chalk, reed pen, 31 × 48 cm ($12\frac{1}{4} \times 18\frac{7}{8}''$)
Collection Mrs. Charles Engelhard, Newark, New Jersey

1432 The Plain of the Crau, F 1448
Reed pen, 30 × 46.5 cm ($11\frac{3}{4} \times 18\frac{1}{2}''$)
Location unknown

1433 Ruins of Montmajour, F 1423
Chalk or pencil, reed pen, violet ink, 47.5 × 31 cm ($18\frac{7}{8} \times 12\frac{1}{4}''$)
Rijksmuseum Vincent van Gogh, Amsterdam

1434 Ruins of Montmajour, F 1417
Chalk or pencil, reed pen, violet ink, 31 × 47.5 cm ($12\frac{1}{4} \times 18\frac{7}{8}''$)
Rijksmuseum Vincent van Gogh, Amsterdam

1435 Landscape with Arles in the Background, F 1475
Pencil, reed pen, 47.5 × 30.5 cm ($18\frac{7}{8} \times 12\frac{1}{4}''$)
Museum Boymans-van Beuningen, Rotterdam

1433

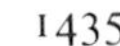

1434

1435

1436

1437

1436 Hill with Bushes, F 1493
Chalk, reed pen, violet ink, 31 × 47.5 cm
($12\frac{1}{4} \times 18\frac{7}{8}''$)
Rijksmuseum Vincent van Gogh, Amsterdam

June 1888
1437 View of Arles from a Hill, F 1452
Pen, 48 × 59 cm ($18\frac{7}{8} \times 23\frac{1}{4}''$)
Nasjonalgalleriet, Oslo

three haystacks in the yard that Vincent depicted in 1443, but this time the scene is viewed from outside the gate. The reed-pen drawing 1444 was perhaps made not before the painting but as a copy of it, like those he would later make of many other paintings. In this instance the letters, which make no mention of 1443 and 1444, do not provide the answer.

The much more sketchy drawing 1445 may have been based on the previous one; the foreground, the low wall, and the path alongside it reveal a remarkable similarity. That is why it has been assigned a place here, although there is no other clue to the dating.

Les Saintes-Maries-de-la-Mer

During the week of June 17 to 22 Vincent made a short trip to the small fishing village of Les Saintes-Maries-de-la-Mer, not far from Arles. A series of important paintings and drawings resulted.

Vincent's report on this outing in Letter 499 makes it evident that he must have worked at a dazzling pace. Within a single week he completed three paintings and a dozen drawings (of which he would later make replicas). He himself was surprised at the assurance he had acquired during his short stay in the South, and it was with a feeling of satisfaction that he wrote Theo: "I have been here only a few months, but tell me, would I have been able in Paris to make the drawing of the little boats *in one hour?* Not even with the perspective frame; well, this was made without measuring, straight onto the paper" (Letter 500). The brilliant drawing of the little boats, which would lead to one of Vincent's most popular paintings, is 1458. On Saturday, June 23, the day he returned to Arles, he immediately sent the drawings he had made to Theo and told him the story of the drawing (and the painting) of the little boats: "In the same mail I am sending you the Stes-Maries drawings. On the point of leaving, very early in the morning, I made the drawing of the little boats and I am working on the painting of them, a size-30 canvas, with more sea and sky on the right-hand side" (Letter 500). There is also a watercolor of the subject, 1459, which has the same composition as the drawing and the painting. The sketch, 1461, that Vincent made in his next letter to Bernard (Letter B6) was done after the painting.

Vincent had written Theo from Saintes-Maries: "I brought three canvases with me and have filled them up—two sea pieces, a view of the village, also drawings that I shall mail to you when I am back in Arles tomorrow" (Letter 499). This tells us that, apart from the view of the beach with the little boats he had painted in Arles, he had done three paintings in Saintes-Maries. The view of the village is the bright, colorful large canvas that presents a powerfully composed, impressive view of the fortified village church and the houses around it, 1447 (colorplate XXV, page 329). The self-contained group of buildings, reduced to simple geometric shapes, makes us think of landscapes by Cézanne, but the extended foreground with its sharply diverging lines and curious violet and green gamut of colors is typically Van Gogh. There is also a drawing of this subject (1446), but it is done in a horizontal format and therefore differs somewhat in composition.

The paintings Vincent called "sea pieces" must be 1452 (a sea with a single boat in the foreground) and 1453 (a fairly rough sea with a number of small boats). The latter appears in the small rough sketch he made for Bernard in Letter B6 (1464). The only drawings of these seascapes that we know of are those that Vincent made from them sometime later, back in Arles. While in Saintes-Maries he made use of the reed pen especially for sketches of the curious houses with their thatched roofs topped by a white ridge and for some landscapes. Among the studies actually made in Saintes-Maries, I include the

1438

1439

1440

1438 Harvest Landscape, F 1484
Pen, watercolor, 39.5 × 52.5 cm (15¾ × 20⅞")
Fogg Art Museum, Harvard University, Cambridge, Massachusetts

1439 Harvest Landscape, F 1483
Pen, watercolor, 48 × 60 cm (18⅞ × 23⅝")
Collection Mrs. J. B. A. Kessler, London

1440 Harvest Landscape, F 412
72.5 × 92 cm (28¾ × 36¼")
Rijksmuseum Vincent van Gogh, Amsterdam

1441 Haystacks near a Farm, F 1425
Pen, watercolor, 50 × 62 cm (19⅝ × 24⅜")
Collection M. Meirowsky, Berlin

1442 Haystacks near a Farm, F 425
73 × 92.5 cm (28¾ × 36⅝")
Rijksmuseum Kröller-Müller, Otterlo

1441

1442

1443

1444

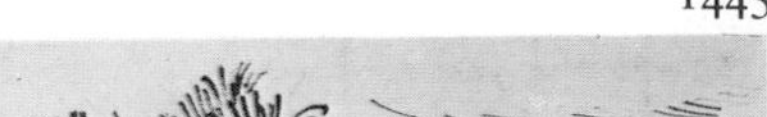

1445

1443 Entrance Gate to a Farm with Haystacks, F565
46×61 cm ($18\frac{1}{8} \times 24''$)
National Gallery of Art, Washington, D.C.

1444 Entrance Gate to a Farm with Haystacks, F1478
Pencil, reed pen, brown ink, 39×53.5 cm ($15\frac{3}{8} \times 21\frac{1}{4}''$)
Stedelijk Museum, Amsterdam (on loan from the Rijksmuseum, Amsterdam)

1445 Landscape with the Wall of a Farm, F1478a
Reed pen, 23×32 cm ($9 \times 12\frac{5}{8}''$)
Private collection, New York

small drawings of narrow streets and individual houses: 1448–51, 1454, and 1456 (the last of these bears the notation "Cimetière de Stes Maries" in Vincent's hand). Also, the sketch of the beach and the boats as seen from between the dunes, 1455, and, perhaps, the drawing of a landscape with the kind of small barn that is typical of the Camargue (the region between Arles and Saintes-Maries), 1457, although this differs somewhat in format from the other drawings. On the last morning of his stay on the coast, Vincent added to these, as mentioned above, the preliminary studies for the painting with the little boats, 1458 and 1459, thus bringing the number of drawings made in one week to eleven.

Once back in Arles, Vincent did not send all these drawings to Theo: "I have three more drawings of cottages which I still need and shall send them along after these" (Letter 500). He used them to make a couple of painted studies; we know of only two, namely painting 1462 from drawing 1449, and painting 1465 from drawing 1448. He must have done this during the first few days after his return, right after doing the painting of the boats on the beach. A few days later, when he wrote to Bernard, he included in the letter not only a rough sketch (1464) of the seascape painted in Saintes-Maries (1453), but also a sketch containing numerous color notes (1463), which had been made from a painting of the typical cottages (1462); the painting must therefore already have been completed at that time. The previously mentioned study 1465, depicting a group of cottages, may likewise have been painted about then.

A girl's head (1467) appeared somewhat unexpectedly in the midst of all these landscapes. Letter 501*a* provides an explanation: after relating that it was harvesttime and that he was spending all his days at work in the fields, Vincent wrote John Russell in a letter that gives a good insight into his personality and way of life: "And when I sit down to write I am so abstracted by recollections of what I have seen that I leave the letter. For instance at the present occasion I was writing to you, and going to say something about Arles as it is—and as it was in the old days of Boccaccio.

"Well, instead of continuing the letter I began to draw on the very paper the head of a dirty little girl I saw this afternoon whilst I was painting a view of the river with a greenish yellow sky.

"This dirty 'mudlark' I thought yet had a vague Florentine sort of figure like the heads in the Monticelli pictures, and reasoning and drawing this wise I worked on the letter I was writing to you."

Vincent had sent the rough draft (1466) along with the letter to Russell, and he must have painted the girl's head later for himself, from memory. Strangely enough, this was his first "portrait" since the one of the old woman from Arles (1357) that he had painted four months earlier, shortly after his arrival in Arles. This one certainly did not come up to the level of the later portraits, which were to be such a significant element in Vincent's work of the Arles period.

The painting of the river landscape men-

1446

1447

1448

1446 View of Saintes-Maries, F 1439
Pen, 43 × 60 cm (16⅞ × 23⅝″)
Collection Oskar Reinhart, Winterthur, Switzerland

1447 View of Saintes-Maries, F 416
64 × 53 cm (25¼ × 20⅞″)
Rijksmuseum Kröller-Müller, Otterlo
Colorplate XXV, opposite

1448 Three Cottages in Saintes-Maries, F 1438
Pencil, reed pen, brown ink, 30 × 47 cm (11¾ × 18½″)
Rijksmuseum Vincent van Gogh, Amsterdam

Note on Illustrations 1446–65

Later research has proved that Van Gogh's stay at Saintes-Maries-de-la-Mer in 1888 took place somewhat earlier than had previously been assumed. The group of works done at Saintes-Marie (1446–65, on pp. 328–35) therefore chronologically belong before drawing 1438 on p. 326.

Colorplate XXV, View of Saintes-Maries, 1447 ›

tioned briefly in the letter has also come down to us. It is 1468, and it is described in much more detail to Theo: "I have a view of the Rhône—the iron Trinquetaille Bridge, in which the sky and the river are the color of absinthe, the quays mauve, the figures leaning against the parapet more or less black, the iron bridge an intense blue, and a background with a deep orange and an intense veronese green accent. Once again an unfinished attempt, but one in which I am seeking eventually [to express] something sadder and thus more oppressive" (Letter 503).

There is also a drawing of this subject with the concentrated short lines and dots characteristic of the Arles style (1469).

Summer in Arles

The study of the bridge must have been more or less incidental. It was midsummer, and Vincent's time was actually taken up with subjects of an entirely different kind. He had sent both Russell (in Letter 501*a*) and Bernard (in Letter B7) a small rough sketch of a painting he was working on, together with a description that made it clear that he considered the project of prime importance not only because of the subject (the figure of the sower appears countless times in his work, starting with his first copies after Millet), but also because of the color (the painting is 1470, and the rough sketches are 1471 and 1472). The most detailed description of the painting (colorplate XXVI, page 330) is to be found in his letter to Theo: "I now have behind me a week of hard and busy work in the wheat fields under the hot sun; as a result, I have studies of wheat fields, landscapes, and—a sketch of a sower. In a plowed field, a big field with violet clods of earth ascending toward the horizon, a sower in blue and white. At the horizon, a field with short ripe stalks of grain. Above all this, a yellow sky with a yellow sun. You feel, just from an enumeration of the tonal values, that *color* plays a very important role in this composition. The sketch as it now is—a size-25 canvas—also bothers me a lot in the sense that I wonder whether I ought not to take it seriously and make an awesome painting of it; God, how much I would like to do that!" (Letter 501).

As a result of the "week of hard and busy work in the wheat fields," we know of no fewer than ten studies of the wheat fields (including one drawing): two with the city in the background, 1473 and 1477; two with a low ridge of hills in the distance, 1475 and 1476; and six in which sheaves of wheat or bundles of wheat stalks dominate the picture, 1478–83. Improbable as it may appear, all, or nearly all, of these studies must have been painted in the last week of June. Vincent had returned from Saintes-Maries on Saturday, June 23, and then painted first the boats on the beach and the cottages. About July 2 he wrote to Bernard: "I have seven studies of wheat fields,* unfortunately all painted quite

*A figure of *ten* studies was given above. The explanation may be that two of the painted studies were made somewhat later in July. Most of them came from Mrs. van Gogh-Bonger's collection—thus, from Theo's—and where this is not the case, we know of drawings made from them confirming that they date from the summer of 1888.

〈 Colorplate XXVI, Sower with Setting Sun, 1470

1449

1450

1451

1449 Street in Saintes-Maries, F 1434
Reed pen, 30.5 × 47 cm (12¼ × 18½″)
Formerly collection Robert von Hirsch, Basel

1450 Row of Cottages in Saintes-Maries, F 1437
Reed pen, 30.5 × 47 cm (12¼ × 18½″)
Rijksmuseum Vincent van Gogh, Amsterdam

1451 Two Houses in Saintes-Maries, F 1440
Pencil, reed pen, 29 × 46 cm (11⅜ × 18⅛″)
Location unknown

grudgingly, nothing but landscapes. Landscapes in yellow and old gold, quick, quick, quickly and hurriedly made, like the mower who toils under the burning sun, intent only on getting the whole lot of it onto the ground" (Letter B9). From the letters written in the meantime it appears certain that he had also painted in the same week the river scene 1468 and *Sower*, 1470, and even that was not all; as will shortly be demonstrated, he had also been working on two portraits that very week! Small wonder then that he had to write to Bernard: "I would make sketches for you if I were not so exhausted" (Letter B8).

A curious feature about most of the pictures with wheat fields is that the horizon is placed very high in the composition. For Vincent the color of the grain was what mattered, and the emptiness of the foreground—as can be seen in 1473, for example—apparently did not bother him. In a letter accompanied by a sketch, 1474, he explained this painting to Bernard as follows: "Here is another landscape: Setting sun? Rising moon? Summer evening in any case. The city violet, the heavenly body yellow, the sky blue-green. All the grain has a tint of old gold, copper, green-gold or reddish gold, yellowish gold, yellow-bronze, green-red. A size-30 canvas, square. I painted it with the mistral going full force" (Letter B7). Meantime, in two other equally fascinating paintings, he saw to it that no such large area of the picture was filled with yellow grain but that this was set off against a more variegated foreground with patches of green and red and blue flowers. Perhaps the most successful of the group, in a daring vertical format that makes the foreground seem still longer, is the painting with the half-mown wheat field and a passing train, 1477, where the sheaves on the left provide an element of variety and accentuate the depth.

Portraits at Last

As I have just mentioned, Vincent had also started doing portraits again; this was what he regarded as his true field of activity. He wrote Theo a detailed account of the important news about June 29: "I have a model at last, a Zouave—he is a lad with a small head, a bull's neck, and the look of a tiger; I began with a portrait and then made another one from it; the bust portrait I painted of him was terribly harsh, in a uniform of the same blue as enameled pans, with faded orange-red piping, and two stars on the chest; an ordinary blue and very difficult to make. I set off the catlike, heavily tanned head covered by a red kepi against a door painted green and the orange-colored stones of a wall. So it is a crude combination of tones, not easy to manage. The study I have made of it seems very harsh to me, and yet I would not mind working all the time on such vulgar and even garish portraits. I learn from them, and that is what I want from my work most of all. Well, the second portrait will be a full-length one with the subject sitting against a white wall" (Letter 501).

A few days later he wrote about this to Bernard: "I would make sketches for you if I were not so exhausted, because for the past three or four days I have been drawing and painting from a model—a Zouave; on the other hand, I find it restful and relaxing when I write. What I have flung onto it is pretty ugly: a drawing of the Zouave seated; a painted sketch of the Zouave against a completely white wall, and finally his portrait against a green door and some orange bricks of a wall. It is harsh and, well, ugly and badly done" (Letter B8). And after thanking Bernard for a sketch he had received from him: "One of these days I will [also] send you a drawing; tonight I am too tired, my eyes are fatigued even if that were not already the case with my brain."

By combining the information provided by these two letters, it becomes clear that Vincent had drawn the Zouave—Second Lieu-

1452

1453

1454

1452 A Fishing Boat at Sea, F415
51 × 64 cm (20⅛ × 25¼")
Rijksmuseum Vincent van Gogh, Amsterdam

1453 Fishing Boats at Sea, F417
44 × 53 cm (17⅜ × 20⅞")
Pushkin Museum, Moscow

1454 Cottages in Saintes-Maries, F1436
Reed pen, 29 × 49 cm (11⅜ × 19¼")
Location unknown

1455 Beach, Sea, and Fishing Boats, F1432
Pen, reed pen, pencil, 30.5 × 47.5 cm (12¼ × 18⅞")
Rijksmuseum Vincent van Gogh, Amsterdam

1456 View of Saintes-Maries with Cemetery, F1479
Pen, reed pen, 29.5 × 47.5 cm (11¾ × 18⅞")
Private collection, Switzerland

1455

1456

1457

1458

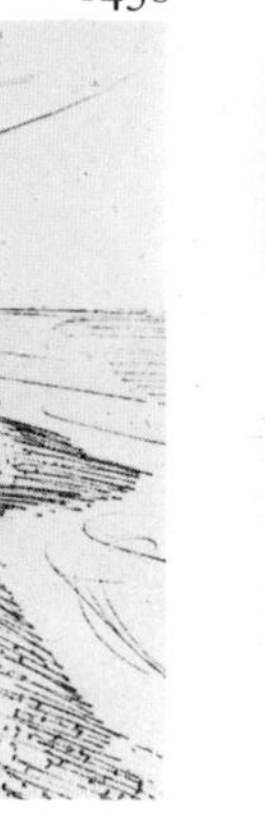

1459

1460

1461

1457 Landscape with Hut in the Camargue, F 1498 (reverse: 1614)
Pencil, pen, reed pen, brown ink, 34.5 × 25.5 cm ($13\frac{3}{4} \times 10\frac{1}{4}$″)
Rijksmuseum Vincent van Gogh, Amsterdam

1458 Fishing Boats on the Beach, F 1428
Reed pen, 39.5 × 53.5 cm ($15\frac{3}{4} \times 21\frac{1}{4}$″)
Collection Dr. Peter Nathan, Zurich

1459 Fishing Boats on the Beach, F 1429
Watercolor, 39 × 54 cm ($15\frac{3}{8} \times 21\frac{1}{4}$″)
Location unknown

1460 Fishing Boats on the Beach, F 413
64.5 × 81 cm ($25\frac{5}{8} \times 31\frac{7}{8}$″)
Rijksmuseum Vincent van Gogh, Amsterdam

1461 Fishing Boats on the Beach
Sketch in Letter B6
Private collection, Paris

tenant Milliet—seated and also had made two painted studies of him, a bust portrait and a full-length portrait against a white wall: drawing 1485 (obviously a first draft, which indeed cannot be regarded as very successful in view of the squat position and strange proportions of the figure) and 1486 and 1488. The full-length portrait was later reworked by Vincent, as appears from Letter 519, August 8. The drawing promised to Bernard must have been the large watercolor 1487, which bears the inscription: "A mon cher copain Emile Bernard" ("To my good pal Emile Bernard") and was probably made from the painted study 1486.

Tensions

For the time being Vincent had just the one model, and he continued to make landscapes. Although the tempo slowed a little, enough drawings and painted studies were made in the first weeks of July to maintain what can justly be called a steady rate of activity. His productivity of the past few weeks must have surprised even Vincent himself, and it is characteristic of him that in some of his letters he considered it necessary to discuss and defend the rapid pace at which he worked: "I have to warn you that everyone will say I work too fast. Don't believe a word of it. Is it not emotion, the genuineness of a feeling for nature that guides us, and when now and then these emotions are so strong that you work without realizing that you work, when now and then the strokes of the brush come in a sequence and relationship one to the other like words in a speech or in a letter, you must remember that it has not always been like that and that in future, too, there will be many trying days without inspiration. So we must strike while the iron is hot and put aside the iron when it has been forged" (Letter 504).

In his next letter* he expanded on this topic still further; painting was, he said, "a sober and calculating kind of thing whereby your mind is strained to the limit, like an actor on the stage in a difficult part, when in less than half an hour you have to think of a thousand things at the same time. After that the only thing that brings relief and relaxation is to besot yourself with a quick glass or to smoke a lot." This is one of the few allusions to the excessive drinking that has been discussed frequently in connection with Van Gogh. It was repeated in Letter 513, when, speaking about artists such as Gauguin, he said that he saw them with their backs to the wall. "Let us hope that there is a way out for him and for us. If I let my thoughts run rampant, if I reflected upon the disastrous possibilities, then I would not be able to do a thing; I throw myself head over heels into my work, I pull myself out of it with my studies; when the thunder rumbles too strongly within me, I drink a glass too many to stupefy myself" (Letter 507).

Roaming in and about Town

According to the letter Vincent sent Theo about July 6 (Letter 503), he had spent a few days reworking the canvas of the sower. About July 7 he reported that he had completed a new painting: "Do you remember among the small drawings a wooden bridge with women washing, with a view of the city in the background? I have just painted this motif in a large format" (Letter 504). The small drawing referred to is 1405, and the painting with the same subject is 1490. A drawing corresponding very closely to the painting must have been made from this study sometime later; it is 1507.

July 12 Vincent wrote: "Yesterday at sunset I was on a rocky moor where there are

*This is Letter 507. In their publication in book form the letters written during these weeks are not arranged exactly in chronological order. They should be read in this sequence: 503, 504, 507, 508, 505, 506.

1462

1463

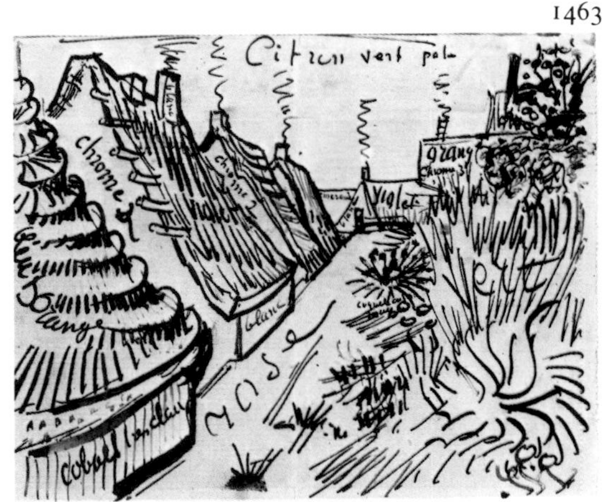

1464

1462 Street in Saintes-Maries, F420
36.5 × 44 cm ($14\frac{5}{8} \times 17\frac{3}{8}$")
Location unknown

1463 Street in Saintes-Maries
Sketch in Letter B6
Private collection, Paris

1464 Fishing Boats at Sea, Landscape with Edge of a Road, and Farm along a Road
Sketches in Letter B6
Private collection, Paris

1465 Three Cottages in Saintes-Maries, F419
33.5 × 41.5 cm ($13\frac{3}{8} \times 16\frac{1}{2}$")
Location unknown

1465

1466

1467

1468

1469

1466 Girl's Head, F 1507a
Sketch belonging with Letter 501a
Reed pen, 15 × 12.5 cm ($5\frac{7}{8} \times 5\frac{1}{8}''$)
Solomon R. Guggenheim Museum, New York

1467 Girl's Head, F 535
35.5 × 24.5 cm ($14\frac{1}{8} \times 9\frac{7}{8}''$)
Private collection, Switzerland

1468 View of a River, Quay, and Bridge, F 426
65 × 81 cm ($25\frac{5}{8} \times 31\frac{7}{8}''$)
Formerly collection André Meyer, New York

1469 View of a River, Quay, and Bridge, F 1507
Pen, 24 × 31 cm ($9\frac{1}{2} \times 12\frac{1}{4}''$)
Metropolitan Museum of Art, New York

very small bent oaks, in the background a ruin on the hill, and in the valley wheat" (Letter 508). This must have been the Montmajour region that we are familiar with from *Harvest Landscape* (1440) and from drawings such as 1437. "Actually I brought a study of it back with me, but it fell far short of what I wanted to do." This study is very probably the rocky landscape with a tree, 1489. We are on firmer ground when it comes to the view of the park mentioned in the same letter (1499) because Vincent enclosed a sketch of it. I assume, moreover, that various drawings of summer landscapes, which cannot be accurately dated, were made during this same period in the course of Vincent's wanderings in the vicinity of Arles. I would also assign to this period the frequently reproduced painted study in which Vincent pictured himself making his way along a road, 1491. (A clue to the dating is the presence of the grain still standing in the field.) The same self-portrait, but in words, is to be found in his letter to Wil, written the last week of June, in which he contrasts his present appearance with that in the last self-portrait he had made in Paris: "From greenish gray, my complexion has become grayish orange, and I am wearing a white suit instead of a blue one, and I am always dusty, moreover always loaded like a porcupine with poles, painter's easel, canvas, and other merchandise" (Letter W4). We know that the road was the one to Tarascon, because when he sent the canvas, along with others, to Theo, he considered it worthy of special mention: "There is, for instance, among them a sketch of myself, loaded with boxes, poles, a canvas, on the sunny road to Tarascon" (Letter 524). This curious self-portrait was unfortunately destroyed by fire in Magdeburg in 1945.

The drawings of summer landscapes just referred to are 1492–95. All show the same style of drawing—notably the use of the stippling technique to indicate the rather full foliage. The tree-lined road in 1493 bears a strong resemblance to the one in the painted study 1491, and the road with a farmhouse in 1495 is recognizable as the one in the earlier painting 1419.

The drawing of the *Landscape with Alphonse Daudet's Windmill*, 1496, which is hard to date, has been included here because of its similar forceful linear style. (The windmill is the one Daudet had rented in Provence and made famous by his *Lettres de mon Moulin*, published in 1869). I have also assigned to this little group the watercolor with another old windmill, 1497, which is somewhat similar to 1496 in both composition and the subject. The letters give no clue to the dating of this drawing, and it might equally have been made later on in the summer.

In the same letter in which Vincent wrote about his trip to the hill country with the ruin, he reported that he had painted a study of the public garden across from the little yellow house: "Here is a new motif—a little corner of the park with rounded shrubs and a weeping tree, and in the background, oleander bushes. And the lawn that has just been mowed, with the long rows of cuttings drying in the sun, a bit of blue-green sky above" (Letter 508).

1470

1471

1472

Identification presents no problem; the accompanying sketch (1500) makes it clear that the painting referred to here was 1499. I assume that the drawing of a weeping tree, 1498, preceded the painting and was made before the tall grass was mowed. The painting, in which the weeping tree is not so centrally placed, strikes us by the simplicity of the "new motif": nothing but the rows of freshly mowed lawn bordered by some shrubs. Therefore, it is surprising that Vincent later tried to achieve an even starker simplicity.

Thoughts of Gauguin

In the following weeks Vincent embarked upon a vigorous program of drawing.

1470 Sower with Setting Sun, F422
64 × 80.5 cm ($25\frac{1}{4} \times 31\frac{7}{8}$")
Rijksmuseum Kröller-Müller, Otterlo
Colorplate XXVI, p. 330

1471 Sower with Setting Sun
Sketch in Letter 501a
Rijksmuseum Vincent van Gogh, Amsterdam

1472 Sower with Setting Sun
Sketch in Letter B7
Private collection, Paris

1473 Wheat Field with Setting Sun, F465
74 × 91 cm ($29\frac{1}{8} \times 35\frac{7}{8}$")
Kunstmuseum, Winterthur, Switzerland

1474 Wheat Field at Dusk
Sketch in Letter B7
Private collection, Paris

1473

1474

1475

1476

1477

1478

1479

1475 Wheat Field, F564
50 × 61 cm (19⅝ × 24″)
P. and N. de Boer Foundation, Amsterdam

1476 Wheat Field, F411
Canvas on cardboard, 54 × 65 cm
(21¼ × 25⅝″)
Rijksmuseum Vincent van Gogh, Amsterdam

1477 Wheat Field with Sheaves and Arles in the Background, F545
73 × 54 cm (28¾ × 21¼″)
Musée Rodin, Paris

1478 Wheat Field with Sheaves (No F Number)
23.5 × 36.5 cm (9½ × 14⅝″)
Collection Mrs. Godet-Druet, Paris

1479 Wheat Field with Sheaves and Mower, F559
73 × 93 cm (28¾ × 36⅝″)
Toledo Museum of Art, Ohio

Strange as this may seem, it stemmed from his ideas about possible collaboration with Paul Gauguin. For an explanation of this whole matter we must go back to earlier correspondence with Theo. When Vincent rented the little yellow house, he had already considered the possibility of sharing it with another artist. In the very first letter in which the house is mentioned he said: "I could if necessary share the new studio with someone else, and that is what I would really like to do. Perhaps Gauguin will come to the South. Perhaps I could arrange it with MacKnight [the American painter Dodge MacKnight]" (Letter 480).

It is July before we learn: "Well, your letter brought me the great news that Gauguin accepts the proposal. It would certainly be best if he made haste to come here at once; instead of getting out of the mess, he might well get into it if he went first to Paris" (Letter 507). Vincent remained concerned about the costs Theo would have to bear to carry out the scheme. In Letter 505, about July 15, we read: "I would be willing right now to send you the thirty studies [that I have], which might perhaps make it somewhat easier to find the money to get Gauguin here." Shortly after he had another thought: "I believe I would do well just now to work mainly on drawings and see to it that I have a supply of paint and linen on hand for the time when Gauguin comes. I wish that one could be as free in the use of paint as with pen and paper. Because I am afraid to waste paint, I sometimes spoil a painted study. With paper, if I am not writing a letter but am making a drawing, it goes all right; so many sheets of Whatman, so many drawings" (Letter 506).

Consequently, he could begin his next letter, about July 18, with the words: "I have just mailed you a roll of five pen-and-ink drawings. You have a sixth of that series of Montmajour: a group of very dark pine trees and the city of Arles in the background. Next I hope to add a general view of the ruin (you have a hasty sketch of it among the small drawings)" (Letter 509).

The drawing of the pine trees with Arles in the background was the large pen-and-ink drawing, 1437, that was done before the trip to Saintes-Maries. Among the small drawings there were two sketches of the ruin, 1433 and 1434, both of which he sent to Theo at the end of May. Four of the large drawings belonging to a "series of Montmajour," which Vincent was now sending, can easily be traced; they are 1501–4. The fifth has probably been lost, for we know of no other drawing of this region in a format of approximately 19$\frac{3}{4}$ by 23$\frac{5}{8}$ inches. (We do know another relatively "large" drawing of the banks of the Rhône in the same precise style, 1497a, but that one was made in town and not at Montmajour.) Vincent was obviously especially attached to the first two. In Letter 509 he expressed this with a feeling of satisfaction which for him was unusual: "In my opinion the two views of the Crau and the country on the banks of the Rhône are the best I have made with my pen." He also made special mention of these two landscapes in a letter to Bernard a few days later: "I have made large pen-and-ink drawings. Two: an immense stretch of country in bird's-eye view from a hill—vineyards, mowed fields of grain. All this multiplied into infinity, stretching out like the surface of a sea to the horizon, bounded by the low hills of the Crau. It does not appear Japanese, and yet it is the most Japanese thing I have ever made; a microscopic little figure of a plowman, a tiny train passing through the fields of grain; that is all the life that is in it" (Letter B10).

Working for Bernard

Avoiding the expense of canvas and paint led Vincent to great productivity in drawing, although it could not, as we shall see, completely stifle the inspiration to work with oils.

1480

1481

1482

1480 Wheat Field with Sheaves, F561
53 × 64 cm (20$\frac{7}{8}$ × 25$\frac{1}{4}$")
Honolulu Academy of Arts

1481 Wheat Field with Sheaves, F558
50 × 60 cm (19$\frac{5}{8}$ × 23$\frac{5}{8}$")
Israel Museum, Jerusalem

1482 Wheat Field with Sheaves and Mower, F560
53 × 66 cm (20$\frac{7}{8}$ × 26")
Nationalmuseum, Stockholm

1483 Ears of Wheat in a Field, F562
54 × 65 cm (21$\frac{1}{4}$ × 25$\frac{5}{8}$")
Israel Museum, Jerusalem

1484 Sheaves of Wheat, F1641
Black chalk, brush, black ink,
47.5 × 62.5 cm (18$\frac{7}{8}$ × 24$\frac{3}{4}$")
Rijksmuseum Vincent van Gogh, Amsterdam

1483

1484

1485

1486

1487

1488

1485 Zouave Sitting, Whole Figure, F1443
Reed pen, 52 × 66 cm ($20\frac{1}{2} \times 26''$)
Location unknown

1486 Zouave, Half-Figure, F423
65 × 54 cm ($25\frac{5}{8} \times 21\frac{1}{4}''$)
Rijksmuseum Vincent van Gogh, Amsterdam

1487 Zouave, Half-Figure, F1482
Black chalk, pen, watercolor, 30 × 23 cm
($11\frac{3}{4} \times 9''$)
Metropolitan Museum of Art, New York

1488 Zouave Sitting, Whole Figure, F424
81 × 65 cm ($31\frac{7}{8} \times 25\frac{5}{8}''$)
Private collection, South America

For a while Vincent devoted himself mainly to making small drawings from the numerous painted studies he had around him in the studio. At the beginning of the month he had thanked Bernard for a sketch he had sent him but was himself too tired to send Bernard one in return (see page 332). This time he took the initiative himself about July 22, when he wrote: "You may be inclined to forgive me for not replying right away to your letter when you see the small batch of sketches I am enclosing" (Letter B10). In doing this, he did ask whether Bernard was willing to send him, in exchange, sketches based on Bernard's Breton studies, with the promise that he would ask Theo to take some of them. Without waiting for an answer, Vincent started again on a new series, and scarcely two days later he reported: "Today I have sent you nine more sketches based on painted studies. In this way you will get to see motifs from the countryside that inspires Cézanne, for the Crau in the vicinity of Aix is the same as around Tarascon and the Crau here" (Letter B11).

From a letter to Theo written at about the same time we learn that the first lot consisted of *six* drawings (Letter 511). This means that within a few days Vincent had made for Bernard no fewer than fifteen small drawings from his own work. The question of which drawings these were and the relationship between Vincent and Bernard in general are matters that have been dealt with by Roskill in a very thorough study already referred to.* This research, with which I am in almost complete agreement, has helped make it possible to identify all but one of the drawings in the long series sent to Bernard. In any case, the following were included (the numbers of the painted studies from which they were made are given in parentheses):

Fishing Boats at Sea 1505 (1453)
Street in Saintes-Maries 1506 (1462)
Canal with Women Washing 1507 (1490)
Sower with Setting Sun 1508 (1470)
Newly Mowed Lawn with Weeping Tree 1509 (1499)
Haystacks near a Farm 1514 (1442)
Wheat Field 1515 (1476)
Wheat Field with Sheaves 1516 (1477)
Sheaves of Wheat 1517 (1480)
Rocks with Tree 1518 (1489)

These are rich little drawings in which the essence of the painted examples has been captured in truly masterful fashion. In general they differ somewhat from the spontaneously done larger drawings because of their greater degree of stylization, which is clearly apparent in the forms of waves and plants, the manner in which the structure of a haystack is made up of small whorls, and especially, the use of many small dots of ink to fill up entire planes (as in 1506, 1507, 1515, and others).

It is obvious that Vincent could not give up painting altogether and it is unlikely that he was able to resist the colorfulness of nature during those weeks. To that temptation we owe two of the most scintillating and typical

*"Van Gogh's Exchanges of Work with Emile Bernard in 1888," *Oud Holland*, vol. LXXXVI, no. 2–3 (1971).

1489

1490

1491

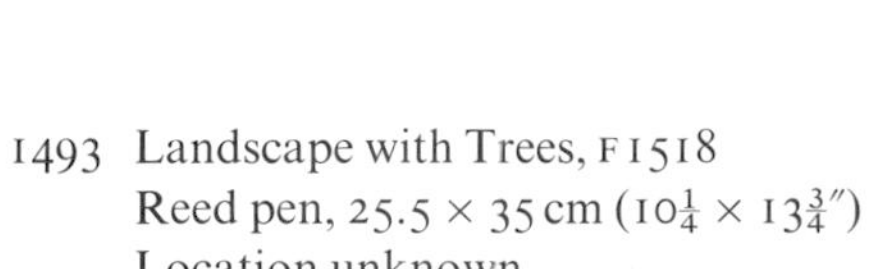

July 1888

1489 Rocks with Tree, F466
54 × 65 cm (21¼ × 25⅝″)
Museum of Fine Arts, Houston

1490 Canal with Women Washing, F427
74 × 60 cm (29⅛ × 23⅝″)
Private collection, New York

1491 The Painter on the Road to Tarascon, F448
48 × 44 cm (18⅞ × 17⅜″)
Destroyed; formerly Kaiser Friedrich Museum, Magdeburg

1492 The Road to Tarascon with a Man Walking, F1502
Pencil, pen, reed pen, 25 × 34 cm (9⅞ × 13⅜″)
Kunsthaus, Zurich

1493 Landscape with Trees, F1518
Reed pen, 25.5 × 35 cm (10¼ × 13¾″)
Location unknown

1494 Landscape with Trees in the Foreground, F1509
Pencil, reed pen, 25 × 34 cm (9⅞ × 13⅜″)
Collection Mrs. George F. Baker, New York

1495 Road with Trees, F1518a
Pencil, reed pen, brown ink, 24 × 34 cm (9½ × 13⅜″)
Albertina, Vienna

1496 Landscape with Alphonse Daudet's Windmill, F1496
Pencil, reed pen, brown ink, 25.5 × 34.5 cm (10¼ × 13¾″)
Rijksmuseum Vincent van Gogh, Amsterdam

1492

1493

1494

1495

1496

1497

1497a

1498

1497 The Old Mill, F 1464
Pen, watercolor, 30 × 50 cm ($11\frac{3}{4} \times 19\frac{5}{8}$″)
Private collection, Zurich

1497a Bank of the Rhône at Arles, F 1472a
Reed pen, lilac ink, 38.5 × 60.5 cm ($14\frac{1}{4} \times 23\frac{3}{4}$″)
Museum Boymans-van Beuningen, Rotterdam

1498 Weeping Tree on a Lawn, F 1468
Chalk, pen, reed pen, 49 × 61.5 cm ($19\frac{1}{4} \times 24\frac{3}{8}$″)
Art Institute of Chicago

pieces of that summer. About July 24 he informed Theo: "I have a new drawing, a garden full of flowers; I have also two painted studies of it" (Letter 512). And after urging Theo to send on quickly a fairly large order of linen and paint, he continued: "This sketch will show you the motif of the new studies; one of them is in a vertical format and the other in a horizontal format of the same motif, size-30 canvases." The study in vertical format was 1510, the horizontal one 1513 (colorplate XXVII, page 347). In the margin of sketch 1511 Vincent made detailed color notes that clearly show how much this work depended on color. Black-and-white reproductions can give only the faintest idea of the significance of Vincent's new canvases.

La Mousmé and Roulin

In addition to landscapes, Vincent informed both Bernard and Theo July 28 or 29 (and he repeated it a few days later to Wil) that he had painted still another portrait: this was 1519. The report to Theo was the most detailed: "Well, if you know what a 'mousmé' is (you will if you have read Loti's *Madame Chrysanthème*), I have just painted one. It took me the whole week, I was not able to do anything else, as once again I have not been feeling very well. . . . A 'mousmé' is a Japanese girl—in this case she is a Provençal—about twelve or fourteen years old. So I now have two figure pieces, the Zouave and her. . . . The portrait of the girl is on a white ground, strongly tinted with veronese green; the bodice is rendered in blood-red and violet stripes. The skirt is royal blue, with large orange-yellow dots. The dull fleshy parts are grayish yellow, the hair violet, the eyebrows and eyelashes black, the eyes orange and prussian blue. A small branch of oleander between the fingers, for the hands are also included" (Letter 514). This description reveals once again what was the most important consideration for Vincent in making this figure piece—the color.

We know of a sensitively rendered drawing of the girl (1520) with color notes in the margin—an indication that it was apparently made after the painting. There is also a smaller, more sketchy rendering on notepaper, which Vincent must have made in a letter to Gauguin. This small drawing was later found pasted into the manuscript of Gauguin's *Noa-Noa* (the description of his voyage to Tahiti) and bearing the notation "du regretté Vincent van Gogh" ("from the lamented Vincent van Gogh"). However, the most carefully executed and most beautiful version (but only of the head and upper part of the body) was the copy he drew a short time later for his friend Russell, 1533.

Scarcely had Vincent completed the portrait of the girl when a new model came on the scene, a figure who was to play an important part in Vincent's life. In Letter 516, beginning of August, he wrote Theo: "At the moment I am working with another model: a postman in blue uniform, trimmed with gold, a thick bearded head, very Socratic." A few days later Vincent described the sittings to Bernard: "I have just made a portrait of a postman, or even two portraits. A Socratic type, no less Socratic because he drinks a

1499

1500

1501

1499 Newly Mowed Lawn with Weeping Tree, F428
60.5 × 73.5 cm (24 × $29\frac{1}{8}$″)
Private collection, Ascona/Zurich

1500 Newly Mowed Lawn with Weeping Tree
Sketch in Letter 508
Rijksmuseum Vincent van Gogh, Amsterdam

1501 The Crau, Seen from Montmajour, F1420
Black chalk, pen, reed pen, brown and black ink, 49 × 61 cm ($19\frac{1}{4}$ × 24″)
Rijksmuseum Vincent van Gogh, Amsterdam

1502 Landscape near Montmajour with Train, F1424
Pen, reed pen, black chalk, 49 × 61 cm ($19\frac{1}{4}$ × 24″)
British Museum, London

1503 Rocks with Trees, F1447
Pencil, pen, reed pen, brush, black ink, 49 × 60 cm ($19\frac{1}{4}$ × $23\frac{5}{8}$″)
Rijksmuseum Vincent van Gogh, Amsterdam

1504 Hill with the Ruins of Montmajour, F1446
Pen, 47.5 × 59 cm ($18\frac{7}{8}$ × $23\frac{1}{4}$″)
Rijksmuseum (Rijksprentenkabinet), Amsterdam

1502

1503

1504

1505

1506

1507

1508

1505 Fishing Boats at Sea, F 1430
Reed pen, 24 × 32 cm ($9\frac{1}{2} \times 12\frac{5}{8}$")
Nationalgalerie, East Berlin

1506 Street in Saintes-Maries, F 1435
Reed pen, 24 × 31 cm ($9\frac{1}{2} \times 12\frac{1}{4}$")
Museum of Modern Art, New York

1507 Canal with Women Washing, F 1444
Pen, 31.5 × 24 cm ($12\frac{3}{8} \times 9\frac{1}{2}$")
Rijksmuseum Kröller-Müller, Otterlo

1508 Sower with Setting Sun, F 1442
Reed pen, 25 × 31 cm ($9\frac{7}{8} \times 12\frac{1}{4}$")
Location unknown

little and thus has a florid complexion. . . . He sat a bit stiffly while posing and that is why I painted him twice, the second time at a single sitting. On the white canvas a blue, off-white background; in the face all the broken tones, yellow, green, violet, pink, and red. The uniform prussian blue, piped with yellow" (Letter B14).

The "postman," as Vincent called him (he himself used the title "entreposeur des postes"—"custodian of the mails"), was a "Socratic" republican named Joseph Roulin, whose wife and children also became Vincent's models—and friends.

From this letter to Bernard and simultaneous reports to Theo (Letters B14, 517, and 518), it can be gathered that Vincent first painted a three-quarter-length portrait, 1522, and then a bust portrait, 1524. In both these impressive works, the forceful blue of the uniform, as might be expected, strikes the dominant note, and Vincent has adapted the background to it: light blue in 1522, turquoise in 1524. Especially in the latter work, the quiet, open face has been rendered with a master's hand, sympathetically and devoid of the almost parodistic style that the flowing beard would later induce Vincent to adopt.

There is a small drawing with color notes, 1523, that was probably made from the three-quarter-length portrait but for what purpose we do not know, and there is a later variant of the bust portrait (1647).

Working for Russell

How it was possible will always astonish us, but while Vincent was working on these portraits, he managed to undertake a whole new series of masterly drawings based on his painted studies (1525–36). This time they were intended for his friend John Russell, who he hoped would buy a painting of Gauguin's in order to help him out. The dates provide the proof. In the same letter, August 1 to 3, in which he reported he was working on the portraits of the postman, he wrote: "I am working hard for Russell; I have had the idea that I should make him a series of drawings based on my painted studies; I am convinced that he will look upon them favorably and that this—at least I hope—will make him so much the more inclined to do business [with us]" (Letter 516). What he meant by this last remark becomes clear a little further on; in a long dissertation he explained that, along with the drawings, he wanted to send Russell a letter that might persuade him to purchase the painting of Gauguin's that Theo had bought. "Well, let me finish the drawings; I have eight of them and will make twelve, and let us then see what he will say." Only a few days later, Vincent wrote: "I have sent Russell twelve drawings made from painted studies and I thus had occasion to speak about it again" (that is, about the fact that Gauguin, from whom he had just received a letter, had no money to come to Arles; see Letter 517).

The twelve drawings that Vincent completed in these few days can be identified with relative certainty because they were in Russell's possession and acquired from him by subsequent owners. These drawings are listed below (the numbers of the studies on

1509

1511

1510

1509 Newly Mowed Lawn with Weeping Tree, F1450
Pen, 22.5 × 31 cm ($9 \times 12\frac{1}{4}$")
Location unknown

1510 Garden with Flowers, F430
95 × 73 cm ($37\frac{3}{8} \times 28\frac{3}{4}$")
Private collection, Zurich

1511 Garden with Flowers
Sketch in Letter 512
Rijksmuseum Vincent van Gogh, Amsterdam

1512 Garden with Flowers, F1455
Pen, 49 × 61 cm ($19\frac{1}{4} \times 24$")
Collection Oskar Reinhart, Winterthur, Switzerland

1513 Garden with Flowers, F429
72 × 91 cm ($28\frac{3}{8} \times 35\frac{7}{8}$")
Gemeentemuseum, The Hague (on loan from the state)
Colorplate XXVII, p. 347

1514 Haystacks near a Farm, F1426
Pen, reed pen, 24 × 31.5 cm ($9\frac{1}{2} \times 12\frac{5}{8}$")
Mücsarnok, Budapest

1512

1513

1514

1515

1516

1517

1518

1515 Wheat Field, F 1481
Pen, reed pen, 24×31.5 cm ($9\frac{1}{2} \times 12\frac{5}{8}''$)
Metropolitan Museum of Art, New York.
Gift of Mrs. Max J. H. Rossbach, 1964

1516 Wheat Field with Sheaves and Arles in the Background, F 1491
Pen, 32×24 cm ($12\frac{5}{8} \times 9\frac{1}{2}''$)
Location unknown

1517 Sheaves of Wheat, F 1488
Pen, 24.5×32 cm ($9\frac{7}{8} \times 12\frac{5}{8}''$)
Nationalgalerie, East Berlin

1518 Rocks with Tree, F 1554
Pen, reed pen, 24×31 cm ($9\frac{1}{2} \times 12\frac{1}{4}''$)
Collection Mrs. M. L. Caturla, Madrid

which they were based are given in parentheses):

Haystacks near a Farm 1525 (1442)
Fishing Boats at Sea 1526 (1453)
Harvest Landscape 1527 (1440)
A Fishing Boat at Sea 1528 (1452)
Wheat Field with Sheaves 1529 (1477)
Wheat Field with Sheaves 1530 (1480)
The Road to Tarascon (without the figure) 1531 (1491)
Garden with Flowers 1532 (1513)
Mousmé 1533 (1519)
Lawn with Weeping Tree (probably from a variant of 1499 that has not been preserved) 1534 (——)
Zouave 1535 (1486)
Joseph Roulin 1536 (1524)

Clearly, Vincent did not make exactly the same series for Russell as he had for Bernard and—as was to be expected—he also wanted to give him an idea of the portraits he had just finished.

—and for Theo

After sending all these drawings to Bernard and Russell, Vincent apparently realized that it was time for him to show Theo, too, some of his work again. In his next letter, August 6, we read: "Did I tell you that I have sent drawings to our friend Russell? Right now I am doing pretty much the same ones over again for you; there will also be twelve of them" (Letter 518). He was dissatisfied with what he called "le hagard" ("the disordered look") of his painted studies, which he blamed on the unrelenting mistral, which "absolutely prevented him from being master of his touch" (Letter 518). He probably did fewer than twelve drawings; when he reported two days later that he had sent the work off, there were three large drawings and "in addition, some others that are smaller" (Letter 519). It can also be gathered from the letter that the large ones were drawings of flower gardens—one of them very probably being the previously mentioned work 1512—and that the harvest landscape and two seascapes were among the smaller drawings. Since these drawings came from the collection of Theo van Gogh, it can almost certainly be assumed that this third group included at least the following:

Garden with Flowers 1512
Garden with Flowers 1537
Garden with Sunflowers 1539
Harvest Landscape (from 1440) 1540
Fishing Boats at Sea (from 1453) 1541
A Fishing Boat at Sea (from 1452) 1542
Sower with Setting Sun (from 1470) 1543
Wheat Field with Sheaves (from 1477) 1544
Newly Mowed Lawn with Weeping Tree (from 1499) 1545
Wheat Field with Setting Sun (from 1473) 1546

Vincent had already written to Theo several times about his portraits of Roulin; August 11 he had sent him a drawing made from one of these, along with another drawing of a portrait. This time they were *large* drawings, and although the one made from the three-quarter-length portrait of Roulin

1519

1520

1521

1519 Mousmé, Sitting in a Cane Chair, Half-Figure, F431
74 × 60 cm ($29\frac{1}{8} \times 23\frac{5}{8}$″)
National Gallery of Art, Washington, D.C.

1520 Mousmé, Sitting in a Cane Chair, Half-Figure, F1504
Pencil, pen, reed pen, 32.5 × 24.5 cm ($13 \times 9\frac{7}{8}$″)
Pushkin Museum, Moscow

1521 Mousmé, Sitting in a Cane Chair, Half-Figure, F1722
Pen, 15 × 13 cm ($5\frac{7}{8} \times 5\frac{1}{8}$″)
The Louvre, Paris

Colorplate XXVII, Garden with Flowers, 1513 〉

(1547) must certainly have given Theo an idea of the composition of the original work (1522), it must be said that the "copy" hardly does justice to its monumental quality.

The letter in which Vincent announced that he was sending these drawings is among the most important he wrote because it contains a detailed explanation of the ideas he had in mind in making his portraits. The occasion for this discussion was that he had begun working with a new model: "You will shortly be making the acquaintance of Mr. Patience Escalier, a kind of 'man with a hoe,'* a former cowherd from the Camargue and now a gardener at a house in the Crau. This very day I am sending you the drawing I made from that painting, also the drawing made from the portrait of the postman Roulin" (Letter 520). He did not expect the people in Paris (for instance, Portier, the art dealer) to have much appreciation for the new portrait; Theo perhaps would, for he had changed, so Vincent thought, and in order to give him some insight into the piece, he made a rather odd comparison: "I do not think that my *Peasant* will come off badly set next to the Lautrec that you have and I even dare to believe that Lautrec will become even more distinguished by reason of their being put side by side and mine will gain through the strangeness of the comparison because the impression of sunniness, of being burned, scorched by the hot sun and open air will become even stronger next to the rice powder and the elegant toilette."

Coloristic Portraits

An awareness that his style was changing began to grow on Vincent. "I believe that what I learned in Paris is *fading away* and that I am returning to the ideas I formed in the country before I became acquainted with the Impressionists. And I would not be very surprised if the Impressionists soon found something to criticize in my manner of doing things, which is nourished more by Delacroix's ideas than by theirs. For instead of trying to depict exactly what I see in front of me, I use color in a more arbitrary way to express myself forcefully."

Then, strangely enough, as an example of what he meant, he described a portrait he obviously had not yet made, but actually did execute shortly afterward—certainly an indication of how much careful deliberation went into what he did despite the speed at which he worked: "I want to make a portrait of an artist I am on friendly terms with who is a great dreamer, who works the same way a lark sings, because that is his nature. That man will be fair-haired. . . . I shall therefore paint him as he is, as faithful to reality as I can, to begin with. But that is not the finished picture. To finish it, I shall become a colorist, working in very arbitrary fashion. I exaggerate the fairness of the hair, I arrive at orange tones, chrome yellow, light lemon yellow. Behind the head I paint—instead of the nondescript wall of the shabby lodgings—the infinite; I make a simple background of the richest, the most intense blue I can con-

*This expression—in French "homme à la houe"—is an allusion to the title of the famous painting by Millet, which Theo would, of course, recognize.

1522

1523

1524

1522 Joseph Roulin, Sitting in a Cane Chair, Three-Quarter-Length, F432
81 × 65 cm ($31\frac{7}{8} \times 25\frac{5}{8}$")
Museum of Fine Arts, Boston

1523 Joseph Roulin, Sitting in a Cane Chair, Three-Quarter-Length, F1723
Pen, 32 × 24 cm ($12\frac{5}{8} \times 9\frac{1}{2}$")
Location unknown

1524 Joseph Roulin, Head, F433
64 × 48 cm ($25\frac{1}{4} \times 18\frac{7}{8}$")
Private collection, Detroit

〈 Colorplate XXVIII, Portrait of Eugène Boch, 1574

1525

1526

1527

trive, and by virtue of this simple combination the fair head, with the light falling on it, takes on, against that rich blue background, a mysterious appearance like that of a star in the deep azure of the sky" (Letter 520).

The painting he had thus conjured up was to become the portrait of the Belgian painter Eugène Boch, who with Dodge MacKnight was staying that summer in the small village of Fontvieille, near Arles. Vincent, on the occasion of various visits to Fontvieille, had become friendly with him. Although it was to look a bit different in the final version, the painting would still exhibit many of the characteristics described here (1574; colorplate XXVIII, page 348).

Vincent used this procedure also in the portrait of Patience Escalier: "I worked in a similar way in the portrait of the peasant, without, of course, wanting in this case to evoke the mysterious gleam of a pale star in infinite space. But by my depicting in the full sea of flames of the harvest, in the full force of the South, the powerful man that I had to paint. That explains the vivid orange tones, like red-hot iron; that explains tones of old gold, casting light in the shadows. Alas, dear brother ... the good folk will see nothing more in that exaggeration than a caricature." It is evident that Van Gogh was fully aware that he had to go his own way, misunderstood by the multitude, and with less and less chance of being appreciated even by the few art dealers from whom he could still expect something.

His work on the portraits did not prevent Vincent from continuing at the same time to paint landscapes outdoors. About August 13 he was able to write that he had four more of them: "I have two studies of thistles on a piece of farmland, thistles white with the fine dust from the road. In addition, a small study of a rest area occupied by the [workers and] performers in a traveling fair, red and green covered wagons; also a small study of [railroad] cars of the Paris–Lyons–Marseilles train" (Letter 522).

These studies—1550 and 1551, 1553 and 1554—while not among the most important Vincent made, nevertheless have a charm of their own. In the latter two, this arises from the unpretentious, "naïve" portrayal of a bit of colorful reality happened upon as it were by chance, and in the studies of the thistles, it emerges from the arbitrary composition that, especially in 1550, strikes us by the way he has allowed the sunny country road with the small figure of a woman and the brow of the hill with the woods to remain half hidden behind the wild growth in the foreground. The same bit of landscape also appears in a small horizontal drawing undoubtedly made at the same time, 1552.

Vincent's faculty for discerning surprising compositions in the multicolored world around him, and his urge to record them immediately in line and color, caused him to take in hand still another everyday subject. On August 14 or 15 he wrote Theo: "I am now working on a study like this [here he drew in the letter the rough sketch 1557], depicting barges seen from above from the quay. The two barges are violet-pink, the water is very green, there is no sky, the tricolor flying from the mast. A workman with a wheelbarrow is unloading sand. I also have a drawing of it" (Letter 524). The very detailed large drawing, 1556, referred to here must have been made first. In fact, Vincent had already sent off the drawing even while he was still working on the study (1558), and it is interesting to note how far he went in trying to simplify it in comparison with the drawing. He left out the small sailboats in the background and the Rhône bridge and the economically observed small figures in the upper left-hand corner of the drawing. In the painting he was particularly concerned with the forceful contrasts in colors, and when he described the canvas for the benefit of Bernard, it was in terms of color: "two barges in a violet pink on water of veronese green, with gray sand, wheelbarrow, planks, a small

August 1888

1525 Haystacks near a Farm, F1427
Pen, 24 × 31 cm (9½ × 12¼″)
Philadelphia Museum of Art

1526 Fishing Boats at Sea, F1430a
Reed pen, 24.5 × 32 cm (9⅞ × 12⅝″)
Solomon R. Guggenheim Museum, New York

1527 Harvest Landscape, F1486
Pen, 24 × 32 cm (9½ × 12⅝″)
Collection Mr. and Mrs. Paul Mellon, Upperville, Virginia

1528 A Fishing Boat at Sea, F1433
Reed pen, 24 × 31.5 cm (9½ × 12⅝″)
Collection Joseph Pulitzer, Jr., St. Louis

1529 Wheat Field with Sheaves and Arles in the Background, F1490
Pen, 31.5 × 23.5 cm (12⅝ × 9½″)
Collection Mr. and Mrs. Leigh B. Block, Chicago

1528

1529

1530

1531

1533

1532

1530 Wheat Field with Sheaves, F 1489
Pen, 24 × 32 cm ($9\frac{1}{2} \times 12\frac{5}{8}''$)
Collection H. R. Hahnloser, Bern

1531 The Road to Tarascon, F 1502a
Pen, reed pen, 24.5 × 32 cm ($9\frac{7}{8} \times 12\frac{5}{8}''$)
Solomon R. Guggenheim Museum, New York

1532 Garden with Flowers, F 1454
Pen, 24 × 31.5 cm ($9\frac{1}{2} \times 12\frac{5}{8}''$)
Location unknown

1533 Mousmé, Half-Figure, F 1503
Pen, reed pen, 31.5 × 24 cm ($12\frac{5}{8} \times 9\frac{1}{2}''$)
Collection Paul M. Hirschland, New York

1534 Lawn with Weeping Tree, F 1449
Pen, 31.5 × 24.5 cm ($12\frac{5}{8} \times 9\frac{7}{8}''$)
Location unknown

1534

blue and yellow figure of a man. All this seen from a high quay in a bird's-eye view. No sky; it is only a sketch or rather a small study, made in the full force of the mistral" (Letter B15). And in a subsequent letter to Bernard, for whom this painting was intended, he stressed the sketchy nature of the work even more forcefully: "a landscape with men unloading sand, which is likewise a plan, an attempt, for a painting with a more mature objective" (Letter B18).

Meanwhile, for the first time since May 10, Vincent again was able to show his brother a number of his painted studies; this must have been an important event. He had already informed Theo in Letter 516 that his friend the Zouave Milliet would be going to Paris on August 17 and had promised he would take the parcel along with him. Now the time had come, and he sent Theo a telegram informing him that Milliet would deliver the paintings on Friday, August 17, in the Cercle Militaire at precisely 7 A.M. He also gave various details about the consignment in a letter that, to him, must have seemed like an interim stocktaking: "The roll he will be bringing with him for you contains thirty-five studies, among which there are many I am desperately dissatisfied with and yet am sending because they will give you at least a vague idea of very fine motifs in nature. There is, for instance, among them a sketch of myself, loaded with boxes, poles, a canvas, on the sunny road to Tarascon. There is a view of the Rhône, in which the sky and the water are the color of absinthe, with a blue bridge and little black figures of idlers loitering about; there is the sower, women washing, and still others, some that did not turn out well and some unfinished, especially a large landscape with underbrush" (Letter 524).

Artists are generally most pleased with their newest works, and thus it is not surprising that at the end of his next letter he wrote: " I have added to this lot a drawing of the study I am now working on—the barges with the men unloading sand" (Letter 525; the drawing, of course, was 1556).

The Sunflowers

A happy inspiration induced Vincent to interrupt his work on landscapes and portraits and turn to making a few still lifes. These were the sunflowers, which have contributed perhaps more than any other of Vincent's paintings to make his name known throughout the world—which are in some cases the *only* works with which he is identified. Curiously, the thought of Gauguin had a decisive influence in this connection too. The first mention of the idea is to be found in a letter to Emile Bernard written about August 18: "I am thinking about hanging a half dozen paintings of sunflowers in my studio, a decoration in which unmixed or broken chromatic yellows will shine forth from various backgrounds, blue, from the palest veronese [*sic*] to *royal blue*, framed with wooden slats painted orange. The same kind of effect as leaded windows in a Gothic church" (Letter B15).

A few days later the sunflowers were already on the easels, and in writing to Theo, Vincent made no secret of the fact that they were intended for Gauguin: "I am painting

1535

1536

1537

1535 Zouave, Half-Figure, F 1482a
Pen, reed pen, 32 × 24.5 cm (12⅝ × 9⅞″)
Solomon R. Guggenheim Museum, New York

1536 Joseph Roulin, Head, F 1458
Pen, 31.5 × 24 cm (12⅜ × 9½″)
Collection H. R. Hahnloser, Bern

1537 Garden with Flowers, F 1456
Reed pen, 61 × 49 cm (24 × 19¼″)
Private collection, Zurich

1538 Garden with Flowers, F 578
65 × 54 cm (25⅝ × 21¼″)
Location unknown

1539 Garden with Sunflowers, F 1457
Pencil, reed pen, brown ink, 60 × 48.5 cm (23⅝ × 19¼″)
Rijksmuseum Vincent van Gogh, Amsterdam

1540 Harvest Landscape, F 1485
Pen, 24 × 32 cm (9½ × 12⅝″)
Nationalgalerie, East Berlin

1541 Fishing Boats at Sea, F 1430b
Reed pen, 24 × 31.5 cm (9½ × 12⅝″)
Musée d'Art Moderne, Musées Royaux des Beaux-Arts de Belgique, Brussels

1539

1540

1541

with the enthusiasm of a Marseillais eating bouillabaisse, which will not surprise you, since what it is all about is painting large sunflowers. I have three canvases on the stocks: 1st, three large flowers in a green vase, light background (size-15 canvas); 2nd, three flowers, one flower which has gone to seed and lost its leaves and one in bud on a background of royal blue (size-25 canvas); 3rd, twelve flowers and buds in a yellow vase (size-30 canvas). The last one is light on light and will, I hope, be the best. I will probably not leave it at that. As I hope to live with Gauguin in a studio of our own, I would like to make a decoration for the walls. Nothing but large sunflowers.... Well, if I carry out that plan, there will be a dozen panels of them. The whole thing will therefore become a symphony in blue and yellow. I work at it every morning from sunrise on, for the flowers wilt quickly and it is a matter of doing the whole thing in one go" (Letter 526).

This clear description leaves no doubt that the first two canvases mentioned must have been 1559 and 1560.* The canvas with the twelve sunflowers on a bluish-green background is more difficult to deal with because Vincent later painted a replica of it. Of the two pieces, 1561 seems, in my view (and in that of the editors of the 1970 *catalogue raisonné*), to be the original on grounds of style.

A few days later Vincent reported: "I am now working on the fourth painting of the sunflowers. This fourth one is a bouquet of fourteen flowers and has a yellow background, just like a still life with quinces and lemons that I did earlier [1339]. But because it is much larger, it is quite impressive, and I believe that this time it is painted with more simplicity than the quinces and lemons" (Letter 527).

As Vincent later made replicas of this piece, too, there is again some room for hesitation in deciding which of the three works is the original. In agreement with the 1970 *catalogue raisonné*, I assume that 1562 is the one painted in 1888.

Experimenting

At the end of August, Vincent wrote that he was once more working with models: a woman from Arles—who, however, failed to put in an appearance after being paid in advance—and the old peasant, who had returned for a second portrait (Letter 529). The blazing, flaming portrait of Patience Escalier, 1563, was the result. In the same letter, Vincent said that he was also talking to other people about sitting for him, and he thereupon made a pronouncement of some significance: "There is something that keeps forcing me to make as many figure studies as possible."

A lack of models may have been responsible for the self-portrait with straw hat and pipe, 1565, which is not mentioned specifically in the letters. I believe this work is best dated to the end of the month.† On the basis of style—if viewed as a rather hasty sketch—it fits in well with the work done during the late summer of 1888; the vivid yellow of the straw hat and the soft bluish green of the painter's smock are strongly reminiscent of the color scheme in the still life of sunflowers 1561, that "symphony in blue and yellow."

In these final days of August, Vincent's subjects went far beyond the human figure

1542

1543

1544

1542 A Fishing Boat at Sea, F 1431
Reed pen, 24 × 32 cm (9½ × 12⅝")
Collection Werner Vowinckel, Cologne

1543 Sower with Setting Sun, F 1441
Reed pen, 24.5 × 32 cm (9⅞ × 12⅝")
Rijksmuseum Vincent van Gogh, Amsterdam

1544 Wheat Field with Sheaves and Arles in the Background, F 1492
Pen, 31.5 × 24 cm (12⅝ × 9½")
Formerly collection Robert von Hirsch, Basel

1545 Newly Mowed Lawn with Weeping Tree, F 1451
Pen, 24 × 31.5 cm (9½ × 12⅝")
Private collection, United States

*The only details that do not tally are "size-15 canvas" and "size-25 canvas," but I assume that Vincent was mistaken in this. This problem is discussed in the commentary to F453 in the 1970 *catalogue raisonné*.

†Since self-portrait 1565 clearly shows the left ear, it must have been painted before the dramatic episode that occurred at the end of 1888. And since it shows Vincent with a beard, it must have been made considerably later than the end of July, when, according to Letter 514, he was clean-shaven. That he afterward grew a beard is apparent from self-portrait 1581, which can be dated with certainty to the middle of September 1888.

1545

1546

1547

1548

1549

1550

1551

1546 Wheat Field with Setting Sun, F 1514
Pen, reed pen, 24 × 31.5 cm ($9\frac{1}{2} \times 12\frac{5}{8}''$)
Kunstmuseum, Winterthur, Switzerland

1547 Joseph Roulin, Three-Quarter-Length, F 1459
Pen, 59 × 44.5 cm ($23\frac{1}{4} \times 17\frac{3}{4}''$)
Los Angeles County Museum of Art, Mr. and Mrs. George Gard de Sylva Collection

1548 The Old Peasant Patience Escalier, F 443
64 × 54 cm ($25\frac{1}{4} \times 21\frac{1}{4}''$)
Norton Simon Foundation, Los Angeles

1549 The Old Peasant Patience Escalier, F 1460
Pencil, pen, reed pen, brown ink,
49.5 × 38 cm ($19\frac{5}{8} \times 15''$)
Fogg Art Museum, Harvard University, Cambridge, Massachusetts

1550 Thistles, F 447
59 × 49 cm ($23\frac{1}{4} \times 19\frac{1}{4}''$)
Stavros S. Niarchos Collection

1551 Thistles, F 447a
55 × 45 cm ($21\frac{5}{8} \times 17\frac{3}{4}''$)
Location unknown

and face. "I am also occupied with a bunch of flowers and with a still life of a pair of old shoes" (Letter 529). Two weeks earlier, in the middle of the month, he had written: "I am hoping now to make a study of oleanders" (Letter 524), and it seems reasonable to assume that canvases 1566 and 1567, which show oleanders in a vase, are the still lifes of flowers he referred to. The still life depicting the same vase, with zinnias this time, is stylistically very closely related and must have been painted at the same time (1568). Still life 1566, which is also the largest of the three, is marked by the presence once again of books on the table. Vincent has pointedly put Emile Zola's novel, with the telling title *La Joie de Vivre*, on top—the same book he had depicted with a Bible in 946.

Vincent made still lifes of "a pair of old shoes" on a number of occasions, as we have seen. This particular piece, 1569, is generally considered to have been painted at this time. This dating seems to me beyond dispute if it is compared with the portrait of the Zouave seated with his legs sprawled out (1488), in which the stone-covered floor of Vincent's studio in the yellow house is portrayed in identical fashion in a striking bird's-eye view perspective. (Vincent resumed work on the Zouave's portrait this month.)

The river views 1570 and 1571 must also have been made at about this time. Vincent does not mention them in his letters, but he had already written twice in August about a coal barge he had seen berthed on the Rhône at the same place where he had painted the scene of sand being unloaded from the barges. "Pure Hokusai" he had called the spectacle of the glimmering barge against the gray water and the violet evening sky (see Letters 516 and 526). "It would be a marvelous subject," he had remarked in Letter 526. The large studies he finally made of this subject must have been thrown on the canvas with great speed; the smaller of the two (1571), in particular, is a very cursory impression.

Accurate dating is equally difficult in the case of the much more carefully painted views of the interior of a restaurant, 1572 and 1573. Why Vincent made two practically identical paintings of the same subject remains a mystery, but one may have been intended for the owner of the restaurant. I do not believe that 1572 is a sketchy preliminary study for the other. But certainly both of them, with their curious, typically Neo-Impressionist composition—that is to say, the anticompositional and, as it were, photographic effect of large empty chairs and tables in the foreground and the diners small in the background—represent a further new element in Vincent's work which he himself must have viewed as an experiment.

September had arrived when Vincent wrote: "I finally have a first sketch for the painting I have been dreaming about for a long time: the 'Poet.'" He had described the painting he envisioned to Theo earlier, but now he revealed that he had found a model, the Belgian painter Eugène Boch (see pages 349–50): "His fine head with the green eyes contrasts in my portrait with a starry sky of deep ultramarine blue; he is wearing a short yellow jacket with a collar of unbleached linen, a multicolored necktie. He sat twice in one day for me" (Letter 531). The expression "a first sketch" implied that Vincent regarded 1574 (colorplate XXVIII, page 348) as just a study and not the final painting. As far as can be gathered from the correspondence, he never made another portrait of Boch, who in any event was leaving the next day for Paris and was then going on to the Borinage to work there. There seems scarcely any reason to want a more finished version; the portrait as it stands ranks as one of the most personal and impressive works Vincent painted. Regardless of how rapidly and nonchalantly he threw onto the canvas the unsmoothed brushstrokes with which, so to speak, he

1552

1553

1554

1552 Thistles along the Road, F 1466
Pencil, pen, brown ink, 24.5 × 32 cm ($9\frac{7}{8} \times 12\frac{5}{8}''$)
Rijksmuseum Vincent van Gogh, Amsterdam

1553 Railway Carriages, F 446
45 × 50 cm ($17\frac{3}{4} \times 19\frac{5}{8}''$)
Location unknown

1554 Traveling Players' Caravans, F 445
45 × 51 cm ($17\frac{3}{4} \times 20\frac{1}{8}''$)
The Louvre, Paris

1555 Road with Telegraph Pole and Crane, F 1495
Pencil, pen, 24 × 32 cm ($9\frac{1}{2} \times 12\frac{5}{8}''$)
Rijksmuseum Vincent van Gogh, Amsterdam

1556 Quay with Men Unloading Sand Barges, F 1462
Pen, reed pen, 48 × 62.5 cm ($18\frac{7}{8} \times 24\frac{3}{4}''$)
Collection Edith Wetmore, New York

1555

1556

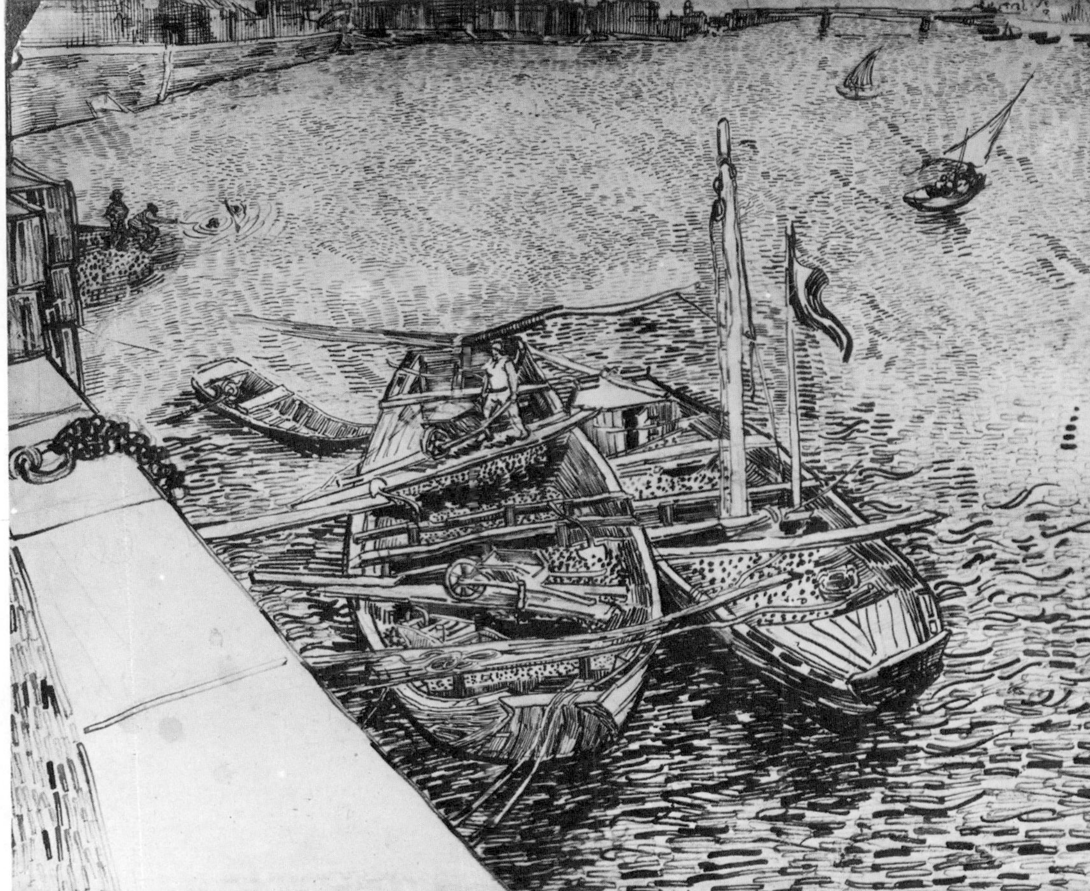

1557

1558

1559

1560

1561

1557 Quay with Men Unloading Sand Barges
Sketch in Letter 524
Rijksmuseum Vincent van Gogh, Amsterdam

1558 Quay with Men Unloading Sand Barges, F449
55 × 66 cm ($21\frac{5}{8}$ × 26″)
Museum Folkwang, Essen

1559 Three Sunflowers in a Vase, F453
73 × 58 cm ($28\frac{3}{4}$ × $22\frac{7}{8}$″)
Private collection, United States

1560 Five Sunflowers in a Vase, F459
98 × 69 cm ($38\frac{5}{8}$ × $27\frac{1}{8}$″)
Destroyed; formerly in Yokohama, Japan

1561 Twelve Sunflowers in a Vase, F456
91 × 71 cm ($35\frac{7}{8}$ × 28″)
Bayerische Staatsgemäldesammlungen, Munich

modeled the narrow head of the artist Boch, it is perhaps precisely because of this spontaneous treatment that the portrait makes such a forceful, well-characterized impression. We get a feeling from all this that Vincent here has already fully achieved what in this same letter he expressed as his ideal: "I would like to paint men and women with something of that eternal quality, formerly symbolized by the halo, that we seek in the radiance, in the vibration of our coloring."

The Night Café

As Vincent was seldom fortunate enough to have friends who would pose for him, portraits were to remain for some time the exception in his work. The following days were taken up by quite a different kind of subject: "Although, in looking back, he now does not seem to be such a bad fellow, I had called the innkeeper names and told him that, in order to get even for all the extra money I had paid him, I would paint his whole dirty joint in such a way that I would be compensated. Now at last, to the great delight of the innkeeper, of the postman whom I have already painted, of the patrons, who are night owls, and of myself, I stayed up three nights to paint, while sleeping during the day" (Letter 533).

Even more interesting than this half-melancholy, half-humorous account of how the painting came about is the exceptionally detailed explanation—which he added to this—of his intentions in the use of the colors: "I have attempted with the red and green to express the terrible passions of man. . . . I am making a copy in watercolors, to send you tomorrow, so as to give you an idea of it" (Letter 533).

And the next day after he had mailed that watercolor (1576), he summed up the symbolic meaning of the colors once again in still other, possibly even stronger terms: "In my painting *The Night Café* I have tried to express the idea that the café is a place where a person can ruin himself, go mad, commit crimes" (Letter 534).

Whether or not one is prepared to call Vincent's use of color symbolic, it was certainly extremely personal and unconventional, as also appears from such paintings, in particular, as *Café Terrace at Night* (1580) and *The Starry Night* (1592). Even a pair of less emotionally inspired studies done before *Café Terrace* are especially striking because of their color: *The Old Mill* (1577), "painted in broken tints" (Letter 535), and *Public Garden* (1578)—the first with a turquoise, and the second with a deep lemon-yellow, sky.

Café Terrace at Night was painted during the same week as this park landscape, which in his letter of September 16 or 17 he called "the first painting of this week." He continued: "The second shows the exterior of a café, the terrace lighted by a big gaslamp in the blue night, with a corner of blue sky studded with stars" (Letter 537). In a letter to Wil he gave a fascinating description of this work, of which a large drawing (1579) also exists: "On the terrace are small figures of people drinking. An immensely large yellow streetlamp illuminates the terrace, the façade, the sidewalk, and even casts a light on the

1562

1563

1564

1562 Fourteen Sunflowers in a Vase, F454
93×73 cm ($36\frac{5}{8} \times 28\frac{3}{4}''$)
Tate Gallery, London

1563 The Old Peasant Patience Escalier, Half-Figure, F444
69×56 cm ($27\frac{1}{8} \times 22''$)
Stavros S. Niarchos Collection

1564 The Old Peasant Patience Escalier, Half-Figure, F1461
Reed pen, 14×13 cm ($5\frac{1}{2} \times 5\frac{1}{8}''$)
Private collection, Switzerland

1565 Self-Portrait with Straw Hat and Pipe, F524
Canvas on cardboard, 42×31 cm ($16\frac{1}{2} \times 12\frac{1}{4}''$)
Rijksmuseum Vincent van Gogh, Amsterdam

1566 Majolica Jar with Branches of Oleander, F593
60×73 cm ($23\frac{5}{8} \times 28\frac{3}{4}''$)
Metropolitan Museum of Art, New York

1567 Majolica Jar with Branches of Oleander, F594
56×36 cm ($22 \times 14\frac{1}{8}''$)
Location unknown

1568 Majolica Jar with Zinnias, F592
64×49.5 cm ($25\frac{1}{4} \times 19\frac{5}{8}''$)
Collection Mr. and Mrs. Basil P. Goulandris, Lausanne

1569 A Pair of Old Shoes, F461
44×53 cm ($17\frac{3}{8} \times 20\frac{7}{8}''$)
Private collection, New York

1565

1566

1567

1568

1569

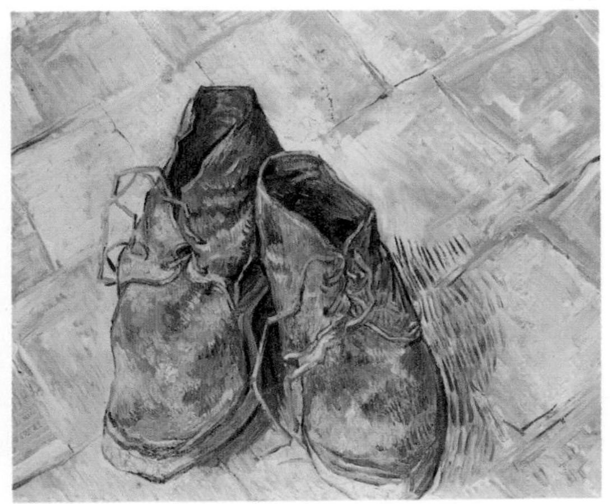

1570

1571

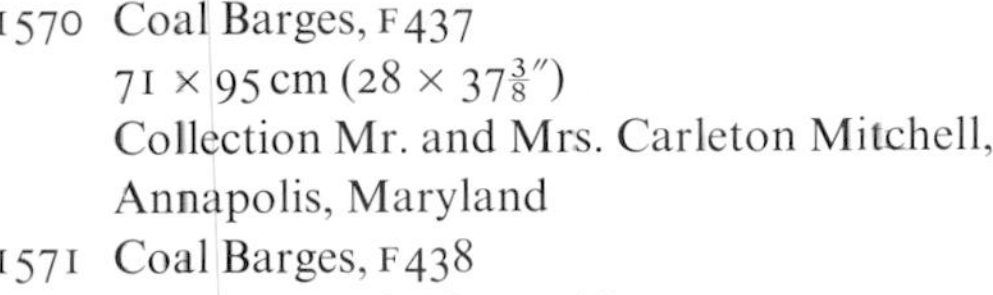

1570 Coal Barges, F437
71 × 95 cm (28 × $37\frac{3}{8}$")
Collection Mr. and Mrs. Carleton Mitchell, Annapolis, Maryland

1571 Coal Barges, F438
53.5 × 64 cm ($21\frac{1}{4}$ × $25\frac{1}{4}$")
Thyssen-Bornemisza Collection, Lugano-Castagnola, Switzerland

paving stones, which take on a violet-pink hue. The fronts of the houses along a street stretching out under the starlit sky are deep blue or violet with a green tree. Here, then, is a night picture without any black, nothing but beautiful blue and violet and green, and in those surroundings the lighted square is colored sulfur yellow and lemon green." And he concluded this description with: "I really enjoy doing a painting on the spot at night" (Letter W7).

The Starry Night
He had also done this when, some ten days later, he sent Theo a rough sketch with the words: "Enclosed a small sketch of a size-30 canvas, square; finally *The Starry Night*, painted at night under a gas lamp.* The sky is bluish-green, the water is royal blue, the earth is mauve. The city is blue and violet, the gaslight is yellow, and the reflections are reddish gold and taper off to bronze green. On the bluish-green field of the sky, the Great Bear, twinkling in green and pink, its modest brilliance contrasting with the strong gold of the gaslight. Two colorful little figures of lovers in the foreground" (Letter 543).

A painting like this one, 1592, especially makes one realize how far Vincent had gone in the "arbitrary" use of colors. The heavy touches, from light blue to the darkest prussian blue, applied almost like a mosaic, form the mysterious background here for the yellow of the stars and the orange of the reflections of light on the water. But not only have the colors been intensified; Vincent's high-pitched mood also found expression in the drawing. Never before had he departed so drastically from reality as in depicting this sky (and the bit of star-filled sky in *The Night Café*).

September 18 Vincent had the satisfaction of being able to report that he had spent his first night in the new house. He drew new strength from the thought that prospects were now good for doing the kind of work that could repay Theo for all he had done for him, and so we see him in the coming weeks producing a large number of very important paintings in quick succession.

Self-Portrait and Landscapes
Once again Vincent felt moved to make a self-portrait: 1581. His own lengthy comment on it is indispensable for an understanding of the strange appearance he gave himself here. He described it to Theo, September 16 or 17, as "the third painting of this week" in the previously mentioned Letter 537—"a self-portrait, *almost without color*, ash-colored tones on a background of pale veronese green"—and he informed Wil that it was a study "in which I look Japanese" (Letter W7). That this was intentional appears from other descriptions he gave. This time he wanted to give the portrait something that transcended the conventional portrayal of external appearance: "I have conceived the portrait as that of a bonze, a simple wor-

*"Under a gas lamp": this is really sufficient to refute the romantic legend that Van Gogh used to paint at night with a wreath of small burning candles affixed to his straw hat. This account is found in many books but is not supported by a single document.

1572

1573

1574

1572 Interior of a Restaurant, F549
54 × 64.5 cm ($21\frac{1}{4} \times 25\frac{5}{8}$")
Collection Murray S. Danforth, Jr., Providence, Rhode Island

1573 Interior of a Restaurant, F549a
65.5 × 81 cm ($26 \times 31\frac{7}{8}$")
Collection V. Margutti, Zurich, and H. Vaucher, Neuchâtel

September 1888

1574 Portrait of Eugène Boch, F462
60 × 45 cm ($23\frac{5}{8} \times 17\frac{3}{4}$")
The Louvre, Paris
Colorplate XXVIII, p. 348

1575 The Night Café, F463
70 × 89 cm ($27\frac{5}{8} \times 35$")
Yale University Art Gallery, New Haven, Connecticut

1575

1576

1577

1578

1576 The Night Café, F 1463
Watercolor, 42 × 61.5 cm ($16\frac{1}{2} \times 24\frac{3}{8}$")
Collection H. R. Hahnloser, Bern

1577 The Old Mill, F 550
64.5 × 54 cm ($25\frac{3}{8} \times 21\frac{1}{4}$")
Albright-Knox Art Gallery, Buffalo, New York

1578 Public Garden with Round Clipped Shrub and Weeping Tree, F 468
73 × 92 cm ($28\frac{3}{4} \times 36\frac{1}{4}$")
Art Institute of Chicago

shiper of the eternal Buddha" (Letter 553*a*).

During the last weeks of September it appears that Vincent was working on several paintings at the same time, just as he had done when the orchards were in bloom. In Letter 544 he reported: "There are now ten size-30 canvases in the works," and a week later he wrote Boch: "I am working on seven size-30 canvases" (Letter 553*b*). He must have been engaged simultaneously in doing the self-portrait and several paintings of the public garden across from the yellow house. September 18 he wrote: "At the moment I am busy with another size-30 canvas (square); once again a garden scene, or rather a footpath under plane trees with a lawn, painted green, and black little fir groves" (Letter 538). The description makes it reasonable to assume that 1582 was the one referred to here.

The speed at which Vincent worked is once more strikingly illustrated by what we read in the next letter, the second to Theo that day: "I already wrote you early this morning, after which I continued on with a painting of a garden in the sun. I then brought that one home and went out again with a fresh canvas and that one, too, is now finished" (Letter 539).

There is one more detail that should be mentioned concerning the public garden scenes. When Vincent realized that he was actually working on historic ground, he tried to introduce something of this into these scenes, which then took on a special, a "poetic," significance for him. Thereafter, in commenting in his letters on various paintings that he had made of the public garden, he would refer to "the poet's garden" ("le jardin du poète"). "And I had wanted to paint this garden in such a way as also to bring to mind Petrarch, the old poet from here (or rather from Avignon) and the new poet from here—Paul Gauguin" (Letter 544*a*).

Apart from various drawings, we know of nine paintings of the small park across from the yellow house. These are 1499 (from July; the previously mentioned sketch of this, 1509, had been sent by Vincent to Bernard), 1578, 1582, 1585, 1598, 1601, 1613, 1615, and 1689. When, however, all the available data are taken into account, it becomes apparent that Vincent considered only *four* paintings to be portrayals of "the poet's garden": 1578, 1601, 1615, and a painting that has been lost but can be visualized from the letter sketches 1583 and 1584.*

1579

1580

1581

Hard and Soft Colors

An important portrait from this period was that of the Zouave Milliet done a few days after the officer returned from Paris (1588). About September 28, Vincent reported to Theo: "Milliet sends you his cordial regards. I have now made his portrait with the red kepi against an emerald-green background on which the insignia of his regiment are represented, the crescent with a five-pointed star" (this is a note on the back of drawing 1590, which was sent with Letter 543). There can be no doubt that this developed into a masterly portrait of what Vincent in Letter 541 called "a fine subject," a portrait in which he was able to do full justice to the "pale, languid face, the red kepi against an emerald-green background" and to achieve a lively characterization of the sympathetically observed personality.

At the same time he was working on a landscape, *Plowed Field* (1586), which, on account of its soft colors, pleased Milliet, who apparently had conservative tastes: "he ordinarily does not like what I make, but because the clods of earth have a soft color

*I have dealt with this question at greater length in "The Poet's Garden," *Vincent*, vol. III, no. 1 (1974), pp. 22–32.

1579 Café Terrace at Night, F1519
Reed pen, 62 × 47 cm ($24\frac{3}{8} \times 18\frac{1}{2}$")
Collection Emery Reves, Roquebrune, France

1580 Café Terrace at Night, F467
81 × 65.5 cm ($31\frac{7}{8} \times 26$")
Rijksmuseum Kröller-Müller, Otterlo

1581 Self-Portrait, F476
62 × 52 cm ($24\frac{3}{8} \times 20\frac{1}{2}$")
Fogg Art Museum, Harvard University, Cambridge, Massachusetts

1582 A Lane in the Public Garden, F470
73 × 92 cm ($28\frac{3}{4} \times 36\frac{1}{4}$")
Rijksmuseum Kröller-Müller, Otterlo

1582

1583

1584

1585

1586

1587

1588

1583 Round Clipped Shrub in the Public Garden, F 1465
Sketch sent with Letter 541
Pen, 13.5 × 17 cm ($5\frac{1}{2} \times 6\frac{3}{4}$″)
Location unknown

1584 Round Clipped Shrub in the Public Garden
Sketch in Letter 553b
Rijksmuseum Vincent van Gogh, Amsterdam

1585 Man Reading a Newspaper in the Public Garden, F 566
72.5 × 91 cm ($28\frac{3}{4} \times 35\frac{7}{8}$″)
Phillips Collection, Washington, D.C.

1586 Plowed Field, F 574
72.5 × 92 cm ($28\frac{3}{4} \times 36\frac{1}{4}$″)
Rijksmuseum Vincent van Gogh, Amsterdam

1587 Plowed Field
Sketch in Letter 541*a*
Rijksmuseum Vincent van Gogh, Amsterdam

1588 Lieutenant Milliet, F 473
60 × 49 cm ($23\frac{5}{8} \times 19\frac{1}{4}$″)
Rijksmuseum Kröller-Müller, Otterlo

like a pair of clogs, it did not bother him, with the forget-me-not-blue sky and the fluffy white clouds" (Letter 541). A few days later he had completed it, and he sent Theo a small sketch (1587).

Scarcely a day or two later, in the same letter in which he sent Theo a small sketch of *The Starry Night*, he also sent him a small rough sketch of the painting he had made of the little yellow house, accompanied by the words: "In addition, [I am sending you] a small sketch of a size-30 canvas, square, that shows the house and its surroundings under a sulfur-yellow sun, under a sky of pure cobalt blue. This motif is really harsh! but precisely because of this I want to conquer it. For it is appalling, those yellow houses in the sun, and then the incomparable freshness of the blue. The ground is also entirely yellow. I will send you a better drawing of it than this small rough draft made from memory" (Letter 543; the "better drawing" was 1591; colorplate XXIX, page 365). It is this picture, 1589, with its simple realism like a "naïve" painting, which has perhaps contributed even more than Vincent's manifold references in his letters to make the little yellow house world famous.

In the meantime Vincent had been working hard on a large painting of a vineyard, 1595 (colorplate XXX, page 366; customarily called *The Green Vineyard* to distinguish it from the somewhat later *Red Vineyard*), and in a letter probably written just before the end of the month he announced: "Alas, my study of the vineyard, it has cost me blood and sweat, but [now] I have it, another size-30 canvas, square, and once again to decorate the wall of the house" (Letter 544). It has taken on the character of a grandiose painting in which, by contrast with the painting of the yellow house, great liberties have been taken with reality, so that, for example, the entire lower half seems more like a decorative, abstract color pattern than a portrayal of vines and tendrils.

A New Outburst of Creativity

At the beginning of October he was still occupied with several canvases he had started earlier, as is evident from his previously noted remark in his letter to Boch (Letter 553*b*, October 4): "I am working on seven size-30 canvases." The first new study we encounter is the small painting 1597, which is striking in its vivid yellow, orange, and light blue, with the large yellow disk of the sun in the picture and three freakish-looking pollard willows in the foreground. I surmise that this is the work Vincent meant when he wrote, October 7: "Yesterday I painted a sunset" (Letter 454). While it certainly cannot be numbered among Van Gogh's most important paintings, it does provide us with a good basis for realizing how far he had moved away from Impressionism.

Quite different in character is the small painting 1599, which was not inspired by nature but by some sketches and poems received from Emile Bernard under the title *Au Bordel* (*In the Brothel*). Vincent's comment on this is significant. Emphatically repeating that his *Night Café* was not a brothel but that a prostitute and her pimp just happened to be in it, he informed Bernard that he had now

1589

1590

1591

1589 Vincent's House, F464
76 × 94 cm (29⅞ × 37″)
Rijksmuseum Vincent van Gogh, Amsterdam

1590 Vincent's House, F1453
Sketch sent with Letter 543
Pen, 13 × 20.5 cm (5⅛ × 8¼″)
Collection N. Dreher, Brienz, Switzerland

1591 Vincent's House, F1413
Chalk, pen, brown ink, watercolor,
25.5 × 31.5 cm (10¼ × 12⅝″)
Rijksmuseum Vincent van Gogh, Amsterdam
Colorplate XXIX, opposite

Colorplate XXIX, Vincent's House, 1591

made a painting for him *from memory* showing a small group like one he had once noticed there.

Meantime, he had made still another small painting which he certainly would not regard as a major work: the portrait of his mother, based on a photograph (1600). "I cannot stand the photograph without any color and I am trying to make a portrait with harmonious colors, just the way I remember her" (Letter 546).

Vincent did not even mention these two small studies when, at the end of the week of October 6 to 13, he wrote: "There are five canvases that I have started on this week" (Letter 552). The first of the five large paintings, the public garden scene, 1598, had been announced in the middle of the week as follows: "I again have a size-30 canvas, 'Park in the Fall,' two cypresses, which are bottle green and bottle shaped, three small chestnut trees with tobacco- and orange-colored foliage. A small yew tree with pale lemon-yellow foliage and a violet trunk, two small bushes with blood-red and scarlet-purple foliage. A little sand, a bit of grass, a bit of blue sky" (Letter 551). This description makes clear how much it meant to Vincent to portray once again the symphony of colors created by fall.

The other four large canvases, 1601 and 1603–5, had been completed by Saturday, October 13, according to Letter 552. The mere description of them shows how incredibly rich and varied had been the harvest of that single week (see also sketches 1602 and 1607). To be sure, one painting, the charming picture of the diligence, may have been left in a somewhat sketchy state, and the one of the railroad bridge reveals perhaps obvious signs of haste. On the other hand, however, a painting like that of the Trinquetaille bridge represents, in my view, a high point in Vincent's *oeuvre* by reason of the color and the daring yet balanced composition, and a park scene like the one with the great blue spruce fir ranks with the best of "the poet's garden" series.

It is not surprising that after such exertion, Vincent had to write that he was exhausted and had to take a few days' rest; in any event a strong mistral was blowing (Letter 553). But on Tuesday, October 16, he was already back at work and was able to send Theo a small sketch of what was to become one of his best-known paintings, his *Bedroom*, 1608. "My eyes are still tired, but well, I had a new idea in my head and here is the sketch of it. Again a size-30 canvas. This time it is simply my bedroom; only now the color must do the job and, as its simplification imparts a greater style to things, must suggest rest or sleep in general."

Vincent's Bedroom, the Books, and the Park

Vincent's Bedroom, the symbol of the definitive, spiritual taking possession of the yellow house, now completely furnished, exists in three versions that we know. One of them, 1793, is smaller than the others (measuring $22\frac{1}{2}$ by $29\frac{1}{8}$ inches) and thus is not a "size-30 canvas." Consequently, it cannot be the original piece. As the two others, differing only in very minor details, are size-30 canvases, one of them must be the replica

1592

1593

1594

1595

1592 The Starry Night, F474
72.5 × 92 cm ($28\frac{3}{4}$ × $36\frac{1}{4}$")
Private collection

1593 The Starry Night, F1515
Sketch sent with Letter 543
Pen, dimensions unknown
Location unknown

1594 The Starry Night
Sketch in Letter 553*b*
Rijksmuseum Vincent van Gogh, Amsterdam

1595 The Green Vineyard, F475
72 × 92 cm ($28\frac{3}{8}$ × $36\frac{1}{4}$")
Rijksmuseum Kröller-Müller, Otterlo
Colorplate XXX, opposite

made in Saint-Rémy. Relying apparently on considerations of style, the editorial committee of the 1970 *catalogue raisonné* has concluded that 1608 is the original piece. In my opinion this is definitely confirmed by a detail in the picture itself. In Letter 553*b*, written October 4—only about ten days before the painting was made—Vincent informed his friend Boch: "Your portrait hangs in my bedroom, together with that of Milliet, the Zouave, which I have just completed." The painting on the extreme right above the bed in 1608 must indeed be what he referred to as the portrait of Milliet, for the bright red of the kepi can be made out against the green of the background just below the upper edge of the picture. In the later replica this painting has been replaced by the portrait of a woman. It is clear that the original painting depicted the situation as Vincent saw it when he painted the work in October 1888. When he made the replicas, including 1793, he took liberties with the subject in this particular regard. The other portrait shown in 1608 is less easily identified, but the blue of the background, the yellow of the jacket, and the trace of a little reddish beard make it reasonable to assume that Vincent was in this way alluding to the portrait of Boch (1574), which tallies with what he said in Letter 553*b*.

I have placed here, after the painting of the bedroom, the still life with piles of books (1612) that is a companion piece to *Piles of French Novels* (1332) painted in Paris.*

Another painting, not mentioned in the letters, which I assume was made at about this time is the park scene, 1613. It fits in with the series of studies that Vincent had devoted to "the poet's garden" across from his house in September and October, and the same is true of the hasty sketch 1614, one of the few drawings we know from the autumn of 1888. We learn that Vincent had gone back to working in the park again from the next report of a new canvas, 1615, which was accompanied by letter sketch 1616: "This is a rather vague little sketch of my latest canvas, a row of green cypresses against a pink sky with the crescent of the moon in light lemon-yellow. In the foreground some ground with sand and some thistles. A pair of lovers, the man pale blue with a yellow hat, the woman with a pink bodice and black dress. This is the fourth canvas of 'the poet's garden'—the wall decoration of Gauguin's room" (Letter 556, October 21 or 22).

1596

1597

1598

Gauguin's Arrival

Vincent learned October 7 that Theo had succeeded in selling some of Gauguin's ceramic art for 300 francs, and we know from a letter Gauguin wrote to Emile Schuffenecker, a close friend and fellow artist, that this had convinced him to leave for Arles at the end of the month. When Vincent heard that Gauguin would not be coming right away because he was ill and reluctant to travel, his reaction was typical—was the trip really so tiring, he asked Gauguin, would he not recover more quickly in Arles than in Brittany, and he added very emphatically in a postscript: "Come at once, unless you are too ill" (see Letter 549). And it goes on this way in subsequent letters until finally, in Letter 555, October 17, he reported to Theo: "Gauguin writes me that he has already shipped his trunk and he promises to come the twentieth of this month, that is, within a few days." For some reason or other it turned out to be the twenty-third, and October 24 Vincent was at last able to announce: "As you already know from my telegram, Gauguin arrived in good health. I even get the impression that he is in better shape than I am" (Letter 557).

*See Carl Nordenfalk, "Van Gogh and Sweden," *Konsthistorisk Tidskrift*, vol. XV, no. 3–4 (1946), pp. 89–96, and compare the treatment of the surface of the table in 1566 with that of 1612, which, in my opinion, was painted from memory. Vincent speaks of the picture of French novels in connection with the *Bedroom* in Letter 555.

1596 Sower, F575a
33 × 40 cm (13 × 15¾")
The Armand Hammer Collection, Los Angeles

October 1888

1597 Pollard Willows with Setting Sun, F572
Canvas on cardboard, 31.5 × 34.5 cm (12⅝ × 13¾")
Rijksmuseum Kröller-Müller, Otterlo

1598 A Lane in the Public Garden, F472
72 × 93 cm (28⅜ × 36⅝")
Private collection

1599 Visitors in the Night Café, F478
33 × 41 cm (13 × 16⅛")
©The Barnes Foundation Museum of Art, Merion, Pennsylvania

1599

1600

1601

1602

1604

1603

1600 Portrait of Van Gogh's Mother (after a photograph), F477
40.5 × 32.5 cm (16$\frac{1}{8}$ × 13″)
Norton Simon Foundation, Los Angeles

1601 Public Garden with a Couple and a Blue Fir Tree, F479
73 × 92 cm (28$\frac{3}{4}$ × 36$\frac{1}{4}$″)
Private collection

1602 Public Garden with a Couple and a Blue Fir Tree
Sketch in Letter 552
Rijksmuseum Vincent van Gogh, Amsterdam

1603 The Viaduct, F480
71 × 92 cm (28 × 36$\frac{1}{4}$″)
Kunsthaus, Zurich (on loan)

1604 The Trinquetaille Bridge, F481
73.5 × 92.5 cm (29$\frac{1}{8}$ × 36$\frac{5}{8}$″)
Private collection, New York

1605 The Tarascon Stagecoach, F478a
72 × 92 cm (28$\frac{3}{8}$ × 36$\frac{1}{4}$″)
Henry and Rose Pearlman Foundation, New York

1605

Exact dating of the paintings Vincent did in November and December 1888 is not possible because the few letters he wrote Theo in those months are themselves hard to date. For most of these works—which in any case number far fewer than during the preceding period—a more general classification will have to suffice. However, for the first landscapes made shortly after Gauguin's arrival (1617 and 1618) we have reliable information. Rough sketches of these (1619) appear in Vincent's letter to Theo, October 28, with the explanation: "This week I have made a new study of a sower, the landscape entirely flat, the figure small and indistinct. I also have a new study of a plowed field with the trunk of an old yew tree" (Letter 558*b*).

Calling this a "new" study of a sower, Vincent was undoubtedly thinking about his last painting of this subject, 1470, done in June. The new version is almost a replica of the earlier one (although the sower is now moving from right to left). With its refined tones, this piece, too, was certainly intended as a color study, but with the absence of striking elements—like the yellow disk of the sun that dominated the picture in 1470—it seems as though what Vincent especially wanted to express this time was simply the endless expanse of space in which the solitary sower, striding along resolutely, is almost lost ("the figure small and indistinct").

The painting of a tree trunk, 1618, with its lemon-yellow sky, can also be seen as primarily a color study. Yet the deciding factor in choosing this unusual subject may have subconsciously been the symbolism of the mighty old tree in the foreground, which, like the small figure of the sower—but in an entirely different way—dominates the wide area of space. In its composition this painting is a sort of prelude to the still much more unusual canvas that would shortly follow it: the sower and an old tree together, seen against a setting sun (1627).

Autumn Landscapes

The colors of autumn determine the character of the next group of landscapes, 1620–23. They are mentioned in early November in letters to both Bernard (Letter B19*a*, probably at the beginning of the month) and Theo (Letter 559, probably about November 11). Vincent wrote Bernard: "I myself have made two studies of falling leaves in an avenue of poplars, and a third study, all in yellow, of that avenue in its entirety." Despite its brevity, this information is important to us, because apart from the two studies of falling leaves—which must have referred to 1620 and 1621—mention is also made of a *third* painting of the same avenue of poplars. That "study, all in yellow," must be painting 1622, which, except for the green sky, matches this description. The fourth painting of the avenue with Roman tombs, called *The Alyscamps*, 1623—in which the yellow was not so predominant—probably did not yet exist when Letter B19*a* was written but must have been made shortly after the other three paintings.

The composition of paintings 1620 and 1621—in which the avenue of tombs is observed from a very high vantage point and from between the trees—is something entirely

1606

1607

1606 The Tarascon Stagecoach
Sketch in Letter 552
Rijksmuseum Vincent van Gogh, Amsterdam

1607 The Viaduct and the Trinquetaille Bridge
Sketches in Letter 552
Rijksmuseum Vincent van Gogh, Amsterdam

1608 Vincent's Bedroom, F482
72 × 90 cm ($28\frac{3}{8} \times 35\frac{3}{8}$")
Rijksmuseum Vincent van Gogh, Amsterdam

1609 Vincent's Bedroom
Sketch in Letter 554
Rijksmuseum Vincent van Gogh, Amsterdam

1610 Vincent's Bedroom
Sketch in Letter B22
Private collection, Paris

1611 Interior of a Restaurant, F1508v (reverse: not included)
Drawn over a sketch of motifs of painting 1608
Pencil, 26 × 43.5 cm ($10\frac{1}{4} \times 17\frac{3}{8}$")
Rijksmuseum Vincent van Gogh, Amsterdam

1612 Piles of French Novels, F358
53 × 72.5 cm ($20\frac{7}{8} \times 28\frac{3}{4}$")
Rijksmuseum Vincent van Gogh, Amsterdam

1608

1609

1610

1611

1612

1613

1614

1613 A Lane in the Public Garden with a Weeping Tree, F471
74 × 62 cm ($29\frac{1}{8} \times 24\frac{3}{8}''$)
Destroyed; formerly collection Eduard Arnhold, Berlin

1614 A Lane in the Public Garden with Three Benches, F1498v (reverse: 1457)
Blue chalk, pen, blue ink, 25.5 × 34.5 cm
($10\frac{1}{4} \times 13\frac{3}{4}''$)
Rijksmuseum Vincent van Gogh, Amsterdam

new in Vincent's *oeuvre*. The first thought that comes to mind is that it was due to some outside influence—for example, that of Gauguin, with whom he had been working for several weeks. However, Gauguin's own portrayals of the Alyscamps, made about the same time, are even more conventional in composition and more closely resemble Vincent's two other paintings of this subject, 1622 and 1623.

Another landscape with typical fall colors is the painting of a vineyard with setting sun—*The Red Vineyard* (1626). This can also be dated fairly accurately because its completion is mentioned in Letter 561, written November 12 at the latest. More important, though, is what Vincent wrote in the preceding letter (Letter 559), in which he not only reported that "at the moment I am working on a completely red and yellow vineyard," but also gave an indirect description of the painting: "But if you had been with us Sunday, when we saw a red vineyard, completely red like red wine. In the distance it tapered off into yellow, and there was also a green sky with the disk of the sun, and the fields, after the rain, violet and here and there glittering yellow, where the setting sun was reflected."

This tallies so exactly with the painted study that Vincent, after seeing this sunset, must have lost no time in putting the scene on canvas from memory. As the Sunday in question was probably November 4, the vineyard must have been painted very soon after that date. The warm colors, the majestic feeling of space, the untrammeled brushwork, and the artist's skill in suggesting bustle and liveliness in the numerous small figures observed in a wide variety of attitudes—all these combine to make this a fascinating canvas. It has achieved the somewhat cheerless renown of being supposedly the only painting of Vincent's that found a buyer during his lifetime.

Madame Ginoux as a Model

An important painting of an entirely different kind must have been made at almost the same time: the famous portrait of Madame Ginoux, the wife of the proprietor of a café who belonged to Vincent's circle of friends in Arles (1624). As appears from the same letter in which Vincent wrote about his studies of the Alyscamps and about the red vineyard, this portrait was made in an incredibly short time: "Next, I finally have a woman from Arles, a figure (size-30 canvas) that I slapped on in one hour ["sabrée dans une heure"], background of light lemon-yellow, the face gray, the clothes black, black, black, unmixed prussian blue. She is resting an elbow on a green table and is sitting in an orange-colored wooden armchair" (Letter 559). Despite the speed at which it was executed (Letter 573 refers to it as "a portrait painted in three-quarters of an hour"), it turned out to be a masterly portrait, striking in the clear characterization of the thoughtful face, as well as in the pronounced silhouette effect of the bluish-black figure against the sharply contrasting yellow of the flat background.

There are two versions of this portrait: the one with the sophisticated still life consisting of a closed vermilion-red book and an open yellow and gray book (1624), and the version with a pair of yellowish-green gloves and a red parasol instead of the books (1625). Both are almost identical so far as the portrait itself is concerned, and the color scheme is about the same. As often happened, Van Gogh did not mention a second version in his letters. The one with the gloves comes from the estate of Mrs. van Gogh-Bonger and is thus presumably the painting that was sent to Theo; the other version must have been done for Madame Ginoux herself.

The influence of the Japanese woodcuts with their flat colors in these portraits has

1615

1616

1617

1615 A Lane of Cypresses with a Couple Walking, F485
75 × 92 cm ($29\frac{1}{2} \times 36\frac{1}{4}$")
Location unknown

1616 A Lane of Cypresses with a Couple Walking
Sketch in Letter 556
Rijksmuseum Vincent van Gogh, Amsterdam

1617 Sower in the Crau, with the Ruins of Montmajour, F494
72 × 91 cm ($28\frac{3}{8} \times 35\frac{7}{8}$")
Collection Mrs. L. Jäggli-Hahnloser, Winterthur, Switzerland

1618

1619

1620

1621

1622

1623

1618 Trunk of an Old Yew Tree, F573
91 × 71 cm ($35\frac{7}{8} \times 28''$)
Collection Mr. and Mrs. Paul Mellon, Upperville, Virginia

1619 Sower and Trunk of an Old Yew Tree
Sketches in Letter 558*b*
Rijksmuseum Vincent van Gogh, Amsterdam

November 1888

1620 The Alyscamps, Avenue at Arles, F486
73 × 92 cm ($28\frac{3}{4} \times 36\frac{1}{4}''$)
Rijksmuseum Kröller-Müller, Otterlo

1621 The Alyscamps, Avenue at Arles, F487
72 × 91 cm ($28\frac{3}{8} \times 35\frac{7}{8}''$)
Stavros S. Niarchos Collection

1622 The Alyscamps, Avenue at Arles, F568
89 × 72 cm ($35 \times 28\frac{3}{8}''$)
Collection Mr. and Mrs. Basil P. Goulandris, Lausanne

1623 The Alyscamps, Avenue at Arles, F569
92 × 73.5 cm ($36\frac{1}{4} \times 29\frac{1}{8}''$)
Collection Mrs. A. Mettler-Weber, Zollikon, Switzerland

been pointed out by Meyer Schapiro.* In any event, in my opinion, Japanese influence must have been responsible in large part for the extraordinary and surprising composition of the painting with the sower against a setting sun, 1627. The dark silhouette of the tree running diagonally across the picture reminds us of the Hiroshige print with the slanting plum tree that Vincent had copied in Paris a year earlier (1296). The dating of this new sower does not present any difficulties. Vincent made a sketch of it in Letter 558*a*, about November 21, and described it in the following brief and objective terms: "This is a sketch of the latest canvas I have been working on, another sower. An immense lemon-yellow disk of the sun. A greenish-yellow sky with pink clouds. The field violet, sower and tree prussian blue. A size-30 canvas." (The sketch is 1628.) He must have been pleased with this study, for he made a small replica of it (1629), and about the middle of December —probably in reaction to a remark by Theo upon receiving the sketch—he wrote: "From time to time a canvas that really is a painting, like the sower in question, which I myself also consider better than the first one" ("the first one" was thus *Sower*, 1617, a sketch of which had been included in Letter 558*b*, written in October).

"A Memory"

As a composition, the painting of three women in a garden, 1630, is even more unusual. Writing to Theo, Vincent called it "a memory of our garden at Etten" (Letter 562, about December 2), and in a simultaneous letter to Wil he supplied a detailed and important description of it: "I have already replied that I am not too keen on Mother's portrait. Now, with the intention of hanging it in my bedroom, I have painted a *Memory of the Garden at Etten*, and here is a small sketch of it" (Letter W9; the sketch is 1631). To us the most important part of his account are the lines about the relation of the picture to reality: "Well, I know that there is perhaps no real likeness at all, but for me the painting reflects the poetic character and style of the garden as I feel it. And so, assuming that those women walking there are you and Mother, assuming that there is no, absolutely no ordinary, meaningless resemblance—Mother's personality is for me suggested by the conscious choice of the color, the somber violet with the sharply contrasting lemon-yellow spots of the dahlias."

It is surprising to read in a somewhat later letter to Theo that Vincent did not consider the painting a "success"; he felt "that work made from the imagination also demands experience" (Letter 560). From our point of view there is little reason to regard the work as inferior. However curious its composition, it is an extremely fascinating, somewhat enigmatic canvas, incredibly rich in subdued but yet sparkling colors, reminiscent of medieval stained-glass windows. It is strange that in this letter Vincent speaks of "that thing I made of the garden in *Nuenen*." We have to assume that this was a slip of the pen, but it confirms how little he had intended this painting to depict a clearly defined actual situation. As a "model" for the painting, he may have relied on Madame Ginoux herself or—what is more likely—the portrait of her he had in his studio, insofar as a model was needed.

Life with Gauguin

The radical changes that now became apparent in Vincent's work have often been attributed to the influence of Gauguin, with whom he had been living and working for a month. Therefore, it is appropriate to examine more closely the relationship between the two artists that was to have such far-

*Schapiro, *Vincent van Gogh* (1950), p. 88.

1624

1625

1626

1624 The Arlésienne (Madame Ginoux), with Books, F488
90 × 72 cm ($35\frac{3}{8} \times 28\frac{3}{8}$″)
Metropolitan Museum of Art, New York

1625 The Arlésienne (Madame Ginoux), with Gloves and Parasol, F489
93 × 74 cm ($36\frac{5}{8} \times 29\frac{1}{8}$″)
The Louvre, Paris

1626 The Red Vineyard, F495
75 × 93 cm ($29\frac{1}{2} \times 36\frac{5}{8}$″)
Pushkin Museum, Moscow

1627 Sower with Setting Sun, F450
Burlap on canvas, 73.5 × 93 cm ($29\frac{1}{8} \times 36\frac{5}{8}$″)
Collection E. G. Bührle, Zurich

1627

1628

1629

1630

1631

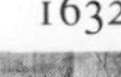

1632

1633

1628 Sower with Setting Sun
Sketch in Letter 558*a*
Rijksmuseum Vincent van Gogh, Amsterdam

1629 Sower with Setting Sun, F451
32 × 40 cm ($12\frac{5}{8} \times 15\frac{3}{4}$″)
Rijksmuseum Vincent van Gogh, Amsterdam

December 1888

1630 Memory of the Garden at Etten, F496
73.5 × 92.5 cm ($29\frac{1}{8} \times 36\frac{5}{8}$″)
The Hermitage, Leningrad

1631 Memory of the Garden at Etten
Sketch in Letter W9
Rijksmuseum Vincent van Gogh, Amsterdam

1632 Woman Reading Novel, F497
73 × 92 cm ($28\frac{3}{4} \times 36\frac{1}{4}$″)
Collection Mr. and Mrs. Louis Franck, Gstaad, Switzerland

1633 Woman Reading Novel
Sketch in Letter W9
Rijksmuseum Vincent van Gogh, Amsterdam

reaching significance for Vincent's life from then on.

From Vincent's letters we get a picture of Gauguin immediately assuming the role of dominating figure toward the admirer who had so urgently insisted on his coming; he showed off his greater experience of life and tried to influence the younger colleague with his new views on art. In these circumstances the relationship between the two men seems to have gone quite smoothly over a period of many weeks, as appears from Vincent's short reports to Theo, Bernard, and Wil. At the beginning of December that was still the way things were: "He is a really great artist and a most excellent friend" (Letter 562).

After this, it is interesting but disturbing to read what Gauguin had to say in his *Avant et Après*:

"At the time I arrived in Arles, Vincent was full of Neo-Impressionism and was in serious trouble [il pataugeait considérablement], which made him very sad; not that this school, like all other schools, was bad, but it simply did not suit his impatient and independent nature. With all his yellow on violet, all his painting with complementary colors, which he did in an unsystematic way, he got no further than incomplete, soft, monotonous harmonies; the clarion call was lacking. I undertook the task of showing him the way, which proved easy, for I found rich and fertile soil. Like all original natures that show the stamp of personality, Vincent knew no fear and no obstinacy. From that day onward Vincent made surprising progress; he appeared to discover what lay within him, hence that whole series of sunflowers after sunflowers in full sunshine."*

The truth of the matter—which scarcely needs any further corroboration here—was that Vincent was at his prime as an artist when Gauguin joined him; that under Gauguin's influence he did make a few "imaginative" paintings but regarded them as a sideline and soon turned away from them to devote all his energy to the painting of portraits; and that the Synthetic style—a merging of Neo-Impressionist theories with Japanese design concepts and Symbolist precepts which Gauguin, together with Bernard, had developed in 1888 in Pont-Aven—is scarcely traceable in the work that Vincent did after Gauguin's departure.†

Portraits continued to occupy Vincent during this period. *Woman Reading Novel*, 1632 (see Letter W9), was made at the beginning of December. Although this time the letters do not provide any definite answer to the dating, I would also place early in December the very characteristic self-portrait, 1634, in yellow suit on a greenish background, which was inscribed to Charles Laval ("à l'ami Laval"). Laval was a painter who had worked with Gauguin and Bernard in Pont-Aven in the summer of 1888. Vincent did not know him personally, but in September, when Bernard had proposed an exchange of paintings on behalf of Laval and a few others, Vincent enthusiastically agreed, adding that he would be happy to have their self-portraits (Letter B19, about October 7). It appears that Laval's self-portrait arrived in Arles at the beginning of December. It was "extraordinarily good," Vincent declared in Letter 562, adding a sketch of it. It seems reasonable to assume that he then started working right away on his own self-portrait for Laval.

*This remark refers to paintings that Vincent had done two months before Gauguin's arrival! *Avant et Après* consists of reminiscences recorded fifteen years later and published in 1918.

†A more detailed treatment of the relationship between Vincent and Gauguin is to be found in the able studies done by John Rewald, *Post-Impressionism* (1978), and Mark Roskill, *Van Gogh, Gauguin and the Impressionist Circle* (1970).

1634

1635

1636

1634 Self-Portrait, F501
46 × 38 cm (18⅛ × 15″)
Metropolitan Museum of Art, New York

1635 Vincent's Chair, F498
93 × 73.5 cm (36⅝ × 29⅛″)
Tate Gallery, London (on loan from the National Gallery)

1636 Gauguin's Chair, F499
90.5 × 72 cm (35⅞ × 28⅜″)
Rijksmuseum Vincent van Gogh, Amsterdam

1637 Augustine Roulin with Baby, F490
92 × 73.5 cm (36¼ × 29⅛″)
Philadelphia Museum of Art

1637

1638

1639

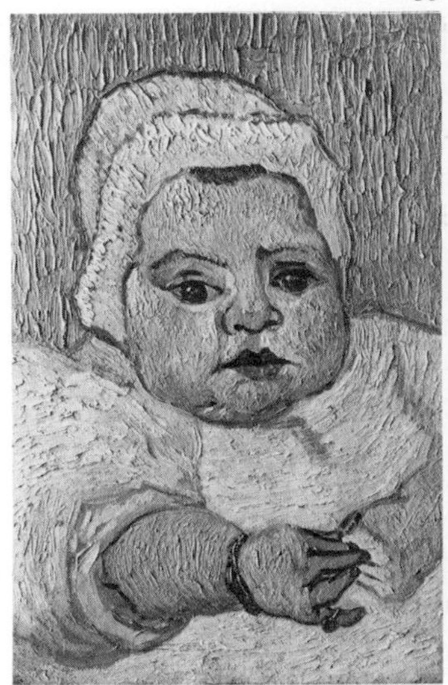

1640

1641

1642

1643

1638 Augustine Roulin with Baby, F491
63.5 × 51 cm ($25\frac{1}{4} \times 20\frac{1}{8}$″)
Metropolitan Museum of Art, New York, Robert Lehman Collection

1639 The Baby Marcelle Roulin, F440
35 × 24 cm ($13\frac{3}{4} \times 9\frac{1}{2}$″)
National Gallery of Art, Washington, D.C.

1640 The Baby Marcelle Roulin, F441a
36 × 25 cm ($14\frac{1}{8} \times 9\frac{7}{8}$″)
Collection Mr. and Mrs. Louis Franck, Gstaad, Switzerland

1641 The Baby Marcelle Roulin, F441
35.5 × 24.5 cm ($14\frac{1}{8} \times 9\frac{7}{8}$″)
Rijksmuseum Vincent van Gogh, Amsterdam

1642 Portrait of Armand Roulin, F492
66 × 55 cm ($26 \times 21\frac{5}{8}$″)
Museum Folkwang, Essen

1643 Portrait of Armand Roulin, F493
65 × 54 cm ($25\frac{5}{8} \times 21\frac{1}{4}$″)
Museum Boymans-van Beuningen, Rotterdam

The Two Chairs

"Quite amusing" was how Vincent modestly described the two studies—the chairs, 1635 and 1636—which he announced in Letter 563, December 2 to 6, little realizing how much cause for discussion he was providing with these two paintings. There are few paintings of Vincent's about which so much was written in later years. Scholars—such as H. R. Graetz (*The Symbolic Language of Vincent van Gogh*, 1963), Humberto Nagera (*Vincent van Gogh*, 1967), and Albert J. Lubin (*Stranger on the Earth*, 1972)—have devoted entire chapters to them in their psychoanalytical studies. And little wonder that this is so, for paintings that have as their subject nothing but a chair with a few small objects on it can hardly escape being called strange. When one learns that Vincent himself called the reddish-brown curved one "Gauguin's chair" and the other one his own chair, it becomes obvious that there is more behind this than the realistic rendering of a piece of furniture. For that matter, he also more or less invited psychological interpretations by what he wrote well over a year later to the art critic G.-Albert Aurier: "A few days before we parted, when my illness forced me to go to an asylum, I tried to paint 'his empty place.' It is a study of his chair, which is dark brownish red, with a greenish cane seat, and in the absent one's place a candlestick with a burning candle and modern novels" (Letter 626*a*). But if a relationship is to be established between the painting of Gauguin's chair and the conscious or unconscious apprehension about his departure, this still does not explain why Vincent, for whom the departure motive was in any case irrelevant, painted a canvas with his *own* empty chair, at the same time, as a companion piece (see Appendix, note 7).

In any case, it is clear that he wanted to express in the two paintings something of the differences between their two personalities: the simple, rough wooden chair was his, as befitted his nature; the elegantly curved chair was naturally that of the admired guest, for whom he had wanted to furnish the best room, dainty as "a woman's boudoir" (Letter 534). And an artistic motif that cannot be ignored, regardless of what psychological interpretation may be given to the paintings, is the contrast that Vincent himself clearly expressed when he wrote: "[one is] a completely yellow chair of wood and cane on red flagstones against a wall (*daytime*). Then Gauguin's chair, red and green, a *nighttime* effect, the wall and the floor also red and green; on the seat two novels and a candle" (Letter 563).

Portraits and Groups

It appears from Letter 560, written about the middle of December, that Vincent had, before then, painted a whole series of portraits in rapid succession. In the preceding letter (Letter 563, written December 2 to 6) there is no mention of this at all. Vincent, who had had enough of working "from the imagination," now wrote: "I have made portraits of *an entire family*, that of the postman whose head I did previously—the husband, the wife, the baby, the younger son, and the sixteen-year-old son; all with a personality and truly French, although they look like Russians. Size-15 canvas. You can imagine how much I am in my element."

If he had made only one portrait of each of these people, that would have totaled five, but we know of more than one for some of them. A few out of the entire series of these portraits, 1637–47, may have been made in the days after Letter 560 had been written. That is very likely, since Vincent himself wrote: "I hope to go on with this and have them pose better ["d'arriver à des poses plus sérieuses"], to be paid for with portraits. And if I succeed in painting that whole family still better, I will at least have a work that is personal and to my liking" (Letter 560). It is, of

1644

1645

1646

1644 Portrait of Camille Roulin, F537
43 × 35 cm (16⅞ × 13¾″)
Philadelphia Museum of Art

1645 Portrait of Camille Roulin, F538
37.5 × 32.5 cm (15 × 13″)
Rijksmuseum Vincent van Gogh, Amsterdam

1646 Portrait of Augustine Roulin, F503
55 × 65 cm (21⅝ × 25⅝″)
Collection Oskar Reinhart, Winterthur, Switzerland

1647 Joseph Roulin, Head, F434
65 × 54 cm (25⅝ × 21¼″)
Kunstmuseum, Winterthur, Switzerland

1648 Boy with Cap, F536
47.5 × 39 cm (18⅞ × 15⅜″)
Private collection, Zurich

1647

1648

1649

1650

1652

1651

1653

1649 Portrait of a Man, F533
65 × 54.5 cm (25⅝ × 21⅝″)
Rijksmuseum Kröller-Müller, Otterlo

1650 Portrait of a One-Eyed Man, F532
56 × 36 cm (22 × 14⅛″)
Rijksmuseum Vincent van Gogh, Amsterdam

1651 Portrait of a Peasant with Pipe, F534
62 × 47 cm (24⅜ × 18½″)
© The Barnes Foundation Museum of Art, Merion, Pennsylvania

1652 The Dance Hall, F547
65 × 81 cm (25⅝ × 31⅞″)
The Louvre, Paris

1653 Spectators in the Arena, F548
73 × 92 cm (28¾ × 36¼″)
The Hermitage, Leningrad

1654

1655

1656

course, impossible to determine in what sequence the portraits were made. Where there are two (or even three) almost identical versions, such as of Madame Augustine Roulin, the baby, or the boy Camille Roulin (1644 and 1645), one of them probably served as "payment," whereas the two completely different portraits of Armand Roulin, the sixteen-year-old son (1642 and 1643), were presumably made at different times.

In view of Vincent's great activity in portrait painting during the second half of December, I have also assigned to this period the four excellent portraits of unknown sitters, 1648–51. No clues to the dating are to be found in the letters.

Exact dating is also impossible in the case of the two other paintings—*The Dance Hall*, 1652, and *Spectators in the Arena*, 1653. Since works with such large groups of people are the exception in Van Gogh's *oeuvre*, the thought of outside influences, here too, naturally comes to mind. One such influence must almost certainly have been Bernard, whose painting of Breton women was constantly before Vincent's eyes since Gauguin had brought it with him. In his very first letter after Gauguin's arrival in Arles, Vincent had written about it enthusiastically: "Gauguin brought a magnificent painting with him that he had obtained in an exchange with Bernard, Breton women in a green meadow—white, black, green and a red note, and the flat flesh tints" (Letter 557). Vincent even made a copy of the admired painting in watercolor, 1654—sometime in November or December. The composition of 1652 and 1653 bears a strong resemblance to this work of Bernard's; there is the same swarming of numerous figures spread out over the entire picture plane, some with their backs toward the spectator, the same decorative use of motifs in the national dress, and particularly, the same characteristic placing of large, arbitrarily truncated figures in the foreground.

Finally, the famous canvas 1655. I shall discuss this at greater length in conjunction with the replicas made in January, but we know from Letter 574, January 28, 1889, as well as from other sources, that Vincent had started this new portrait of Madame Roulin, which he called *La Berceuse*, when he was interrupted by his illness, as he put it in his mild-mannered way.

Conflict with Gauguin

In discussing the background of the conflict with Gauguin, which was the cause of the "interruption," I shall be as brief as possible. So much has already been written about the pathological aspects of Van Gogh's illness in the more or less romanticized biographies and the more or less scientific studies that it will suffice here to mention a few of the main points.

It is only in the last two letters of Vincent's we know from 1888 that there are signs of tension. In Letter 564, written after he and Gauguin had paid a visit to the museum in nearby Montpellier, he told Theo: "Gauguin and I talk a lot about Delacroix, Rembrandt, etc. The discussion is highly charged; we sometimes stop with a brain exhausted like an electric battery that has run out." And finally Letter 565: "I believe that Gauguin was a bit disappointed in the good city of Arles, in the little yellow house where we work and particularly in me. . . . All in all I believe that he will either definitely leave or definitely stay. I have told him to think it over carefully and to weigh one thing against the other again before acting. Gauguin is very strong, very creative, but for that very reason he needs quiet. Will he find that somewhere else if he does not find it here?" This was probably written December 23, to judge from what is said in Letter 571.

The evening of that same day there occurred suddenly and completely unexpectedly the dramatic event that brought an end to their work together and to Gauguin's stay in

1654 Breton Women and Children (after Emile Bernard), F 1422
Watercolor, 47.5 × 62 cm ($18\frac{7}{8} \times 24\frac{3}{8}$″)
Civica Galleria d'Arte Moderna, Milan

1655 Augustine Roulin (La Berceuse), F 504
92 × 73 cm ($36\frac{1}{4} \times 28\frac{3}{4}$″)
Rijksmuseum Kröller-Müller, Otterlo

January 1889

1656 Plate with Onions, *Annuaire de la Santé*, and Other Objects, F 604
50 × 64 cm ($19\frac{5}{8} \times 25\frac{1}{4}$″)
Rijksmuseum Kröller-Müller, Otterlo

1657 Self-Portrait with Bandaged Ear, F 527
60 × 49 cm ($23\frac{5}{8} \times 19\frac{1}{4}$″)
Courtauld Institute Galleries, London

1657

1658

1659

1660

1662

1661

1663

1658 Self-Portrait with Bandaged Ear and Pipe, F529
51×45 cm ($20\frac{1}{8} \times 17\frac{3}{4}''$)
Private collection
Colorplate XXXI, p. 383

1659 Doctor Félix Rey, Bust, F500
64×53 cm ($25\frac{1}{4} \times 20\frac{7}{8}''$)
Pushkin Museum, Moscow

1660 Table with Two Red Herrings, F283a
33×47 cm ($13 \times 18\frac{1}{2}''$)
Collection Francis Junker, France

1661 Plate with Two Red Herrings, F510
33×41 cm ($13 \times 16\frac{1}{8}''$)
Collection Mrs. G. Signac, Paris

1662 Two Crabs, F606
47×61 cm ($18\frac{1}{2} \times 24''$)
Location unknown

1663 A Crab Upside Down, F605
38×45.5 cm ($15 \times 18\frac{1}{8}''$)
Rijksmuseum Vincent van Gogh, Amsterdam

Arles. What happened can best be told by quoting the tersely worded item that appeared a week later, December 30, in a local Sunday paper, *Le Forum Républicain*: "Last Sunday night at half past eleven a painter named Vincent Vangogh, a native of Holland, appeared at the *maison de tolérance* No. 1, asked for a girl called Rachel, and handed her . . . his ear with these words: 'Keep this object like a treasure.' Then he disappeared. The police, informed of these events, which could only be the work of an unfortunate madman, looked the next morning for this individual, whom they found in bed with scarcely a sign of life.

"The poor man was taken to the hospital without delay."

We know that Vincent was no "unfortunate madman"—the letter he wrote earlier in the day is sufficient proof of that. On the other hand, the wound he had inflicted upon himself by cutting off part of his left ear was undeniably the expression of a latent mental illness that was to manifest itself repeatedly during the next year and a half in the form of periods of extreme depression and even complete apathy.

The events of the following days can be recounted in a few words. Although Joseph Roulin, who visited Vincent in the hospital every day, initially viewed the situation as critical, there was an improvement within a remarkably short time. As early as December 31, the Reverend Frédéric Salles, who had taken Vincent's case to heart, was able to write Theo that, upon visiting Vincent, he had found him calm, "in a state revealing nothing abnormal." And January 2, in the office of Dr. Félix Rey, the attending physician, Vincent himself was able to write Theo a reassuring note. Roulin wrote January 4 that he had been in the yellow house with Vincent, and Vincent on that occasion sent penciled notes to Theo and Gauguin. In the note to Theo he expressed regret that Theo had made the journey to Arles for his sake, especially at that inclement time of year, for "after all, nothing serious has happened to me."

1889

The amazing speed of Vincent's recovery from the effects of his serious wound and the psychic shock was matched by the amazing speed of the recovery in his productivity and his ability to attain once again the high level he had achieved before his illness. Even in his first letter after being discharged from the hospital, he wrote: "I am thinking of making Dr. Rey's portrait and possibly other portraits as soon as I get a bit used to painting again" (Letter 568, January 7), and in a second letter, written the same day: "I am going back to working again tomorrow; I shall start by making one or two still lifes in order to get back into the habit of painting" (Letter 569).

He was able to carry out these intentions, for on January 17 he wrote: "Despite all that [namely, a lack of money and proper food] I am back working again and have already made three studies in the studio, plus Dr. Rey's portrait which I have given him as a memento" (Letter 571). Four studies in these first nine days, including the masterly portrait

1664

1665

1666

1664 Blue Gloves and a Basket with Oranges and Lemons, F502
48×62 cm ($18\frac{7}{8} \times 24\frac{3}{8}$″)
Collection Mr. and Mrs. Paul Mellon, Upperville, Virginia

1665 Self-Portrait with Clean-Shaven Face, F525
40×31 cm ($15\frac{3}{4} \times 12\frac{1}{4}$″)
Collection J. Körfer, Bollingen, Switzerland

1666 Vase with Fourteen Sunflowers, F457
100×76 cm ($39\frac{3}{8} \times 29\frac{7}{8}$″)
Collection Edith Beatty, London

Colorplate XXXI, Self-Portrait with Bandaged Ear and Pipe, 1658 〉

of Dr. Rey (1659)—well may we say that Vincent succeeded in getting used to painting again.

What were the other new studies he had in the studio on January 17? One of them—one of the still lifes he intended to start making—must have been the painting with the table (a drawing table?) on which there are a dish with onions, a candlestick, and various other objects, 1656. Several writers (including Nordenfalk in his biography) have pointed out the appropriateness of the subject; the book shown is a volume of the health yearbook *Annuaire de la Santé*, by F.V. Raspail, whose modern views on medicine—a kind of nature therapy—were fully subscribed to by Vincent.

We also know of two self-portraits with bandaged ear, 1657 and 1658, which must have been made shortly after he was discharged from the hospital and still had to wear the bandage. In Letter 570, January 9, he reported: "This morning I had the dressing changed at the hospital" and "the wound is healing very nicely." I therefore assume that the two self-portraits were made during the short period between January 8 and 17, when he had finished four studies. And of the four studies, more than one is a masterpiece: these two bold self-portraits are among Van Gogh's most widely discussed and most widely reproduced paintings. No more need be said here than that his controlled handling of his medium corresponds with the resigned composure evident in these self-portraits, especially the one in which he is calmly smoking his beloved pipe.

Another Collapse

Although Vincent seemed to have made a rapid recovery physically, after a month he suffered another mental breakdown; there can be no question that in January he had forced the pace too much in going back to work. On February 7 he was apparently committed to a special cell in the hospital by order of the superintendent of police.

After February 17 he was home for a few days, but by February 26 the Reverend Mr. Salles was compelled to write Theo: "Your poor brother has once more been confined to the hospital." And further: "A petition, signed by some thirty neighbors, brings to the attention of the mayor the objections against allowing this man to be at large and cites facts to support this opinion. The superintendent of police, to whom this document was delivered, had your brother taken immediately to the hospital, with express instructions not to let him leave." Although Vincent remained in the hospital, he was able to return to his work again a few weeks later. In Letter 583 (beginning of April) for the first time he again wrote triumphantly: "I am working." What he had on the easel was a festive painting: blossoming peach trees with the peaks of the Alpilles in the background.

In addition to the four studies Vincent spoke of on January 17 there is another still life, mentioned in a letter written after a short visit by Signac: "As a memento I gave him a painting that had annoyed the good gendarmes of Arles because it showed two herrings, which, as you know, are called 'gendarmes' " (Letter 581). The piece referred to here is 1661, which was part of Signac's es-

1667

1668

1669

1667 Vase with Fourteen Sunflowers, F458
95 × 73cm ($37\frac{3}{8} \times 28\frac{3}{4}$″)
Rijksmuseum Vincent van Gogh, Amsterdam

1668 Vase with Twelve Sunflowers, F455
92 × 72.5cm ($36\frac{1}{4} \times 28\frac{3}{4}$″)
Philadelphia Museum of Art

1669 Augustine Roulin (La Berceuse), F505
93 × 74cm ($36\frac{5}{8} \times 29\frac{1}{8}$″)
Collection Walter Annenberg, Rancho Mirage, California

〈 Colorplate XXXII, Orchard in Bloom with Poplars in the Foreground, 1685

tate. I assume that still life 1660—which, although a more tranquil composition, was painted with the same boldly hatched brushstrokes—was done at about the same time. The dating of still life 1664 is much more certain since immediately after its completion, it was mentioned in Letter 573, January 23: "I have just finished a new canvas which has what you might almost call chic, a rush basket with lemons and oranges—a sprig of cypress green and a pair of blue gloves; you have already seen others of those baskets of fruit of mine."

The still lifes of crabs, 1662 and 1663, done from exactly the same vantage point as 1661, are generally assumed to date from this period, too, although they are not mentioned in the letters.

The still lifes of this period also include the vases with sunflowers, 1666, 1667, and 1668, which are replicas of the canvases made in August. Also in Letter 573, January 23, in which he mentioned the still life with oranges and lemons, Vincent said that he was going to do one of the paintings with sunflowers over again because Gauguin wanted one, and in the next letter he referred to *both*.

Still another work—also a replica—dating from these months was mentioned by Vincent in Letter 574, where he made this important statement: "I believe I already told you that, in addition, I have a canvas of a *berceuse*, which I happened to be working on when I was interrupted by my illness. At the moment I have two versions of that canvas as well." This work is 1655.

Although Vincent called this portrait of Augustine Roulin too harsh, it turned out to be an imposing figure piece, and he spent a long time working on it, not only for the sake of its artistic qualities but undoubtedly also because of what Roulin and his wife meant to him (see Appendix, note 8). There are no fewer than five virtually identical versions of this work, 1655 and 1669–72. The flowered background in 1655 is clearly different from the other backgrounds. Not only do the pink and white flowers look more like real flowers (even though what is depicted is wallpaper, whether real or imaginary), but careful inspection shows that the entire pattern was differently constructed. In the four other versions, the background flowers and design are all similar, apparently having been copied from one canvas to the other with painstaking attention to detail.

January 30—after relating that Roulin had paid him a visit and he had shown him the two copies of his wife's portrait—Vincent wrote: "Today I have started on a third *berceuse*" (Letter 575). Since he was able to write by February 3 that he had let Madame Roulin select one of the three copies on hand, we can assume that the third copy was also made in January 1889 and had been completed no later than February 1 or 2. The fourth copy, which on February 3 was "in the works," was not completed right away. February 7, as we have seen, Vincent was taken to the hospital for the second time, and a few weeks later, when he had been able to resume work for a few days, this fourth *berceuse* was apparently what he was working on. Madame Roulin, he wrote, "had a good eye and took the best; however, I am doing that over at the moment

1670

1671

1672

1673

1670 Augustine Roulin (La Berceuse), F506
93 × 73cm (36⅝ × 28¾″)
Art Institute of Chicago

February 1889

1671 Augustine Roulin (La Berceuse), F508
92 × 72cm (36¼ × 28⅜″)
Museum of Fine Arts, Boston

March 1889

1672 Augustine Roulin (La Berceuse), F507
91 × 71.5cm (35⅞ × 28⅜″)
Stedelijk Museum, Amsterdam

April 1889

1673 Joseph Roulin, Bust, F439
65 × 54cm (25⅝ × 21¼″)
Rijksmuseum Kröller-Müller, Otterlo

1674 Joseph Roulin, Bust, F435
67.5 × 56cm (26¾ × 22″)
©The Barnes Foundation Museum of Art, Merion, Pennsylvania

1675 Joseph Roulin, Bust, F436
64 × 54.5cm (25¼ × 21⅝″)
Private collection, Ascona/Zurich

1676 Corner of a Garden with Flowers and Butterflies, F460
51 × 61cm (20⅛ × 24″)
Private collection, Paris

1677 Corner of a Garden with Flowers and Butterflies, F402
54 × 46cm (21¼ × 18⅛″)
Rijksmuseum Vincent van Gogh, Amsterdam

1678 Clumps of Grass, F582
44.5 × 49cm (17¾ × 19¼″)
Location unknown

1679 Flowering Rosebushes, F580
33 × 42cm (13 × 16½″)
National Museum of Western Art, Tokyo

1680 A Field of Yellow Flowers, F584
Canvas on cardboard, 34.5 × 53cm (13¾ × 20⅞″)
Location unknown

1674

1675

1676

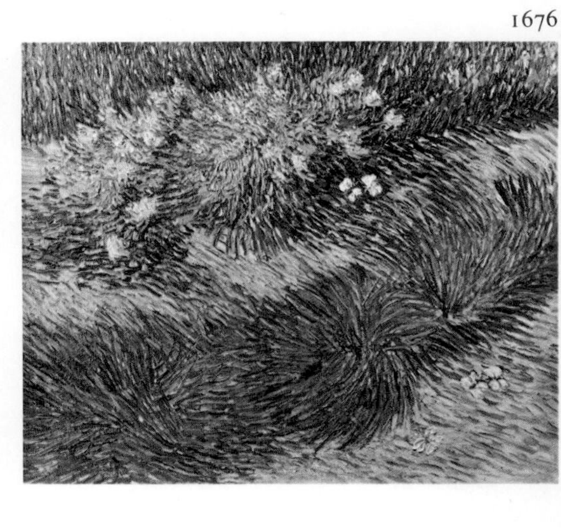

1677

1678

1679

1680

and do not want that [replica] to be inferior" (Letter 578). Several weeks later Vincent made still another copy. It was March 29 when he wrote: "And now I am doing my figure piece of the *berceuse* again for the fifth time" (Letter 582).

Self-portrait 1665 also dates from this period. Despite its small size, it is an impressive portrait in which Vincent looks at us intently, as in so many of the Paris self-portraits, but with an expression of suffering in his face more marked than in the portraits of that period (see Appendix, note 9).

The fact that he portrayed himself here with a clean-shaven face is of decisive importance for the dating. His beard was shaved off when he was admitted to the hospital on account of the mutilation of his ear; this is apparent from the self-portraits with the bandage around his face, 1657 and 1658.

Final Works

The fifth replica of the *berceuse*, 1672, is the first of the canvases that can be dated with certainty among those that Vincent painted after taking up his work again in the final days of March. Although he did not mention them in his letters, it is generally taken for granted that the three versions of a bust portrait of Roulin, 1673, 1674, and 1675, also date from the first months of 1889, since they exhibit almost the same decorative backgrounds as the portraits of his wife and the portrait of Dr. Rey, 1659.

By April, Vincent was sufficiently recovered to be allowed to work outside the hospital, where he still resided. The peach orchard in bloom, 1681, was one of the first results of that outdoor work. Vincent wrote about this in some detail in a letter to his friend Signac, in which he also mentioned landscape 1683 and included exceptionally evocative sketches of both (1682 and 1684) in the letter; in these, too, he displayed great virtuosity.

Although landscape 1685 is not mentioned in the letters written at this time, Vincent referred to it later on several occasions because he had designated this canvas—"the blossoming orchard with the poplars intersecting the canvas" (Letter 614)—for entry in the exhibition of the Belgian group Les XX.

Shortly before Theo's marriage, which took place April 17, Vincent wrote again, but he devoted only a few words to his work: "I have six studies of spring, two of them large orchards. There is little time because these effects are so short-lived" (Letter 584). The two large orchards must have been 1681 and 1685; the third orchard, 1683, was somewhat smaller. Although there is no way of knowing definitely what the other studies of spring were, I assume that they must have included at least some of the paintings of grasses and plants (1676–80)—a group of simple but charming canvases.

From a letter to Wil (Letter W11) we learn something about two remarkable paintings which Vincent—perhaps as a farewell?—had made of the hospital: 1686 and 1687. There is also a fairly large drawing of the hospital garden, 1688, but this cannot be regarded as a preliminary study for the painting.

The last painting mentioned by Vincent before his departure from Arles was the lane in the city park with several people, 1689. He wrote about it May 2: "I am working on an avenue of chestnut trees with pink blossoms with a small flowering cherry tree and a wistaria and the avenue splashed with spots of sun and shadow" (Letter 589). As he had by that time already sent off to Theo the two boxes containing his most recent work, this must have been one of the few of the very last canvases remaining behind (see Letter 600).

One of those paintings was *Road with Pollard Willows* (1690), and for anyone looking for conscious or unconscious symbolism in his paintings, this picture of an empty road—bordered by a wall and ghostlike trees and trailing off into the distance around a bend—speaks in unmistakable terms, when it is considered that it was painted at a time when Vincent was leaving an eventful period in Arles behind him and was on his way to meet a new and unknown fate in Saint-Rémy.

1681

1682

1683

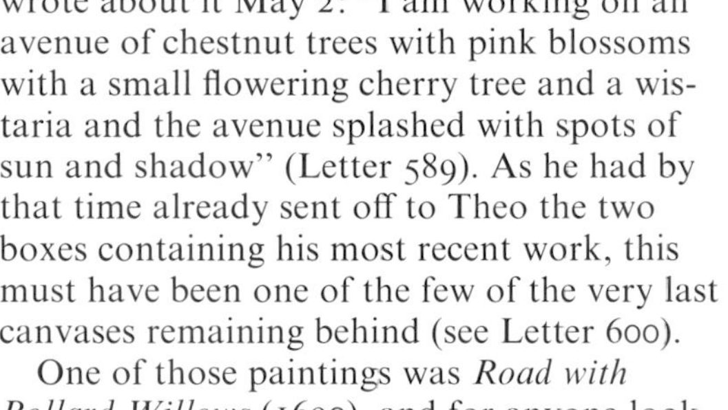

1684

1685

1686

1687

1688

1689

1690

1681 The Crau with Peach Trees in Bloom, F514
65.5 × 81.5 cm (26 × 32¼″)
Courtauld Institute Galleries, London

1682 The Crau with Peach Trees in Bloom
Sketch in Letter 583*b*
Rijksmuseum Vincent van Gogh, Amsterdam

1683 Orchard in Bloom with View of Arles, F515
50.5 × 65 cm (20⅛ × 25⅝″)
Rijksmuseum Vincent van Gogh, Amsterdam

1684 Orchard in Bloom with View of Arles
Sketch in Letter 583*b*
Rijksmuseum Vincent van Gogh, Amsterdam

1685 Orchard in Bloom with Poplars in the Foreground, F516
72 × 92 cm (28⅜ × 36¼″)
Bayerische Staatsgemäldesammlungen, Munich
Colorplate XXXII, p. 384

1686 Dormitory in the Hospital, F646
74 × 92 cm (29⅛ × 36¼″)
Collection Oskar Reinhart, Winterthur, Switzerland

1687 The Courtyard of the Hospital, F519
73 × 92 cm (28¾ × 36¼″)
Collection Oskar Reinhart, Winterthur, Switzerland

1688 The Courtyard of the Hospital, F1467
Pencil, reed pen, brown ink, 45.5 × 59 cm (18⅛ × 23¼″)
Rijksmuseum Vincent van Gogh, Amsterdam

May 1889

1689 Lane with Chestnut Trees in Bloom, F517
72.5 × 92 cm (28¾ × 36¼″)
Private collection, United States

1690 Road with Pollard Willows, F520
55 × 65 cm (21⅝ × 25⅝″)
Stavros S. Niarchos Collection

Saint-Rémy

After his wound had healed, Vincent did not go back to live in the yellow house. Although he was free to work out of doors, he continued to spend the nights in the hospital. He acknowledged that he did not feel capable of taking care of himself: "It would mean trouble for others as well as for myself if I left the hospital, for I feel—and am—paralyzed as it were when it comes to acting or fending for myself" (Letter 586).

The Reverend Mr. Salles took care of the rest. He asked Theo's consent to have Vincent committed to the asylum of Saint-Rémy-de-Provence (about fifteen miles northeast of Arles), which was housed in the twelfth-century monastery of Saint-Paul-de-Mausole. May 8, after receiving 200 francs by telegraph from Theo, Salles accompanied Vincent to the asylum. Two days later he reported to Theo: "Our trip to Saint-Rémy went off perfectly. Mr. Vincent was completely calm and explained his problem himself to the director just like someone who is fully aware of his condition. He stayed with me until I left, and when I took leave of him, he thanked me cordially and seemed somewhat affected by the thought of the completely new life he was going to lead in this home."

1691

Many books and articles have offered theories about the nature of Van Gogh's mental illness, but it appears impossible to give one simple diagnosis of it. The opinions of specialists vary from epilepsy to schizophrenia. At the end of Vincent's stay in Saint-Rémy, the doctor who had treated him for an entire year wrote in the register of the asylum that the patient had been perfectly calm and lucid most of the time and had then worked at his painting, but that he had had several attacks, lasting from two weeks to two months, during which he was tormented by horrible terrors. With the exception of a short period in the beginning of 1890 (see page 440), Vincent's illness had hardly any effect on his art, but it finally caused his death by suicide at a very early age.

The Monastery Garden

The monastery at Saint-Rémy is a rambling two-story structure in which Vincent, in addition to the cell where he slept, had a room at his disposal for use as a studio. The cell was on the second floor, and the studio on the first floor. Since some of the paintings of the view from the building seem to have been made from a somewhat higher vantage point, Vincent must, I believe, have done these scenes from one of the corner sections of the structure, where there was an extra story.*

The building was surrounded by a large garden with flowers and pine trees and looked out in the rear onto a walled plot of ground with a field of grain that was the subject of many paintings and drawings that Vincent made from his cell.

He appears to have started on work in the garden immediately. In his first letter to Theo, written a few days after his arrival, he reported: "I am working on two [paintings]: violet irises and a lilac bush, two motifs I have found in the garden" (Letter 592). They are the important canvases 1691 and 1692, neither of which shows any signs of depression.

Other paintings dating from the first days—also made in the garden but very different in color and composition—were 1693 and (probably) 1698. The former was described in Letter 592 as "one of those eternal little love nests in the greenery," and a small sketch (1694) gave an idea of the subject: "Sturdy, ivy-covered trunks, the ground also covered

*Visible in a photograph in Marc Edo Tralbaut, *Van Gogh: Eine Bildbiographie* (1958), p. 111.

1692

1693

1694

1695

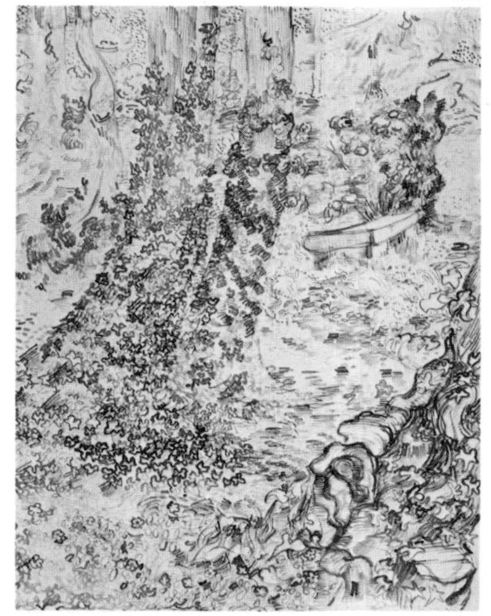

1696

1697

1698

May 1889

1691 Irises, F608
71 × 93 cm (28 × 36⅝″)
Joan Whitney Payson Gallery of Art, Westbrook College, Portland, Maine

1692 Lilacs, F579
73 × 92 cm (28¾ × 36¼″)
The Hermitage, Leningrad

1693 Trees with Ivy, F609
92 × 72 cm (36¼ × 28⅜″)
Location unknown

1694 Trees with Ivy
Sketch in Letter 592
Location unknown

1695 Trees with Ivy, F1522
Pencil, reed pen, brown ink, 62 × 47 cm (24⅜ × 18½″)
Rijksmuseum Vincent van Gogh, Amsterdam

1696 Tree with Ivy, F1532
Pencil, reed pen, washed with brown ink, 60.5 × 47 cm (24 × 18½″)
Rijksmuseum Vincent van Gogh, Amsterdam

1697 Trees in the Garden, F1505
Charcoal, brush, pen, brown ink, 45.5 × 60.5 cm (18⅛ × 24″)
Rijksmuseum Kröller-Müller, Otterlo

1698 Asylum and Garden, F734
95 × 75.5 cm (37⅜ × 29⅞″)
Rijksmuseum Kröller-Müller, Otterlo

over with ivy and periwinkle, a stone bench, and a bush with roses in the cool shade." In addition to the sketch, there is also a drawing of the subject (1695), which is one of the series he sent to Theo at the end of June or beginning of July with the announcement: "To give you an idea of what I have in hand, I am sending you some ten drawings, all based on canvases I am working on" (Letter 597).* Each of those drawings is reproduced here together with the corresponding painting, but it is also possible that Vincent did all of them together in June from the existing paintings shortly before shipping them, just as he had done in similar cases in Arles.

A chance observation in the garden led to a picture of a large moth, which he called *Death's-Head Moth* (1700, and letter sketch 1701). "The colors," he wrote in Letter 592, "are astonishingly subdued, black, gray, white, shading off into reddish or faintly olive-green reflections." It is not surprising that he also painted the moth, 1702, although he regretted that he had to kill it to do so.

An ivy-covered tree appears in a second drawing, 1696, which is very similar to 1695 and probably made at the same time. I also ascribe to these first weeks of Vincent's stay in the asylum the impression he did of a larger portion of the garden, 1697, which exhibits the same technique but a somewhat more relaxed style. The same applies to the charming canvas of a single iris plant, 1699, which is closely related to the very first painting done at this time, 1691. Vincent might well write: "Life is not quite so sad when you consider that it takes place mostly in the garden" (Letter 592).

Reconnaissance in Chalk and Watercolor

His view of the countryside was nevertheless limited essentially to what he could see through barred windows, as he put it in the same letter: "Through the windows with iron bars I see an enclosed wheat field, a prospect à la Van Goyen, above which I see the sun rise in all its glory in the morning." He recorded this scene in the majestic drawing 1706, which I date earlier than does the 1970 *catalogue raisonné* by reason of the precise topographically accurate style characteristic of Vincent's initial reconnaissance of his surroundings. In this same early group I include, in addition to the drawings of the ivy-covered trees, the masterly, frequently reproduced drawing of the fountain in the asylum garden, 1705. Both this drawing and 1706 display vigorous hatching over the entire sheet. When Vincent drew or painted the view across the wheat field, he omitted the bars, as in 1706 and in other works, but there is one sheet on which he has depicted the forbidding windows as if his aim was to accustom himself to them (1704).

The garden in spring offered still other motifs in abundance to which black and white could not do full justice. Watercolor was the medium of seven drawings (1707–13) in which Vincent succeeded in rendering the luxuriant world of the garden in a highly personal, original manner with a facile touch that he had seldom achieved previously. The strokes of color come in swarms in a limited

*In Letter W13 it is "a dozen drawings."

1699

1700

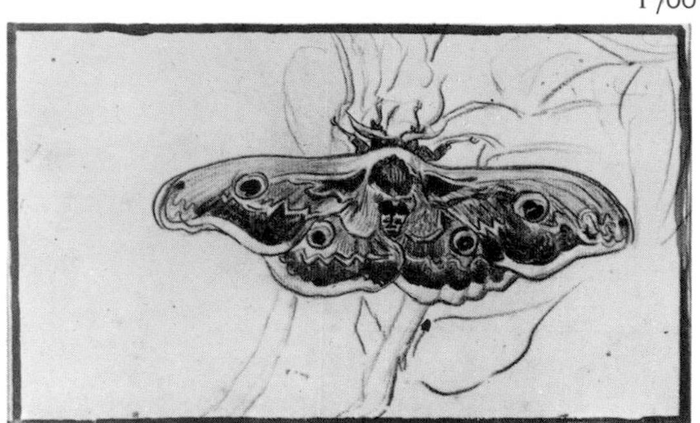

1701

1699 Irises, F601
Paper on canvas, 62.5 × 48 cm ($24\frac{3}{4} \times 18\frac{7}{8}$")
National Gallery of Canada, Ottawa

1700 Death's-Head Moth, F1523
Black chalk, pen, brown ink, 16 × 26 cm ($6\frac{1}{4} \times 10\frac{1}{4}$")
Rijksmuseum Vincent van Gogh, Amsterdam

1701 Death's-Head Moth
Sketch in Letter 592
Location unknown

1702 Death's-Head Moth on an Arum, F610
33 × 24 cm ($13 \times 9\frac{1}{2}$")
Rijksmuseum Vincent van Gogh, Amsterdam

1703 Arums, F1613
Pen, reed pen, brown ink, 31 × 41 cm ($12\frac{1}{4} \times 16\frac{1}{8}$")
Rijksmuseum Vincent van Gogh, Amsterdam

1704 Barred Windows, F1605v (reverse: 1935)
Black chalk, 24 × 32 cm ($9\frac{1}{2} \times 12\frac{5}{8}$")
Rijksmuseum Vincent van Gogh, Amsterdam

1705 Fountain in the Garden of the Asylum, F1531
Black chalk, pen, reed pen, brown ink, 49.5 × 46 cm ($19\frac{5}{8} \times 18\frac{1}{8}$")
Rijksmuseum Vincent van Gogh, Amsterdam

1702

1703

1704

1705

1706

1707

1708

1709

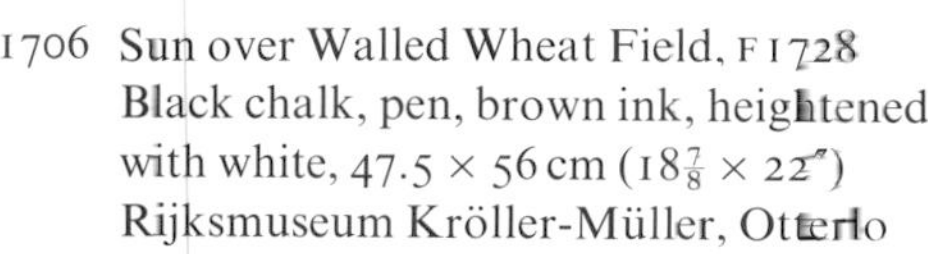

1706 Sun over Walled Wheat Field, F 1728
Black chalk, pen, brown ink, heightened with white, 47.5 × 56 cm ($18\frac{7}{8} \times 22''$)
Rijksmuseum Kröller-Müller, Otterlo

1707 Flowering Shrubs, F 1526
Watercolor, 61 × 47 cm ($24 \times 18\frac{1}{2}''$)
Location unknown

1708 Flowering Shrubs, F 1527
Watercolor, 62 × 47 cm ($24\frac{3}{8} \times 18\frac{1}{2}''$)
Rijksmuseum Kröller-Müller, Otterlo

1709 Trees and Shrubs, F 1534
Black chalk, pencil, pen, brown ink, watercolor, 47.5 × 61.5 cm ($18\frac{7}{8} \times 24\frac{3}{8}''$)
Location unknown

1710

1711

1712

range of yellows, greens, and blues, with only a single light red accent here and there to indicate the oleander blossoms, with almost a complete absence of perspective and depth, but strongly suggestive of thick, compact vegetation. The brushstrokes whirl about the paper here so freely and nonchalantly that large sections of the sheet, sometimes virtually its entire surface (as in 1707 and 1708), are covered with what becomes an almost abstract, fascinating color pattern.

A series of rough, hasty pencil sketches of the enclosed wheat field behind the asylum must have been done by Vincent at this time in his room (1714–19). They can be regarded as finger exercises for the many studies he later devoted to this spot, such as the more carefully executed black chalk drawing 1721, sketch 1720, and the small canvas 1722.

The first full-scale rendering of the enclosed wheat field then follows; it is 1723. The dating of this work is based on Vincent's description of it, written about June 9: "I am working on two landscapes (size-30 canvas), distant views of the hills: one is the field I see from the window of my bedroom. In the foreground a wheat field, battered and beaten flat after a storm. A dividing wall and cottages and hills beyond the gray foliage of a few olive trees. Finally, at the top of the canvas a great white and gray cloud, drowned in blue. It is a landscape marked by extreme simplicity, also in its color" (Letter 594).

We might add that it is marked not only by extreme simplicity, but also by extreme subtlety in the color, in the shading off of yellowish greens and bluish greens into the light blue of the hills and the sky. The great white cloud is essential, not only to the balance of the composition, but also because the play of its lines, combined with the undulations of the wheat, gives expression to the emotion experienced by Vincent in relation to nature that would increasingly come to dominate his landscapes. (There is a variant of this canvas that is not mentioned in the letters, 1727.)

Outside the Walls

It is clear that the paintings 1723 and 1727 represent the view from Vincent's window, but he had also been at work in the neighborhood outside the asylum for the past few days. As Vincent himself indicated, this was not entirely without risk: "I would not have the courage to begin again in the outside world. I have been to the village once—and then with an escort—and just the sight of people and things made me almost faint and I felt very upset. Amid nature it is a feeling for the work that keeps me going" (Letter 594).

The first result of this work outside was 1725, the second canvas he must have been referring to when he wrote about June 9 that he was working on two landscapes. This can be gathered from the description "a ripening field of grain surrounded by green bushes" that he gave in a letter to Wil, continuing: "At the end of the field a little pink house with a tall, dark cypress standing out against the purplish and bluish hills in the distance and against a sky of forget-me-not blue with pink streaks, whose pure tints present a contrast to the heavy ears of grain with tints warm as a crust of bread, given them by the burning sun" (Letter W12).

As regards color, this impressive canvas has much in common with the picture of the enclosed field, 1723, but the composition of 1725 is both more balanced and more surprising. The grain, although already turning yellow, is not yet fully ripened, and that is equally true of some of the other paintings of these surroundings, which I assign to the same period—early June. I have mentioned 1723 and 1727, and now add canvases 1728, 1744, and 1745, all depicting the wheat field behind the asylum or the hills, the Alpilles, directly behind it.

These latter three canvases were previously dated spring 1890. I shall explain later why, in my opinion, they could not have been done in May of 1890 (March and April of that year are completely ruled out by reason of Vincent's illness). However, it can be pointed out here that there is no need to seek the stylistic parallels of these three paintings in works done in the spring of 1890. The wheat field in 1728 has stylistic counterparts in landscapes 1723 and 1725, which must for sound reasons be ascribed to the early summer of 1889. Similarly, the rolling hills rendered in deep blue with dark outlines in 1744 are to be found also in the early canvas 1723 and in the painting of *Olive Trees in a Mountain Landscape*, which dates from the middle of June 1889 (1740).

Reality Intensified

How difficult it is to work with stylistic com-

1713

1714

1715

1716

1717

1718

1710 Trees and Shrubs, F 1533
Black chalk, pencil, pen, brown ink, watercolor, 47 × 62 cm (18½ × 24⅜″)
Rijksmuseum Vincent van Gogh, Amsterdam

1711 Stone Bench in the Garden of the Asylum, F 1537
Black chalk, watercolor, gouache, 37 × 61 cm (14⅝ × 24″)
Rijksmuseum Vincent van Gogh, Amsterdam

1712 Trees in the Garden of the Asylum, F 1536
Watercolor, 46.5 × 61.5 cm (18½ × 24⅜″)
Location unknown

1713 Stone Steps in the Garden of the Asylum, F 1535
Black chalk, pencil, brown ink, watercolor, 63 × 45 cm (24¾ × 17¾″)
Rijksmuseum Vincent van Gogh, Amsterdam

1714 Enclosed Field, F 1556
Pencil, 25.5 × 32.5 cm (10¼ × 13″)
Rijksmuseum Vincent van Gogh, Amsterdam

1715 Enclosed Field, F 1557
Pencil, black chalk, 25 × 32.5 cm (9⅞ × 13″)
Rijksmuseum Vincent van Gogh, Amsterdam

1716 Enclosed Field, F 1558
Pencil, black chalk, 25 × 32.5 cm (9⅞ × 13″)
Rijksmuseum Vincent van Gogh, Amsterdam

1717 Enclosed Field, F 1559
Pencil, 25 × 33 cm (9⅞ × 13″)
Rijksmuseum Vincent van Gogh, Amsterdam

1718 Enclosed Field, F 1560
Pencil, 25 × 33 cm (9⅞ × 13″)
Rijksmuseum Vincent van Gogh, Amsterdam

1719 Enclosed Field, F 1561
Pencil, 25 × 32.5 cm (9⅞ × 13″)
Rijksmuseum Vincent van Gogh, Amsterdam

1719

parisons in the Saint-Rémy period becomes evident when one realizes that during the same weeks in which these generally well-balanced landscapes of the wheat field and the hills were made, Vincent also produced a painting such as the vibrating, frenzied—and subsequently famous—*Starry Night*, 1731 (colorplate XXXIII, page 401; see also the drawing, 1732, and the preliminary studies, 1729 and 1730). The dating is beyond question: Vincent mentioned *The Starry Night* together with the mountain landscape, 1740, in Letter 595, written June 17 or 18. The announcement of two canvases that in our eyes are so spectacular seems almost too restrained and simple: "At last I have a landscape with olive trees and also a new study of a starry sky." But what he said after that made it evident that they also had a special significance for him, even though he apparently was not able to formulate his intentions very concretely. The important thing—he seems to have meant—was to follow in the footsteps of Delacroix and arrive at a true presentation of nature with the aid of color and drawing that deliberately depart from reality ("un dessin plus volontaire que l'exactitude trompe-l'oeil").

It cannot be said that canvases like *The Starry Night* and *Olive Trees* represented the high point and final stage of a gradual development of Vincent's artistic genius. There was nothing in the immediately preceding works to indicate that he would, from one day to the next, arrive at such a majestic, Expressionistic vocabulary. Landscapes painted not much later the same month—specifically 1753 and 1755, which can be accurately dated—exhibit a much more tranquil representation of reality.

Meyer Schapiro characterized the mountain landscape 1740 as "more powerful and imaginative than anything in later Expressionistic art, which proceeded from a similar, emotionally charged vision of nature."* And it was truly a master stroke, for not only had he effectively rendered the typical twisted tangle of branches of the trees, but by letting their rhythm be transmitted to the heaving earth and the tormented silhouette of the mountains, he imparted a rare dynamic force to the entire landscape. In the drawing (1741) made from the painting, the pattern of wavy lines, within which the olive trees become almost unrecognizable, is even more pronounced, but this in turn also makes it clear how much the original work owes to the subdued but fascinating harmony of the sea green of the olive trees and the blues of the sky and the mountaintops, ranging from a soft to a deep blue tone.

There is a curious, somewhat mysterious group of six sketches (1733–38), rough drafts of attempts to render an Egyptian head. No precise dating is possible, but I have placed them in June 1889, following the 1970 *catalogue raisonné*, which states rather vaguely, "June 1889 or later." Reference was made in that connection to Letter 594, written at the beginning of June, where there is a short passage containing comments by Vincent on what makes Egyptian art extraordinary: "Isn't it that these serene, calm kings, wise

*Schapiro, *Vincent van Gogh* (1950), p. 108.

1720

1721

1722

June 1889

1720 Motifs of the Mountain Landscape behind the Walls, F1602 (reverse: 1927)
Black chalk, 23.5 × 32 cm (9½ × 12⅝″)
Rijksmuseum Vincent van Gogh, Amsterdam

1721 Mountain Landscape Seen across the Walls, F1549v (reverse: 1965)
Black chalk, 31 × 23.5 cm (12¼ × 9½″)
Rijksmuseum Vincent van Gogh, Amsterdam

1722 Mountain Landscape Seen across the Walls, F723
37.5 × 30.5 cm (15 × 12¼″)
Collection E. Ribbius Peletier, The Hague

1723 Mountain Landscape Seen across the Walls, F611
70.5 × 88.5 cm (28 × 35″)
Ny Carlsberg Glyptotek, Copenhagen

1724 Mountain Landscape Seen across the Walls, F1547
Pen, reed pen, brown ink, 47 × 62 cm (18½ × 24⅜″)
Rijksmuseum Vincent van Gogh, Amsterdam

1725 Green Wheat Field with Cypress, F719
73.5 × 92.5 cm (29⅛ × 36⅝″)
Národni Galerie, Prague

1726 Wheat Field with Cypress, F1548
Pen, 46 × 61 cm (18⅛ × 24″)
Pierpont Morgan Library, New York

1723

1725

1724

1726

1727

1728

1729

1727 Mountain Landscape Seen across the Walls; Green Field, F718
73 × 92 cm ($28\frac{3}{4} \times 36\frac{1}{4}$")
Location unknown

1728 Mountain Landscape Seen across the Walls with Rising Sun and Green Field, F720
72 × 92 cm ($28\frac{3}{8} \times 36\frac{1}{4}$")
Rijksmuseum Kröller-Müller, Otterlo

1729 Bird's-Eye View of the Village, F1541v (reverse: 1730; on the same sheet: 2091)
Pencil, pen, washed, 16.5 × 30 cm ($6\frac{3}{4} \times 11\frac{3}{4}$")
Rijksmuseum Vincent van Gogh, Amsterdam

and gentle, patient and kind, look as though they could never be other than what they are, eternal tillers of the soil, worshipers of the sun?" These sketches, however, do not resemble the style of the work he did in June 1889, and the small rough sketches he made next to heads 1733 and 1738 seem to me in any case to date from 1890; the girl's head was almost certainly made in July 1890 (see, for example, 2074).

Several much more important drawings, also not done from paintings but from nature, must surely be assigned to June 1889—1739, 1742, and 1743. The sort of carefree, rapid technique employed by Vincent in these works—which gives the impression that mobility and the interplay of lines meant more to him than fidelity of depiction—is strongly reminiscent of the treatment in drawings 1732 and 1741. A detail such as the whimsically jagged rocks in 1740 and 1741 is seen again in stylized form in the upper left-hand corner of the pen-and-ink drawing 1742, which, for the rest, depicts only a confused mass of leaves.

Cypresses and Olive Trees

This decorative, almost abstract pattern of semicircular or slightly curved short lines is also seen in the drawings of cypresses, 1747 and 1749, made from paintings 1746 and 1748. The cypress, along with the olive, was Vincent's favorite tree, and he had in masterly fashion worked it into the paintings *The Starry Night*, 1731, and *Green Wheat Field*, 1725. Here the cypress has become the principal, almost the sole, motif.

In Letter 596 he said explicitly that of the twelve size-30 canvases he was working on (!), two were paintings of cypresses, and he described one of these, 1746, in some detail: "I believe that of the two canvases of cypresses the one in the sketch [1750 was enclosed] will be the best. The trees in it are very tall and massive. The foreground very low with blackberries and bushes. Behind the violet hills a green and pink sky with a crescent moon. The foreground particularly is in heavy impasto, blackberry bushes with yellow, violet, and green reflections."

What these paintings and the ones immediately preceding them—such as *The Starry Night*, 1731, and *Olive Trees*, 1740—have in common are mainly the whirling skies, with their forceful, almost wild, strokes of color, and—so far as 1746 is concerned—the tormented brushwork in the foreground and the "unnatural" crescent of the moon, quite apart from the fact that the cypresses, because Vincent has rendered them in the shape of flames, are themselves an expression of inner emotion.

In *Cypresses*, 1748, Vincent originally did not include the two female figures in the foreground, which is also apparent in the corresponding drawing 1749. He added them half a year later when he designated the painting for the art critic G.-Albert Aurier, who at the end of January 1890 had devoted a laudatory article to Vincent's work (see page 436). Before sending it, he wrote Aurier: "At the moment I am still working on it, as I want to put a figure in it" (Letter 626*a*). The canvas is also mainly a color study; Vincent himself put it aptly when he said that it was "like a multicolored Scottish cloth" (Letter

1730

1731

1732

1730 Landscape with Cypresses, F 1541 (reverse: 1729; on the same sheet: 2058)
Pencil, 24 × 32 cm (9½ × 12⅝")
Rijksmuseum Vincent van Gogh, Amsterdam

1731 The Starry Night, F 612
73 × 92 cm (28¾ × 36¼")
Museum of Modern Art, New York
Colorplate XXXIII, p. 401

1732 The Starry Night, F 1540
Pen, 47 × 62.5 cm (18½ × 24¾")
Destroyed; formerly Kunsthalle, Bremen

1733 Head of an Egyptian King (Mummy?), F 1520 (reverse: 1734)
Black chalk, 35.5 × 31 cm (14⅛ × 12¼")
Rijksmuseum Vincent van Gogh, Amsterdam

1734 Head of an Egyptian King (Mummy?), F 1520v (reverse: 1733)
Black chalk, 35.5 × 31 cm (14⅛ × 12¼")
Rijksmuseum Vincent van Gogh, Amsterdam

1735 Head of an Egyptian King (Mummy?), F 1521 (reverse: 1736)
Black chalk, 31 × 23.5 cm (12¼ × 9½")
Rijksmuseum Vincent van Gogh, Amsterdam

1736 Head of an Egyptian King (Mummy?), F 1521v (reverse: 1735)
Blue chalk, 31 × 23.5 cm (12¼ × 9½")
Rijksmuseum Vincent van Gogh, Amsterdam

1737 Head of an Egyptian King (Mummy?), F 1635 (reverse: 2086)
Blue and black chalk, 31 × 23.5 cm (12¼ × 9½")
Rijksmuseum Vincent van Gogh, Amsterdam

1738 Head of an Egyptian King (Mummy?), F 1596a (reverse: 1942)
Blue chalk, 31.5 × 23.5 cm (12⅝ × 9½")
Rijksmuseum Vincent van Gogh, Amsterdam

1739 Trees in the Garden of the Asylum, F 1501
Pencil, reed pen, 47 × 60 cm (18½ × 23⅝")
Rijksmuseum Vincent van Gogh, Amsterdam

1733

1734

1735

1736

1737

1738

1739

597), a simile he repeated several months later in his letter to Aurier.

He could also have used the same expression for the colorful landscape 1751, in which an abundance of poppies and a few red roofs provide the contrast. The poppies and the fresh colors of the vegetation supply a basis for placing this work, too, early in the summer, even though it is not mentioned by Vincent in his letters at that time. We know definitely that it was sent to Theo in September; it was referred to at the time of the shipment as "Study of Fields" in Letter 607, and as "Poppies" in Letter 608.

The studies of cypresses Vincent was working on during the last days of June, according to Letters 596 and 597, must have included the important canvas 1755, which he always referred to in later letters as *Wheat Field with Cypresses* (colorplate XXXIV, page 402). In addition to the almost identical replica, 1756, and drawing 1757, there is also a smaller version that he made for his mother and sister in September (1790).

In a sense even more remarkable, perhaps not so much for its aesthetic as for its biographical and "symbolic" significance, is the third canvas referred to in Letter 596—1753. Here, too, the subject was the now ripened grain, this time in the small field behind the asylum. The first mention of it was again quite short and simple: "I have made a wheat field, all very yellow and all very light, perhaps the lightest canvas I have yet made" (Letter 596). He provided a somewhat more detailed description in the letter written a few days later to accompany the shipment of drawings (Letter 597), and it is clear that the description was intended to apply to two of these drawings: "The latest [canvas] I have started is the wheat field, in which you see a little reaper and a big sun. The canvas is completely yellow except for the wall and the background of purplish hills. The canvas that is almost identical in motif is different in color, as it is grayish green with a white and blue sky." These last words clearly refer to painting 1723, and if a comparison is made of the corresponding drawings (1724 and 1754) sent to Theo, it will be seen that they are in fact "almost identical in motif" (see Appendix, note 10).

I have also assigned to the second half of June the olive orchards 1758, 1759, and 1760, even though, in the Van Gogh literature—and in the 1970 *catalogue raisonné*—they have always been dated late fall 1889 (see also Appendix, note 11).

Works in July

We have little firm information about the studies Vincent did in the first half of July. We do know the painting mentioned in Letter 603, July 6, with a rising moon above the field behind the asylum "where sheaves have replaced the grain, dull yellow-ocher and violet." This is without doubt canvas 1761, which displays an artificial-looking regularity in the brushstrokes that produces a sort of hatching effect over the entire picture plane, including the area depicting the evening sky.

When Vincent, in a letter of July 6, made a poetic digression about the "small emotions," which he called "the great direction givers of life," he enclosed a triple sketch of cicadas or

1740

1741

1742

1740 Olive Trees in a Mountain Landscape, F712
72.5 × 92 cm ($28\frac{3}{4} \times 36\frac{1}{4}''$)
Collection Mr. and Mrs. John Hay Whitney, New York

1741 Olive Trees in a Mountain Landscape, F1544
Pencil, pen, reed pen, 47 × 62.5 cm
($18\frac{1}{2} \times 24\frac{3}{4}''$)
Nationalgalerie, East Berlin

1742 Wild Vegetation in the Mountains, F1542
Reed pen, brown ink, 47 × 62 cm
($18\frac{1}{2} \times 24\frac{3}{8}''$)
Rijksmuseum Vincent van Gogh, Amsterdam

Colorplate XXXIII, The Starry Night, 1731 ›

grasshoppers (1765), and wrote: "Their song in the intense heat has the same charm for me as that of the cricket in the farmer's hearth at home" (Letter 603)—an indication that he had not forgotten his native land.

He mentioned in the same letter that he had also started on "a new canvas with ivy." Although the reference is rather vague, I assume that what he meant was the large study 1762, a companion piece of sorts to the painting done in May, 1693, but somewhat less "realistic" and illustrational. A very similar, but smaller, replica, 1763, and another small variant, 1764, were probably made at about the same time or a little later.

A major work that we can definitely place in the first half of July is the powerful *Mountains with Dark Hut*, 1766. The genesis of this piece—strongly reminiscent of the equally emotionally charged painting *Olive Trees in a Mountain Landscape*, 1740—is indicated in the letters. According to Letter 596, June 25, his sisters Lies and Wil had sent Vincent the book *Le Sens de la Vie* (The Meaning of Life) by the Swiss novelist Edouard Rod, which had greatly impressed them, but, as Vincent said, "little women and books are two different things," and it had told him absolutely nothing about the meaning of life. In a later letter, however, he wrote: "Although I am not too fond of Rod's book, I have nevertheless made a canvas of the passage where he speaks of the mountains and the blackish huts" (Letter 601). Although the painting bears little relation to "the meaning of life" or to the novel of that name, it turned out to be a new, grandiose metamorphosis of the landscape we already know as the background of *Olive Trees in a Mountain Landscape* —now re-created to become, in Vincent's words, "a somber mountain country where one noticed hidden dark goatsheds and sunflowers blooming" (Letter 607).

A final canvas from the first half of July, in the same spirit as *Mountains with Dark Hut*, is *Entrance to a Quarry*, 1767, a work that Vincent called "a more sober attempt, of a dull, unobtrusive color, broken greens, iron-red, and yellow ocher, corresponding to what I told you, that at times I feel like starting again with a palette as in the North" (Letter 601).

Another Attack

When Theo wrote Vincent July 16 to thank him for his letters and drawings, and excused himself for not having done so sooner because of the intense heat and extreme fatigue, he received no reply. Only after writing again July 29 and sending a telegram to the director of the asylum, Dr. Théophile Peyron, about the middle of August asking for information were his fears confirmed. The only question is why Dr. Peyron had not informed him sooner: Vincent had had another relapse.

What this terrible fact meant to Vincent he related in moving terms August 22, when he was able to write Theo:* "You understand that I am deeply distressed about the attacks returning again, I was beginning to hope that

*We know the date of this letter from a letter Jo van Gogh-Bonger, Theo's wife, wrote to her sister-in-law Wil informing her that Vincent's letter had arrived August 23 (see *Vincent*, vol. III, no. 2 [1974], p. 20).

‹ Colorplate XXXIV, Wheat Field with Cypresses, 1755

1743

1744

1745

1743 Olive Trees in a Mountain Landscape, F 1543
Black chalk, brush, brown ink, 50 × 65 cm (19⅝ × 25⅝")
Rijksmuseum Vincent van Gogh, Amsterdam

1744 Mountain Landscape Seen across the Walls, F 725
53 × 70 cm (20⅞ × 27⅝")
Private collection, London

1745 Mountain Landscape Seen across the Walls, F 724
59 × 72 cm (23¼ × 28⅜")
Rijksmuseum Kröller-Müller, Otterlo

this would not happen any more. You might do well to write a few words to Dr. Peyron to say that working on my paintings is quite necessary for my recovery, for these days without anything to do, and without being able to go to the room he had assigned to me for painting, are almost unbearable." As appears from this letter, 601, and Letter 607, this new crisis had come upon Vincent when he was outside on a windy day painting the *Entrance to a Quarry*, 1767, which, despite the attack, he was able to complete. For the time being, however, there could be no further question of any activity, and since Vincent did not write until the beginning of September that he had again started to do a little work (Letter 602), we know that his production was *completely interrupted for at least a month and a half* that summer.

Although Vincent speedily recovered from the physical aftermath of his illness, the new attack had the fatal effect of convincing him that from then on the crises were bound to recur. A few weeks later, when he announced that he was thinking about going north after Christmas, he added: "To leave now, when I consider a new crisis to be likely in the winter, that is to say, in three months, would perhaps be too imprudent" (Letter 604). It is all the more astounding, therefore, that his creative powers—after a complete collapse over a period of six weeks—could revive almost at once.

New Activity

When we delve into the chronology and background of the work produced in these weeks, we encounter another of those enigmas that this highly gifted and inspired artist presents at regular intervals during his career. The number and the quality of works he produced almost immediately after his recovery are well-nigh incredible. Yet all doubt is dispelled when the reports in his letters are checked and dated as accurately as possible. By September 7, not even two weeks after he had started working again, Vincent had completed at least *nine* paintings, including several of his most famous works. Or to take another date, by September 19, twelve days later, he had completed a total of at least eighteen, and perhaps twenty-one, paintings.

The group of works mentioned in Letters 604 and 605 (the latter dated September 7) includes:

Enclosed Field with Plowman	1768
Self-Portrait	1770
Vincent's Bedroom	1771
Self-Portrait	1772
Enclosed Field with Reaper at Sunrise	1773
Portrait of the Chief Orderly (Trabu)	1774 (in duplicate)
Pietà (after Delacroix)	1775, 1776

The first *Self-Portrait*, showing the artist's palette (colorplate XXXV, page 419), was an extremely important work from the outset. Vincent wrote: "I started it the first day I got up [from my sickbed]. I was thin, pale as the devil. It is dark bluish violet and the head whitish with yellow hair, thus a color effect" (Letter 604). For us there is a good deal more

1746

1747

1748

1746 Cypresses, F613
95 × 73 cm ($37\frac{3}{8} \times 28\frac{3}{4}''$)
Metropolitan Museum of Art, New York

1747 Cypresses, F1525
Pen, reed pen, 62.5 × 47 cm ($24\frac{3}{4} \times 18\frac{1}{2}''$)
Brooklyn Museum, New York

1748 Cypresses, F620
92 × 73 cm ($36\frac{1}{4} \times 28\frac{3}{4}''$)
Rijksmuseum Kröller-Müller, Otterlo

1749 Cypresses, F1524
Pen, reed pen, 62.5 × 46.5 cm ($24\frac{3}{4} \times 18\frac{1}{2}''$)
Art Institute of Chicago

1750 Cypresses
Sketch in Letter 596
Rijksmuseum Vincent van Gogh, Amsterdam

1751 Fields with Poppies, F581
71 × 91 cm ($28 \times 35\frac{7}{8}''$)
Kunsthalle, Bremen

1752 Fields with Poppies, F1494
Reed pen, 48 × 64 cm ($18\frac{7}{8} \times 25\frac{1}{4}''$)
Collection Mrs. Mark C. Steinberg, St. Louis

1753 Enclosed Wheat Field with Reaper, F617
72 × 92 cm ($28\frac{3}{8} \times 36\frac{1}{4}''$)
Rijksmuseum Kröller-Müller, Otterlo

1749

1751

1750

1752

1753

1754

1755

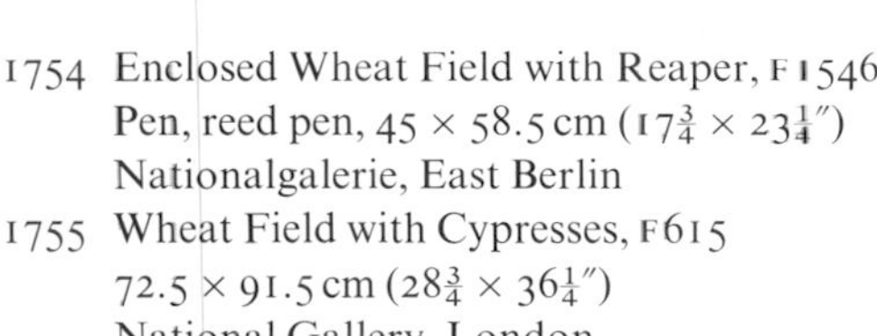

1754 Enclosed Wheat Field with Reaper, F 1546
Pen, reed pen, 45 × 58.5 cm (17¾ × 23¼″)
Nationalgalerie, East Berlin

1755 Wheat Field with Cypresses, F 615
72.5 × 91.5 cm (28¾ × 36¼″)
National Gallery, London
Colorplate XXXIV, p. 402

than a color effect. This is a tremendously spontaneous, powerful, penetrating self-portrait that, more than anything that he says in the letters, expresses the force of the pent-up energy with which a person just recovering from an illness throws himself back into his work.

Vincent's Bedroom (1771) is an almost identical replica, even in size, of the original painting, 1608, that was done in the Arles period. The history of this replica can be traced in the correspondence. Vincent had sent the original to Theo in April 1889 but had pasted newspapers over it because, as he reported in Letter 588, the dampness in the yellow house during his illness had made it peel. And he explained further in Letter 604 that it had been painted and dried so quickly that the paint had not adhered well to the canvas. Theo had sent it back with the request not to touch it up but to *copy* it; Theo was then going to have the original painting relined (Letter T10). In Letter 604 Vincent reported: "So now I have redone the canvas of the bedroom" ("ainsi j'ai refait la toile de la chambre à coucher").*

About the same time as he did the painting of the bedroom, Vincent must have been working on a second self-portrait. In Letter 604 he wrote: "So at the moment—and not having another model—I am working on two self-portraits because it is high time I did a bit of portrait painting." And after he had described the self-portrait, 1770, he said: "But after that I started again with another, three-quarter on a light background."

A striking aspect of this self-portrait—deservedly one of the most frequently reproduced and most frequently described portraits of the artist—is the background with the bluish-white, light blue, and light green swirling lines which continue on even into the wrinkles of the grayish-blue suit with the light mauve reflections. Although not alluded to by Vincent (this was one of the matters never mentioned in his letters), that flaming background must clearly be seen as the expression—conscious or unconscious—of the turmoil, the maelstrom of feelings and thoughts that threatened his mind, or rather from which his personality now emerged healed and resolute. For Vincent himself made an unequivocal distinction between the self-portrait with palette, "from when I was ill" (Letter 607), and this somewhat later one: "You will see, if you put the portrait with light background, which I have just completed, next to the self-portraits from Paris, that I *now* look healthier than then, and even much healthier" (Letter 604).

Landscapes and Portraits

The feverish pace of Vincent's resumed activity at this time is perhaps best reflected in the way in which the landscape with reaper, 1773, came into being. Vincent had painted a similar landscape, *Enclosed Wheat Field with Reaper* (1753) shortly before his illness. The origin of the later landscape can be traced at close hand, as it were, in Letter 604. Vincent

*The English translation of this in *The Complete Letters* is incorrect and very misleading: "So I have gone over the canvas of my bedroom" (vol. III, p. 201). Vincent did not merely "go over" the painting or touch it up, but made a copy of it.

1756

1757

1758

1756 Wheat Field with Cypresses, F717
73 × 93.5 cm ($28\frac{3}{4} \times 37''$)
Private collection, Switzerland

1757 Wheat Field with Cypresses, F1538
Black chalk, pen, reed pen, brown ink,
47 × 62 cm ($18\frac{1}{2} \times 24\frac{3}{8}''$)
Rijksmuseum Vincent van Gogh, Amsterdam

1758 Olive Orchard, F585
72 × 92 cm ($28\frac{3}{8} \times 36\frac{1}{4}''$)
Rijksmuseum Kröller-Müller, Otterlo

1759 Olive Orchard, F715
73 × 93 cm ($28\frac{3}{4} \times 36\frac{5}{8}''$)
William Rockhill Nelson Gallery and Atkins Museum of Fine Arts, Kansas City, Missouri

1760 Olive Orchard, F709
44 × 59 cm ($17\frac{3}{8} \times 23\frac{1}{4}''$)
Rijksmuseum Vincent van Gogh, Amsterdam
July 1889

1761 Enclosed Field with Sheaves and Rising Moon, F735
72 × 92 cm ($28\frac{3}{8} \times 36\frac{1}{4}''$)
Rijksmuseum Kröller-Müller, Otterlo

1762 Trunks of Trees with Ivy, F746
74 × 92 cm ($29\frac{1}{8} \times 36\frac{1}{4}''$)
Rijksmuseum Vincent van Gogh, Amsterdam

1763 Trunks of Trees with Ivy, F747
45 × 60 cm ($17\frac{3}{4} \times 23\frac{5}{8}''$)
Rijksmuseum Kröller-Müller, Otterlo

1764 Trunks of Trees with Ivy, F745
47 × 61 cm ($18\frac{1}{2} \times 24''$)
Rijksmuseum Vincent van Gogh, Amsterdam

1765 Three Cicadas, F1445
Sketch belonging with Letter 603
Pen, 20.5 × 18 cm ($8\frac{1}{4} \times 7\frac{1}{8}''$)
Rijksmuseum Vincent van Gogh, Amsterdam

1759

1760

1761

1762

·1763

1764

1765

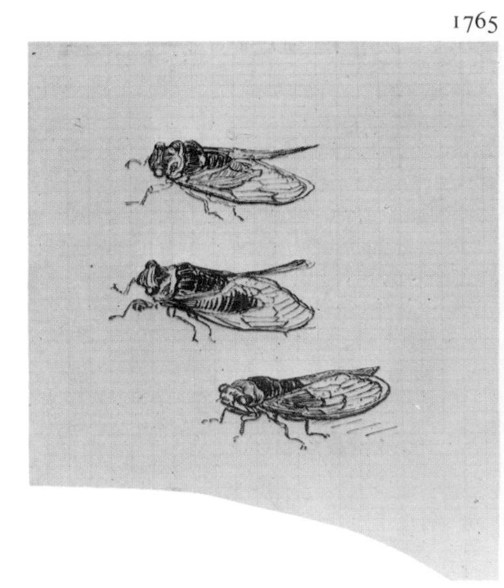

first appears to have started work again on the canvas done in July: "The work is going fairly well—I am struggling with a canvas that I had started a few days before my illness, a reaper; the study is entirely yellow, the paint put on terribly thick, but the motif was fine and simple." And then he goes on: "Well, I am working on it again, I won't let go, and I will try it again on a new canvas." The letter goes on to deal with various other subjects, and then, obviously after an interruption, we read: "Well the reaper is done, I believe that that is one you will hang in your home—it is a picture of death as it is told to us in the great book of nature."

The masterly portrait of the chief orderly, Trabu, 1774, is very close in style to the self-portrait with a light background, 1772. Vincent wrote in Letter 604 that he had started on the portrait, "and perhaps I shall also paint his wife, for he is married and lives in a small house close by the asylum." And further on in the same letter: "I have been working on the portrait of the orderly this afternoon and made some progress with it. If it were not considerably softened—completely softened—by an intelligent look and a good-natured expression, it would look like a real bird of prey."

The portrait that we know, 1774, is probably not, however, the original canvas, but a copy, for a few days later he wrote: "I have made the portrait of the orderly and I have a copy of it for you" (Letter 605, September 7). The same applies to the portrait of Trabu's wife, 1777, which he did in fact make a few days later.

Before Vincent started on the portrait of Madame Trabu, a picture of quite a different kind had been made, 1775 (colorplate XXXVI, page 420). September 5—and this shows how fast he continued to work—he wrote: "During my illness there was a slight accident—that Delacroix lithograph, the *Pietà*, along with some other sheets, fell into some oil and paint and was ruined. I was upset about it—so I made myself sit down to paint it and you will see it one fine day: I made a copy of it on a size-5 or -6 canvas, which, I believe, has feeling" (Letter 605).

Significance of the Pietà

Religious subjects are rare in Vincent's *oeuvre*; the *Pietà* constitutes an important exception. The way he put it in Letter 605 makes it apparent that in this case, however, it was not only his admiration for the work of Delacroix but also the religious nature of the subject that played a part in his decision to copy the print. The letter contains a bitter indictment of his pious surroundings and those in charge of the asylum "who willingly foster those sickly religious aberrations, whereas something ought to be done to cure them." But earlier in the letter he had said: "I am not indifferent, and when I suffer, religious thoughts sometimes give me great consolation."

Some viewers profess to see in the Christ a self-portrait because of his short brownish-red beard. In my view this is wrong, for as far as the likeness is concerned, Vincent very strictly followed the work he was copying, Célestin-François Nanteuil's lithograph after Delacroix. On the other hand, the color, of course, was Vincent's own addition. Another question is whether the painting as a whole may not be regarded as a self-portrait in the sense that the choice of the model may have unconsciously been influenced by an imagined similarity with his own situation: the suffering (strictly speaking, dead) human being behind whom a female figure rises up, with compassionate gesture and countenance.

This painting is the first in a long series of copies that occupied Vincent both this and the following year, when he would have to spend much of his time in his room. Using a metaphor borrowed from music, he explained somewhat later that he conceived them as "improvisations" in color of the black-and-white composition of a Delacroix or a Millet which he had before him: "I started doing

1766

1767

1766 Mountains with Dark Hut, F622
73 × 93 cm ($28\frac{3}{4} \times 36\frac{5}{8}$")
Justin K. Thannhauser Collection, Solomon R. Guggenheim Museum, New York

1767 Entrance to a Quarry, F635
52 × 64 cm ($20\frac{1}{2} \times 25\frac{1}{4}$")
Location unknown

September 1889

1768 Enclosed Field with Plowman, F625
49 × 62 cm ($19\frac{1}{4} \times 24\frac{3}{8}$")
Location unknown

1769 Enclosed Field with Plowman
Sketch in Letter 602
Rijksmuseum Vincent van Gogh, Amsterdam

1768

1769

1770

1771

1772

1773

1774

1770 Self-Portrait, F626
57 × 43.5 cm (22½ × 17⅜″)
Collection Mr. and Mrs. John Hay Whitney, New York
Colorplate XXXV, p. 419

1771 Vincent's Bedroom, F484
73 × 92 cm (28¾ × 36¼″)
Art Institute of Chicago

1772 Self-Portrait, F627
65 × 54 cm (25⅝ × 21¼″)
The Louvre, Paris

1773 Enclosed Field with Reaper at Sunrise, F618
74 × 92 cm (29⅛ × 36¼″)
Rijksmuseum Vincent van Gogh, Amsterdam

1774 Portrait of the Chief Orderly (Trabu), F629
61 × 46 cm (24 × 18⅛″)
Collection Mrs. G. Dübi-Müller, Solothurn, Switzerland

this by chance and I find that you learn something from it and especially that it is sometimes a consolation. In doing this my brush then moves between my fingers like a bow on a violin, and entirely for my own pleasure" (Letter 607).

As a final note on the *Pietà*, there is a replica, in a smaller size, 1776, which has always been erroneously taken to be a painting from the Auvers period (see Appendix, note 12).

Three September Works
Although none of the three following works is mentioned in the letters, there are various reasons that lead me to assume that they were made in September at about the same time as the portraits just discussed and as the copies made after Millet that will be dealt with shortly.

The painting *Half-Figure of an Angel* (1778) is a reproduction in color of an engraving Theo had sent Vincent in July or August. It fits in well with the works done during these weeks as regards color, for this, too, is another study in blue and yellow (the angel's halo and face are yellow, the background and the added side strips are bluish green to cobalt blue).

Portrait of a Farmer (1779) is one of countless paintings of Van Gogh's that one must see firsthand—or at least in color reproduction—in order to appreciate them fully. A delightful painting, which in its freshness and simplicity radiates health and joy in living, although by the expression of the eyes and mouth, Vincent characterizes the farmer as a difficult fellow. "As often as I get the opportunity to do so, I work on portraits, which I sometimes think myself are better and more serious than the rest of my work," Vincent wrote September 19 (Letter 606).*

One of the portraits alluded to here could also have been the small *Self-Portrait*, 1780. This is a very problematical work, and no further details about it can be found in Vincent's letters. Although I certainly do not find September 1889 unacceptable as a date, I am not inclined to agree with the *catalogue raisonné* in linking this small painting with the references in the letters (for example, Letters 608 and 612) to a "small self-portrait" that Vincent had intended for his mother and sister. The present work looks as though it was abandoned in an unfinished state and, both as a painting and as a portrait, is far from being attractive enough for the family "collection."

Copies and Smaller Replicas
In September, Vincent must have worked intensively and rapidly on copies—in addition to that of the *Pietà*. September 19 he was able to write Theo: "At the moment I have seven copies out of the ten of *Les Travaux des Champs* [*The Labors of the Field*] by Millet" (Letter 607). He had made those copies from wood engravings by Jacques-Adrien Lavieille sent to him by Theo. We do not know exactly which of the ten he had

*The 1970 *catalogue raisonné* dates the painting April 1889, and earlier authorities give May or June, but there is nothing to indicate that Vincent made any portraits at that time.

1775

1776

1777

1775 Pietà (after Delacroix), F630
73 × 60.5 cm (28¾ × 24″)
Rijksmuseum Vincent van Gogh, Amsterdam
Colorplate XXXVI, p. 420

1776 Pietà (after Delacroix), F757
42 × 34 cm (16½ × 13⅜″)
Private collection, Los Angeles

1777 Portrait of the Wife of the Chief Orderly, F631
Canvas on panel, 64 × 49 cm (25¼ × 19¼″)
Location unknown

1778 Half-Figure of an Angel (after an etching), F624
54 × 64 cm (21¼ × 25¼″)
Location unknown

1779 Portrait of a Farmer, F531
61 × 50 cm (24 × 19⅝″)
Civica Galleria d'Arte Moderna, Milan

1780 Self-Portrait, F528
51 × 45 cm (20⅛ × 17¾″)
Nasjonalgalleriet, Oslo

1778

1779

1780

1781

1782

1783

1784

1781 Woman Binding Sheaves (after Millet), F 700
43.5×33.5 cm ($17\frac{3}{8} \times 13\frac{3}{8}''$)
Rijksmuseum Vincent van Gogh, Amsterdam

1782 Reaper with Sickle (after Millet), F 687
43.5×33.5 cm ($17\frac{3}{8} \times 13\frac{3}{8}''$)
Rijksmuseum Vincent van Gogh, Amsterdam

1783 Reaper with Scythe (after Millet), F 688
43.5×25 cm ($17\frac{3}{8} \times 9\frac{7}{8}''$)
Location unknown

1784 Thresher (after Millet), F 692
44×27 cm ($17\frac{3}{8} \times 10\frac{5}{8}''$)
Rijksmuseum Vincent van Gogh, Amsterdam

then completed; in Letter 607 only the small painting *Sheepshearers*, 1787, is mentioned by name as the last one he was working on at that particular time. We know that he did not get around to doing one of the ten until much later, in February 1890 (Letter 626), but I assume that, with this single exception, he did the series in sequence and thus had completed nine copies after Millet, all small paintings, soon after September 19: 1781–89.

Later, in January 1890, Vincent wrote: "Those copies now—you will see them some time—I have not sent to you, because, more than the present ones, they were only hesitant attempts ["*des tâtonnements*"] but they have still greatly helped me with *Les* [*Quatre*] *Heures de la Journée* [*The Four Hours of the Day*, on which he was then working]" (Letter 623). There is no denying that this group does not have the same standing in Vincent's *oeuvre* as do some of the other copies, such as the *Pietà*, 1775, or the *Good Samaritan*, 1974, but they are nevertheless charming little paintings in which Millet had not, in fact, been simply copied by Vincent but, as he put it, had been "translated into another language" (Letter 613).

The range of colors, however typical of Van Gogh, is quite limited here: it has been reduced to a simple clear contrast, that of the primary colors yellow and blue. Vincent has achieved this by putting all his figures in clothes of a cool blue, varying from pale to deep, which, together with the predominantly blue skies, sets off the warm golden yellow of the grain.

All the work that Vincent had done since his illness had been accomplished entirely in his bedroom or studio. Even September 7 he had written: "I have not been in the open air for two months" (Letter 605), and the copies after Millet had also, of course, been done indoors. It is not entirely clear whether he stayed indoors by choice or by order of Dr. Peyron. Somewhat ambiguously he says: "That semifreedom often prevents you from doing what you feel you are quite capable of doing" (Letter 608). And while he confessed to Theo that he could not stand the company of the other patients and therefore "did not go downstairs" (Letter 605), he wrote to his mother in a more positive vein: "These last weeks have gone very well for me as far as my health is concerned, and I work from morning to night almost without a break, day in and day out, and I shut myself up in the studio to avoid being distracted" (Letter 606).

In this manner, four more small works were produced within the walls of the asylum: 1790–93. This time they were copies, not of the work of others, but of his own work, done on a smaller scale for his mother and Wil. From indications in the letters, they appear to have been made in the latter part of September. They were smaller versions of the paintings already known to us—*Wheat Field with Cypresses*, 1755, *Olive Orchard*, 1758, *Enclosed Field with Reaper at Sunrise*, 1773, and *Vincent's Bedroom*, 1608—and it is therefore understandable that Vincent, having no further use for these larger canvases, also sent them to Theo in December, together with the smaller ones for his mother and sister.

Just one further comment: Once Mother

1785

1786

1787

1785 Sheaf Binder (after Millet), F693
44 × 32.5 cm ($17\frac{3}{8} \times 13''$)
Rijksmuseum Vincent van Gogh, Amsterdam

1786 Woman Spinning (after Millet), F696
40 × 25.5 cm ($15\frac{3}{4} \times 10\frac{1}{4}''$)
Private collection

1787 Sheepshearers (after Millet), F634
43 × 29 cm ($16\frac{7}{8} \times 11\frac{3}{8}''$)
Rijksmuseum Vincent van Gogh, Amsterdam

1788 Peasant Woman Cutting Straw (after Millet), F697
40.5 × 26.5 cm ($16\frac{1}{8} \times 10\frac{5}{8}''$)
Rijksmuseum Vincent van Gogh, Amsterdam

1789 Peasant Woman with Rake (after Millet), F698
39 × 24 cm ($15\frac{3}{8} \times 9\frac{1}{2}''$)
Location unknown

1790 Wheat Field with Cypresses, F743
52 × 65 cm ($20\frac{1}{2} \times 25\frac{5}{8}''$)
Location unknown

1791 Olive Orchard, F711
53.5 × 64.5 cm ($21\frac{1}{4} \times 25\frac{5}{8}''$)
Private collection, Switzerland

1792 Enclosed Field with Reaper at Sunrise, F619
59.5 × 73 cm ($23\frac{5}{8} \times 28\frac{3}{4}''$)
Museum Folkwang, Essen

1788

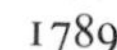

1789

1790

1791

1792

1793

1794

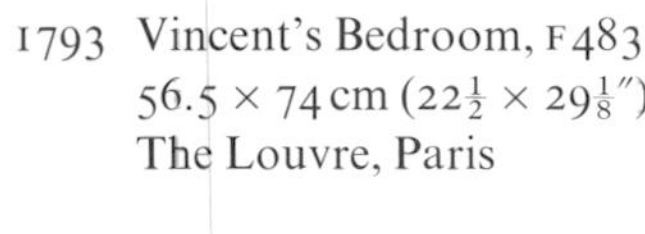

1793 Vincent's Bedroom, F483
56.5 × 74 cm ($22\frac{1}{2} \times 29\frac{1}{8}$")
The Louvre, Paris

October 1889

1794 Landscape with Plowman, F706
54 × 67 cm ($21\frac{1}{4} \times 26\frac{3}{8}$")
Collection W. A. Coolidge, Cambridge, Massachusetts

van Gogh and Sister Wil had received the small paintings, they seem to have attached little importance to them. According, at least, to the data in the 1970 *catalogue raisonné*, these all ended up in the hands of various foreign owners at a very early stage.

Outdoors Again

The indoor period must have come to an end in the final days of September. Vincent's first letters from October mention paintings that he had done outdoors, some of them even outside the asylum walls. Thus, in Letter 609, October 5: the *Mulberry Tree*, 1796, and *Two Poplars with a Background of Mountains*, 1797. His own comments on these canvases, in which yellow is strongly predominant, are somewhat surprising because he connects them with Monticelli: "I have a few studies, including a completely yellow *Mulberry Tree* on stony ground, which stands out against the blue of the sky, and you will see, I believe, in this study that I have picked up the trail of Monticelli." In the same letter he mentions once again "a garden scene, a fall effect, in which the drawing is a bit more naïve and ... more domestic."

A few days later, even two of these are mentioned: "I also have two views of the garden and the asylum in which the place looks quite pleasant. I have tried to reconstruct the whole thing as it might have been by simplifying and by accentuating the proud and unchanging character of the pine trees and cedar groves against the blue sky" (Letter 610).

Although 1798 and 1799 must have been the paintings referred to here, the studies of trees, 1800 and 1801, which were also made in the monastery garden, were probably done at about the same time.

One of the next landscapes mentioned must actually have been started earlier. In Letter 610 Vincent wrote: "I have just brought back a canvas on which I have been working for some time, once again representing the same field as that of the reaper." The description makes it clear that 1795 is the landscape meant here, and even though Vincent called it "again a rough study" ("une étude rude"), he was rather pleased with it. He wrote Bernard regarding this work: "I have gotten better control of myself in these recent studies because my state of health has become more stable" (Letter B20).

The last remark also referred to 1802, a painting which he announced, also in Letter 610, as follows: "This week I also made the *Entrance to a Quarry*, which looks like something Japanese; you remember, of course, that there are Japanese drawings of rocks where here and there herbs and small trees are growing."

It was a rather cryptic landscape, and the subject can scarcely be discerned in a black-and-white reproduction, but it does seem to have something Japanese about it and fascinates by the simple contrast of the somewhat somber green and reddish brown and by the interplay of the wavy lines of the branches of the pine trees.

Even less easily decipherable as to subject is 1803, a landscape which is almost an abstract color composition: violet to soft mauve rocks surrounding a rust-brown, green-spotted central portion. Fortunately there is a canvas presenting a clearer picture of (probably) the same spot, the much more important painting 1804, always referred to by Vincent as "the ravine."

Comparing the two studies, one recognizes in the blue-striped patch at the bottom of 1803 the small brook that is crossed by a footbridge in the larger canvas.

In Letter 610, Vincent further reports that he had also worked indoors, and we may assume that this occurred, too, during that productive first week of October: "I have made an almost entirely violet copy of that

1795

1796

1797

1795 Enclosed Field with Farmer Carrying a Bundle of Straw, F641
73 × 92 cm ($28\frac{3}{4} \times 36\frac{1}{4}''$)
Indianapolis Museum of Art

1796 Mulberry Tree, F637
54 × 65 cm ($21\frac{1}{4} \times 25\frac{5}{8}''$)
Norton Simon Foundation, Los Angeles

1797 Two Poplars with a Background of Mountains, F638
61 × 45.5 cm ($24 \times 18\frac{1}{8}''$)
Cleveland Museum of Art

1798 Trees in the Garden of the Asylum, F64
73 × 60 cm ($28\frac{3}{4} \times 23\frac{5}{8}''$)
Private collection, Switzerland

1798

1799

1800

1801

1802

1803

1804

1799 Trees in Front of the Entrance to the Asylum, F643
90 × 71 cm (35⅜ × 28″)
The Armand Hammer Collection, Los Angeles

1800 Trees in the Garden of the Asylum, F640
64.5 × 49 cm (25⅝ × 19¼″)
Private collection, Geneva

1801 Trees in the Garden of the Asylum, F731
42 × 32 cm (16½ × 12⅝″)
Private collection, Switzerland

1802 Entrance to a Quarry, F744
60 × 72.5 cm (23⅝ × 28¾″)
Rijksmuseum Vincent van Gogh, Amsterdam

1803 A Small Stream in the Mountains, F645
31 × 40 cm (12¼ × 15¾″)
Rijksmuseum Vincent van Gogh, Amsterdam

1804 A Path through the Ravine, F662
73 × 92 cm (28¾ × 36¼″)
Museum of Fine Arts, Boston

woman with a child seated by a hearth by Madame Demont-Breton." Virginie Demont-Breton's painting had been exhibited that year at the Paris Salon, and Vincent must have read about it. His own "violet" copy was naturally made from a black-and-white reproduction, which he must have found in a magazine or which had been sent by Theo (1805).

One further canvas that might be ascribed to October is the fairly large *Landscape with Plowman*, 1794, of which there is no trace in the letters.

No More Canvas

After the intensive activity at the beginning of October, Vincent experienced an unexpected setback which interfered with his work as seriously as sickness would have. He had already asked Theo October 5 for zinc white and canvas (Letter 609), and a few days later he had to follow this up with: "If you have not yet sent off the canvas and paint, then I must tell you that at this moment I am without any canvas at all," and this is repeated with great emphasis at the end of the letter (Letter 610). Unfortunately it took a considerable time on this occasion—for reasons we do not know—before Theo helped him out, and thus it appears that from October 5 to about October 23, more than half a month, Vincent was unable, for lack of canvas, to make a single painting (see also Letter 611).

But lack of canvas would not prevent him from finding an outlet for his creative urge in drawing, and we can be sure that a fairly large number of drawings, mainly of trees in the garden during the fall, originated in these two weeks, to the extent that he did not spend the time walking. These are the drawings 1809–31, all done in the same style and all variations of more or less the same subject.

It also seems likely to me that the three remarkable and well-known gouaches that Vincent made of one of the corridors of the monastery, 1808 (colorplate XXXVII, page 437), of the entrance hall, 1806, and of the room where he customarily worked, 1807, must date from this time when he was unable to paint. They are powerful drawings—marked by a quietly controlled perspective—in which, for the first time, Vincent has been able to provide us also with a vivid impression of the interior of the monastery.*

There was a similar problem with canvas three to four weeks later. About November 20, Vincent again wrote Theo: "I have used up all my canvas," and he asked him to send ten yards as soon as possible. "Then I am going to attack the cypresses and the mountains" (Letter 615).

It was December 7 before he wrote Theo again: "I want to thank you very much for the ten yards of canvas which have just arrived" (Letter 618). We must therefore assume that between about November 20 and December 7, too, Vincent had been able to do little or no painting. There may, however, have been one canvas, for in that same letter, written when the canvas had "just arrived," he spoke about the painting of the road menders in Saint-Rémy (1860 or 1861) as "the last study he had made."

An Admirer

October 22 Theo sent Vincent some papers and periodicals, including a short, but very forcefully worded note about Van Gogh's work—the first public appreciation it received, half a year before G.-Albert Aurier's subsequently famous article in the *Mercure de France*.

*The picture shown on the upper right wall of Vincent's room apparently represents the painting of trees, dating from October (1801); this is an indication that the watercolor was done later.

1805

1806

1807

1805 Woman with Baby, Sitting at the Fireside (after Virginie Demont-Breton), F644
66 × 51 cm (26 × 20⅛″)
Location unknown

1806 The Vestibule of the Asylum, F1530
Black chalk, gouache, 61.5 × 47 cm (24⅜ × 18½″)
Rijksmuseum Vincent van Gogh, Amsterdam

1807 Window of Vincent's Studio at the Asylum, F1528
Black chalk, gouache, 61.5 × 47 cm (24⅜ × 18½″)
Rijksmuseum Vincent van Gogh, Amsterdam

1808

1809

1810

1811

1812

1813

1814

1808 A Passageway at the Asylum, F 1529
Black chalk, gouache, 65 × 49 cm ($25\frac{5}{8} \times 19\frac{1}{4}''$)
Museum of Modern Art, New York
Colorplate XXXVII, p. 437

1809 Two Trunks of Pine Trees, F 1579
Pencil, 30 × 20.5 cm ($11\frac{3}{4} \times 8\frac{1}{4}''$)
Rijksmuseum Vincent van Gogh, Amsterdam

1810 Treetop Seen against the Wall of the Asylum, F 1580
Pencil, 30 × 20.5 cm ($11\frac{3}{4} \times 8\frac{1}{4}''$)
Rijksmuseum Vincent van Gogh, Amsterdam

1811 Pine Trees in the Garden of the Asylum, F 1581
Pencil, 30 × 20 cm ($11\frac{3}{4} \times 7\frac{7}{8}''$)
Rijksmuseum Vincent van Gogh, Amsterdam

1812 A Pine Tree and Cypresses in the Garden of the Asylum, F 1574
Pencil, 33 × 25.5 cm ($13 \times 10\frac{1}{4}''$)
Collection Fraukje Wezelaar, Sydney, Australia

1813 Field with Bare Tree, F 1562
Pencil, 23.5 × 32.5 cm ($9\frac{1}{4} \times 13''$)
Rijksmuseum Vincent van Gogh, Amsterdam

1814 Path between Pine Trees, F 1582
Black chalk, 20.5 × 30 cm ($8\frac{1}{4} \times 11\frac{3}{4}''$)
Rijksmuseum Vincent van Gogh, Amsterdam

The author was J.J. Isaäcson, a Dutch painter who lived for a while in Paris and, with Jacob Meyer de Haan, belonged to Theo's circle of friends. He must therefore have been very well informed about Vincent's work and the circumstances of his life.

Vincent reacted: "No need to tell you that I find what he said in a footnote about me to be highly exaggerated, and with all the more reason I would prefer that he say *nothing* about me" (Letter 611). This does not mean that Vincent did not appreciate the article itself. He expressed himself with feeling in writing about it, saying: "In what he says one feels very strongly that he is a very troubled and very good person who is happy when he can admire."

What had Isaäcson written about him? In the article, entitled "Gevoelens over de Nederlandsche kunst op de Parijsche Wereldtentoonstelling" ("Opinions about Dutch Art at the Paris World's Fair"), Isaäcson had written these prophetic words: "Who interprets for us in forms and colors the mighty life, the great life once more becoming aware of itself in this nineteenth century? One I know, a solitary pioneer, he stands alone struggling in the deep night, his name, Vincent, is for posterity." And the footnote to this read: "About this remarkable hero—he is a Dutchman—I hope to be able to say something later."* It was like the clarion call of a herald.

Once Vincent had canvas again, he immediately set to work, and his first theme was one of the etchings by Millet that Theo had sent. This time he made a large copy (1833). Writing about October 25 to acknowledge receipt of the shipment from Theo, he said: "This morning I started on the diggers, using a size-30 canvas" (Letter 611).

Although this painting may look simple, Vincent spent a good deal of time on it. He was still working on it at the beginning of November (Letter 613), and it was not until December 7 that he wrote: "I have also completed the copy of *Men Digging*, or almost" (Letter 618). The work, entitled *Two Diggers* here, must actually have been finished in December, for it was among the paintings that were sent to Theo January 3 (Letter 621).

The only information we have about the portrait of a man, 1832, comes from a letter that Vincent wrote to his mother about October 23: "At the moment I am working on a portrait of one of the patients here." And this is followed by a reflection that makes us think again about the atmosphere in which he worked: "It is funny, but after you have been with them for a while and have gotten used to them, you no longer think of them as being crazy" (Letter 612).

In Letter 613, the works by Millet are again discussed. After *Two Diggers*, the next in line were two works from the series *Les Quatre Heures de la Journée—La Veillée (The Family at Night)* and *Fin de la Journée (The End of the Day)*, 1834 and 1835. At Vincent's request, Theo had also sent him

*Apparently as a result of Vincent's letter to Isaäcson, which has not been preserved, the contemplated article was not written. However, they did correspond at a later date; see Vincent's Letter 614*a*, beginning of June 1890.

1815

1816

1817

1818

1819

1820

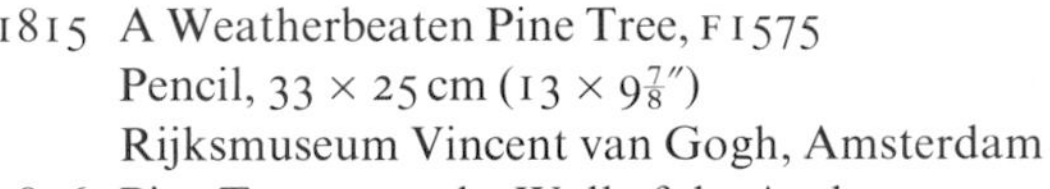

1815 A Weatherbeaten Pine Tree, F 1575
Pencil, 33 × 25 cm ($13 \times 9\frac{7}{8}''$)
Rijksmuseum Vincent van Gogh, Amsterdam

1816 Pine Trees near the Wall of the Asylum, F 1576v (reverse: 1817)
Pencil, 30 × 16.5 cm ($11\frac{3}{4} \times 6\frac{3}{4}''$)
Rijksmuseum Vincent van Gogh, Amsterdam

1817 A Bare Treetop in the Garden of the Asylum, F 1576 (reverse: 1816)
Pencil, 30 × 16.5 cm ($11\frac{3}{4} \times 6\frac{3}{4}''$)
Rijksmuseum Vincent van Gogh, Amsterdam

1818 Pine Trees Seen against the Wall of the Asylum, F 1571
Pencil, 30 × 20.5 cm ($11\frac{3}{4} \times 8\frac{1}{4}''$)
Rijksmuseum Vincent van Gogh, Amsterdam

1819 A Row of Bare Trees, F 1578
Black chalk, 23.5 × 30.5 cm ($9\frac{1}{2} \times 12\frac{1}{4}''$)
Rijksmuseum Vincent van Gogh, Amsterdam

1820 Garden of the Asylum with Tree Trunks and a Stone Bench, F 1577
Pencil, 19.5 × 29 cm ($7\frac{7}{8} \times 11\frac{3}{8}''$)
Rijksmuseum Vincent van Gogh, Amsterdam

Colorplate XXXV, Self-Portrait, 1770 ›

wood engravings of these by Jacques-Adrien Lavieille. In the letter, Vincent wrote: "I have *The Family at Night* and am working on the *Diggers* and the *Man Putting on His Jacket*, size-30 canvases, and the *Sower*, smaller. *The Family at Night* is a gamut of violets and soft mauves with pale lemon-yellow light from the lamp, also the orange-colored glow of the fire and the man in red ocher." To this Vincent added: "I would like Jo to see *The Family at Night*"—obviously thinking about her approaching motherhood.

Since we are confronted in Letter 613 alone—in the above passages and others—with no fewer than eight different subjects, we can safely assume that his method of procedure was once again to work on a number of canvases simultaneously. While most of the subjects—such as *The Family at Night*, *The End of the Day*, and *Sower*—are easy to identify, there are a few problems. *Sower*, a very old acquaintance of Vincent's, seems to have been made in two versions, although he mentions only one: 1836 and 1837. *The Shepherdess* (1838), after Millet's so-called *Grande Bergère*—which he turned into a symphony of blue—is not mentioned at all in Vincent's list. I have included it in this series because it clearly fits in, but it may also have been done somewhat later, since Vincent continued making copies until the end of the year.

This was undoubtedly connected with the weather, which was becoming less and less favorable for working out of doors. On one occasion a rainstorm seems to have kept him indoors and to have enticed him into making yet another of the countless paintings of the view from his window, now transformed into bluish-gray and brown hues by the streaming rain (1839). He mentions this in Letter 613, along with a number of subjects which the garden provided for him and which now, after all his enforced drawing, he was finally able to render in the glowing autumn colors he was so fond of: "Besides that, I am working on a rain effect and an evening effect with big pine trees. And also on a landscape with falling leaves. . . . I have also done a canvas for Dr. Peyron; a view of the building with a large pine tree. . . . Finally, you will see that in a large landscape with pine trees—red-ocher trunks outlined in black—there is more character than in the previous ones."

It requires no great effort of imagination to conclude that the description "evening effect with big pine trees" was meant to apply to 1843, an impressive painting done in virtually only two colors. Apart from some red of the setting sun and the black outlines, there is only the olive-green of the bizarre pine trees and their branches and the yellow of the evening sky, reflected on the trunks and the patches of light on the ground.

The "landscape with falling leaves" ("une chute des feuilles," literally, "a fall of leaves," in the artistic phrase used by Vincent) must be 1844, a painting in which one can actually see the yellow leaves fluttering down along the red-brown and green trunks. The composition of this canvas is rather curious also because of the way that the two trunks in the foreground divide the picture plane, seen from a high vantage point, into two sections. There is a strong temptation to see a

1821

1822

1823

1824

1825

1826

1821 Pine Trees near the Wall of the Asylum, F 1570
Pencil, black chalk, 25 × 32 cm ($9\frac{7}{8} \times 12\frac{5}{8}$″)
Rijksmuseum Vincent van Gogh, Amsterdam

1822 Trees and a Stone Bench in the Garden of the Asylum, F 1572v (reverse: 1830)
Pencil, black chalk, 18.5 × 29 cm ($7\frac{1}{2} \times 11\frac{3}{8}$″)
Rijksmuseum Vincent van Gogh, Amsterdam

1823 A Group of Pine Trees near a House, F 1573
Black chalk, 25 × 32.5 cm ($9\frac{7}{8} \times 13$″)
Rijksmuseum Vincent van Gogh, Amsterdam

1824 Pine Trees Seen against the Wall of the Asylum, F 1563
Pencil, 20.5 × 30 cm ($8\frac{1}{4} \times 11\frac{3}{4}$″)
Rijksmuseum Vincent van Gogh, Amsterdam

1825 Pine Trees in Front of the Wall of the Asylum, F 1564
Pencil, 25 × 32.5 cm ($9\frac{7}{8} \times 13$″)
Collection D. de Wolff Peereboom, Bergen, The Netherlands

1826 Pine Trees in Front of the Wall of the Asylum, F 1565
Pencil, 21 × 30 cm ($8\frac{1}{4} \times 13\frac{3}{4}$″)
Rijksmuseum Vincent van Gogh, Amsterdam

self-portrait in the solitary figure walking along the forest path, and also in the figure listlessly reclining on a bench in the counterpart to this painting, 1845, and in the small figure of a stroller in 1846.

Finally, the "canvas for Dr. Peyron" mentioned in Letter 613 must certainly have been the painting in which the entrance area of the asylum is depicted in a rather naïve picturebook manner and, actually, "with a large pine tree," 1840. It does not seem too farfetched to suggest that the somewhat self-satisfied figure standing with his hands in his pockets in front of the building represents Dr. Peyron himself, for whom the canvas was intended. Yet no attempt has been made to endow the face with individual features.

A pair of fall studies not referred to in any letter but similar in treatment to canvases such as 1845, the one with the reclining figure, are 1847 and 1848. The impressive, colorful, yet controlled canvas showing a sawed-off tree, 1849, is described in considerable detail by Vincent in Letter B21. An almost identical replica, 1850, was probably made at about the same time, but it is impossible to determine which is the original and which the copy. The only difference is in the color of sky, which is predominantly yellow in 1850, but tempered by a pink cloud in the other work. When Vincent, in Letter 618, written when he was sending off a number of paintings, referred to "the study of the institution and garden, of which there are two variants," he probably meant these two similar large canvases. Among other studies to which that same description would be applicable (1798, 1799, 1840, and 1841), there are no two so similar as to qualify as "two variants."

Vincent also made—either as a preliminary study or as a "copy"—the fairly large reed-pen drawing of this subject, 1851; and, in my opinion, the reed-pen drawing of the wind-blown pine trees in the garden, 1852, is most closely allied to this by reason of its autumnal character.

Olive Trees Once More

In June, Vincent had done work on several occasions in the olive orchards surrounding the monastery of Saint-Paul, and he now was impelled to return to this subject. After receiving photographs of work by Bernard, including a *Christ in the Garden of Olives*, which he thought appalling, and after reading a letter from Gauguin, in which he announced that he was dealing with this subject and enclosed a sketch of the work, Vincent burst forth: "I have been working in the olive orchards this month, for they made me furious with their *Christ in the Garden of Olives*, in which nothing had been observed.... To shake this off, I have been spending these clear and cold days, with, however, a fine and radiant sun, toiling away every morning and afternoon in the olive orchards, and the result is five size-30 canvases, which, together with the three studies of olive trees that you have, at least constitute an attack on the difficult problem."

Vincent van Gogh's olive orchards are ranked, and with good reason, among his most famous subjects. As many biographies and descriptions of his work point out, this theme was one that clearly enabled him to express what was most personal in his make-up as an artist. Although his own explanation of his obsession with the olive trees was that they were in his view extremely characteristic of the southern landscape, it is hard to disagree with the writers who see in the gnarled trunks and the twisted branches a reflection of his own tormented psyche. The bizarre shapes of these trees must certainly have played their part as a subconscious motive for the continual harking back to this subject.

The new olive orchards, however, differ sharply from the earlier ones, and—while this is naturally a subjective judgment—it seems

1827

1828

1829

1830

1831

1827 Pine Trees along a Road to a House, F 1569
Black chalk, 25 × 32.5 cm ($9\frac{7}{8} \times 13''$)
Rijksmuseum Vincent van Gogh, Amsterdam

1828 A Group of Pine Trees, F 1567
Pencil, 25.5 × 32.5 cm ($10\frac{1}{4} \times 13''$)
Rijksmuseum Vincent van Gogh, Amsterdam

1829 Pine Trees in Front of the Wall of the Asylum, F 1568
Pencil, 33 × 25 cm ($13 \times 9\frac{7}{8}''$)
Rijksmuseum Vincent van Gogh, Amsterdam

1830 Pine Trees Seen against the Wall of the Asylum, F 1572 (reverse: 1822)
Pencil, 29 × 18.5 cm ($11\frac{3}{8} \times 7\frac{1}{2}''$)
Rijksmuseum Vincent van Gogh, Amsterdam

1832

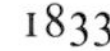

1833

1834

1835

1836

1837

1838

1831 Pine Trees in Front of the Wall of the Asylum, F1566
Pencil, 25 × 32.5 cm ($9\frac{7}{8}$ × 13″)
Private collection, Amsterdam

1832 Portrait of a Patient, F703
32 × 23.5 cm ($12\frac{5}{8}$ × $9\frac{1}{2}$″)
Rijksmuseum Vincent van Gogh, Amsterdam

1833 Two Diggers (after Millet), F648
72 × 92 cm ($28\frac{3}{8}$ × $36\frac{1}{4}$″)
Stedelijk Museum, Amsterdam

November 1889

1834 The Family at Night (after Millet), F647
72.5 × 92 cm ($28\frac{3}{4}$ × $36\frac{1}{4}$″)
Rijksmuseum Vincent van Gogh, Amsterdam

1835 The End of the Day (after Millet), F649
72 × 92 cm ($28\frac{3}{8}$ × $36\frac{1}{4}$″)
Collection Walter P. Chrysler, Jr., New York

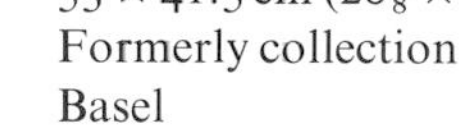

1836 Sower (after Millet), F689
64 × 55 cm ($25\frac{1}{4}$ × $21\frac{5}{8}$″)
Rijksmuseum Kröller-Müller, Otterlo

1837 Sower (after Millet), F690
81 × 65 cm ($31\frac{7}{8}$ × $25\frac{5}{8}$″)
Stavros S. Niarchos Collection

1838 The Shepherdess (after Millet), F699
53 × 41.5 cm ($20\frac{7}{8}$ × $16\frac{1}{2}$″)
Formerly collection Robert von Hirsch, Basel

to me that Vincent was here unable to achieve the beauty and power of those done earlier. In these later pictures, 1853–57, there is a formalistic element and an element of labored repetition-in-variation that detracts considerably from the spontaneous power of the canvases done in June.

To be sure, in 1853 the composition is somewhat enlivened by the presence of the figures of the olive pickers, and, in 1856 in particular, there is no lack of expressive force because here the deep-yellow sky with the yellow disk of the sun above the bluish-gray mountains strongly counterbalances the brownish-red earth and the bluish-green foliage. Generally speaking, however, these five landscapes add little to the varied picture Vincent had already been able to give of the olive trees.

Finally, there is also a *smaller* canvas of the olive trees, as seen against a blue sky with white clouds, 1858. While there is no external evidence for dating this work, in my opinion it was most likely made in connection with the five size-30 canvases depicting this subject. The treatment of the ground, for example, with its little blocks of paint in many colors, bears a close resemblance to that series. There is a striking reed-pen drawing in brown ink of the same scene, 1859, which exhibits a masterly technique of rapid independent short strokes characteristic of the few other pen-and-ink drawings of these months.

Exhibitions

In a letter dated May 21, Theo told Vincent that before long there was to be an exhibition of the Indépendants and asked him which paintings he thought were most suitable to be shown (Letter T9). Vincent answered that it was all one to him ("just act as if I weren't here"), but nevertheless suggested *The Starry Night* as a possibility. In September, when the exhibition of the Indépendants was open, Theo reported that of the two important canvases he had sent in on Vincent's behalf—*The Starry Night* (1592) and *Irises* (1691)—the first was hung less favorably, but the latter was much admired (Letter T16, September 5). In the meantime another possibility of showing Vincent's work had presented itself. In July, Octave Maus, the secretary of Les XX (Les Vingt), in Brussels, had invited Vincent—through Theo as intermediary—to take part in an exhibition of his group, but due to his illness Vincent had not been able to reply to the letter Theo had sent him (Letter T12, July 16).

This invitation can certainly be taken as a sign that Vincent's extremely individualistic and unorthodox work was beginning to achieve a certain amount of fame even beyond the very small circle of Paris colleagues who had thus far seen something of it. Vincent must have realized this. In November, when Theo came back to the request (Letter T20) and forwarded a letter from Octave Maus himself, Vincent made a fairly large selection of works to show with Les XX—six large canvases—which in itself gave evidence of much self-confidence. Writing to Theo, he put it this way: "This is what I would like to show at the Vingtistes [exhibition]: the two companion pieces of the *Sunflowers;* the *Ivy*, vertical format; the *Orchard in Bloom* (which Tanguy is showing right now) with the poplars that intersect the canvas; *The Red Vineyard; Wheat Field with Rising Sun*, on which I am now working" (Letter 614). These were, respectively, 1561, 1562, 1693, 1685, 1626, and 1862.

When the public went to view his entries, they caused something of an uproar but—more important still—at this exhibition one of his paintings was finally sold.

Busy Again

When Vincent, after having to do without canvas for some three weeks, received an-

1839

1840

1841

1839 Enclosed Field in the Rain, F650
73.5 × 92.5 cm ($29\frac{1}{8} \times 36\frac{5}{8}$")
Collection Henry P. McIlhenny, Philadelphia

1840 Pine Tree in Front of the Entrance to the Asylum, F653
58 × 45 cm ($22\frac{7}{8} \times 17\frac{3}{4}$")
The Louvre, Paris

1841 Trees in the Garden of the Asylum, F730
50 × 63 cm ($19\frac{5}{8} \times 24\frac{3}{4}$")
Private collection

1842 Stone Bench in the Garden of the Asylum, F732
39 × 46 cm ($15\frac{3}{8} \times 18\frac{1}{8}$")
Museu de Arte, São Paulo

1842

1843

1844

1845

1846

1847

1848

1843 Weatherbeaten Pine Trees against the Setting Sun, F652
92 × 73 cm (36¼ × 28¾″)
Rijksmuseum Kröller-Müller, Otterlo

1844 Man Walking in a Wood with Falling Leaves, F651
73.5 × 60 cm (29⅛ × 23⅝″)
Rijksmuseum Vincent van Gogh, Amsterdam

1845 Path in a Wood with Sitting Figure, F733
61 × 50 cm (24 × 19⅝″)
Rijksmuseum Kröller-Müller, Otterlo

1846 Man Walking among the Trees, F742
46 × 51 cm (18⅛ × 20⅛″)
Rijksmuseum Kröller-Müller, Otterlo

1847 Two Men Digging among the Trees, F701
62 × 44 cm (24⅜ × 17⅜″)
Detroit Institute of Arts

1848 Woman Walking under the Trees, F818
50 × 65.5 cm (19⅝ × 26″)
Baltimore Museum of Art

other ten yards December 7, he went back to work with a vengeance. He wrote to Theo that day: "The last study I did is a view of the village where they are working—underneath enormous plane trees—repairing the pavement. So there are piles of sand, stones, and gigantic trunks" (Letter 618). It may reasonably be assumed that for this purpose he used some of the old canvas that had been left over—in other words, that the study had been started some weeks before, especially as there are *two* almost identical versions of this important canvas, 1860 and 1861. When Vincent sent one of these to Theo at the beginning of January he mentioned the replica also: "'The Large Plane Trees'—the principal street or boulevard of Saint-Rémy, study from nature: I have a replica of it here which is perhaps more finished" (Letter 621).

They are large canvases, lacking all conventional charm but striking by reason of the fall colors and particularly the bizarre composition: the gigantic plane trees—rendered by bold brushstrokes in bluish gray, beige, brown, and red—dominate the picture with their orange-red fall foliage to such a degree that the façades in the background, the women of Arles in their national dress, and the summarily sketched road workers are scarcely noticed.

A few days later, as appears from a letter to Wil, Vincent was working on an even more important landscape, a canvas to which he gave the title "Field of Young Wheat at Sunrise."

This painting, 1862, which, as we have seen, he had intended for the exhibition of Les XX in Brussels, he had taken up again, and he now told Wil: "At the moment I am reworking this canvas; it is (together with the *Orchard in Bloom*, which Theo said he liked) the loveliest thing I have made" (Letter W16). This new canvas has a richness of color that is unprecedented, far surpassing the forced yellow of the painting of the enclosed field, 1753, and even the more varied palette apparent in the replica 1773. The mosaiclike technique with small blocks of paint in contrasting colors (applied in a much more sensitive and natural manner than in the latest olive orchards) imparts both to the field, shining in the rising sun, and to the multicolored morning sky a luster such as Vincent had rarely achieved before.

In drawing 1863 he has laid out the composition of this work, with its curious crossing diagonals and perspective lines, in the same way as he had done in June and July with the most important of his canvases of that time.

Other December Landscapes

Even if we assume that the work on *Enclosed Field with Young Wheat and Rising Sun* had for the most part been done in November, it is still remarkable that Vincent was able to make something like a dozen pantings—all of them landscapes, despite the cold—during the few weeks left to him in December (he again became ill before Christmas).

Several of these twelve, however, cannot with any certainty be ascribed to December, and most of them are undoubtedly of less significance than the somewhat earlier works such as the street scene in Saint-Rémy and the landscape at sunrise, which have just been mentioned. In the effort to determine which of them date from December, indirect references can also be helpful. A case in point is Vincent's description of paintings that he sent to Theo at the beginning of January and must therefore have completed at least a few weeks earlier. A whole list of such works is given in Letter 621, January 3, and, in Letter 622, written the next day, he mentioned two other canvases he had sent to his old friend Roulin in Marseilles.

Among the works discussed in Letter 621 is "*Fields*—fields of young wheat, a background of mauve mountains, and a yellowish sky."

1849

1850

1851

1849 A Corner of the Asylum and the Garden with a Heavy, Sawed-Off Tree, F660
73.5 × 92 cm (29⅛ × 36¼")
Museum Folkwang, Essen

1850 A Corner of the Asylum and the Garden with a Heavy, Sawed-Off Tree, F659
71.5 × 90.5 cm (28⅜ × 35⅞")
Rijksmuseum Vincent van Gogh, Amsterdam

1851 A Corner of the Asylum and the Garden with a Heavy, Sawed-Off Tree, F1545
Black chalk, pen, reed pen, 47 × 61 cm (18½ × 24")
The Armand Hammer Collection, Los Angeles

1852

1853

1854

1855

1856

1857

1858

1852 Pine Trees near the Wall of the Asylum, F 1497
Reed pen, 63.5 × 48 cm (25¼ × 18⅞″)
Tate Gallery, London

1853 Olive Orchard with a Man and a Woman Picking Fruit, F 587
73 × 92 cm (28¾ × 36¼″)
Rijksmuseum Kröller-Müller, Otterlo

1854 Olive Orchard, F 586
74 × 93 cm (29⅛ × 36⅝″)
Konstmuseum, Göteborg

1855 Olive Orchard, F 708
73.5 × 91.5 cm (29⅛ × 36¼″)
Collection Walter Annenberg, Rancho Mirage, California

1856 Olive Orchard with Mountains and the Disk of the Sun, F 710
74 × 93 cm (29⅛ × 36⅝″)
Minneapolis Institute of Arts

1857 Olive Orchard, F 707
73 × 92.5 cm (28¾ × 36⅝″)
Rijksmuseum Vincent van Gogh, Amsterdam

1858 Olive Orchard, F 714
49 × 63 cm (19¼ × 24¾″)
National Gallery of Scotland, Edinburgh

And in Letter 622 the two canvases sent to Roulin are described as "a *White House among the Olive Trees* and a *Wheat Field with a Background of Mauve Mountains, and a Black Tree*, as in the large canvas I sent you."

The first canvas referred to, *Fields with Pollard Tree and Mountainous Background*, can hardly have been anything but 1864, which indeed depicts a fresh green field with a mountain background under a yellow sky. We know of no other painting that matches this description.

The two smaller canvases sent to Roulin are obviously 1865 and 1866. The first is clearly the white house among the olive trees, and the other is indeed a wheat field with young—therefore, green—wheat, "with a background of mauve mountains, and a black [read, of course: dark] tree." The added words "as in the large canvas I sent you" become clear when they are applied to the canvas *Fields*, 1864, sent to Theo, which is in fact a large painting ($28\frac{3}{4}$ by $36\frac{1}{4}$ inches), portraying almost the same scene and featuring a tree standing rather prominently in the foreground, its trunk contrasting darkly with the light green.

Women Picking Olives

There is definitely no need for uncertainty with regard to the three almost identical paintings of olive orchards with women picking olives, 1868, 1869, and 1870; there is also a quick sketchbook note of this, 1867. On several occasions, Vincent wrote in some detail about these canvases, which, according to Letters 617 and 619, kept him occupied rather intensely for some time. Although his information is somewhat confusing, the gist of it is that, working in the groves, he had made a large study with small pink figures and a pink sky, and that, when he wrote Theo about it December 18, he was busy making a replica in softer hues: "It is a canvas I am doing from memory on the basis of the study made on the spot, because I want something that is far away like a vague memory, softened by time. There are only two tones, pink and green, which form a harmony, neutralize each other, act as opposites. I shall probably make two or three copies of it, for it is, after all, the result of half a dozen studies of olive trees" (Letter 617). And more, we would be inclined to add.

The three paintings with the women picking olives differ from the earlier olive orchards because of an element of charm and dignity attributable to the soft colors and the pyramidal composition with the carefully placed female figures in the center. One seems to detect here something of the admiration Vincent expressed in many letters for the work of the French painter Pierre Puvis de Chavannes, which often gives an impression of lofty tranquillity (see, for example, Letter W22).

Variants and Small Studies

In canvas 1871 we meet an old friend. This scene of a ravine in which two small female figures are ascending a mountain path had been painted by Vincent back in October (see 1804). It appears from a letter to his mother that he had taken up this subject again in the

1859

1860

1861

1859 Olive Orchard, F1555
Reed pen, brown ink, 50 × 65 cm
($19\frac{5}{8} \times 25\frac{5}{8}''$)
Rijksmuseum Vincent van Gogh, Amsterdam

December 1889

1860 Road Menders in a Lane with Heavy Plane Trees, F657
74 × 93 cm ($29\frac{1}{8} \times 36\frac{5}{8}''$)
Cleveland Museum of Art

1861 Road Menders in a Lane with Heavy Plane Trees, F658
73.5 × 92.5 cm ($29\frac{1}{8} \times 36\frac{5}{8}''$)
Phillips Collection, Washington, D.C.

1862 Enclosed Field with Young Wheat and Rising Sun, F737
71 × 90.5 cm ($28 \times 35\frac{7}{8}''$)
Formerly collection Mrs. J. Robert Oppenheimer, Princeton, New Jersey

1863 Enclosed Field with Rising Sun, F1552
Black chalk, reed pen, 47 × 62 cm
($18\frac{1}{2} \times 24\frac{3}{8}''$)
Staatliche Graphische Sammlung, Munich

1864 Fields with Pollard Tree and Mountainous Background, F721
73 × 91.5 cm ($28\frac{3}{4} \times 36\frac{1}{4}''$)
Rijksmuseum Kröller-Müller, Otterlo

1862

1863

1864

1865

1866

1867

1868

1865 White House between Olive Trees, F664
70 × 60 cm ($27\frac{5}{8} \times 23\frac{5}{8}$")
Location unknown

1866 Fields with Bare Tree and Mountainous Background, F663
45 × 55 cm ($17\frac{3}{4} \times 21\frac{5}{8}$")
Location unknown

1867 Women Picking Olives, F1729
Black chalk, 8 × 13 cm ($3\frac{1}{8} \times 5\frac{1}{8}$")
Rijksmuseum Vincent van Gogh, Amsterdam

1868 Women Picking Olives, F654
73 × 92 cm ($28\frac{3}{4} \times 36\frac{1}{4}$")
Metropolitan Museum of Art, New York

second half of December: "I am now working on a painting of a path between the mountains and a little brook that winds its way between the stones" (Letter 619). The letter, January 3, accompanying the shipment of paintings reveals that this work was a *replica*; thus, there are two variants that have been preserved.

It is quite possible that the weather did not permit any work out of doors, and as a result a second replica of an older canvas may also have been made: the small painting of the field behind the asylum, 1872.

There are, finally, a few landscapes—of lesser importance—that, even though not referred to in the letters, should, I believe, be assigned to the month of December solely for reasons of style: canvases 1873–78. The study of the plowed fields with the Alpilles in the background (1874) fits in best with 1864 and 1866, but is a smaller and more sketchy variation of them. A somewhat more finished work is the canvas depicting the houses among cypresses, 1873, which strongly resembles the painting sent to Roulin, 1865, in which the house among the olive trees has a more inviting look.

The remaining four, 1875–78, have all been done in the very small format of landscape 1874 (a canvas 13 by 16⅛ inches). They are probably random notes, made during Vincent's ramblings about the hills of the Alpilles, and most of them very sketchy, such as the one of the woman on the path between the trees, 1875, and the one of the little field with a couple of rabbits, 1876.

A Brief Crisis

Before the year 1889 ended, still another dramatic event disturbed Vincent's life: he was suddenly struck by a crisis again. In simple and clear terms he himself explained what had happened in a letter to his friends in Arles—the Ginouxes: "Just before Christmas I was in a rather bad way for a few days again this year, but it was over very quickly; it held me in its grip for less than a week" (Letter 622*a*). The exceptionally moving letter containing this passage had been written because Madame Ginoux was also ill, and Vincent had realized with some emotion that exactly one year before he had gone through a similar crisis and that she had also been ill at the same time. In order to console her—and certainly himself as well—he pondered, as he so often did, the mysteries of health and sickness: "What makes us ill and bowed down by our despondency today is the same thing that gives us the strength to get up next day—when the illness has passed—with the will to recover." For himself he knew it to be true: "As far as I am concerned, illness has done me good—it would be ungrateful not to admit it. It has made me calmer, and far different from what I had imagined, I have had more good fortune this year than I had dared hope for." A more striking proof of Vincent's greatness of mind and his readiness to accept his burdensome lot would, it seems to me, be hard to find.

Although Vincent had "recovered" once again, the new year had begun under ominous circumstances, and the work he managed to complete in January demanded more time and effort than was customary for him.

1869

1870

1871

The first few days of the month he must have been engaged mainly in sending off the paintings for Theo and Roulin, as he mentioned in Letters 621 and 622. Yet in the latter letter, January 4, he was also able to write: "I have just now made a small portrait of one of the boys here, which he wanted to send to his mother." It is generally believed that this referred to canvas 1879, showing a boy in a blue school uniform with school cap against a background half dark red and half orange (curiously, Vincent had used the same rather unusual combination of background colors exactly one year earlier, for his self-portrait with bandaged ear, 1658).

1869 Women Picking Olives, F655
73 × 89 cm (28¾ × 35″)
Collection Mr. and Mrs. Basil P. Goulandris, Lausanne

1870 Women Picking Olives, F656
73 × 92 cm (28¾ × 36¼″)
National Gallery of Art, Washington, D.C.

1871 A Path through the Ravine, F661
72 × 92 cm (28⅜ × 36¼″)
Rijksmuseum Kröller-Müller, Otterlo

1872 Mountain Landscape Seen across the Walls, F722
21.5 × 32.5 cm (8⅝ × 13″)
Location unknown

1872

1873

1874

1875

1876

1877

1878

1873 Wooden Sheds amid Olive Trees and Cypresses, F623
45.5 × 60 cm ($18\frac{1}{8} \times 23\frac{5}{8}''$)
Location unknown

1874 Landscape with a House and Mountains in the Background, F726
33 × 41 cm ($13 \times 16\frac{1}{8}''$)
Museum of Modern Art, New York

1875 Woman on a Road among Trees, F728
32.5 × 40.5 cm ($13 \times 16\frac{1}{8}''$)
Private collection, Lausanne

1876 Field with Two Rabbits, F739
33 × 40.5 cm ($13 \times 16\frac{1}{8}''$)
Rijksmuseum Vincent van Gogh, Amsterdam

1877 Landscape with a House and a Plowman (Bird's-Eye View), F727
33 × 41 cm ($13 \times 16\frac{1}{8}''$)
Location unknown

1878 Olive Orchard (Bird's-Eye View), F716
33 × 40 cm ($13 \times 15\frac{3}{4}''$)
Rijksmuseum Vincent van Gogh, Amsterdam

About the middle of January he wrote: "I have enough ideas for paintings in my head for when the weather makes it possible to work outside" (Letter 623). In the meantime he just made copies. Theo had had kind words to say about *The Family at Night*, after Millet (it was one of the things he liked best out of the entire shipment dispatched at the beginning of January), and now Vincent wrote: "So I have now finished the other three [of the series] *Heures de la Journée* after Lavieille's wood engravings." These were *Morning: Going Out to Work*, 1880, *Noon: Rest*, 1881, and *The End of the Day*, 1835 (the last of these had been started earlier; see page 421). These were the copies that prompted Vincent to say that this kind of copying should be regarded as "translating into another language, the language of colors."

Here again he sought, in soft blues and lavender, colors with which the complementary yellow—especially, of course, in the painting with the haystacks, 1881—plays an important part. "It has cost me much time and trouble," he admitted, and that must also have been the case with two other copies mentioned in this letter: "This week I am going to start on 'The Snow-Covered Field' and *The First Steps* by Millet, in the same size as the others. There will then be six canvases forming a series, and I assure you that I have worked on them, on those last three *Heures de la Journée*, with deliberation to calculate the colors."

The reason that the six canvases seemed in Vincent's mind to form a series was probably that they were all done in the large format of size-30 canvases; in subject they differ too widely for any connection between them to be seen, although they are mostly pictures of rural life. Apart from the four *Hours of the Day* (1834, 1880, 1881, and 1835), the series consisted of *Plow and Harrow*, 1882 (called by Vincent "The Snow-Covered Field"), and *The First Steps*, 1883.

Vincent has again carefully and sensitively "translated" these much admired works by Millet into his own scale of colors, but in my opinion they add little to his own *oeuvre*. Theo, however, thought otherwise; when he acknowledged receipt of Vincent's next voluminous shipment, he was again profuse in praise of these particular copies: "The copies after Millet are perhaps the most beautiful thing you have done, and they make me believe that on the day you set yourself to making compositions of figures, there will be great surprises in store for us" (Letter T33). We can only hope that this praise for paintings that were not essentially his own work did not cause Vincent too much hurt.

1879

1880

1881

Vincent's Crises and Their Causes

No more than five paintings, four of them copies, were produced in the first three weeks of January. On Saturday or Sunday, January 18 or 19, Vincent finally considered himself equal to making a short trip to Arles again to visit his sick friend, Madame Ginoux. Exactly how long he was there we do not know, but after his return, about January 20, he wrote a letter to Wil, who had come to stay with Theo and his wife, Jo, in Paris and had arrived with a cold: "I visited a sick woman suffering from a rather alarming complication of a nervous character and going through the change of life" (Letter W19). Shortly afterward he must have had another relapse. Theo, not suspecting anything, sent a letter January 22, in which he said he was glad that Vincent was none the worse for the trip to Arles (he was aware, of course, of what Vincent had said in his letter to Wil), but actually the trip to Arles—or seeing Madame Ginoux again—just seemed, once more, to be extremely risky.

The attack again did not last long. January 31 Vincent was able to write Jo in reply to her letter of the twenty-ninth: "I am better,

January 1890

1879 Boy with Uniform Cap, F665
63.5 × 54 cm (25¼ × 21¼")
Museu de Arte, São Paulo

1880 Morning: Going Out to Work (after Millet), F684
73 × 92 cm (28¾ × 36¼")
Location unknown

1881 Noon: Rest (after Millet), F686
73 × 91 cm (28¾ × 35⅞")
The Louvre, Paris

1882 Plow and Harrow (after Millet), F632
72 × 92 cm (28⅜ × 36¼")
Rijksmuseum Vincent van Gogh, Amsterdam

1882

1883

1884

1885

1886

1887

1888

1883 The First Steps (after Millet), F668
73 × 92 cm (28¾ × 36¼″)
Metropolitan Museum of Art, New York

February 1890

1884 Men Drinking (after Daumier), F667
60 × 73 cm (23⅝ × 28¾″)
Art Institute of Chicago

1885 Prisoners' Round (after Gustave Doré), F669
80 × 64 cm (31½ × 25¼″)
Pushkin Museum, Moscow

1886 The Woodcutter (after Millet), F670
43.5 × 25 cm (17⅜ × 9⅞″)
Rijksmuseum Vincent van Gogh, Amsterdam

1887 Cypresses with Two Women in the Foreground, F1525a
Black chalk, reed pen, 31 × 23 cm (12¼ × 9″)
Rijksmuseum Kröller-Müller, Otterlo

1888 Cypresses with Two Women in the Foreground, F621
42 × 26 cm (16½ × 10¼″)
Rijksmuseum Vincent van Gogh, Amsterdam

but have again had a few days like the others, being upset and not exactly knowing what was the matter with me. But you see that I am regaining my composure" (Letter 624, written in Dutch, as was Jo's letter).

It has been conjectured that Vincent's periods of illness were connected with events in Theo's life—his engagement, his marriage, and so on. The facts reported add to the evidence militating against this theory. Vincent's latest crisis occurred, not after, but just before an extremely important event in the life of Theo and Jo. Jo had written Vincent the night of January 29, while awaiting her confinement, and Vincent had immediately answered in the most heartfelt terms: "I am quite moved that you should write me and that you are so calm and in control of yourself on one of your difficult nights. How I am longing to hear that you have come safely through it and that your child is alive. How happy Theo will be, and a new ray of sunshine will beam within him when he sees you recovering" (Letter 624).

The big event was not long in coming. The birth took place January 31, and the very same day Theo wrote Vincent about it, adding that the only thing to mar their happiness was that they had received the report from Dr. Peyron about Vincent's new crisis (Letter T27). For them it went without saying: "We shall give him your name, and my wish is that he will have the same perseverance and will be just as courageous as you."

1889

1890

1891

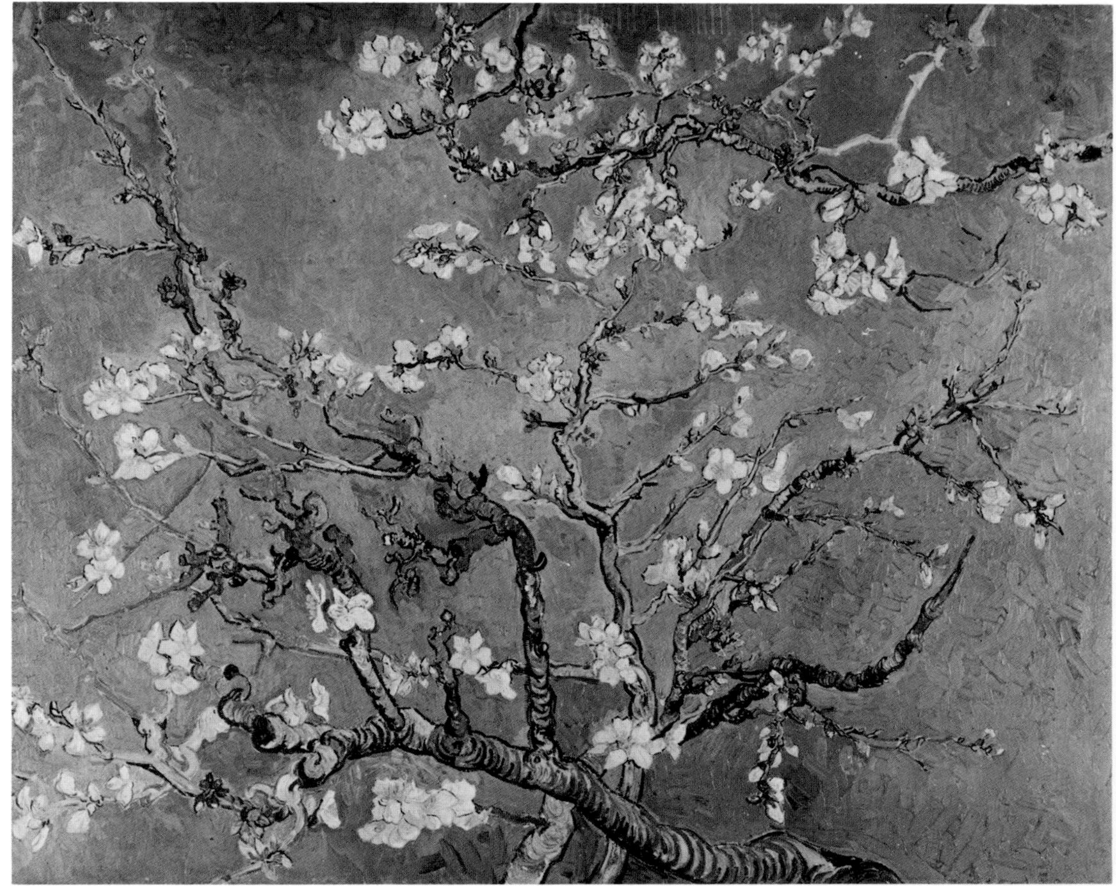

Confined to the Asylum

It must have taken some time before Vincent could resume his ordinary work. There was still no question of painting out of doors, and for the time being he would not be capable of great productivity. In Letter 623, about the middle of January, he had written: "I am thinking of making a painting of *Men Drinking* by Daumier and *The Prison* by Régamey; you will find them among the wood engravings." The last remark probably meant: "Will you try to find them for me," and Theo seems to have done this, although instead of Régamey he sent a wood engraving by Gustave Doré. After his illness, Vincent wrote, February 10 or 11: "I have tried making copies of *Men Drinking* by Daumier and *The Prison* by Doré; it is very difficult" (Letter 626).

What prompted Vincent in the middle of January to start thinking about copying such unlikely subjects as *Men Drinking* or *The Prison*? That question may never be answered without a considerable amount of guesswork. Daumier's caricatural fantasy (1884), in particular, is far removed from Vincent's normal sphere of interest, and the copy is a somewhat bewildering and isolated element in his *oeuvre*. Much more fascinating is the copy of *Prisoners' Round* (also called *Newgate Prison Exercise Yard*), after Gustave Doré, 1885. This subject is also an unusual one for Van Gogh, although his choice of it can perhaps be explained by his interest, during The Hague period, in English prints depicting social themes. There is, however, considerable support for the view that an element of biographical association is to be found here. Can it really be that *Prisoners' Round* embodies an unspoken criticism of the deadly monotony of the life of the patients of Saint-Paul-de-Mausole?

Although the foremost prisoner has been rendered by Vincent with reddish-brown hair, it is my opinion that he copied the features of this figure—who is, moreover, beardless—with scrupulous care, just as he did with the rest of the picture. There is accordingly no reason that I can see to assert, as some have done, that an effort was knowingly made to transform this figure into a self-portrait.

Praise from Aurier

As Vincent kept working, in almost perfunctory fashion, on the copies of *Men Drinking* and *Prisoners' Round*, his mind must have

1889 Cypresses with Four People Working in the Field, F1539 (reverse: not included)
Black chalk, 32 × 23.5 cm ($12\frac{5}{8} \times 9\frac{1}{2}$")
Museum Folkwang, Essen

1890 Studies of a Man Digging and a Landscape with Cypresses, F1593v (reverse: 1906)
Pencil, 23.5 × 31.5 cm ($9\frac{1}{2} \times 12\frac{5}{8}$")
Rijksmuseum Vincent van Gogh, Amsterdam

1891 Branches of an Almond Tree in Blossom, F671
73 × 92 cm ($28\frac{3}{4} \times 36\frac{1}{4}$")
Rijksmuseum Vincent van Gogh, Amsterdam

1892 The Arlésienne (Madame Ginoux), with Cherry-Colored Background, F540
60 × 50 cm ($23\frac{5}{8} \times 19\frac{5}{8}$")
Galleria Nazionale d'Arte Moderna, Rome

1892

1893

1894

1895

1896

1893 The Arlésienne (Madame Ginoux), with Light Pink Background, F 541
65×49 cm ($25\frac{5}{8} \times 19\frac{1}{4}''$)
Rijksmuseum Kröller-Müller, Otterlo

1894 The Arlésienne (Madame Ginoux), with Pink Background, F 542
65×54 cm ($25\frac{5}{8} \times 21\frac{1}{4}''$)
Museu de Arte, São Paulo

1895 The Arlésienne (Madame Ginoux) in Light-Colored Dress and with Cream-Colored Background, F 543
66×54 cm ($26 \times 21\frac{1}{4}''$)
Collection Dr. Ruth Bakwin, New York

1896 The Arlésienne (Madame Ginoux), in Light-Colored Dress
Sketch in Letter W 22
Rijksmuseum Vincent van Gogh, Amsterdam

been occupied with entirely different matters. Although Theo did not specifically mention it in his letter January 31 (Letter T22), he must have enclosed an article by the young critic G.-Albert Aurier about Vincent that had appeared in the *Mercure de France* at the end of January—the first detailed and laudatory treatment of his work ever published. Influenced by the currents of fashion dominating Symbolist literature, Aurier wrote in affected and turgid prose that must certainly have rendered his article inaccessible to the general reading public.

Despite its high-flown language, the article was the warm testimony of a kindred spirit in a periodical highly regarded by intellectuals and artists of that time, and it must have whetted the curiosity of many regarding Vincent's almost completely unknown *oeuvre*.

It is difficult to imagine the emotions felt by Vincent, who had thus far certainly not been spoiled by praise, when he read this article, for in comparison with this even Isaäcson's words about a solitary hero struggling alone—which he considered exaggerated—paled into insignificance. His reaction probably was not so much joy and satisfaction—although those cannot have been absent—as rather defensiveness, confusion, and even fear. (He wrote somewhat later to his mother, in Letter 629*a*, April 30, that he had immediately feared "that he would rue the day.")

"I was very much surprised by the article about my paintings that you sent me," he wrote Theo; "no need to say that I hope to keep on thinking that I do not paint like that, but I see it rather as indicating how I ought to paint. For the article is very right in the sense that it points out the gap that must be filled, and I believe that basically the author wrote it to give guidance not only to me, but also to the other Impressionists, and even more so to bring about the breakthrough at the right place" (Letter 625).

More Copies

Let us return to Vincent's work, to the little work that he was able to do. About the same time that he was copying *Men Drinking* and *Prisoners' Round*, he must also have made the copy of *The Woodcutter*, after Millet, 1886. "I hope one of these days to start on Delacroix's *Good Samaritan* and Millet's *Woodcutter*," he had written in Letter 626, and although he did not get around to the *Good Samaritan* for some time, he seems to have carried out his intentions as far as *The Woodcutter* is concerned, although there is no further comment on it. It was the last of the series *Les Travaux des Champs*, the other nine having presumably all been copied the previous September.

In Letter 625 he also spoke about a painting of a sower he was working on. My feeling is that he had again taken up one of the two copies he had made or had at least started on in November, 1836 and 1837.

Even though the following works, 1887–90, are landscapes with cypresses, this does not mean that Vincent was again working out of doors, for that was certainly not the case. The second one, 1888, a very small canvas with cypresses and two tiny female figures

1897

1898

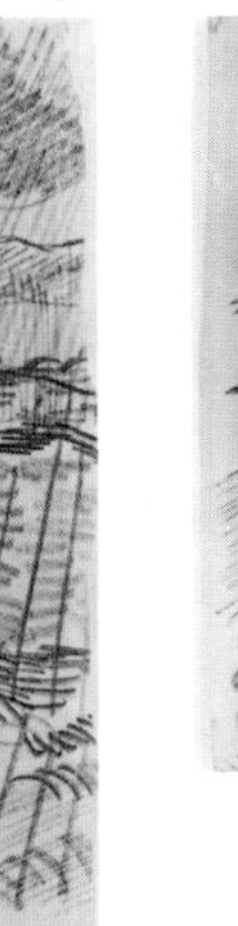

1899

March–April 1890

1897 Enclosed Field with a Sower in the Rain, F 1550
Pencil, black chalk, 23.5 × 31.5 cm (9½ × 12⅝″)
Museum Folkwang, Essen

1898 Enclosed Field with a Sower in the Rain, F 1551 (reverse: 1947)
Black chalk, 24 × 27.5 cm (9½ × 11″)
Rijksmuseum Vincent van Gogh, Amsterdam

1899 Field with a Sower, F 1592v (reverse: 1910)
Pencil, 24 × 32 cm (9½ × 12⅝″)
Rijksmuseum Vincent van Gogh, Amsterdam

Colorplate XXXVII, A Passageway at the Asylum, 1808 ›

($16\frac{1}{2}$ by $10\frac{1}{4}$ inches), is merely a copy, in reduced size, of the painting intended for Aurier, 1748, and must therefore surely have been done in the studio. The presence of the figures indicates that it must have been painted after Vincent had added them to the large canvas (see page 398). Vincent obviously made the copy for himself or for Theo in order to have some kind of reminder of the painting he was so fond of that was to go to Aurier.

The same thing is true of the *drawing* of the same subject, 1887, in which the details of the earlier painting, 1748, are rendered even more clearly. As the copy that was drawn is closer in detail to the original than is the painted copy, we can assume that Vincent started with the drawing. Another point to note in the small painting is that he has introduced a cloudy sky that differs markedly from the one in the canvas made for Aurier: strange tatters of clouds with colored edges, the likes of which he had never painted in June 1889 but are to be met with again in some of the disconcerting canvases of the next few months.

On the basis of their quiet and controlled treatment, I have placed drawings 1889 and 1890 here rather than with the numerous sketchbook sheets dating from the following period when Vincent was ill.

A Painting as a Birthday Present

The large canvas we are about to consider (1891) occupies a very special place in Vincent's *oeuvre* because of its subject and composition—both unique for him—and its biographical significance. This painting of blossoming almond boughs against a sky-blue background, symbol of budding new life, is the best evidence of the feelings of joy that he experienced upon hearing the news of the birth in Paris of his nephew and namesake, Vincent Willem van Gogh.

For the time being, he said nothing to Theo about the painting he was starting to work on for that occasion, probably because he wanted it to be a surprise for Jo and him, but in letters to his mother (Letter 627) and to Wil (Letter W20) he mentioned it in almost identical terms. These two letters, as careful investigation has shown, were both written about February 20. Therefore, sometime between February 1, when Vincent had received the news of the birth, and February 20, the painting of the almond blossom (which in the Arles period Vincent would probably have finished in one day) must have come into being after he had worked on it—as far as can be gathered from the various letters—in bits and pieces over a fairly long time, up to shortly before his new crisis, on February 22 or 23.

There is a curious anomaly about *Branches of an Almond Tree in Blossom*. Although the background is naturally intended to represent a blue sky, as Vincent confirmed in the letter to his mother, I believe that there are firm grounds for assuming that—despite what one would expect—this painting was not made out of doors, but rather *indoors* with cut branches as the model or perhaps branches that he could observe from a window. It is not just by chance that no part of the trunk of the little almond tree is shown here, in

1900

1901

1902

1903

1904

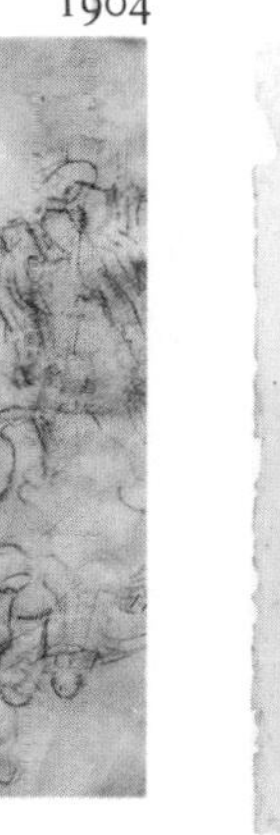

1905

1900 Sun Disk above a Path between Shrubs, F 1553
Pen, reed pen, brush, 63 × 48 cm ($24\frac{3}{4} \times 18\frac{7}{8}$″)
Location unknown

1901 Field with Two Sowers and Trees, F 1618
Black chalk, 28.5 × 22 cm ($11\frac{3}{8} \times 8\frac{5}{8}$″)
Collection Mr. and Mrs. Joram Piatigorski (address unknown)

1902 A Sower and a Man with a Spade, F 1645 (reverse: 1903)
Black chalk, 31 × 25 cm ($12\frac{1}{4} \times 9\frac{7}{8}$″)
Collection Jacques Dubourg, Paris

1903 Two Sowers, F 1645v (reverse: 1902)
Pencil, 31 × 25 cm ($12\frac{1}{4} \times 9\frac{7}{8}$″)
Collection Jacques Dubourg, Paris

1904 Sketches of a Cottage and Figures, F 1649v (reverse: 1926)
Black chalk, 23 × 30.5 cm ($9 \times 12\frac{1}{4}$″)
Location unknown

1905 Sketches of a Cottage and Figures, F 1600v (reverse: 1928)
Pencil, black chalk, 23.5 × 32 cm ($9\frac{1}{4} \times 12\frac{5}{8}$″)
Rijksmuseum Vincent van Gogh, Amsterdam

〈 Colorplate XXXVIII, Two Peasant Women Digging in a Snow-Covered Field at Sunset, 1923

contrast to the blossoming fruit trees he had painted in Arles in the fall.

Madame Ginoux Again

During these few weeks in February 1890, in addition to the copies mentioned so far and the canvas of the almond blossoms, Vincent must have worked on no fewer than five versions of a portrait of Madame Ginoux (1892–95 and one piece that has been lost). Naturally she did not pose for this portrait herself; Madame Ginoux was living in Arles and was ill besides, but Vincent worked from a drawing by Gauguin (see Appendix, note 13). Of the five versions, one was intended for Madame Ginoux, one for Gauguin, one for Theo, and one for himself (which he later took with him to Auvers to show to Dr. Gachet). Concerning the fifth piece, now in the Rijksmuseum Kröller-Müller, we know only that it was previously owned by G.-Albert Aurier, who presumably got it from Vincent or from his estate.

Madame Ginoux must have greatly occupied Vincent's thoughts at this time, and working on her portrait affected him deeply. In the curious unfinished letter to Gauguin (Letter 643), which was never sent, we read: "I have paid for making it with another month of illness."

This is what actually happened, and it leaves us in no doubt about the emotional effect that the making of the portrait and the model had on Vincent. When, on Saturday, February 22, he went to Arles to take Madame Ginoux the copy of the portrait he had intended for her, he was setting the stage for a new attack of his illness. The facts, as far as they could be ascertained, are given in a letter Dr. Peyron sent Theo February 24: "I was obliged to send two men with a carriage to Arles to pick him up, and there is no way of knowing where he spent the night between Saturday and Sunday. He had taken the portrait of a woman of Arles with him; it has not been recovered."*

Much as we would like to know exactly what happened, there is no chance that anything more will ever be known than what Dr. Peyron has disclosed. It is not even clear whether Vincent ever saw the Ginouxes this time.

Although Vincent had said that the portrait was based exactly on Gauguin's drawing, there was still a personal addition: the books on the table. This is not an entirely unexpected addition, for in the portrait he had painted of Madame Ginoux in Arles in an hour (1624), he had also placed a pair of books in front of her. This time the titles are legible: *Uncle Tom's Cabin* by Harriet Beecher Stowe and *A Christmas Carol* by Charles Dickens, and it is rather pathetic to think that Madame Ginoux probably never read these books, although we know from his letters that Vincent had translations in French.

A Period of Illness

The crisis of February 22, 1890, was the starting point for one of the saddest episodes in a life already rife with sad events. The period of illness it ushered in lasted longer than any

Vincent, vol. I, no. 2 (1971), p. 43.

1906

1907

1908

1909

1910

1911

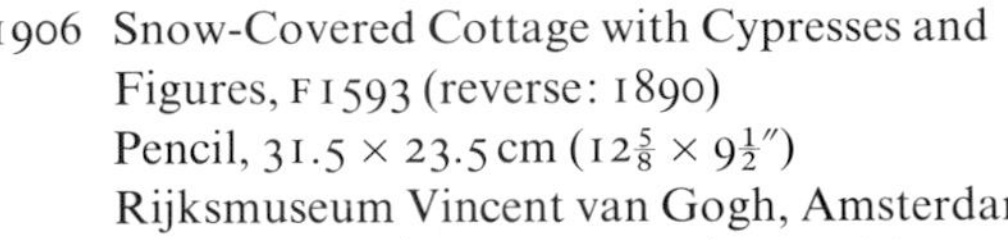

1906 Snow-Covered Cottage with Cypresses and Figures, F 1593 (reverse: 1890)
Pencil, 31.5 × 23.5 cm ($12\frac{5}{8} \times 9\frac{1}{2}$″)
Rijksmuseum Vincent van Gogh, Amsterdam

1907 Snow-Covered Cottages, a Couple with a Child, and Other Walkers, F 1591 (reverse: 1908)
Pencil, 24 × 32 cm ($9\frac{1}{2} \times 12\frac{5}{8}$″)
Rijksmuseum Vincent van Gogh, Amsterdam

1908 Cottages with Three Figures, F 1591V (reverse: 1907)
Pencil, 24 × 32 cm ($9\frac{1}{2} \times 12\frac{5}{8}$″)
Rijksmuseum Vincent van Gogh, Amsterdam

1909 Couple Walking in Front of Snow-Covered Cottage, F 1585 (reverse: 1961)
Pencil, 24.5 × 32 cm ($9\frac{5}{8} \times 12\frac{5}{8}$″)
Rijksmuseum Vincent van Gogh, Amsterdam

1910 People Walking in Front of Snow-Covered Cottage, F 1592 (reverse: 1899)
Pencil, 24 × 32 cm ($9\frac{1}{2} \times 12\frac{5}{8}$″)
Rijksmuseum Vincent van Gogh, Amsterdam

1911 Sketch of Diggers and Other Figures, F 1620 (reverse: 1934)
Pencil, black chalk, 23 × 31 cm ($9 \times 12\frac{1}{4}$″)
Collection T. E. Hanley, Bradford, Pennsylvania

1912 Landscape with Cottage and Two Figures, F 1597V (reverse: 1949)
Pencil, 23.5 × 32 cm ($9\frac{1}{2} \times 12\frac{5}{8}$″)
Rijksmuseum Vincent van Gogh, Amsterdam

1912

1913

1914

1915

1916

1917

1918

1919

1920

1913 Snow-Covered Cottages with Figures, F 1648 (reverse: 1914)
Pencil, 23.5 × 31 cm ($9\frac{1}{4} \times 12\frac{1}{4}''$)
Collection Ernesto Blohm, Caracas

1914 Cottages and Trees, F 1648v (reverse: 1913)
Pencil, 31 × 23.5 cm ($12\frac{1}{4} \times 9\frac{1}{4}''$)
Collection Ernesto Blohm, Caracas

1915 Farmers Digging and Cottages, F 1594 (reverse: 1958)
Pencil, 23.5 × 32 cm ($9\frac{1}{4} \times 12\frac{5}{8}''$)
Rijksmuseum Vincent van Gogh, Amsterdam

1916 Diggers and Road with Cottages, F 1595 (reverse: 1957)
Pencil, 24 × 32 cm ($9\frac{1}{2} \times 12\frac{5}{8}''$)
Location unknown

1917 Sketch of a Tree against Clouds with Color Annotations, F 1583
Pencil, black chalk, 25 × 32.5 cm ($9\frac{7}{8} \times 13''$)
Rijksmuseum Vincent van Gogh, Amsterdam

1918 Sketch of Clouds with Color Annotations, F 1584
Pencil, 25 × 32.5 cm ($9\frac{7}{8} \times 13''$)
Rijksmuseum Vincent van Gogh, Amsterdam

1919 Cottages and Setting Sun, F 673
45.5 × 43 cm ($18\frac{1}{8} \times 16\frac{7}{8}''$)
Private collection, Switzerland

1920 Cottages and Setting Sun, F 674
50 × 39 cm ($19\frac{5}{8} \times 15\frac{3}{8}''$)
©The Barnes Foundation Museum of Art, Merion, Pennsylvania

he had gone through so far, longer even than that exactly one year earlier, in February and March 1889. Not until the end of April could Vincent say: "This is the first time after two months of indisposition that I have brought myself to write" (Letter 629*a*).

The illness, which must have been a torment for Vincent, was not the only cause of the terrible sadness of this period; what he produced—despite his statement that he had not been able to work for these two months—was equally sad. There are, in fact, a great number of drawings and study sheets that can have been made only during these two months, even though Vincent himself does not mention them in his letters. This is the only logical conclusion, because they are closely related to several painted studies that he did write about, referring to them as "souvenirs du nord." He wrote Theo: "While I was ill, I did make a few small canvases from memory that you will see later, 'reminiscences of the North'" (Letter 629). In a letter to his mother and sister he went into somewhat greater detail: "Even while my illness was at its worst, I kept painting, among other things a reminiscence of Brabant, cottages with moss roofs and beech hedges, on a fall evening with a stormy sky, a red sun setting amid reddish clouds. Also a turnip field with women pulling out the green tops in the snow" (Letter 629*a*).

It is not difficult to recognize the canvases referred to here, painted *from memory* during his worst period of illness; they are the landscapes with peasant cottages under heavy skies, 1919, 1920, and 1921, and the one with the women digging in a snow-covered field, 1923 (colorplate XXXVIII, page 438), with, as a companion piece, the landscape in which men are digging, 1922. What is depressing is that these works—and they are virtually the only ones in his entire voluminous *oeuvre* of which this is true—unmistakably show the signs of his mental collapse in this period.

That these canvases were indeed "a reminiscence of Brabant" is quite clear. The typical farmhouses with their "moss roofs" point in that direction, but even more indicative is the coating of snow seen in painting 1923, as well as in many of the drawings. The snow-covered field of turnips was an old motif with Vincent, and it is evident how intensely his mind was concentrated on the past when we consider that we have to go back five years to find out which memory had risen to the surface in his mind; there is a sentence in Letter 418 (from the Nuenen period, July 1885) which gives the explanation: "I am slogging away these days at a drawing of a woman I saw last winter pulling up carrots in the snow."

This small group of paintings formed a sort of nucleus for a large number of drawings and study sheets depicting landscapes and figures that Vincent apparently worked on throughout the two months of his illness in an attempt to kill time and to keep his head more or less clear. Lack of external evidence makes it impossible to say with certainty which works were made in this period, but for various reasons I have concluded that 1897–1918 and 1924–69, almost exclusively drawings and sketches, belong here.

1921

1922

1923

In nearly all these drawings the kinds of human figures depicted have peculiar shapes that differentiate them from the kinds of figures appearing in Vincent's earlier drawings and paintings. These later men and women have abnormally long arms and often walk with bowed heads and bent knees. The trunk of the body and the joints of arms and legs are represented by bulging ellipses. The dummylike figures in the drawings are not infrequently monstrously misshapen (an example of this is the man seated at the table, 1953). It is especially in these gawky, often pathetic figures, such as in 1948 or 1952, that I see a reflection of Vincent's mental state in these months.

What is striking in several of the individual

1921 Cottages and Cypresses at Sunset with Stormy Sky, F675
Canvas on panel, 29 × 36.5 cm ($11\frac{3}{8} \times 14\frac{5}{8}$")
Rijksmuseum Vincent van Gogh, Amsterdam

1922 Two Diggers (after Millet), F694
32 × 40.5 cm ($12\frac{5}{8} \times 16\frac{1}{8}$")
Justin K. Thannhauser Collection, Solomon R. Guggenheim Museum, New York

1923 Two Peasant Women Digging in a Snow-Covered Field at Sunset, F695
50 × 64 cm ($19\frac{5}{8} \times 25\frac{1}{4}$")
Collection E. G. Bührle, Zurich
Colorplate XXXVIII, p. 438

1924 Peasant Women Digging, F1586v (reverse: 1945)
Black chalk, 23.5 × 28 cm ($9\frac{1}{2} \times 11$")
Rijksmuseum Vincent van Gogh, Amsterdam

1924

1925

1926

1927

1929

1928

1925 Landscape with Cottages, F 1598 (reverse: 1932)
Pencil, 23.5 × 32 cm ($9\frac{1}{2} \times 12\frac{5}{8}''$)
Rijksmuseum Vincent van Gogh, Amsterdam

1926 Sheet with Numerous Figure Sketches, F 1649 (reverse: 1904)
Pencil, 23 × 30.5 cm ($9 \times 12\frac{1}{4}''$)
Location unknown

1927 Sheet with Sketches of Diggers and Other Figures, F 1602v (reverse: 1720)
Black chalk, 23.5 × 32 cm ($9\frac{1}{2} \times 12\frac{5}{8}''$)
Rijksmuseum Vincent van Gogh, Amsterdam

1928 Sheet with Sketches of Diggers and Other Figures, F 1600 (reverse: 1905)
Black chalk, 23.5 × 32 cm ($9\frac{1}{2} \times 12\frac{5}{8}''$)
Rijksmuseum Vincent van Gogh, Amsterdam

1929 Sheet with Sketches of Working People, F 1599 (reverse: 1933)
Pencil, 24 × 31.5 cm ($9\frac{1}{2} \times 12\frac{5}{8}''$)
Rijksmuseum Vincent van Gogh, Amsterdam

drawings is that there is a strange mix of memories of Brabant and impressions from his immediate Provençal environment. In 1906, the snow-covered Brabant cottage is surrounded by *cypresses*, and in other similar drawings, such as 1911, the cottage is surrounded by *southern* pines. Although drawings 1897, 1898, and 1899 cannot be considered "reminiscences of the North," their treatment in general, and the strangely distorted figures of the sowers in particular, cause me to regard them as belonging to the group of works dating from the period of illness in March and April. The scene portrayed here is clearly the enclosed field behind the asylum that Vincent had depicted in so many paintings from the Saint-Rémy period. Sketches 1917 and 1918, dated "autumn 1889" in the 1970 *catalogue raisonné*, should in my opinion be assigned to this March–April period, because I see in these notes for multicolored cloudy skies preliminary studies for canvases such as 1919–23, with their colored tatters of clouds, rather than for the paintings done in the fall.

A sheet like 1936 must be one of those cases where a piece of drawing paper used by Vincent in the Nuenen period for studies of hands has been used by him again to make rough sketches in the remaining blank spaces. As the more important element here consists of the little figures clearly typical of the work done in March and April 1890, I have placed the sheet in this period and have done the same with 1937 and 1956. A similar drawing, in which the hands seem to be more important than a small figure added by Vincent in Saint-Rémy, has, as we have seen, been assigned to the Nuenen period (618). I further assume that the sheet in 1930 and 1931 is a comparable case. On the right half we see an academic rendering of a plate, bowl, and spoon, which I also assume dates from the Nuenen period and was perhaps one of the preliminary studies for *The Potato Eaters* (similar objects are to be seen, for example, in a drawing such as 732). The other half of the sheet was then used by Vincent for figure studies in Saint-Rémy.

During this period he was bent on filling every little blank space, whether because he really did not have enough paper or whether he was under some compulsion to do so by reason of his mental state at the time. The lengths to which he went are visible in various amusing sheets on which barely adequate spaces are filled with little drawings in a sort of inset that separates them from the rest of the sheet. Good examples of this are 1929, 1935, and 1936. A similar case was 1890, but because of the disciplined treatment of the drawing in the inset, I dated it before the period of illness.

Another unmistakable remembrance of times long past was the important and striking painting of an old man with his head in his hands, 1967. Here again, Vincent has copied himself, or as he would say, "translated" his image into the language of colors. The original was the drawing from The Hague years, 267, of which Vincent had also made a lithograph that he had inscribed "At Eternity's gate" (268). It is possible that he had a copy of the lithograph in Saint-Rémy. If that was not the case, and if Theo had not

1930

1931

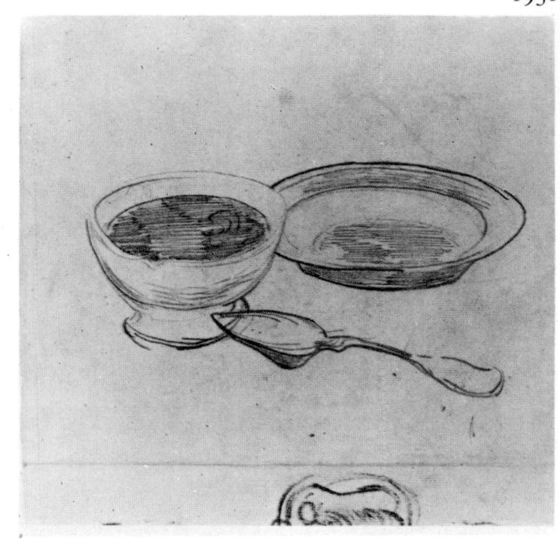

1932

1933

1934

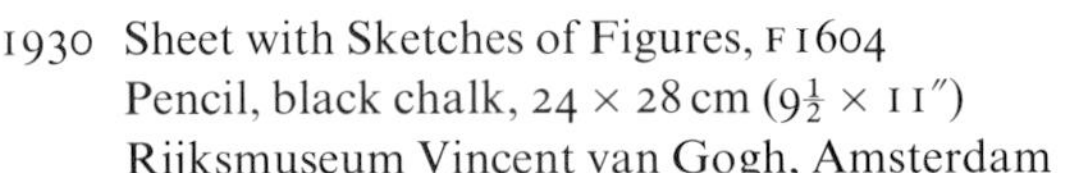

1935

1930 Sheet with Sketches of Figures, F 1604
Pencil, black chalk, 24 × 28 cm (9½ × 11″)
Rijksmuseum Vincent van Gogh, Amsterdam

1931 Drawing of Cup, Plate, and Spoons, F 1604
(on the same sheet as 1930, but made earlier)
Pencil, black chalk, 24 × 28 cm (9½ × 11″)
Rijksmuseum Vincent van Gogh, Amsterdam

1932 Sheet with Numerous Sketches of Working People, F 1598v (reverse: 1925)
Pencil, 23.5 × 32 cm (9½ × 12⅝″)
Rijksmuseum Vincent van Gogh, Amsterdam

1933 Sheet with Sketches of Peasants, F 1599v
(reverse: 1929)
Pencil, black chalk, 24 × 31.5 cm
(9½ × 12⅝″)
Rijksmuseum Vincent van Gogh, Amsterdam

1934 Sheet with Sketches of a Digger and Other Figures, F 1620v (reverse: 1911)
Pencil, black chalk, 23 × 31 cm (9 × 12¼″)
Collection T. E. Hanley, Bradford, Pennsylvania

1935 Sheet with Sketches of Working People, F 1605 (reverse: 1704)
Black chalk, 24 × 32 cm (9½ × 12⅝″)
Rijksmuseum Vincent van Gogh, Amsterdam

1936 Sheet with Two Sowers and Hands, F 1603
(reverse: 1937)
Pencil, black chalk, 23.5 × 32 cm
(9½ × 12⅝″)
Rijksmuseum Vincent van Gogh, Amsterdam

1936

1937

1938

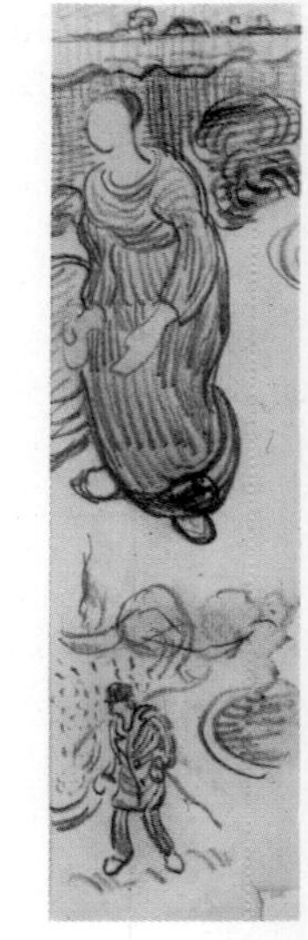

1939

1940

1941

1942

1943

1944

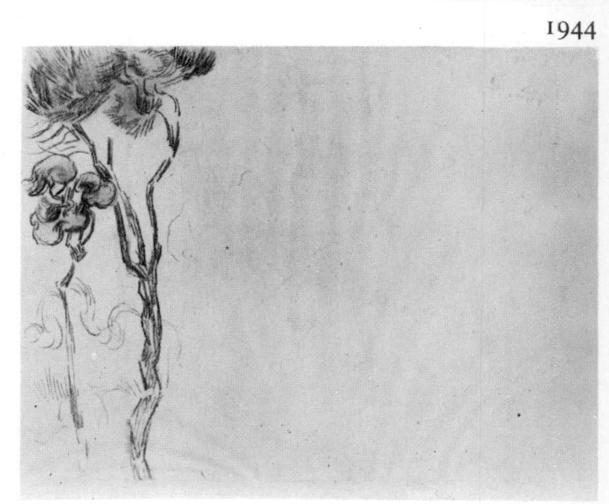

1937 Sheet with Hands and Several Figures, F 1603v (reverse: 1936)
Pencil, black chalk, 23.5 × 32 cm (9½ × 12⅝″)
Rijksmuseum Vincent van Gogh, Amsterdam

1938 Sheet with Walking Woman and Walking Man, F 1607 (reverse: 1939)
Pencil, 23.5 × 7.5 cm (9½ × 3⅛″)
Rijksmuseum Vincent van Gogh, Amsterdam

1939 Sheet with Two Women Doing Laundry, F 1607v (reverse: 1938)
Pencil, 23.5 × 7.5 cm (9½ × 3⅛″)
Rijksmuseum Vincent van Gogh, Amsterdam

1940 Sheet with a Woman at a Table and a Woman Walking, F 1606 (reverse: 1941)
Pencil, 23.5 × 7 cm (9½ × 2¾″)
Rijksmuseum Vincent van Gogh, Amsterdam

1941 Sheet with a Digger and a Dog (?), F 1606v (reverse: 1940)
Pencil, 23.5 × 7 cm (9½ × 2¾″)
Rijksmuseum Vincent van Gogh, Amsterdam

1942 Sketch of a Stooping Man, F 1596av (reverse: 1738)
Black chalk, 31.5 × 23.5 cm (12⅝ × 9½″)
Rijksmuseum Vincent van Gogh, Amsterdam

1943 Couple Arm in Arm and Other Figures, with a Mill in the Background, F 1596 (reverse: 1959)
Pencil, 24.5 × 25 cm (9⅝ × 9⅞″)
Rijksmuseum Vincent van Gogh, Amsterdam

1944 Two Trees, F 1590 (reverse: 1946)
Black chalk, 24 × 32.5 cm (9½ × 13″)
Rijksmuseum Vincent van Gogh, Amsterdam

sent him the old drawing 267, then it would have been something of a miracle for Vincent, after a lapse of seven and a half years, to be able to reconstruct the subject so accurately, down to the smallest details, even allowing for minor differences such as in the attitude of the head.

The sheer number of drawings produced in the months of March and April 1890 is apt to give the impression that Vincent was continuously active during this period. In reality, one period of activity did not just blend gradually into another. He himself saw the crisis of February 22 as a total collapse. Looking back upon it, he wrote Theo: "The work was progressing well; the last canvas of the blossoming branches—you will see, it is perhaps the most patiently and most competently done of all my work, painted with calm and with a greater sureness of touch. And the next day: *fichu comme une brute* [roughly: "everything went to pieces"]. Hard to understand a thing like that, but alas, that is how it is" (Letter 628).

In March and April, Vincent was really very ill, "*totalement abruti*," as he expressed it in Letter 628 ["completely stupefied"]. Only once, in the middle of March, did he break the silence in order to reply to Theo's letters (this was again in Letter 628), but the very first sentence shows how sad his condition was: "Today I tried to read the letters that had come for me, but I was still not lucid enough to be able to understand them. Yet I am trying to answer you, and I am hoping that in a few days it will pass."

Even the end of the period of illness did not mean a gradual transition to more regular work, but as on previous occasions, there was a sudden return of his intellectual capacity and creative mastery. This is apparent from Letters 629 and 629*a*, April 30, and especially from Letter 630, written two days later: "Now that I have been outside a bit in the park, I am able to think quite clearly again about my work; I have more ideas in my head than I could ever carry out, but without its worrying me." What is also very significant is that as soon as he was able to write, he could also report that "for several days" he had been working on a painting of a meadow with dandelions, 1970, a painting that, as we shall see, was the first of a series of well-balanced and important canvases.

For a proper understanding of how this group of works was produced, we must bear in mind that Vincent's stay in Saint-Rémy came to an end in May. For months he had been writing to Theo about his desire to leave the asylum, where life was "very wearisome because of its monotony" (Letter 614) and where he sometimes felt "overwhelmed with boredom and grief" (Letter 631). He was almost certain that in the North (meaning the environs of Paris, not the Netherlands) he would "get well quickly, at least for a fairly long time" (Letter 630). In March, on the advice of the painter Camille Pissarro, Theo had found an address in the village of Auvers-sur-Oise, thirty miles north of Paris, where Vincent would be able to work under the supervision of a doctor, Paul-Ferdinand Gachet, who was a painter himself and a friend of painters. Dr. Peyron gave his consent, and finally, on Friday evening, May 16,

1945

1946

1947

1948

1949

1950

1945 Two Men on a Road with Pine Trees, F1586 (reverse: 1924)
Black chalk, 23.5 × 28 cm (9½ × 11″)
Rijksmuseum Vincent van Gogh, Amsterdam

1946 Four Men on a Road with Pine Trees, F1590v (reverse: 1944)
Pencil, 24 × 32.5 cm (9½ × 13″)
Rijksmuseum Vincent van Gogh, Amsterdam

1947 Sketch of a Peasant Working, F1551v (reverse: 1898)
Black chalk, 24 × 27.5 cm (9½ × 11″)
Rijksmuseum Vincent van Gogh, Amsterdam

1948 Peasant Digging, F1587v (reverse: 1969)
Black chalk, 28.5 × 23.5 cm (11⅜ × 9½″)
Rijksmuseum Vincent van Gogh, Amsterdam

1949 Three Peasants with Spades on a Road in the Rain, F1597 (reverse: 1912)
Pencil, 32 × 23.5 cm (12⅝ × 9½″)
Rijksmuseum Vincent van Gogh, Amsterdam

1950 Two Men Walking in a Landscape with Trees, F1647 (reverse: 1968)
Pencil, black chalk, 29.5 × 20.5 cm (11¾ × 8¼″)
Collection Mr. and Mrs. Sydney M. Schoenberg, St. Louis

1951 Couple Walking Arm in Arm with a Child in the Rain, F1589 (reverse: 1960)
Pencil, 24.5 × 25 cm (9⅝ × 9⅞″)
Rijksmuseum Vincent van Gogh, Amsterdam

1951

1952

1953

1954

1955

1956

1957

1952 Sketches of People Sitting on Chairs, F 1601v (reverse: 1953)
Pencil, 32 × 23.5 cm ($12\frac{5}{8} \times 9\frac{1}{2}''$)
Rijksmuseum Vincent van Gogh, Amsterdam

1953 Sheet with People Sitting on Chairs, F 1601 (reverse: 1952)
Pencil, 32 × 23.5 cm ($12\frac{5}{8} \times 9\frac{1}{2}''$)
Rijksmuseum Vincent van Gogh, Amsterdam

1954 Sheet with Two Groups of Peasants at a Meal and Other Figures, F 1588
Black chalk, 34 × 50 cm ($13\frac{3}{8} \times 19\frac{5}{8}''$)
Rijksmuseum Vincent van Gogh, Amsterdam

1955 Sheet with Figures at a Table, a Sower, Clogs, etc., F 1651 (reverse: 1956)
Black chalk, 31 × 23 cm ($12\frac{1}{4} \times 9''$)
Private collection, New York

1956 Sheet with Figures and Hands, F 1651v (reverse: 1955)
Black chalk, 23 × 31 cm ($9 \times 12\frac{1}{4}''$)
Private collection, New York

1957 Sheet with Peasants Eating and Other Figures, F 1595v (reverse: 1916)
Pencil, 24 × 32 cm ($9\frac{1}{2} \times 12\frac{5}{8}''$)
Location unknown

1958

1959

1960

1961

1962

Vincent left for Paris on his way to Auvers-sur-Oise.

The eight letters Vincent is known to have written during the last two weeks of his stay in Saint-Rémy enable us to follow his production step by step. Since on April 30 he was working in the garden on *Field of Grass with Dandelions*, the first painting after his illness, all eleven canvases mentioned in these letters must have been made in the unbelievably short time of sixteen to eighteen days, a few of which must have been spent packing and shipping his trunk.

Field of Grass with Dandelions, 1970, which opens the series, is a bright, charming garden scene that Vincent himself described as being "of extreme simplicity" in Letter 631, in which he made a sketch of it (1971). In this work he had taken up again the theme that one year before, in Arles, he had introduced into canvases 1676–80, with which the new painting is also closely allied stylistically. This applies also to another view of the garden of the asylum, 1975, made a few days later, which has been kept within the same quiet range of yellows, greens, and blues as the companion piece 1970.

The two copies done by Vincent in this short period—one after Rembrandt, 1972, and one after Delacroix, 1974—differ considerably in approach to the subject. The painting after Delacroix is a true copy in the sense of being a "translation in color"; in it Vincent faithfully followed the original, as he had done when making the copies after Millet the previous year and in January and February. Here, too, of course, the vigorous brushwork is characteristic of his own style; in particular, the parallel lines of the foreground in this piece are common to other work done at this time (they are so heavy and uniform on the yellowish-green range of hills that the depth perspective is impaired). The color is enchantingly beautiful; while there is still a reminder of the primary yellow, blue, and red of Delacroix, these accents are everywhere incorporated into a subtle harmony with the subdued intermediate colors that predominate in this painting.

In the copy after Rembrandt, Vincent has in contrast taken great liberties in his approach to the subject. Did he hesitate to depict the figure of Christ? It is really going too far simply to say, as has been done, that he replaced the Christ by a *sun*—in an expression of the allegedly typical pagan attitude of the painter. In the Rembrandt etching, too, a bright light shines from the left side into the grotto where the miracle takes place. In Vincent's conception, the shining sun has a meaning all its own in the new composition, which resulted, as Vincent himself wrote, from restricting himself to "the three figures in the background of the etching": the pathetic male figure who was brought back to life and the two women bending over him with expansive gestures. Vincent eliminated not only the figure of Christ, but also the figure of the man prominently placed in the background of the etching. Can it have been for any other reason than that in this little group he wanted to portray his own recent resurrection?

Nothing was heard from Vincent in the week of May 4 to 11, but when on Monday, May 12, he wrote again, it became apparent what he had been doing: "I am working on a canvas with roses on a light green background, and two canvases depicting large bouquets of violet irises. One bouquet is set off against a pink background, and here the effect is harmonious and soft because of the combination of green, pink, and violet colors. On the other hand, the second violet bouquet (going as far as carmine and pure prussian blue) stands out against a deep lemon-yellow background with other yellow tones in the vase and the pedestal on which it rests, and the effect is one of terribly glaring contrasts that enhance each other by their juxtaposition" (Letter 633). And the next day he

1958 Sketch of the Painting The Potato Eaters, F 1594v (reverse: 1915)
Pencil, black chalk, 23.5 × 32 cm ($9\frac{1}{4} \times 12\frac{5}{8}$″)
Rijksmuseum Vincent van Gogh, Amsterdam

1959 Three Peasants at a Meal, F 1596v (reverse: 1943)
Pencil, 24.5 × 25 cm ($9\frac{5}{8} \times 9\frac{7}{8}$″)
Rijksmuseum Vincent van Gogh, Amsterdam

1960 Child and Woman Pouring Coffee (from The Potato Eaters) and Woman Sitting, F 1589v (reverse: 1951)
Black chalk, 25 × 24.5 cm ($9\frac{7}{8} \times 9\frac{5}{8}$″)
Rijksmuseum Vincent van Gogh, Amsterdam

1961 Interior of a Farm with Two Figures, F 1585v (reverse: 1909)
Pencil, 24.5 × 32 cm ($9\frac{5}{8} \times 12\frac{5}{8}$″)
Rijksmuseum Vincent van Gogh, Amsterdam

1963

1964

1965

1966

1968

1967

1969

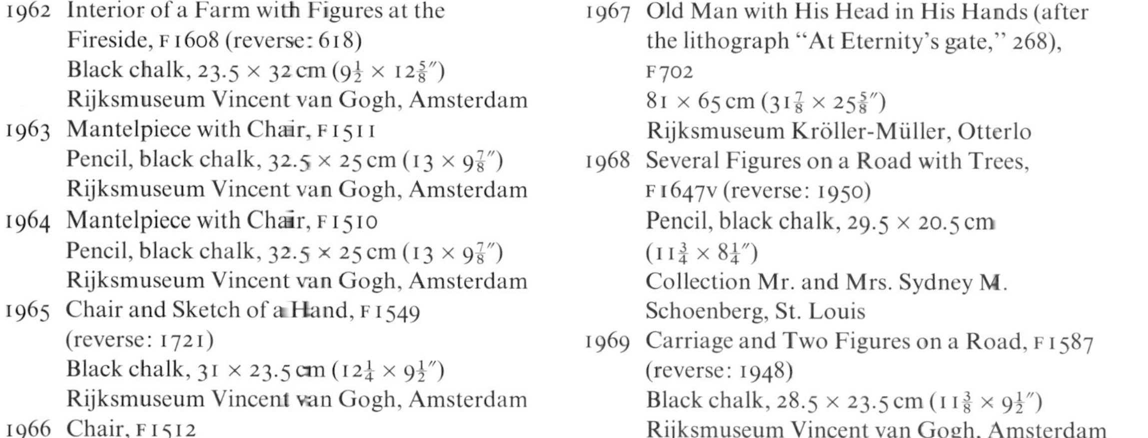

1962 Interior of a Farm with Figures at the Fireside, F 1608 (reverse: 618)
Black chalk, 23.5 × 32 cm (9½ × 12⅝″)
Rijksmuseum Vincent van Gogh, Amsterdam

1963 Mantelpiece with Chair, F 1511
Pencil, black chalk, 32.5 × 25 cm (13 × 9⅞″)
Rijksmuseum Vincent van Gogh, Amsterdam

1964 Mantelpiece with Chair, F 1510
Pencil, black chalk, 32.5 × 25 cm (13 × 9⅞″)
Rijksmuseum Vincent van Gogh, Amsterdam

1965 Chair and Sketch of a Hand, F 1549 (reverse: 1721)
Black chalk, 31 × 23.5 cm (12¼ × 9½″)
Rijksmuseum Vincent van Gogh, Amsterdam

1966 Chair, F 1512
Pencil, 33 × 24.5 cm (13 × 9⅝″)
Rijksmuseum Vincent van Gogh, Amsterdam

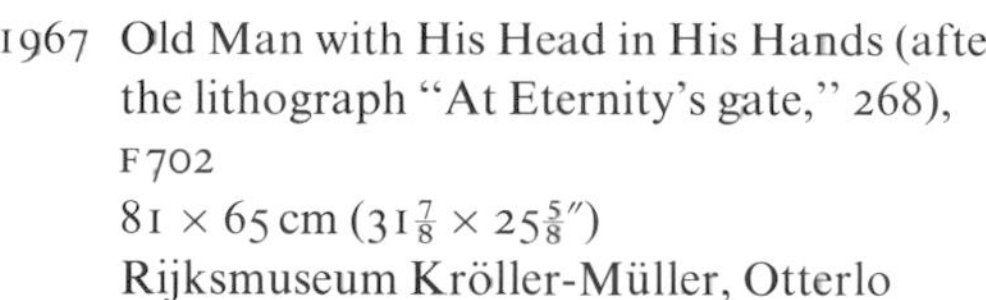

1967 Old Man with His Head in His Hands (after the lithograph "At Eternity's gate," 268), F 702
81 × 65 cm (31⅞ × 25⅝″)
Rijksmuseum Kröller-Müller, Otterlo

1968 Several Figures on a Road with Trees, F 1647v (reverse: 1950)
Pencil, black chalk, 29.5 × 20.5 cm (11¾ × 8¼″)
Collection Mr. and Mrs. Sydney M. Schoenberg, St. Louis

1969 Carriage and Two Figures on a Road, F 1587 (reverse: 1948)
Black chalk, 28.5 × 23.5 cm (11⅜ × 9½″)
Rijksmuseum Vincent van Gogh, Amsterdam

wrote again: "I have just completed another canvas of roses against a yellowish-green background in a green vase" (Letter 634).

These four large flower pieces, 1976–79, made within one week, are confirmation of a regained sense of assurance and probably also a sign of a rebirth of optimism on Vincent's part.

The still lifes of flowers were the last paintings mentioned in Vincent's letters to Theo from Saint-Rémy, but not the last ones he made there. After a final talk with Dr. Peyron, he was given permission to pack his trunk, and on May 13, the day he wrote Letter 634, he went to the station to ship his trunk by freight. We must assume that he had not been outside the walls of the monastery for some time, and therefore it is not surprising to detect a note of wistfulness when we read: "I saw the country again, fresh and full of flowers after the rain—how many things there were I still could have made."

There were three more days before he could actually leave, and Vincent was certainly not idle during that time. We know this in the first place from what he said in the letters to his mother and Wil. To his mother he wrote: "During the last two or three weeks I was in Saint-Rémy I kept working from early morning until night without letup" (Letter 639). His letter to Wil (W22) was worded almost identically, and the first draft of that letter (W21), which was not mailed, was even more explicit: "The last days in Saint-Rémy I still worked like a madman. Great bouquets of flowers, violet-colored irises, great bouquets of roses, landscapes." More exact information, however, is only to be found in the letter Vincent wrote June 24 or 25 from Auvers, when the paintings he had been obliged to leave behind in Saint-Rémy, because they were not yet dry, had been forwarded to him there. Here he mentions subjects that are new to us: "The canvases from there have now arrived; the *Irises* are quite dry and I dare to hope you will see something in them, and there are also *Roses*, a *Wheat Field*, a small canvas with mountains, and finally a *Cypress with a Star*" (Letter 644).

To begin with the last one, this is the frequently reproduced canvas *Road with Men Walking, Carriage, Cypress, Star, and Crescent Moon*, 1982, and its dating in the last days of the Saint-Rémy period is firmly established by this reference. There is also confirmation of this in a letter to Gauguin (Letter 643)—written shortly before this but never sent—in which Vincent had also made a *sketch* (1983) of the painting. Apart from the somewhat clumsily rendered walkers, the small rough sketch differs little from the painting, but it must be borne in mind that it was made by Vincent from memory a week before the canvas itself arrived. Even more interesting therefore is his description in words: "I also have from there a *Cypress with a Star*, a last attempt; a night sky with a lackluster moon, the slender crescent only just emerging from the opaque shadow of the earth—a star with an exaggerated radiance, if you will; a radiance of soft pink and green in the ultramarine sky with drifting clouds. Below, a road bordered with tall yellow cane, behind this the low, blue Alps, an old inn with orange lighted windows, and a very tall cypress, straight as an arrow, very dark. On the road, a yellow carriage with a white horse in front, and two late walkers." The words "a last attempt" must probably be interpreted to mean "the last thing I made in Saint-Rémy." Therefore, this enigmatic, strongly Expressionist painting marks the end of a yearlong period of extremely varied production, and it is striking that it is very closely related to an equally fascinating piece done at the beginning of the Saint-Rémy period—*The Starry Night*, dating from June 1889 (1731).

Identification of the paintings referred to by Vincent as a *Wheat Field* and "a small canvas with mountains" presents greater difficulties. With regard to the first, I have come to the conclusion, after considering every possibility, that the work most probably meant is *Field with Green Wheat*, 1980. In the 1970 *catalogue raisonné*, this canvas is dated "early July 1890" and is consequently ascribed to Auvers. In any event July seems too late to me, because even in Auvers the wheat was yellow by then, as witness, for example, the well-known canvas with the crows. In Saint-Rémy the wheat would still have been green in the middle of May, and the style of painting seems to me to have more in common with a canvas such as *Road with Cypress and Star* (1982) than with the generally more tranquil landscapes done in Auvers. What I find especially noteworthy is the similarity between the seemingly steep and winding road on the right-hand side of the painting and the virtually identical road in *Road with Cypress and Star*. (What looks like a yellow wheat field in the latter painting is actually, according to Vincent's description, "tall yellow cane.")

The vague description "a small canvas with mountains" could refer to any number of small-sized paintings from Saint-Rémy. The 1970 *catalogue raisonné* attaches the

1970

1971

1972

1973

1974

1975

May 1890

1970 Field of Grass with Dandelions and Tree Trunks, F676
72 × 90 cm ($28\frac{3}{8} \times 35\frac{3}{8}$″)
Rijksmuseum Kröller-Müller, Otterlo

1971 Field of Grass with Dandelions and Tree Trunks
Sketch in Letter 631
Rijksmuseum Vincent van Gogh, Amsterdam

1972 The Raising of Lazarus (after a detail from an etching by Rembrandt), F677
48.5 × 63 cm ($19\frac{1}{4} \times 24\frac{3}{4}$″)
Rijksmuseum Vincent van Gogh, Amsterdam

1973 The Raising of Lazarus
Sketch in Letter 632
Rijksmuseum Vincent van Gogh, Amsterdam

1974 The Good Samaritan (after Delacroix), F633
73 × 60 cm ($28\frac{3}{4} \times 23\frac{5}{8}$″)
Rijksmuseum Kröller-Müller, Otterlo

1975 Field of Grass with Flowers and Butterflies, F672
64.5 × 81 cm ($25\frac{5}{8} \times 31\frac{7}{8}$″)
National Gallery, London

quotation to the small landscape 1874, which is accordingly dated "spring 1890." An examination of the many mountain landscapes can leave little doubt, it seems to me, that the small painting of the couple walking among the olive trees, 1981, is the canvas referred to in Letter 644. The other landscape (1874), a much quieter treatment of the subject than the canvas *Road with Cypress and Star*, fits in better, in my view, with the landscapes done in December 1889. In contrast, the sketch depicting the walking couple shows obvious signs of having been painted extremely fast, with great impetuosity. Therefore, it exhibits much more of the highly tense character of the large canvas *Road with Cypress and Star*, which must have been completed a day or two later and, as a "last attempt," was surely made with greater care, and must also have been intended much more as a "painting," in the sense in which Vincent used that term. Although the star is missing in the small canvas, we do find here again the cypresses and the crescent moon and the blue range of hills in the distance.*

One can only guess what Vincent's intentions were with regard to this subject. There is now more reason than ever to see in the strongly accentuated red hair and red beard of the figure in the foreground a self-portrayal, and temptation is then great to attach a symbolic meaning to the figure of the woman in yellow, who, with a grand gesture, seems to be leading her companion away from the area of the olive trees and the mountains. Whether it was meant to imply that we shall never know; in any case it is clear that the motif did have a part to play in Vincent's subconscious at this time. It appears also in one of the small rough sketches that I assigned to the period of illness (1968). That sketch shows a similar couple in the foreground, and there as well the woman with upraised arm seems to be showing the man the way.

On Friday evening, May 16, 1890, Vincent set out for Paris, on the way to Auvers, where he hoped he could live his own life in complete freedom. While there, too, he would display great activity, he had indeed, during the last weeks in Saint-Rémy, "worked like a madman." If we recapitulate what he had painted since April 28 or 29, the results appear to be:

Two copies:	
The Raising of Lazarus	1972
The Good Samaritan	1974
Two garden scenes:	
Field of Grass with Dandelions and Tree Trunks	1970
Field of Grass with Flowers and Butterflies	1975
Four still lifes of flowers	1976–79
Three landscapes	1980–82
(See also Appendix, note 14.)	

Mentally and physically it was an almost superhuman achievement.

*The canvas with the walking couple is dated October 1889 in the 1970 *catalogue raisonné*. In my opinion it is not related in any way to the few canvases that Vincent made in that month.

1976

1977

1978

1976 Vase with Pink Roses, F681
71 × 90 cm (28 × 35⅜″)
Collection Mr. and Mrs. W. Averell Harriman, New York

1977 Vase with Violet Irises against a Yellow Background, F678
92 × 73.5 cm (36¼ × 29⅛″)
Rijksmuseum Vincent van Gogh, Amsterdam

1978 Vase with Violet Irises against a Pink Background, F680
73 × 93 cm (28¾ × 36⅝″)
Metropolitan Museum of Art, New York

1979 Vase with Pink Roses, F682
93 × 72 cm (36⅝ × 28⅜″)
Collection Walter Annenberg, Rancho Mirage, California

1980 Field with Green Wheat, F807
73 × 93 cm (28¾ × 36⅝″)
Collection Mr. and Mrs. Paul Mellon, Upperville, Virginia

1981 Couple Walking among Olive Trees in Mountainous Landscape with Crescent Moon, F704
49.5 × 45.5 cm (19⅝ × 18⅛″)
Museu de Arte, São Paulo

1982 Road with Men Walking, Carriage, Cypress, Star, and Crescent Moon, F683
92 × 73 cm (36¼ × 28¾″)
Rijksmuseum Kröller-Müller, Otterlo

1983 Road with Men Walking, Carriage, Cypress, Star, and Crescent Moon
Sketch in Letter 643
Rijksmuseum Vincent van Gogh, Amsterdam

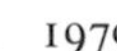

1979

1980

1981

1982

1983

Auvers-sur-Oise

1984

1985

1986

1987

"I had expected a sick man, but here was a sturdy, broad-shouldered man, with a healthy color, a smile on his face, and a very resolute appearance"; thus Jo van Gogh-Bonger described Vincent's arrival in Paris. There is no other information about the few days he spent with Theo and his little family than her brief account of it in her "Memoir" to *The Complete Letters*, and it therefore seems to me proper to reproduce her narrative in her own words:

"He stayed with us three days, and was cheerful and lively all the time. St. Rémy was not mentioned. He went out by himself to buy olives, which he used to eat every day and which he insisted on our eating too. The first morning he was up very early and was standing in his shirt sleeves looking at his pictures, of which our apartment was full. The walls were covered with them—in the bedroom, the 'Orchards in Bloom'; in the dining room over the mantelpiece, the 'Potato Eaters'; in the sitting room (salon was too solemn a name for that cosy little room), the great 'Landscape from Arles' and the 'Night View on the Rhône.' Besides, to the great despair of our *femme de ménage*, there were under the bed, under the sofa, under the cupboards in the little spare room, huge piles of unframed canvases; they were now spread out on the ground and studied with great attention.

"We also had many visitors, but Vincent soon perceived that the bustle of Paris did him no good, and he longed to set to work again. So he started on May 21 for Auvers,* with an introduction to Dr. Gachet, whose faithful friendship was to become his greatest support during the short time he spent at Auvers" (vol. I, pages l–li).

We have Vincent's own account of his arrival in Auvers (Letter 635). He had visited Paul Gachet and found him rather eccentric and just as much affected by nervous trouble as he himself. The inn Dr. Gachet had taken him to he found too high at 6 francs a day, but he had found one himself for 3.50 francs and had taken up his lodgings there. The inn, which was owned by Arthur Gustave Ravoux, was opposite the little town hall of the village; it is still in existence and is now called La Maison de Van Gogh. Vincent thought that he would be able to do a lot of work and do it well in Auvers.

A survey of the drawings and paintings he made in Auvers reveals an almost unbelievable productivity, even allowing for some unevenness in quality. We find a large number of truly masterful and matchless works next to many slipshod and hasty sketches in oils, and a small group of important drawings next to dozens of sketchbook sheets in pencil and chalk. The letters give an accounting of no fewer than thirty-one paintings.

More or less identical variants were made of some of the paintings mentioned in the letters, and Vincent in most cases probably did these immediately after the original work. There are thus two copies of the portrait of

*This must have been May 20; Vincent also wrote (in Letter 643) that he had been in Paris only three days.

May 1890

1984 A Group of Cottages, F 750
60 × 73 cm (23⅝ × 28¾″)
The Hermitage, Leningrad

1985 Old Vineyard with Peasant Woman, F 1624
Pencil, washed, blue, red, and white gouache, 43.5 × 54 cm (17⅜ × 21¼″)
Rijksmuseum Vincent van Gogh, Amsterdam

1986 Landscape with Cottages, F 1640
(reverse: 1990)
Pencil, washed, blue watercolor, 45 × 54.5 cm (17¾ × 21⅝″)
Rijksmuseum Vincent van Gogh, Amsterdam

1987 Cottages with Thatched Roofs, F 792
72 × 91 cm (28⅜ × 35⅞″)
The Louvre, Paris

Colorplate XXXIX, The Church in Auvers, 2006 〉

Dr. Gachet, three of Adeline Ravoux (daughter of the innkeeper), two of a peasant girl among wheat stalks, and two of "Daubigny's garden."* If we add the painting of the little town hall in festive array—certainly done on Bastille Day, July 14—then the number of paintings that can be dated with certainty comes to thirty-six.

Just this group of thirty-one canvases alone, or thirty-six with the variants included, averages out over the two-month period to one painting every other day, and even if, out of the remaining fifty ascribed to this period in the 1970 *catalogue raisonné*, some might date from before Auvers and some might not be authentic, the conclusion would still have to be that the work was done at a dazzling tempo.

A casual remark by Vincent himself points in this direction. In a letter probably written on the *fourth* day of his stay in Auvers, we read: "I am working hard, have four painted studies and two drawings" (Letter 648).

The sketchbooks from this period were no longer kept together in book form, as had been the case with some of the very early sketchbooks. The sheets have become detached or have been torn out, and some of them are no longer with the others that are kept in the Rijksmuseum Vincent van Gogh (there are a few in the Louvre and in the United States). To provide an overview of these sketches, I have arranged them together at the beginning of July (in the 1970 *catalogue raisonné* they are all dated June, July, or June/July 1890). In doing this, I am not, of course, suggesting that they were all made one after the other at the beginning of July; rather, they were produced gradually throughout Vincent's stay in Auvers in company with his other work, but it is impossible to put them in any kind of chronological order with even the remotest semblance of credibility.

May 1890

In my opinion the works 1984–2004 represent Vincent's production between his arrival in Auvers, May 20, and the remainder of the month. The subject of all these paintings and drawings was the new and inspiring surroundings in which he would be working from then on. "Auvers is very beautiful," he wrote in his very first letter (Letter 635), "among other things, many old thatched roofs, something that is becoming rare . . . really, it is strikingly beautiful, it is the true countryside, typical and picturesque."

His first subject (1984) was just such an old farmhouse with a thatched roof, "with a field of flowering peas and wheat in the foreground, hills in the background" (Letter 636). In the glaring blue of the sky, in the yellowish green and orange-yellow of the foreground, and in the strong red of one roof, we immediately see in this painting the bright colors that, generally speaking, are characteristic of the work of the Auvers period and differentiate them somewhat from the paintings done in Saint-Rémy—although there is naturally no question of a real break

*The French landscape painter Charles Daubigny lived for a number of years in a large house in Auvers quite near the Ravoux inn, where Vincent was staying.

1988

1989

1990

1988 A Group of Cottages, F759
61 × 73 cm (24 × 28¾″)
Toledo Museum of Art, Ohio

1989 A Group of Cottages, F805
73 × 60.5 cm (28¾ × 24″)
Museum of Fine Arts, Boston

1990 Houses and Chestnut Trees, F1640v
(reverse: 1986)
Black chalk, 45 × 54.5 cm (17¾ × 21⅝″)
Rijksmuseum Vincent van Gogh, Amsterdam

‹ Colorplate XL, Wheat Fields, 2099

with the past from one week to the next.

Similar painted studies of houses in Auvers or farmhouses in the surrounding area are to be found in 1987–89, 1995, and others, and here, too, we see how time and again the lively color accents give the landscape a cheerful appearance. Typical examples in this regard are *Landscape with Trees and Houses*, 2000, with a foreground rendered in brick red and bright green, and *Village Street*, 2001, with orange roofs under a blue and white sky.

Even the watercolor drawings 1985 and 1986, hastily put down on paper with extraordinary verve, take part in this enthusiastic interplay of movement and color with their bright blue and red brushstrokes.

In a letter May 25, Vincent mentioned that he was working on the drawing of a vineyard (1985) and two paintings of chestnut trees, 1991 (carefully prepared for by a drawing, 1990) and 1992: "I have a drawing of an old vineyard of which I intend to make a size-30 canvas*; also, a study of pink chestnut trees (in bloom) and another of white ones" (Letter 637).

Some rather extensive groups of farm buildings inspired him to make the detailed and carefully executed larger drawings 1993 and 1994. Landscapes 2003 and 2004—conceived as views of large parts of the village—differ quite sharply from the other studies of farmhouses in the use of unmodulated colors, and as a result they are difficult to date with any accuracy. On the other hand, they are related to the paintings of the farmhouses in the freshness of their colors, and the difference here, in my opinion, can be explained by the fact that they are sketches in oil that were made very quickly and had not yet been developed into finished paintings.

A special case is the intense, overwrought study of a garden, 1999, which is distinguished, on the one hand, by the agitated interplay of lines of the pointed and curving leaves and the threatening sky and, on the other hand, by the unusually sharp color contrast between the green of the plants and the glowing red of the roof before which they stand. The painting was an impression of Dr. Gachet's garden as Vincent had seen it on his first visit there. This is borne out by what he wrote his sister June 3: "I shall spend one or two days at his place each week in order to work in his garden. I have already painted two studies of it, one with plants from the south, aloes, cypresses, marigolds, the other with white roses, grapevines, and a little figure; also a bouquet of ranunculus"† (Letter W22).

June

The flaming cypresses against red roofs appear again in the second painting made in Dr. Gachet's garden, the canvas with "roses, grapevines, and a little white figure" that Vincent, according to a letter to Theo (Letter 638), had painted "last Sunday," that is, June 1 (2005). The girl in white with a yellow sun hat seen standing among the roses was most likely Gachet's nineteen-year-old daughter. Marguerite. This is an attractive little painting, but the composition is somewhat unclear and overloaded.

The large painting of the Gothic-style village church, 2006 (colorplate XXXIX, page 455), which, in contrast, is imposing precisely because of the simplicity of its concept, was probably painted as soon as the next day, for Vincent was able to describe it in detail in the previously mentioned letter to Wil, written June 3: "What is more, I have a larger painting of the village church, an effect derived from the contrast of the violet-blue structure against a sky of deep and simple blue, pure cobalt; the stained-glass windows

*As far as we know, this intention was never carried out.

†No painting of this subject from this period is known.

1991

1992

1993

1991 Flowering Chestnut Tree, F752
63 × 50.5 cm ($24\frac{3}{4} \times 20\frac{1}{8}$")
Rijksmuseum Kröller-Müller, Otterlo

1992 Flowering Chestnut Trees, F751
70 × 58 cm ($27\frac{5}{8} \times 22\frac{7}{8}$")
Location unknown

1993 Cottages with a Woman Working in the Foreground, F1653
Pencil, pen, 47 × 61.5 cm ($18\frac{1}{2} \times 24\frac{3}{8}$")
The Louvre, Paris

1994 Cottages with a Woman Working in the Foreground, F1642
Charcoal, reed pen, pastel, 47 × 62.5 cm ($18\frac{1}{2} \times 24\frac{3}{4}$")
Art Institute of Chicago

1994

1995

1996

1997

1998

1999

2000

1995 Village Street, F791
49 × 70 cm ($19\frac{1}{4} \times 27\frac{5}{8}''$)
Stavros S. Niarchos Collection

1996 Village Street, F1638 (reverse: 1998)
Pencil, pen, brown ink, 44.5 × 55 cm
($17\frac{3}{4} \times 21\frac{5}{8}''$)
Rijksmuseum Vincent van Gogh, Amsterdam

1997 A Group of Cottages with Two Women in the Foreground, F1640a
Black chalk, 44 × 46.5 cm ($17\frac{3}{8} \times 18\frac{1}{2}''$)
Location unknown

1998 Village Street, Sketch, F1638v (reverse: 1996)
Black chalk, 30.5 × 23.5 cm ($12\frac{1}{4} \times 9\frac{1}{2}''$)
Rijksmuseum Vincent van Gogh, Amsterdam

1999 Doctor Gachet's Garden, F755
73 × 51.5 cm ($28\frac{3}{4} \times 20\frac{1}{2}''$)
The Louvre, Paris

2000 Landscape with Trees and Houses, F815
64 × 78 cm ($25\frac{1}{4} \times 30\frac{3}{4}''$)
Rijksmuseum Kröller-Müller, Otterlo

are like patches of ultramarine; the roof is violet and partly orange. In the foreground a bit of greenery and flowers and sand with pink sunlight [shining] on it."

It is interesting to note that this work reminded him of the studies he had made of the old tower and the graveyard in Nuenen, and as a matter of fact the heavy bulk of the old tower in studies such as 490 and 772 did fill the picture plane in the same way as the massive church of Auvers does in this later canvas, but Vincent could with justice add: "only now the color is probably richer and more expressive." The "probably" is one of those understatements typical of him, for the color here is not merely very expressive, but even overwhelmingly emotionally charged—to an extent that was only sporadically seen in the long series of paintings from the Saint-Rémy period (*The Starry Night*, 1731, is perhaps the only painting that is comparable in this respect).

It is almost inconceivable that Vincent could have made the penetrating portrait of Dr. Gachet at almost the same time as the painting of the church, although the same hand has, of course, left its mark in such recognizable characteristics as the mosaiclike structure of the painted surface (mainly in the foreground of the painting of the church, in the background of the portrait), and both paintings have in common the deep and radiant blue. Yet the letters leave no doubt about the dating. In the previously mentioned Letter 638, June 3—which included the small rough sketch 2008—Vincent wrote: "I am working on his portrait, the head with a white cap, very fair, very light, the hands also in a light flesh color, a blue suit, and a cobalt-blue background; he is leaning on a red table; on which there is a yellow book and a sprig of digitalis."* The description and the little sketch make it apparent that Vincent is here referring to 2007. There is a variant of this portrait, 2014, which in most respects is identical (although the expression is somewhat different), but it does not include the books. The authenticity of this portrait, which is not mentioned in the letters, is difficult to disprove, as Dr. Gachet's son, who later donated it to the Louvre, has stated that he saw it being painted when he was seventeen years old.†

Understandably Vincent set great store by the portrait of Dr. Gachet, probably primarily because of the subject's importance to him as a fatherly friend and medical adviser, but certainly also because of the work's success as a portrait. He adverted to it several times (Letters W22, W23, and 643), laying particular stress on the *expression*—"a melancholy expression" (Letter W23), "the heartrending expression of our time" (Letter 643). Especially noteworthy is the comparison he made with the *Self-Portrait*, 1772,

*The digitalis, a remedy for the treatment of heart disease, was an allusion to the sitter's profession. The books served mainly to introduce a note of yellow into the composition, but by taking pains to make the titles legible (*Manette Salomon* and *Germinie Lacerteux*, both by Jules and Edmond de Goncourt), Vincent let it be known that he was still an admirer of French naturalistic novels, and perhaps that Gachet shared this admiration.

†To Marc E. Tralbaut; see his *Vincent van Gogh* (1969), p. 312.

2001

2002

2003

2001 Village Street, F802
73×92 cm ($28\frac{3}{4} \times 36\frac{1}{4}$")
Ateneumin Taidemuseo, Helsinki

2002 A Group of Houses, F794
51×58 cm ($20\frac{1}{8} \times 22\frac{7}{8}$")
Location unknown

2003 A Group of Houses in a Landscape, F797
55×65 cm ($21\frac{5}{8} \times 25\frac{5}{8}$")
Thyssen-Bornemisza Collection, Lugano-Castagnola, Switzerland

2004 A Group of Houses in a Landscape, F799
50×52 cm ($19\frac{5}{8} \times 20\frac{1}{2}$")
Rijksmuseum Vincent van Gogh, Amsterdam
June 1890

2005 Marguerite Gachet in the Garden, F756
46×55 cm ($18\frac{1}{8} \times 21\frac{5}{8}$")
The Louvre, Paris

2006 The Church in Auvers, F789
94×74 cm ($37 \times 29\frac{1}{8}$")
The Louvre, Paris
Colorplate XXXIX, p. 455

2007 Doctor Gachet Sitting at a Table with Books and a Glass with Sprigs of Foxglove, F753
66×57 cm ($26 \times 22\frac{1}{2}$")
Private collection, New York

2004

2005

2006

2007

2008

2009

2010

2008 Doctor Gachet Sitting at a Table with Books and a Glass with Sprigs of Foxglove
Sketch in Letter 638
Rijksmuseum Vincent van Gogh, Amsterdam

2009 Pink Roses, F595
32 × 40.5 cm ($12\frac{5}{8} \times 16\frac{1}{8}$")
Ny Carlsberg Glyptotek, Copenhagen

2010 Blossoming Chestnut Branches, F820
72 × 91 cm ($28\frac{3}{8} \times 35\frac{7}{8}$")
Collection E. G. Bührle, Zurich

which, although quite different, must have served more or less as an example: "It is in the same vein as the *Self-Portrait* that I brought with me [from Paris] when I left to come here. Mr. [sic] Gachet is absolutely *fanatical* about that portrait and absolutely wants me to make one just like it for him, if I can, and that is what I want to do" (Letter 638). (See also Appendix, note 15.)

On the same Saturday, June 7, that Vincent gave the finishing touches to the second portrait of Gachet, he must very quickly have painted the beautiful little *Branches of Flowering Acacia*, 2015.* Therefore, it seems reasonable to suppose that similar flower studies were also made at this time—*Blossoming Chestnut Branches* (2010), the three *Roses* (2009, 2011, and 2012), and *Poppies with Butterflies* (2013). Of these five canvases, *Blossoming Chestnut Branches* is by far the most important, even in size, and had it been part of a public collection, it might very well have become just as famous as, for example, *Branches of an Almond Tree*, 1891. The deep ultramarine blue of the background links it to works such as *The Church in Auvers*, 2006, and the portrait of Dr. Gachet, 2007.

Anecdotal Landscapes

Sunday, June 8, the day after Vincent had finished these two important works, Theo, accompanied by his wife and baby, came out from Paris and had dinner with Vincent at Dr. Gachet's—a visit that is described in lively detail in Jo van Gogh-Bonger's "Memoir." After this Vincent went back to work again with such vigor that by Tuesday, June 10, he could write: "Since Sunday I have made two studies of houses in the greenery" (Letter 640). This somewhat vague description could fit several paintings of peasant dwellings, but to me it seems most probable that the two small canvases 2016 and 2017 were the ones referred to here.

Although these are charming little works, they are less important than the larger landscapes that immediately followed (2018, 2019, and 2020). Vincent wrote about them in a letter to his sister: "Yesterday in the square I painted a large landscape showing endless fields seen from a height, different kinds of green, a dark-green potato field, the earth rich and purple between the rectangular beds, a white field of beans in flower to the side, a field of clover with pink flowers, and the little figure of a mower, a field of tall full-grown grass in a pinkish tint; also grain, poplars, a last range of blue hills on the horizon, and at the foot of these a train passing by with a huge cloud of white smoke trailing behind it in the greenery. A white road crosses the canvas. On the road a little carriage and beside the road white houses with bright red roofs. A fine rain leaves blue and gray streaks over the whole scene. There is another landscape with vines and meadows in the foreground and behind them the roofs of the village. And yet another one, with nothing but a green wheat field extending as far as a white country house surrounded by a white wall, with a single tree" (Letter W23, June 10 or 11).

*Ibid., p. 314.

2011

2012

2013

2011 Branches with Wild Roses, F597
23.5 × 32 cm ($9\frac{1}{2} \times 12\frac{5}{8}$")
Rijksmuseum Vincent van Gogh, Amsterdam

2012 Wild Roses with a Beetle, F749
32.5 × 23.5 cm ($13 \times 9\frac{1}{2}$")
Rijksmuseum Vincent van Gogh, Amsterdam

2013 Poppies with Butterflies, F748
33.5 × 24.5 cm ($13\frac{3}{8} \times 9\frac{7}{8}$")
Rijksmuseum Vincent van Gogh, Amsterdam

2014 Doctor Gachet at a Table with a Sprig of Foxglove in His Hand, F754
68 × 57 cm ($26\frac{3}{4} \times 22\frac{1}{2}$")
The Louvre, Paris

2015 Branches of Flowering Acacia, F821
33 × 24 cm ($13 \times 9\frac{1}{2}$")
Nationalmuseum, Stockholm

2016 Group of Houses with a Little Figure, F758
33 × 40.5 cm ($13 \times 16\frac{1}{8}$")
Private collection, New York

2017 A House and Two Figures, F806
38 × 45 cm ($15 \times 17\frac{3}{4}$")
Rijksmuseum Vincent van Gogh, Amsterdam

2018 Wheat Field and White Country House, F804
48.5 × 63 cm ($19\frac{1}{4} \times 24\frac{3}{4}$")
Phillips Collection, Washington, D.C.

2014

2015

2016

2017

2019

2018

2020

2019 Landscape with Carriage and Train in the Distance, F760
72 × 90 cm ($28\frac{3}{8} \times 35\frac{3}{8}$")
Pushkin Museum, Moscow

2020 Vineyard with a Group of Houses, F762
64 × 80 cm ($25\frac{1}{4} \times 31\frac{1}{2}$")
The St. Louis Art Museum

We see that Vincent, especially in the painting he mentioned here first, 2019, had reverted to the type of wide landscape, also seen "from a height" and containing many anecdotal details, that he had drawn and painted on numerous occasions in the Arles period. In one of them, the wheat field, 1477, a long train with a great cloud of smoke is also shown passing through the picture. Vincent himself must have been reminded of the earlier landscapes. In the letter to Theo in which he mentioned painting 2019, he expressed himself as follows: "I also have a study in the style of the *Harvest Landscape* [1440], which you have in the room where the piano is: fields, seen from a height, with a little carriage on a road" (Letter 641).

Paintings 2021 and 2022 are, respectively, a large and a small river view, which in style are typical of the Auvers period but which because of a lack of external evidence are difficult to date. In the 1970 *catalogue raisonné* the large canvas with the small boats, 2021, which is given the title *The Bank of the Oise*, is dated June 1890, but a comment adds that "the possibility must not be excluded that this work was executed in Paris during the summer of 1887." In my opinion, however, the heavy, mosaiclike brushstrokes make the latter hypothesis highly improbable. *The Little Stream*, as the small and very sketchy painting 2022 is referred to in the *catalogue raisonné*, is dated May 1890 in that work.

The drawing with watercolor and gouache, 2023, is clearly a view of the Oise with the Auvers bridge. The panoramic view and the somewhat naïve quantity of detail give it something in common with painted studies such as *Landscape with Carriage and Train*, 2019, and thus also with some of the drawings of distant views from the Arles period, but the forceful brushwork in 2023 is typical of the impetuosity of Auvers. The lively, vivid green, blue, and bright red colors give a sense of cheerfulness.

There are also three much less important pencil sketches of the Oise landscape, all of them obviously done very quickly, 2024, 2025, and 2026; 2026 is actually nothing more than a very hasty note of a particular site.

Another large, colorful landscape is 2027, a canvas which Vincent mentioned in his letter June 14: "At the moment I am working on a *Field with Poppies* in the clover" (Letter 641).

The more intimate small study of a garden, 2029, must date from about the same time, for even in his letter June 17 he wrote: "I am thinking about making a more important canvas of Daubigny's house and garden,* of which I already have a small study" (Letter 642). This is a charming and sunny landscape that bespeaks a moment of tranquillity, and in it the animation of *Field with Poppies*, 2027, and certainly the intense emotionalism of *The Church in Auvers*, 2006, seem to have been forgotten.

An Etched Portrait

Quite suddenly and unexpectedly, Vincent seems to have turned his attention at this time to a technique that was entirely new for him—etching. The reason for this was that Dr. Gachet happened to have an etching press, and Vincent started thinking about making some motifs from the South, because, as he said, "I can print them without cost at Mr. Gachet's, who can certainly print them for nothing if I make them" (Letter 642). As far as we know, only one etching was made, a new portrait of Dr. Gachet. The dating of the etching, 2028, has given rise to considerable discussion because of the inscription, which, although seemingly reading "15 Mai 90," has been interpreted by some authorities as "25 Mai 90" because the figure "15," written, of course, in reverse on the etching plate, is not clear. As Vincent had not yet arrived in Auvers by May 15, he must himself have made a mistake either in this figure or in the month.

*See note on p. 457.

2021

2022

2023

2021 Riverbank with Rowboats and Three Figures, F798
72 × 92 cm ($28\frac{3}{8} \times 36\frac{1}{4}$″)
Detroit Institute of Arts

2022 Little Stream Surrounded by Bushes, F740
25.5 × 40 cm ($10\frac{1}{4} \times 15\frac{3}{4}$″)
Estate of C. V. Starr, New York

2023 Landscape with Bridge across the Oise, F1639
Pencil, watercolor, gouache, 47.5 × 63 cm
($18\frac{7}{8} \times 24\frac{3}{4}$″)
Tate Gallery, London

2024 Landscape with the Oise, F1627
Pencil, black chalk, 23.5 × 30.5 cm
($9\frac{1}{2} \times 12\frac{1}{4}$″)
Rijksmuseum Vincent van Gogh, Amsterdam

2025 Landscape with the Oise, F1629
Pencil, black chalk, 23.5 × 30.5 cm
($9\frac{1}{2} \times 12\frac{1}{4}$″)
Rijksmuseum Vincent van Gogh, Amsterdam

2024

2025

2026

2027

2028

2029

2030

2026 Little Stream Surrounded by Bushes, F 1628
Pencil, black chalk, 23.5×30.5 cm
($9\frac{1}{2} \times 12\frac{1}{4}$″)
Rijksmuseum Vincent van Gogh, Amsterdam

2027 Field with Poppies, F636
73×91.5 cm ($28\frac{3}{4} \times 36\frac{1}{4}$″)
Gemeentemuseum, The Hague (on loan from the state)

2028 Portrait of Doctor Gachet with Pipe, F 1664
Etching, 18×15 cm ($7\frac{1}{8} \times 5\frac{7}{8}$″)
Various collections

2029 Corner of Daubigny's Garden, F765
51×51 cm ($20\frac{1}{8} \times 2c\frac{1}{8}$″)
Rijksmuseum Vincent van Gogh, Amsterdam

2030 Vase with Field Flowers and Thistles, F763
Paper on canvas, 66×45 cm ($26 \times 17\frac{3}{4}$″)
Formerly collection André Meyer, New York

The latter interpretation seems to me more probable,* which would mean that the etching was made on June 15, 1890. This seems even more reasonable since there are letters by both Theo van Gogh and Gauguin acknowledging the receipt of an etching, although unfortunately neither of them mentions the subject of the etching. Theo's letter was written June 23 (Letter T38), and Gauguin's must have been written at about the same time (Letter G39, manuscript in the Rijksmuseum Vincent van Gogh). Theo called it "a genuine painter's etching," and while this really says very little, we must admit that Vincent, in this first attempt to apply the etching technique, succeeded in making an impressive portrait of his friend, even though the model's hand must be regarded as poorly drawn—as indeed was also often the case with Vincent's painted portraits.

June 17 Vincent wrote Theo: "I am working on two studies. The first a bouquet of wild plants, thistles, stalks of wheat, leaves of different kinds of green: some almost red, others all green, others tending toward yellow. The second study, a white house among the trees with a star in the night sky and an orange light shining through the window and black foliage and a dark pink note" (Letter 642). The descriptions make clear that what he was referring to were the still life of flowers, 2030, and the somewhat larger, and relatively tranquil, painting of a white house with several figures, 2031. The latter work is a night scene in which the star with an enormous halo—reminiscent of canvases such as *The Starry Night*, 1731, and *Road with Cypress and Star*, 1982—seems in some strange manner to have gone astray.

The simple still lifes of flowers, 2032 and 2033, which are not mentioned in the letters, have been placed here because of several points of similarity with the flower piece 2030.

A work that is mentioned in the letters is a painting whose entire surface is covered with an almost abstract pattern of wheat stalks and a few pink and blue flowers—2034. Vincent even made a couple of sketches of it in a letter to Gauguin, written about June 17 but never mailed: "I am trying to make studies of wheat, like this (I just can't seem to draw it), nothing but blue-green stalks, long leaves like ribbons, green and pink in the reflection, ears turning light yellow, bordered with the soft pink of the dusty bloom—a pink bindweed down below twisted around a stem. Against such a very lively yet restful background, I would like to paint portraits" (Letter 643).

While painting 2034 may not have great significance in itself, it was important as a source of inspiration, for Vincent's idea of using such patterning as a background for portraits was translated into fact a short time later. It was against stalks of wheat like these that he painted a peasant girl—in one pose standing, with a white dress, 2055, and in another, seated, with the same wide-brimmed yellow straw hat, but wearing a violet blouse with red polka dots, 2053. The latter portrait,

*If the inscription actually did originate with Van Gogh, May 25 was the date of his *first* visit at Gachet's and therefore seems highly unlikely.

2031

2032

2033

2031 White House in the Night with Figures and a Star, F766
59.5 × 73 cm ($23\frac{5}{8} \times 28\frac{3}{4}''$)
Location unknown

2032 Vase with Cornflowers and Poppies, F280
65 × 50 cm ($25\frac{5}{8} \times 19\frac{5}{8}''$)
Albright-Knox Art Gallery, Buffalo, New York

2033 Vase with Field Flowers, F589
41 × 34 cm ($16\frac{1}{8} \times 13\frac{3}{8}''$)
Location unknown

2034 Ears of Wheat, F767
64.5 × 47 cm ($25\frac{5}{8} \times 18\frac{1}{2}''$)
Rijksmuseum Vincent van Gogh, Amsterdam

2035 Adeline Ravoux, Half-Figure, F768
67 × 55 cm ($26\frac{3}{8} \times 21\frac{5}{8}''$)
Private collection, Switzerland

2036 Adeline Ravoux, Head, F786
52 × 52 cm ($20\frac{1}{2} \times 20\frac{1}{2}''$)
Cleveland Museum of Art

2037 Adeline Ravoux, Half-Figure, F769
71.5 × 53 cm ($28\frac{3}{8} \times 20\frac{7}{8}''$)
Private collection

2038 Wheat Fields, F775
50 × 101 cm ($19\frac{5}{8} \times 39\frac{3}{4}''$)
Neue Galerie in der Stallburg, Kunsthistorisches Museum, Vienna

2034

2035

2036

2037

2038

2039

2040

2039 Wheat Fields
Sketch in Letter 646
Rijksmuseum Vincent van Gogh, Amsterdam

2040 Field with Trees and the Château of Auvers at Sunset, F770
50 × 100 cm ($19\frac{5}{8} \times 39\frac{3}{8}''$)
Rijksmuseum Vincent van Gogh, Amsterdam

in particular, with its forceful color contrasts which Vincent himself feared might seem "a little coarse" (Letter 646), has resulted in a very original and, for him, unusually "cheerful" painting, a synthesis of all the pastoral beauty and joy of living Auvers had meant to him.

More Portraits and Landscapes
"This week I made a portrait of a girl of about sixteen, in blue against a blue background, the daughter of the people at whose place I am living," Vincent wrote, June 24 or 25. "I have given her this portrait, but I have made a variant of it for you, a size-15 canvas" (Letter 644). He was referring to the portrait in full profile of Adeline Ravoux, the blond daughter of the innkeeper (she was actually thirteen years old). This portrait, 2035, shows her in a blue dress, seated, against a striped background of ultramarine blue. In addition to an almost identical companion piece, 2037, there is also a bust-length portrait of her in three-quarter view 2036 (see Appendix, note 16).

An anecdote told about portrait 2035 has it that a few years after Van Gogh's death, Ravoux sold it, together with the painting *The Town Hall of Auvers*, 2108, to some foreigners for 40 francs, thereby imagining that he had made a shrewd deal.* Adeline Ravoux, to whom we owe this anecdote—recounted by her years later—has also contended that portraits 2036 and 2037 were unknown to her. However, her memory may have deceived her here, for while it might possibly be assumed, by stretching things a bit, that 2037 is a copy made by Vincent in his room, the other portrait, 2036, could not have been made by him from memory. In any case, all three portraits are remarkable in color and composition and probably constitute a good likeness of the subject.

A New Format
That same week Vincent had also been working on landscapes, and more important, he had turned to an unusual new elongated format that he would frequently be using from then on: "I furthermore have a canvas that is a yard long but only eighteen inches high, of wheat fields, and a similar one of trees, violet trunks of poplars, and beneath them grass with little flowers, pink, yellow, white, and various kinds of green. Finally, an evening effect: two pear trees very dark against a yellowish sky, with wheat fields, and on the violet background, the château surrounded by dark foliage" (Letter 644). Here Vincent did not go beyond an announcement, but in Letter 646 he made small sketches of two of the three landscapes, 2039 and 2042, which, especially in the case of the canvas with the vague description "of wheat fields," provide a welcome means of identification.

As a group, the paintings that correspond to these sketches are uneven. The forest scene, 2041, with its violet trees and elongated figures, is perhaps more odd than attractive, but *Wheat Fields* (2038) and *Château*

*Adeline Carrié (née Ravoux), "Les souvenirs d'Adeline Ravoux sur le séjour de Vincent van Gogh à Auvers-sur-Oise," *Les Cahiers de Van Gogh*, no. 1 (1956), pp. 7–17.

2041

2042

2043

2041 Couple Walking between Rows of Trees, F 773
50 × 100 cm ($19\frac{5}{8} \times 39\frac{3}{8}''$)
Cincinnati Art Museum

2042 Couple Walking between Rows of Trees
Sketch in Letter 646
Rijksmuseum Vincent van Gogh, Amsterdam

2043 Glass with Flowers, F 598
41 × 32 cm ($16\frac{1}{8} \times 12\frac{5}{8}''$)
Collection A. Peralta-Ramos, New York

2044 Vase with Flowers and Thistles, F 599
41 × 34 cm ($16\frac{1}{8} \times 13\frac{3}{8}''$)
Collection J. Blair MacAulay, Oakville, Ontario

2045 Japanese Vase with Roses and Anemones, F 764
51 × 51 cm ($20\frac{1}{8} \times 20\frac{1}{8}''$)
The Louvre, Paris

2046 Vase with Flowers, F 764a
42 × 29 cm ($16\frac{1}{2} \times 11\frac{3}{8}''$)
Rijksmuseum Vincent van Gogh, Amsterdam

2047 Marguerite Gachet at the Piano, F 1623 (reverse: 2094)
Black chalk, 30 × 19 cm ($11\frac{3}{4} \times 7\frac{1}{2}''$)
Rijksmuseum Vincent van Gogh, Amsterdam

2044

2045

2046

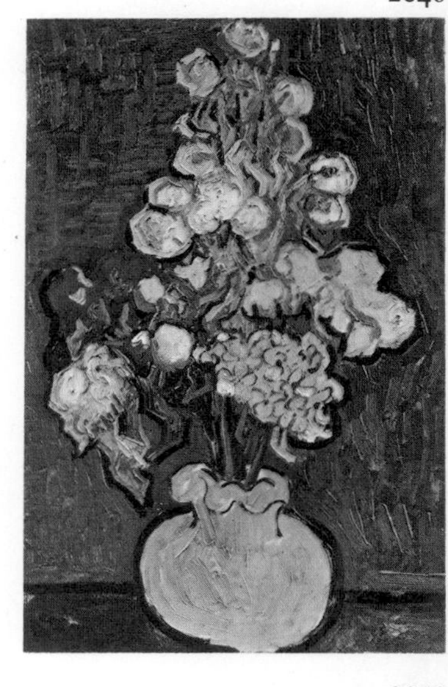

2047

2048

2049

2050

2048 Marguerite Gachet at the Piano, F772
102 × 50 cm ($40\frac{1}{8} \times 19\frac{5}{8}$″)
Kunstmuseum, Basel
2049 Marguerite Gachet at the Piano
Sketch in Letter 645
Location unknown
2050 Head of a Boy with a Carnation between His Teeth, F787
39 × 30.5 cm ($15\frac{3}{8} \times 12\frac{1}{4}$″)
Location unknown

of Auvers at Sunset* (2040) are certainly among the finest canvases of the Auvers period. The landscape with extensive fields, 2038, is very similar in treatment to several paintings done a few weeks later that Vincent described as "immense expanses of grain under an overcast sky" (Letter 649). However, the colorful alternation of yellow, grayish-green, and bright green fields, the yellow haystack, and the countless red poppies in the foreground give 2038 a much gayer look, although even here the absence of workers in the fields adds a touch of loneliness to the countryside. In the large landscape in which the château of Auvers appears in the background, Vincent has succeeded, by means of a bold profusion of yellow and orange brushstrokes, in rendering the glowing sky of a summer evening as seen behind a silhouette of dark green trees, while at the same time the house and even the surrounding trees have been made to sparkle like blue gems. Despite the absence of human figures, there certainly is no question of loneliness or gloom here.

Canvases 2043–46, like 2032 and 2033, belong to the group of still lifes of flowers that Vincent apparently kept working on at the same time as he was doing landscapes and portraits, and they can be dated only roughly as belonging to this period. They differ widely in treatment and quality. Some—such as the celadon *Japanese Vase with Roses and Anemones*, 2045—are more carefully done and more traditional in composition, whereas in others Vincent seems to have aimed at a certain capriciousness of line (2043 and 2044) or else has laid great stress on color but given only scant attention to form and matter (2046).

The portrait of Marguerite Gachet, 2047–49, is considerably more important, and Vincent sketched it and described it in detail with evident satisfaction: "Yesterday and the day before, I painted Miss Gachet's portrait, which, I hope, you will soon see; the dress is pink, the wall in the background green with orange dots, the carpet red with green dots, the piano dark violet; it is a yard high by eighteen inches in width. It is a figure I enjoyed painting, but a difficult one" (Letter 645, June 28 or 29). Though he wrote that he intended making a copy of this portrait for Theo, nothing seems to have come of this, nor did he make a second portrait of Marguerite Gachet at a small organ as he had proposed to do.

The double portrait of a pair of peasant tots, of which there are two versions, 2051 and 2052, and the head of a young man with a carnation between his teeth and an unruly mop of hair, 2050 (the youth was probably a sort of "village idiot"), cannot be accurately dated but were presumably done during the same weeks as the many other portraits. I think that we must regard them as hasty studies in oils, which, with their heavy, violet-blue wavy lines and contours, certainly exhibit some of the characteristics of Vincent's other portraits, but which, because of their sketchy treatment and the poorly rendered facial expressions, fail to come up to the level of the others.

Vincent was more fortunate with the portrait of a little girl sitting in a flowery field,

2051

2052

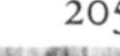

2053

2051 Two Children, F783
51.5 × 51.5 cm (20½ × 20½")
The Louvre, Paris

2052 Two Children, F784
51.5 × 46.5 cm (20½ × 18½")
Collection Mr. and Mrs. Basil P. Goulandris, Lausanne

2053 Girl with Straw Hat, Sitting in the Wheat, F774
92 × 73 cm (36¼ × 28¾")
Collection H. R. Hahnloser, Bern

2054 Girl with Straw Hat, Sitting in the Wheat
Sketch in Letter 646
Rijksmuseum Vincent van Gogh, Amsterdam

2055 Girl, Standing in the Wheat, F788
66 × 45 cm (26 × 17¾")
National Gallery of Art, Washington, D.C.

2056 Head of a Girl, F518
51 × 49 cm (20⅛ × 19¼")
Rijksmuseum Kröller-Müller, Otterlo

2057 Child, Sitting in the Grass with an Orange, F785
51 × 50 cm (20⅛ × 19⅝")
Collection Mrs. L. Jäggli-Hahnloser, Winterthur, Switzerland

2058 Dead Leaf and Pod, F1611 (on the same sheet: 1730)
Black chalk, 24 × 31.5 cm (9½ × 12⅝")
Rijksmuseum Vincent van Gogh, Amsterdam

2054

2055

2056

2057

2058

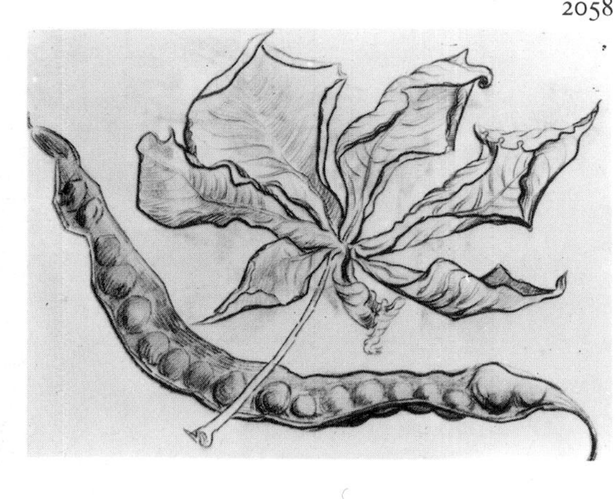

2059

2060

2061

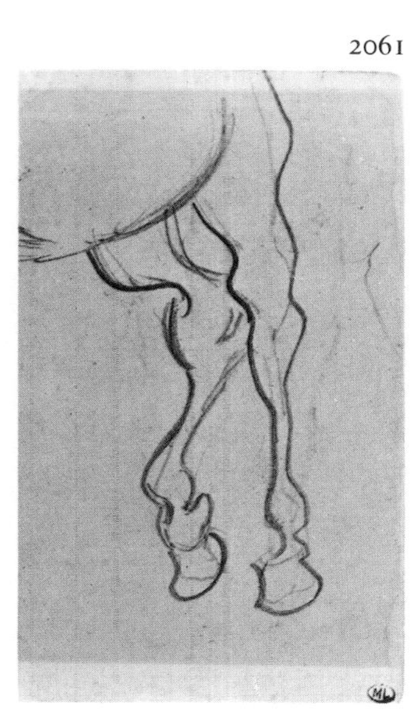

2062

2063

2059 Blossoming Branches, F 1612
Pencil, reed pen, brown ink, 41 × 31 cm ($16\frac{1}{8} \times 12\frac{1}{4}''$)
Rijksmuseum Vincent van Gogh, Amsterdam

2060 Branch with Leaves, F 1614
Black chalk, brush, ink, 47.5 × 40 cm ($18\frac{7}{8} \times 15\frac{3}{4}''$)
Rijksmuseum Vincent van Gogh, Amsterdam

July 1890

2061 Hind Legs of a Horse, F 1622 (reverse: 2075)
Black chalk, 13.5 × 8.5 cm ($5\frac{1}{2} \times 3\frac{1}{2}''$)
The Louvre, Paris

2062 Horse and Carriage, F 1730
Black chalk, pencil, 13 × 8 cm ($5\frac{1}{8} \times 3\frac{1}{8}''$)
Rijksmuseum Vincent van Gogh, Amsterdam

2063 Sketch of a Donkey, F 1631
Black chalk, 21.5 × 47 cm ($8\frac{5}{8} \times 18\frac{1}{2}''$)
Rijksmuseum Vincent van Gogh, Amsterdam

2057. Here the fiery orange the child is holding in her hand makes for a cheerful contrast with the blond hair, the light blue blouse, the little blue-striped skirt, and the bright green grass with the little yellow flowers. The facial expression comes off much better this time, and the charming portrait of this toddler with her rosy cheeks forms a worthy companion piece to the equally colorful painting of the older peasant girl seated among the wheat stalks and poppies, 2053 (see page 466).

To this small group I have added the attractive little portrait 2056, which in the 1970 *catalogue raisonné* has been ascribed to the Arles period and has become known as "the little Arlésienne." Although the catalogue of the Rijksmuseum Kröller-Müller remarks on its stylistic similarity to the portrait of Marguerite Gachet, 2048, a change in the dating from Arles to Auvers is considered "too drastic." To me, the style seems more typical of Auvers than of Arles, and a further argument against Arles, in my opinion, is that the dress the girl is wearing is unlike the local dress of virtually all the women whose portraits were done by Vincent in Arles, except for the portrait of the child, 1519. The dress, on the contrary, closely resembles that of the girl in 2053, and except for the marked difference in complexion, one might even assume, on the basis of the long dark hair, that paintings 2053, 2055, and 2056 all portray the same person.

July

We have come to the final month of Vincent's life. Only four letters to his brother—the second of which was very short—and one letter to his mother have come down to us from this month. Although providing few details about the events of these weeks, they do suggest moments of great nervous tension—moments that undoubtedly served to hasten the fatal ending.

The short letter, written after a visit by Vincent to Paris (Letter 647), sounds almost like a cry of despair, while the next letter makes it apparent that a reply received in the meantime from Jo had relieved him of a great anxiety. What it was all about is clear from the following sentence: "It is no small matter when all of us see our daily bread in jeopardy, no small matter when for other reasons as well we sense the fragility of our existence" (Letter 649). As virtually nothing more specific is revealed by the letters, we must rely for further information on what Jo van Gogh-Bonger related in her "Memoir": "Early in July, Vincent visited us once more in Paris. We were exhausted by a serious illness of the baby; Theo was again considering the old plan of leaving Goupil and setting up in business for himself; Vincent was not satisfied with the space where the pictures were kept, and our removal to a larger apartment was talked of—so those were days of much worry and anxiety. Many friends came to visit Vincent—among others Aurier, who had recently written his famous article about Vincent and now came again to look at the pictures with the painter himself. Toulouse Lautrec stayed for lunch and made many jokes with Vincent about an undertaker's man they had met on the stairs. Guillaumin was also expected, but it became too much

2064

2065

2066

2067

2068

2069

2064 Sketch of Cows and Children, F 1632
Pencil, 23.5 × 20 cm ($9\frac{1}{2} \times 7\frac{7}{8}$")
Rijksmuseum Vincent van Gogh, Amsterdam

2065 Woman with Striped Skirt, F 1644
(reverse: 2066)
Pencil, 13.5 × 8.5 cm ($5\frac{1}{2} \times 3\frac{1}{2}$")
The Louvre, Paris

2066 Lady with Checked Dress and Hat, F 1644v
(reverse: 2065)
Black chalk, 13.5 × 8.5 cm ($5\frac{1}{2} \times 3\frac{1}{2}$")
The Louvre, Paris

2067 Sketch of Two Women, F 1634
Black chalk, pen, violet ink, 23.5 × 30 cm ($9\frac{1}{2} \times 11\frac{3}{4}$")
Rijksmuseum Vincent van Gogh, Amsterdam

2068 Sketch of a Hen, F 1731
Pencil, black chalk, 8 × 13 cm ($3\frac{1}{8} \times 5\frac{1}{8}$")
Rijksmuseum Vincent van Gogh, Amsterdam

2069 Men in Front of the Counter in a Café, F 1654
(reverse: 2070)
Pencil, 8 × 13 cm ($3\frac{1}{8} \times 5\frac{1}{8}$")
Collection E. Buckman, Richmond, Virginia

2070 Sketches of a Hen and a Cock, F 1654v
(reverse: 2069)
Pencil, 13 × 8 cm ($5\frac{1}{8} \times 3\frac{1}{8}$")
Collection E. Buckman, Richmond, Virginia

2071 Sheet with Many Sketches of Figures, F 1652
(reverse: 2074)
Black chalk, 43.5 × 27 cm ($17\frac{3}{8} \times 10\frac{5}{8}$")
Collection Mr. and Mrs. Harry M. Goldblatt, New York

2072 Sketch of a Lady with Striped Dress and Hat and of Another Lady, Half-Figure, F 1619
(reverse: not included)
Pencil, 22 × 18.5 cm ($8\frac{5}{8} \times 7\frac{1}{2}$")
Vassar College Art Gallery, Poughkeepsie, New York

2070

2071

2072

2073

2074

2075

2076

2077

2078

2079

2073 Couple Walking, F 1650v (reverse: not included)
Pencil, chalk, 27 × 44 cm ($10\frac{5}{8} \times 17\frac{3}{8}$")
Location unknown

2074 Sheet with a Few Sketches of Figures, F 1652v (reverse: 2071)
Pencil, black chalk, 27 × 43.5 cm ($10\frac{5}{8} \times 17\frac{3}{8}$")
Collection Mr. and Mrs. Harry M. Goldblatt, New York

2075 Head of a Boy with Broad-Brimmed Hat, F 1622v (reverse: 2061)
Black chalk, 13.5 × 8.5 cm ($5\frac{1}{2} \times 3\frac{1}{2}$")
The Louvre, Paris

2076 Sketch of a Woman with a Baby in Her Lap, F 1617
Black chalk, 13.5 × 8.5 cm ($5\frac{1}{2} \times 3\frac{1}{2}$")
The Louvre, Paris (?)

2077 Sketch of a Couple Walking with a Child, F 1616
Black chalk, 13.5 × 8.5 cm ($5\frac{1}{2} \times 3\frac{1}{2}$")
The Louvre, Paris

2078 Landscape with Houses among Trees and a Figure, F 1589a
Charcoal, washed and heightened with white, 30 × 40 cm ($11\frac{3}{4} \times 15\frac{3}{4}$")
Fine Arts Museums of San Francisco

2079 Woman with a Spade on a Road with Houses in the Background, F 1636
Pencil, black chalk, 44.5 × 27 cm ($17\frac{3}{4} \times 10\frac{5}{8}$")
Rijksmuseum Vincent van Gogh, Amsterdam

for Vincent, so he did not wait for this visit but hurried back to Auvers—overtired and excited, as is evident in his last letters and pictures, in which the threatening catastrophe seems approaching like the ominous black birds that dart through the storm over the wheat fields" (page lii).

Final Work

Although the letters are even less informative about the work done in July, this does not mean that Vincent was less productive during these weeks than he had been previously. The reason for bringing together here a large number of sketchbook sketches and other small drawings has already been explained (see page 457). These hasty little sketches—which taken individually are of no great importance—do not in my view require much comment. They can be recognized as small preparatory studies for paintings or details of paintings, tentative sketches of people in action, topographical notes, and so on. One single sheet that has been entirely covered with little human figures, 2071, is reminiscent of similar study sheets from the early months of the year in Saint-Rémy, but it could not have been part of that series. Some of the figures are clearly the same as those to be found in paintings from the Auvers period, and there is also a difference in style. The somewhat more important drawings 2078 and 2079 are sketches of houses in the rural surroundings of Auvers similar to others that Vincent had made in May. The freer dynamic linear style explains why they have here been assigned to a somewhat later phase of the work done in Auvers, although no really accurate dating is possible.

The small drawing of the town hall, 2080, deserves special attention because Vincent also made a painting of the subject. The painting, 2108, gives a colorful picture of the small building as it must have looked on Bastille Day, decorated with many little flags and Chinese lanterns. Vincent probably painted it very early in the morning before the square became filled with people; since no merrymakers are present here, he obviously avoided them deliberately. The drawing, 2080, should not be seen as a preparatory study for the painting; it could have been made at any other time, for it depicts a spot that Vincent saw daily from where he lived.

The simple frontal composition of the canvas depicting the decorated town hall is somewhat reminiscent of the painting *The Church in Auvers*, 2006, with which, in fact, it has in common the mosaiclike treatment of the foreground with its separate brushstrokes. But how much less imposing than *The Church in Auvers* is the doll-like little structure in the later canvas, in which the treatment of the meager festive trimmings seems to be ironic or even bordering on caricature.

For want of any other means of dating than style, I have also placed the small canvas of the bony cows, 2095, at the beginning of Vincent's production in July. It is a copy by Vincent in color of an etching made by Dr. Gachet after a painting by Jordaens.

Symbolic Landscapes

Generally, of Vincent's work in the final weeks of his life, it is the landscapes that have

2080

2081

2082

2083

2084

2085

2080 Town Hall of Auvers with a Man Walking, F 1630 (reverse: 2081)
Black chalk, 23.5 × 31 cm ($9\frac{1}{2} \times 12\frac{1}{4}$")
Rijksmuseum Vincent van Gogh, Amsterdam

2081 Sketch of Houses among Trees with a Figure, F 1630v (reverse: 2080)
Blue chalk, 23.5 × 31 cm ($9\frac{1}{2} \times 12\frac{1}{4}$")
Rijksmuseum Vincent van Gogh, Amsterdam

2082 Head of a Man with a Hat, a Perspective Frame, and Other Sketches, F 1637v (reverse: 2083)
Blue chalk, 31 × 24 cm ($12\frac{1}{4} \times 9\frac{1}{2}$")
Rijksmuseum Vincent van Gogh, Amsterdam

2083 Houses among Trees, F 1637 (reverse: 2082)
Black and blue chalk, pen, violet ink, 24 × 31 cm ($9\frac{1}{2} \times 12\frac{1}{4}$")
Rijksmuseum Vincent van Gogh, Amsterdam

2084 Man with Scythe in Wheat Field and Other Figures, F 1615 (reverse: 2085)
Black and blue chalk, 23.5 × 31 cm ($9\frac{1}{2} \times 12\frac{1}{4}$")
Rijksmuseum Vincent van Gogh, Amsterdam

2085 Women Working in Wheat Field, F 1615v (reverse: 2084)
Black and blue chalk, 23.5 × 31 cm ($9\frac{1}{2} \times 12\frac{1}{4}$")
Rijksmuseum Vincent van Gogh, Amsterdam

2086

2087

2088

2089

2090

2091

2092

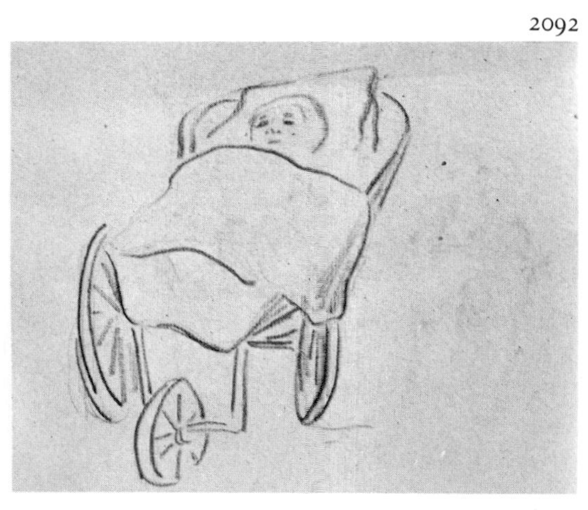

2093

2094

2086 Man with Scythe in Wheat Field, F 1635v (reverse: 1737)
Blue chalk, 31 × 23.5 cm ($12\frac{1}{4} \times 9\frac{1}{2}$″)
Rijksmuseum Vincent van Gogh, Amsterdam

2087 Woman Working in Wheat Field, F 1626 (reverse: 2088)
Black chalk, 30.5 × 23.5 cm ($12\frac{1}{4} \times 9\frac{1}{2}$″)
Rijksmuseum Vincent van Gogh, Amsterdam

2088 Two Women Working in Wheat Field, F 1626v (reverse: 2087)
Black chalk, 23.5 × 30.5 cm ($9\frac{1}{2} \times 12\frac{1}{4}$″)
Rijksmuseum Vincent van Gogh, Amsterdam

2089 A Carriage with a Horse, F 1609 (reverse: not included)
Pencil, 27 × 43.5 cm ($10\frac{5}{8} \times 17\frac{3}{8}$″)
Rijksmuseum Vincent van Gogh, Amsterdam

2090 Carriage, F 1610 (reverse: 2091)
Pencil, black chalk, 21.5 × 23.5 cm ($8\frac{5}{8} \times 9\frac{1}{2}$″)
Rijksmuseum Vincent van Gogh, Amsterdam

2091 Sketch of Women in a Field, F 1610v (reverse:2090; on the same sheet: 1729)
Black chalk, 21.5 × 23.5 cm ($8\frac{5}{8} \times 9\frac{1}{2}$″)
Rijksmuseum Vincent van Gogh, Amsterdam

2092 Baby in a Carriage, F 1633
Black chalk, 21.5 × 23.5 cm ($8\frac{5}{8} \times 9\frac{1}{2}$″)
Rijksmuseum Vincent van Gogh, Amsterdam

2093 A Woman Picking Up a Stick in Front of Trees, F 1732
Black chalk, 13 × 8 cm ($5\frac{1}{8} \times 3\frac{1}{8}$″)
Rijksmuseum Vincent van Gogh, Amsterdam

2094 A Tree in a Field, F 1623v (reverse: 2047)
Black chalk, 27 × 24 cm ($10\frac{5}{8} \times 9\frac{1}{2}$″)
Rijksmuseum Vincent van Gogh, Amsterdam

proved to be most important—although even among these there are some (such as 2122–24*) that were not, I think, carried beyond the stage of a first sketchy draft. Spacious landscapes were often represented in the recently adopted format twice as long as it was high (about 40 by 20 inches). An experiment in which Vincent used this format to depict the village as it appeared during a heavy rainstorm, 2096, was not very successful. However, an impressive example of its use is the simple landscape 2097. While basically this is nothing more than a green strip and a somewhat wider blue strip, in reality it is a panorama built up, with a fine sense of color, of yellow, yellowish-green, and bluish-green fields under a threatening blue-white overcast sky. In 2098, the landscape has been rendered by means of a swirl of heavy brushstrokes; it is dominated by two large haystacks. And there are several other variations of the landscape theme.

The most original and most intriguing of these elongated canvases is the one in which the viewer thinks he can recognize tree trunks and roots painted blue, and green branches, but is hard put to identify the subject as a whole, 2113. Among the views of the village, the painting of a group of houses seen from a distance, 2114, is especially noteworthy as a charming scene of pastoral tranquillity, well-balanced in color and composition.

In the case of painting 2111, we have the small preparatory sketch, as well—2110. The larger, more detailed painting exhibits the deep, bright primary colors typical of the Auvers period, but it reveals also the nervous tensions that seem to have manifested themselves in the undulating or, as it were, exploding movements in almost all parts of the composition.

In subject the highly simplified landscape 2112—depicting two women walking—stands in a class by itself. This painting was probably done from memory in an attempt to record the occasion of a meeting with a pair of colorfully and elegantly dressed women, a meeting that was described by Vincent in Letter 645, June 28 or 29.

I have waited until now to comment on two important landscapes done in July that Vincent discussed in his letters and that can therefore be precisely dated: the large canvases 2099 (colorplate XL, page 456) and 2102, corresponding to letter sketches 2100 and 2103. Wednesday, July 9, immediately after receiving Jo's letter, Vincent wrote to say what a relief that letter had been for him after the Sunday spent in Paris, and he added: "Back here, I set to work again, though the brush almost fell from my hands. I knew exactly what I wanted, and I have painted three big canvases since then. They are immense expanses of grain under clouded skies, and I have not hesitated to try to express melancholy and extreme loneliness. . . . The third canvas is Daubigny's garden, a painting I have been thinking about doing since I have been here" (Letter 649). With the exception of *Daubigny's Garden*, 2104, those "big canvases" did not refer to the elongated 40-by-20-inch size but to the usual "size-30 canvas." This is obvious from Letter 651, Vincent's last letter, in which he referred again to these paintings and made sketches of all three, together with the sketch of a fourth canvas that he must have been working on in the final weeks, the painting of thatched roofs being repaired, 2115. (The sketches are, respectively, 2100, 2103, 2106, and 2116.)

The landscapes are among Vincent's most beautiful works from this time. They have clearly been done quickly and without hesitation, and despite their vast, stately emptiness, they exhibit considerable variety in the gradation of their few colors. The maze of little colored strokes making up the fore-

*The little tower in the painting *Group of Houses and Church*, 2124, was identified by John Rewald as belonging to the church of the Saint-Rémy asylum (see *Post-Impressionism*, 3d edition [1978], p. 339). In consequence, the canvas has to be dated earlier than the Auvers period, possibly October 1889.

2095

2096

2097

2095 Cows (after Jordaens), F822
55 × 65 cm ($21\frac{5}{8} \times 25\frac{5}{8}$")
Musée des Beaux-Arts, Lille

2096 Landscape in the Rain, F811
50 × 100 cm ($19\frac{5}{8} \times 39\frac{3}{8}$")
National Museum of Wales, Cardiff

2097 Wheat Field under Clouded Skies, F778
50 × 100 cm ($19\frac{5}{8} \times 39\frac{3}{8}$")
Rijksmuseum Vincent van Gogh, Amsterdam

2098 Field with Two Stacks of Wheat or Hay, F809
50 × 100 cm ($19\frac{5}{8} \times 39\frac{3}{8}$")
Collection H. R. Hahnloser, Bern

2099 Wheat Fields, F782
73.5 × 92 cm ($29\frac{1}{8} \times 36\frac{1}{4}$")
Bayerische Staatsgemäldesammlungen, Munich
Colorplate XL, p. 456

2098

2099

2100

2101

2103

2102

2104

2100 Wheat Fields
Sketch in Letter 651
Rijksmuseum Vincent van Gogh, Amsterdam

2101 Wheat Fields, F812
50 × 40 cm ($19\frac{5}{8} \times 15\frac{3}{4}''$)
Phillips Collection, Washington, D.C.

2102 Wheat Fields, F781
73 × 92 cm ($28\frac{3}{4} \times 36\frac{1}{4}''$)
Museum of Art, Carnegie Institute, Pittsburgh

2103 Wheat Fields
Sketch in Letter 651
Rijksmuseum Vincent van Gogh, Amsterdam

2104 Daubigny's Garden, F776
53 × 104 cm ($20\frac{7}{8} \times 41''$)
Hiroshima Castle Museum

grounds—hard to define and yet suggestive of luxuriant vegetation—sets them somewhat apart from the previously mentioned landscape of the no less immense grain fields, 2038, with which they still have much in common, although they make a much less spirited impression.

Wheat Field with Crows

At this time Vincent was certainly working on the landscape that is one of his best-known paintings—*Wheat Field under Threatening Skies with Crows*, 2117, which is also alluded to by Jo van Gogh-Bonger in the passage quoted from her "Memoir." Curiously, this painting has always been linked in the Van Gogh literature with the passage from Letter 649 quoted above. The words "melancholy and extreme loneliness" ("de la tristesse, de la solitude extrême") consequently appear time and again with reproductions of painting 2117 and of the other landscape under threatening skies usually mentioned in the same breath with it, 2097. Yet on closer inspection, *Wheat Field ... with Crows*, for all its somber and threatening aspect, does not at all fit Vincent's description in Letter 649. The two large canvases he was speaking about depicted "immense expanses of grain under an overcast sky" ("d'immenses étendues de blés sous de ciels troublés"). Even "ciels troublés" seems too weak a term for the bluish-black stormy skies of painting 2117, but apart from that, the mass of wheat that obstructs the view like a wall, and in which a winding path seems to be able to penetrate only part way, cannot be compatible with a description like "immense expanses of grain."

It is also curious that the atmosphere of *Wheat Field ... with Crows* seems at odds with the description of the fields given by Vincent at precisely the same time in a letter to his mother—although it is not clear whether his thoughts were directed to the fields themselves or to the manner in which they were depicted in the painting. His words were: "I myself am completely absorbed in that interminable plain with fields of grain against the hills, vast as a sea, delicate yellow, delicate soft green, delicate violet of a plowed and weeded piece of ground, regularly speckled with the green of potato plants in flower, all this under a sky with delicate blue, white, pink, violet tones. I am wholly in a mood of almost too great calm, in a mood to paint this" (Letter 650).

But there is still something else, something that more than anything else convinced me that this was *not* the wheat field Vincent had referred to earlier. Although Vincent had indeed written that he wanted in these two paintings to express "melancholy and extreme loneliness," he added after this: "You will see this soon, I hope, as I intend to take them to you in Paris as soon as possible, because I almost dare to believe that these canvases will tell you what I cannot express in words, [namely,] what I see in the countryside that is wholesome and invigorating." It is inconceivable that Vincent would have wanted to take the painting with the crows along with him in order to show what he saw in the countryside that was "wholesome and invigorating."

2105

2106

2107

2105 Daubigny's Garden with Black Cat, F777
56 × 101.5 cm (22 × $40\frac{1}{8}$″)
Kunstmuseum, Basel (on loan from the Rudolf Staechelin Collection)

2106 Daubigny's Garden with Black Cat
Sketch in Letter 651
Rijksmuseum Vincent van Gogh, Amsterdam

2107 Garden, F814
64 × 80 cm ($25\frac{1}{4}$ × $31\frac{1}{2}$″)
Collection Jacques Walter, Paris

2108 The Town Hall of Auvers on Bastille Day, F790
72 × 93 cm ($28\frac{3}{8}$ × $36\frac{5}{8}$″)
Collection Mr. and Mrs. Leigh B. Block, Chicago

2109 A Garden with Sunflowers, F810
Panel, 31.5 × 41 cm ($12\frac{5}{8}$ × $16\frac{1}{8}$″)
Collection A. C. M. Baronesse de Rothschild, Paris

2110 Street and Stairs with Two Figures, F796
20.5 × 26 cm ($8\frac{1}{4}$ × $10\frac{1}{4}$″)
Collection Mr. Loebb, Tiegenhof, Germany

2111 Street and Stairs with Five Figures, F795
51 × 71 cm ($20\frac{1}{8}$ × 28″)
The St. Louis Art Museum

2108

2109

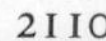

2110

2111

Because of the tendency to romanticize Van Gogh, this dramatic painting has often been regarded in the past as his last work. Although I cannot say with certainty that it was *not* his last painting, I am convinced that the painting with crows was not one of the two landscapes made between July 7 and 9. That it must have originated in the final weeks of the Auvers period seems apparent from the fact that a field of fully ripened grain is depicted here. In the earliest paintings from this period the grain was still green. There is one painting by Vincent in which the grain has been cut and bound in sheaves. This is 2125, and it is unquestionably much less striking than *Wheat Field ... with Crows*. However, if we are looking for some kind of symbol in the painting marking the end of this artist's life, then I would think that a picture of grain that has been harvested and sheaved would serve as well as the doom-filled painting with the threatening skies and the ill-omened crows, regardless of how much more powerful and expressive the latter might be.

Life's End

The end of Vincent's life has been described so often that I will be as brief as possible in dealing with it here. There are several eyewitness accounts of his death and burial, and though they differ somewhat in details, they all give a moving portrayal of the events that took place in Auvers in the last days of July 1890.

Sunday, July 27, Vincent returned to the Ravoux inn toward evening, later than expected, and went straight to his attic room. When one of the lodgers, who had become worried, looked in on him, he found Vincent lying in bed wounded, after having tried to take his life with a pistol somewhere outside the village. The bullet had lodged in his side instead of his heart, and he had been able to walk home. The local physician was called, but Vincent asked for Dr. Gachet, who was also sent for. The two doctors came to the conclusion that it was impossible to remove the bullet and that matters must be allowed to run their course. Theo, who could not be reached until the next morning, came out from Paris and remained at Vincent's bedside while Vincent quietly lay there smoking his pipe. The end came the next night—according to the death certificate at half-past one, and thus on July 29. August 5, Theo described the event in a letter to his sister Elisabeth: "He himself desired to die. While I was sitting by him, trying to persuade him that we would heal him, and that we hoped he would be saved from further attacks, he answered: 'La tristesse durera toujours.' I felt I understood what he wished to say.

"Shortly afterward he was seized with another attack, and the next minute closed his eyes."*

Vincent seems to have said nothing about the reasons for his deed; in any case, Theo did not report anything of this nature. Attempts to find specific demonstrable motives

*This letter is quoted by Elisabeth du Quesne-van Gogh in her *Personal Recollections of Vincent van Gogh* (1913), p. 52. Vincent's last words, as she reported them, were: "The sadness will always remain."

2112

2113

2112 Two Ladies Walking in a Landscape, F819
Paper on canvas, 32 × 61 cm (12⅝ × 24″)
Marion Koogler McNay Art Institute, San Antonio

2113 Roots and Trunks of Trees, F816
50.5 × 100.5 cm (20⅛ × 39⅝″)
Rijksmuseum Vincent van Gogh, Amsterdam

2114 Group of Houses Seen against a Hill, F793
50 × 100 cm (19⅝ × 39⅜″)
Tate Gallery, London

2115 Cottages with Thatched Roofs and Figures, F780
65 × 81 cm (25⅝ × 31⅞″)
Kunsthaus, Zurich

2116 Cottages with Thatched Roofs and Figures
Sketch in Letter 651
Rijksmuseum Vincent van Gogh, Amsterdam

2117 Wheat Field under Threatening Skies with Crows, F779
50.5 × 100.5 cm (20⅛ × 39¾″)
Rijksmuseum Vincent van Gogh, Amsterdam

2114

2115

2116

2117

Rosendale Library
PO Box 482
Rosendale, NY 12472

have been made, but to no avail, and in my opinion without good cause. A suicidal tendency fitted into the picture of his illness, as was apparent from the events in Saint-Rémy. His latent melancholy had certainly been fed by his growing anxiety about the threat to his existence now that Theo's own worries had intensified, but nonetheless I have no doubt that this suicide attempt, just like the earlier ones mentioned by Dr. Peyron in the register of the asylum,* resulted from a momentary impulse. The fact that he carried a pistol seems to contradict this statement, and it is indeed an ominous symptom, but according to what people in Auvers said at the time, he had borrowed it from Ravoux only "a few days before" (the added words "to keep the crows away from him while he was painting" seem a rather unconvincing reason for his doing so). There is nothing in the last letters that points toward thoughts of suicide, though their tone is not exactly cheerful. On the contrary, a weighty argument for the view that he had acted on impulse can be drawn from the fact that even July 24, in his very last letter (Letter 651), he mentioned that he wanted to replenish his stock of paint and asked Theo's help to this end.

The funeral took place July 30. Immediately afterward Emile Bernard gave a detailed account of it to G.-Albert Aurier in a letter that contains this moving passage: "All his most recent paintings had been hung on the walls of the room where the corpse was laid out, surrounding him as it were with a halo, and to the artists they made his death still more painful by the brilliance of the genius they revealed. On the bier a simple white sheet, in addition an abundance of flowers, the sunflowers he loved so much, dahlias, everywhere yellow flowers. It was, as you will remember, his favorite color, symbol of the light he dreamed of, in the hearts and in the works."†

Among the friends who had paid him this tribute were the painters Anton Hirschig (a Dutchman who also lived at Ravoux's), Charles Laval, and Lucien Pissarro; besides there were, of course, Theo van Gogh and his brother-in-law Andries Bonger, Dr. Gachet, and Ravoux. Also, Julien Tanguy—Père Tanguy—had come from Paris. Together they brought him, under the hot July sun, to the cemetery of Auvers, on the hill behind the old church he had portrayed with magnificence and amid the wheat fields he loved.

Theo van Gogh, as Emile Bernard wrote, was "grief-stricken," and his already precarious health never recovered from the shock. In August and September he went to great trouble to organize an exhibition of his brother's work, but all he could do was to arrange a small showing in his own apartment of works selected and hung with the help of Bernard. In October he became seriously ill, and when a few days later his mind also failed him, he had to be taken to Holland, where he died January 25, 1891.

It was only after Theo's death that the first retrospective exhibitions were actually held. Small groups of Vincent's paintings were shown at the exhibition of Les XX in Brussels in February 1891, at the exhibition of the Indépendants in Paris in March 1891, and at a small Paris gallery, Le Barc de Boutteville, in April 1891, but it was not until 1901 that a larger exhibition could be held in Paris—at Bernheim-Jeune, where seventy-one works were shown.

In Holland, where Jo van Gogh-Bonger had gone, taking her husband's enormous collection, interest developed more quickly. Paintings by Van Gogh were to be seen at Buffa's gallery in Amsterdam in February 1892, at Oldenzeel's in Rotterdam in March of that year, and at The Hague Art Society in May and June, when forty-five paintings and forty-five drawings were on view. The first comprehensive exhibition was organized by Jo van Gogh-Bonger, with the aid of the artist R.N. Roland Holst, and held in Amsterdam from December 1892 to February 1893. Articles that showed genuine appreciation for Van Gogh's completely original talent also began to appear more often—in Holland as well as abroad. Emile Bernard took in hand the publication of a selection of Vincent's letters to himself and to Theo in the *Mercure de France* between April 1893 and February 1895. And so it was that fairly soon after his death Vincent van Gogh was acknowledged, no longer as "a solitary pioneer ... struggling" alone—as Isaäcson had put it—but as one of the most famous artists of modern times.

2118

2119

2120

*See Victor Doiteau and Edgar Leroy, *La Folie de Vincent van Gogh* (1928), in which the register is reproduced opposite p. 85.

†Quoted in Michel-Ange Bernard, "Emile Bernard et Vincent van Gogh," *Art Documents*, no. 29 (1953).

2121

2122

2123

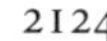

2124

2125

2118 Wheat Field with Cornflowers, F808
60 × 81 cm ($23\frac{5}{8} \times 31\frac{7}{8}$″)
Private collection

2119 Wheat Field with a Stack of Wheat or Hay, F1643
Brown watercolor, washed, 46.5 × 61 cm ($18\frac{1}{2} \times 24$″)
Whitworth Art Gallery, University of Manchester, England

2120 Wheat Field, F761
50 × 65 cm ($19\frac{5}{8} \times 25\frac{5}{8}$″)
Private collection, Zurich

2121 Field with a Stack of Wheat or Hay, F563
64 × 52.5 cm ($25\frac{1}{4} \times 20\frac{7}{8}$″)
Rijksmuseum Kröller-Müller, Otterlo

2122 Group of Houses and Church, F800
34 × 42 cm ($13\frac{3}{8} \times 16\frac{1}{2}$″)
Museum of Art, Rhode Island School of Design, Providence

2123 Group of Houses and Church, F801
43 × 50 cm ($16\frac{7}{8} \times 19\frac{5}{8}$″)
Private collection, Switzerland

2124 Group of Houses and Church, F803
44.5 × 60 cm ($17\frac{3}{4} \times 23\frac{5}{8}$″)
Collection Mrs. Elizabeth Taylor, United States

2125 Field with Stacks of Wheat, F771
50.5 × 101 cm ($20\frac{1}{8} \times 39\frac{3}{4}$″)
Collection Mrs. Charles Beatty, London

Notes

1. In her edition of the letters Mrs. van Gogh-Bonger had replaced the name Margo Begemann in the manuscript by "Miss X," just as she had changed Kee Vos to "K." in the Etten letters. In the later Dutch editions these changes were retained. In the English edition of 1958 the full names were reinstated, but in the French edition of 1960 this had still not been done.

2. The head of the old peasant (563 and 564) is dated April 1885 in the 1970 *catalogue raisonné* and described as "study for *The Potato Eaters*." The pen-and-ink drawing 564, which fits neatly into the series Vincent sent Theo at the end of December, makes me think that he had already painted the elder De Groot in December and that when he gave *The Potato Eaters* its final form, at the end of April, he used his study in order to ensure that the head of the man would be a good likeness. He did, after all, write that the definitive version was not painted on the spot but done in his studio, and "mostly from memory" adding, "you know yourself how many times I have painted the heads!" (p. 166). The figure of old De Groot has thus clearly been "painted in" and seems to be floating in space.

3. Vanbeselaere, misled by the fact that sketch 960 was erroneously published together with Letter 383, dated this canvas October 1884 and assumed that it had been heavily retouched in Paris. Following his lead, Annet Tellegen, who did change the dating to November 1885, also believed that the piece had been retouched in Paris ("Vincent van Goghs Appelboomgaard," *Bulletin Museum Boymans-van Beuningen*, vol XVIII, no. 1 [1967], pp. 2-33), and the editors of the 1970 *catalogue raisonné* came to the same conclusion. Yet I am not convinced of the need to assume that any retouching was done in Paris. In any case, Vanbeselaere's "half reworked in stipple technique" is highly exaggerated. He was obviously surprised at the colorfulness of the canvas, but at the same time had not seen the connection with Letter 434. Vincent referred to the yellow leaves in his painting as many as five times in writing about it, and they must accordingly have been very decidedly yellow. He also wrote about the "reddish-brown leaves" of the tree to the right, and he described the red roofs, which Vanbeselaere ascribed to retouching, as "specks of red." If Vincent really had intensified some touches of color at a later date, the appearance of the painting can hardly have been changed to any great extent.

4. The instances of hesitation apparent in Vincent's letters from Antwerp can easily cause his main objective to be misinterpreted. His original plan was to live with Theo and to set up a real "painter's studio . . . where, if need be, people could come and see him" (Letter 448), but he very soon abandoned that idea. As he wished to devote himself during the first year to drawing from "the nude and the antique" (meaning plaster casts)—which he could do equally well at Cormon's, at the Ecole des Beaux-Arts, or at the Louvre—he did not need a big studio and might just as well live in a small attic room for the time being.

Another hesitation centered on when he should go to Cormon's, and here it is easy to be misled. He kept stressing the need to draw from "the nude and the antique" because he did not want to be sent back to Nuenen between March and June. The question of where he could continue his study of drawing was of secondary importance, but Cormon's studio was certainly his first choice. This could even be combined with other possibilities: "I hear they work for four hours in the morning at Cormon's; then in the evening one can go and work at the Louvre or at the Ecole des Beaux-Arts or in some other atelier where drawing is done" (Letter 448). This explains the frequently repeated, almost unvarying refrain: "I also like the idea of staying here [in Antwerp] without going back, and then *from here to Cormon's* whenever you want" (Letter 448); "you can be sure that I would be very glad if I could work about a year at Cormon's" (Letter 451); and short and to the point in Letter 454: "Let me draw for a year at Cormon's."

He had also thought about the possibility of going to Paris right away and living in an attic room, but not starting at Cormon's immediately, that is, not before June. As his letters indicate, he would then want to "finish what was most pressing, those studies from the antique that will certainly help me in the event that I should go to Cormon's" (Letter 452). He could then start drawing in the Louvre or the Ecole des Beaux-Arts. The implication is always: better an attic room in Paris and making shift with drawing than going to Nuenen. He was not afraid of being denied admission to Cormon's; he just knew that some preliminary study would be very useful. "At Cormon's I shall have to paint some thing or other as a test, probably a nude figure from nature, and the more I have mastered the structure beforehand, the more able and willing he will be to tell me things" (Letter 456).

The main objective was and continued to be to go and work at Cormon's, and to do so as soon as possible. He realized that objective by going to Paris unexpectedly at the end of February.

5. The text of this book had been written when, in July 1976, Bogomila Welsh-Ovcharov took her doctor's degree (cum laude) at Utrecht University with a dissertation entitled *Vincent van Gogh: His Paris Period, 1886-1888* (thesis supervisor, Professor J.G. van Gelder). At this stage I have preferred not to try and revise my own study with the use of some of Welsh-Ovcharov's conclusions and documentary data, but can most heartily recommend her very thorough study of this little-known period. It consists of three main sections: a biographical survey, an extensive inquiry into Vincent's color theory, and an examination of the stylistic and iconographic influences he experienced during this period. There is also a chronological list of the Paris paintings, grouped according to subject; as could be expected, this list does not completely agree with my own chronology.

Welsh-Ovcharov departs significantly from the opinion generally held up to this time in asserting that Van Gogh did not enter Cormon's studio in the first months after his arrival in Paris, but did so only in the fall of 1886, or at any rate divided his time there between the spring and fall. She formed this conviction on the basis of remarks by Emile Bernard in some of his scattered recollections of Vincent. Bernard would not have seen Vincent at work at Cormon's until after his return from Brittany, that is, in the fall of 1886.

I, for my part, attach more value than she does to what has been said by Mrs. van Gogh-Bonger and especially by Hartrick, who have made it clear that Vincent was working at Cormon's in the *spring*. My main argument for the spring is a psychological one. Why would Vincent, who was so eager to go to work at Cormon's (see also note 4), have put this off until the fall?

It is clear that a shift in the Cormon period would quite radically alter the chronology of the works.

6. In the 1970 *catalogue raisonné* the portrait of Tanguy, 1351, is dated "autumn 1887"; it is thus earlier than 1352, which is dated "late 1887." In my opinion, the two portraits were probably made in very quick succession, for Vincent must have had to give one copy to Tanguy, who was undoubtedly an unpaid model. It is more than likely that he left 1351 with Tanguy; this can be gathered from Letter 506, and as a matter of fact, Rodin later bought it from Tanguy's daughter. The other version, 1352, remained with Theo and later found its way back into the art market from the holdings of Mrs. van Gogh-Bonger.

Vincent himself described a similar procedure in connection with the portrait of the chief orderly of the asylum in Saint-Rémy (Letters 604 and 607) and the portrait of Roulin's wife, *La Berceuse* (Letter 576).

7. As a source of inspiration for the painting *Gauguin's Chair*, reference is often made to a wood engraving by Luke Fildes published in *The Graphic* after the death of Charles Dickens. The void left by the great author had been indicated allegorically by an empty chair in front of a desk. Van Gogh was familiar with this illustration; he had commented on it in a letter to Theo (Letter 252), written six years earlier. However, if he wanted to depict "an empty place," he did not need Fildes's example for such an obvious symbol, and what is more, the English print was much too closely associated with the thought of *death* to connect it with the friend he worked with every day.

8. Vincent spoke about his "intention" in regard to the *berceuse* in various letters. To quote just one passage: "In a letter to Gauguin, I had just written, in reference to this canvas, that I, as a result of our talks about the Icelandic fishermen who, in melancholy isolation, exposed to all dangers, are alone on the doleful sea—that I, as a result of those intimate talks, had hit upon the idea of making the kind of painting that would engender in seafarers, who are children as well as martyrs, seeing it in the cabin of an Icelandic fishing boat, a feeling of being rocked in a cradle that would bring back to them the memory of the little lullaby sung by their own mothers" (Letter 574). His reading must also have played a part; *Pêcheur d'Islande* (*Iceland Fisherman*), by Pierre Loti, was a novel he greatly admired. Still preoccupied with theories about complementary colors, he also saw this painting largely as a color study, but one with the "strident contrasts" of a colored print from a cheap shop: "a woman in green with orange hair stands out against a green background with pink flowers" (Letter 574).

9. The date September 1888 given in the 1970 *catalogue raisonné* for the self-portrait 1665 is based on the erroneous belief that there is a connection between it and Letter 540, written in that month. The self-portrait "with an ashen tint" that is referred to is rather the one depicting Vincent as a Japanese, 1581. At the end of June 1888 Vincent had written Wil that his hair and beard were then "still clean-shaven," but in the self-portrait 1581 (dating from September) he already had a short beard again and in the self-portrait 1565 (probably dating from August) an even somewhat heavier beard. I am also unable to accept the view that the self-portrait 1665 was painted in the summer of

1888, because at that time Vincent was reporting on almost every work he had in hand. This was certainly true of the portraits, sometimes even the numbers of these being mentioned; thus, in August, the figure of the Zouave, 1488, was called "the fifth figure study" (Letter 519).

According to the reminiscences of Gustave Coquiot, Paul Signac had told him that when he paid Vincent a visit, at the end of March 1889, Vincent was wearing "the famous bandage and the fur cap." This would be an argument against dating the self-portrait 1665 at the end of January but it is, of course, unthinkable that Vincent would still have had a bandage around his ear at the end of March.

10. There has always been some uncertainty about which of the two versions of the enclosed wheat field with reaper is the original. The 1970 *catalogue raisonné* opted for 1773 ("done directly from nature"). The catalogue of the Rijksmuseum Kröller-Müller, on the other hand, states, even in the editions after 1970, that the other version, 1753, which it owns, is the older of the two—started in June 1889, completed in September. The question is not particularly important in itself, as Vincent, according to Letter 604, was still doing some work on the original on the same day that he was making the replica. To my mind, however, there can be no doubt that 1753 is the original canvas. The drawing made from the painting, 1754, is clear evidence of this, for it corresponds with 1753, but not with 1773—there is a difference in the position of the sun, the location of the wheat sheaves, and the shape of the ridge of the mountain. It appears that after Vincent had made the all-yellow canvas, he became disenchanted with it and decided to try another color scheme. This takes on even more significance in the light of what he wrote sometime later: "As regards the reaper, I thought at first that the large-size replica I am sending you was not bad—but later on, when the days of mistral and rain had come, I began to prefer the canvas done from nature, which I found rather amusing" (Letter 608). That was, in fact, a picture of summer heat.

11. Up to now it has always been assumed that no chronological sequence could be arrived at for the fifteen known canvases by Vincent of olive orchards. However, information in the letters and comparisons of style provide a solid basis for the sequence given here.

a. First, there is a group of four "early" canvases, those dating from June, or possibly the beginning of July, 1889. The key factor here is the date of the consignments: one canvas depicting olive trees was sent to Theo about July 9 (Letter 600), two on September 19 (Letter 607), and one on September 28 (Letter 608). As Vincent suffered a breakdown about the middle of July and did not resume working out of doors again until the end of September, these four must have been made before mid-July and probably, according to the reports in the letters, in June. The first was 1740, the canvas with the white cloud (see Letter W12). In Letter 608 he announced that he was going to send a smaller replica of one of the olive orchards; this small work, made in September, was 1791. The original of this, 1758, was thus also one of the early works. The closest to this in style is 1759. Since, according to Letter 600, the painting sent in July was not a size-30 canvas, the smaller canvas 1760 must be the one referred to here. The first group thus comprises 1740, 1758, 1759, and 1760, together with the replica in reduced size, 1791, made in September.

b. Among the remaining size-30 canvases were three paintings with women picking olives that, according to Letter 617, were in hand during December: 1868, 1869, and 1870.

c. The size-30 canvases still to be accounted for that depict olive orchards, 1853-57, may therefore be identified as the five size-30 canvases that Vincent said he was working on when he wrote about them in November (Letters B21 and 615).

d. Of the two smaller canvases that still remain, 1858 and 1878, the first comes closer to those done in November—especially because of the dark, colorful brushstrokes by which the earth is rendered—and the second, by reason of its extreme stylistic technique, must surely have been done in late December 1889.

12. The reason that the smaller *Pietà*, 1776, has always been assumed to have been painted in Auvers is a statement by Vincent in Letter 638, June 1890: "Gachet also told me that if I wanted to do him a great favor, he would like me to make him a replica of the copy of the *Pietà* by Delacroix." There is nothing, however, to show that Vincent actually did this. On the other hand, writing to Wil, Vincent made it unmistakably clear that the small copy was made in September 1889. In Letter W14 Vincent gave a detailed description of the painting, and then added: "I thought I should send you a sketch of it in order to give you an idea of what Delacroix is. That small copy does not, of course, have any value from any point of view." The words "that small copy" cannot, of course, refer to a canvas measuring 28¾ by 24 inches.

Paul Gachet, Jr.—seemingly a reliable source—stated in his book *Deux amis des impressionnistes* (Two Friends of the Impressionists) that the small *Pietà* was painted in September 1889 and the large one in Auvers. He asserts that he, in the company of his father, saw the latter canvas at Vincent's "when it was still wet" (p. 119). He must have been mistaken (his book, published in 1956, was written when he was very old), for the large canvas comes from Theo's collection, and that seems to be at odds with the idea that it was painted for Gachet at his request.

After stating in Letter 605 that the lithograph had been ruined by oil and paint, Vincent had added: "So I made myself sit down to paint it and you will see it one fine day: I made a copy of it on a size-5 or -6 canvas." This must be taken to mean: The painting was done on a canvas measuring 28¾ by 24 inches, thus "a size-20 canvas," and a smaller copy was made from this. That replica measures 16½ by 13⅜ inches and is, in fact, "a size-6 canvas." Vincent seems later to have had second thoughts about giving the small copy to Wil, for the *Pietà* is not mentioned among the small paintings he sent to his mother and Wil through Theo in December.

13. It is important for a proper understanding of Vincent's portraits of Madame Ginoux to know about a large canvas that was painted in early November 1888 by Gauguin in the café owned by Ginoux. In this painting (in the Pushkin Museum, Moscow), Gauguin, following his theories, had relied on his imagination, for Vincent wrote about it to Bernard: "At the moment Gauguin is working on a canvas of the same night café that I painted, too, but with persons he has seen in the brothels" (Letter B19*a*). Probably this refers to the three women who appear in the background in the company of the postman Roulin. In this painting Madame Ginoux is seen in the foreground sitting at a café table, her head resting on her left hand, and thus in exactly the same posture as Vincent painted her in the portraits 1624 and 1625. It is my conviction that the two painters worked here *simultaneously*, Van Gogh somewhat more to the right, finishing his portrait at great speed, while Gauguin was working on his large scene.

Gauguin also made a drawing of Madame Ginoux in this position, probably as a preliminary study for the painting, and this drawing, which he had apparently given to Vincent, was in turn used again as a model for the portrait paintings 1892-95 made by Vincent in February 1890. In this drawing Gauguin had given Madame Ginoux a rather curious, enigmatic expression, which became even more pronounced in Vincent's later "copies," with the result that one hardly recognizes here the woman of the charming portraits 1624 and 1625.

In 1892, 1894, and 1895 the book titles are in French: *Contes de Noël* and *La Case de l'Oncle Tom;* in 1893 the titles are: *Uncle Tom's Cabin* and *Christmas Tales.* In some cases there was no room for the authors' names.

14. Some other paintings dated April, May, or "spring 1890" in the 1970 *catalogue raisonné* could not, in my opinion, have been done between the end of April and May 16 simply for lack of time. Furthermore, from the point of view of style they do not seem to fit into the series of eleven pictures I previously mentioned. The works whose dates I have revised are:

Corner of a Garden	1677	April 1889
Mountain Landscape	1728	June 1889
Mountain Landscape	1744	June 1889
Mountain Landscape	1745	June 1889
Fields with Poppies	1751	June 1889
Woman Walking under the Trees	1848	November 1889
Landscape with a House	1874	December 1889
Woman on a Road	1875	December 1889
Landscape with a House and a Plowman	1877	December 1889
The Arlésienne (Madame Ginoux)	1895	February 1890

15. As far as I have been able to determine, the quotation "It [the portrait of Dr. Gachet] is in the same vein as the *Self-Portrait* that I brought with me when I left to come here" has been interpreted in all the literature on Van Gogh as meaning "brought with me from Saint-Rémy" rather than "brought with me from Paris when I left to come here" (that is, to Auvers). In my *Van Gogh door Van Gogh* (p. 188), I had assumed that Vincent was referring to the self-portrait with the palette (1770) when he wrote in September: "Today I am sending you my self-portrait" (Letter 607). It became clear to me later that the portrait he sent to Paris at that time must have been the self-portrait with the light background, 1772. The other one he kept for himself. It later came into the possession of J.J. Isaäcson, probably as a gift from Vincent himself or from Theo.

16. It has generally been assumed up to now—even in the 1970 *catalogue raisonné*—that the bust-length portrait of Adeline Ravoux, 2036, was the variant for Theo referred to by Vincent in Letter 644, "even though [it is] not exactly a size-15 canvas." This is, however, a curious misunderstanding. The bust-length portrait, measuring 20½ by 20½ inches, is by no means a size-15 canvas (the theoretical dimensions of which are 25⅝ by 21¼ inches). On the other hand, the portraits 2035 and 2037—measuring, respectively, 26⅜ by 21⅝ inches and 28⅜ by 20⅞ inches—can both be regarded as size-15 canvases, although the latter is a little higher, probably for compositional reasons. There can be no doubt that the variant for Theo referred to by Vincent was this canvas 2037, which, in fact, appears to have come from Theo's collection.

Concordance of De la Faille and Hulsker Numbers

The heading F in the columns below designates the catalogue number in the 1970 *catalogue raisonné* by J.-B. de la Faille. The heading JH designates the corresponding number in the present work by Jan Hulsker. A list of colorplates follows, with the respective F and JH numbers.

n: not reproduced; works originally given a number by De la Faille but later rejected or considered doubtful by himself or the editors of the 1970 *catalogue raisonné*, or works that are no more than insignificant scribbles or drafts.
juv.: juvenilia C.B.: Cuesmes-Brussels

F	JH	F	JH	F	JH	F	JH	F	JH
1	81	62	922	120	519	178v	1198	224	1112
1a	82	63	920	121	956	179	786	225	1110
1b	388	64	537	122	522	179v	1300	226	1172
1c	389	65	627	123	518	180	1194	227	1170
2	173	66	743	124	955	181	1090	228	1171
2a	176	67	604	125	525	182	948	229	1176
3	186	67a	602	126	800	183	952	230	1177
4	187	68	495	126a	655	184	458	231	1099
5	188	69	724	127	651	185	484	232	1113
6	189	70	715	128	697	185a	761	233	1180
7	178	70a	716	129	876	186	361	234	1168
8	182	71	719	129a	727	187	808	235	1136
8a	180	72	718	130	692	188	413	235a	n.
9	385	73	717	131	685	189	386	236	1130
10	384	74	648	132	574	190	492	237	1131
11	392	75	550	133	584	191	762	238	1178
12	185	76	542	134	684	191a	950	239	1267
13	179	77	686	135	585	192	184	240	1268
14	1193	77v	1304	136	683	193	914	241	1134
15	387	77a	n.	136a	548	194	603	242	1147
15a	393	78	734	137	593	195	961	243	1129
16	391	79	763	138	644	196	957	243a	1106
17	395	80	681	139	905	197	1167	244	1093
18	397	80a	682	140	745	198	1125	245	1145
19	409	81	695	141	783	199	1091	246	1133
20	417	82	764	142	807	200	541	246a	n.
21	415	83	777	143	546			247	1149
22	421	84	772	144	561	201	1139	248	1146
23	n.	85	693	144a	704	202	738	248a	1148
24	500	85a	694	145	653	203	1123	248b	1150
25	521	86	785	146	551	203a	n.	249	1105
26	450	87	600	146a	565	204	190	250	1166
27	503	88	490	147	891	205	971	251	1142
28	1191	89	803	148	908	206	972	252	1140
29	471	90	823	149	690	207	979	253	1121
30	479	91	809	150	650	207a	1204	253a	1232
31	477	92	810	151	649	208	1195	254	1342
32	480	92a	806	152	656	208a	1089	255	1124
33	489	93	805	153	587	209	1201	256	1169
34	459	94	893	153a	586	210	947	257	n.
35	478	95	827	154	608	211	973	258	1141
36	698	95a	899	155	787	212	999	259	1132
37	501	96	878	156	569	212a	929	260	970
38	504	97	876	157	712	213	1247	261	1101
39	505	98	901	158	946	214	1092	262	1102
40	507	99	930	159	n.	215	1045	263	1202
41	513	100	831	160	722	215a	n.	263a	1199
42	517			160a	563	215b	1205	264	1179
43	516	101	927	161	788	215c	n.	264a	1306
44	962	102	937	162	457	215d	n.	265	1100
45	959	103	928	163	687	216	1348	266	1175
46	524	104	923	164	558	216a	1054	266a	1223
47	526	104a	924	165	688	216b	1060	267	1224
48	527	105	926	166	850	216c	1082	268	1299
48a	488	106	936	167	689	216d	1071	269	725
49	534	107	933	168	632	216e	1078	269v	1301
50	529	108	990	169	633	216f	1076	270	1207
51	925	109	942	169a	583	216g	1055	270a	1272
52	535	109v	1303	170	824	216h	1058	271	1186
53	538	110	941	171	658	216i	1072	272	1183
54	536	111	939	171a	657	216j	1059	273	1116
55	532	112	938	172	514	217	1164	274	1115
56	530	113	944	173	n.	218	1144	275	1278
57	539	114	945	174	978	219	1117	276	1259
58	531	115	935	175	497	220	1138	277	1316
59	921	116	934	176	799	221	1109	278	1103
60	540	117	946	177	543	221a	n.	279	1104
61	533	118	932	177a	1192	222	1108	280	2032
61v	1302	119	949	178	528	223	1111	281	1143

F	JH	F	JH	F	JH	F	JH	F	JH
282	1165	348	1182	421	n.	495	1626	570	1421
283	1120	348a	1221	422	1470	496	1630	571	1392
283a	1660	349	1184	423	1486	497	1632	572	1597
283b	1230	350	1245	424	1488	498	1635	573	1618
284	n.	351	1255	425	1442	499	1636	574	1586
285	1118	352	1321	426	1468	500	1659	575	1422
286	1127	353	1271	427	1490			575a	1596
286a	1128	354	1270	428	1499	501	1634	576	1423
286b	1294	355	1266	429	1513	502	1664	577	n.
287	1231	356	1248	430	1510	503	1646	578	1538
288	1200	357	1216	431	1519	504	1655	579	1692
289	1203	358	1612	432	1522	505	1669	580	1679
290	1360	359	1332	433	1524	506	1670	581	1751
291	1314	360	1349	434	1647	507	1672	582	1678
292	1219	361	1260	435	1674	508	1671	583	1263
293	1269	362	1264	436	1675	509	n.	584	1680
294	1209	363	1351	437	1570	510	1661	585	1758
295	1211	364	1352	438	1571	511	1386	586	1854
296	1210	365	654	439	1673	512	n.	587	1853
297	1346	365v	1354	440	1639	513	1389	588	1335
297a	1347	366	1345	441	1641	514	1681	589	2033
298	1257	367	1261	441a	1640	515	1683	590	n.
299	1254	368	1262	442	n.	516	1685	591	1429
300	1275	369	1206	443	1548	517	1689	592	1568
		370	1208	444	1563	518	2056	593	1566
301	1327	371	1296	445	1554	519	1687	594	1567
302	1322	372	1297	446	1553	520	1690	595	2009
303	1323	373	1298	447	1550	521	n.	596	1135
304	1326	374	1338	447a	1551	522	1356	597	2011
305	1265	375	1328	448	1491	523	n.	598	2043
306	1317	376	1331	449	1558	524	1565	599	2044
307	1318	377	1329	450	1627	525	1665	600	1424
308	1313	378	1340	451	1629	526	1309		
309	1315	379	1341	452	1330	527	1657	601	1699
309a	1312	380	1225	453	1559	528	1780	602	1343
310	1274	381	1355	454	1562	529	1658	603	1336
310a	1273	382	1337	455	1668	530	n.	604	1656
311	1325	383	1339	456	1561	531	1779	605	1663
312	1253	384	1425	457	1666	532	1650	606	1662
313	1251	385	n.	458	1667	533	1649	607	1364
314	1258	386	1365	459	1560	534	1651	608	1691
315	1320	387	n.	460	1676	535	1467	609	1693
316	1246	388	782	461	1569	536	1648	610	1702
317	1287	388v	1307	462	1574	537	1644	611	1723
318	1288	389	1359	463	1575	538	1645	612	1731
319	1333	390	1357	464	1589	539	n.	613	1746
320	1334	391	1358	465	1473	540	1892	614	n.
321	1311	392	1361	466	1489	541	1893	615	1755
322	1292	393	1362	467	1580	542	1894	616	n.
323	1295	394	1379	468	1578	543	1895	617	1753
324	1293	395	1363	469	1310	544	1369	618	1773
324a	1137	396	1367	470	1582	545	1477	619	1792
325	n.	397	1368	471	1613	546	n.	620	1748
326	n.	398	1366	472	1598	547	1652	621	1888
327	1126	399	1398	473	1588	548	1653	622	1766
328	1212	400	1371	474	1592	549	1572	623	1873
329	1215			475	1595	549a	1573	624	1778
330	1214	401	n.	476	1581	550	1577	625	1768
331	1235	402	1677	477	1600	551	1396	626	1770
332	1234	403	1378	478	1599	552	1381	627	1772
332a	1233	404	1391	478a	1605	553	1387	628	n.
333	1236	405	1394	479	1601	554	1388	629	1774
334	1228	406	1399	480	1603	555	1380	630	1775
335	1226	407	1402	481	1604	556	1383	631	1777
336	1227	408	1417	482	1608	557	1397	632	1882
337	1229	409	1416	483	1793	558	1481	633	1974
338	1237	410	1426	484	1771	559	1479	634	1787
339	1238	411	1476	485	1615	560	1482	635	1767
340	1239	412	1440	486	1620	561	1480	636	2027
341	1242	413	1460	487	1621	562	1483	637	1796
341a	1243	414	n.	488	1624	563	2121	638	1797
342	1256	415	1452	489	1625	564	1475	639	n.
343	1250	416	1447	490	1637	565	1443	640	1800
344	1353	417	1453	491	1638	566	1585	641	1795
345	1249	418	n.	492	1642	567	1419	642	1798
346	1244	419	1465	493	1643	568	1622	643	1799
347	1241	420	1462	494	1617	569	1623	644	1805

F	JH
645	1803
646	1686
647	1834
648	1833
649	1835
650	1839
651	1844
652	1843
653	1840
654	1868
655	1869
656	1870
657	1860
658	1861
659	1850
660	1849
661	1871
662	1804
663	1866
664	1865
665	1879
666	1094
666a	1107
667	1884
668	1883
669	1885
670	1886
671	1891
672	1975
673	1919
674	1920
675	1921
676	1970
677	1972
678	1977
679	n.
680	1978
681	1976
682	1979
683	1982
684	1880
685	n.
686	1881
687	1782
688	1783
689	1836
690	1837
691	n.
692	1784
693	1785
694	1922
695	1923
696	1786
697	1788
698	1789
699	1838
700	1781
701	1847
702	1967
703	1832
704	1981
705	n.
706	1794
707	1857
708	1855
709	1760
710	1856
711	1791
712	1740
713	n.
714	1858
715	1759
716	1878
717	1756
718	1727
719	1725
720	1728
721	1864
722	1872
723	1722
724	1745
725	1744
726	1874
727	1877
728	1875
729	n.
730	1841
731	1801
732	1842
733	1845
734	1698
735	1761
736	n.
737	1862
738	n.
739	1876
740	2022
741	n.
742	1846
743	1790
744	1802
745	1764
746	1762
747	1763
748	2013

F	JH
749	2012
750	1984
751	1992
752	1991
753	2007
754	2014
755	1999
756	2005
757	1776
758	2016
759	1988
760	2019
761	2120
762	2020
763	2030
764	2045
764a	2046
765	2029
766	2031
767	2034
768	2035
769	2037
770	2040
771	2125
772	2048
773	2041
774	2053
775	2038
776	2104
777	2105
778	2097
779	2117
780	2115
781	2102
782	2099
783	2051
784	2052
785	2057
786	2036
787	2050
788	2055
789	2006
790	2108
791	1995
792	1987
793	2114
794	2002
795	2111
796	2110
797	2003
798	2021
799	2004
800	2122
801	2123
802	2001
803	2124
804	2018
805	1989
806	2017
807	1980
808	2118
809	2098
810	2109
811	2096
812	2101
813	n.
814	2107
815	2000
816	2113
817	1319
818	1848
819	2112
820	2010
821	2015
822	2095
823	n.
824	n.
825	juv.
826	juv.
827	C.B.
828	C.B.
829	C.B.
830	1
831	C.B.
832	C.B.
833	13
834	C.B.
835	juv.
836	juv.
836v	n.
837	juv.
838	juv.
839	juv.
840	103
841	359
842	5
843	6
844	59
845	7
846	8
847	C.B.
848	C.B.
849	11
850	15
851	51

F	JH
852	275
853	274
854	66
855	43
856	17
857	32
858	18
859	29
860	38
860a	42
861	40
862	31
863	34
864	51
865	25
866	54
866a	27
867	67
868	80
869	83
870	84
871	85
872	334
873	79
874	C.B.
874v	3
875	4
876	14
877	423
878	16
879	62
880	76
881	77
882	350
883	53
884	57
885	71
886	69
887	73
888	68
888v	65
889	75
890	45
891	24
892	72
893	19
894	20
895	21
896	78
897	63
898	141
899	105
900	47
901	136
902	9
902a	10
903	12
904	98
905	juv.
906	260
907	261
908	258
909	94
910	99
910a	90
911	319
911v	320
912	318
913	109
914	112
915	122
916	162
917	115
918	111
919	123
920	113
921	116
922	114
922a	119
923	125
924	118
925	117
926	166
927	161
928	199
929	129
929a	130
930	138
930a	131
931	291
932	145
933	142
933v	371
934	255
935	143
936	140
937	144
937v	n.
938	152
939	150
939a	120
940	154
941	146
942	147
943	156

F	JH
944	153
945	160
946	158
946v	95
946a	151
947	164
948	171
949	169
950	170
951	197
952	194
952v	193
953	234
954	287
954a	288
955	355
956	245
956a	210
957	242
958	251
959	244
960	241
961	284
962	212
963	297
964	273
964a	340
964b	345
965	298
966	280
967	225
968	213
969	211
970	222
971	250
972	237
972a	239
973	236
974	246
975	235
976	265
977	243
978	238
978a	240
979	314
979a	257
980	204
981	317
982	247
983	107
984	108
985	286
986	231
987	303
988	232
988a	148
989	315
990	172
991	233
992	1029
993	254
994	253
995	56
996	283
996a	264
997	267
998	269
999	277
1000	276
1001	278
1002	281
1003	285
1004	289
1005	292
1006	295
1007	299
1008	301
1009	335
1009a	106
1010	306
1011	309
1012	308
1013	305
1014	310
1015	307
1016	304
1017	302
1018	316
1019	311
1020	333
1020a	330
1020b	331
1021	362
1022	344
1023	343
1024	336
1025	346
1026	347
1026a	360
1027	354
1028	367
1029	366
1030	364
1031	363
1032	368

F	JH
1033	353
1034	372
1035	374
1035a	375
1036	377
1037	390
1038	228
1039	196
1040	100
1041	167
1042	207
1043	206
1044	208
1045	209
1046	282
1047	329
1048	102
1049	312
1050	149
1051	215
1052	101
1053	357
1053a	358
1054	293
1055	290
1056	365
1057	294
1057a	296
1058	348
1059	352
1060	326
1061	220
1062	216
1063	218
1064	221
1065	217
1066	322
1067	356
1068	219
1069	325
1070	74
1071	104
1072	341
1073	404
1074	249
1075	224
1076	142
1077	135
1078	134
1078a	127
1079	192
1080	349
1081	515
1082	201
1083	313
1084	137
1085	C.B.
1086	C.B.
1087	200
1088	168
1089	124
1090	1406
1091	252
1092	270
1093	965
1094	398
1095	406
1096	411
1097	418
1098	425
1099	399
1100	400
1101	401
1102	402
1103	403
1104	424
1105	C.B.
1106	460
1107	445
1108	451
1109	439
1110	437
1111	483
1112	768
1112v	774
1113	438
1114	444
1115	502
1116	462
1116a	139
1116av	499
1117	446
1118	452
1119	449
1120	443
1121	453
1122	454
1123	455
1124	456
1125	448
1126	605
1127	426
1127a	n.
1128	466
1129	461

F	JH
1130	465
1131	427
1132	463
1133	485
1134	481
1135	468
1136	496
1137	493
1138	486
1139	494
1140	487
1141	510
1142	512
1143	509
1144	511
1144a	523
1145	581
1146	580
1147	578
1148	567
1149	647
1150	575
1150v	n.
1151	576
1152	749
1152v	665
1153	741
1153v	733
1154	612
1155	744
1156	613
1156v	582
1157	739
1158	626
1158v	n.
1159	614
1159v	742
1160	1005
1160v	1004
1161	746
1161v	760
1162	622
1163	n.
1164	615
1164v	611
1165	624
1166	751
1167	625
1167v	623
1168	666
1168v	664
1169	631
1170	630
1171	570
1172	571
1173	572
1174	562
1175	645
1176	549
1177	609
1178	594
1179	324
1180	545
1181	679
1182	590
1183	596
1184	597
1185	595
1186	748
1187	812
1187v	813
1188	820
1189	677
1190	676
1191	547
1192	544
1193	566
1193a	552
1194	588
1194a	747
1195	818
1195v	819
1196	816
1197	817
1198	564
1199	579
1200	560
1201	778
1201v	779
1202	229
1203	710
1204	708
1205	711
1206	705
1207	706
1207a	707
1208	652
1209	22
1210	709
1211	791
1212	790
1213	23
1214	702
1215	798
1216	64

F	JH
1217	700
1218	701
1219	720
1219v	721
1220	703
1221	70
1222	895
1223	894
1224	678
1225	729
1226	736
1227	672
1227v	811
1228	730
1229	740
1229v	775
1230	770
1231	769
1231v	771
1232	429
1233	430
1233v	434
1234	954
1235	C.B.
1236	432
1236v	436
1237	.433
1238	435
1239	464
1240	469
1240a	467
1241	470
1242	474
1243	472
1244	1289
1244v	1290
1244a	1154
1244av	1156
1244b	1155
1244bv	1151
1244c	1157
1244cv	1153
1244d	1158
1244dv	1159
1245	230
1246	520
1247	953
1248	407
1249	473
1250	842
1251	841
1252	890
1253	898
1254	888
1255	826
1256	897
1257	829
1257v	830
1258	892
1259	887
1260	884
1261	872
1262	831
1262a	838
1262b	840
1263	871
1264	869
1265	833
1265a	834
1266	868
1267	870
1268	881
1269	832
1270	821
1271	n.
1272	910
1272a	822
1273	909
1274	n.
1275	n.
1275a	873
1276	900
1276v	837
1277	880
1278	889
1279	836
1280	839
1281	843
1282	906
1283	828
1283v	846
1284	907
1285	n.
1286	n.
1287	789
1288	797
1289	814
1289v	815
1290	696
1290a	699
1291	796
1292	882
1293	896
1294	321
1295	875
1296	877

F	JH
1297	491
1297v	795
1297a	793
1297av	794
1298	765
1298v	766
1299	874
1300	n.
1301	917
1301v	886
1302	859
1303	860
1304	847
1305	849
1306	851
1307	853
1308	844
1309	855
1310	852
1311	848
1312	854
1313	864
1314	861
1315	856
1316	858
1317	863
1318	866
1319	857
1319v	911
1320	867
1321	915
1321v	885
1322	916
1322v	865
1323	862
1324	n.
1325	903
1326	904
1327	902
1328	754
1328v	757
1329	756
1329v	755
1330	780
1330v	750
1331	759
1332	758
1332v	781
1333	753
1333v	752
1334	n.
1335	883
1336	767
1336v	773
1337	506
1338	964
1339	912
1340	913
1341	918
1342	919
1343	475
1343a	951
1344	801
1345	802
1346	804
1347	408
1348	958
1349	731
1349v	732
1350	976
1350v	967
1350a	968
1350b	969
1351	977
1352	975
1353	1016
1354	963
1354a	997
1354av	996
1355	966
1356	974
1357	981
1357a	985
1358	980
1359	984
1360	619
1360v	621
1361	998
1362	1009
1363a	1014
1363av	1063
1363b	1069
1363c	1070
1363cv	1079
1363d	1075
1363e	1049
1363f	1051
1363fv	1036
1363g	1052
1364I	1007
1364II	1008
1364a	1041
1364b	1046
1364bv	1042
1364c	1084

F	JH
1364d	1047
1364dv	1040
1364e	1080
1365	1086
1366	1039
1366v	1044
1367	1043
1368	1015
1369	1017
1369v	1018
1370	1087
1371	1068
1371v	n.
1372	982
1372v	983
1373	1190
1373v	1189
1374	1291
1375	n.
1376	1162
1377	1033
1378	1197
1378v	n.
1379	1196
1380	1019
1380v	1020
1381	1023
1381v	1024
1382	1027
1383	1025
1384	1021
1385	1030
1386	1022
1387	1098
1388	1095
1389	1096
1390	1097
1391	1220
1392	1218
1393	1217
1394	1181
1395	1188
1396	1222
1396a	1185
1397	1173
1398	1174
1399	1031
1399a	1032
1400	1283
1401	1284
1402	1280
1403	1281
1404	1213
1405	1187
1406	1277
1407	1034
1408	1252
1409	1276
1410	1286
1411	1305
1412	1350
1413	1591
1414	1385
1415	1408
1416	1415
1417	1434
1418	1431
1419	1430
1420	1501
1421	1414
1422	1654
1423	1433
1424	1502
1425	1441
1426	1514
1427	1525
1428	1458
1429	1459
1430	1505
1430a	1526
1430b	1541
1431	1542
1432	1455
1433	1528
1434	1449
1435	1506
1436	1454
1437	1450
1438	1448
1439	1446
1440	1451
1441	1543
1442	1508
1443	1485
1444	1507
1445	1765
1446	1504
1447	1503
1448	1432
1449	1534
1450	1509
1451	1545
1452	1437
1453	1590
1454	1532

F	JH
1455	1512
1456	1537
1457	1539
1458	1536
1459	1547
1460	1549
1461	1564
1462	1556
1463	1576
1464	1497
1465	1583
1466	1552
1467	1688
1468	1498
1469	1384
1470	1377
1471	1420
1472	1404
1472a	1497a
1473	1405
1474	1407
1475	1435
1476	1409
1477	1411
1478	1444
1478a	1445
1479	1456
1480	1382
1480a	1403
1481	1515
1482	1487
1482a	1535
1483	1439
1484	1438
1485	1540
1486	1527
1487	1410
1488	1517
1489	1530
1490	1529
1491	1516
1492	1544
1493	1436
1494	1752
1495	1555
1496	1496
1497	1852
1498	1457
1498v	1614
1499	1372
1500	1373
1501	1739
1502	1492
1502a	1531
1503	1533
1504	1520
1505	1697
1506	1375
1507	1469
1507a	1466
1508	n.
1508v	1611
1509	1494
1510	1964
1511	1963
1512	1966
1513	1412
1514	1546
1515	1593
1516	1376
1517	1374
1518	1493
1518a	1495
1519	1579
1520	1733
1520v	1734
1521	1735
1521v	1736
1522	1695
1523	1700
1524	1749
1525	1747
1525a	1887
1526	1707
1527	1708
1528	1807
1529	1808
1530	1806
1531	1705
1532	1696
1533	1710
1534	1709
1535	1713
1536	1712
1537	1711
1538	1757
1539	1889
1539v	n.
1540	1732
1541	1730
1541v	1729
1542	1742
1543	1743
1544	1741
1545	1851
1546	1754

F	JH
1547	1724
1548	1726
1549	1965
1549v	1721
1550	1897
1551	1898
1551v	1947
1552	1863
1553	1900
1554	1518
1555	1859
1556	1714
1557	1715
1558	1716
1559	1717
1560	1718
1561	1719
1562	1813
1563	1824
1564	1825
1565	1826
1566	1831
1567	1828
1568	1829
1569	1827
1570	1821
1571	1818
1572	1830
1572v	1822
1573	1823
1574	1812
1575	1815
1576	1817
1576v	1816
1577	1820
1578	1819
1578a	n.
1579	1809
1580	1810
1581	1811
1582	1814
1583	1917
1584	1918
1585	1909
1585v	1961
1586	1945
1586v	1924
1587	1969
1587v	1948
1588	1954
1589	1951
1589v	1960
1589a	2078
1590	1944
1590v	1946
1591	1907
1591v	1908
1592	1910
1592v	1899
1593	1906
1593v	1890
1594	1915
1594v	1958
1595	1916
1595v	1957
1596	1943
1596v	1959
1596a	1738
1596av	1942
1597	1949
1597v	1912
1598	1925
1598v	1932
1599	1929
1599v	1933
1600	1928
1600v	1905
1601	1953
1601v	1952
1602	1720
1602v	1927
1603	1936
1603v	1937
1604	1930 1931
1604v	n.
1605	1935
1605v	1704
1606	1940
1606v	1941
1607	1938
1607v	1939
1608	1962
1608v	618
1609	2089
1610	2090
1610v	2091
1611	2058
1612	2059
1613	1703
1614	2060
1615	2084
1615v	2085
1616	2077
1617	2076

F	JH
1618	1901
1619	2072
1619v	n.
1620	1911
1620v	1934
1621	n.
1621v	n.
1622	2061
1622v	2075
1623	2047
1623v	2094
1624	1985
1625	n.
1626	2087
1626v	2088
1627	2024
1628	2026
1629	2025
1630	2080
1630v	2081
1631	2063
1631v	n.
1632	2064
1633	2092
1634	2067
1634v	n.
1635	1737
1635v	2086
1636	2079
1637	2083
1637v	2082
1638	1996
1638v	1998
1639	2023
1640	1986
1640v	1990
1640a	1997
1641	1484
1642	1994
1643	2119
1644	2065
1644v	2066
1645	1902
1645v	1903
1646	n.
1646v	n.
1647	1950
1647v	1968
1648	1913
1648v	1914
1649	1926
1649v	1904
1650	n.
1650v	2073
1651	1955
1651v	1956
1652	2071
1652v	2074
1653	1993
1654	2069
1654v	2070
1655	259
1656	262
1657	266
1658	256
1659	379
1660	377
1661	737
1662	268
1663	272
1664	2028
1665	181
1666	383
1667	629
1668	691
1669	825
1670	1119
1671	1122
1672	1114
1672a	1344
1673	C.B.
1674	2
1675	26
1676	36
1677	52
1678	46
1679	121
1680	97
1681	202
1682	263
1683	279
1684	351
1685	300
1686	431
1687	428
1688	482
1689	n.
1690	845
1691	835
1692	993
1693a	992
1693b	991
1693c	987
1693d	988
1693e	986
1693f	989

F	JH
1693g	990
1693h	1002
1693i	1003
1693j	1006
1694	995
1695	994
1696	1011
1697	1000
1697v	1001
1698	1012
1699	1013
1700	1010
1701	1081
1701v	1085
1702	1037
1702v	1038
1703	1083
1703v	1026
1704	1035
1705	1028
1705v	n.
1706	1088
1707	1067
1708	1064
1708v	1065
1709	1066
1709v	1050
1710	1036
1710v	1048
1711	1062
1711v	1057
1712	1056
1712v	1053
1713	1061
1713v	1077
1714	1160
1715	1161
1716	1073
1716v	1074
1717	1163
1718	1152
1719	1279
1719v	1285
1720	1308
1721	n.
1722	1521
1723	1523
1724	620
1724v	n.
1725	617
1726	616
1727	610
1728	1706
1729	1867
1730	2062
1731	2068
1732	2093

List of Colorplates

Picture Credits

Black-and-white illustrations other than those in the possession of the publisher were produced from photographs lent by the Rijksbureau voor Kunsthistorische Documentatie, The Hague. Color reproductions, other than those of the publisher, were made from color photographs originating from:

Museum Boymans-van Beuningen, Rotterdam: page 102

Rijksmuseum Kröller-Müller, Otterlo: pages 49, 68, 240, 257, 311, 329

Stedelijk Museum, Amsterdam: pages 67, 101, 120, 170, 187, 222, 239, 275, 293, 312

Selected Bibliography

Arranged in chronological order

I. Catalogues Raisonnés

Faille, J.-B. de la. *L'oeuvre de Vincent van Gogh: catalogue raisonné*. 4 vols. Paris and Brussels: G. van Oest, 1928.

———. *Les faux van Gogh*. Paris and Brussels: G. van Oest, 1930.

Scherjon, W. *Catalogue des tableaux par Vincent van Gogh décrits dans ses lettres. Périodes: St. Rémy et Auvers sur Oise*. Utrecht: Société d'Editions A. Oosthoek, 1932.

———, and de Gruyter, W. J. *Vincent van Gogh's Great Period: Arles, St. Rémy and Auvers sur Oise (Complete Catalogue)*. Amsterdam: De Spieghel, 1937.

Faille, J.-B. de la. *The Works of Vincent van Gogh: His Paintings and Drawings*. Amsterdam: Meulenhoff; New York: Reynal, in association with William Morrow, 1970.

Hulsker, Jan. *Van Gogh en zijn weg*. Amsterdam: Meulenhoff, 1977. Original Dutch edition of this volume.

II. Major Exhibition Catalogues

Paris, Musée de l'Orangerie. *Van Gogh et les peintres d'Auvers-sur-Oise*. Introduction by L. van Ryssel [Paul Gachet, Jr.]. Preface by Germain Bazin. Notes by Albert Châtelet. Paris: Editions des Musées nationaux, 1954.

Marlborough Fine Art Ltd., London. *Van Gogh Self Portraits*. Essays by A. M. Hammacher and Oskar Kokoschka. 1960.

Paris, Institut néerlandais. *Exposition Les amis de van Gogh*. Introductory remarks by A. M. Hammacher. 1960.

Marlborough Fine Art Ltd., London. *Van Gogh's Life in His Drawings/Van Gogh's Relationship with Signac*. Texts by A. M. Hammacher. 1962.

London, Hayward Gallery. *Vincent van Gogh*. Compiled by Alan Bowness. London: The Arts Council of Great Britain, 1968.

Brooklyn, The Brooklyn Museum. *Van Gogh's Sources of Inspiration: 100 Prints from His Personal Collection*. Introduction by Jo Miller. Prints selected by Vincent W. van Gogh. 1971.

Nottingham, University of Nottingham, Fine Art Department. *English Influences on Vincent van Gogh*. Text by Ronald Pickvance. London: The Arts Council of Great Britain, 1974.

Paris, Institut néerlandais. *Oeuvres écrites de Gauguin et Van Gogh*. Text by Vincent W. van Gogh. 1975.

III. Letters

A. Complete editions

Brieven aan zijn broeder. 3 vols. Amsterdam: Mij. voor Goede en Goedkoope Lectuur, 1914.
This first extensive publication of letters was edited by Johanna Gesina van Gogh-Bonger, the widow of Theo van Gogh, who also wrote a biographical introduction. The letters were published in the languages in which they were originally written: French, Dutch, and English. Many letters and parts of letters were omitted in this edition, and it was not until 1952 that the editor's son, Vincent Willem van Gogh, began publication of the complete correspondence, which included, in addition to Theo's letters to Vincent, Vincent's letters to Wilhelmina van Gogh, Anthon van Rappard, and Emile Bernard.

Verzamelde brieven van Vincent van Gogh. Foreword by V. W. van Gogh. Reprinted forewords and introduction by J. van Gogh-Bonger. 4 vols. Amsterdam and Antwerp: Wereldbibliotheek, 1952–54.

The Complete Letters of Vincent van Gogh. Introduction by V. W. van Gogh. Preface and Memoir by J. van Gogh-Bonger. 3 vols. Greenwich, Conn.: New York Graphic Society, 1958.

Correspondance complète enrichie de tous les dessins originaux. Preface and notes by Georges Charensol. Translated by M. Beerblock and L. Roelandt. 3 vols. Paris: Gallimard, 1960.

Van Gogh: Pisma. Preface by P. V. Melkovoy. Revised by J. I. Kusnetsov. Moscow, 1966.

Letters of Vincent van Gogh, 1886–1890: A Facsimile Edition. London: Scolar Press, 1977.

B. Selections

Van Gogh: Raconté par lui-même et par ses amis, ses contemporains, sa postérité. Vésenaz and Geneva: Pierre Cailler, 1947.

Als Mensch unter Menschen: Vincent van Gogh in seinen Briefen an den Bruder Theo. 2 vols. Selected by Fritz Erpel. Berlin: Henschelverlag, 1959.

Van Gogh: A Self-Portrait. Selected by W. H. Auden. Greenwich, Conn.: New York Graphic Society, 1961.

The Letters of Vincent van Gogh. Selected and edited by Mark W. Roskill. New York: Atheneum, 1963.

Vincent: Bulletin of the Rijksmuseum Vincent van Gogh, Amsterdam, vol. I, no. 1–2 (1970).
Unpublished letters from the postman, Joseph Roulin, the Reverend Frédéric Salles, and Dr. Théophile Peyron to Theo van Gogh.

Van Gogh's "Diary": The Artist's Life in His Own Words and Art. Edited by Jan Hulsker. New York: William Morrow, 1971.

Vincent: Bulletin of the Rijksmuseum Vincent van Gogh, Amsterdam, vol. III, no. 2–3 (1974).
Unpublished letters from Theo van Gogh to his relatives and letters he received from them.

IV. Books

Bernard, Emile. *Lettres de Vincent van Gogh à Emile Bernard*. Paris: A. Vollard, 1911. Includes introductions by Bernard compiled from articles he published in *Les Hommes d'Aujourd'hui* (1880) and *Mercure de France* (1893).

du Quesne-van Gogh, Elisabeth. *Personal Recollections of Vincent van Gogh*. Translated by Katherine S. Dreier, with a foreword by Arthur B. Davies. Boston: Houghton Mifflin, 1913.

Jaspers, Karl. *Strindberg und Van Gogh: Versuch einer pathographischen Analyse unter vergleichender Heranziehung von Swedenborg und Hölderlin*. Bern: E. Bircher, 1922.
English translation: *Strindberg and Van Gogh: An Attempt at a Pathographic Analysis with Reference to Parallel Cases of Swedenborg and Hölderlin*. Translated by Oskar Grunow and David Woloshin. Tucson: University of Arizona Press, 1977.

Meier-Graefe, Julius. *Vincent van Gogh*. Translated by John Holroyd Reece. 2 vols. London: Medici Society, 1922.

Coquiot, Gustave. *Vincent van Gogh*. Paris: Ollendorff, 1923.

Piérard, Louis. *The Tragic Life of Vincent van Gogh*. Translated by Herbert Garland. London: John Castle, 1925.

Stokvis, Benno J. *Nasporingen omtrent Vincent van Gogh in Brabant*. Amsterdam: S. L. van Looy, 1926.

Doiteau, Victor, and Leroy, Edgar. *La folie de Vincent van Gogh*. Paris: Aesculape, 1928.

Fels, Florent. *Vincent van Gogh*. Paris: H. Floury, 1928.

Beer, François Joachim. "Essai sur les rapports de l'art et de la maladie de Vincent van Gogh." Thesis. Strasbourg, 1936.

Pach, Walter. *Vincent van Gogh, 1853–1890: A Study of the Artist in Relation to His Times*. New York: Artbook Museum, 1936.

Florisoone, Michel. *Van Gogh*. Paris: Librairie Plon, 1937.

Vanbeselaere, Walther. *De Hollandsche periode (1880–1885) in het werk van Vincent van Gogh (1853–1890)*. Foreword by August Vermeylen. Amsterdam and Antwerp: De Sikkel, 1937.

Rose, Marguerite, and Mannheim, M. J. *Vincent van Gogh im Spiegel seiner Handschrift*. Basel: S. Karger, 1938.

Hartrick, A. S. *A Painter's Pilgrimage through Fifty Years*. Cambridge: At the University Press, 1939.

Goldscheider, Ludwig, ed. *Vincent van Gogh*. Introduction by Wilhelm Uhde. New York: Oxford University Press, Phaidon Press edition, 1941.

Parronchi, Alessandro. *Van Gogh*. 2d ed. Florence: Arnaud, 1947.

Tralbaut, Marc Edo. *Vincent van Gogh in zijn Antwerpsche periode*. Amsterdam: A. J. G. Strengholt, 1948.

Buchmann, Mark. *Die Farbe bei Vincent van Gogh*. Zurich: Bibliander-Verlag, 1948.

Weisbach, Werner. *Vincent van Gogh, Kunst und Schicksal*. Basel: Amerbach-Verlag, 1949–51.

Schapiro, Meyer. *Vincent van Gogh*. New York: Harry N. Abrams, 1950.

Leymarie, Jean. *Van Gogh*. Paris: P. Tisné, 1951.

Nordenfalk, Carl. *The Life and Work of Van Gogh*. Translated by Lawrence Wolfe. New York: Philosophical Library, 1953.

Cooper, Douglas. *Drawings and Watercolors by Vincent van Gogh*. New York: Macmillan, 1955.

Bromig-Kolleritz, K. "Die Selbstbildnisse Vincent van Goghs; Versuch einer kunsthistorischen Erfassung der Darstellungen." Thesis. Munich, 1955.

Perruchot, Henri. *La vie de Van Gogh*. Paris: Hachette, 1955.

Gachet, Paul. *Deux amis des impressionnistes: le docteur Gachet et Murer*. Paris: Editions des Musées nationaux, 1956.

Gauzi, François. *My Friend Toulouse-Lautrec*. Translated by Paul Dinnage. London: Neville Spearman, 1957.

Marois, Pierre. *Le secret de Van Gogh*. Paris: Librairie Stock, 1957.

Elgar, Frank. *Van Gogh: A Study of His Life and Work*. Translated by James Cleugh. New York: Frederick A. Praeger, 1958.

Huyghe, René. *Vincent van Gogh*. Translated by Helen C. Slonim. New York: Crown, 1958.

Tralbaut, Marc Edo. *Van Gogh: Eine Bildbiographie*. Munich: Kindler Verlag, 1958.
English translation: *Van Gogh: A Pictorial Biography*. Translated by Margaret Shenfield. London: Thames and Hudson; New York: Viking Press, 1959.

———. *Vincent van Gogh in Drenthe*. Assen: De Torenlaan, 1959.

Cogniat, Raymond. *Van Gogh*. Translated by James Cleugh. New York: Harry N. Abrams, 1959.

Mauron, Charles. *Van Gogh au seuil de la Provence: Arles, février à octobre 1888*. Marseilles: Impr. Sauquet, [1959?].

Stellingwerff, Johannes. *Werkelijkheid en grondmotief bij Vincent Willem van Gogh*. Amsterdam: Swets & Zeitlinger, 1959.

Hammacher, A. M. *Selbstbildnisse*. Stuttgart: Reklambücher, 1960.
Nizon, Paul. *Die Anfänge Vincent van Goghs: Der Zeichnungsstil der holländischen Zeit: Untersuchung über die künstlerische Beziehung zur Psychologie und Weltanschauung des Künstlers*. Bern: Walter Fischer, 1960.
Badt, Kurt. *Die Farbenlehre Van Goghs*. Cologne: M. DuMont Schauberg, 1961.
Cabanne, Pierre. *Van Gogh*. Translated by Mary I. Martin. Englewood Cliffs, N.J.: Prentice-Hall, 1963.
Graetz, H. R. *The Symbolic Language of Vincent van Gogh*. New York: McGraw-Hill, 1963.
Longstreet, Stephen. *The Drawings of Vincent van Gogh*. Los Angeles: Borden, 1963.
Minkowska, Françoise. *Van Gogh, sa vie, sa maladie et son oeuvre*. Paris: Presses du Temps Présent, 1963.
Tralbaut, Marc Edo. *Van Goghiana*, vols. I–X. A selection of articles by the author. Antwerp, 1963–70.
Nagera, Humberto. *Vincent van Gogh: A Psychological Study*. Foreword by Anna Freud. New York: International Universities Press, 1967.
Gogh, V. W. van, ed. *Vincent van Gogh on England*. Amsterdam: NV 't Landhuys, 1968.
Leymarie, Jean. *Who Was Van Gogh?* Translated by James Emmons. Geneva: Albert Skira, 1968; distributed by World Publishing Company, Cleveland.
Novotny, Fritz. *Über das "Elementare" in der Kunstgeschichte und andere Aufsätze*. Vienna: Verlag Brüder Rosenbaum, 1968.
Szymańska, Anna. *Unbekannte Jugendzeichnungen Vincent van Goghs und das Schaffen des Künstlers in den Jahren 1870–1880*. Berlin: Henschelverlag, 1968.
Erpel, Fritz. *Van Gogh: The Self-Portraits*. Preface by H. Gerson. Translated by Doris Edwards. Greenwich, Conn.: New York Graphic Society, 1969.
Hammacher, A. M. *Genius and Disaster: The Ten Creative Years of Vincent van Gogh*. New York: Harry N. Abrams, 1969.
Keller, Horst. *Vincent van Gogh: The Final Years*. New York: Harry N. Abrams, 1969.
Tralbaut, Marc Edo, *Vincent van Gogh*. New York: Viking Press, Studio Books, 1969.
Wallace, Robert, and the Editors of Time-Life Books. *The World of Van Gogh, 1853–1890*. New York: Time-Life Books, 1969.
Roskill, Mark W. *Van Gogh, Gauguin and the Impressionist Circle*. Greenwich, Conn.: New York Graphic Society, 1970.
Lecaldano, Paolo. *L'opera pittorica completa di van Gogh e i suoi nessi grafici*. 2 vols. Milan: Rizzoli, 1971.
Welsh-Ovcharov, Bogomila M. *The Early Work of Charles Angrand and His Contact with Vincent van Gogh*. Utrecht and The Hague: Editions Victorine, 1971.
Leprohon, Pierre. *Vincent van Gogh*. Cannes: Editions Corymbe, 1972.
Revised and enlarged edition of the author's *Tel fut van Gogh*. Paris: Editions du Sud, 1964.
Lubin, Albert J. *Stranger on the Earth: A Psychological Biography of Vincent van Gogh*. New York: Holt, Rinehart and Winston, 1972.
Hulsker, Jan. *Van Gogh door Van Gogh*. Amsterdam: Meulenhoff, 1973.
Welsh-Ovcharov, Bogomila M. *Van Gogh in Perspective*. Englewood Cliffs, N.J.: Prentice-Hall, 1974.
Treble, Rosemary. *Van Gogh and His Art*. New York: Galahad Books, 1975.
Welsh-Ovcharov, Bogomila M. *Vincent van Gogh: His Paris Period, 1886–1888*. Utrecht and The Hague: Editions Victorine, 1976.
Chetham, Charles Scott. *The Role of Vincent van Gogh's Copies in the Development of His Art*. New York: Garland, 1976.
Secretan-Rollier, Pierre. *Van Gogh chez les gueules noires: l'homme de l'espoir*. Lausanne: L'Age d'homme, 1977.
Rewald, John. *Post-Impressionism from Van Gogh to Gauguin*. 3d ed. New York: Museum of Modern Art, 1978.

V. Articles

Doiteau, Victor. "La curieuse figure du dr. Gachet." *Aesculape*, vol. XIII (1923), vol. XIV (1924).
Bernard, Emile. "Souvenirs sur Van Gogh." *L'amour de l'art*, vol. V (December 1924), pp. 393–400.
Westerman Holstijn, A. J. "Die psychologische Entwicklung Vincent van Goghs." *Imago*, vol. X, no. 4 (1924), pp. 389–417.
Möbius, M. R. "Vincent van Gogh: Zum Selbstbildnis von 1899." *Der Cicerone*, vol. XVIII (August 1926), pp. 512–23.
Hentzen, Alfred. "Der Garten Daubignys von Vincent van Gogh." *Zeitschrift für Kunstgeschichte*, vol. IV (1935), pp. 325–33.
———, "Nochmals: Der Garten Daubignys von Vincent van Gogh." *Zeitschrift für Kunstgeschichte*, vol. V (1936), pp. 252–59.
Doiteau, Victor, and Leroy, Edgar. "Van Gogh et le portrait du dr. Rey." *Aesculape*, vol. XXIX (1939), pp. 42–47, 50–55.
Kraus, Gerard. "Vincent van Gogh en de psychiatrie." *Psychiatrische en Neurologische Bladen*, vol. XLV (1941), pp. 985–1034.
Gelder, J. G. van. "De genesis van de Aardappeleters (1885) van Vincent van Gogh." *Beeldende Kunst*, vol. XXVIII, no. 1 (1942), pp. 1–8.
Republished as *Vincent van Gogh/The Potato Eaters (in the collection V. W. van Gogh, Amsterdam)*. English adaption by A. D. B. Sylvester, London: Percy Lund Humphries, Gallery Books, n.d.
Seuphor, Michel. "Vincent van Gogh: esquisse pour un portrait spirituel." *Tout Dire* (1945), pp. 195–210.
Derkert, Carlo. "Theory and Practice in van Gogh's Dutch Painting." *Konsthistorisk Tidskrift*, vol. XV, no. 3–4 (1946), pp. 97–120.
———; Eklund, Hans; and Reutersvärd, Oscar. "Van Gogh's Landscape with Corn Shocks: With Discussion of Variants and Replicas in the Artist's Oeuvre." *Konsthistorisk Tidskrift*, vol. XV, no. 3–4 (1946), pp. 121–30.
Nordenfalk, Carl. "Van Gogh and Sweden." *Konsthistorisk Tidskrift*, vol. XV, no. 3–4 (1946), pp. 89–96.
———, and Meyerson, Åke. "The Date of the Stockhom Landscape with Corn Shocks." *Konsthistorisk Tidskrift*, vol. XV, no. 3–4 (1946), pp. 130–33.
Langui, Emile. "Vincent van Gogh: la technique." *Les arts plastiques*, vol. I (1947), pp. 29–38.
Nordenfalk, Carl. "Van Gogh and Literature." *Journal of the Warburg and Courtauld Institutes*, vol. X (1947), pp. 132–47.
Honeyman, T. J. "Van Gogh: A Link with Glasgow." *Scottish Art Review*, vol. II, no. 2 (1948), pp. 16–23.
Florisoone, Michel. "Deux grands chefs-d'oeuvre de Van Gogh entrent au Musée du Louvre." *Bulletin des Musées de France*, vol. VI (1949), pp. 139–50.
Bonger, F. "Vincent van Gogh als lezer." *Maandblad voor Beeldende Kunsten*, vol. XXVI (March 1950), pp. 53–66.
Bernard, Michel-Ange. "Emile Bernard et Vincent van Gogh." *Art Documents*, no. 16–18, 21, 27 (1952); no. 29 (1953).
Cooper, Douglas. "The Yellow House and Its Significance." Gemeentemuseum, The Hague, *Mededelingen*, vol. VIII, no. 5–6 (1953), pp. 94–106.
Hammacher, A. M. "Van Gogh en de Maatschappij." Gemeentemuseum, The Hague, *Mededelingen*, vol. VIII, no. 5–6 (1953), pp. 74–79.
Kraus, Gerard. "De relatie tussen mens en kunstenaar." Gemeentemuseum, The Hague, *Mededelingen*, vol. VIII, no. 5–6 (1953), pp. 82–93.
Mauron, Charles. "Vincent et Théo van Gogh: une symbiose." Lecture. Amsterdam: Instituut voor moderne kunst, 1953.
Aigrisse, Gilberte. "L'évolution du symbole chez Van Gogh. *Psyché* (Paris), vol. IX, no. 92 (1954), pp. 310–18.
Leymarie, Jean. "Symbole et réalité chez Van Gogh." Gemeentemuseum, The Hague, *Mededelingen*, vol. IX, no. 1–2 (1954), pp. 41–49.
Tralbaut, Marc Edo. "Van Gogh's Japanisme." Gemeentemuseum, The Hague, *Mededelingen*, vol. IX, no. 1–2 (1954), pp. 6–40.
———. "Vincent van Gogh en de keramiek." *Mededelingen Vrienden van de Nederlandse Ceramiek*, no. 2 (1955), pp. 2–40.
———. "Vincent van Gogh in het Caf' conc' of het raakpunt met Raffaëlli." Stedelijk Museum, Amsterdam, 1955.
Carrié (née Ravoux), Adeline. "Les souvenirs d'Adeline Ravoux sur le séjour de Vincent van Gogh à Auvers-sur-Oise." *Les Cahiers de Van Gogh*, no. 1 (1956), pp. 7–17.
Charensol, Georges. "Van Gogh à Marseille." *Revue des Deux Mondes*, vol. III (1957), pp. 1944–51.
Blum, Hélène P. "Les chaises de Van Gogh." *Revue française de Psychoanalyse*, vol. XXI, no. 1 (1958), pp. 82–93.
Gans, Louis. "Vincent van Gogh en de schilders van de Petit Boulevard." *Museumjournaal*, vol. IV, no. 5–6 (1958), pp. 85–93.
Charensol, Georges. "Van Gogh en Provence." *Revue des Deux Mondes*, vol. VI (1959), pp. 336–44.
Joosten, E. "Het rijke begrip 'invloed.'" *Museumjournaal*, vol. V, no. 4 (1959), pp. 73–76.
Hulsker, Jan. "Van Gogh's Dutch Years." *Delta*, vol. III, no. 1 (Spring 1960), pp. 31–46.
Plüss, Eduard. "Ungemalte Bilder von Vincent van Gogh." in *Festschrift Kurt Badt zum siebzigsten Geburtstage*, edited by Martin Gosebruch, pp. 231–59. Berlin: Walter de Gruyter, 1961.
Meerloo, J. A. M. "Vincent van Gogh's Quest for Identity." *Nederlands Kunsthistorisch Jaarboek*, vol. XIV (1963), pp. 183–97.
Novotny, Fritz. "Die Zeichnungen van Goghs in der Albertina." *Albertina Studien*, vol. I (1963), pp. 15–20.
Tellegen, Annet. "Geen panoramalandschap bij Van Gogh." *Bulletin Rijksmuseum*, vol. XII, no. 2 (1964), pp. 57–61.
Roskill, Mark W. "Van Gogh's Blue Cart and His Creative Process." *Oud Holland*, vol. LXXXI, no. 1 (1966), pp. 3–19.
Tellegen, Annet. "Vincent van Goghs Appelboomgaard: De populierenlaan bij Vincent van Gogh: Van Gogh en Montmajour." *Bulletin Museum Boymans-van Beuningen*, vol. XVIII, no. 1 (1967), pp. 2–33.
Jaffé, Hans L. C. "Vincent van Gogh en G. H. Breitner, een parallel?" *Miscellanea Joseph Duverger*. Bijdragen tot de kunstgeschiedenis der Nederlanden, I, Ghent (1968), pp. 383–88.
Joosten, Joop M. "Van Gogh publicaties." *Museumjournaal*, vols. XIV–XV (1969–70).
Vincent: Bulletin of the Rijksmuseum Vincent van Gogh, Amsterdam, vols. I–IV (1970–76).
Approximately 75 articles about Vincent van Gogh appeared in this special quarterly.
Wylie, Anne Stiles. "An Investigation of the Vocabulary of Line in Vincent van Gogh's Expression of Space." *Oud Holland*, vol. LXXXV, no. 4 (1970), pp. 210–35.
Eerenbeemt, H. F. J. M. van den. "Van Gogh in Tilburg." *Brabantia*, vol. XX, no. 6 (November 1971).
Roskill, Mark W. "Van Gogh's Exchanges of Work with Emile Bernard in 1888." *Oud Holland*, vol. LXXXVI, no. 2–3 (1971), pp. 142–79.
Heelan, Patrick A. "Toward a New Analysis of the Pictorial Space of Vincent van Gogh." *The Art Bulletin*, vol. LIV, no. 4 (1972), pp. 478–92.
Pickvance, Ronald. "The New De La Faille." *The Burlington Magazine*, vol. CXV, no. 840 (1973), pp. 174–80.
Rewald, John. "Theo van Gogh, Goupil and the Impressionists." *Gazette des Beaux-Arts*, vol. LXXXI (January–February 1973), pp. 1–108.
Visser, W. J. A. "Vincent van Gogh en 's-Gravenhage." *Jaarboek Die Haghe*, 1973.
Holland Herald, vol. VIII, no. 2 (1973).
A special issue containing, among other articles, findings by Paul Chalcroft and Ken Wilkie on the Loyer family and Vincent's relationship with them in England.
Op de Coul, Martha. "The Entrance to the Pawnshop in The Hague Drawn by Vincent van Gogh." *Oud Holland*, vol. XC, no. 1 (1976), pp. 65–69.

Biographical Chronology

1853 Vincent Willem is born in Zundert, in the south of Holland, the eldest son of the Reverend Mr. Theodorus van Gogh (1822 – 85) and Anna Cornelia Carbentus (1819 – 1907)

1857 His brother Theodorus is born

1866 After having attended the village school in Zundert and a boarding school in Zevenbergen, he enters the new grammar school in Tilburg

1868 He leaves the Tilburg school in March

1869 He starts work in March as an apprentice at Goupil & Co., art dealers, in The Hague

1873 He is transferred to Goupil's London branch in May

1875 He is transferred to Goupil's main gallery, in Paris, in May

1876 He is dismissed April 1; he goes to England, where he works as a teacher and later also as an assistant preacher, in Ramsgate and Isleworth

1877 He returns to Holland and works in a bookshop in Dordrecht from January to April; he moves to Amsterdam in May to prepare for study at the Theological Seminary

1878 He abandons this study in July; he then enrolls in a three-month course for evangelists in Brussels

1878 – 80 He works as an evangelist in the Borinage

1880 He decides to become an artist and moves to Brussels

1881 He lives with his parents, now in Etten, from April to Christmas; he falls in love with his cousin Kee Vos

1882 – 83 He returns to The Hague; his model, Sien Hoornik, becomes his mistress

1883 He works in Drenthe, in the north of Holland, from September to December

1883 – 85 In December he goes to Nuenen, in the south of Holland, living first in his parents' home, later alone

1884 He has a dramatic love affair with Margot Begemann

1885 His father dies suddenly, March 26; Vincent moves to Antwerp in November

1886 He works at the Royal Academy of Fine Arts for about six weeks; he leaves for Paris at the end of February

1886 – 88 He lives with his brother Theo in Paris; he works at Cormon's studio for a few months; several Paris painters — Emile Bernard, Paul Signac, and Paul Gauguin — become his friends; his palette becomes brighter

1888 In February he leaves for Arles; he moves into his own studio ("the yellow house") in May; Gauguin joins him in October; quarrels with Gauguin lead to Vincent's internment in the Arles hospital

1889 Theo marries Johanna Bonger (1862 – 1925), April 17; in May, Vincent decides to enter the mental asylum in Saint-Remy

1890 January 31, Theo and Johanna's child is born; he is called Vincent Willem after his uncle; Vincent moves to Auvers-sur-Oise in May; he commits suicide here at the end of July at the age of thirty-seven

1891 Theo dies, January 21

Index

Page numbers are in roman type. Colorplate numbers are given as roman numerals, in roman type. Black-and-white illustrations are designated by arabic numerals, in *italic type*.

Q

R

S